CO-AZM-737

PAGES PACKED WITH ESSENTIAL INFORMATION

"Value-packed, unbeatable, accurate, and comprehensive."

—The Los Angeles Times

"The guides are aimed not only at young budget travelers but at the independent traveler; a sort of streetwise cookbook for traveling alone."

—The New York Times

"Unbeatable; good sight-seeing advice; up-to-date info on restaurants, hotels, and inns; a commitment to money-saving travel; and a wry style that brightens nearly every page."

—The Washington Post

THE BEST TRAVEL BARGAINS IN YOUR BUDGET

"All the dirt, dirt cheap."

—People

"Let's Go follows the creed that you don't have to toss your life's savings to the wind to travel—unless you want to."

—The Salt Lake Tribune

REAL ADVICE FOR REAL EXPERIENCES

"The writers seem to have experienced every rooster-packed bus and lunar-surfaced mattress about which they write."

—The New York Times

"[Let's Go's] devoted updaters really walk the walk (and thumb the ride, and trek the trail). Learn how to fish, haggle, find work—anywhere."

—Food & Wine

"A world-wise traveling companion—always ready with friendly advice and helpful hints, all sprinkled with a bit of wit."

—The Philadelphia Inquirer

A GUIDE WITH A SPIRIT AND A SOCIAL CONSCIENCE

"Lighthearted and sophisticated, informative and fun to read. [Let's Go] helps the novice traveler navigate like a knowledgeable old hand."

—Atlanta Journal-Constitution

"The serious mission at the book's core reveals itself in exhortations to respect the culture and the environment—and, if possible, to visit as a volunteer, a student, or a teacher rather than a tourist."

—San Francisco Chronicle

LET'S GO PUBLICATIONS

TRAVEL GUIDES

Australia
Austria & Switzerland
Brazil
Britain
California
Central America
Chile
China
Costa Rica
Costa Rica, Nicaragua & Panama
Eastern Europe
Ecuador
Egypt
Europe
France
Germany
Greece
Guatemala & Belize
Hawaii
India & Nepal
Ireland
Israel
Italy
Japan
Mexico
New Zealand
Peru
Puerto Rico
Southeast Asia
Spain & Portugal with Morocco
Thailand
USA
Vietnam
Western Europe
Yucatán Peninsula

ROADTRIP GUIDE

Roadtripping USA

ADVENTURE GUIDES

Alaska
Pacific Northwest
Southwest USA

CITY GUIDES

Amsterdam
Barcelona
Berlin, Prague & Budapest
Boston
Buenos Aires
Florence
London
London, Oxford, Cambridge & Edinburgh
New York City
Paris
Rome
San Francisco
Washington, DC

POCKET CITY GUIDES

Amsterdam
Berlin
Boston
Chicago
London
New York City
Paris
San Francisco
Venice
Washington, DC

COSTA RICA, NICARAGUA & PANAMA

RESEARCHERS
ASA BUSH **MARYAM JANANI**
ETHAN WAXMAN

ASHLEY LAPORTE MANAGING EDITOR
JOSEPH MOLIMOCK RESEARCH MANAGER
CLAIRE SHEPRO RESEARCH MANAGER

EDITORS
COURTNEY A. FISKE **RUSSELL FORD RENNIE**
SARA PLANA **CHARLIE E. RIGGS**
OLGA I. ZHULINA

HOW TO USE THIS BOOK

COVERAGE LAYOUT. *Let's Go Costa Rica, Nicaragua & Panama* begins in Costa Rica, moves on to Nicaragua, and finishes in Panama. The coverage in each individual country chapter is organized geographically, to facilitate linking transportation from place to place. For connections between destinations, information is generally listed under both the arrival and departure cities. Parentheticals usually provide the trip duration followed by frequency, then the price. For more general information on travel, consult Essentials (p. 5).

COVERING THE BASICS. The first chapter, **Discover Costa Rica, Nicaragua & Panama** (p. 1), contains highlights of the country, complete with **Suggested Itineraries**. The **Essentials** (p. 5) section contains practical information on planning a budget, making reservations, and other useful tips for traveling throughout these countries. Take some time to peruse the **Life and Times** (Nicaragua p. 168, Costa Rica p. 48, Panama p. 232) sections and brush up on your Latin American history. The **Appendix** (p. 315) features climate information, a list of national holidays for each country, measurement conversions, and a glossary. For study abroad, volunteer, and work opportunities throughout the region, the **Beyond Tourism** (p. 35) chapter has all the resources you need.

RANKINGS, TIP BOXES, AND FEATURES. Our Researchers list establishments in order of value from best to worst, with absolute favorites denoted by the *Let's Go* thumbpick (🖐). Since the lowest price does not always equal the best value, we've incorporated a system of price ranges (❶-❺) for food and accommodations—the ranges are different for each country, and you will find price diversity charts for all three in the **Life and Times** sections (Nicaragua p. 168, Costa Rica p. 48, Panama p. 232). Tip boxes come in a variety of flavors: warnings (🖐), helpful hints and resources (🖐), inside scoops (🖐), and a variety of other things you should know. When you want a break from transportation info and listings, check out our features for unique opportunities, surprising insights, and fascinating stories.

PHONE CODES AND TELEPHONE NUMBERS. 505 is the area code for all of Nicaragua, 506 for Costa Rica, and 507 for Panama, but when calling within the country, it is not necessary to use these numbers. Phone numbers are all preceded by the ☎ icon.

A NOTE TO OUR READERS. The information for this book was gathered by Let's Go researchers from May through August of 2009. Each listing is based on one researcher's opinion, formed during his or her visit at a particular time. Those traveling at other times may have different experiences since prices, dates, hours, and conditions are always subject to change. You are urged to check the facts presented in this book beforehand to avoid inconvenience and surprises.

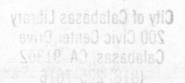

CONTENTS

RESEARCHERS

Asa E. Bush
Nicaragua

A first-time Researcher, Asa coped with 15 hour ferry rides in the rain, hostile taxi drivers, and two-story climbs with the calm and determination of an old hand. This Idaho native conquered volcano craters and jungle hikes with the same focus that he devoted to finding the best deals and the safest routes for our readers. His hilarious blogs and penchant for adventure kept us on the edge of our seats, while his ability to get out of a sticky situation continually impressed even the toughest of Let's Go veterans.

Maryam Janani
Costa Rica

This neurobio major from San Antonio spent much of her time in Costa Rica trying to avoid overly forward men, and the rest of it keeping her distance from, as she puts it, Costa Rica's "animal-infested rainforest." Character-istically one who avoids animals not in cages, Maryam put her best foot forward in this country known for its wildlife, traveling all over the country from Golfito to Tortuguero to Nicoya. Her attention to detail made for meticulous coverage, but she still managed to have some fun—going ziplining and bungee jumping in her free time, making those of us in the office green with envy.

Ethan Waxman
Panama

Given that his favorite book is *The Three Musketeers*, we knew from the outset that Ethan would be a great fit for the wild jungles of Panama. He forged his way through the overgrown and unexplored Darién, island-hopped via boats filled with leaky gasoline tanks in the San Blas archipelago, and got chased by wild dogs in Panama City. With an eye for adventure, and an enthusi-asm for getting to know locals, we knew we could trust Ethan to give us honest coverage.

STAFF WRITERS

Charlotte Alter   Lauren Brown   C. Harker Rhodes   Megan Amram

Charles Fisher-Post   Allison Averill   Meg Popkin

ACKNOWLEDGMENTS

JOSEPH THANKS: Ashley, for letting me get her coffee and be her stay-at-home dad. But really for being a great boss and friend—never simma down. Asa, for being the man. The other RM's for keeping the office fun and the poetry erotic. The Eds for their hard work/summer UnFun. The whole LG office for being quaint, Bohemian, and tasty. My friends for letting me stay in on the weekends and stay here for the summer. Florence, NJ for still being home, and Mom, Dad, Jim, Mike, and Russ for keeping it that way.

CLAIRE THANKS: Let's Go's 9-5 work day for helping me maintain a normal sleep schedule for the first time since middle school, Maryam and Ethan for all their hard work, my fellow Research Managers for all the bonding and fun times in the pod, Kavita for the swine flu piglet that sat on my desk all summer, Molly for being my aloe buddy and putting up with my many whackings of the snooze button in the morning, my family (and little brother) for their guidance with my various cooking experiments, and my friends for an adventure-packed and fun-filled summer.

EDITORS THANKS: The Ed Team would first and foremost like to thank our lord (Jay-C) and savior (Starbucks, Terry's Chocolate Orange). We also owe gratitude to Barack Obama (peace be upon Him), the Oxford comma, the water cooler, bagel/payday Fridays, the HSA "Summer-Fun" team for being so inclusive, Rotio (where-fore art thou Rotio?), the real Robinson Crusoe, the Cambridge weather and defective umbrellas, BoltBus, Henry Louis Gates, Jr. (sorry 'bout the phone call), the office blog, gratuitous nudity, the 20-20-20 rule and bananas (no more eye twitches), the Portuguese flag, trips to the beach (ha!), sunbathing recently-married Mormon final club alums, non-existent free food in the square, dog-star puns, and last but not least, America. The local time in Tehran is 1:21am.

But seriously, to the MEs and RMs, our Researchers (and all their wisdom on table-cloths and hipsters), LGHQ, HSA, our significant others (future, Canadian, and otherwise), and families (thanks Mom).

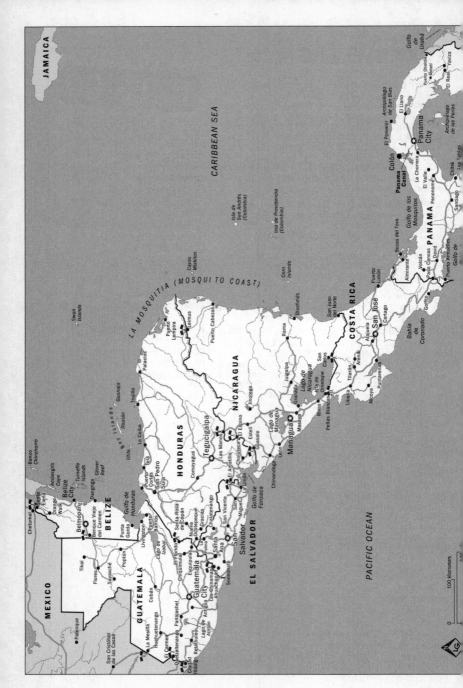

DISCOVER COSTA RICA, NICARAGUA & PANAMA

Spider monkeys, camouflaged vine snakes, and lizards that walk on water. Vibrant, thundering waterfalls and tropical rainstorms. From their green mountains and white-sand beaches to their expansive coffee fields and active volcanoes, Nicaragua, Costa Rica, and Panama await exploration. Grab your hiking shoes and go explore the worn cobblestone streets of Granada and León in Nicaragua. Tan on the Caribbean coast, hike in lush jungles, and watch Tico farmers grow coffee in Costa Rica. In Panama, visit the famous Canal, brave the streets of Panama City, and catch a wave off the coast of Isla Grande. These three Central American countries are home to some of the region's greatest adventures.

Our Researchers have pulled together the very best advice on how to get around, how to stay safe, what to eat, where to sleep, and how to plan your trip. Whether you're interested in spending a week surfing along the Pacific coast, or looking for a whirlwind tour of the region in a month, we've got you covered.

WHEN TO GO

The most important factor to consider when planning a trip to Central America is the **rainy season,** or *invierno* (winter). Central America's rainy season generally occurs between May and November. Predictably, the rest of the year is called the **dry season,** or *verano* (summer). The seasons are particulary distinct on the Pacific Coast, while on the Carribbean Coast, some rain should be expected regardless of the season. The temperature in Central America is determined by altitude rather than season; the highlands experience moderate highs and pleasantly cool nights, while the costal and jungle lowlands swelter. For a country-specific temperature chart, see the **Appendix** (p. 315).

The dry season is the tourist "high season," meaning crazy crowds and elevated prices. Budget travelers should consider a rainy season trip. Access roads and trains can be washed out for weeks during the rainy season. Even then, the sun generally shines all day, with the exception of the furious but fleeting afternoon rainstorms. Dry season travel is for those in search or a tan. The region's best parties are usually during **Semana Santa,** the week-long Easter holiday. For more destination-specific info, see the specific country introductions.

WHAT TO DO

✪ DIVING AND SNORKELING

If you're looking for a place to explore the deep blue, a trip to any or all of the three countries in this region is the way to go. With the Caribbean Sea to the east and the Pacific Ocean to the west, Costa Rica, Nicaragua, and Panama are literally surrounded by some of the best snorkeling and diving sites in the

DISCOVER

world. We know there is a bit more to diving and snorkeling than just jumping in, so we've singled out some great budget options in the sea of tourist traps.

DIVE RIGHT IN	SNORKEL SHMORKEL
PLAYA HERMOSA (P. 115). Swim with eels, octopi, and seahorses in Costa Rica's Nicoya Peninsula.	**ISLA GRANDE (P. 265).** Explore the reef right of the shore; try and find the white crucifix.
SAN BLAS ISLANDS (P. 270). Explore the archipelago just off Panama's coast.	**CORN ISLANDS (P. 222).** This Nicaraguan island is a snorkeler's paradise.
ISLA COIBA (P. 288). Head to this island in southeastern Panama for underwater adventure.	**PLAYA HERMOSA (P. 115).** The waters surrounding this Costa Rican island offer great views of sea life.

HISTORICAL SITES

Over 2000 years ago, the inhabitants of Northern Guatemala begin hauling huge slabs of limestone out of the ground in order to construct temples and palaces more than 70m high. The structures embody the mystery and grandeur of the great Maya cities, whose earliest remnants may date back more than 4000 years. The awesome temples, hieroglyphics, carvings, and statues that immortalize the ancients can be visited today in areas all over Nicaragua, Costa Rica, and Panama. Below are just a few of the incredible sites we cover in this guide.

HISTORICAL SITES
ISLA ZAPATERA(P. 195). Take a boat to this small island off the coast of Granada to see ancient petroglyphs and visit an important archaeological site.
COLÓN (P. 257). This Panamanian city plays host to a number of impressive ruins, including La Trinchera.
LEÓN VIEJO (P. 189). The site of Hernándo Córdoba's beheading, this was Nicaragua's colonial capital until 1610 when it was destroyed by an earthquake.
GRANADA (P. 190). One of Nicaragua's most famous cities, Granada offers a glimpse into colonial Central America.

SURFING

In August 2009, 35 different countries participated in the ICA Surfing Championships at Playa Hermosa in Costa Rica. The pros know what's up: the surfing in this region is some of the greatest in the world. Whether you're looking to find the best hidden spots where only the seasoned dare tear it up, or simply looking to stand up on a board for the first time, Central America is the place to be. And when it comes to finding the best beaches, surfing lessons, and rentals, we've got you covered.

SURF AND SPLASH
☒**ISLA GRANDE (P. 263).** The eastern part of this Panamanian island offers prime waves for surfing.
☒**JACÓ (P. 130).** After a long day of on your board, enjoy a drink with fellow surfers at this partygoing paradise.
☒**BOCAS DEL TORO (P. 303).** There are many places to surf at this mecca in Panama; we recommend north of Carenero Key.
☒**PLAYA MAL PAÍS (P. 128).** Despite its name, this really is a good place to surf.

⚑ PROTECTED AREAS

Blessed with one of the most breathtaking and extensive park systems in the world, Central America is a nature-lover's paradise. The diversity of the region caters to every whim—whether you're looking to stroll along well-maintained trails or to machete your way through thousands of kilometers of jungle, Central America will not disappoint.

ALWAYS USE PROTECTION	
☒ **SAN RAMÓN WATERFALL (P. 203).** On Isle de Ometepe, the cool waters of this waterfall are a prefect reward after a 1½hr. hike through pristine jungle.	☒**SAN CRISTOBAL VOLCANO (P. 199).** One of the most impressive peaks in Nicaragua, this volcano affords incredible views of the surrounding area.
☒ **VOLCÁN MOMBACHO (P. 195).** Hike in and around craters at this volcano in Nicaragua.	☒**RESERVA BIOLÓGICA MONTEVERDE (P. 101).** This reserve in Costa Rica is home to an impressive array of wildlife.
☒ **VOLCÁN POÁS (P. 78).** Come hike this volcano situated in one of Costa Rica's cloud forests.	☒**REFUGIO NACIONAL CAÑO NEGRO (P. 90).** This lush reserve in Costa Rica is home to 160 different species of mammals and over 315 species of birds.

⚑ BEACH BUMMING

Okay, so maybe ripping tasty waves isn't for you. Perhaps the idea of trekking through jungles makes you nauseous. Maybe you're one of those who gets claustrophobic in a snorkel mask. Don't worry, we're not judging, and we've thought of you, too. Here is a list of some of the best beaches in Central America. From the shores of the Caribbean Sea in Nicaragua to the quiet coasts of the Pacific in Costa Rica, we've found the best places to lay out with a mixed drink in hand. All you have to do is remember sunscreen.

BEACH IT
☒ **PLAYA PANAMÁ (P. 118).** This beach is a convenient daytrip from Costa Rica's famous Playa Hermosa.
☒**SAN JUAN DEL SUR (P. 195).** This welcoming town in Nicaragua offers just about every ocean adventure you can think of.
☒**PLAYA VENADO (P. 296).** Just a short thirty minute trip from Pedasí on Panama's Azuero Peninsula.

DISCOVER

CULTURAL AWESOMENESS

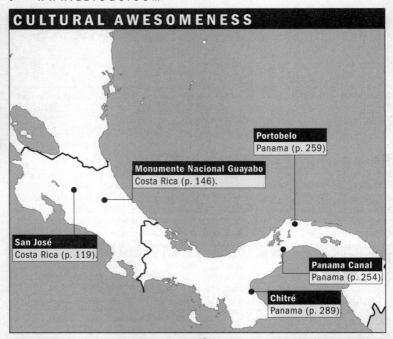

Portobelo
Panama (p. 259)

Monumente Nacional Guayabo
Costa Rica (p. 146).

San José
Costa Rica (p. 119).

Panama Canal
Panama (p. 254).

Chitré
Panama (p. 289).

ISLANDS (2 WEEKS)

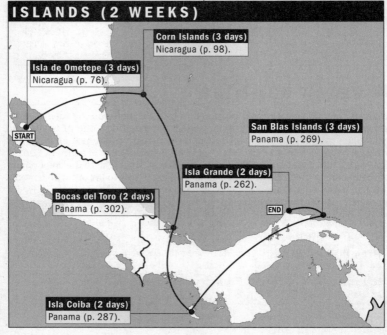

Corn Islands (3 days)
Nicaragua (p. 98).

Isla de Ometepe (3 days)
Nicaragua (p. 76).

San Blas Islands (3 days)
Panama (p. 269).

Isla Grande (2 days)
Panama (p. 262).

Bocas del Toro (2 days)
Panama (p. 302).

START

END

Isla Coiba (2 days)
Panama (p. 287).

ESSENTIALS

PLANNING YOUR TRIP

ENTRANCE REQUIREMENTS
Passport (p. 5). Required for all visitors.
Visa (p. 6). See specific country chapters for visa-specific entrance info.
Inoculations (p. 13). Travelers who have visited nations with endemic yellow fever must present proof of vaccination.
Work Permit. Required for all foreigners planning to work in Nicaragua, Costa Rica, and Panama.

DOCUMENTS AND FORMALITIES

See individual country chapters for specific info on **Consular Services** and **Tourist Offices**.

PASSPORTS

REQUIREMENTS

Citizens of Australia, Canada, Ireland, New Zealand, the UK, and the US need valid passports to enter Nicaragua, Costa Rica, and Panama; these nationalities also need their passports to re-enter their home countries. Nicaragua, Costa Rica, and Panama generally do not allow entrance if the holder's passport expires in under three months; returning home with an expired passport is illegal and may result in a fine.

NEW PASSPORTS

Citizens of Australia, Canada, Ireland, New Zealand, the UK, and the US can apply for a passport at any passport office or at selected post offices and courts of law. Citizens of these countries may also download passport applications from the official website of their country's government or passport office. Any new passport or renewal applications must be filed well in advance of the departure date, though most passport offices offer rush services for a steep fee. Note, however, that "rushed" passports still take up to two weeks to arrive.

PASSPORT MAINTENANCE

Make photocopies of the page of your passport that has your photo on it. Be sure to also make copies your visas, traveler's check serial numbers, and any other important documents. Carry one set of these copies in a safe place, apart from the originals, and leave another set at home. Consulates also recommend that you carry an expired passport or an official copy of your birth certificate separate from other documents.

If you lose your passport, immediately notify the local police and your home country's nearest embassy or consulate. To expedite its replacement, you must show photo ID and proof of citizenship; it also helps to know all information previously recorded in the passport. In some cases, a replacement may take weeks to process, and it may be valid only for a limited time. Any visas stamped in your old passport will be lost forever. In an emergency, ask for immediate temporary traveling papers that will permit you to re-enter your home country.

VISAS

See specific country chapters for **visa** specific entrance information. Entering Central America to study or work requires a special visa. For more information on these visas, see **Beyond Tourism,** p. 35.

IDENTIFICATION

Always carry at least two forms of identification on your person, including a photo ID. A passport and a driver's license will usually suffice. Never carry all of your IDs together; instead, split them up in case of theft or loss and keep photocopies in your luggage and at home.

STUDENT, TEACHER, AND YOUTH IDENTIFICATION

The **International Student Identity Card (ISIC),** the most widely accepted form of student ID, provides discounts on some sights, accommodations, food, and transportation, access to a 24hr. emergency help line, and insurance benefits for US cardholders. In Central America, most ISIC discounts will be found in the major cities, and usually apply at hotels or restaurants, with the odd boat cruise in there. Applicants must be full-time secondary or post-secondary school students, and at least 12 years old. Because of the proliferation of fake ISICs, some services (particularly airlines) require additional proof of student identity. For travelers who are under 26 years old and are not students, the **International Youth Travel Card (IYTC)** also offers similar benefits to the ISIC.

Each of these identity cards costs US$22. ISICs and IYTCs are valid for one year from the date of issue. To learn more about ISICs and IYTCs, visit www. myisic.com. Many student travel agencies (p. 18) issue these cards; for a list of issuing agencies and more information, see the **International Student Travel Confederation (ISTC)** website at www.istc.org.

The **International Student Exchange Card (ISE Card)** is a similar identification card available to students, faculty, and children aged 12 to 26. The card provides discounts, medical benefits, access to a 24hr. emergency help line, and the ability to purchase discounted airfares. An ISE Card costs US$25; visit www.isecard. com for more info. The ISE is only accepted in Costa Rica and Nicaragua.

CUSTOMS

Upon entering Nicaragua, Costa Rica, and Panama, you must declare certain items from abroad and pay a duty on the value of those articles if they exceed the allowance established by the country's customs service. These include alcohol, cigarettes, perfume and cash. Contact the nearest consulate to determine the allowance amounts. Jot down a list of any valuables brought from home and register them with customs before traveling abroad. It's a good idea to keep receipts for all goods acquired abroad. Goods and gifts purchased at duty-free shops abroad are not exempt from duty or sales tax; "duty-free" means that you won't pay tax in the country of purchase. Upon returning home, you must likewise declare all articles acquired abroad and pay a duty on the value of articles in excess of your home country's allowance.

MONEY

CURRENCY AND EXCHANGE

Check the currency converter on websites like www.xe.com or www. bloomberg.com for the latest exchange rates.

As a general rule, it's cheaper to convert money in Nicaragua, Costa Rica, and Panama than at home. While currency exchange will probably be available in your arrival airport, it's wise to bring enough foreign currency to last for at least 24-72hr.

When changing money abroad, try to go only to banks or *casas de cambio* that have at most a 5% margin between their buy and sell prices. Since you lose money with every transaction, it makes sense to convert large sums at one time (unless the currency is depreciating rapidly).

If you use traveler's checks or bills, carry some in small denominations (the equivalent of US$50 or less) for times when you are forced to exchange money at poor rates. Bring a range of denominations since charges may be applied per check cashed. Store your money in a variety of forms. Ideally, at any given time you will be carrying some cash, some traveler's checks, and an ATM and/or credit card. All travelers should also consider carrying some US dollars (about US$50 worth), which are often preferred by local tellers.

TRAVELER'S CHECKS

Traveler's checks are one of the safest and most convenient means of carrying funds. American Express and Visa are the best-recognized brands. Many banks and agencies sell them for a small commission. Check issuers provide refunds if the checks are lost or stolen, and many provide additional services, such as toll-free refund hotlines abroad, emergency message services, and assistance with lost or stolen credit cards or passports. In Central America, traveler's checks are accepted in most capitals and in larger cities. Note that they are only accepted in US dollars, and that American Express is heavily preferred to Visa. Nicaragua is a notoriously bad place for traveler's checks.

American Express: Checks available with commission at AmEx offices and select banks (www.americanexpress.com). AmEx cardholders can also purchase checks by phone (☎+1-800-528-4800). Cheques for Two can be signed by either of 2 people traveling together. For purchase locations or more information, contact AmEx's service centers: in Australia ☎2 9271 8666, in Canada and the US 800-528-4800, in New Zealand 9 583 8300, in the UK 1273 571 600.

Visa: Checks available at banks worldwide. For the location of the nearest office, call the Visa Travelers Cheque Global Refund and Assistance Center: in the UK ☎800 895 078, in the US 800-227-6811; elsewhere, call the UK collect at +44 2079 378 091. Checks available in American, British, Canadian, European, and Japanese currencies, among others. Visa also offers TravelMoney, a prepaid debit card that can be reloaded online or by phone. For more information on Visa travel services, see http://usa.visa.com/personal/using_visa/travel_with_visa.html.

CREDIT, DEBIT, AND ATM CARDS

Where they are accepted, credit cards often offer superior exchange rates—up to 5% better than the retail rate used by banks and other currency-exchange establishments. Credit cards may also offer services such as insurance or emergency help and are sometimes required to reserve hotel rooms or rental cars. **MasterCard** and **Visa** are the most frequently accepted in Nicaragua, Costa Rica, and Panama; **American Express** cards work at some ATMs, AmEx offices, and at major airports. Credit cards are widely accepted in the capitals and larger cities in Nicaragua, Costa Rica, and Panama, especially at major hotels and restaurants. In particular, Nicaragua is surprisingly credit card-friendly in rural areas. Outside the cities, count on using cash.

The use of **ATM cards** is increasingly common in Nicaragua, Costa Rica, and Panama. ATM machines are ubiquitous in larger cities and generally available in towns with banks. Still, err on the side of caution; even if there is an ATM, it might not work or accept your card. The safest bet is to withdraw cash in larger cities. Depending on the system that your bank at home uses, you can most likely access your personal bank account from abroad. ATMs get the same wholesale exchange rate as credit cards, but there is often a limit on the amount of money you can withdraw per day (usually around US$500). There is also typically a surcharge of US$1-5 per withdrawal, so it pays to be efficient.

Debit cards are as convenient as credit cards but withdraw money directly from the holder's checking account. A debit card can be used wherever its associated credit card company (usually MasterCard or Visa) is accepted.

The two major international money networks are **MasterCard/Maestro/Cirrus** (for ATM locations ☎+1-800-424-7787; www.mastercard.com) and **Visa/PLUS** (for ATM locations visit http://visa.via.infonow.net/locator/global/). In Nicaragua, Costa Rica, and Panama, **Visa** is heavily preferred, and MasterCard might not be accepted at local ATMs. Most ATMs charge a transaction fee that is paid to the bank that owns the ATM. It is a good idea to contact your bank or credit card company before going abroad; frequent charges in a foreign country can sometimes prompt a fraud alert, which will freeze your account.

GETTING MONEY FROM HOME

If you run out of money while traveling, the easiest and cheapest solution is to have someone back home make a deposit to your bank account. Otherwise, consider one of the following options.

WIRING MONEY

It is possible to arrange a **bank money transfer,** which means asking a bank back home to wire money to a bank in Nicaragua, Costa Rica, or Panama. This is the cheapest way to transfer cash, but it's also the slowest, usually taking several days or more. Note that some banks may only release your funds in local currency, potentially sticking you with a poor exchange rate; inquire about this in advance. Money transfer services like **Western Union** are faster and more convenient than bank transfers—but also much pricier. Western Union has many locations worldwide. To find one, visit www.westernunion.com, or in Australia call ☎1800 173 833, in Canada and the US 800-325-6000, in the UK 0800 735 1815. There is no number to call from Central America. To find agent locations, check the website instead. To wire money using a credit card, in Canada and the US call ☎800-CALL-CASH (800-2255-2274), in the UK 0800 833 833. Money transfer services, like remittances and access to emergency funds, are also available to **American Express** cardholders at selected travel offices in Central America; check www.amextravelresources.com before leaving.

US STATE DEPARTMENT (US CITIZENS ONLY)

In serious emergencies only, the US State Department will forward money within hours to the nearest consular office, which will then disburse it according to instructions for a US$30 fee. If you wish to use this service, you must contact the **Overseas Citizens Services** division of the **US State Department** (☎+1-202-501-4444, from the US 888-407-4747).

COSTS

The cost of your trip will vary considerably depending on where you visit, how you travel, and where you stay. For more on expenses, see the individual country chapters. The most significant expenses will probably be your round-trip (return) airfare to Central America (see **Getting to Nicaragua, Costa Rica, and Panama: By Plane,** p. 18).

TIPPING AND BARGAINING

Tipping and bargaining in the developing world is a quite different and much more common practice than you may be accustomed to, and there are many unspoken rules to which tourists must adhere.

THE ART OF THE DEAL. Bargaining in Nicaragua, Costa Rica, and Panama is a given: no price is set in stone, and vendors and drivers will automatically quote you a price that is several times too high. It's up to you to get them down to a reasonable rate. With the following tips and some finesse, you might be able to impress even the most hardened hawkers:

1. **Bargaining needn't be a fierce struggle laced with barbs.** Quite the opposite—good-natured, cheerful wrangling may prove your best weapon.
2. **Use your poker face.** The less your face betrays your interest in the item the better. If you touch an item to inspect it, the vendor will be sure to "encourage" you to name a price or make a purchase. Coming back again and again to admire a trinket is a good way of ensuring that you pay a ridiculously high price. Never get too enthusiastic about the object in question; point out flaws in workmanship and design. Be cool.
3. **Know when to bargain.** In most cases, it's quite clear when it's appropriate to bargain. Most private transportation fares and things for sale in outdoor markets are all fair game. Don't bargain on prepared or pre-packaged foods on the street or in restaurants. In some stores, signs will indicate whether "fixed prices" prevail. When in doubt, ask tactfully, "Is that your lowest price?" or whether discounts are given.
4. **Never underestimate the power of peer pressure.** Try having a friend make a show of discouraging you from your purchase—if you seem to be reluctant, the merchant will want to drop the price to interest you again.
5. **Know when to turn away.** Feel free to refuse any vendor or driver who bargains rudely and don't hesitate to move on to another vendor if one will not be reasonable about his final price. However, to start bargaining without an intention to buy is a major faux pas. Agreeing on a price and declining it is also poor form. Turn away slowly with a smile and "thank you" upon hearing a ridiculous price—it may plummet.
6. **Start low.** Never feel guilty offering a ludicrously low price. Your starting price should be no more than one third to one half of the asking price.

TAXES

Nicaragua, Costa Rica, and Panama all have either a **sales tax** or a **value-added tax (VAT)** that is assessed based on the price of the item. The rate is 5% in Panama, 13% in Costa Rica, and 15% in Nicaragua. Some businesses and menus list prices without tax, so make sure you know how much you'll be paying before you purchase.

PACKING

Pack lightly: lay out only what you think you absolutely need, then pack half of the clothes and twice the money. If you plan to do a lot of hiking, also consult **The Great Outdoors,** p. 29.

> **Converters and adapters:** All of the countries in Central America run on 110V/60Hz electricity, the same kind as in the United States. Appliances use North American two- and three-prong plugs. Travelers from outside the US will need both an adapter (to change the plug) and a converter (to change the voltage).

> **First-aid kit:** For a basic first-aid kit, pack bandages, a pain reliever, antibiotic cream, a thermometer, a multifunction pocketknife, tweezers, moleskin, decongestant, motion-sickness remedy, diarrhea or upset-stomach medication (Pepto Bismol® or Imodium®), an antihistamine, sunscreen, insect repellent, and burn ointment.

> **Important documents:** Don't forget your passport, traveler's checks, ATM and/or credit cards, adequate ID, and photocopies of all of the aforementioned in case these documents are lost or stolen. Also check that you have any of the following that might apply to you: a hostelling membership card, driver's license, travel insurance forms, ISIC, and/or bus pass.

SAFETY AND HEALTH

LOCAL LAWS AND POLICE

Central American legal systems are notorious for being ineffective and police often succumb to bribery, although this seems to be less true in Panama and Costa Rica. Tourist police are present in tourist friendly cities and towns for peacekeeping and informational purposes. To learn which towns have tourist police, contact the **tourism bureau** in each country, listed in the respective country chapters. Aggressive campaigns against sexual tourism exist in most Central American countries and sexual activity with a minor is usually punishable by imprisonment.

DRUGS AND ALCOHOL

Because of Central America's serious narcotics problems, penalties are severe for drug possession. Your home embassy will be of minimal assistance should you get into trouble. Remember that you are subject to the laws of the country in which you travel, not those of your home country; it is your responsibility to familiarize yourself with these laws before leaving. If you carry **prescription**

drugs while you travel, have a copy of the prescriptions themselves and a note from your doctor. Avoid public drunkenness; in certain areas it is against the law and can also jeopardize your safety and earn the disdain of locals.

SPECIFIC CONCERNS

NATURAL DISASTERS

FLOODS. The rainy season in Nicaragua, Costa Rica, and Panama runs from May to November. Many countries in Central America see over 200cm (80 inches) of rainfall annually. This causes extensive flooding, which can destroy bridges and roads, making travel dangerous and often impossible. Areas along the Caribbean coast and near rivers are most prone to flooding. Resulting **mudslides** are a real danger in the mountainous areas of Nicaragua, Costa Rica, and Panama. In recent years, they have caused the destruction of entire villages. Exercise caution when traveling during the rainy season; check the weather and know your route before heading out.

SEISMIC ACTIVITY. Most of Central America lies along the boundary of several tectonic plates, making it the sight of frequent and often unpredictable earthquakes. Tremors are more common, but large-scale quakes are still a danger. If an earthquake occurs, be sure to stay away from anything that could fall on you. If indoors, stand in a doorway or go under a desk. If you are driving, pull over to the side of the road until the quake passes. Nicaragua, Costa Rica, and Panama are also sites of active **volcanoes.** Stay away when they're erupting.

CRIME

Unfortunately, crime rates are extremely high in Nicaragua, Costa Rica, and Panama, and pose very real risks for travelers. Petty theft and pickpocketing (see **Possessions and Valuables, p. 12**). Carjackings and armed robberies targeted at tourists have risen to alarmingly high levels in recent years. Foreigners are assumed to have money, making them instant (and often easy) targets for thieves. If you are held up, do not attempt to resist, since robbers will not hesitate to shoot. Many tourist murders in recent years have stemmed from resistance to robbers.

DEMONSTRATIONS AND POLITICAL GATHERINGS

Political demonstrations are a frequent sight in Nicaragua, Costa Rica, and Panama, often due to labor problems or electoral results. While demonstrations are usually nonviolent, groups will often block roads or airports. These areas are obviously better avoided during times of political unrest.

TERRORISM

While crime is a major problem, terrorism is limited in Nicaragua, Costa Rica, and Panama. Drug and street gangs exist, especially in capital cities, but their activity is generally local and financial in nature. See below for more information.

ESSENTIALS

PERSONAL SAFETY

EXPLORING AND TRAVELING

To avoid unwanted attention, try to blend in as much as possible. Respecting local customs (in many cases, dressing more conservatively than you would at home) may ward off would-be hecklers. Familiarize yourself with your surroundings before setting out and carry yourself with confidence. Check maps in shops and restaurants rather than on the street. If you are traveling alone, be sure someone at home knows your itinerary. Never tell anyone you meet that you're by yourself. When walking at night, stick to busy, well-lit streets and avoid dark alleyways. There is no sure-fire way to avoid all the threatening situations that you might encounter while traveling, but a good **self-defense course** will give you concrete ways to react to unwanted advances. **Impact, Prepare,** and **Model Mugging** (www.modelmugging.org) can refer you to local self-defense courses in Australia, Canada, Switzerland, and the US.

POSSESSIONS AND VALUABLES

Never leave your belongings unattended; crime can occur in even the most safe-looking hostel or hotel. Bring your own padlock for hostel lockers. Be particularly careful on **buses** and **trains;** horror stories abound about determined thieves who wait for travelers to fall asleep. Carry your bag or purse in front of you where you can see it. When traveling with others, sleep in alternate shifts. When alone, be careful in selecting a train compartment: never sit in an empty one and always use a lock to secure your pack to the luggage rack. Use extra caution if traveling at night or on overnight trains. Try to sleep on top bunks with your luggage stored above you (if not in bed with you) and keep important documents and other valuables on you at all times.

Bring as little with you as possible. Buy a few combination **padlocks** to secure your belongings. Next, **carry as little cash as possible.** Keep your traveler's checks and ATM/credit cards in a **money belt** along with your passport and

ID cards. Lastly, **keep a small cash reserve separate from your primary stash.** This should be about US$50 (US dollars are best) sewn into or stored in the depths of your pack, along with your traveler's check numbers and photocopies of your important documents.

In large cities, **con artists** often work in groups and may involve children in their schemes. Beware of certain classics: sob stories that require money, rolls of bills "found" on the street, mustard spilled (or saliva spit) onto your shoulder to distract you while they snatch your bag. **Never let your passport or your bags out of your sight.** Hostel workers will sometimes stand at bus and train arrival points to recruit tired and disoriented travelers to their hostel; never believe strangers who tell you that theirs is the only hostel open. Beware of **pickpockets** in city crowds, especially on public transportation. Also, be alert in public telephone booths. If you must say your calling-card number, do so very quietly; if you punch it in, make sure no one can look over your shoulder.

If you will be traveling with electronic devices, such as a laptop computer, check whether your homeowner's insurance covers loss, theft, or damage when you travel. If not, you might consider purchasing a separate, low-cost insurance policy. **Safeware** (☎+1-800-800-1492; www.safeware.com) specializes in covering computers and charges US$90 for 90-day comprehensive international travel coverage up to US$4000.

PRE-DEPARTURE HEALTH

In your passport, write the names of people you wish to be contacted in case of a medical emergency and list any allergies or medical conditions. Matching a prescription to a foreign equivalent is not always easy, safe, or possible, so, if you take **prescription drugs,** carry up-to-date prescriptions or a statement from your doctor stating the medications' trade names, manufacturers, chemical names, and dosages. While traveling, be sure to keep all medication with you in your carry-on luggage.

The names in Nicaragua, Costa Rica, and Panama for common drugs are: *aspirina* (aspirin), *paracetamol* or *acetaminofén* (acetaminophen), *penicilina* (penicillin), *ibuprofeno* (ibuprofen), and *antihistamínico* (antihistamine/allergy medicine). Brand names like Tylenol®, Advil®, and Pepto Bismol® are also well known.

IMMUNIZATIONS AND PRECAUTIONS

Travelers over two years old should make sure that the following vaccines are up to date: **MMR** (for measles, mumps, and rubella), **DTaP** or **Td** (for diphtheria, tetanus, and pertussis), **IPV** (for polio), **Hib** (for *Haemophilus influenzae* B), and **HepB** (for Hepatitis B). See **Inoculation Recommendations, p. 13,** for details on inoculation.

ESSENTIALS

INOCULATION RECOMMENDATIONS

There are several inoculations recommended for travel in Nicaragua, Costa Rica, and Panama. Yellow fever inoculations are required throughout Central American for visitors who have previously visited nations where it is endemic. Panama is the only nation in which yellow fever is a health risk:

Hepatitis A, or immunoglobulin (IG), is a series of shots, so consult your doctor a few weeks in advance.

Hepatitis B, particularly if you expect to be exposed to blood (e.g. healthcare workers), have sexual contact, stay longer than 6 months, or undergo medical treatment. The Hepatitis B vaccine is now recommended for all infants and for children 12 years old or younger who did not receive the series as infants.

Rabies, for travel in rural areas or anticipated contact with animals.

Typhoid, for travel in rural areas.

Yellow fever, if traveling to rural areas in Panama.

For recommendations on immunizations and prevention, consult the **Centers for Disease Control and Prevention** (CDC; below) in the US or the equivalent in your home country, and check with a doctor for guidance. For country-specific information about malaria and other vaccinations, see the **Health** section for each country chapter.

INSURANCE

Travel insurance covers four basic areas: medical and health problems, property loss, trip cancellation/interruption, and emergency evacuation. Though regular insurance policies may well extend to travel-related accidents, you may consider purchasing separate travel insurance if the cost of potential trip cancellation, interruption, or emergency medical evacuation is greater than you can afford. Prices for travel insurance generally run about US$50 per week for full coverage, while trip cancellation and interruption coverage may be purchased separately at a rate of US$3-5 per day, depending on length of stay.

Medical insurance often covers costs incurred abroad; check with your provider. **Homeowners' insurance** (or your family's coverage) often covers theft during travel and loss of travel documents (passport, plane ticket, railpass, etc.) up to US$500. **American Express** (☎+1-800-528-4800) grants most cardholders automatic collision and theft car-rental insurance on rentals.

USEFUL ORGANIZATIONS AND PUBLICATIONS

The American **Centers for Disease Control and Prevention** (CDC; ☎+1-800-CDC-INFO/232-4636; www.cdc.gov/travel) maintains an international travelers' hotline and an informative website. Consult the appropriate government agency in your home country for consular information on health, entry requirements, and other issues for various countries. See **Travel Advisories,** p. 12. For quick information on health and other travel warnings, call the **Overseas Citizens Services** (☎+1-202-647-5225) or contact a passport agency, embassy, or consulate abroad. For information on medical evacuation services and travel insurance firms, see the US government's website at http://travel.state.gov/travel/abroad_health.html or the **British Foreign and Commonwealth Office** (www.fco.gov.uk). For general health information, contact the **American Red Cross** (☎+1-202-303-5000; www.redcross.org).

STAYING HEALTHY

ONCE IN COSTA RICA, NICARAGUA, AND PANAMA

ENVIRONMENTAL HAZARDS

Heat exhaustion and dehydration: Avoid heat exhaustion and heatstroke by drinking plenty of fluids, eating salty foods (e.g. crackers), abstaining from dehydrating beverages (e.g. alcohol, coffee, and tea), and wearing sunscreen. Cool off victims with wet towels and see a doctor.

Hypothermia: A rapid drop in body temperature, shivering, exhaustion, and hallucinations are the clearest sign of overexposure to cold. Do not let hypothermia victims fall asleep. To avoid it, keep dry, wear layers, and use common sense.

Sunburn: Always wear sunscreen (SPF 30 or higher) when spending significant amounts of time outdoors. If you get sunburned, apply some aloe and wear more sunblock the next time out.

INSECT-BORNE DISEASES

Many diseases are transmitted by insects—mainly mosquitoes, fleas, ticks, and lice. Be aware of insects in wet or forested areas, especially while hiking and camping. Wear long pants and long sleeves, tuck your pants into your socks, and use a mosquito net. Use insect repellents such as DEET and soak or spray your gear with permethrin (licensed in the US only for use on clothing). **Mosquitoes**—responsible for malaria, dengue fever, and yellow fever—can be particularly abundant in wet, swampy, or wooded areas.

Dengue fever: An "urban viral infection" transmitted by Aedes mosquitoes that bite during the day. The incubation period is usually 4-7 days. Early symptoms include a high fever, severe headaches, swollen lymph nodes, and muscle aches. Patients also suffer from nausea, vomiting, and rash. To reduce the risk of contracting Dengue fever, use mosquito repellent and wear clothing that covers the arms and legs. See a doctor immediately upon noticing symptoms, drink plenty of liquids, and take a fever-reducing medication such as acetaminophen (Tylenol®).

Malaria: Transmitted by *Anopheles* mosquitoes that bite at night. The incubation period varies anywhere between 10 days and 4 weeks. Early symptoms include fever, chills, aches, and fatigue, followed by high fever and sweating, sometimes with vomiting and diarrhea. See a doctor if you experience flu-like symptoms after traveling in a risk area. To reduce the risk of contracting malaria, use mosquito repellent, particularly in the evenings and when visiting forested areas. See a doctor at least 4-6 weeks before a trip to a high-risk area to get up-to-date malaria prescriptions and recommendations. A doctor may prescribe oral prophylactics, like mefloquine or doxycycline. Know that mefloquine can have serious side effects, including paranoia, psychosis, and nightmares. Halofantrine (often marketed as Halfan) is commonly prescribed overseas, but be aware that it has serious heart-related side effects.

Other insect-borne diseases: Lymphatic filariasis is a roundworm transmitted by mosquitoes. Infection causes lymphedema and enlargement of extremities. **Leishmaniasis,** a parasite transmitted by sand flies, usually occurs in rural Central America. Symptoms include fever, weakness, swelling of the spleen, and skin sores weeks to months after the bite. **Chagas' disease (American trypanomiasis)** is a relatively common parasite transmitted by the cone nose or "kissing" bug, which infest mud, adobe, and thatch. Its immediate symptoms include fever, fatigue, headache, and nausea. If untreated in the long term, Chagas' can lead to fatal, debilitating conditions of the heart and intestines. There are no vaccines for these ailments, and tropical specialists offer the only (limited) treatment available.

FOOD- AND WATER-BORNE DISEASES

Prevention is the best cure: be sure that your food is properly cooked and that the water you drink is clean. Watch out for food from markets or street vendors that may have been cooked in unhygienic conditions. Other culprits are raw shellfish, unpasteurized milk, and sauces containing raw eggs. Buy bottled water or purify your own water by bringing it to a rolling boil or treating it with **iodine tablets.**

Dysentery: Results from an intestinal infection caused by bacteria in contaminated food or water. Common symptoms include bloody diarrhea, fever, and abdominal pain and tenderness. The most common type of dysentery generally only lasts a week, but it is highly contagious. Seek medical help immediately. Dysentery can be treated with the drugs norfloxacin or ciprofloxacin (commonly known as Cipro). If you are traveling in high-risk (especially rural) regions, consider obtaining a prescription before you leave.

Giardiasis: Transmitted through parasites and acquired by drinking untreated water from streams or lakes. Symptoms include diarrhea, cramps, bloating, fatigue, weight loss, and nausea. If untreated, it can lead to severe dehydration. Giardiasis occurs worldwide.

Hepatitis A: A viral infection of the liver acquired through contaminated water or shellfish from contaminated water. Symptoms include fatigue, fever, loss of appetite, nausea, dark urine, jaundice, vomiting, aches and pains, and light stools. The risk is highest in rural areas and the countryside, but Hepatitis A is also present in urban areas. Ask your doctor about the Hepatitis A vaccine or an injection of immunoglobulin.

Traveler's diarrhea: Results from drinking fecally contaminated water or eating uncooked and contaminated foods. Symptoms include nausea, bloating, and urgency. Try non-sugary foods with protein and carbohydrates to keep your strength up. Over-the-counter anti-diarrheals (e.g., Imodium®) may counteract the problem. The most dangerous side effect is dehydration; drink uncaffeinated soft drinks and eat salted crackers. If you develop a fever or your symptoms don't go away after 4-5 days, consult a doctor. For treatment of diarrhea in children, consult a doctor immediately.

Typhoid fever: Caused by the salmonella bacteria, which are common in villages and rural areas in Nicaragua, Costa Rica, and Panama. Mostly transmitted through contaminated food and water, typhoid may also be acquired by direct contact with another person. Early symptoms include high fever, headaches, fatigue, appetite loss, constipation, and a rash on the abdomen or chest. Antibiotics can treat typhoid, but a vaccination (70-90% effective) is recommended.

OTHER INFECTIOUS DISEASES

The following diseases exist all over the world. Travelers should know how to recognize them and what to do if they suspect they have been infected.

AIDS and HIV: For detailed information on Acquired Immune Deficiency Syndrome (AIDS) in Central America, call the CDC's 24hr. National AIDS Hotline at ☎+1-800-232-4636. Nicaragua and Panama require HIV test results for those applying for extended residency, and only rarely grant residency to people with positive tests. Provisions exist in Panama to deport those with HIV/AIDS, but they do not screen visitors.

Hepatitis B: A viral liver infection transmitted via blood or other bodily fluids. Symptoms, which may not surface until years after infection, include jaundice, appetite loss, fever, and joint pain. Hepatitis B is transmitted through unprotected sex and unclean needles. A 3-shot vaccination sequence is recommended for sexually active travelers and anyone planning to seek medical treatment abroad. The vaccine series must begin 6 months before traveling.

Rabies: Transmitted through the saliva of infected animals (often dogs and bats); fatal if untreated. By the time symptoms (thirst and muscle spasms) appear, the disease is in its terminal stage. Wash the wound, seek immediate medical care, and try to have the animal located. There is a vaccine, but it is only semi-effective.

Sexually transmitted infections (STIs): Gonorrhea, chlamydia, genital warts, syphilis, herpes, HPV, and other STIs are easier to catch than HIV and can be just as serious. Though condoms may protect you from some STIs, oral or even tactile contact can lead to transmission. If you think you may have contracted an STI, see a doctor immediately.

Swine influenza: "Swine flu", also known by its subtype H1N1, is a highly infectious strain of flu that originated in Mexico in 2009. Cases have been reported in Central America, but have been rarely fatal. Symptoms include fever, fatigue, chills, muscle pain, and congestion. Wash your hands and go to the hospital if you have symptoms. There is currently no vaccine.

OTHER HEALTH CONCERNS

MEDICAL CARE ON THE ROAD

In general, medical facilities in Nicaragua, Costa Rica, and Panama are fairly basic. Only in the capital cities are you likely to find facilities equipped for advanced surgery or trauma treatment. In some countries, namely Nicaragua, you'll have trouble finding adequate care anywhere. Most hospitals and doctors expect to be paid upfront in cash. Public hospitals are often crowded, and can't provide appropriate care in many cases. Private hospitals are better, but not comprehensive, and are much more expensive (though a far cry from what you'd pay in the US). Ambulance services, available in cities, are often just transportation to the hospital. It is important to let the driver know which kind of hospital you'd like to go to. While some countries like Panama have many English-speaking personnel, don't count on receiving adequate care unless you can communicate your needs in Spanish. Check with your embassy or consulate to see if they have a list of local doctors.

If you are concerned about obtaining medical assistance while traveling, you may wish to employ special support services. The **International Association for Medical Assistance to Travelers** (**IAMAT;** US ☎+1-716-754-4883, Canada +1-416-652-0137; www.iamat.org) has free membership, lists English-speaking doctors worldwide, and offers details on immunization requirements and sanitation. For those whose insurance doesn't apply abroad, it is possible to purchase additional coverage (see **Insurance, p. 14**).

Those with medical conditions (such as diabetes, allergies to antibiotics, epilepsy, or heart conditions) may want to obtain a **MedicAlert** membership (US$40 per year), which includes, among other things, a stainless-steel ID tag and a 24hr. collect-call number. Contact the MedicAlert Foundation International (from the US ☎888-633-4298, outside the US +1-209-668-3333; www.medicalert.org).

WOMEN'S HEALTH

Women traveling in unsanitary conditions are vulnerable to **urinary tract (including bladder and kidney) infections. Vaginal yeast infections** may flare up in hot and humid climates. Wearing loosely-fitting trousers or a skirt and cotton underwear will help, as will over-the-counter remedies like Monistat or Gyne-Lotrimin. If symptoms persist, see a doctor. Bring supplies from home if you are prone to infection, along with tampons, pads, and reliable contraceptive devices, as they may be difficult to find on the road. **Abortion** is not legal in Costa Rica or Panama except when the mother's life is endangered. It is illegal in all cases in Nicaragua.

TOILETS
Toilets are often subpar in Nicaragua, Costa Rica, and Panama, especially outside of the cities. Make sure to bring toilet paper with you everywhere, and remember that the plumbing systems are not, as a rule, equipped to handle paper waste.

GETTING TO COSTA RICA, NICARAGUA, AND PANAMA

BY PLANE
When it comes to airfare, a little effort can save you a bundle. Last-minute specials, airfare wars, and charter flights are often the best. The key is to hunt around, be flexible, and ask about discounts. Students, seniors, and those under 26 should never pay full price for a ticket.

AIRFARES
Airfares to Nicaragua, Costa Rica, and Panama peak between December and April. Holidays, especially Christmas and *Semana Santa* (the week before Easter), are also expensive. The cheapest times to travel are late spring and November. Midweek (M-Th morning) round-trip flights run cheaper than weekend flights, but they are generally more crowded and less likely to permit frequent-flier upgrades. Not fixing a return date ("open return") or arriving in and departing from different cities ("open-jaw") can be pricier than round-trip flights. Patching one-way flights together is the most expensive way to travel. Flights between Central American capitals tend to be cheaper than overseas flights.

If these countries are only one stop on a more extensive globe-hop, consider a **round-the-world (RTW) ticket.** Tickets usually include at least five stops and are valid for about a year; prices range US$3000-8000. Try the airline consortiums **Oneworld** (www.oneworld.com), **Skyteam** (www.skyteam.com), and **Star Alliance** (www.staralliance.com).

Fares for round-trip flights to capital cities from the US or Canada's east coast cost around US$250-300 in the low season. From the US or Canada's west coast, flights are around US$200-300; from the UK, UK£400-600; from Australia AUS$3000-3500; from New Zealand NZ$4000-4500.

BUDGET AND STUDENT TRAVEL AGENCIES
Travelers holding **ISICs** and **IYTCs** (p. 6) qualify for big discounts from student travel agencies. Most flights from budget agencies are on major airlines, but note that in high season some may sell seats on less reliable chartered aircraft.

STA Travel, 2871 Broadway, New York City, NY 10025, USA (24hr. reservations and info ☎+1-800-781-4040; www.statravel.com). A student and youth travel organization with offices worldwide, including US offices in Los Angeles, New York City, Seattle, Washington, DC, and a number of other college towns. Ticket booking, travel insurance, railpasses, and more. Walk-in offices are located throughout Australia (☎+61 134 782), New Zealand (☎+0800 474 400), and the UK (☎+44 8712 230 0040).

FLIGHT PLANNING ON THE INTERNET. The internet may be the budget traveler's dream when it comes to finding and booking bargain fares, but the array of options can be overwhelming. Many airline sites offer special last-minute deals on the web. Check the websites of **Taca** (www.taca.com) and **Copa** (www.copaair.com) for sweet fares.

STA (www.statravel.com) and **StudentUniverse** (www.studentuniverse. com) provide quotes on student tickets, while **Orbitz** (www.orbitz.com), **Expedia** (www.expedia.com), and **Travelocity** (www.travelocity.com) offer full travel services. **Priceline** (www.priceline.com) lets you specify a price and obligates you to buy any ticket that meets or beats it; **Hotwire** (www.hotwire. com) offers bargain fares but won't reveal the airline or flight times until you buy. Other sites that compile deals include www.bestfares.com, www.flights. com, www.lowestfare.com, www.onetravel.com, and www.travelzoo.com.

Cheapflights (www.cheapflights.co.uk) is a useful search engine for finding—you guessed it—cheap flights. **Booking Buddy** (www.bookingbuddy.com), **Kayak** (www.kayak.com), and **SideStep** (www.sidestep.com) are online tools that let you enter your trip information and search multiple sites at once. *Let's Go* does not endorse any of these websites. As always, be cautious and research companies before you hand over your credit card number.

COMMERCIAL AIRLINES

TRAVELING FROM NORTH AMERICA

Standard commercial carriers like **American** (☎+1-800-433-7300; www.aa.com), **Continental** (☎+1-800-231-0856; www.continental.com), and **United** (☎+1-800-538-2929; www.ual.com) will probably offer the most convenient flights, but they may not be the cheapest, unless you snag a special promotion or airfare-war ticket. You will probably find flying one of the following "discount" airlines a better deal, if any of their limited departure points is convenient for you.

Copa: from US ☎1-800-359-2672; www.copaair.com. Flies into smaller cities throughout Central America. Flights from Miami and Los Angeles start at US$250. Includes **Lacsa,** the Costa Rican airline.

Taca: from US ☎1-800-400-8222; www.taca.com. Offers flights starting at US$250 from most major US cities to Central America. Check the website for incredibly cheap deals.

TRAVELING FROM IRELAND AND THE UK

There are no affordable flights on British or Irish carriers; the best bets are other European airlines.

Iberia: from the UK ☎0870 609 0500; www.iberia.com. From London to Panama City (UK£400).

KLM Royal Dutch Airlines: from the UK ☎0871 222 7740; www.klm.com. From London to Panama City (UK£600).

TRAVELING FROM AUSTRALIA AND NEW ZEALAND

Qantas (+1-800-227-4500; www.qantas.com) is the only carrier from Down Under that flies to the Americas, with flights to destinations all over the US, as well as to

Mexico City and Cancún. The cheapest options, which run around US$2500 for most of the year, are still **American** and **United**. There are no direct flights.

BY BUS

Getting to Nicaragua, Costa Rica, and Panama is possible by bus via Mexico and the rest of Central America. Buses leave from the border town of **Chetumal** and continue on to points south. For more information, see **Getting Around** below.

BORDER CROSSINGS

Coming overland from North America means traveling through Mexico via bus (see above) or car. If driving, remember that Mexican insurance should be obtained before heading into Mexico. Preparation and planning is essential. Traveling to Panama from Colombia is impossible—to do so you must cross the **Darién gap,** an often dangerous jungle with no roads or trails. For specific border crossings, see the **Transportation** section for each country chapter.

GETTING AROUND COSTA RICA, NICARAGUA, AND PANAMA

BY PLANE

Copa Airlines and **Taca** (see above) offer flights between the capitals and major cities of Nicaragua, Costa Rica, and Panama (usually US$100-200). Check the airlines' websites for last-minute deals and special offers.

AIRCRAFT SAFETY. The airlines of developing-world nations do not always meet safety standards. The **Official Airline Guide** (www.oag.com) and many travel agencies can tell you the type and age of aircraft on a particular route. This can be especially useful in Nicaragua, Costa Rica, and Panama, where less reliable equipment is often used for internal flights. The **International Airline Passengers Association** (www.iapa.com) provides region-specific safety information to its members. The **Federal Aviation Administration** (www.faa.gov/passengers/international_travel) reviews the airline authorities for countries whose airlines enter the US. **US State Department** travel advisories (www.travel.state.gov) sometimes involve foreign carriers, especially when terrorist bombings or hijackings may be a threat., though it hasn't been a problem in Nicaragua, Costa Rica, and Panama.

BY BUS

INTERNATIONAL BUSES

The cheapest way to get from country to country in Central America is by **international coach bus.** There are two main lines that serve Central America. These buses feature amenities like air-conditioning and reclining seats that you won't find on local buses, but these comforts at a higher price.

King Quality (☎+502 2369 7070; www.king-qualityca.com). Offers coach trips from Tapachula, Mexico through all of Central America (except for Belize and Panama). Also coordinates hotel stays in the destination countries. Mexico to Costa Rica, one-way US$98; round-trip US$181.

Tica Bus (www.ticabus.com). Travels to multiple destinations all the way from Tapachula, Mexico to Panama City. Tickets allow you to hop on and off at the stops along the way—a nice way to see several countries. Mexico to Panama City, one-way US$105; round-trip US$210.

LOCAL BUSES

Buses are the only way to get around in a cheap and relatively reliable way. In intercity travel, the beastly Toyota Coaster is the vehicle of choice; people far in excess of the theoretical capacity (21) cram into these white beauties. In rural areas you'll most often ride the famous **"chicken buses"**—garishly painted American school buses. Worn shocks feel every bump in the rough, unpaved roads. Drivers have few qualms about putting it into high gear down hills. Keep in mind that those who travel by bus in Nicaragua, Costa Rica, and Panama occasionally fall prey to hijackers and roadside bandits. Traveling by bus at night can be particularly dangerous. Buses are not the easiest: they often seem to run without a schedule, even if there is one posted. Buses may run on time or may take twice as long, or they may break down.

BY CAR

Driving in Nicaragua, Costa Rica, and Panama frees you from cramped, overheated buses never will, but also promises bad roads and bad conditions. Getting around Nicaragua, Costa Rica, and Panama by car is a challenge—make sure to do your homework beforehand. Visit the **Association for Safe International Road Travel** (☎1-301-983-5252; www.asirt.org) for more information if you're planning to drive.

DRIVING PERMITS AND CAR INSURANCE

INTERNATIONAL DRIVING PERMIT (IDP)

If you plan to drive a car while in Nicaragua, Costa Rica, or Panama, you must be over 18 and have an **International Driving Permit (IDP),** though all the countries in Central America allow travelers to drive for a limited number of months with a valid license from your home country. It may be a good idea to get an IDP anyway, in case you're in a situation (e.g., an accident or stranded in a small town) where the police do not know English.

Your IDP, valid for one year, must be issued in your own country before you depart. An application for an IDP usually requires one or two photos, a current local license, an additional form of photo identification. You will also be charged a fee. To apply, contact your home country's automobile association. Be vigilant when purchasing an IDP online or anywhere other than your home automobile association. Many vendors sell permits of questionable legitimacy for higher prices.

CAR INSURANCE

Most credit cards cover standard car insurance. If you rent, lease, or borrow a car, you will need a **green card,** or **International Insurance Certificate,** to certify that you have liability insurance and that it applies abroad. Green cards can be obtained at car-rental agencies, car dealers (for those leasing cars), some travel agents, and some border crossings. Rental agencies may require you to purchase theft insurance in countries in which they believe there is a high risk of auto theft.

RENTING

While renting a car in Nicaragua, Costa Rica, or Panama allows you to travel comfortably and at your own pace, it comes with its own set of hassles. In general, the cheaper the car, the less reliable and more difficult it is to handle, which can pose problems on the often dangerous roads.

With reliable public transportation in most cities, it is often unnecessary to rent a car. Parking and city driving are often exhausting, and rental cars are often a target for theft in cities.

While regular cars might suffice during the dry season (November to April), four-wheel-drive (4WD) vehicles are often essential in the rainy season, especially in rural areas. Less expensive 4WDs, however, tend to be more top heavy and can topple over when navigating particularly bumpy roads.

RENTAL AGENCIES

You can generally make reservations before you leave by calling major international offices in your home country. It's a good idea to cross-check this information with local agencies as well. *Let's Go* includes local desk numbers in town listings.

To rent a car from most establishments in Central America, you need to be at least 21 years old. Some agencies require renters to be 25, and most charge those aged 21-24 an additional insurance fee (around US$10 per day). Small local operations occasionally rent to people under 21, but be sure to ask about the insurance coverage and deductible. Always check the fine print.

Budget: ☎+1-800-472-3325; www.budgetcentroamerica.com. Rental cars available in Costa Rica (US$25), Nicaragua (US$20), and Panama (US$20). Insurance is another US$10/day. 24hr. roadside assistance in Nicaragua.

National: ☎+1-877-222-9058; www.nationalcar.com. Rental cars available in Costa Rica (US$20 per day), Nicaragua (US$40), and Panama (US$20). US$25 surcharge for those under 25.

Thrifty: ☎+1-918-669-2168; www.thrifty.com. Rental cars available in Costa Rica (US$30-40 per day), Nicaragua (US$20), and Panama (US$15-20). Surcharges apply to drivers under 25.

COSTS AND INSURANCE

Rental-car prices start at around US$20 per day for national companies. Local agencies start around US$25. Expect to pay more for larger cars and for four-wheel-drive. Cars with **automatic transmission** can cost up to US$20 more per day than cars with manual transmission (stick shift), and, in some places, cars with automatic transmission, especially four-wheel-drive, are nearly impossible to find in the first place.

Remember that if you are driving a conventional rental vehicle on an unpaved road in a rental car, you are almost never covered by insurance. Be aware that cars rented on an **American Express** or **Visa/MasterCard Gold** or **Platinum** credit card in Central America might not carry the automatic insurance that they would in some other countries; check with your credit card company before renting. Insurance plans from rental companies almost always come with a **deductible** (or excess) of around US$750-1000 for conventional vehicles; excess can reach US$1500 for younger drivers and for four-wheel-drive vehicles. This means that the insurance purchased from the rental company only applies to damages over the deductible; damages below that amount must be covered by your existing insurance plan. Some rental companies in Central America require you to buy a **collision damage waiver (CDW)**, which will waive the deductible in the case of a collision. **Loss damage waivers (LDWs)** do the same in the case of theft or vandalism. It is important to note that CDWs only cover collisions with other cars.

National chains often allow one-way rentals (picking up in one city and dropping off in another). There is usually a minimum hire period and sometimes an extra drop-off charge of several hundred dollars.

ON THE ROAD

In Nicaragua, Costa Rica, and Panama, defensive driving is imperative. The rules of the road (those that exist) are rarely enforced and rarely obeyed. Speed limits are often not posted, and thus somewhat discretionary. Passing on blind corners is not uncommon. In addition, roads outside of cities are unpaved, unlit, poorly maintained, and seasonally damaged by flooding and other natural disasters.

Gasoline (petrol) generally costs US$3-5 per gallon. Unleaded gas is available in most places, but not everywhere.

DANGERS

The biggest driving danger in Nicaragua, Costa Rica, and Panama is the road itself. Urban roads and highways are generally well-paved, but outside of these areas the roads are not. Be careful driving during the rainy season (May-Oct.), when roads are often in poor condition and **landslides** are common. In many areas the luxury of a 4WD vehicle may be well worth the extra rental cost. When approaching a one-lane bridge, labeled "*puente angosto*" or "*solo carril*," the first driver to flash headlights has the right of way.

Carjacking and **armed vehicular robbery** are becoming problems in many parts of Central America. Robbers target tourists, often at night, on highways, small roads, and crowded urban streets. It is advisable to avoid these areas at night, and to ask locals about the safest routes to take. Foreign brands and sports cars—anything that will signal to strangers you are foreign or have money—should be avoided.

CAR ASSISTANCE

There are few resources to help out in case of a breakdown or accident in Nicaragua, Costa Rica, and Panama. Some rental agencies offer 24hr. roadside assistance—ask about this when you're shopping around. Your best bet is to make sure your vehicle is ready for the road. Parts, gas, and service stations are hard to come by, so be prepared for every possible occurrence. Mechanically savvy drivers might want to bring tools for any problems that arise.

ESSENTIALS

If you are involved in an accident, you should wait until the police arrive to move your vehicle so that an officer can prepare a report. Unless this is done immediately and reported to insurers; otherwise, it is difficult or impossible to file claims and receive coverage.

BY THUMB

 LET'S NOT GO. *Let's Go* strongly urges you to consider the risks before you choose to hitch. We do not recommend hitching as a safe means of transportation, though it is common in Nicaragua, Costa Rica, and Panama.

KEEPING IN TOUCH

BY EMAIL AND INTERNET

Internet is widely available in Nicaragua, Costa Rica, and Panama. In the capitals and larger cities, internet cafes are ubiquitous and fairly cheap. In smaller cities and towns, internet access is slower and spottier but still available. In general, large hotels offer internet to their guests. Some larger restaurants, as well as American chains like McDonalds, have it as well. Travelers with wireless-enabled computers may be able to take advantage of an increasing number of "hotspots," where they can get online for free or for a small fee. Nicaragua, Costa Rica, and Panama are short on free Wi-Fi hotspots; the best bet is large hotels and restaurants and some hostels.

Connection speed varies greatly from place to place, but in the cities broadband and other high-speed connections are common. It gets slower as you move into rural areas, where dial-up and DSL are more likely to be found. Prices vary by region, but internet generally costs US$1-3 per hr.

Although in some places it's possible to forge a remote link with your home server, in most cases this is a much slower (and thus more expensive) option than taking advantage of free **web-based email accounts** (e.g., www.gmail.com). **Internet cafes** and the occasional free internet terminal at a public library are listed in the **Practical Information** sections of major cities. For lists of additional cybercafes in Central America, check out www.cybercaptive.com or www.travel-island.com/internet.cafes/CyberCafes.

 WARY WI-FI. Wireless hot spots make internet access possible in public and remote places. Unfortunately, they also pose **security risks.** Hot spots are public, open networks that use unencrypted, unsecured connections. They are susceptible to hacks and "packet sniffing"—the theft of passwords and other private information. To prevent problems, disable "ad hoc" mode, turn off file sharing and network discovery, encrypt your email, turn on your firewall, beware of phony networks, and watch for over-the-shoulder creeps.

BY TELEPHONE

CALLING HOME FROM NICARAGUA, COSTA RICA, AND PANAMA

Prepaid phone cards are a common and relatively inexpensive means of calling abroad. Each one comes with a Personal Identification Number (PIN) and a toll-free access number. Call the access number and then follow the directions for dialing your PIN. To purchase prepaid phone cards, check online for the best rates; www.callingcards.com is a good place to start. Online providers generally send your access number and PIN via email, with no actual "card" involved. You can also call home with prepaid phone cards purchased in Central America (see **Calling Within,** p. 25).

PLACING INTERNATIONAL CALLS. To call from home or to call home from Nicaragua, Costa Rica, and Panama, dial:

1. The **international dialing prefix.** To call from **Australia,** dial ☎0011; **Canada** or the **US,** ☎011; **Ireland, New Zealand,** or the **UK,** ☎00; **Costa Rica,** ☎00; **Panama,** ☎0.
2. The **country code** of the country you want to call. To call **Australia,** dial ☎61; **Canada** or the **US,** ☎1; **Ireland,** ☎353; **New Zealand,** ☎64; the **UK,** ☎44; **Costa Rica,** ☎506; **Nicaragua,** ☎505; **Panama,** ☎507.
3. The **city/area code.** *Let's Go* lists the city/area codes for cities and towns in Central America opposite the city or town name, next to a ☎, as well as in every phone number. If there's no number, then there's no area code.
4. The **local number.**

Another option is to purchase a **calling card,** linked to a major national telecommunications service in your home country. Calls are billed collect or to your account. Cards generally come with instructions for dialing both domestically and internationally.

Placing a **collect call** through an international operator can be expensive but may be necessary in case of an emergency. You can frequently call collect without even possessing a company's calling card just by calling its access number and following the instructions.

CALLING WITHIN NICARAGUA, COSTA RICA, AND PANAMA

The simplest way to call within the country is to use a **card-based telephone,** as coin-based phones are increasingly unavailable. Prepaid phone cards, available at newspaper kiosks and convenience stores, usually save time and money in the long run. Phone rates typically tend to be highest in the morning, lower in the evening, and lowest on Sundays and late at night. International calls are best made using special phone cards or on internet call providers like Skype, who offer the best rates of all, though this requires internet. Cell phones (see below) are a good option if you make a lot of local calls or need to be contacted.

CELL PHONES

Cell phone service is reliable and widely available in Central America. The best option is to buy a cell phone when you arrive—they're often just US$20-

30—and buy minutes in prepaid increments. The rates on the prepaid cards are comparable to the rates of payphones. If you need to make lots of local calls, or need people to be able to contact you, this is the best option. Cellular rates for international calls can be prohibitively expensive. Still, phone cards are a better option for calling abroad. It is possible to bring your own cell phone, as long as it is not SIM-locked and operates on the same band as the country you are in. Be aware that expensive cell phones are ostentatious in Latin America and are begging to be stolen.

The international standard for cell phones is **Global System for Mobile Communication (GSM).** To make and receive calls in Central America, you will need a GSM-compatible phone and a **SIM (Subscriber Identity Module) card,** a country-specific, thumbnail-size chip that gives you a local phone number and plugs you into the local network. Many SIM cards are prepaid, and incoming calls are frequently free. You can buy additional cards or vouchers (usually available at convenience stores) to "top up" your phone. For more information on GSM phones, see below and check out www.telestial.com. Companies like **Cellular Abroad** (www.cellularabroad.com) rent cell phones that work in a variety of destinations around the world.

> **GSM PHONES.** Just having a GSM phone doesn't mean you're necessarily good to go when you travel abroad. The majority of GSM phones sold in the US operate on a different frequency (1900) than international phones (900/1800) and will not work abroad. Tri-band phones work on all three frequencies (900/1800/1900) and will operate through most of the world. Additionally, some GSM phones are SIM-locked and will only accept SIM cards from a single carrier. You'll need a SIM-unlocked phone to use a SIM card from a local carrier when you travel. Central America is a patchwork of GSM frequencies. Costa Rica operates at 1800 MHz (like most European phones), while the other countries use the 850/1900 MHz bands. In Panama, you'll need to buy a phone, since the carriers there only operate at 850.

TIME DIFFERENCES

Nicaragua and Costa Rica are 6hr. behind Greenwich Mean Time (GMT), while Panama is 5hr. behind. None of the countries observe Daylight Saving Time.

BY MAIL

SENDING MAIL HOME FROM NICARAGUA, COSTA RICA, AND PANAMA

Airmail is the best way to send mail home from Central America, though quality and timeliness of service varies within the region. Costa Rica's is quite efficient, while the others are less reliable. Surface mail is by far the cheapest and slowest way to send mail. It takes one to two months to cross the Atlantic and one to three to cross the Pacific.

SENDING MAIL TO NICARAGUA, COSTA RICA, AND PANAMA

To ensure timely delivery, mark envelopes "airmail," *"par avion,"* or *"por avión."* In addition to the standard postage system whose rates are listed below, **Federal Express** (☎+1-800-463-3339; www.fedex.com) handles express mail services from most countries to Central America. Sending a postcard within Central America costs about US$0.20, while sending letters locally should not exceed US$0.50. Mail theft is not uncommon, so avoid sending expensive items or money through the mail. In general, mail sent to and from cities has a better chance of arriving.

There are several ways to arrange pick-up of letters sent to you by friends and relatives while you are abroad. Mail can be sent via **Poste Restante** (*"Lista de Correos"* in most of Central America, *"Entrega General"* in Panama) to almost any city or town with a post office. Address these letters like so:

Louis Caputo
Lista de Correos
Correo Central
City, Country

The mail will go to a special desk in the central post office, unless you specify a post office by street address or postal code. It's best to use the largest post office, since mail may be sent there regardless. It is usually safer and quicker, though more expensive, to send mail express or registered. Bring your passport (or other photo ID) for pickup. You may be charged a small fee. If the clerks insist that there is nothing for you, ask them to check under your first name as well. *Let's Go* lists post offices in the **Practical Information** section for each city and most towns.

ACCOMMODATIONS

HOTELS AND HOSPEDAJES

Hotels are the most common kind of accommodation in Nicaragua, Costa Rica, and Panama. Hotels go by many different names. *Hospedajes* or *casas de huéspedes* are usually the cheapest. *Hoteles*, *pensiones*, and *posadas* are slightly more expensive. Standards vary greatly, but generally speaking a basic room includes nothing more than a bed, a light bulb, and perhaps a fan; other amenities are a bonus. The very cheapest places may not provide towel, soap, or toilet paper. Spending a little more gets you a room with a private bath, and if you're lucky, hot water. For a modest amount more you might find a place with some character and charm.

Hotel singles in Nicaragua, Costa Rica, and Panama cost about US$15 per night; doubles are around US$30. Prices are generally higher in the high season and around certain Central American holidays. *Let's Go* quotes room prices with and without private bath. Note that "with bath" means a sink, toilet, and basic shower in the room, not an actual tub. Communal baths are typically the same sort of thing, just off the hall. **Hot shower** is a relative term in Central America, as "hot" can often be tepid at best. In rural areas and sometimes in cities, the water heating device can be electric coils in the shower head. Such devices work best at low water pressure.

In sea level areas, try to get a room with a fan or a window with a nice coastal breeze. In more upscale hotels, air-conditioning will probably be available. Look for screens and mosquito netting in more tropical areas. At higher elevations, hot showers and extra blankets are a must.

HOSTELS

Many hostels are laid out dorm-style, often with large single-sex rooms and bunk beds. Private rooms that sleep from two to four are becoming more common. Hostels sometimes provide kitchens and utensils for your use, breakfast and other meals, storage areas, laundry facilities, internet, transportation to airports, and bike or moped rentals. Some hostels impose a maximum stay, close during certain daytime "lockout" hours, have a curfew, don't accept reservations, or, less frequently, require that you do chores. In Nicaragua, Costa Rica, and Panama, a dorm bed in a hostel will average around US$8-10 and a private room around US$15-20.

OTHER TYPES OF ACCOMMODATIONS

LONG-TERM ACCOMMODATIONS

Travelers planning to stay in Nicaragua, Costa Rica, and Panama for extended periods of time may find it most cost-effective to rent an **apartment.** A basic one-bedroom (or studio) apartment in a capital city will be less than US$200 per month. For US$300-400, you can often find more comfortable two-bedroom digs with a kitchen, full bath, and other amenities. There are plenty of luxury condos for rent, especially beachfront properties, but unless you have a few thousand to blow per month and are so inclined, it's not worth it. Besides the rent itself, prospective tenants are typically required to front a security deposit (frequently one month's rent) and the last month's rent.

The biggest hurdles to overcome when renting an apartment in Nicaragua, Costa Rica, and Panama are learning the local laws related to property rental, hammering the contract out, and surmounting the language barrier. Consult your consulate, talk to locals about your rights and responsibilities as a tenant, and ask around to see if you are getting a good price.

CAMPING

Camping in Nicaragua, Costa Rica, and Panama is a pleasant way to save money and sleep a little closer to nature. That said, there are few proper campgrounds, public or private. Many hotels and hostels will let you sleep on their property for a nominal fee, a fraction of what a room costs. Some travelers report that many residents will let you sleep on their land for free or for a small fee, as long as you ask beforehand. Some national park services (e.g., Costa Rica's) will allow you to sleep in certain parks for free.

Lugging your camping gear with you is unnecessary. Tents, hammocks, and mosquito nets are widely available at cheap rates. In addition to having to carry any equipment you bring with you, customs officials may disinfect it at the airport, adding travel time to your trip. For more information on outdoor activities in Nicaragua, Costa Rica, and Panama, see **The Great Outdoors, p. 29**.

THE GREAT OUTDOORS

The **Great Outdoor Recreation Page** (www.gorp.com) provides excellent general information for travelers planning on camping or enjoying the outdoors.

 LEAVE NO TRACE. *Let's Go* encourages travelers to embrace the "leave no trace" ethic, minimizing their impact on natural environments and protecting them for future generations. Trekkers and wilderness enthusiasts should set up camp on durable surfaces, use cookstoves instead of campfires, bury human waste away from water supplies, bag trash and carry it out with them, and respect wildlife. For more detailed information, contact the **Leave No Trace Center for Outdoor Ethics**, P.O. Box 997, Boulder, CO 80306, USA (☎+1-800-332-4100 or 303-442-8222; www.lnt.org).

NATIONAL PARKS

Ecotourism is becoming a major economic force in Nicaragua, Costa Rica, and Panama thanks to the abundance of natural beauty and biodiversity in the area, best maintained in nature reserves in each country. National Park systems in this region vary in quality, upkeep, and regulations. Some National Parks have regulations they follow stringently, with a good ranger force and plenty of financial support to assure upkeep and protection. Costa Rica has by far the best system of protected land. The country's effort is repaid by the droves of visitors that visit and pay for the parks' maintenance. Other countries have less financial support and lack upkeep of paths and hiking trails, as well as maintenance of roads and entrances.

Not all parks and reserves are open to the public. Admission is generally US$5-10, though some charge more for tourists. Costa Rica is the only country whose conservation department, *Sistema Nacional de Areas de Conservacion* (SINAC), has a dedicated website (www.sinac.go.cr), which provides comprehensive information about services, prices, and hours. For information about national parks in Nicaragua and Panama, the best bet is to go to the tourist office or visit their websites—see **Tourist Offices** in each country chapter.

WILDLIFE

The jungles and streets of Central America are home to a variety of poisonous and harmful critters that will ruin your day

THINGS WITH STINGS. Venomous snakes inhabit the jungles of the isthmus. The most dangerous is the fer-de-lance (*terciopelo* in Spanish), a nocturnal snake that lives in and around settled areas. Snakebites are uncommon and usually accidental, but to minimize the risk, always wear shoes and avoid stepping off the path. Bites can be fatal if left untreated. **Tarantulas** also prowl the jungles of Central America. Bites are usually not fatal, but should be treated immediately. More common are **scorpions** (*alacranes*), some of which can grow up to 8 inches in length. To avoid these guys, shake out your shoes before putting them on and watch where you walk.

BUGGIN' OUT. Mosquitoes and other bugs can be a huge, highly infectious bother. Yellow fever, malaria, and dengue fever are all transmitted through mosquito bites. Mosquitoes can bite through thin fabric, so cover up as much as possible with thicker material. **100% DEET** is useful, but mosquitoes are so ravenous that nothing short of a mosquito hood and netting really stops every jab. Another villain is the "kissing bug," which causes **Chagas disease** in humans. Sleeping inside and using a mosquito net are your defense. See **Staying Healthy** (p. 15) for more information.

NOT YOUR BEST FRIEND. Stay away from dogs, especially the stray variety. **Rabies** is frighteningly prevalent in Central America. If bitten, get treatment immediately. By the time you're foaming at the mouth, it's too late.

ORGANIZED ADVENTURE TRIPS

Organized adventure tours offer another way to explore the wild. Activities include archaeological digs, biking, canoeing, climbing, hiking, kayaking, photo safaris, rafting, and skiing. Tourism bureaus can often suggest parks, trails, and outfitters. Organizations that specialize in camping and outdoor equipment like REI and EMS (above) also are good sources of info.

> **Specialty Travel Index,** P.O. Box 458, San Anselmo, CA 94979, USA (in the US ☎888-624-4030, elsewhere +1-415-455-1643; www.specialtytravel.com).

> **Quetzaltrekkers,** ☎+505 2311 6695; www.quetzaltrekkers.com. Offers guided trips through Nicaragua and Guatemala, and donates all of its profits to help impoverished children. Minimum donations run around US$20/day.

SPECIFIC CONCERNS

SUSTAINABLE TRAVEL

As the number of travelers on the road rises, the detrimental effect they can have on natural environments is an increasing concern. With this in mind, *Let's Go* promotes the philosophy of sustainable travel. Through sensitivity to issues of ecology and sustainability, today's travelers can be a powerful force in preserving and restoring the places they visit.

Ecotourism, a rising trend in sustainable travel, focuses on the conservation of natural habitats—mainly, on how to use them to build up the economy without exploitation or overdevelopment. Travelers can make a difference by doing advance research, by supporting organizations and establishments that pay attention to their carbon footprint, and by patronizing establishments that strive to be environmentally friendly.

Deforestation and **biodiversity loss** are the greatest ecological problems facing Nicaragua, Costa Rica, and Panama. It is estimated that Central America has lost 20% of its forest cover in the past 20 years, most of it converted to pasture to graze cattle for the North American beef market. Deforestation causes soil erosion, loss of wildlife and their habitats, and greater carbon dioxide emissions. As a consumer, there are plenty of ways to combat this, from using recycled paper to eating fewer hamburgers. On the road, you can help by visiting the national parks and reserves. The admission fee and any donations you make will go toward the upkeep of the parks, and your visit will educate you about the specific environmental concerns of the country. You can also ensure that any tours you go on follow environmentally friendly practices.

The **illegal wildlife trade** is also a problem in Nicaragua, Costa Rica, and Panama. Be conscious of what animal products you might be buying, as it may be processed from an endangered species. Seaturtle eggs, though illegal, are sold in many places in Central America (Panama especially), and tortoise shells are often peddled as souvenirs. It's also illegal to traffic in these items. If you're caught at customs, you might be thrown in jail.

For opportunities to volunteer and work toward sustainable travel and conservation in Nicaragua, Costa Rica, and Panama, see **Beyond Tourism,** (p. 35).

ECOTOURISM RESOURCES. For more information on environmentally responsible tourism, contact one of the organizations below:

Conservation International, 2011 Crystal Dr., Ste. 500, Arlington, VA 22202, USA (☎+1-800-429-5660 or 703-341-2400; www.conservation.org).

Green Globe 21, Green Globe vof, Verbenalaan 1, 2111 ZL Aerdenhout, the Netherlands (☎+31 23 544 0306; www.greenglobe.com).

International Ecotourism Society, 1301 Clifton St. NW, Ste. 200, Washington, DC 20009, USA (☎+1-202-506-5033; www.ecotourism.org).

United Nations Environment Program (**UNEP;** www.unep.org).

RESPONSIBLE TRAVEL

Your tourist dollars can make a big impact on the destinations you visit. The choices you make during your trip can have powerful effects on local communities—for better or for worse. Travelers who care about the destinations and environments they explore should make themselves aware of the social and cultural implications of their choices. Simple decisions such as buying local products, paying fair prices for products or services, and attempting to speak the local language can have a strong, positive effect on the community.

Community-based tourism aims to channel tourist dollars into the local economy by emphasizing tours and cultural programs that are run by members of the host community. This type of tourism also benefits the tourists themselves, as it often takes them beyond the traditional tours of the region.

Because the Central American economy is so dependent on tourism, it is especially important to be conscious of your actions as a tourist. Commodification of tradition, loss of authenticity, and income inequality are all issues that have been exacerbated by tourism here in the last decades. Strive to practice **minimum-impact travel.** Leave the land and the cultural landscape the way you found it. Be conscious of all of your transactions and what they mean for both parties.

WOMEN TRAVELERS

Women exploring on their own inevitably face some additional safety concerns. Single women can consider staying in hostels that offer single rooms that lock from the inside. It's a good idea to stick to centrally located accommodations and to avoid solitary late-night treks or bus rides. Always carry extra cash for a phone call, bus, or taxi. **Hitchhiking** is never safe for lone women or even for two women traveling together. Look as if you know where you're going and approach older women or couples for directions if you're lost or feeling uncomfortable in your surroundings.

Generally, the less you look like a tourist, the better off you'll be. Women in in this region seldom travel without the company of men; foreign women who travel alone often draw attention. Awareness of social standards and dress codes may help to minimize unwanted attention. More traditional areas of the country generally require conservative dress; wear a long skirt and sleeved blouses in churches or religious towns. If you are traveling with a male friend, it may help to pose as a couple; this will make it easier to share rooms and will also chill the blood of potential Romeos. Wearing a conspicuous **wedding band** sometimes helps to prevent unwanted advances.

Your best answer to verbal harassment is no answer at all; feigning deafness, sitting motionless, and staring straight ahead at nothing in particular will usually do the trick. The extremely persistent can sometimes be dissuaded by a firm, loud, and very public "Go away!"—in Spanish, *"¡Vete!"* or *"¡Déjame en paz!"* Don't hesitate to seek out a police officer, a store clerk, or a passerby if you are being harassed. Some countries have a **policía turística** specifically geared toward travelers. Memorize the emergency numbers in places you visit and consider carrying a whistle on your keychain. A **self-defense course** will both prepare you for a potential attack and raise your level of awareness of your surroundings (see **Personal Safety,** p. 12). Also, it might be a good idea to talk with your doctor about the health concerns that women face when traveling (p. 17).

GLBT TRAVELERS

Attitudes toward gay, lesbian, bisexual, and transgender (GLBT) travelers can vary drastically from region to region in these three countries. In many places it is socially unacceptable, while the cities of San Jose, Manuel Antonio, and Quepos in **Costa Rica** are surprisingly tolerant. While Costa Rica has the most travel-friendly infrastructure for GLBT travelers, Nicaragua and Panama are becoming increasingly tolerant and gay bars are beginning to open in major cities and touristy areas. This is a very recent development, however—be careful about open association and realize that *machismo* and very strict gender role expectations are the norm. Although bisexual, gay, and lesbian communities may exist and even thrive in larger cities, the governments there still have a rather unfavorable outlook toward homosexuality, so keeping a low profile about your sexuality is probably your best bet. **Homosociality** (camaraderie between members of the same sex, particularly men) is much more common than you may be accustomed to. Handholding between two men, for example, is quite common.

Listed below are contact organizations, mail-order catalogs, and publishers that offer materials addressing some specific concerns. **Out and About** (www.planetout.com) offers a comprehensive website and a weekly newsletter addressing gay travel concerns.

International Lesbian and Gay Association (ILGA), 17 Rue de la Charité, 1210 Brussels, Belgium (☎+32 2 502 2471; www.ilga.org). Provides political information, such as homosexuality laws of individual countries.

TRAVELERS WITH DISABILITIES

Traveling in Nicaragua, Costa Rica, and Panama with disabilities can be very difficult, especially for travelers on a budget. Sidewalks are narrow and in disrepair; streets are busy and disorganized. Transportation is generally not wheelchair accessible, so planning with a tour group, though expensive, may be the best (or only) option.

Travelers with disabilities should inform airlines and hotels of their disabilities when making reservations, as some time may be needed to prepare special accommodations. Call ahead to restaurants, museums, and other facilities to find out if they are wheelchair accessible. Guide-dog owners should inquire as to the quarantine policies of each country.

For those who wish to rent cars, some major car-rental agencies (e.g., Hertz) offer hand-controlled vehicles. The listings below are some organizations that can help plan your trip.

> **Mobility International USA (MIUSA)**, 132 E. Broadway, Ste. 343, Eugene, OR 97401, USA (☎+1-541-343-1284; www.miusa.org). Provides a variety of books and other publications containing information for travelers with disabilities.

> **Society for Accessible Travel and Hospitality (SATH)**, 347 5th Ave., Ste. 605, New York City, NY 10016, USA (☎+1-212-447-7284; www.sath.org). An advocacy group that publishes free online travel information. Annual membership US$49, students and seniors US$29.

MINORITY TRAVELERS

More likely than not, if you are a tourist in Nicaragua, Costa Rica, or Panama, you are the minority, especially if you are white. No matter what you may try to do to disguise it, locals can spot a "*gringo*" from miles away. This is not necessarily a bad thing; tourism is an important industry in many of the countries in the region and locals often go out of their way to cater to foreigners.

Travelers with darker skin should be aware that they are an uncommon sight in Nicaragua, Costa Rica, and Panama, and will attract curious stares and attention, but probably not any outright racism. *Chinita, negra,* and *india* are terms that will be thrown out, often inaccurately, at minority travelers. Understand that in Central America these are considered descriptive terms. These terms, along with other misperceptions, stem from unfamiliarity with people of different backgrounds. Reports of racism and discrimination from minority travelers are far from the norm.

Tourists are at an especially high risk in some of the region's more dangerous areas. Anti-Western, and especially anti-American sentiment may still be strong in some of the more war-torn countries, where the US funded and trained brutal military forces during the Cold War. Travelers need to always be aware of the fact that they not only stick out, but are a prime target for Central America's less scrupulous residents.

DIETARY CONCERNS

The cuisine in Nicaragua, Costa Rica, and Panama does not always cater to the traveler with specific eating concerns. **Vegetarian cuisine** is not hard to find in the more touristed, cosmopolitan cities, but in more remote areas, beans and rice may be the only option. Many eateries in Nicaragua, Costa Rica, and Panama do not consider pork or chicken to be "meat," so make sure to ask for *vegetariano* food, not just a meal *sin carne*. If you are concerned about the specific ingredients of dishes listed on the menu, be sure to ask very specific questions.

Travelers who keep **kosher** should contact synagogues in larger cities for information on kosher restaurants, which are a rare sight in Nicaragua, Costa Rica, and Panama. Your own synagogue or college Hillel should have access to lists of Jewish institutions across the nation. If you are strict in your observance, you may have to prepare your own food on the road. Travelers looking for **halal** restaurants may find www.zabihah.com a useful resource.

BEYOND TOURISM

A PHILOSOPHY FOR TRAVELERS

> ### HIGHLIGHTS OF BEYOND TOURISM IN CENTRAL AMERICA
>
> **REHABILITATE** macaws and parrots in Atenas, Costa Rica.
>
> **SPEND** the summer perfecting your Spanish in Panama (p. 38).
>
> **NAVIGATE** to 🖥 www.letsgo.com to find more information about Beyond Tourism opportunities in other parts of Central America.

As a tourist, you are always a foreigner. Sure, hostel-hopping and sightseeing can be great fun, but connecting with a foreign country through studying, volunteering, or working can extend your travels beyond tourist traps. We don't like to brag, but this is what's different about a *Let's Go* traveler. Instead of feeling like a stranger in a strange land, you can understand Central America like a local. Instead of being that tourist asking for directions, you can be the one who gives them (and correctly!). All the while, you get the satisfaction of leaving Central America in better shape than you found it. It's not wishful thinking—it's Beyond Tourism.

As a **volunteer** Central America, you can roll up your sleeves, cinch down your Captain Planet belt, and get your hands dirty doing anything from learning the language of the ancient Mayas to cleaning up after endangered jaguars. This chapter is chock-full of ideas to get involved, whether you're looking to pitch in for a day or run away from home for a whole new life in activism.

Ahh, to **study** abroad! It's a student's dream, and when you find yourself deciphering 2000 year old Mayan hieroglyphics, it actually makes you feel sorry for those poor tourists who don't get to do any homework while they're here. Not surprisingly, archaeology, zoology, Latin American studies, and urban development programs are common in the region.

Working abroad is one of the best ways to immerse yourself in a new culture, meet locals, and learn to appreciate a non-US currency. Yes, we know you're on vacation, but we're not talking about normal desk jobs. However, *Let's Go* strongly encourages those considering employment in developing countries to only pursue positions that do not involve competing for jobs with locals. Teaching English or helping to develop small businesses allow travelers to utilize their unique skills and aid development in Belize or Guatemala rather than hinder it.

VOLUNTEERING

Feel like saving the world this week? Volunteering can be a powerful and fulfilling experience, especially when combined with the thrill of traveling in a new place. Central America is full of chances to make a difference—whether in a school, a zoo, or a protected nature reserve. Social causes and ecological initiatives make up the bulk of volunteer opportunities in the region, so travelers interested in education, healthcare, and environmental issues are sure to find the perfect cause.

Most people who volunteer in Central America do so on a short-term basis at organizations that make use of drop-in or once-a-week volunteers. The best way to find opportunities that match your interests and schedule may be to go through intermediary organizations designed to connect volunteers with local NGO's and community service organizations. **Global Vision International** (☎+440 1727 250 250; www.gvi.gov.uk) offers wide-range of volunteer opportunities in Central America, from working with children in Guatemala to embarking on a wildlife expedition in Costa Rica. **The International Volunteer Programs Association** (☎646 505 8209; www.volunteerinternational.org) provides an up-to-date database of hundreds of volunteer and internship opportunities around the world. **The Institute for Field Research Expeditions** (☎+1 214-666-3169; www.ifrevolunteers. org) offers a variety of volunteer opportunities in Central America for a fee. As always, read up before heading out.

Those looking for longer, more intensive volunteer opportunities usually choose to go through a parent organization that takes care of logistical details and often provides a group environment and support system—for a fee. There are two main types of organizations—religious and secular—although there are rarely restrictions on participation for either. Websites like **www.volunteerabroad.com**, **www.servenet.org**, and **www.idealist.org** allow you to search for volunteer openings both in your country and abroad.

ENVIRONMENTAL AND WILDLIFE CONSERVATION

It isn't always easy being green, but volunteers in Central America help to make it a whole lot easier. In a region known for its natural beauty and biodiversity, environmental and wildlife conservation are essential to preserving the unique, indigenous flora and fauna. These organizations are committed to doing just that and are always in need of volunteers.

> **Center for Ecological Living and Learning (CELL).** An organization in partnership with Lesley University, CELL offers a 12-week sustainability project that takes place in 3 countries: Nicaragua, Honduras, and Costa Rica. Help develop renewable energy in Nicaragua, teach a Honduran community how to achieve environmental sustainability, and learn about the conservation of natural resources in a Costa Rican rainforest. College credit granted through Lesley University. US$12,500 (airfare not included).

> **Go Eco** (☎972 3647 4208; www.goeco.org). Save sea turtles in Costa Rica, befriend iguanas in Honduras. Go Eco offers wildlife conservation volunteer opportunities in Central America and around the world.

> **Involvement Volunteers,** P. O. Box 218 Port Melbourne, VIC 3207 Australia (☎+613 9646 9392; www.volunteering.org.au). Volunteer for 4-12 weeks for various conservation projects. Park maintenance, trail building, reforestation, helping in a tree nursery, and teaching about environmental conservation in addition to optional US$5 per hr. Spanish lessons. US$350 per month includes food and accommodation.

> **Rainforest and Reef,** P.O. Box 141543, Grand Rapids, Michigan 49514-1543, USA (☎ +1 877-255-3721; rainforestandreef.org). An organization dedicated to marine and rainforest ecology. Offers field courses in Belize, Costa Rica, Nicaragua, and Panama. Semester abroad experiences are offered at several field course sites.

EDUCATION AND RURAL DEVELOPMENT

What better way to make an impact on a country than to work directly with its people? Youth outreach initiatives, work in orphanages and domestic violence shelters, and non-profit organizations working to reduce poverty await do-gooders of all backgrounds in Central America.

Amigos de las Américas, 5618 Star Lane, Houston, Texas 77057 (☎+1 713-782-5290; www.amigoslink.org/Amigos). Programs in Honduras, Panama, and Nicaragua for high school and college-aged students. Teach young people about leadership and environmental health. Programs fill up fast, so apply early.

MEDICAL OUTREACH

Health-related concerns plague many areas of Central America, especially in impoverished rural areas and within indigenous communities. Volunteers in rural clinics and hospitals often provide the only medical care to which many people have access.

Global Crossroad, (☎+1-866-387-7816; www.globalcrossroad.com). Volunteer programs around the world, including medical projects in Guatemala, Costa Rica, and Honduras. Participants assist at a clinic and hospital and engage in health-related community education. Healthcare background and Spanish skills necessary. Application fee of US$350, prices vary depending on length of stay but room and board are included with fee.

STUDYING

 VISA INFORMATION. Country-specific visa information is available in the introduction chapters of Costa Rica (p. 41), Nicaragua (p. 164), and Panama (p. 227).

It's completely natural to want to play hookey on the first day of school when it's raining and first period Trigonometry is meeting in the old cafeteria, but when your campus is Antigua, Guatemala and your meal plan revolves around warm, hand-rolled burritos and a refreshing midday mojito, what could be better than the student life?

A growing number of students report that studying abroad is the highlight of their learning careers. If you've never studied abroad, you don't know what you're missing—and, if you have studied abroad, you know not to miss it.

Study-abroad programs range from basic language and culture courses to university-level classes, often for college credit (sweet, right?). In order to choose a program that best fits your needs, research as much as you can before making your decision—determine costs and duration as well as what kinds of students participate in the program and what sorts of accommodations are provided. Don't forget to read up on the city or town where the program takes place too—rural Central American villages aren't exactly known for the wild all-night keggers that some students might be used to at home.

In programs that have large groups of students who speak English, there is a trade-off. You may feel more comfortable in the community, but you will not have the same opportunity to practice a foreign language or to befriend other international students. For accommodations, dorm life provides a better opportunity to mingle with fellow students, but there is less of a chance to experience the local scene. If you live with a family, you could potentially build lifelong friendships with natives and experience day-to-day life in more depth, but you might also get stuck sharing a room with their pet iguana. Conditions can vary greatly from family to family.

UNIVERSITIES

Most university-level study-abroad programs are conducted in Spanish, although many programs offer classes in English as well as lower-level language courses. Savvy linguists may find it cheaper to enroll directly in a university abroad, although getting college credit may be more difficult. You can search **www.studyabroad.com** for various semester-abroad programs that meet your criteria, including your desired location and focus of study. If you're a college student, your friendly neighborhood study-abroad office is often the best place to start. For university programs in Central America, check individual curriculum and course offerings before paying application fees or a deposit.

AMERICAN PROGRAMS

AFS International Programs, 71 West 23rd St., 17th fl., New York, NY 10010-4102, USA (☎+1 800-237-4636 or 212-807-8668; www.afs.org). Runs study abroad and community service programs for high school and college students as well as educators in countries around the world, including Guatemala, Honduras, Panama, and Costa Rica. Volunteers live with host families and programs last from several months to one year. Cost varies based on the program type and duration.

Center for Global Education at Augsburg College, 2211 Riverside Avenue, Minneapolis, MN 55454 USA (☎+1 800-299-8889 or 612-330-1159; www.augsburg.edu/global). Offers a semester long program for college students called Sustainable Development and Social Change in Central America. Participants spend five weeks in Guatemala, four in El Salvador, and six in Nicaragua for the equivalent of 4 courses or 16 credits. Basic Spanish knowledge required. Costs US$16,375 and includes tuition, room and board, medical/emergency insurance, travel within Central America, and in-country costs.

CENTRAL AMERICAN PROGRAMS

No matter what your interests are, you're likely to find an exciting study abroad opportunity in Central America. There are two universities within Belizean borders, both of which are eager to include visiting students for study abroad semesters or summers. The capital cities of both Honduras and Nicaragua—Tegucigalpa and Managua, respectively—are home to several universities, some of which offer study abroad and exchange programs. Costa Rica has a wide variety of study abroad opportunities, whether you'd prefer to live in a bustling metropolis, on a deserted beach, or in a tropical rainforest. Some programs specialize in Spanish and academics, while others focus more heavily on field research. The Universidad Tecnológica de Panamá is just one of many schools in Panama that offer study abroad opportunities.

LANGUAGE SCHOOLS

Old lady making snarky comments to you in the plaza? Imprudent cashier at the mercado? Cute moped girl that is totally into you? To communicate is to be human, and without the local language in your tool belt, you're up a creek without a *pala*. Fear not! Language school is here to help—and particular regions of Central America are chock full of them.

While language school courses rarely count for college credit, they do offer a unique way to get acquainted with Guatemalan culture and language. Schools can be independently run or university affiliated, local or international, youth-oriented or full of old people—the opportunities are endless. Many language schools are part of a package deal including meals and accommodation, often a homestay with a local family, about 5 hours of instruction five or six days per week, and group activities or community service opportunities. From the bustling streets of Guatemala City to the quietest highland village, it seems that Spanish (and an occasional Mayan dialect!) is being taught in every setting imaginable. Local language schools can be found under Beyond Tourism in the Practical Information sections of most cities and towns throughout the book. US embassy websites also offers an extensive list of Spanish language schools; the site for Guatemela, for instance, is http://guatemala.usembassy.gov. Below are a couple places to begin your search; sites may take a commission or have booking fees:

A2Z Languages, 3219 East Camelback Road 806, Phoenix, AZ 85018, USA (☎+1-800-496-4596; www.a2zlanguages.com). Helps students find suitable language immersion programs in several countries, including Costa Rica and Guatemala.

AmeriSpan Study Abroad, 1334 Walnut St, 6th Floor, Philadelphia, PA 19107, USA (☎+1 215-751-1100; www.amerispan.com). Offers language immersion programs in Costa Rica, Honduras, Nicaragua, Guatemala, and Panama.

Language Immersion Institute, State University of New York at New Paltz, 1 Hawk Dr., New Paltz, NY 12561, USA (☎+1 845-257-3500; www.newpaltz.edu/lii). Short, intensive summer language courses and some overseas courses in Spanish. Program fees are around US$1000 for a 2-week course, not including accommodations.

Languages Abroad, (☎+1 800-219-9924; www.languagesabroad.com). Offers 1- to 12-week standard and intensive language programs for all levels in Costa Rica, Guatemala, Honduras, and Panama.

http://www.learn-spanish.com
E-mail: crlang@crlang.co.cr

In the USA, Call Toll Free
1-866-230-6361
In Costa Rica - 2280-1739

- Convenient Location in San Jose - San Pedro Area
- Costa Rican Owned and Operated
- Individual Instruction in Small Groups (3-6)
- Instructors have University Degrees in Spanish
- Homestays - A Unique Experience Living with a Tico Family
- Open and Flexible Schedule - Start Anytime
- 24 Hour Airport Transportation
- Excursions, Tour Discounts, Free Coffee, Refreshments, and Internet Access
- LOW RATES - ALL INCLUSIVE: Includes Afternoon Latin Dance, Costa Rican Cooking, Latin Music Classes, Conversation Hour, and Cultural Activities.

P.O. Box 1966-2050
San Jose, Costa Rica
Central America

Spanish and More

CRLA

Costa Rican Language Academy

WORKING

Some travelers want **long-term** jobs that enable them to get to know another part of the world while immersing themselves in another culture and developing international connections. Most of these jobs are confined to the tourist industry or involve teaching English. Others seek **short-term** employment to finance their travel. However, *Let's Go* does not recommend competing for employment in developing countries where jobs for locals may already be scarce. Instead, English speakers and those with a particular area of expertise (education, healthcare, small business development) can use their unique skills to positively impact Belize or Guatemala through teaching or some other under-served field. **Transitions Abroad** (www.transitionsabroad.com) offers updated online listings for work over any time period.

Note: working abroad often requires a special work visa.

MORE VISA INFORMATION. Due to high unemployment rates in many Central American countries, natives are wary of allowing foreign workers to come in and contribute to those discouraging statistics. Still, finding work as a foreigner is not impossible. Work permit requirements vary widely in different countries. In Guatemala, the company intending to hire you must receive permission from immigration authorities. In order to obtain a job in Nicaragua, you have to seek extended residency; to do so, you must be able to present your birth certificate and police record, among other official documents. Websites offer conflicting information about working in Central American countries, and so your best option is to contact a country's embassy in Washington, DC for employment details.

LONG-TERM WORK

If you're planning on spending a substantial amount of time (more than 3 months) working in Central America, search for a job well in advance. International placement agencies are often the easiest way to find employment abroad, especially for those interested in teaching. Although they are often only available to college students, **internships** are a good way to ease into working abroad. Many students say the interning experience is well worth it, despite low pay (if you're lucky enough to get paid at all). Be wary of advertisements for companies offering to get you a job abroad for a fee—oftentimes, these same listings are available online or in newspapers.

TEACHING ENGLISH

Suffice it to say that teaching jobs abroad pay more in personal satisfaction and emotional fulfillment than in actual cash. Nevertheless, even volunteer teachers often receive some sort of a daily stipend to help with living expenses. Salaries may be low for English teachers, but, considering the low cost of living in Central America, your Quetzals could go a long way. Most legitimate schools will only hire long-term teachers with a bachelor's degree or equivalent, although college undergraduates can sometimes get special summer positions teaching or tutoring. Many schools require teachers to have a **Teaching English as a Foreign Language (TEFL)** certificate. You may still be able to find a teaching job without one, but certified teachers often find higher-paying jobs.

The Spanish-impaired don't have to give up their dream of teaching, either. Private schools usually hire native English speakers for English-immersion classrooms where no Spanish is spoken. (Teachers in public schools will more likely work in both English and Spanish.) Placement agencies or university fellowship programs are the best resources for finding teaching jobs. The alternatives are to contact schools directly or try your luck once you arrive. In the latter case, the best time to look is several weeks before the start of the school year.

COSTA RICA

The Spanish explorers who first arrived at this "rich coast" in 1502 named the region for the decorative gold bands worn by its native inhabitants and for the fortunes they hoped to attain there. Despite this optimistic view, later explorers found no gold—or material riches of any sort—anywhere along the coast. Indeed, the country's only riches seemed to be its endless armies of mosquitoes and its unforgiving jungles, neither of which colonial settlers found in short supply. These days, however, most visitors to Costa Rica would probably attest that its initial name was not such a misnomer after all. Its well-oiled tourist industry is only too happy to recount the country's impressive statistics: though it covers only 0.03% of the world's territory, Costa Rica is home to 6% of its plant and animal species. From camouflaged vine snakes to Jesucristo lizards that "walk on water" in fantastic 50 yd. dashes, the wildlife here is truly entertaining. Many Costa Rican creatures come off as performers, and there is something decidedly exhibitionist about their homeland as well. The terrain seems to include all possible landforms: volcanoes, jungles, beaches, coral reefs, hidden caves, and deserted islands all lie within a day's (or even an hour's) travel of one another.

Sometimes it feels like the only thing this country can't offer is a corner that travelers haven't already found and conquered—leaving fusion bistros and high-tech canopy tours in their wake. Fortunately, rustic spots never lie too far away, and Costa Rica's national character has remained surprisingly visible beneath the trappings of its tourist infrastructure. Though you'll find plenty of gringos lounging on the beaches of the Pacific, you'll find vacationing *tico* families enjoying them as well. Their *tico* friendliness only adds to the charm of the country.

ESSENTIALS

PASSPORTS, VISAS, AND CUSTOMS.

Passport. Required of all visitors. Must be valid for a full 6 months after arrival.

Visa (p. 6). Not required of citizens from the US, UK, EU, Canada, Australia, NZ and many other countries. Valid for 90 days.

Onward Ticket. Required of all visitors.

Work Permit. Required for all foreigners planning to work in Costa Rica for more than a year.

Required Vaccinations. Travelers who have visited nations with endemic yellow fever need proof of vaccination.

Driving Permit. International Driving Permit or valid American or Canadian driver's license and passport required.

Departure Tax. US$26.

EMBASSIES AND CONSULATES

For a list of embassies in Costa Rica, see the **Practical Information** section for San José (p. 62). The following are Costa Rican embassies and consulates abroad.

COSTA RICA

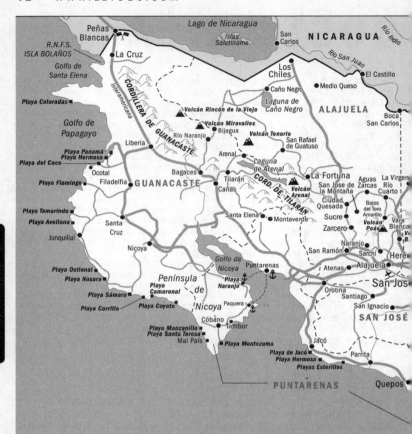

Costa Rica

| 0 | 30 kilometers |
| 0 | 30 miles |

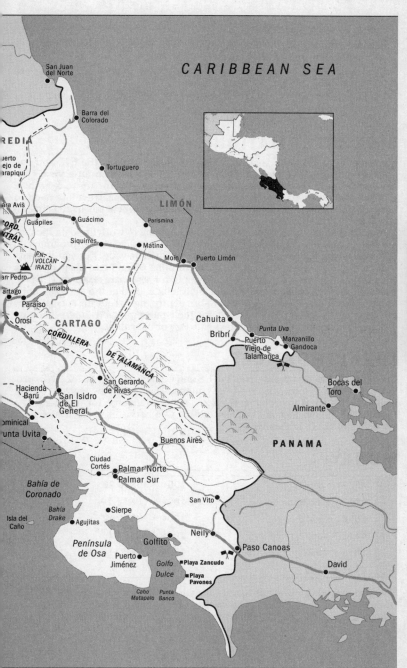

CARIBBEAN SEA

San Juan
del Norte

Barra del
Colorado

REDIA

uerto
ejo de
arapiquí

ara Avís

Tortuguero

LIMÓN

RO·
TRAL

Guápiles

Guácimo

Parismina

Siquirres

Matina

P.N.·
VOLCÁN·
IRAZÚ

Moín

Puerto Limón

an Pedro

artago

Turrialba

Paraíso

Cahuita

Orosi

CARTAGO

Punta Uva

Bribrí

CORDILLERA

Puerto
Viejo de
Talamanca

Manzanillo
Gandoca

DE TALAMANCA

Bocas del
Toro

Hacienda
Barú

San Gerardo
de Rivas

Almirante

San Isidro
de El
General

ominical

unta Uvita

Buenos Aires

PANAMA

Ciudad
Cortés

Palmar Norte

Palmar Sur

Bahía de
Coronado

San Vito

Bahía
Drake

Sierpe

Isla del
Caño

Agujitas

Neily

Península
de Osa

Golfito

Paso Canoas

David

Puerto
Jiménez

Golfo
Dulce

Playa Zancudo

Playa
Pavones

Cabo
Matapalo

Punta
Banco

Australia: Consulate, De la Sala House, Piso 11, 30 Clarence Street, New South Wales, 2000 (☎+61 29261 1177).

Canada: Embassy, 325 Dalhousie Street, Suite 407, Ottawa, Ontario, K1N 7G2 (☎+1 613-562-2855). Open M-F 9am-5pm.

UK: Embassy, Flat 1, 14 Lancaster Gate London W2 3LH (☎+44 020 7706 8844). Open M-F 10am-3pm.

US: Embassy, 2114 "S" Street NW, Washington, DC 20008 (☎+1 202-234-2945 or 2946). Open M-F 10am-6pm.

VISA INFORMATION

Citizens of the US, UK, Australia, New Zealand, Canada, the EU, and Ireland are permitted to stay in Costa Rica for 90 days without a visa. Citizens of other select nations can stay without a visa for up to a month. Everyone else must apply for a visa. For a **visa extension,** travelers need to contact the **Office of Temporary Permits** in the **Department of Immigration** in San José (☎+506 2299 8026; www.migracion.go.cr).

A **work permit** is required for all foreigners planning to work in Costa Rica for more than one year. Most short-term study, work, and volunteer programs do not require special visas. Standard tourist visas will be valid. Foreign students registered in recognized educational institutions planning to **study** in Costa Rica for more than six months should apply for **temporary residence** (US$100 deposit required, waived under special circumstances) at the embassy upon entering the country. Long-term study-abroad programs requiring special entry documentation often process forms for their participants. Double-check on entrance requirements at the nearest embassy or consulate.

TOURIST OFFICES

The **Costa Rica Tourism Board** (from the US and Canada ☎1-866-26782 7422) provides a wealth of information on the country. The spiffy new website (www.visitcostarica.com) is probably the most helpful resource for travelers. The **tourist office,** in San José at Plaza de Cultura, C. 5 between Av. Central & Av. 2 (☎+506 223 1733), is also helpful.

MONEY

AUS$1 = ₡462	100₡ = AUS$0.22
CDN$1 = ₡529	100₡ = CDN$0.19
EUR€1 = ₡815	100₡ = EUR€0.12
NZ$1 = ₡369	100₡ = NZ$0.27
UK£1 = ₡933	100₡ = UK£0.11
US$1 = ₡576	100₡ = US$0.17

The currency chart above is based on August 2009 exchange rates. The unit of currency in Costa Rica is the **colón,** which is divided into 100 *céntimos,* though these coins are becoming increasingly less useful as Costa Rican currency depreciates on the global market. Paper notes circulate in the following amounts: 50, 100, 500, 1000, 2000, 5000, and 10,000. You might hear them referred to as *rojo* (1000) or *tucán* (5000). Travelers should take care to retain credit card receipts and check accounts regularly. Many of Costa Rica's more touristed destinations (large nature reserves, the Nicoya Peninsula, much of the Central Valley) are full of establishments that prefer US dollars

Costa Rica's streets (particularly in San José) are full of money vendors who will pass off counterfeit US dollars and *colones*. Visitors should also be sensitive to the possibility of credit card fraud, which is widespread.

Costa Rica levies a 13% **sales tax** on all purchases. In addition, restaurants add a 10% **service charge** on all bills. Usually these charges are included in the prices posted, but ask beforehand to be sure. Checks in Costa Rican restaurants often include two price columns: one with tax-inclusive prices and one without.

COSTS

Trip cost will vary considerably, depending on where you go, how you travel, and where you stay. The rainy season (May-Nov.) typically brings the best deals. Transportation in remote areas can be expensive. The most significant expenses will probably be your round-trip (return) airfare to Costa Rica. To give you a general idea, a bare-bones day in Costa Rica (camping or sleeping in hostels, buying food at supermarkets) costs about US$15 (¢6500); a slightly more comfortable day (sleeping in hostels or guest houses and the occasional budget hotel, eating one meal per day at a restaurant, going out at night) would cost US$30 (¢13,000). For a luxurious day, the sky's the limit. Don't forget to factor in emergency reserve funds (at least US$200) when planning out how much money you'll need.

PRICE DIVERSITY

We list establishments in order of value from best to worst, honoring our favorites with the *Let's Go* thumbs-up (⚄). Because the cheapest *price* is not always the best *value*, we have incorporated a system of price ranges based on a rough expectation of what you will spend. For **accommodations,** we base our ranges on the cheapest price for which a single traveler can stay for one night. For **restaurants,** we estimate the average amount one traveler will spend in one sitting. The table below tells you what you'll typically find in Costa Rica at the corresponding price range, but keep in mind that no system can accommodate the quirks of individual establishments.

ACCOMMODATIONS	RANGE	WHAT YOU'RE LIKELY TO FIND
❶	Under ¢7500 (US$1-13)	Campgrounds, dorm rooms, and very rustic *cabinas*. Expect bunk beds and a communal bath, but you might get lucky with private baths and singles. You may have to bring your own or rent towels and sheets.
❷	¢7600-14,500 (US$14-25)	Upscale hostels, small hotels, and *cabinas*. You may have a private bathroom with cold or warm water, or a sink in your room and a communal shower in the hall. Most include fans and TVs.
❸	¢14,600-29,000 (US$26-50)	A small room with a private hot-water bath or a *cabina* with a full kitchen. Should have decent amenities, such as phone, A/C, and TV. Breakfast may be included in the price of the room.
❹	¢29,100-46,400 (US$51-80)	Similar to a ❸, with more amenities or a more convenient location.

COSTA RICA

ACCOMMODATIONS	RANGE	WHAT YOU'RE LIKELY TO FIND
❺	Over ¢46,500 (Over US$80)	Large hotels, lodges, or upscale chains, usually found in heavily touristed areas. If it's a ❺ and it doesn't have the perks you want, you've paid too much.

FOOD	RANGE	WHAT YOU'RE LIKELY TO FIND
❶	¢Under 2900 (US$1-5)	Mostly *sodas* serving inexpensive *comida típica*, street food, or fast-food, but also university cafeterias and bakeries. May be only takeout, though limited seating is often available.
❷	¢2900-5800 (US$6-10)	Some high end *sodas*, sandwiches, pizza, appetizers at a bar, or low-priced entrees. Most ethnic eateries are a ❷. Either takeout or a sit-down meal, but only slightly more fashionable decor.
❸	¢5900-10,400 (US$11-18)	Mid-priced entrees, seafood, and exotic pasta dishes. A bit more expensive, but chances are you're paying for a change from *comida típica*. More upscale ethnic eateries. Since you'll have the luxury of a waiter, tip will set you back a little extra.
❹	¢11,000-14,500 (US$19-25)	A somewhat fancy restaurant. Entrees may be heartier or more elaborate, but you're really paying for decor and ambience. Few restaurants in this range have a dress code, but some may look down on t-shirts and sandals. These places tend to be in more-touristed areas.
❺	Over ¢14,500 (Over US$25)	Your meal might cost more than your room, but there's a reason—it's something fabulous, famous, or both. Expect delicious food with great service and a spectacular view. Otherwise, you're paying for nothing more than hype. Don't order a PB&J!

TRANSPORTATION

Domestic air travel is more expensive but also more convenient than traveling by bus. Smaller, less regulated airlines do offer domestic flights, but it is recommended that you use the two larger airlines: **Sansa** (from the US ☎877-767-2672, in Costa Rica 506-2290-4100; www.flysansa.com) and the pricier but more reliable **NatureAir** (toll-free ☎1-800-235-9272; www.natureair.com), have flights connecting San José with destinations throughout Costa Rica (p. 57).

The **bus** system in Costa Rica is thorough, cheap, and reliable. From San José, you can travel almost anywhere in the country for under US$6. However, it's not always immediately clear where the buses arrive, when they leave, or how much they cost. Costa Rica's bus system is labyrinthine; every destination is served by a different company, and each company is located in a different part of town. You can find the most accurate bus information, including detailed schedules and maps, at the **Instituto Costarricense de Turismo** (**ICT**; ☎+506 223 1733, from the US 800-343-6332). You can find ICT representatives at the base of the stairs just before you exit the airport in San José (p. 57).

Boats are a fairly common mode of transportation along the Caribbean Lowlands, ranging from *lanchas* (water taxis) to larger ferries. These modes of transportation are just as reliable and much more quaint than a bus ride. On the other hand, boats are almost always open to the elements, with little shelter from bad weather. Public boat transport is available daily out of Limón, but it might be easier to stick to pre-arranged packages set up by a hotel or by tour operators.

For information on **driving**, see **Essentials,** p. 5.

BORDER CROSSINGS

Travelers can cross into Costa Rica by land or sea. Remember to carry enough money to pay any entrance or exit fees.

NICARAGUA. There is one land crossing at **Peñas Blancas/Sapoá,** 75km north of Liberia and near Rivas, Nicaragua. There is a more pleasant **boat crossing** at **Los Chiles** that goes to San Carlos, Nicaragua.

PANAMA. There are three land crossings. **Paso Canoas** (p. 302) is 18km southeast of Ciudad Neily, near David, Panama; it is sometimes blocked by protesting banana workers. **Sixaola/Guabito** (p. 313) is on the Caribbean coast 1½hr. from Puerto Viejo de Talamanca, near Changuinola, Panama. A third crossing at **Río Sereno,** east of San Vito, is rarely used.

SAFETY

LOCAL LAWS AND POLICE. Costa Rica is a democratic republic and maintains a strong emphasis on human rights and democracy. Costa Rican law requires that all foreigners carry their passports with them at all times and be able to demonstrate proof of legal entry. The country's police force is domestic; there is no military. The **Practical Information** section for each town lists the location and number of the local police station. In case of an emergency, dial ☎**911.**

NATURAL DISASTERS. The rainy season in Costa Rica occurs between May and November, contributing to an average rainfall of 250cm per year. There are often **floods** during this time, especially near the Caribbean coast and areas surrounding major rivers. For more information on volcanoes and earthquakes, see **Essentials, p. 5**.

HEALTH

Malaria is especially common in the Alajuela, Limón, Guanacaste, and Heredia provinces. Travelers going to these places should seek preventive treatment.

THE OUTDOORS

Costa Rica's extensive national park system provides good hiking and camping opportunities. If camping, be sure to do your research ahead of time as some parks do not offer camping facilities. There are restrictions on how many people can be in a given park at the same time. Camping outside of official camping areas is usually not permitted. The **Ministerio del Ambiente y Energía** (Ministry of Atmosphere and Energy), commonly known as **MINAE,** is a government organization devoted to encouraging sustainable development in Costa Rica. MINAE has a strong presence in many of the natural sights of Costa Rica. In some cases it is required that you have a guide; inquire at the local MINAE office.

The *parques nacionales* are the foundation of the ecotourism industry in Costa Rica. There are twenty national parks spread across the country that draw visitors from all over the world. While attracting large crowds every year, the national park system still manages to preserve most parks from significant human impact. Entrance fees vary by park, but are generally US$5-10. Not all parks are easily accessible by foot.

LIFE AND TIMES

HISTORY

BEFORE COLUMBUS

Costa Rica's development actually follows a dynamic timeline that both mirrors and defies the typical story of Central America. Spanish explorers arrived in Costa Rica at the dawn of the 16th century and found upwards of 25,000 people from five distinct native groups. The history of the country predates their arrival by several hundred years, with the oldest archeological site in Costa Rica dating back to 1000 BC. The area that is now Costa Rica played an important historical role as a meeting place for various pre-Columbian civilizations, such as the Mesoamericans to the north and the Andeans to the South. The Spanish conquest, while often characterized as a peaceful settlement, was in fact especially destructive to the native cultures and peoples. Following Columbus' arrival in Costa Rica in 1502, new settlements and diseases reduced the native population to 120,000 by 1521, to 10,000 by 1611, and to only 500 by 1675. Today, only 1% of Costa Rica's population is descended from its original indigenous inhabitants.

THE COLONIAL PERIOD

Costa Rica was not settled until explorer Gil Gonzalez Davila set off from Panama to settle the region in 1522. The golden bands the natives wore in their ears and noses inspired him to name the region Costa Rica, or the "Rich Coast." The early settlement years were tumultuous, marked by ongoing conflict between European settlers and native residents as well as recurring attacks from British pirates along both coasts. In 1564, Juan Vásquez de Coronado finally managed to establish himself in the Central Valley and proclaimed the city of Cartago as his capital. Due to its status as a remote outpost within the Spanish colonial kingdom, Costa Rica had the opportunity to develop under weaker colonial influence than that of many of its neighbors.

LIBERATION AND "EL GRANO DE ORO"

Although Central America officially gained independence from Spain on September 15, 1821, Costa Ricans didn't hear about it until a month later, when the news arrived by mule from Mexico. Predictably, liberation led to a power struggle. While Costa Rica's four largest cities (San José, Cartago, Heredia, and Alajuela) vied to govern the country from within its borders, nearby nations (Guatemala, Mexico, and Nicaragua) vied to govern it from beyond them. Costa Rica eventually became a member of the United Provinces of Central America and was one of the first to become its own country when the collective dissolved in 1838.

Much of Costa Rica's socio-economic development during the 19th century was defined by the export of coffee and bananas, two fruits that, surprisingly, were not native to the country. For 70 years, coffee was the country's only major export, obstructing the growth of even basic foods. It remained dominant until the 1870s, when Minor Keith, an American engineer building a railroad connecting San José and Puerto Limón, began to plant banana trees along the sides of the train tracks.

INVASION AND DICTATORSHIP

The only serious external threat to Costa Rican national security during the late 19th century came from William Walker, a rogue gold miner from Tennessee who wanted to annex the country as a slave-holding American state. The Costa Rican people had been asked by an enemy of Walker's, Cornelius Vanderbilt, to stop Walker's mission. The Costa Rican army invaded Guanacaste in 1856. Fueled by a newly forged sense of territorial pride, the Costa Rican army drove Walker's forces back to Rivas, Nicaragua, where a drummer boy and precocious military strategist named Juan Santamaría set fire to Walker's troops' impromptu barracks, ending their deluded campaign and launching Santamaría into the sparsely populated ranks of Costa Rican national heroes. Costa Ricans now celebrate the day Juan Santamaría sacrificed his life to burn the Mesón de Guerra and secure national freedom on April 11.

General Tomás Guardia, one of Costa Rica's only dictators, seized power soon after in 1870 in order to end the rule of the coffee barons. During Guardia's 12 years in power, his ambitious, iron-fisted policies modernized the country in important ways, though they cost Costa Ricans their civil liberties and accrued a sizable deficit. After his dictatorship, the country saw a peaceful transition back to democracy. In 1889, Costa Rica conducted the first legitimate large-scale elections in Central American history, though women and African descendants were not allowed to vote.

DOMESTIC REFORM AND CIVIL WAR

Costa Rica underwent a rather ungraceful transition into the 20th century. These years were marked by border disputes with Panama and another dangerous flirtation with autocracy. In the 1914 elections, the people of Costa Rica were unable to give a majority vote to any candidate. As a result, congress chose Alfredo González as a compromise, but he was soon overthrown by the reactionary General Federico Tinoco. The dictatorship was unpopular and brief, however, and the decades to follow were smooth and prosperous. A powerful, probably highly caffeinated coffee elite continued to ensure that income taxes were low (as they still are today), though social discontent grew among laborers and radicals. Moderate president Rafael Ángel Calderón Guardia implemented important labor reforms, including health care and minimum wage for laborers, but he lost popular support soon after World War II. In 1944, he annulled the results of the election and installed a puppet president instead.

A disaffected middle class rose up against this puppet regime during the War of National Liberation in 1948 under the leadership of José Figueres Ferrer. Widely known as "Don Pepe," Figueres appealed to a popular distrust of communism's foreign ideology and called for the renewal of Costa Rican democracy. Backed by US CIA forces looking to stop communism, Figueres defeated the government's machete-clad forces in six weeks before inaugurating the Founding Junta of the Second Republic and instituting a wide range of political reforms. In 1949, he banned the Communist party and wrote a new constitution that gave women and African descendents the right to vote. It abolished the

Costa Rican military, making Costa Rica the first country ever to operate under a democratic system without an army.

GLOBAL ROLES AND NOBEL LAURELS

Since dissolving its army in 1949, Costa Rica has enjoyed peace, political stability, and a relatively high degree of economic comfort, earning the nickname "Switzerland of the Americas." It has not, however, been unaffected by civil strife in nearby nations. Thousands of refugees (some Salvadorean, most Nicaraguan) have crossed the border each year since the late 1970s, causing unemployment and tensions to rise.

The 1980s were a tough period for Costa Rica. In addition to the internal crises of currency devaluation and soaring welfare and oil costs, the country faced plummeting prices in the coffee, sugar, and banana markets, as well as a nearby civil war in Nicaragua. In 1987, however, former president Oscar Arias earned the Nobel Peace Prize when he achieved a consensus among Central America leaders with the Plan de Paz Arias, negotiated a cease-fire agreement, and laid the groundwork for a unified Central American Parliament. In 1988, he increased his commitment to democracy by creating the Arias Foundation for Peace and Human Progress.

TODAY

Today, Costa Rica is one of the most prosperous countries in Latin America. Its well-educated population maintains a strong democratic spirit and displays an admirable level of collective sensitivity to issues surrounding ecological conservation, democratic development, and commercial vitality. In 2006, following the passage of a constitutional amendment that allowed for the re-election of presidents, former president and Nobel Laureate Oscar Arias was re-elected as president in one of the closest elections in Costa Rican history. Economically, the country has experienced relatively stable growth and a slow reduction in inflation. Though unemployment, poverty, and the management of an emerging welfare state are still pressing issues, Costa Rica has consistently managed to sustain generally positive economic trends.

ECONOMY

Costa Rica has a strong agricultural history, and its economy has traditionally been based on the export of bananas and coffee. Today, though agriculture continues to be important to the economy, with the addition of pineapples to the export market, the economy has been greatly diversified. After economic trouble in the 1980s, the economy has begun to turn around, and Costa Rican wealth is fairly well distributed among the different social classes.

In order to protect Costa Rica's environment and its ecotourism industry, the government has banned all open-pit mining. In 2004, Costa Rica became an observer in the Asia-Pacific Economic Cooperation Forum and began to widely increase its trading with Southeast Asia.

Today, Costa Rica's export-oriented economy relies primarily on tourism, and the industry is growing. Statistics have recorded a significant increase in tourism from year to year, making it even more important. Governmental development strategies for Costa Rica have been geared increasingly toward environmental and social sustainability, as tourists mainly come to Costa Rica for two reasons: its wilderness and its reputation for convenience and safety.

ECOTOURISM

The official slogan of Costa Rica's tourist industry—"Costa Rica: No Artificial Ingredients"—reveals just how intentional the country has been about furthering its reputation as a natural and eco-friendly tourist environment. Ecotourism has made Costa Rica famous worldwide. It remains a huge draw for foreign tourists, promoting sustainable, responsible travel to natural sites, as well as encouraging low-impact cultural and environmental exploration that will generate income for farther conservation. In fact, Costa Rica has been awarded and honored by the Sustainable Tourism Certification program for its sustainable approach to tourism.

Some of the unique elements of Costa Rica's ecotourism industry are its opportunities for turtle-watching. Visitors come from all over the world to watch turtles come ashore to lay their eggs at night on various Pacific and Caribbean beaches. Some of the most important nesting sites for turtles in the western hemisphere are located in Tortuguero (p. 156) and Parismina, a smaller, less-touristed town 50km south, home to a turtle conservation organization that draws hundreds of volunteers each year to protect the eggs from poachers.

Though proponents of the industry maintain that it benefits the environment and travelers alike, Costa Rican ecotourism remains a delicate endeavor. While there has been a push to move tourism toward luxury ecotourism in order to attract wealthier travelers seeking comfortable wilderness adventures, conservation groups are concerned that larger facilities will put an unreasonably heavy burden on the nation's ecosystems.

COSTA RICA AND NICARAGUA

Two issues continue to strain Costa Rica-Nicaragua relations: conflicts over use of the San Juan River and illegal immigration from Nicaragua. Dating back to 1858, the **Cañas-Juarez Treaty** holds that the San Juan River constitutes the border between Costa Rica and Nicaragua but belongs to Nicaragua, though Costa Rica was granted perpetual free commercial access to its waters. Negotiations continue as both countries try to reach a consensus about what constitutes "commercial use." The borders of both countries are paying the price for this tension, as the political conflict impedes investment and development.

The issue of migration between these two countries also remains an urgent one. Because Costa Rica is prosperous and economically stable, it has drawn massive numbers of illegal immigrants from Nicaragua. Many come to work, and a significant portion of the Costa Rican population is made up of Nicaraguans. Both the Costa Rican and the Nicaraguan governments have made attempts to resolve the disputes, but their isolation and political pride have made resolution elusive. In the midst of this tension, *ticos* tend to look down upon their Nicaraguan neighbors, commonly known as *nicas*. Immigrant *nicas* are accused of stealing jobs, bringing violent crime, and using up many of the country's social resources.

PEOPLE

DEMOGRAPHICS

Out of nearly 4.3 million inhabitants, indigenous people compose less than 1% of the population, while individuals of African descent make up only 3% and are concentrated on the Caribbean coast. A staggering 94% of the population is of European and *mestizo* descent, making Costa Rica one of the most racially homogeneous countries in Latin America.

Most of the eight groups of *indígenas* in Costa Rica who wish to protect their traditional lifestyles and languages do so on one of the 22 reserves scattered throughout the country. Reserve boundaries are often disrespected, however, and indigenous lands are constantly threatened. Other ethnic groups, including Germans, Americans, Italians, Britons, Chinese, and other Latin Americans, have immigrated to Costa Rica over the past 150 years and have established communities. The town of Monteverde, for example, was founded by Quakers and is now home to a community that supports itself with cheese production.

LANGUAGE

Spanish is the official language, though Costa Ricans speak with a characteristic *tico* twist in accent and usage. Rare in other regions of the country, English is common along the Caribbean coast, where a Caribbean Creole dialect is used. Indigenous groups maintain their traditional languages.

Costa Rica has more country-specific vocabulary than many larger nations, generally known as *tiquismo*, which is characterized by the addition of the diminutive "-ito" or "-ico" to words in order to make them more friendly. They have ventured into the realms of the phonetically implausible by turning the word *chiquito* (small) into *chiquitico*, and they use this ending so often that *"ticos"* has come to refer to Costa Ricans in general. The country's most popular phrase, *pura vida* (literally "pure life"), is extremely versatile and may be used to mean "hello," "goodbye," "awesome," or "good luck." While the phrase is not used too often in major cities, it is kept alive by rural communities, enthusiastic tourists, and a thriving souvenir industry. Some other common words include: *tuanis*, the spanglish pronunciation of the English phrase "too nice"; *mae* (dude); and *rico/a*, an adjective often used to describe excellent food.

RELIGION

Costa Rica is a politically secular country with weak links between church and state. Though the constitution provides for religious freedom, **Roman Catholicism** is the official religion, practiced by nearly 77% of the population. As such, only Catholic marriages receive state recognition—all others must have a civil ceremony. Semana Santa (Holy Week), a national holiday culminating on Easter Sunday, is a balance of piety and partying. Protestantism has a presence, though it has yet to gain the ubiquity it has in other Central American countries. There are small numbers of Jehovah's Witnesses, Jews, Mennonites, Quakers, and people of other denominations throughout the country.

CULTURE

FOOD AND DRINK

If it doesn't have **rice and beans,** it isn't **tico.** Rice and black beans infiltrate almost every meal. In one day, it's possible to have them for breakfast as **gallo pinto** (literally, "spotted rooster"; rice and beans fried with spices and served with meat or eggs), then take a **casado** for lunch and have a hearty bowl of black bean soup for dinner. "Casado" literally means "married," and it refers to the hearty combination plates (usually rice and beans with meat, plantains, cabbage, and tomato). *Tamales*, *empanadas*, and *tortas* are also typical dishes.

Comida típica (native dishes) in Costa Rica are usually mild and can even be bland. As if to answer this need for flavor, *lizano salsa*, a slightly sweet and spicy sauce of vegetables, has become Costa Rica's most popular condiment.

Informal restaurants called *sodas*, which serve flavorful, home-style cooking at inexpensive prices, dominate the landscape. Larger and generally more expensive *restaurantes* are slightly less common. If you're far from the city, you may find yourself at a small *soda* where they only offer you a spoon. This is because *campesinos* (rural field workers) often eat only with this utensil. Don't be embarrassed to ask for a fork and knife. Many meals come with bread or corn tortillas, both of which you can use as utensils.

In terms of popularity, nothing can compete with the widespread appeal of Costa Rica's world-class **coffee**. *Ticos* young and old enjoy a big mug of *café* (usually mixed with milk) multiple times a day. Despite the high quality of Costa Rican blends, most *ticos* seem to prefer a sweetened brew. For a stronger cup of joe, look for restaurants and cafes that cater to tourists, or buy your own beans. Ask for *café sin leche* or *café negro* to skip the cream and sugar.

Though coffee has captured the hearts of Costa Ricans, alcohol is still putting up a fight for their livers. **Guaro,** made from sugar cane and similar to rum, is the national liquor. It mixes well with anything, though *coco loco* (*guaro* with coconut juice) is a popular choice. When it comes to lower proof options, Imperial, Pilsen, and Bavaria beers are popular among *ticos*.

CUSTOMS AND ETIQUETTE

BEING COSTA RICAN. *Ticos* are very family oriented. Kids live with their parents through their college years and generally don't leave home before marriage. Close extended families are common and contribute to fairly cohesive communities, particularly in rural areas. Costa Ricans are known for their relaxed temperament, as well as their willingness to lend a hand — or even a home—in times of need. The phrase *quedar bien*, which means "stay on good terms," is one of the essential tenets of Costa Rican values. Costa Ricans will often want to *quedar bien* by saying "yes" when they mean "no" in order to avoid conflict. This may also mean that promises made during face-to-face interactions are more symbolic than authentic; a friendly gesture is emphasized over a desire for particularly deep or intimate friendship.

BEING POLITE. When speaking Spanish in Costa Rica, you'll find an important distinction between the *usted*, *vos*, and *tú* forms of verbs. Use *usted*, the third person singular, or *ustedes*, the third person plural, when speaking to a stranger or someone older; it is more formal and respectful. Costa Ricans are distinct for using *usted* very broadly: with family, friends, children, and even pets. It is important to use *Don* or *Doña* before an older person's name; call a friend's father Don Alberto and not just Alberto.

Machismo has left a mark on Costa Rican gender relations. Out of tradition, men are very chivalrous, often assuming a protective role, though women might also find themselves subjected to unwanted male attention on the streets. It is considered good manners for men to open doors and help carry bags.

DRESS CODE. Costa Ricans are always very conscious about looking presentable and tidy when they go out. People often dress much more conservatively than the warm weather would call for. Men usually wear slacks, jeans, t-shirts, polo shirts, or button-down shirts. Women usually wear pants, jeans, or skirts in the city. Travelers should try not to wear shorts in the city; shorts are acceptable in more rural areas and at the beach. When in doubt, it's a good idea for visitors to present themselves in a fairly conservative manner.

COSTA RICA

TICO TIME. People in Costa Rica tend to be very laid-back—being on time is not a major point of concern. *Ticos* can be late for almost everything, which often comes as a surprise to foreigners accustomed to punctuality. While it is usual for people to be 15-30min. late for business appointments, a meeting with friends can be delayed by up to several hours.

THE ARTS

Unlike some of its other Central American neighbors, Costa Rica is not known for its artistic heritage. Typical artifacts include **statues** in gold, jade, and stone, as well as breastplates featuring stylized jaguars, crocodiles, and hook-beaked birds from the Pre-Columbian era. Some of the most famous and mysterious artifacts are the more than 300 almost perfectly spherical **Diquis stones,** called *Las Bolas* by locals, which are found in the southern territories. The stones are arranged in geometric formations that point to earth's magnetic north and are estimated to be around 1600 years old. Archaeologists still are confounded by their origin. With the arrival of Spanish colonial rulers, Costa Rica's arts and culture were dominated by European norms for centuries. In the modern era, Costa Ricans have begun to take an active interest in their pre-Columbian history and culture, and excavations have fueled this process of rediscovery.

While periodicals rule the reading market, Costa Rica does have a colorful literary history. Before the 20th century, Costa Rican literature drew largely on European models, though it also gained inspiration from folk tales and colloquial expression in a movement known as *costumbrismo.* Despite the strength of this early movement, Costa Rican literature didn't find its expressive voice until the 20th century, when it began dedicating itself to political and social criticism. **José Marín Cañas's** *Inferno verde*, a depiction of the Chaco War between Paraguay and Bolivia, bolstered anti-imperialist sentiment. **Oreamuni's** *La ruta de su evasión* explored inter-generational tensions and the subtleties of Latin American *machismo.* Writer **Fabián Dobles,** winner of the Premio Nacional, Costa Rica's highest distinction for artistic and intellectual achievement, has also gained recognition beyond the borders of the country; and **Carlos Salazar Herrera** is one of the nation's premier artists, a painter, poet, and professor. Costa Rica also serves as a haven for expat writers and artists from around the world, offering inspiration or simply a secluded backdrop.

BEYOND TOURISM

VOLUNTEERING

SAVE THE ANIMALS

With an increasing number of tourists visiting Costa Rica every year, there is a greater need to protect the wildlife. Programs mainly focus on protecting turtles from poachers or helping out in a wildlife refuges.

Earthwatch, 3 Clock Tower Pl., Ste. 100, Box 75, Maynard, MA 021754, USA (☎+1 800-776-0188 or +1 978-461-0081; www.earthwatch.org). Arranges eco-friendly programs in Costa Rica and provides the opportunity to participate in cutting-edge scientific research. Volunteers have the opportunity to gather data about the effects of climate change on leatherback turtles or caterpillars; alternatively, volunteers can help

Costa Rican coffee farmers develop environmentally friendly methods of production. Fees vary; average US$2800.

Volunteer Visions, Casa Roja de Dos Pisos, Playa Samara, Guancaste, Costa Rica (US ☎+1 330-871-4511; www.volunteervisions.org). Provides affordable volunteer opportunities for adventurous individuals. Based in Costa Rica, Volunteer Visions's wildlife conservation project in the Guancaste region of Costa Rica strives to reintroduce birds, monkeys, and other animals to the wild. Volunteers help to care for the animals. Trips range from 2 weeks (US$650) to 26 weeks (US$3340). Fee includes food, accommodations (homestay or dorm), orientation, and excursions.

World Endeavors, 3015 E Franklin Ave., Minneapolis, MN 5540, USA (☎+1 612-729-3400 or +1 866-802-9678; www.worldendeavors.com). Opportunities for volunteers to rescue and rehabilitate parrots, macaws, and other native tropical birds in Atenas. Programs range from 2 weeks (US$1455) to 3 months (US$2877), including housing, 3 meals per day with a family, and cultural activities. Placements longer than 1 month receive 2 weeks of Spanish language classes.

SAVE THE TREES

Costa Rica is one of the most environmentally diverse places on earth. Numerous organizations work to protect the national parks, tropical forests, and beaches from unsustainable farming practices and tourist practices. The following programs offer volunteer opportunities ranging from trail maintenance and reforestation to teaching sustainable farming techniques.

Punta Mona Center (www. puntamona.org), located 5km south of Manzanillo. A huge organic farm and educational center dedicated to sustainable agriculture. Interns live in houses built completely of fallen trees, and using solar-powered, eco-friendly energy. 100+ varieties of tropical fruits, vegetables, and medicinal herbs are grown at the farm. Meals (mostly vegetarian) included. Internships (US$600 per month) begin the first day of each month.

Asociación Preservacionista de Flora y Fauna Silvestre (APREFLOLFAS), P.O. Box 917 2150, San José, Costa Rica (☎2240 6087; www.apreflofas.or.cr). This non-profit volunteer organization, also called "The Raccoon," provides a wealth of information on ecotourism in Costa Rica's parks. The organization promotes reforestation and works to guard Costa Rica's natural resources from illegal exploitation.

Asocianción de Voluntario de Areas Protegias Silvestres (ASVO), Apdo. 11384-1000, San José (☎2258 4430; www.asvocr.org). Your link to virtually every national park in Costa Rica. Although some parks prefer that volunteers contact their conservation areas directly, you can always reach a specific park through this office. Live and work in the same conditions as the park rangers. US$17 per day to cover lodging and meals.

FARMING

The export of crops if an important part of Costa Rica's economy, and there is a plethora of opportunities for involvement in this industry.

Finca Lomas, (☎506 2224 6090 or 506 2224-0911; ww.anaicr.org). An environmentally friendly farm in the Talamancan Lowland Rainforest. Works to establish sustainable economic and environmental groups and encourage community self-sufficiency.

uVolunteer (Volunteer Costa Rica), Apartado 280-4250, San Ramon, Alajuela, Costa Rica (☎+1 971 252 1334; www.uvolunteer.org). Strives to create a sustainable, conservative method of farming that is realistic for Costa Rican farming communities. Volunteers' responsibilities may include organic gardening, constucting nature trails, and caring for animals.

World-Wide Opportunities on Organic Farms (WWOOF), P.O. Box 2154, Winslow, Buckingham MK18 3WS, England, UK (www.wwoof.org). A network that connects volunteers with organic farms in Costa Rica and around the world. Promotes sustainable, organic farming by providing travelers with information on farms that will host them for free. Membership fee (US$16) buys a book of host farms from which you can choose.

STUDYING

AMERICAN PROGRAMS

American Field Service (AFS), 198 Madison Ave., 8th fl., New York, NY 10016, USA (☎+1 800-237-4636; www.usa.afs.org). Offers homestay exchange programs in Costa Rica primarily for high school students and graduating seniors planning on taking a gap year. Summer US$5900-6900; semester US$7900; full year US$8900.

American Institute for Foreign Study (AIFS), River Plaza, 9 W. Broad St., Stamford, CT 06902, USA (☎+1-866-906-2437; www.aifs.com). Organizes programs for college students through Veritas Unviersity in San José. 12-week program without airfare US$7495; 16-week program without airfare US$8995.

Council on International Educational Exchange (CIEE), 300 Fore St., Portland, ME 04101, USA (☎+1-207-553-4000 or 800-40-STUDY/407-8839; www.ciee.org). One of the most comprehensive resources for work, academic, and internship programs around the world, including Costa Rica, where you can study ecology in Monteverde. Summer fee US$6,500; semester fee US$12,900.

COSTA RICAN PROGRAMS

Instituto Monteverde, Apdo. 69-5655, Monteverde, Puntarenas, Costa Rica (☎2645 5053 or 2645 5365; www.mvinstitute.org). This non-profit association provides educational and cultural resources for the local community. Learn about sustainability and community health, as well as Spanish language and culture. Email info@mvinstitute.org for further details.

University of Costa Rica Rainforest Adventure, World Class Adventures in Education 17812 SH 16 S, Pipe Creek, TX, 78063, USA (☎+1 800-321-7625; www.educationabroad.com). A tropical field ecology program for English-speaking undergraduates at Costa Rica's main national university. Students take Spanish lessons and stay with Costa Rican families. Credit accepted by many US universities. US$8500.

SAN JOSÉ

At first, Costa Rica's capital is sure to frustrate the tourists eager to experience the country's natural beauty. Modern concrete structures encroach on the city's surviving examples of colonial architecture. Smog and grime dominate the capital, while piercing car horns never stop blaring. During the summer rainy season, travelers should expect daily downpours.

Still, San José is filled with the energy of a young and bustling city. As irritating as the fast-food joints on every corner may be for someone attempting to escape civilization, the neon facades demonstrate how rapidly the city is modernizing. Internet cafes have sprung up on nearly every corner. Luxury hotels and restaurants offering international cuisine provide the discerning traveler with a plethora of culinary options. But have no fear, loyal lovers of *comida típica*—the authentic *casado* can still be found just about anywhere.

For those seeking nightlife, bars and clubs in San Pedro and El Pueblo are alive with energy and music until the wee hours of morning. San José is home to approximately 300,000 people (over 1 million including the suburbs), and most of them will show you up on the dance floor—the speed and elegance of *salsa* takes most gringos by surprise.

The transportation and economic hub of Costa Rica, San José offers a glimpse into the country's future. Surrounded by mountains and perched 1132m above sea level, San José was first settled in 1736, though it spent much of the colonial era as a tobacco-farming town. In 1823, San José replaced Cartago as the capital of Costa Rica and came into its own as the nexus of the coffee trade. As an ever-changing city, it is a worthy stop between the two coasts. Be sure to give yourself enough time; there's plenty to see here in bustling San José.

◪ INTERCITY TRANSPORTATION

FLIGHTS

International Flights: Juan Santa María International Airport (SJO), about 15km northwest of San José in Alajuela. Most cheaply accessible by bus from San José to Alajuela. Official **airport taxis** to and from San José charge ¢13,366 (US$23). The taxi driver will meet you at the airport exit to confirm a price and will then take you to the window on your left to pay the fare. **Grayline Tours** (☎2291 2222; www.graylinecostarica.com) runs an **airport shuttle** that picks up travelers across the street and upstairs from the airport exit and drops off at many mid-range and top-end hotels around town for ¢5,811 (US$10). Online booking available. Airlines include: **American** (☎2223 5426); **Continental** (☎2296 4911 or 0800 044 0005); **Copa** (☎295 7400); **Delta** (☎2257 4141 or 1-800-221-1212); **Iberia** (☎2441 2591); **Mexicana** (☎2257 6334); **Taca,** through **Sansa** (☎2221 9414); **United** (☎2220 4844 or 2441 8025). Arriving at the airport 2½hr. early is recommended for all international flights. **Sansa** (☎2666 0307; www.flysansa.com) offers the cheapest domestic flights from a terminal just to the left of the international terminal (¢39,514-56,947/US$68-98). Departures and one-way fares on Sansa: **Barra de Colorado** (1 per day M, F, Sa; ¢45,907/US$79); **Drake Bay** (2 per day, ¢56,367/US$97); **Golfito** (4 per day, ¢55,205/US$95); **Liberia** (6 per day, ¢55,205/US$95); **Nosara** (1 per day, ¢55,205/US$95); **Palmar Sur** (3 per day, ¢50,555/US$87); **Puerto Jimenez** (6 per day, ¢55,205/US$95); **Quepos** (9 per day, ¢32,541/US$56); **Samara** (1 per day, ¢56,948/US$98); **Tamarindo** (6 per day, ¢55,205/US$95); **Tambor** (5 per day, ¢43,583/US$75); **Tortuguero** (1 per day, ¢45,907/US$79).

Tobías Bolaños Airport, in Pavas, 20min. from San José by taxi. Serves **NatureAir** (☎2229 6000, US reservations +1-800-235-9272; www.natureair.net).

Domestic Flights: Online reservations available. Departures and one-way fares for NatureAir: **Arenal** (1 per day, ¢43,001/US$74); **Bocas del Toro** (1-2 per day M, W, F, Su; ¢76,705/US$132); **Drake Bay** (2 per day, ¢63,340/US$109); **Golfito** (1 per day, ¢61,597/US$106); **Liberia** (4 per day, ¢61,597/US$106); **Limón** (1 per day M, W, F, Su; ¢47,650/US$82); **Nosara** (1-2 per day, ¢61,597/US$106); **Palmar Sur, Dominical** (1 per day, ¢55,785/$96); **Puerto Jiménez** (5 per day, ¢63,340/US$109); **Punta Islita** (1 per day, ¢63,340/US$109); **Quepos** (3 per day, ¢35,447/US$61), **Tamarindo** (3 per day, ¢61,597/US$106); **Tambor** (2 per day, ¢45,907/US$79); **Tortuguero** (1 per day, ¢50,556/US$87). When booking online, you may find cheaper deals with more restrictions.

BUSES

Buses to almost everywhere in the country arrive and depart from the city's stops and terminals. Many depart from around **Terminal Coca-Cola,** between Av. 1/3, C. 16/18. The schedule is available at the **Instituto Costarricense de Turismo (ICT)** at the **Museo de Oro.** Times often change, so double-check with your hostel. Fares for domestic trips are not listed and change frequently, but expect rides under 4hr. to cost ¢2000 or less, with longer trips under ¢4000. **All fares must be paid in colones, so carry small bills or change.**

Domestic Buses:

Alajuela-Airport: TUASA, Av. 2, C.12/14 (☎2442 6900). 35min.; every 10min. 4:30am-10pm, every 30min. 10-11pm.

Cahuita: Terminal Caribe, Av. 13, C. Central (☎2257 8129). 4hr.; 6, 10am, 2, 4pm.

Cariari: Terminal Caribe, Av. 13, C. Central (☎2222 0610). 2hr., 9 per day 6:30am-8:30pm.

Cartago: Empresa Lumaca, Av. 10, C. 5 (☎2537 2320). 45min., every 10min. 5:05am-midnight.

Fortuna: Auto Transportes, Av. 7/9, C. 12 (☎2255 0567). 4hr.; 6:15, 8:40, 11:30am.

Golfito: Tracopa, Av. 18/20, C. 5 (☎2221 4214). 8hr.; Su 7am, 3:30pm.

Guápiles: Empresarios Guapileños, Av. 13, C. Central. 1½hr., every hr. 5:30am-7pm.

Heredia: Transportes Unidos 400, Av. 7/9, C. 1. Other locations at Av. Central, C. 8 and Av. 5/7, C. 4. 30min., every 10min. 5am-11pm (5am-3am from Av. 7/9, C. 1).

Jacó: Transportes Morales, Terminal Coca-Cola, Av. 3, C. 16 (☎2223 1109). 2hr.; 6am, every 2hr. 7am-7pm.

Liberia: Pulmitan, Av. 5/7, C. 24 (☎2256 9552). 4½hr., 8 per day 6am-10pm.

Limón: Caribeños, Terminal Caribe, Av. 13, C. Central (☎2221 0610). 2½hr., every hr. 5am-7pm.

Monteverde: Autotransportes Tilarán, Atlántico Nte. Terminal, Av. 7/9, C.12 (☎2222 3854). 5hr.; 6:30am and 2:30pm.

Playa Nosara and Garza: Tracopa-Alfaro, Av. 3/5, C. 14 (☎2222 2666). 6hr., 5:30am.

Playa Panamá: Tralapa, Av. 1/3, C. 20 (☎2221 7202). 6hr.; 3:30pm. Return 3pm.

Playa Tamarindo: Tracopa-Alfaro, Av 5, C. 14/16 (☎2222 2666). 5hr., 11:30am and 3:30pm. Tralapa, Av. 3/5, C. 20 (☎2221 7202), 4pm.

Playas del Coco: Av. 5/7, C. 24 (☎2222 1650). 5hr.; 8am, 2, 4pm. Return 4, 8am, 2pm.

Puntarenas: Empresarios Unidos de Puntarenas, Av.12, C. 16 (☎2222 8231). 2hr.; every hr. 6am-7pm; return every hr. 4-7pm.

Quepos and Manuel Antonio: Transportes Morales, Terminal Coca Cola, Av. 3, C. 16 (☎2223 5567). Direct 3hr.; 6, 9am, noon, 2:30, 6, 7:30pm. Return 4, 6, 9:30am, noon, 2:30, 5pm. Indirect 5hr.; 7, 10am, 2, 3, 4pm. Return 5, 8am, 2, 4pm. Only direct buses continue to Manuel Antonio.

Siquirres: Terminal Caribe, Av. 13, C. Central (☎2222 0610). 1hr.; 11 per day 6:30am-6pm.

Turrialba: Transtusa, Av. 6, C. 13 (☎2222 4464). 1hr.; every hr. 5:15am-10pm; return 7am, 9pm.

San José Overview

Volcán Irazú: Av. 2, C. 1/3. 2hr.; Sa-Su 8am. Return Sa-Su 12:30pm.

Volcán Poás: TUASA, Av. 2, C. 12/14 (☎2222 5325). 2hr.; 8:30am. Return 2:30pm.

International Buses:

El Salvador: TicaBus, Av. 2/4, C. 9 (☎2221 8954; www.ticabus.com/ingles). 48hr. with 1 night in Managua; 6, 7:30am, 12:30; ¢23,244 (US$40).

Guatemala: TicaBus, Av. 26, C. 3. 60hr. with 1 night in Nicaragua and 1 night in El Salvador; 6, 7:30am, 12:30pm; ¢32,541 (US$56).

Tegucigalpa, Honduras: TicaBus, Av. 2/4, C. 9. 48hr. with 1 night in Managua; 6, 7:30am, 12:30pm; ¢20,338 (US$35).

San Pedro Sula, Honduras: TicaBus, Av. 2/4, C. 9. 48hr. with 1 night in Managua; 6, 7:30am, 12:30pm; ¢27,311 (US$47).

Nicaragua: TicaBus, Av. 26, C. 3. 8hr.; 6, 7:30am, 12:30pm; ¢8,135 (US$14).

Panamá City: TicaBus, Av. 26, C. 3 (☎2221 8954). 20hr., midnight and 11pm, US$26. Panaline, Av. 3/5, C. 16 (☎2256 8721, www.panalinecr.com). 18hr., 1pm, ¢13,365 (US$23).

ORIENTATION

San José's design follows a typical Costa Rican grid: *avenidas* run east-west and *calles* run north-south. Directions in San José, as well as in other large

SAN JOSÉ

San José Center

♦ ACCOMMODATIONS
Casa León, **25**
Casa Ridgway, **28**
Costa Rica Backpackers
  Hostel, **26**
Hostel Pangea, **6**
Hotel Boston, **21**
Hotel El Descanso, **17**
Hotel Fleur de Lys, **24**
Hotel Nuevo Alameda, **9**
Hotel Príncipe, **19**
Hotel Otoya Pensión, **7**
Kabata Hostel, **5**
Toruma Youth Hostel, **14**
Tranquilo Backpackers, **4**

♦ FOOD
La Grand Ma, **11**
Nuestra Tierra, **23**
Restaurante Grano de Oro, **22**
Rest. Vishnu Vegetariano, **10**
Shakti, **29**
Soda el Parque, **18**
Taquería la Moderna, **20**
Tin Jo, **27**

♦ NIGHTLIFE
Av. 2 Bar/Restaurant, **15**
Bongo's, **2**
Ebony 56, **1**
El Cuartel de la Boca del
  Monte, **13**
Salidas Orbital 2000, **12**
Salsa 54, **8**
Twister Club, **3**

◯ GOVERNMENT BUILDINGS
Asamblea Legislativa, **16**
Corte Suprema de Justicia, **32**
Organismo de Investigación, **31**
Tribunales de Justicia, **30**

cities, are usually given by listing the street and cross street where a destination is located. For example, a building located at Av. 2, C. 5/7 would be located on Av. 2, somewhere in the block between C. 5 and 7. **Avenida Central** (called Paseo Colón north of C. 22) is the main drag, with a shopping and eating area blocked off to traffic between C. 2 and C. 5. Just west of the city center is the frantic **Mercado Central,** bordered by Av. Central/1 and C. 6/8. Four blocks farther west of the market is **Terminal Coca-Cola,** on Av. 1, C. 16/18. Many streets are not labeled; the staff at stores rarely knows its own address, so counting blocks between destinations and relying on landmarks is necessary.

Barrio Amón, northeast of Av. 5 and C. 1, and **Barrio Otoya,** slightly east of Amón, are the most architecturally interesting neighborhoods in the city center, housing Spanish colonial buildings dating back to the 19th century. West of downtown, past C. 42, **La Sabana** contains the large **Parque Metropolitano La Sabana.** Five kilometers farther west, the quiet suburb of **Escazú** is home to gorgeous B&Bs and some of San José's most posh restaurants. Other upscale regions include **Los Yoses,** east of downtown past C. 3, and **San Pedro,** home to the University of Costa Rica and some of the city's best entertainment.

 WATCH OUT! Although San José is relatively safe, theft, prostitution, and drugs make some areas a bit risky. Problem spots include: **Terminal Coca-Cola,** south of Av. 8 between C. 2 and 14, Av. 4 to 6 between C. 4 and 12, areas north of the **Mercado Central,** and areas around the mall and C. de la Amargura in **San Pedro.** Generally, areas beyond a few blocks from San José's center pose a greater threat after dark. The city's parks and crowded streets can present the risk of pickpockets and grab-and-run thiefs, so hold on to your belongings. After sunset, the safest way to get around is by taxi, especially for women traveling alone.

LOCAL TRANSPORTATION

Buses: Local buses run every 5-10min. from 5am to 10pm and travel all over San José, including to the suburbs and the airport. There are no official printed schedules and timing is generally approximate. Ask locals and drivers for info or check bus fronts. Most bus stops are marked with the destination they serve. As local destinations generally run no more than ¢300, it's best to carry small change. Major bus stops include **Escazú** (Av. 1/Central and C. 16), **Guadalupe** and **Moravia** (Av. 3, C. 3/5), and **San Pedro** (Av. 2, C. 11/13 and Av. Central, C. 9/11).

Private Buses: Grayline Tours (☎2220 2126; www.graylinecostarica.com). Offers **buses** to and from popular destinations throughout Costa Rica (one-way ¢14,527-24,987/US$25-43). Buses run once or twice daily between **San José** and **Arenal, Conchal, Golfo Papagayo, Jacó, Manuel Antonio, Monteverde, Playa Hermosa, Playa Tamarindo, Puerto Viejo de Talamanca, Rincón,** and **Sámara.** Most leave daily 7:30-10:30am. AmEx/D/MC/V.

Car Rental: Prices range from ¢11,622/US$20 (for a small manual sedan) to ¢61,015/US$105 (for a 4x4) per day. Avis and Economy tend to offer some of the lowest rates. Minimum rental age is 21, although a few companies require drivers to be at least 23 or 25. Some companies will rent to those 18-21 with double or triple the deposit. A passport, valid driver's license, and major credit card are required; International Driver's Permits are not necessary for rentals of less than 3 months. Online reservations available with the following companies:

Avis (☎2232 9922; www.avis.co.cr), at the Hotel Corobicí, north of the Parque La Sabana on C. 42, and at the airport (☎2442 1321). Minimum rental of 48hr. Minimum age 23.

Budget, Paseo Colón, C. 28/30 (☎2255 4240; www.budget.co.cr), and at the airport (☎2440 4412). Open M-Sa 7am-6pm, Su 7am-4pm; airport office open daily 6am-10pm. 21+. Offers combination packages with specific hotels. Rents to ages 18-21 for surcharge.

Economy (☎2299 2000; www.economyrentacar.com), in Sabana Nte. and at the airport (☎2442 8100). Open daily 7am-10pm, airport office open 5am-2am. Rents to ages 18-21 for surcharge.

Europcar, Paseo Colón, C. 36/38 (☎2257 1158; www.europcar.co.cr), and at the airport (☎2440 9990). Open daily 8am-6pm; airport office open daily 5am-midnight. Surcharge 5-6am and 10pm-midnight.

Hertz, Paseo Colón, C. 38 (☎2221 1818; www.hertz.com). Open M-F 7am-6pm, Sa-Su 7am-5pm. 25+.

National Car Rental, Av. 7, C. 36 and (☎ 2242 7878, toll-free from US +1 800-227-7368; www.natcar.com), at the airport (☎2440 0085). Also at the Hotel Irazu and Hotel Real Intercontinental in San José. Main office open daily 7:30am-6pm; airport 6am-10pm. 21+.

🔼 PRACTICAL INFORMATION

TOURIST AND FINANCIAL SERVICES

Tourist Offices: Instituto Costarricense de Turismo (☎2299 5800, from US or Costa Rica 1-866-COSTARICA/267-8274). Offices located at Av. Central/2, C. 5 (☎2222 1090; open M-F 9am-1pm and 2-5pm), next to El Museo del Oro, and Av. Central/1, C. 5, 2nd fl. (☎2257 8064; open M-F 8:30am-5:30pm). Free country and city maps, intracity bus schedules, and brochures. Another office in the post office (Oficina de Correos). **OTEC Viajes,** an office of **STA Travel,** Av. 1/3, C. 3 (☎2256 0633, www.otecviajes.com), can help you makes changes to your STA ticket, but cannot book new ones. ISIC card available for purchase. Open M-F 8am-6pm, Sa 9am-1pm.

Tours:

Costa Rica Expeditions, Av. 3, C. Central/2 (☎2257 0766 or 2222 0333; www.costaricaexpeditions.com), 1 block east of the post office. Tours throughout the country in collaboration with other companies. Class III and IV whitewater rafting on the Río Pacuare ¢86,584 (US$149) per person. 2-day rafting trip ¢165,614 (US$285). 10% student discount. English spoken. Open daily 8am-5pm. AmEx/D/MC/V.

Costa Rica Nature Escape, Av. Central/1, C. 5, 2nd fl. (☎2257 8064, 24hr. line 8381 7178; www.crnature.com). Student rates for all sorts of adventure, relaxation, and ecotourism packages. One-day Tortuguero tour ¢79,030 (US$136), students ¢74,380 (US$128). Class III whitewater rafting on the Río Reventazón or Río Sarapiquí ¢43,582 (US$75), students ¢40,677 (US$70). Class IV whitewater rafting on the Río Pacuare from ¢57,529 (US$99), students from ¢48,812 (US$84). Open M-F 8:30am-5:30pm. Cash only for student discounts. MC/V.

Ecole Travel, Av. Central, C. 5/7 (☎2223 2240; www.ecoletravel.com), inside Edificio Plaza de la Cultura, 2nd fl. A reputable and relatively inexpensive tour company. Tours to Tortuguero (2 days from ¢121,450/US$209, 3 days from ¢167,937/US$289) and Volcán Arenal and Monteverde (4 days from ¢188,857/US$325). Online booking available. Open M-F 8am-5pm, Sa 9am-1pm.

Ecoscape Nature Tours (☎2297 0664, US and Canada +1 866-887-2764; www.ecoscapetours.com). The Highlights Tour for travelers short on time (¢49,393/US$85). The 1-day tour involves visits to Volcán Poás and its surrounding cloud forest, La Paz, San Fernando Waterfalls, Selva Verde Rainforest Lodge, a boat ride on the Río Sarapiquí, and a drive through Braulio Carillo National Park. A 2-day tour is available as well (¢122,030/US$210, with rafting ¢139,464/US$240).

Embassies: See **Essentials,** p. 5.

Currency Exchange and Banks: There are dozens of banks all over San José; nearly all of them have Cirrus/Plus/V **24hr. ATMs,** sometimes labeled "ATH." All require photo ID to exchange currency, and most require passport and charge 1% commission to cash travelers' checks. Listed below are the main offices.

Banco Central, Av. Central/1, C. 2/4 (☎2243 3333). Open M-F 9:20am-4pm.

Banco de Costa Rica, Av. Central/2, C. 4/6 (☎2287 9000). Open M-F 8:30am-6pm.

Banco Nacional, Av. 1/3, C. 4 (☎2212 2000). Open M-F 10:45am-3:45pm. **ATM** daily 5am-10pm.

Banco de San José, Av. 3/5, C. Central (☎2295 9797). Open M-F 8am-7pm.

BANCO B.C.T., Av. Central/1, C. Central (☎2212 8000). Open M-F 8:15am-5pm.

Banco Popular, Av. 2 and C. 1 (☎2202 2020). Open M-F 8:15am-7pm, Sa 8:15-11:30am. **ATM** open daily 6am-11pm.

HSBC, Av. 1, C. Central (☎2287 1111). M-F 9am-6:30pm, Sa 9am-6pm. **24hr. ATM,** Av. 2, C. Central/2, next to KFC, across from the *parque central.*

American Express: Sabana Sur, Edeficio #1 (☎2242 8585). Passport required to cash traveler's checks. M-F 8am-6pm.

Western Union: Av. 2/4, C. 9 (☎+1 800-777-7777). International ID needed. **Currency exchange.** Open M-F 8:30am-5pm, Sa 9am-12:30pm.

Beyond Tourism: For complete listings, see p. 35.

 WORK IT OUT. Crowded streets, small parks, and cars that don't stop for pedestrians make the San José center a terrible place for jogging. If you want to get some exercise, take the bus from Av. 2, C. 3 (¢140) to the huge Parque Metropolitano in La Sabana. While there, check out the new national soccer stadium, scheduled to be completed in late 2009.

LOCAL SERVICES

English-Language Bookstore: 7th Street Books, Av. Central/1, C. 7 (☎2256 8251). Sells a selection of new and used fiction and nonfiction English-language books. Foreign newspapers and maps available. New books ¢5000-10,000, used ¢900-2500. Open M-Sa 9am-6pm, Su 10am-5pm. AmEx/MC/V. **Librería Lehmann,** Av. Central, C. 1/3 (☎2522 4848). Large selection of reading and stationery supplies. Second-floor **Café Latino** is a delightful spot to read while sipping a cappuccino. Open M-F 8am-6:30pm, Sa 9am-5pm, Su 11am-4pm.

Pasajes Plazavenidos: Av. Central, C. 7/9, diagonally across from Fiesta Casino. Two levels of souvenir shops, ATMs, and fast food restaurants. Bathrooms located upstairs in the back (¢150).

Laundromat: Leavened Lavandería, Av. Central/1, C. 8 (☎2258 0621), to the left of the Gran Hotel Imperial. ¢4000-¢6000 per load. Open M-F 8am-6pm. **Sixaola,** Av. 2, C. 7/9 (☎2221 2111). ¢1000 per kg. Same-day service if in by 10am. Open M-F 8am-6pm, Sa 8am-noon. AmEx/MC/V.

Public Toilets: There are sparkling restrooms on Av. Central, C. 5, underground at the Plaza de la Cultura, next to the Museo de Oro. Some fast food restaurants along Av. Central will allow non-customers to use the *sanitarios,* but they have long lines. **Librería Lehmann** (see above), 1 block north from the Museo de Oro on Av. Central, has a free bathroom in its cafe.

EMERGENCY AND COMMUNICATIONS

Emergency: ☎911.

Police: ☎911. To report a theft, contact the **Organismo de Investigación Judicial (OIJ),** Av. 6/8, C. 15/17 (☎2295 3643). To report a theft in person, proceed east on Av. 6, then turn right onto the walkway paved with square tiles. The entrance is on the right, at the ATM. Follow the signs to the Oficina Denuncias. Ask for an English speaker if necessary. Open 24hr. During business hours, contact the **Crime Victims Assistance**

Office (☎2295 3565), on the 1st floor of OIJ. Open M-F 7:30am-noon and 1-4:30pm. To report a sexual or life-threatening assault, call ☎2295 3493.

Pharmacy: Farmacia Fischel, Av. 3, C. 2 (☎2275 7659), near the center of town. Large selection of pharmaceutical and beauty products. ATM inside. Open daily 7am-8pm. AmEx/D/MC/V. Smaller location at Av. 2, C. 5. (☎2233 0231). Open M-F 7:30am-7:30pm, Sa-Su 8am-7pm.

Medical Services: Hospital San Juan de Dios,Paseo Colón, C. 14/16 (☎2257 6282), in the building where Av. Central becomes Paseo Colón, after C. 14. **Clínica Bíblica,** Av. 14/16, C. 1 (☎2522 1000). English spoken. **24hr. emergency service** and pharmacy.

Telephones: Card and coin phones are all over town, especially along Av. Central. Most phones accept ¢5 and ¢10 coins. Most *ticos* buy phone cards from street vendors. Cards charge around ¢5 per min. for local calls and ¢100 per min. for calls to the US. **Radiográphica,** Av. 5, C. Central/1 (☎2287 0087; www.racsa.co.cr). Collect calls ¢1,743 (US$3). Also has AT&T Direct, MCI, and Sprint service. Sells prepaid internet cards. Open M-F 7:30am-4:30pm, Sa 9am-1pm. Directory assistance ☎113.

> **PHONE HOME.** The easiest way to make both domestic and international calls from a pay phone in Costa Rica is by using a **phone card.** Pick one up at the airport, pharmacy, or from a street vendor, scratch off the silver backing to find your phone card number, and follow the instructions on the back of the card. The cheapest way to reach home is to use a VoIP phone service, such as **Skype,** to place calls from either your computer or one of the many internet cafes around San José.

Internet Access: Internet cafes abound in San José. Here are 2 near the city center:

Café Digital, C. 7, Av. Central/1, 2nd fl. (☎2248 0701). New computers. Internet ¢400 per hr. Scanner, printing, and copies ¢100-200 per page. Skype and webcams available. Calls to the US ¢60 per min. Open M-Sa 8am-9pm, Su 9am-8pm.

Cybernético, on the corner of Av. Central and C. 4, 4th fl. Internet, video, faxing, scanning, and international internet calls. Internet ¢350 per hr. Copies ¢90. Open daily 7am-10pm.

Post Office: Av. 1/3, C. 2 (☎2223 9766), in the large green building. San José has no street mailboxes, so all mail must be sent from here. Open M-F 8am-6pm, Sa 7:30am-noon. Letter to the US ¢160. **Postal Code:** 1000.

ACCOMMODATIONS

San José has hundreds of accommodations for every budget, from bare-bones hostels to Holiday Inns. That said, it's best to steer clear of the cheapest lodgings; paying the relatively "pricey" ¢5000-6800 (US$10-13) for a dormitory bed is worth it for clean, comfortable lodgings, relatively hot water, and a friendly atmosphere. Avoid the city center to escape from noisy crowds. The accommodations listed below are divided into four categories by location. Staying east of the *parque central* is highly recommended, as accommodations here tend to be safe and comfortable. Hotels south of the *parque central* are generally reasonably priced but are often louder because of their proximity to bars. Though they are often the cheapest options, try to avoid places north and west of the *parque*, as these tend to be the areas with the highest concentration of prostitutes, drunken bar patrons, and criminal activities. Pleasant alternatives to staying downtown are found in **San Pedro,** a 10min. bus ride from San José, and the suburb of **Escazú,** a 20min. bus ride, which offers splurge-worthy B&Bs.

EAST OF PARQUE CENTRAL

Hostel Pangea, Av. 7, C. 3/5 (☎2221 1992; www.hostelpangea.com). Walls with dark jungle colors, metal accents, and a location near the city center create an urban feel. Plenty of social space makes this a great place to meet travelers. Free lockers with deposit, unlimited coffee, and international calling available. The staff is extremely helpful, especially in arranging tours. Potential downsides are the wristbands guests must wear at all times and the lack of outlets in the dorm rooms. Breakfast ¢2900 (US$5). Laundry ¢5220 (US$9). Free internet and Wi-Fi. 24hr. airport transport on the hostel's shuttle (¢10,440/US$18). Reception 24hr. Dorms ¢6960; private rooms ¢17,400. Additional locations at Av. 11, C. 3/5 with fewer amenities, and a resort in Arenal. ❶

Costa Rica Backpackers Hostel, Av. 6, C. 21/23 (☎2221 6191; www.costaricabackpackers.com). Packed with young, swim suit-clad vacationers, this inexpensive backpacker magnet adds tropical flair to what feels like a spacious college dorm. Though it's a walk from the city center, the spotless rooms, shared hot-water bathrooms, night guard, communal kitchen, flat-screen TVs with cable, tourist info, free Wi-Fi, and swimming pool will make you want to stay forever. Guests often spend their mornings laying out under the sun or swinging in hammocks near the pool while munching on breakfast. Laundry ¢3,486 (US$6). Reception 24hr. Check-out 11am. Dorms ¢7004; doubles ¢16,342. ¢2,334 key deposit. MC/V with ¢11,673 minimum. ❶

Casa Ridgway, Av. 6/8, C. 15 (☎2233 2693; www.amigosparalapaz.org), on a quiet cul-de-sac off C.15 between Av. 6 and 8. Owned by Quakers, Casa Ridgway offers the best value for peaceful, beautifully decorated accommodations. Each room is unique and most are painted with quotes representative of the establishment's ideals. Guests have access to the communal kitchen, dining area, meeting room, and library. An active Quaker peace center is attached. Breakfast included. Public phone (☎2255 6399). Storage available. Laundry ¢2,905 (US$5). Internet. Reception 7am-10pm. Dorms ¢8171; singles ¢11,090; doubles ¢17,510. MC/V. ❷

Kabata Hostel, Av. 9/11, C. 7 (☎2255 0355; www.kabatahostel.com). Clean, quiet accommodations just blocks from some of San José's nicest parks. Shared hot-water baths, cable TV in the lobby, and free use of kitchen and dining room. Downstairs rooms have large windows and get the most sunlight. The owners are attentive to each guest's needs. Breakfast included. Free Wi-Fi. Free parking. Check-out 10am. Dorms ¢7004, group of 5 or more ¢6420; singles with shared bathroom ¢9338; doubles ¢18,676. Cash only. ❶

Tranquilo Backpackers, Av. 9/11, C. 7 (☎2223 3189 or 2222 2493; www.tranquilobackpackers.com). Bright rooms with hot showers, cable TVs, and access to a communal kitchen. Dorm rooms contain tall plain-wood bunk beds and ceiling windows. Open and sunny common room. Pancake breakfast included. Laundry ¢3000. Free internet. Reception 24hr. Dorms ¢7004; doubles ¢15,175. 2nd location in Santa Teresa/Mal País. Cash only. ❶

Casa León, Av. 6, C. 13/15 (☎2221 1651). Traveling east along Av. 2, turn right onto C. 13 and take a left to follow the train tracks; it's on the left. Casa León is a quiet and comfortable house. Internet and communal kitchen. Laundry available. Up to 6 people per dorm. Dorms ¢8171; singles ¢14,007, with private bath ¢17,510; doubles ¢17,510-23,346. Cash only. ❷

SOUTH OF PARQUE CENTRAL

Hotel Boston, Av. 8, C. Central/2 (☎2221 0563). Spacious, mint-green rooms have sturdy beds, cable TV, and clean private baths with hot water. A good choice south of the city center and San José's thriving bar scene. Reception 24hr. Singles ¢5000; doubles ¢8000; triples ¢10,000. AmEx/MC/V. ❶

SAN JOSÉ

NORTH OF PARQUE CENTRAL

Hotel Otoya Pensión, Av. 5, C 1 (☎2221 3925 or 2221 6017). On the second floor; shares entrance with an internet cafe. The Pensión is located only a couple of blocks south of one of San José's less desirable neighborhoods. Minimal amenities include tvs and fans. Backpackers congregate in a smoky sitting area inconveniently located behind the reception desk. Microwave, fridge, and coffeemaker available for use. Laundry service available. Reception 24hr. Check-out 1pm. All rooms with shared baths. Singles ¢5000; doubles ¢8000; triples ¢10,000. Cash only. ❶

WEST OF PARQUE CENTRAL

Hotel Nuevo Alameda, Av. Central/1, C. 12 (☎2233 3551; www.hotelnuevoalameda.com). Housed in a yellow building on C. 12 near the corner of Av. Central and the *mercado central*. Clean rooms for 1-4 people with large windows, TVs, and private hot-water baths. Ask to be on the west side for a better view. Inner rooms are quieter. A volcano mural decorates the lobby. Wheelchair-accessible. Reception 24hr. Check-out noon. Singles ¢8,716 (US$15) per person. Cash only. ❷

Hotel El Descanso, Av. 4, C. 6 (☎2221 9941), entrance on C. 6. Safe, clean lodgings close to the *parque central*. Upstairs, the carved wooden doors, multicolored walls, and spacious hallways create a comfortable and private atmosphere. Some rooms are not well-maintained. Reception 24hr. Check-out noon. Singles ¢8755; doubles ¢17,510; triples ¢26,264. Cash only. ❷

SAN PEDRO

🏠 **Toruma Youth Hostel (HI),** Av. Central, C. 29/31 (☎2234 8186), between San José and San Pedro. Take the San Pedro bus (¢190) from Av. Central, C. 9/11, and get off at Kentucky Fried Chicken; it's the yellow building across the street. Run by the same brothers who own Hostel Pangea, Toruma's offers an escape from the city. Be prepared to walk 1½km or to take a taxi to get to San Pedro or San José. Has a restaurant, pool, cable TV, and computers with free high-speed internet. Shared hot-water baths. Airport shuttle ¢10,505. Dorms ¢7004; singles and doubles ¢20,427. ❶

◧ FOOD

Black beans, white rice, and chicken remain staples, though American fast food joints have found their way into the mix. Vegetarian and international cuisines are popular, offering respite from the monotony of chain-dining and *comida típica*. Authentic *tico* fare like *casados* and *gallo pinto* are sold in *sodas* throughout the city. Most have cheap lunch and dinner specials (¢1400-2200). Take advantage of the various options and consider doing a little diner-hopping.

SAN JOSÉ

The *mercado central* sells cheaper meals that you can cook in your own hostel kitchen. For a more extensive selection, head to the local supermarkets like **Más X Menos,** Av. Central, C. 11/13 (open daily 6:30am-midnight; AmEx/MC/V) and **Automercado,** at Av. 3, C. 3, on the other side of town (☎2233 5511; open M-Sa 7am-8pm, Su 8am-3pm). Most of the higher-quality, more pleasant *sodas* and restaurants are in the vicinity of Av. Central.

🏠 **Restaurante Grano de Oro,** Av. 2/4, C. 30 (☎2255 3322). An international dining experience at one of San José's best hotels. The pleasant meal begins with attentive service and ends just as sweetly with a chocolate truffle. Start with an arugula, spinach, and parmesan salad (¢3300), then continue with filet mignon (¢12,100) or ravioli with spinach and goat cheese (¢6500). For an undeniably romantic setting, dine at dusk in the garden courtyard. Open daily 6am-10pm. AmEx/D/MC/V. ❸

Nuestra Tierra, Av. 2, C. 15 (☎2258 6500). Candle-lit wooden tables decorated with newspapers from the early 1900s, *vaquero*-uniformed waiters, and meals served on palm leaves. Try the *gallo pinto* breakfast with delicious fried eggs (¢2500). For lunch or dinner, order the house cocktail (¢4900) and a steak (¢6800). There are no vegetarian options. Service is temperamental. Parking available across C. 15. Menu in Spanish and English. Open 24hr. AmEx/D/MC/V. ❸

Restaurant Tin Jo, Av. 6/8, C. 11. (☎2221 7605; www.tinjo.com). Broad selection of exotic Asian fusion cuisine, and an elegant ambience composed of an indoor fountain and warm-colored tapestries on the walls. Vegetarian-friendly menu. Unique desserts include fried banana tempura with vanilla or coconut ice cream (¢2200) and lemon cheesecake with blackberry sauce. The waitstaff is friendly and attentive. Start out with satay (¢2800) or sushi (¢3300-5600). Curries and pad thai ¢4200-7800. Open M-Th 11:30am-3pm and 5:30-10pm, F-Sa 11:30am-3pm and 5:30-11pm, Su 11:30am-10pm. AmEx/D/MC/V. ❷

Shakti, Av. 8, C. 13 (☎2222 4475). This haven of healthy goodness serves only vegetarian dishes and white meat, a change from the typical fare of *gallo pinto* and fried meat. Frutas Shakti offers a light mix of fruit, yogurt, and granola (¢2200). *El Vampiro* (the vampire) combines oranges, sugar beets, and carrots (¢750). The avocado sandwich is delicious and comes with salad (¢1800). In keeping with its health-minded mission, no alcohol is served. While waiting for your food, read up on the healthy and sanitary processes used to produce your meal. Various herbal supplements, breads, and cookies sold at the counter. *Especiál* (main dish, soup, salad, and drink) ¢2400. Open M-F 7:30am-7pm, Sa 7:30am-6pm. D/MC/V. ❶

Cafe Mundo (☎2233 6272). A romantic restaurant that won't break the bank. The Italian fare is served by candlelight and the outside setting overlooks a small pond (look closely for the large fish). Pastas ¢2800-5500. Chicken dishes ¢4200-5000. Desserts include crepes with strawberries, flan, and tiramisu (¢1200-2200). Open M-Th 11am-10:30pm, F 11am-11:30pm, Sa 5-11:30pm. AmEx/D/MC/V. ❶

La Grand Ma, Av. 1, C. 1/3 (☎2221 3996). Packed with locals on their lunch breaks, La Grand Ma serves a wide variety of Costa Rican comfort foods. *Casados* with chicken, beef, and fried fish (¢2250) are popular, as is the selection of *almuerzos caribeñoes,* all of which come with rice and beans (¢3150-3650). Plate of the day with drink ¢2000. Open M-F 8am-5:30pm, Sa 9am-4pm. MC/V. ❶

Restaurant Vishnu Vegetariano, Av. 1, C. Central/1 (☎2256 6063). A variety of appetizing salads available (¢2100-3000). The *ensalada de frutas,* a tropical fruit salad with granola and ice cream or yogurt, is a favorite. Veggie burger combos (¢1700) and vegetarian pizza (¢2500). Don't leave without trying the yogurt smoothie, *morir soñando* ("to die dreaming"; ¢1400). Open M-Sa 7am-9pm, Su 9am-7pm. Other locations include Av. 4, C. 1 (next to the Banco Popular), Av. 8, C. 11/13, and Av. Central, C. 14. AmEx/MC/V. ❶

Soda El Parque, Av. 4/6, C. 2 (☎2258 3681). El Parque's round-the-clock hours draw suit-clad businessmen for lunch and late-night revelers just before dawn. Everyone comes for the same reason: cheap and tasty *comida típica.* The spacious seating area with large ceiling fans provides an escape from the heat or rain. Breakfast ¢700-3000. *Casados* ¢2500-7000. Sandwiches ¢1650-4200. Open 24hr. AmEx/MC/V. ❶

Jicaras del Campo (☎2520 1757). Take a taxi or the Escazú bus to the south side of La Sabana, 150m west from La Contrabría. Enjoy a gigantic selection of *casados* (¢2495) or go for one of the many chicken dishes (¢950). Spacious seating, arched windows, and music from a *marimba* add to the pleasant *tico* ambience. Beer ¢880. Open daily 1-10pm, buffet 1-3pm. AmEx/MC/V. ❶

SAN JOSÉ

ON THE MENU

COMPONENTS OF A CASADO

Although Costa Rica offers various cheap meals, the best for your stomach is the *casado*. Traditionally, wives would prepare this traditional *campesino* dish for their husbands to take to the fields. Today, the dish is enjoyed all over Costa Rica, in basic *sodas* and gourmet restaurants. Most often a lunch option, *casados* are also filling enough for dinner. They include a combination of the following:

Meat: The most common type used is steak, although chicken and fish are almost always available as substitutes. A *casado mexicano* features spicy steak or pulled pork. Vegetarians can ask for any casado "sin carne."

Rice and Beans: These Costa Rican staples—black or red beans and fried or steamed white rice—are sometimes mixed together as *gallo pinto*, or served separately. If you're lucky, your rice and beans may be spiced up with some sauéed onions or scallions.

Fried Plantains: Known as *plátano maduro* or *plátano dorado*, this delicious side is perhaps the best part of the casado. Sometimes served whole, sometimes served sliced, *plátano maduro* is always delicious.

Salad: Loosely interpreted, the salad can be anything—a sliced cole slaw-like concoction, or an elaborate array of local produce dressed in zesty lemon sauce.

Taquería La Moderna, C. 2, Av. 6/8 (☎2223 0513), near the corner of Av. 6. This tiny restaurant is easily missed—look for the line of benches with bright fruit tablecloths and a colorful mural inside. Offers incredibly cheap eats, but the portions are just as small as the prices. Tacos ¢400. Hot dogs ¢450. *Casados* ¢1500. *Empanadas* ¢350. Open M-Sa 7am-9pm, Su 8am-7:30pm. ❶

SAN PEDRO

The heart of San José's student scene, San Pedro is full of inexpensive cafes and restaurants. From San José, catch a bus to San Pedro from Av. Central, C. 9/11 (10min., every 5-10min., ¢190), pass **Mall San Pedro,** and get off when you see the outlet mall to your right. The main drag into San Pedro is **Avenida Central.** The street running perpendicular next to the outlet mall is **Calle Central.** Walk north down C. Central with the **Parque John F. Kennedy** to your left and the outlet mall behind you. The first street on your right leads to C. de la Amargura; a left on C. 3 leads to the University, and a right leads back down to Av. Central. This loop is packed with students all year.

▨ **Jazz Cafe** (☎2253 8933; www.jazzcafecostarica.com), 200m east of C. 3 on Av. Central. An upscale place with live performances every night and meals named after jazz singers and their songs. "Round Midnight" is the filet mignon (¢6300). The food is tasty, but it's the mixed drinks (¢1750-2750), like the Jazz Cocktail (a mix of rum and fruit juice), that really attract large late-night crowds. A different Costa Rican jazz or blues band performs every night. Cover ¢2500-3000. Open daily 6pm-2am. AmEx/MC/V. ❸

▨ **La Oliva Verde** (☎2280 2908), Av. Central, near OmniLife, 300m west of JFK Park. Fresh salads and wraps are made before your eyes in this Mediterranean sandwich shop. Try the Pita Oliva Verde (¢2500), with grilled vegetables, feta cheese, olives, and pesto sauce on soft pita bread. Salad ¢3375. Reduced calorie sauces and nutritional information on every meal. Fruit smoothies from ¢975. Shots of vitamins and minerals from ¢450. Open M-Sa 11am-7:30pm. AmEx/MC/V. ❷

Pizzería Il Pomodoro (☎2224 0966), 25m north of JFK Park on C. Central. The aroma of garlic drifts into the street, drawing those tired of rice and beans into this welcoming Italian eatery. Generous portions of crispy thin-crust pizzas (¢2200-4200) and pastas (¢2000-3500). Beer ¢950. Wine ¢1250. Open M and W-Su 11:30am-11pm. Only pastas and salads are available between 2:30pm and 6pm. AmEx/D/MC/V. ❶

Restaurante Vegetariano (☎2224 1163), 150m north of JFK Park on C. Central. Identifiable only by a worn sign over the entrance, this small restaurant offers a surprisingly comprehensive selection of healthy vegetarian meals. Try one of the 8 different vegetable soups on the menu (from ₡1550) or go for the house special *"Plato Fuerte,"* with brown rice, salad, and avocados (₡2200). MC/V. ❶

👁 SIGHTS

▨TEATRO NACIONAL. Small but exquisite, the National Theater is a must-see. In 1897, the construction of the theater was inspired (and funded) by Costa Rican citizens clamoring for more cultural venues. Because it was originally a product of their interest and money, *ticos* take a great deal of pride in this site. The theater is graced with sculpted banisters overlaid in gold, marble floors, and frescoes. Designed by sculptor Pitro Bulgarelli, statues representing Dance, Music, and Fame adorn its facade. The lobby features Costa Rica's most famous mural, a collage of the crops that brought the country its prosperity—bananas and coffee. A grand staircase inspired by the Paris Opera ascends toward bright overhead reliefs. Performances include ballet, drama, classical music, and opera. *(Av. 2, C. 3, southwest corner of the Plaza de la Cultura. ☎ 2258 5135; www.teatronacional.go.cr. Open M-Sa 9am-4pm. 30min. tours available in English or Spanish on the hr., except at noon; ₡2909/US$5. Ask about performances—often 3 per week—and ticket prices at the ticket window.)*

MUSEO NACIONAL. This museum offers an overview of Costa Rican history and early Costa Rican life. The building has been transformed from a military headquarters (the Cuarto Bellarista) into the home of a collection of artifacts. Though the front is still riddled with bullet-marks from the 1948 Revolution, the interior is full of pre-Columbian art, along with exhibits on Costa Rican history, archaeology, and geology. Don't miss the view of San José from the fort's highest point or the butterfly garden on the lowest level. *(Av. Central/2, C. 17. ☎ 2257 1433 or 2256 4139. Open M-Sa 8:30am-5pm, Su 9am-4:30pm. ₡2325/US$4, students ₡1,162/US$2.)*

MUSEO DE JADE. Costa Rica's Social Security building is an unlikely location for, reportedly, the world's largest collection of American jade. The emerald-colored mineral was of particular importance to Costa Rica's indigenous groups, who used it for jewelry and talismans. The museum also has a small collection of tools and weapons dating back to pre-Columbian times. The exhibits have English and Spanish explanations; ask the security guards for more in-depth information. *(Av. 7, C. 9/1. ☎ 2287 6034. Open M-F 8:30am-3pm, Sa 9am-1pm. ₡1162/US$2. MC/V.)*

PARQUE DE ESPAÑA AND PARQUE MORAZÁN. Complete with well-manicured lawns, benches, and a majestic dome that appears to have been taken straight from a Shakespearean play, these neighboring parks are a tranquil place to rest aching feet. Sudden downpours draw crowds of students, couples, and businessmen looking to stay dry under Morazán's dome. You might even get to see some locals practicing their juggling skills. *(Av. 3/7, C. 5/13. Free.)*

MUSEO DE ARTE COSTARRICENSE. Housed in a terminal of San José's old airport, this small museum is filled with temporary modern art exhibitions and a permanent collection of Costa Rican nationalist art from the 19th and 20th centuries. Those with time on their hands can explore the walls of the Salón Dorado, carved and painted to look like gold, with the history of Costa Rica depicted across all four sides. Check out the sculpture garden behind the museum. For a better view of the stone courtyard and Parque La Sabana, go out on the terrace. *(Paseo Colón, C. 42, on the eastern edge of Parque La Sabana. ☎ 2222 7155; www.musarco.go.cr. Open M-F 9am-5pm, Sa-Su 10am-4pm. M-Sa ¢2909/US$5, students ¢1743/US$3; Su free.)*

 SNEAK PEAK. The **Centro Nacional** houses the national Companies of Dance and Theater. Even if there are no performances scheduled during your visit, you will likely see the dancers, actors, or gymnasts practicing if you quietly and unobtrusively enter the building from the **Parque de España.**

CENTRO NACIONAL DE ARTE Y CULTURA. This impressive fortress of the arts, between Parque de España and the National Library, offers cultural events in some of Costa Rica's oldest edifices. These buildings that have survived everything from earthquakes to civil unrest. Two active theaters share space with the Museo de Arte y Diseño Contemporaneo, which hosts rotating exhibits by contemporary artists in a warehouse-like space. Stop by to see if a performance is running; schedules are on the lowest level near the press office and at the airport. *(Av. 3, C. 15/17. Enter from the southeast corner for the museum and the west side for performances. ☎ 2257 7202; www.mad.ac.cr. Open M-F 10:30am-5:30pm. Tu-Su ¢1162/US$2, students ¢300, M free. Performance prices vary.)*

🛍 SHOPPING

San José's size and high concentration of tourists make buying everything from basic necessities to souvenirs easier—and sometimes cheaper—than in other Costa Rican towns. You'll find the best selection of Costa Rican art, woodwork, jewelry, clothing, hammocks, and other souvenirs at a strip of vendors on Av. Central/2, C. 13/15, near the **Plaza de la Democracia.** (Most vendors open M-Sa 8am-6pm, some open Su.) Another option is **La Casona,** C. Central, Av. Central/1, where several souvenir stores are clustered under one roof. (Most stores open daily M-Sa 9:30am-6:30pm, some open Su.) Serious art collectors should check out San José's wonderful art galleries, many along Av. 1 between C. 5 and 13. **Las Arcadas,** with an entrance on C. 3 between Av. Central/2, and on Av. 2 between C. 3/5, houses clothing stores, beauty salons, an ICT office, and internet and laundry facilities in a two-story plaza. For a standard Western selection of clothing and sportswear (not to mention food courts), take a San Pedro-bound bus to **Mall San Pedro** or the **Outlet Mall.** (Both open daily 10am-8pm.)

📷 **Galería Namu,** Av. 7, C. 5/7 (☎ 2256 3412; www.galerianamu.com). For authentic crafts, visit the only fair-trade gallery in Costa Rica. Namu purchases works from the country's 8 indigenous groups and from folk artists. Check out the carved wood masks (from ¢70,038), colorful tiles (¢11,673), and paintings (¢81,711). Each piece comes with a page on its origins. Ships internationally. Open M-Sa 9am-6:30pm, Su 1:15-4:30pm. MC/V.

🎭 ENTERTAINMENT

A number of 24hr. casinos have opened in San José, many in hotels on Av. 1 near C. 5. Movie theaters throughout San José show US releases with Spanish subtitles.

Fiesta Casino, Av. Central, C. 7/9. Tables and slots if you want to try your luck. You must be 18 or older to gamble.

Cine Variedades, Av. Central/1, C. 5 (☎ 2222 6108), downtown. M-Tu and Th-Su ¢1000, W ¢500. MC/V.

Sala Garbo (☎2223 1960) and **Teatro Laurence Olivier** (☎2222 1034), both on Av. 2, C. 28, 100m south of the Paseo Colón Pizza Hut. Show a varied selection of older films from Latin and North America (¢2000).

Multicines San Pedro (☎2280 0490), on the 3rd floor of San Pedro Mall. Modern theaters with digital sound (¢1800, children ¢1500). MC/V.

Salón de Patines Music, 200m west of JFK Park in San Pedro. Rollerskate (¢2000 with rental skates) and listen to pop music. Skating for kids and parents Sa-Su 10am-12:30pm. Open daily 7-10pm.

▓ NIGHTLIFE

San Pedro pulses with life at night: the dances are *salsa* and *merengue*, and the drinks are *cervezas* and *guaro* cocktails. The scenes range from karaoke bars full of *ticos* belting Latin tunes to American sports bars packed with tourists playing pool and swapping gringo wit. **Calle de la Amargura** is always hopping and is the best place to meet young *ticos*. Most establishments have ¢1000-1500 covers (sometimes more for men), though they are somewhat negotiable and typically include drinks. Dress is casual; a t-shirt is fine in San Pedro bars, but you might want to throw on some dressier threads to go to the El Pueblo and San José clubs. It's a good idea to bring your ISIC card or passport out with you, as most clubs and bars require a valid ID for entrance.

CENTRO COMERCIAL EL PUEBLO

A 15min. ride north of San José center, El Pueblo is the place to find wild nights of dancing and drinking. The gift shops, bars, and dance clubs usually pick up after 11pm. El Pueblo is easily accessible by taxi (¢800-1200). Since the complex is saturated with tourists, petty crime is not uncommon. Beware of thieves who target drunken revelers as they exit. Likewise, be wary of cab drivers who charge too much for pick-ups inside the complex. Walk out to the road for a taxi, but be cautious.

Ebony 56 (☎2223 2195), on your right in the main parking lot. This sleek, ultra-modern club attracts a mix of travelers and locals, mostly in their 20s. Brave revelers dance on a silver stage while the rest watch from space-age couches made of leather and metal piping. Music ranges from reggae and rave to *salsa* and pop, depending on the night and mood. Th Ladies' night. Beer ¢800. Mixed drinks ¢1500. Cover ¢1000-2000. Open daily 6pm-6am.

Twister Club (☎2222 5746), toward the back and on the left of El Pueblo. Attracts a late-20s crowd that gets hot and heavy on the dance floor. Crowds form early, but house beats pumping loud enough to hear from the end of the line keep bodies moving. Gringos are welcomed and may be pleased with the American music selection. Beer ¢800. Mixed drinks ¢1000-1500. Open daily 6:30pm-3am.

Bongo's (☎2222 5746), around the corner from its sister club, Twister. A mixed-age crowd gathers to socialize and dance to house music. Bongo's offers TVs and foosball tables; more seating but less dancing than Twister. Beer ¢800. Mixed drinks ¢2000. Cover ¢1000-2000. Open daily 5pm-4am.

NEAR THE CITY CENTER

San José's center is crawling with bars and clubs, many of them hidden between *sodas* and shops. Bars and clubs often remain shuttered during the day, only to emerge at night with lit signs, loud music, and raucous laughter. Many host a wide range of ages chatting over drinks, while others blast popular Latin hits for expert dancers; most places have a little bit of both.

Salsa 54, Av. 1/3, C. 3 (☎2223 3814). A meeting place for seasoned dance veterans. The soundtrack is a hodgepodge of love songs, 60s hits, *salsa,* and reggae. Many of the dancers are experts, but don't let that stop you from joining them on the floor. Beer ¢800. Mixed drinks ¢1200-1800. Cover around ¢1500. Open M-Sa 7pm-late, Su 2-9pm.

Salidas Orbital 2000, Av. 1/3, C. 3 (☎2233 3814), above Salsa 54. A younger crowd of 20-somethings grooves to pop, tango, *salsa,* and *merengue* on 3 small stages amid a sea of plush red cocktail tables. Male and female models wearing almost nothing dance in the Model Revue. Karaoke depending on the mood. Cover ¢1500. Beer ¢800. Mixed drinks ¢1200-1800. Open F-Sa 7pm-late.

El Cuartel de la Boca del Monte, Av. 1, C. 21/23 (☎2221 0327). Restaurant by day and party spot by night. A good place for large groups—VIP area and lots of seating. Features local bands on M and occasionally on weekends. Rock on Sa. Cover ¢2000 for live music; M women no cover. Beer ¢800. Mixed drinks ¢1500. Open daily 11:30am-3pm and 6pm-3am.

SAN PEDRO

The enormous bar scene near the University in San Pedro is student-oriented and casual. People and music overflow into the streets, making the area relatively safe, though partiers should still take precautions. C. 3, north of Av. Central, known as **Calle de la Amargura,** is the heart of the college scene. There are fewer tourists, making it easier to meet outgoing *tico* students. All bars on C. de la Amargura may close early on weeknights, depending on turnout.

Caccio's. Contains a breezy outdoor patio. Beer ¢800. No cover. Open M-Sa 11am-1am.

Bar Tavarúa. A surf and skate bar that opens up a back room for dancing on crowded nights. Beer ¢650. Open M-Sa 11am-2am.

Terra U. A large student hangout often blasting reggaeton. Beer ¢650. Pitchers ¢1550 before 6:15pm, ¢2000 after. Open daily 10:30am-2am. AmEx/MC/V.

CENTRAL VALLEY

The Central Valley, or *Meseta Central*, makes up the heart of Costa Rica, forming its demographic as well as geographic center. Cordoned off by the two great volcanic ranges that divide the country, this valley is home to four of the nation's five largest cities and almost two-thirds of the entire *tico* population. But the cities and coffee fields cover up the explosive truth: two of the region's towering volcanoes (Irazú and Poás) are still active and have caused the valley's residents heartache on multiple occasions. And yet, residual volcanic ash has secured much of the region's livelihood, blessing these temperate plains and rolling hills with enough fertile soil to cultivate crops and rich coffee.

ALAJUELA

Alajuela, 3km from the international airport and 17km northwest of San José, is perhaps the cleanest and calmest of Costa Rica's cities. Small restaurants and B&Bs anchor the city's family-oriented environment. The town is a good base for pleasant wildlife excursions. For those who simply want to stay put and soak up the scenery, Alajuela's *parque central*, which spreads out in front of a colonial red-domed cathedral, is a good place to sit and relax. As is generally the case, the area closest to the *parque central* is the safest. Tourists should avoid wandering too far afield at night. Still, Alajuela maintains a sunny character with inviting, friendly people, and is a perfect final destination before a flight out of the country.

▣ TRANSPORTATION

Buses: From the **TUASA station,** Av. Central/1, C. 8 (☎2442 6900), 350m west of the southwest corner of the *parque central,* buses go to **San José** (45min., every 5min. 4am-10pm, ₡370) and **Volcán Poás** (1hr.; M-Sa 9:15am, return 2:30pm; ₡1750 round-trip). Buses to **Sarchí** depart 200m west of the *mercado central* (1hr.; M-Sa every 25-30min. 4:55am-10:15pm, Su every 25min. 5:15am-10:15pm; ₡605).

Taxis: A ride to or from the airport should cost no more than ₡1500.

◆ ▣ ORIENTATION AND PRACTICAL INFORMATION

Arriving at the TUASA bus station, turn right onto the *avenida* at the top of the station, then walk 350m until you reach the **parque central,** boxed in by **Avenida Central/Avenida 1** and **Calle Central/Calle 2.** Look for the white **cathedral** on the far end and a white dome-like shelter over a stage. The streets of Alajuela form the standard Costa Rican grid, but street signs are rare, so it's best to count the blocks or use landmarks, as locals do.

Banks: Banco Nacional, Av. Central/1, C. 2 (☎2440 9200). Open M-F 8:30am-3:45pm. **Scotiabank,** Av. 1/3, C. 2 (☎2441 1131). Open M-F 8:30am-6pm. Both have MC/V **ATMs** open 5am-10pm. Scotiabank changes Citibank and V traveler's checks; 1% commission. **Bac San José,** Av. 3, C. Central/1 (☎2443 4380), changes AmEx Travelers

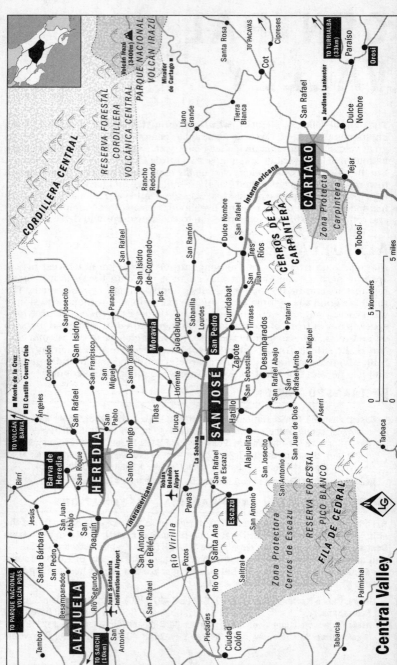

Central Valley

Cheques for a 1% commission. Open M-F 9am-7pm, Sa 9am-1pm. There is a **BCAC/ Bancrédito 24hr. ATM** on Av. Central/2, C. 2, and **24hr. ATMs** inside both Palí and MegaSuper. Open M-F 10am-6:30pm, Sa 9am-5pm. **Western Union** (☎2442 6392) is inside Palí. Open M-Sa 8:30am-1pm and 2-7pm, Su 10am-1:30pm and 2-5pm.

Bookstore: Goodlight Books, Av. 3, C. 3/5 (☎2430 4083; www.goodlightbooks.com). Enjoy *espresso* (¢400) or a dessert (¢350-500) while browsing the selection of new and used English-language books and maps. Internet ¢500 per hr. Free map of the city. Open daily 9am-6pm. **Libros Chiloé,** Av. 5, C. 2/4 (☎2242 7419), across from Hotel Cortez Azul. Buys and sells used books (¢500-3000). Open M-Sa 8:30am-6pm.

Laundry: La Batea, Av. 5/7, C.4 (☎2440 2691). Open M-F 7am-5pm, Sa 7am-4pm. AmEx/D/MC/V.

Public toilets: At the *mercado central.* ¢100.

Police: (☎2440 8889, or 911), 1 block north and 4 blocks east of the *parque's* north-east corner, around the corner from the fire station. Some English spoken. Open M-F 9am-5pm. Emergencies 24hr.

Pharmacy: Farmacia Santa Lucía, Av. Central/2, C. 1 (☎2440 0404). Open M-F 8am-8pm, Sa 9am-6pm. MC/V.

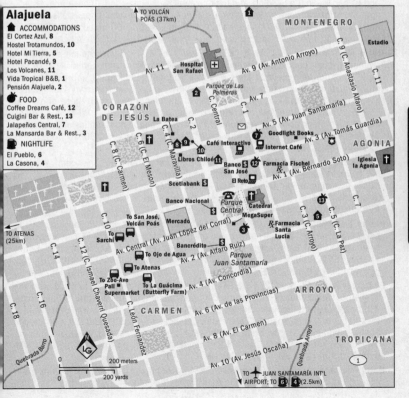

Hospital: Av. 9, C. Central/1 (☎2436 1001), 5 blocks north of the northeast corner of the *parque*, facing Parque de las Palmeras. Open 24hr.

Telephones: Both coin- and card-operated phones are available around the *parque.*

Internet Access: El Reto, Av. 1, C. Central/1 (www.elretocr.com). New computers with Skype and headsets. Internet ¢250 per 30min., ¢350 per hr. Calls to the US ¢50 per min. M-Sa 8am-10pm, Su 10am-7pm. **Conexion,** Av. 3/5, C. 1. Computers with headsets as well as private international calling booths with fans. Internet ¢350 per hr. Calls to the US ¢60 per min. Open daily 7am-7pm. AmEx/D/MC/V. **Café Interactivo,** Av. 3, C. Central/1 (☎2431 1984), is small with older computers. Internet ¢250 per 30min., ¢350 per hr. Open M-Sa 9am-9pm.

Post Office: Av. 5, C. 1 (☎2443 2653), 2 blocks north and 1 block east of the northeast corner of the *parque.* Open M-F 8am-5:30pm, Sa 7:30am-noon. **Postal Code:** 2101. MC/V.

ACCOMMODATIONS

Vida Tropical B&B (☎2443 9576; www.vidatropical.com), 100m east and 300m north of the hospital, across from the Academia de Natación. Decorated in bright tropical colors, this comfortable B&B feels just like home. Five cozy rooms share 2 beautiful baths; 1 room at the back of the garden has a private bath. Guests enjoy pleasant 1st- and 2nd-floor sitting areas with TV, hammocks, and a balcony. The managers, Norman and Isabel, live in the building, and their hospitality is unmatched. Choose from breads, eggs, and tropical fruits for breakfast. Laundry ¢1740. Free local phone calls, internet, and Wi-Fi. Singles ¢17,400; doubles ¢26,100; triples ¢31,900; quads ¢37,700. Children under 12 free. Ask about reduced rates for extended stays. Cash only. ❸

Hotel Mi Tierra, Av. 2, C. 3/5 (☎2441 1974 or 4022; www.hotelmitierra.net). A swimming pool, communal kitchen, and cozy sitting room with cable TV make this hotel a comfortable place to hang out. When he isn't landscaping and painting, the multilingual owner, Roberto, provides a wealth of info about the town. Personalized kayaking and rafting tours available, often at a cheaper price than those offered by large companies. Breakfast and airport transportation included. Wi-Fi in common area. Free parking and luggage storage. Package discounts for families and students. Singles and doubles ¢20,300, with bath ¢23,200; triples ¢23,200/29,000; quads ¢29,000/31,900. AmEx/MC/V. ❸

Los Volcanes, Av. 3, C. Central/2 (☎2441 0525; www.hotellosvolcanes.com). Welcoming fountains and cream-colored walls accentuate the subtle sophistication of this classy accommodation. Breakfast and airport transportation included. Free Wi-Fi and local calls. Singles ¢20,300 (US$35), with hot-water bath ¢26,680 (US$46); doubles ¢26,680/34,800 (US$46/60); triples ¢34,800/42,920 (US$60/74). MC/V. ❸

Hostel Trotamundos, Av. 5, C. 2/4 (☎2430 5832; www.hosteltrotamundos.com). This backpacker hangout is family-owned and offers free internet, cable TV in all rooms, and a communal kitchen. Breakfast included. Free baggage storage and tour information. Dorms ¢6960 (US$12); singles ¢14,500 (US$25), with hot-water bath ¢20,300 (US$35); doubles ¢14,500/20,300 (US$25/35); triples ¢23,200/26,100 (US$40/45). MC/V. ❷

El Cortez Azul, Av. 5, C. 2/4 (☎2443 6145). The common area is filled with the English-speaking manager's artwork. Common kitchen, small backyard, clean rooms, 2 sitting areas with modern couches and cable TV. Services include whitewater rafting trips, tours to Volcán Poás, Volcán Arenal, the La Paz Waterfalls, and the area around Alajuela. Wi-Fi in common area. Tour info at his brother's website, www.hotelmitierra.com. Single-sex dorms ¢5800 (US$10); singles and doubles ¢14,500 (US$25), with bath ¢20,300 (US$35). AmEx/MC/V. ❶

Hotel Pacandé, Av. 5, C. 2/4 (☎2443 8481; www.hotelpacande.com). A spiral staircase at the back of this hotel leads to a brightly painted loft (with private bath) that can house up to 4 people (US$40-60/¢23,200-34,800, depending on group size). Outside common area is surrounded by flower bushes. Breakfast of fruit and coffee is served on the patio. All rooms have mirrors and towels. Free internet, local calls, and transportation from the airport. Singles and doubles ¢16,240 (US$28), with bath ¢23,200 (US$40). Their second location, Pacandé Villa, is located 2.5km north of town toward Volcan Poás. AmEx/MC/V. ❷

▊ FOOD

The largest supermarket in town is **Palí,** four blocks west and one block south of the southwest corner of the *parque.* (☎2442 6392. Open M-Th 8:30am-7pm, F-Sa 8am-8pm, Su 8:30am-6pm.) **MegaSuper,** on the south side of the *parque* at Av. Central, C. Central/2, is smaller but closer to the town center. (☎2441 1384. Open M-Th 8am-9pm, F-Sa 7am-9pm, Su 7am-8pm.) The *mercado central,* two blocks west of the *parque,* is a crowded collection of meat, cheese, fruit, and vegetable stands. (Open M-F 7am-6pm, Sa 6am-6pm.)

▩ **Cuigini Bar and Restaurant,** Av. Central, C. 5 (☎2440 6893). Photos of Italian celebrities line the walls of this 2nd floor restaurant. Menu mixes Southern Italian with American classics. Appetizers range from french fries (¢1150) to Sicilian shrimp (¢3560). Entrees include pasta (¢2200-6500) and the Frank Sinatra burger (¢2670). Live *troba* 3 nights per week. Extensive liquor selection from the bar. Open M-W 11:30am-10pm, F-Sa 11:30am-11pm, Su 4-10pm. Bar open until midnight or later. AmEx/MC/V. ❶

▩ **Coffee Dreams Café,** Av. 1/3, C. 1 (☎2430 3970). It's not just the coffee that's a dream in this homey cafe. Dark wood tables and chairs and black-and-white photos of coffee farmers blend European style with Costa Rican authenticity. Choose from several satisfying entrees, such as the chicken lasagna, served with salad, garlic bread, *refresco natural,* and a delicious dessert (¢2500). Large selection of vegetarian dishes including salads, pies, and crepes (¢1800). Broccoli quiche ¢2500. A wide variety of coffee drinks (¢1400, without liquor ¢900) go great with the *tres leches* (¢1100) or strawberry cheesecake (¢1300). Open M-F 8am-8pm. MC/V. ❶

▩ **Jalapeños Central,** Av. 3/5, C. 1 (☎2430 4027), 50m south of the post office. Mexican *ponchos* and *sombreros* decorate the walls of this popular tourist restaurant. The Columbian owner, Norman, grew up in New York City and serves delicious Tex-Mex food, including burritos (¢1750) and quesadillas (¢1800). Try the excellent *sopa Azteca* (¢2000), with cheese, guacamole, and tortillas. Taco salad ¢3250. Takeout and vegetarian options available. Open M-Sa 11:30am-9pm. AmEx/MC/V. ❶

La Mansarda Bar and Restaurant (☎2441 4390), 25m south of the southeast corner of the *parque.* A large 2nd floor restaurant whose dining area has plenty of tables with balcony seating. No Costa Rican meal is complete without *ceviche* (¢4010-5290) or steamy *sopa de mariscos* (seafood soup ¢5450). Chicken dishes ¢3200-5950. Wine ¢2000 per glass, ¢6000 per bottle. Open daily 11:30am-1am. AmEx/D/MC/V minimum ¢3000. ❷

▊ ♫ NIGHTLIFE AND ENTERTAINMENT

The center of town is relatively deserted at night, and there are few nightlife options. Relax at the bar of one of the neighborhood restaurants or take a taxi (¢1300) to one of the lively, expensive bars across the street from the airport, which are packed with tourists. Though Alajuela is considered one of Costa Rica's safer cities, it is best to travel in a group or take a taxi after 9pm.

Cuigini Bar and Restaurant (☎2440 6893). Many of the waiters and patrons here speak English. Enormous selection of local and imported liquors. The restaurant upstairs serves delicious Italian-American and Southern cuisine. Don't miss the owner's special piña colada. Beer ¢700-900. Mixed drinks ¢1200-4200. Open Tu-Sa 11:30am-midnight or later, Su 4pm-midnight. AmEx/MC/V.

La Mansarda Bar and Restaurant (☎2441 4390), 25m south of the southeast corner of the *parque*, on the right. Primarily a restaurant, but the bar here sees some local action at night. Sa-Su live alternative rock music. Beer ¢700. Mixed drinks ¢1500. Open daily 11:30am-1am. AmEx/MC/V.

El Pueblo (☎2442 4270), past Fiesta Casino, on the road from the airport to Alajuela. Karaoke M-Sa 10pm, Su 4pm. Ask about the Bacardi 2-for-1 offer. Beer ¢1000. Mixed drinks ¢1500. Open M-Th and Su 9am-1am, F-Sa 9am-2:30am.

La Casona (☎2442 0066), on the road between Alajuela and the airport, across the street from El Pueblo. Popular with both tourists and locals, this spacious bar has a fountain and a big-screen TV. A large back room is sometimes used for live music and private functions. The menu includes seafood entrees (¢2600-7300) and a few Peruvian soups and *ceviches* (¢2500). Beer ¢1162. Mixed drinks ¢1740-2320. Open M-Th and Su 11am-midnight, F-Sa 11am-1am.

▶ DAYTRIPS FROM ALAJUELA

VOLCÁN POÁS

Take a taxi and arrive when the park first opens (1hr., ¢20,000 round-trip). Buses depart daily from San José's TUASA station, Av. 2, C. 12/14 (2hr., 8:30am, round-trip ¢22,250). They stop at the TUASA station in Alajuela at 9:15am (1hr., round-trip ¢1750) and arrive at Volcán Poás around 10:30am. The return bus leaves the park at 2:30pm. You may be done seeing the park before the return bus arrives; bring something to amuse yourself. Park open daily Dec.-Apr. 8am-4:30pm, May-Nov. 8am-3:30pm. ¢5800 (US$10), kids ¢11,600 (US$20).

Fifty-five kilometers northwest of San José, Parque Nacional Volcán Poás is a cloud forest accessible by trails lined with moss, orchids, and dangling bromeliads. Poás is the most-visited national park between Mexico and Panama because of its proximity to San José and Alajuela. A steam-belching crater at the top of active Volcán Poás (2574m) forms the park's main attraction. Inside the massive crater (1320m across and 300m deep) is a turquoise acid pool and *fumaroles* (vents in the earth's crust) that release bursts of volcanic steam. The cone looks like a rainbow carved into the terrain, with vibrantly colored layers of gray, white, and red earth that trace the history of the volcano's eruptions.

The **visitor center** features a small **museum** that educates guests about sustainability and eco-friendly practices. There is also a souvenir shop and a cafe with more than 20 flavors of cappuccino (¢900) and a smattering of lunch items and pastries (¢700-1000).

The most direct route to the crater is a 10min. walk up a gentle, paved path from the visitor center. **Laguna Botos,** the water-filled collapsed cone of a former volcano, is a 15min. walk beyond the crater. Look for the paved trail marked "Laguna Botos" just before the crater viewing area. It is an easy uphill walk. From there, return to the main trail or follow the more indirect Sendero Escalonia back to the parking area. Poás is most enjoyable in the morning, especially from May to November, as clouds and rain obscure the view by noon. Try to avoid visiting on Sundays, when the park is usually packed. The path to the crater is wheelchair-accessible and an ambulance is available.

TURRIALBA

Those who visit Turrialba love its down-to-earth feel and its location amid world-class rivers and stunning mountains. Nearby Ríos Reventazón and Pacuare have brought the town international fame; both are packed with Class

III-V rapids and some of the world's best river runs. Whitewater rafters and kayakers of all abilities ride the waters during the rainy season; other travelers stay here on their way to Costa Rica's most significant archaeological site, Monumento Nacional Guayabo. But those uninterested in adventure tours should also consider paying Turrialba a visit; it retains a small-town feel while offering the comforts of a city. During the day, locals hang out in the attractive *parque central*, and at night they fill the restaurants and bars singing. Due to Costa Rica's economic development projects, an increasing number of rivers may soon be dammed for hydroelectric power. Adventurers should take advantage of these natural resources while they still can.

TRANSPORTATION

Buses: Turrialba's bus terminal (☎2557 5050), 350m southwest of the *parque central*, on Av. 4. Tickets may be purchased at the terminal window prior to departure. Leave for **San José** (direct 1hr., indirect 2hr.; every hr. 5:15am-9pm; ¢1105) and pass through **Cartago** (1hr., ¢660). Available to **Siquirres** (2hr.; M-Th every hr. 6am-6:15pm, F-Su every hr. 6am-7pm; ¢920); **La Suiza** (30min.; M-F 5:30, 9, 11:20am, 1, 2, 2:30, 3:30, 3:50, 5, 6pm; Sa 9, 11:30am, 1, 2:30, 3:30pm, every hr. 5-10pm, Su 3:50, 4:50pm; ¢220); **Santa Cruz/Parque Nacional Volcán Turrialba** (1hr., ¢320). On weekends and

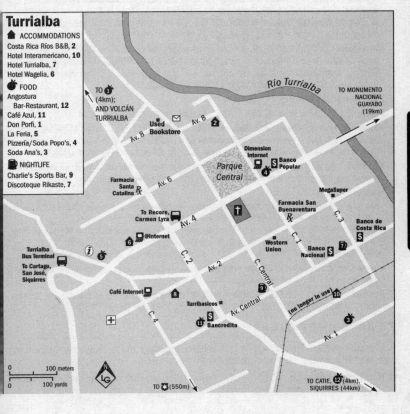

Turrialba

🛏 **ACCOMMODATIONS**
Costa Rica Ríos B&B, **2**
Hotel Interamericano, **10**
Hotel Turrialba, **7**
Hotel Wagelia, **6**

🍴 **FOOD**
Angostura
  Bar-Restaurant, **12**
Café Azul, **11**
Don Porfi, **1**
La Feria, **5**
Pizzería/Soda Popo's, **4**
Soda Ana's, **3**

🌙 **NIGHTLIFE**
Charlie's Sports Bar, **9**
Discoteque Rikaste, **7**

Río Turrialba

TO ❶
(4km);
AND VOLCÁN
TURRIALBA

TO MONUMENTO
NACIONAL
GUAYABO
(19km)

Used
Bookstore

Dimension
Internet

Banco
Popular

Parque
Central

MegaSuper

Farmacia
Santa
Catalina

Farmacia San
Buenaventura

To Recore,
Carmen Lyra

Banco de
Costa Rica

@Internet

Western
Union

Banco
Nacional

Turrialba
Bus Terminal

To Cartago,
San José,
Siquirres

Café Internet

Turribasicos

(no longer in use)

Bancredito

0   100 meters
0   100 yards

TO 🏕(550m)

TO CATIE, ❶❷(4km),
SIQUIRRES (44km)

CENTRAL VALLEY

in the high season you might have to buy tickets to San José a day or so in advance to grab a seat. Buses also leave from the terminal for **Monumento Nacional Guayabo** (1hr.; M-Sa 11:15am, 3:10, 5:30pm; return 5:15, 6:30am, 12:30, 4pm; Su 9am, 3, 6pm, return 6:30am, 12:30, 4pm).

Taxis: (☎2556 7070). Line up at the corner of Av. Central and C. Central. One-way ¢7000; round-trip (includes 1hr. wait) ¢15,000.

ORIENTATION AND PRACTICAL INFORMATION

In Turrialba, 62km east of San José, *calles* run perpendicular to *avenidas*, but none of the streets run exactly north-south or east-west. With the **parque central** as a reference point, most businesses and sights aren't too tough to find.

Tourist Office: There is a tourist office located next to La Feria, but it has variable hours. Patricia or Luis at **Hotel Interamericano** (below) are also able to provide information about the town and nearby sights in English.

Banks: All banks listed have **24hr. ATMs. Banco de Costa Rica** (☎2556 0472), 2 blocks south and 2 blocks east of the park. Open M-F 9am-4pm. **Banco Nacional** (☎2556 1211), a few meters west of Banco de Costa Rica. Open M-F 8:30am-3:45pm. Long lines tend to build up at the tellers. **Banco Popular** (☎2556 6098), on Av. 4, just east of Popo's. Open M-F 8:45am-4:30pm, Sa 8:15-11:30am. **BanCredito** (☎2556 4141), next to Cafe Azul and across the street from Turribasicos. Open M-F 8am-4pm, Sa 8am-11:30pm. **Western Union** (☎2556 0439), 100m south and 50m east of the south corner of the *parque,* is inside of Tienda La Moda. Open M-Sa 8am-6:30pm.

Bookstore: (☎2556 1697), diagonally across from the post office, north of the *parque* on C. Central. A wide selection of second-hand books (¢2000-5000) in English, French, German, Portuguese, and Spanish are sold in this tiny bookstore. Owner speaks English. Hours are flexible; usually M-F 8:30-11:30am and 2:30-5:30pm.

Emergency: ☎911.

Police: (☎2556 0030 or 8265), 500m south of the town center on C. 4.

Pharmacy: Farmacia Santa Catalina (☎2556 8983), Av. 6 and C. 2. Open M-Sa 8am-8pm, Su 4pm-7pm. MC/V. **Farmacia San Buenaventura** (☎2556 0379), Av. 2 and C. 1, one block west of the *parque* on Av. 6. Open M-Sa 8am-7:30pm, Su 8:30am-1pm. AmEx/MC/V.

Hospital: (☎2558 1311). Walk up the stairs at the west end of Av. 2, or drive west on Av. 4 past the bus station and turn left into the hospital. Open 24hr.

Internet:

   Eca Internet, across C. 1 from the *parque,* upstairs past Mama Mía's. Internet ¢300 per hr. Skype and webcams are available. Open M-F 8:30am-10pm, Sa-Su 9am-9pm.

   @Internet (☎2556 2857), just east of Hotel Wagelia on Av. 4. Internet ¢300 per hr. Black-and-white copying ¢20. Printing ¢100-600. Open M-F 8am-10pm, Sa-Su 9am-9pm.

   Cafe Internet (☎2256 4575), Av. 2 and C. 4. Modern computers, A/C. Internet ¢300 per hr.

Phone Cards: Available at **Pague aquí su Luz y Teléfono,** across the street from BanCredito. Open M-F 7:30am-5:30pm, Sa 8am-5pm.

Post Office: (☎2556 1679), 200m northwest of the north corner of the *parque,* across from the bookstore. Open M-F 8am-5:30pm. MC/V. **Postal Code:** 7150.

ACCOMMODATIONS

Although most of Turrialba's hotels are pricier, they may offer a nice place to rest and will arrange trips to nearby sights.

▨ **Hotel Interamericano** (☎2556 0142; www.hotelinteramericano.com), bright coral-and-orange building 3 blocks south and 1 block east of the *parque,* just behind the row of palm trees. The owners speak English and have a wealth of info about sights, guides, and restaurants. Amenities include hot-water showers, Wi-Fi (best near the balcony), and a large sitting area with cable TV. Breakfast and laundry service (wash ¢1500 per kg, dry ¢1000 per load) available. Towels are included, but bring your own for rafting. Reception 24hr. Singles ¢6380, with bath ¢14,500; doubles ¢12,800/20,300; triples ¢19,100/31,900; quads ¢25,500/37,700. V. Traveler's checks accepted. ❶

Costa Rica Ríos Bed and Breakfast (☎2256 6651; www.hotelturrialba.com). Renovated in a Spanish colonial style, Costa Rica Ríos primarily houses those on the week-long adventure tour (p. 83), but all are welcome. Named after surrounding rivers, the 10 airy rooms come with private hot-water baths, parking, free international calls, free self-service laundry, full breakfast, and Wi-Fi. Dinner can be requested for ¢8700. A few hang-out areas include a living room with board games, hot-tub, pool table, computer with internet, and mini-library. The rooftop deck has an amazing view of Volcán Turrialba. Reception 8am-6pm. Singles¢20,300; doubles ¢31,900; triples ¢43,500. AmEx/MC/V. ❸

Volcán Turrialba Lodge (☎2273 4335 or 0194; www.volcanturrialbalodge.com), about 1hr. from Turrialba and only a few km from the volcano's summit. Incredible views of the volcano and the valley from any of their lovely, cabin-style rooms. Perfect for those more interested in the outdoors than the town. Take advantage of the horseback, birdwatching, and hiking tours (p. 83). Common room with TV and comfortable couches. Electric heaters provided. One meal included. Homey singles, doubles, and triples, as well as a 4-bedroom cabin. ¢26,100 per person per night for any room combination. Busiest June-Oct.; reserve in advance. AmEx/MC/V. ❸

Hotel Wagelia (☎2556 1596; www.hotelwageliaturrialbacom), 1 block south of park, 1½ blocks west on Av. 2. 18 comfortable rooms surrounding a mini-garden and a bright outdoor common area. All rooms come with private hot-water baths with soap dispensers, A/C, and cable TV. A phone and safe deposit box are available. The attached restaurant-bar serves moderately priced entrees. Breakfast included. Laundry and tour service available. Wi-Fi. Check-in 2pm. Check-out noon. Singles ¢31,900; doubles ¢45,200; triples ¢48,700. AmEx/MC/V. Traveler's checks accepted. ❹

Hotel Turrialba (☎2556 6654), 100m south and 150m west of the *parque*. Murals decorate the hallways. All the rooms are simple, with wood-paneled walls, clean private hot-water baths, TVs, and ceiling and floor fans. Some rooms lack windows. Reception 24hr. Can place international calls. A/C ¢3000. Singles ¢7500; doubles ¢12,000; triples ¢15,000. AmEx/MC/V. ❷

🍴 FOOD

Dining options are limited to pizza, *comida típica*, and a few less-than-authentic Chinese restaurants. For fresh produce, check out the **farmer's market** along Av. Central. (Open every F and Sa.) The local **MegaSuper** (☎2556 1242) is 100m south and 100m east of the west corner of the *parque*. (Open M-Sa 7am-9pm, Su 7am-7pm. AmEx/D/MC/V.) **Turribasicos**, on C. 2, near the corner of Av. Central/C. 2, has a pharmacy and bakery inside. (☎2556 0933. Open M-Sa 7am-9pm, Su 8am-4pm.)

Restaurante Don Porfi (☎2556 9797), 4km outside of town on the road to Volcán Turrialba. Well worth the ¢2000 cab ride. Up the hill from Turrialba, Don Porfi is popular with locals but generally unknown to tourists. Excellent dishes include mixed seafood platters (¢3850-7000), beef tenderloin (7 varieties; ¢6200-6900), and chicken in garlic sauce (¢3600). The *batidos* are large and the service is highly professional. Try the house dessert, a fried banana crepe with ice cream (¢2000). Open M-Sa 11am-11pm, Su 11am-8pm. Reservations recommended during the high-season, especially on weekends. D/MC/V. ❸

La Feria (☎2557 5550), 200m west of the south corner of the *parque* past Hotel Wagelia, at intersection of Av. 2 and C. 4. Run by a superb chef in a charming set-

CENTRAL VALLEY

ting—local artists' work decorates the walls along with maps of Costa Rica and Turrialba, and soothing jazz plays in the background. Ancient Costa Rican artifacts are
on display as well. Affordable gourmet fare includes filet mignon (¢5150), *casados*
(¢1700), club sandwiches (¢2250), Fish La Feria (¢4850) and a wide variety of fruit
drinks (¢575) and milkshakes (¢750). Plenty of veggie options, like the fantastic
cream of tomato soup with toast (¢1900). Open M and W-Su 11:30am-9:30pm, Tu
11:30am-2:30pm. AmEx/MC/V. ❶

Soda Ana (☎2557 2397), behind Hotel Interamericano on Av. 1. Though this soda
has only a few tables and a very short menu, you most likely will not find a better
casado (¢2000) in town. Rice and beans (¢2000) served F-Su. Ask one of Ana's
sons to pull out their guitar from behind the counter and serenade you with classic
Latin tunes. Open daily 6am-10pm. Cash only. ❶

Angostura Bar-Restaurant (☎2556 5757), 4km outside of town in the opposite
direction of Don Porfi. Though not as elegant or well-established as Don Porfi, this
restaurant with similar prices does dish out some nice plates. With a bottle of wine
ready at each table, you can have the filet mignon (¢3800) or chicken in a cream
mushroom sauce (¢4000). It can get cool in the open-air seating during the rainy
season so consider bringing a light jacket. Taxi to the restaurant ¢2500-3000. Open
M and W-Sa 11am-10pm. Su 11am-9pm. MC/V. ❸

Pizzería/Soda Popo's (☎2556 0064), on the east side of the *parque*. Known for its simple
fare. If rafting has left you too tired to walk, you can order delivery until 11pm. Pizzas ¢2800-
4000, ¢700 per slice. You may have to wait approximately 20min. for a small pizza. Burritos
topped with ketchup, mustard, and mayo ¢600-850. Open daily 7am-11pm. V. ❶

👁 SIGHTS

VOLCÁN TURRIALBA. The scenic road to the summit is steep and winding, and
it becomes especially rocky after the town of Santa Cruz. Previously impassable by automobile, the last few kilometers have recently been repaved, so that
it is now possible, though not exactly easy, to drive all the way up the volcano.
The road, still bumpy and narrow, is most safely tackled in a four-wheel-drive
taxi. (From Turrialba 1-2hr.; roundtrip ¢25,000, includes wait time). The Santa
Cruz bus stops at the entrance to the park, 18km from the summit (1hr., ¢320).
It is best to make the trip early in the morning to avoid mid-day rains and to
catch the sun rising over the valley. Bring a sweatshirt and pants, since it is
often surprisingly cold at the summit.

Turrialba stands out among Costa Rica's volcanoes. Unfortunately, the path
down into the crater is now closed, as the volcano is still active, but you can
look down into the crater as the smoke blows away in the opposite direction. It
is relatively untouched, and there is no information station or entrance fee. For
a guided tour by horseback or on foot, check out **Volcán Turrialba Lodge** (p. 83).

🎭 🎵 NIGHTLIFE AND ENTERTAINMENT

Discoteque Rikaste (☎2556 8081), Av. Central, C. 1/3, beside Banco Nacional,
2nd floor. Dance the night away with locals and tourists on Sa. Cover depends
on time and size of crowd, but may be up to ¢1500. *Ticos* come to sit in the
outside area and drink beer with friends during the day. *Cervezas* ¢600. Sandwiches ¢1000-1500. *Platos fuertes* ¢1700-3000. Restaurant/bar open M-F and
Su 11am-12:30am, Sa 11am-2:30am. AmEx/D/MC/V.

Charlie's Sports Bar (☎2557 6565), Av. Central, C. Central, at the back of the complex.
Modern neon lighting, loud Latin music, and TVs make this new sports bar the perfect
place to catch a *fútbol* game. Buffalo wings ¢3700-5900. Hamburgers and sandwiches

Check Out Receipt

City of Calabasas Library
818-225-7616
www.calabasaslibrary.org

Tuesday, October 17, 2017 1:04:43 PM
27124

Title: Deep into dusk : a Gabriel McRay novel
Material: Books
Due: 11/07/2017

Title: Frommer's easyguide to Costa Rica
Material: Books
Due: 11/07/2017

Title: Let's go. Costa Rica, Nicaragua & Panama
Material: Books
Due: 11/07/2017

Total items: 3

    * Please Renew or Return Items by the
      Due Date to Avoid Fines *

¢2150-4490. Mixed drinks ¢2000. Shots ¢1500. Th Ladies' night. Open M-W and Su 4pm-midnight, Th-Sa 4pm-late.

Pocho's, on the main road in La Suiza. A bus goes to La Suiza every hr. until 10pm (30min., ¢205), but you'll have to take a taxi back if you're staying out later. This popular local bar draws *ticos* and tourists alike. The energetic owner entertains customers by juggling beer bottles and a machete. Look for signs in Turrialba that advertise periodic Sa night disco parties with Costa Rica's most popular DJs. Beer ¢700. Open daily 11am-late.

 TAKE COVER! During the rainy season, the lack of tourists means that those who brave the daily afternoon showers can often get into bars and clubs without paying a cover.

OUTDOOR ACTIVITIES AND GUIDED TOURS

Capitalizing on Turrialba's legendary rafting and kayaking opportunities, tour operators offer adventure trips for all abilities. A day on the rapids is expensive, but the experience is unforgettable, especially on the Pacuare, the most popular and beautiful of the area's rivers. If you have your own equipment or rent from one of the tour companies, your hotel should be able to arrange transportation to a nearby river. Ask about the nearby serpent farm (**Serpentario Viborana;** 10km away; ☎2538 1510), Volcán Turrialba, and the Aquiares waterfall.

Ríos Locos (☎2556 6035; www.whiteh20.com). Not one of Turrialba's largest companies, but it is one of the friendliest. 12 years of experience. These self-proclaimed Río Pacuare specialists offer rafting trips, horseback rides, and boat tours. They prefer small groups but will accommodate groups of up to 36 with advance notice. Class III-IV rafting on the Pacuare, Pejibaye, and Reventazón (half-day ¢29000, full-day ¢49,300). Photographer accompanies raft down river; photos available for negotiated price. Full day horseback tours along a jungle train line near the Peralta River (¢31,900). Can arrange a trip to Monumento Nacional Guayabo (¢23,200). Cash only.

Tico's River Adventures (☎2556 1231; www.ticoriver.com). A small local company that offers friendly service and years of experience. Specializing in rafting trips, Tico arranges day trips to the Pacuare (Class IV), Reventazón (Class II, III, or IV depending on trip), and Pascua (Class IV). Single-day trips ¢43,500 (US$75), include lunch. Special student rate of ¢34,800 (US$60) per person for groups of 10 or more. An all-inclusive 2-day Pacuare trip is also available (¢162,400/US$280 per person, includes hiking). Cash only.

Costa Rica Ríos (☎2556 9617; www.costaricarios.com), 10m north of the *parque*. Considered the most reputable rafting and kayaking operator and owns the largest fleet of water sports equipment in Central America. Offers exclusively pre-booked, all-inclusive, week-long adventure tours. Eight-day adventure (includes rafting, kayaking, canopy tour, and snorkeling) trip from ¢1,043,420 (US$1799); 8-day river-only (rafting and kayaking) trip from ¢927,420 (US$1599). The B&B provides a good place to relax after a week's worth of adventures. AmEx/MC/V.

Volcán Turrialba Lodge (☎2273 4335; www.volcanturrialbalodge.com). Offers a horseback tour to the top of Volcán Turrialba for ¢20,300 (US$35; 4-5hr. includes horse, guide, and snack). 2hr. hiking and birdwatching tours available (¢11,600/US$20). Mountain biking ¢17,400 (US$30). Rates do not include park entrance fees. AmEx/MC/V.

⬧ DAYTRIP FROM TURRIALBA

MONUMENTO NACIONAL GUAYABO

Buses to the entrance leave from the Turrialba bus terminal on Av. 4. (1hr.; M-Sa 11:15am, 3:10, 5:30pm; return 5:15, 6:30am, 12:30, 4pm; Su 9am, 3, 6:30pm; return 6:30am, 12:30, 4pm). Taxis are available (☎ 2556 7070); one-way ¢7000; round-trip ¢15,000, includes 1hr. wait. ☎ 2559 0117. Open daily 8am-3:30pm. US$6, children under 12 ¢580/US$1. Guided tour in English 1-3 people ¢5800 (US$10), 4-10 people ¢14,500 (US$25), 11-20 people ¢17,400 (US$30); in Spanish, ¢4000/7000/11,000.

Located 19km northeast of Turrialba, Monumento Nacional Guayabo is Costa Rica's most important archaeological site and the country's only National Monument. The park covers 218 hectares, although the archaeological site is just 20 hectares, and only four of those 20 have been excavated. Much remains unknown about the civilization that built and abandoned the site, though current estimates suggest that approximately 10,000 people lived here from 1500 BC to AD 1400, with most of the construction occurring after AD 800. Some say that the Guayabo people migrated to Colombia; in fact, many indigenous Columbians claim to have ancestors with similar traditions. The mysterious first inhabitants left records of their sophistication: their houses were built on large *montículos* (circular foundations), and they constructed *calzadas* (long causeways), a bridge, and an aqueduct system that still works today. The remnants of these structures can be found at the end of an easy 1½km trail called **Los Monticulous Path.** The path leads through rainforest to the focal point of the site, though you will pass a monolith, coffin graves, and several intricate petroglyphs along the way. **El Cando de Agua** (1km) leads from the park entrance to a rushing stream. Both trails, especially the shorter one, are very muddy in the rainy season; be sure to bring boots and rain gear. Take a copy of the pamphlet and ask if a guide can give a tour. The ruins are interesting, but there's not much else to see. There's a campsite (¢2320/US$4 per person) that has a toilet and a cold-water shower.

If you find yourself waiting for the bus, head down the road 500m to the **Guayabo Butterfly Garden.** Check out the meshed enclosure filled with 15 different specides of colorful butterflies, caterpillars, and cocoons. Osvaldo Salazar, the owner, can point out camouflaged butterflies and explain the entire growth process (30min.). There is also a guesthouse at the garden with access to a living room and fully equipped kitchen (☎8832 3586; open daily 8am-4pm; ¢2320. Guesthouse ¢17,400 per person). Also visit the neighboring restaurant **La Calzada Guayobo ❶** (☎2559 0437, open M-Tu, and Th-Su 8am-6pm). It is a bright and cheery place, decorated with farm implements leaning against the walls and painted wagon wheels hanging from the ceiling. Go for the grilled chicken breast (¢1950) or the rice and beans (¢1995).

NORTHERN LOWLANDS

Though it lacks the beachside glamour of other tourist hot spots, Costa Rica's mountainous northern region is home to a plethora of climates and travel destinations, from mountains and rolling green pastures to tropical rainforests and lagoons. Visitors to the lowlands will encounter a staggeringly diverse collection of wildlife, and those interested in more extreme adventure will find opportunities for windsurfing, rappelling, spelunking, and white-water rafting. Plus, while areas like Fortuna and Arenal see a huge influx of tourists every year, other parts of the lowlands are surprisingly untouristed, with a rich *campesino* culture mixed with city life in towns like Ciudad Quesada and Los Chiles. A gateway to Nicaragua and both the Atlantic and Caribbean coasts, the lowlands contain some of Costa Rica's most well-conserved examples of tropical rainforests, cloud forests, and marshlands. You can hike through the pristine jungles of Tirimbina Reserve or La Selva, drift along the swampy mangroves of Refugio Nacional Caño Negro, watch the lava flow on Volcán Arenal, and climb through the winding, bat-filled tunnels of the Venado Caves. Whether in search of extreme sports or a morning of relaxing sportfishing or birdwatching, visitors to the Northern Lowlands can strike a balance between tourism opportunities and authentic rural culture in an area distinguished for the richness and diversity of its natural wonders.

PUERTO VIEJO DE SARAPIQUÍ

Puerto Viejo de Sarapiquí is rapidly becoming a top destination for nature-lovers and thrill-seekers alike. The Río Sarapiquí, which runs just 200m from the main road, has opportunities for both wildlife sightings and river rafting. Numerous adventure ranches offer mountain biking and canopy trips for those who prefer land-based action. Despite the myriad outdoor opportunities available, the influx of tourists to the former banana town have had a minimal impact on the town itself; Puerto Viejo remains very small, with one main street and only a handful of hotels and restaurants. With world-class wildlife reserves such as Tirimbina and La Estación Biológica La Selva less than 30min. from town, Puerto Viejo is an ideal base for budget travelers looking to experience the natural wonders of the region.

▐ TRANSPORTATION

Buses: All leave from the station opposite the northwest corner of the soccer field. A schedule is posted inside next to the ticket counter. To: **Ciudad Quesada** (2hr., 12 per day 4:40am-8pm, ¢1230); **Guápiles** (1hr., 11 per day 5:30am-6:30pm, ¢785); **La Virgen** (30min., every hr. 6am-6pm, ¢350); **Río Frío** (1hr., 10 per day 7am-6pm, ¢500); **San José** (10 per day 5am-5:30pm, ¢1610) via **El Tunel Zurquí** or via **Vara Blanca** (5, 7:30, 11:30am, 4:30pm). Tell the cashier at the ticket counter if you want to get off before the final stop; some express buses do not stop at intermediate destinations.

Taxis: Line up along the main street just north of the soccer field. To La Virgen ¢5000.

◢ ▐ ORIENTATION AND PRACTICAL INFORMATION

Puerto Viejo extends along one main street for about 300m. A **soccer field** bordering this street marks the town center. The **bus station** marks the northwest side of this field, while the large stucco **church** sits on the southwest corner.

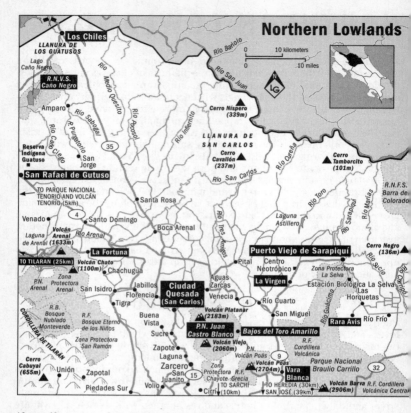

Northern Lowlands

10 kilometers
10 miles

NORTHERN LOWLANDS

About 1km west of town, the main road forks south toward Guápiles and the entrance of **Estación Biológica La Selva**, and southwest toward La Virgen and the entrances of the **Centro Neotrópico Sarapiquís** and the **Serpentario**. About 150m east of the bus station, a small road to the right leads to the **Super Sarapiquí** supermarket. Two hundred and fifty meters east along the main road from the bus station, the road splits yet again, heading northwest on the left and toward the Río Sarapiquí port on the right.

Tourist Information: For the most comprehensive tourist info, talk to William Rojas of ▨**Oasis Nature Tours** (☎2766 6108 or 6260; www.oasisnaturetours.com), 50m west of the soccer field through a green doorway just a couple doors past the bus station. Don William arranges scenic river trips of the Río Sarapiquí all the way to Tortuguero and Nicaragua. Alex Martínez, the owner of **Posada Andrea Cristina** (see opposite page), is a former hunter considered by many to be the region's most knowledgeable and passionate naturalist. He is a good source for info on birdwatching and other nature tours.

Banks: Exchange travelers' checks and US dollars at the **Banco Nacional** (☎2766 6012), at the intersection of the main road and the road to the port. Open M-F 8:30am-3:45pm. **Banco Popular** is 20m east of the soccer field. Open M-F 8:45am-3pm, Sa 8:15am-11:30am. Both have **24hr. ATMs.**

Police: (☎2766 6575 or 2766 6485, emergencies 911), just off the main street along the port turnoff, next to the post office.

Pharmacy: Farmacia Alfa (☎2766 6348), 1 block east of the soccer field on the left. Open M-Sa 8am-8pm. MC/V.

Red Cross: (☎2766 6212 or 2766 6254), 250m west of the soccer field. Open 24hr.

Internet: Sarapiquí Internet (☎2766 6223), 300m west of the soccer field, past the Red Cross. Internet ¢400 per hr. Open daily 8am-8pm. Internet is available in **Mi Lindo Sarapiquí** (p. 87) for ¢400 per hr. Open daily 7am-10pm. Wi-Fi is available at **Restaurante El Surco.**

Post Office: (☎2766 6509), across from Banco Nacional at the port turn off. Open M-F 8am-noon and 1-5:30pm. **Postal Code:** 31001.

ACCOMMODATIONS

Although the area around Puerto Viejo has become a popular destination, the town itself does not have many options for travelers. Luckily, the few hotels that do exist are within walking distance of the bus station, making them convenient choices for those looking to take daytrips to the many attractions just outside of town.

Posada Andrea Cristina (☎2766 6265; www.andreacristina.com), 1km west of the town center. From the bus station, follow the road west toward La Virgen for about 1km; the B&B is on the right. With spacious wood bungalows scattered throughout a beautifully landscaped garden, Andrea Cristina offers a unique and peaceful lodging option for those who don't mind being a bit of a walk from town. The cabins share communal cold-water baths, but the comfy beds and tasty vegetarian-friendly breakfast make up for it. Breakfast included. Singles ¢14,500 (US$25); doubles ¢26,100 (US$45); each additional person ¢8700 (US$15). 10% discount on stays longer than 4 nights. Camp on the grounds for ¢5800 (US$10). MC/V. ●

Mi Lindo Sarapiquí (☎2766 6281), west of the soccer field and directly opposite the bus station. This conveniently located restaurant-hotel-internet-cafe offers sunny, spacious rooms that each have a twin and double bed, ceiling and wall fans, a TV, and private hot-water baths. Laundry ¢150 per item. Singles ¢9500; doubles ¢15,000; triples ¢22,100. AmEx/D/MC/V. ❷

Cabinas Laura (☎2766 6316), 100m down the road to the port. Though its location down a dark alley next to a casket store is less than ideal, this hotel has good prices for those traveling in pairs; A/C and cable TV make it even better. Singles and doubles ¢8000; doubles and triples with A/C ¢10,000-14,000. MC/V. ❷

FOOD

While many of the resorts a few kilometers outside of town serve mouth-watering cuisine, the options in town are limited. Aside from the restaurants at hotels Mi Lindo Sarapiquí and Restaurante El Surco, the only other eating spots available are *sodas* and ice cream shops.

Restaurante Mi Lindo Sarapiquí, attached to the hotel of the same name. Provides tasty *comida típica* to a busy crowd of locals. Though all of the dishes are reasonably priced, the *bocas* menu offers some particularly good deals (¢700-1500). Rice dishes ¢1600-3900. Breakfast ¢950-2500. Open daily 8am-10pm. AmEx/D/MC/V. ●

Restaurante El Surco (☎2766 6005), in Hotel Bambú. With vaulted fan-filled ceilings under a tin roof, El Surco is the closest Sarapiquí gets to fine dining. The dishes are standard Costa Rican fare, but the atmosphere is casually elegant. *Bocas* ¢1100-1800. *Casados* ¢1850-4250. Seafood dishes ¢4800-9000. Pastas ¢1700-4000. Free Wi-Fi. Open daily 6am-10pm. AmEx/MC/V. ❷

Mister Pizza (☎2766 6138), on the east end of the soccer field. This small, fast food and pizza joint offers escape from *comida típica* in town. The pizza crust has an oddly sweet flavor, but the topping options are extensive, ranging from Hawaiian to veggie. Don't miss the combo menu (¢1400). Pizzas ¢1400-5000. Open daily 8am-10pm. ❷

🏔 OUTDOOR ACTIVITIES

🏞 **Hacienda Pozo Azul** (☎2438 2616; www.haciendapozoazul.com), at the bridge in La Virgen. One of the most comprehensive adventure destinations in Puerto Viejo. The sprawling ranch offers canopy tours (US$45), horseback rides (2hr., US$35), rappelling (US$28), rafting (Class II and III rapids US$50, Class IV rapids US$70), mountain biking (half-day US$45), and guided hiking treks (US$15). The ranch was originally a dairy farm, and you can still take a tour of the ranch (US$10) or camp at the on-site facilities (US$25 plus US$20 for 3 meals per person). Alternatively, stay at the pricier jungle lodge (US$60 per person).

Aventuras del Sarapiquí (☎2766 6768 or 8399 3509; www.sarapiqui.com), 15min. west of town on the bus toward La Virgen. These guys opened the first rafting company in the region nearly 20 years ago. The fun-loving group of experienced, bilingual guides leads daily Class II and III rafting trips down the Río Sarapiquí (US$50, includes fruit snack). One of the owners, Pongo, organizes the annual Sarapiquí Adventure Race (www.sarapiquiadventurerace.com), a 2-day competition in Oct. that brings participants to raft, hike, and mountain bike 60km for a charitable cause. (Entrance fee US$50 per person, equipment included.)

Aguas Bravas (☎2292 2072; www.aguas-bravas.co.cr), on the road between Puerto Viejo and La Virgen. Offers a Class II and III rafting trip (US$65) and a Class IV trip for more experienced rafters (US$85).

🏞 DAYTRIPS FROM PUERTO VIEJO

🏞 TIRIMBINA RAINFOREST PRESERVE

From Puerto Viejo, take a bus to La Virgen and ask the driver to let you off at the entrance to Tirimbina (30min., ¢320). Buses returning to Puerto Viejo stop at the Preserve approx. on the hour. A taxi from Puerto Viejo costs ¢5000. On foot from La Virgen, walk 1.6km north along the road to Puerto Viejo de Sarapiquí; the entrance to the park is on the right, 300m past the Serpentario. ☎2761 1579 or 1576; www.tirimbina.org. Self-guided tour ¢8700 (US$15), students ¢5800 (US$10); guided tour ¢12,760/9860 (US$22/17); approx. 2hr. Several tours leave each day (8, 10am, 1:30, 3pm), though it is recommended to call in advance. Chocolate tour ¢11,600 (US$20), students ¢8700 (US$15); offered in the morning and afternoon. Reservations required.

Although about 90% of its land remains pristinely undeveloped, without even the most basic trails, the 350-hectare Tirimbina Rainforest Preserve offers one of the most varied selections of tourism opportunities in the Sarapiquí area. Its 9km of paved trail and more extensive collection of rougher trails can be explored with or without a guide, and the views of primary forest and the Sarapiquí River afforded by the 266m **Puente Colgante** (Hanging Bridge) are some of the best around. The 4km that can be explored without a guide takes approximately 2hr. to properly hike; the other 5km requires a guide given that dangerous animals including snakes, tapirs, and even lions have been known to chow down along the path. A spiral staircase descending from El Puente Colgante, leads to an island formed by **Río Sarapiquí**, where adventurers can take a swim when the river isn't too high. A few trails cross the island, and otters and kingfishers are often spotted on the riverbanks.

For those tired of the usual wildlife-spotting, the Preserve offers several specialized tours, which must be booked in advance. The **bat tour** is a hit with those seeking a glimpse of these nocturnal rainforest residents (7:30pm), and chocoholics' mouths will water on the chocolate tour, which takes guests through a natural chocolate plantation, demonstrates traditional methods of producing chocolate, and concludes with a tasting. Insect repellent, long pants, and hiking boots are recommended for all hikes or walks. An open-air **restaurant** serves meals to guests at the lodge and will also make lunch or dinner for large groups; call the Preserve in advance to arrange a meal before or after a tour.

Though most visitors to the center stop by for only a day or two, Tirimbina also accepts volunteers and researchers for long-term stays of at least two weeks. The Preserve has lodging space for ten volunteers, most of whom help out in the general day-to-day operations of the Preserve, though Spanish speakers may also have the opportunity to help in conservation and ecology classes taught for local primary school kids. Researchers interested in studying the wildlife at Tirimbina are also welcome to stay at the Preserve. Room and board for volunteers and researchers is US$10 per night, though some financial assistance is available. Contact the Preserve for more information on current volunteer and research openings.

Tirimbina also has 12 **rooms** on the grounds available for visitors. The rooms have either a double and twin bed or three twin beds as well as private hot-water baths, Wi-Fi, and A/C. Lodging includes free access to the trails as well as breakfast in the park's restaurant. (Singles and doubles ₡34,800/US$60, students ₡29,000/US$50.)

ESTACIÓN BIOLÓGICA LA SELVA
From Puerto Viejo, take the 6:45am or 12:15pm bus headed to Río Frío (15min., ₡260) to make the 8am or 1:30pm tours. Buses to Guápiles also pass this way. Ask the driver to let you off at the Estación Biológica La Selva. From this stop, follow the dirt road on your right 1km to the station's gates; signs mark the way. To get back to Puerto Viejo, have the station call you a cab (₡3000) or wait at the bus stop on the main road for one of the buses that passes by about every 30min. (less often on Su) on their way back to Puerto Viejo. ☎ 2524 0628; www.ots.ac.cr. Private tours 2hr. Birdwatching tours begin at 5:45am, night tours 6pm; ₡18,560-22,040 (US$32-38). Make reservations online or by phone several days in advance for any of the tours.

Only 6km south of Puerto Viejo, La Selva is one of the three centers of the **Organization for Tropical Studies (OTS)**, a non-profit consortium of universities and research institutions founded on the principles of investigation, education, and conservation. La Selva borders **Parque Nacional Braulio Carrillo** to the south; the park boasts 1614 hectares of primary and secondary rainforest. Hundreds of scientists and students come to La Selva each year to study the staggering number of plants and animals here, several of which the Estación has helped bring back from the edge of extinction. Though the station has an extensive collection of concrete and dirt trails, the paths can only be accessed without a guide by those staying at the lodge. The station has many guided walks and workshops to offer. Two 3½hr. walking tours leave each day (8am, 1:30pm; ₡16,240-18,560/US$28-32). Some trails are accessible to those with physical disabilities. The station also offers private tours, including a birdwatching tour, a night tour, and a workshop on rainforest photography, all of which must be arranged several days in advance.

CENTRO NEOTRÓPICO SARAPIQUÍS
Next to Tirimbina (p. 88). ☎ 2761 1004; fax 2761 1415; www.sarapiquis.org. Open daily 9am-5pm. The tour schedule varies; call ahead for reservations. Entry to museum, archaeological site, and botanical gardens ₡4640 (US$8). Reception open daily 6am-8:30pm.

NORTHERN LOWLANDS

Archaeological site and gardens open 6am-4pm. Museum open 6am-6pm. Tour of museum with guide ¢8700 (US$15), archaeological site ¢5220 (US$9).

The non-profit, private Centro Neotrópico Sarapiquís is a preserve dedicated to interactive cultural, biological, and ecological awareness and conservation. The center offers **three exhibits** to tourists: a **museum** on pre-Columbian culture, an **archaeological dig** with reconstructed 15th-century pre-Columbian buildings, and a **botanical garden** featuring medicinal and edible plants. The museum is well-kept, with neat displays of masks, shamanic implements, and a film on the relationship between man and nature in pre-Columbian societies. Unfortunately, the rest of the center is not as well-organized. Much of the writing on the signs identifying the plants in the botanical gardens has been washed away by the frequent rains, and the archaeological site is quite small, with a sample home, funerary site, and replica statues constituting the majority of the exhibit. Visitors should also beware of the rock pathways in the botanical gardens and archaeological site: the stones get quite slippery when wet, making walking in the rain feel a bit like ice skating in tennis shoes.

The Center was built in a pre-Columbian village style using sustainable technologies like solar power, local natural materials, and a waste-water treatment system. The on-site ecolodge, restaurant, and bar overlook the preserve and follow the *Palenque* architectural style. Large, round huts each house eight **cabins,** all with private hot-water baths, fans, and phones. Safe deposit boxes and laundry services are also available. Eight of the 40 rooms have A/C. (High-season singles and doubles ¢60,320/US$104, triples ¢74,820/US$129; low-season ¢56,260/60,320, US$97/104.) The center runs an extensive **education program** with over 2000 local children and hundreds of foreign volunteers, teachers, and ecologists; for information on getting involved, contact the center (see the information above). Spanish skills are helpful for most jobs, though not necessary.

REFUGIO NACIONAL CAÑO NEGRO

Where there's water, there's life, and Refugio Caño Negro has plenty of both. The refuge gets 3.5m of rain every year, and 85% of its land (100 sq. km) is flooded during the rainy season from May to December. In the heart of this aquatic wonderland is the enormous **Laguna Caño Negro,** a 9 sq. km lake that refills every summer when the banks of the Río Frío and Río Caño Negro overflow. The labyrinth of mangroves, rivers, and harbors here has been declared the world's fourth most important biological zone, with 160 species of mammals and over 315 species of birds. Reptiles like crocodiles, iguanas, turtles, and snakes abound, and rare fish, including the prehistoric gaspar, swim the waters. On the banks of the *laguna*, 23km southwest of Los Chiles, lies the village of Caño Negro. Despite its small size and remote location down a gravel road, this town is the gateway to the Refugio Caño Negro. Caño Negro is part of the protected area of the **Conservación Arenal Huetar Norte,** an organization that focuses on the improvement of the socioeconomic conditions of the community by creating sustainable development programs. Tourism in the area is largely dictated by the water; during the dry season (February to April), you can explore the *laguna* on foot. When the lake is filled, there are two options for exploring. When rains are sufficient, the park can be explored by boat. Otherwise, the easiest way to explore the park is on the consistently accessible **Río Frio.** To find out what is available, ask at the entrance or check with tour operators. (Park open daily 8am-4pm. US$10.)

◰ TRANSPORTATION

By **car**, the best way to get to Caño Negro from San José is to head north on the road toward Los Chiles. The entrance is 1km after the Tanques Gas Zeta (19km before Los Chiles); then take the 19km unpaved road. The entire trip should take around 4hr. Despite the road conditions, **buses** leave from Los Chiles to **Upala** through **Caño Negro** (1½hr.; M-F 5am, noon, 4pm; Sa 5am, 2pm; Su 5am; ¢1100). Buses leave for **Los Chiles** (1½hr.; 3 per day M-F 6am, 12:30pm, and 5pm; Sa 6am, 5pm; Su 12:30pm; ¢1100). Buses leave for **Upala** daily at 11:30am, or approximately 1½hr. after they leave from Los Chiles. The best place to wait for the bus is in front of the mini-super, where you can see traffic coming in and out of town. Buses also stop in front of the hotels along the road to the town's entrance.

◰ ◱ ORIENTATION AND PRACTICAL INFORMATION

The bus enters the village on the **main road,** making a loop around the **parque central** before heading back out at the northwest corner of the *parque*, next to the **school.** Just north of the school is the church and, 25m to the north, a **mini-super** (☎2461 1500; open M-Sa 7am-7pm, Su 7am-5pm.) The refuge entrance is on the southeast corner of the *parque*.

The **MINAE** office (☎2471 1309, open daily 8am-4pm), 200m west of the mini-super, provides tourist information. There is **no bank,** and the nearest medical facility is **Hospital Ebais** (☎2471 1531), a small clinic 50m east from the mini-super. The **police station** (☎2471 1802) is on the southeast side of the *parque*. The town has two **public telephones,** at the mini-super and in front of the police station.

◰ ◱ ACCOMMODATIONS AND CAMPING

It is possible to **camp** on the grounds of the Caño Negro MINAE office, which have access to cold-water showers and bathrooms. (¢1000 per person.)

Albergue Caño Negro (☎2471 2029), 200m north of the northwest corner of the *parque,* on a grassy *finca* on the banks of the Laguna Caño Negra. Simple cabins on stilts come with two twin beds, wall fans, linens, and padlocked doors. Communal cold-water baths located downstairs. Each cabin has a porch overlooking the *finca* and the *laguna*. ¢7000 per person. ❸

Cabinas Martín Pescador (☎2471 1369 or 1116), 100m past the MINAE office, in the field at the end of the road. The reception is across the street from the north side of the *parque* in the small goods store next to the *Cabinas Martín* sign. Cabins with covered porches and hot-water baths; some also have A/C and cable TV. Singles ¢11,600 (US$20); doubles ¢17,400 (US$30); each additional person ¢5800 (US$10). ❸

Natural Lodge Caño Negro (☎2471 1426; www.canonegrolodge.com), 300m north and 50m west of the mini-super. Elegant rooms decorated with abstract paintings have queen beds, A/C, safe deposit boxes, and spacious bathrooms. Amenities include a pool and hot tub. Breakfast included. Helpful and informed staff can schedule various tours. High-season doubles ¢58,000 (US$100), low-season ¢46,400 (US$80); triples ¢63,8000/¢52,220 (US$110/90); quads ¢69,600/¢58,000 (US$120/100); each additional person ¢5,800 (US$10). AmEx/D/MC/V. ❺

Hotel de Campo (☎2471 1012; www.hoteldecampo.com), on the *laguna* side of the road to the village, 400m before Albergue Caño Negro. Tidy, well-equipped rooms in stucco cottages. A manicured garden leads to the lagoon. Hot water and A/C. Breakfast included. Pool for guest use. Rooms ¢49,300 (US$85). Ask about the ecological and fishing tours. AmEx/D/MC/V. ❺

THE LOCAL STORY

MUCHAS MARIPOSAS

Over a decade ago, the **Women's Association of Caño Negro** started the mariposario project. The project aimed to grow colonies of butterflies and sell them. Today, you can visit four different mariposarios in Caño Negro.

1. **La Asociación de Mujeres de Cano Negro** offers one of the biggest, most accessible gardens in town, and sells fresh bread and pastries in its bakery next door.

2. **Dona Claris** has a smaller atrium that features the beautiful blue morpho butterfly. (☎2471 1450. ¢1000.)

3. **Belsis Gracia** has the newest, best constructed mariposario in town. (☎2471 1315. ¢1000.)

4. **La Reinata's** convenient garden has brightly colored mariposas that flutter around lush vegetation. (☎2471 1301. ¢1000.)

🍴 FOOD

Soda la Palmera (☎2471 1045), on the southeast corner of the *parque*. Though the menu offers few options, La Palmera cooks up tasty *comida típica* for a local clientele in its cottage-style dining area. *Gallo pinto* with eggs, an avocado slice, and coffee ¢1200. Entrees ¢2000 with drink. Bathroom use ¢100. Open daily 7am-8pm. ❶

Restaurante Danubio Azul (☎2471 1295), on the southeast side of the *parque*. A quiet spot during low season. In high season, its eating area overlooking the *laguna* becomes a popular disco. *Guapote* fish ¢3600. *Casados* of gaspar (the special lake fish) come with rice, beans, and salad ¢3500. Entrees from ¢2000. Open daily 10am-2am. ❷

Restaurante Jabirú (☎2471 1426), located in the Natural Lodge Caño Negro. The fanciest and priciest food in town. Pasta entrees (fettucine with broccoli sauce, ¢2800). Meat and seafood dishes ¢3500-5800. Imported beer ¢1300-2600. Mango juice ¢600. Continental breakfast with bread, marmalade, coffee/tea, and orange juice ¢2800. Open daily 6am-10pm. ❷

Restaurante El Pueblo (☎2471 1419), located right before the rooms of Cabinas Martín Pescador. This restaurant serves large breakfasts for ¢3500. *Casados* (chicken, fish, or steak, includes salad and bread) ¢4000. Open daily 7am-6pm. ❷

🏞 VISITING THE REFUGE

The park is easily reached from Caño Negro village and is best seen by boat. A 1½km trail starts near the office; others emerge as the lake dries up. **Pantanal Tours,** a small unlabeled office across from Soda La Palmera (above), offers several tours in Spanish and English. (Kayaks ¢17,4000/US$30 per 4 hr.; Fish and ecological tours for 2-3 people ¢29,000/US$50 per 2hr.; horseback riding ¢11,600/US$20 per 2hr.) Open daily 6am-5pm. Antonio at **Cabinas Martín Pescador** (p. 91) takes people fishing on his canopied *lancha.* (1-4 people, ¢29,000/US$50 per 2hr.; each additional person ¢5800/US$10.) **Natural Lodge Caño Negro** runs tours of turtle and butterfly farms (¢14,5000/US$25) and 3 hr. tours of the lake (¢25,520/US$44, includes park entrance fee). There is also the **Tour and Fishing Info Office** (☎8823 4026) shortly past the Natural Lodge Caño Negro which offers fishing, butterfly and turtle tours, camping, trails, and horseback riding. Larger tour operations run out of **La Fortuna** and **Los Chiles.** Prices typically do not include park entrance (¢5800, US$10 per day) or fishing licenses (2 months ¢17,400, US$30). You can pay the ranger for park entry in the kiosk at the entrance on the southeast corner of the *parque*. **Fishing** is prohibited April through July. A license requires a photocopy of your passport and two passport-size photos. To get one, pay ¢17,400 (US$30) in any Banco Nacional and pick up your package at any MINAE office; there is one 100m north and 200m west of the northwest corner of the *parque* in Caño Negro (p. 91). You can also pay at the office. Licenses purchased within the last two months are accepted at Caño Negro. Call the **Area de Conservación Huetar Norte** with questions (☎2471 1309).

Bring waterproof boots—biting ants and 10 of Costa Rica's 17 types of venomous snakes await. For more on **Wilderness Safety,** see p. 47.

👁 SIGHTS BEYOND THE REFUGE

There are five *mariposarios* (butterfly farms) in Caño Negro. **La Asociación de Mujeres de Caño Negro (The Women's Association of Caño Negro; ASOMUCAN)** founded the original, located 50m south and 200m west of the mini-super. They also have a *Panadería* and Deli, **Pan y Café Caño Negro,** where you can get fresh bread. (☎2471 1450. Open daily 6am-6pm. Farm entrance ¢1000.)

NORTHWESTERN COSTA RICA

The two mountain chains that stretch across northwestern Costa Rica guard some of the country's most famous attractions. The world-renowned Monteverde Reserve protects what remains of the cloud forests that once covered all of the Cordillera de Tilarán, while the Cordillera de Guanacaste holds three spectacular national parks farther north. Volcán Arenal, Central America's most active volcano, oozes magma at a cratered peak nestled between these two majestic ranges. Though the arid lowlands of Guanacaste cannot offer such natural beauty, they have a *sabanero* (cowboy) charm all their own. They serve as good base camps for nearby attractions like Volcán Tenorio, Volcán Miravalles, and the national parks that make up the Area de Conservación de Guanacaste,

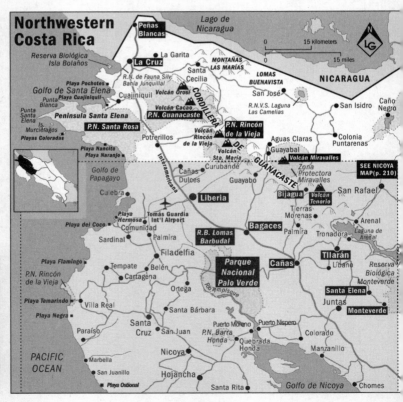

SEE NICOYA MAP(p. 210)

which holds 65% of Costa Rica's species. The region has witnessed everything from annexation to invasions, and its dynamic history fosters a rich folkloric tradition that is constantly unfolding and expanding. While larger numbers of Nicaraguan immigrants have made diversity a source of regional pride and tension in more southern cities like San José, Guanacastan towns have managed to thrive on the harmony and vitality of their mixed populations.

MONTEVERDE AND SANTA ELENA

The Monteverde region, located 184km northwest of San José and due north of Puntarenas, is the reason that many travelers come to Costa Rica in the first place. Dry season guarantees more animal sightings and fewer lightning cancellations, but it also attracts many more tourists, making reservations a must for almost everything. Conversely, the rainy season offers a leisurely schedule and more exhilarating adventures as the ziplines are significantly faster in the rain. Private reserves in the area, including the famous **Monteverde Cloud Forest Reserve**, protect some of the country's last remaining primary cloud forest, which provides refuge for iridescent *quetzals*, foraging *coatis*, and a host of other creatures. Tourists flock to Monteverde to observe its array of flora and fauna. Others travel to these forests longing to fly through canopies on ziplines and watch sunsets on horses. Still others seek retreat, finding peace in the hikes, waterfalls, and art galleries that the region has to offer.

The town of **Monteverde** was founded in 1951 when a group of American Quakers, many of whom had served jail time for refusing to enlist in the armed forces, exiled themselves to the region. They used existing oxcart trails to bring in cows and to start up a successful cheese business. Though the largely English-speaking town has retained a sense of its roots, its population these days is as diverse as the nearby wildlife. There is a mix of *ticos*, tourists, eco-friendly expats, artists, biologists, and students gathered together in a sundry array of jungle lodges, local dives, and ordinary residential communities. The small town of **Santa Elena** hosts many of the area's tourist facilities and practical amenities while retaining an intimate ambience. Its central location provides a launching point to nearby reserves, including **Monteverde Reserve, Santa Elena Reserve,** and **El Bosque Eterno de los Niños.** Most are connected by dirt roads, preserving a dependent community throughout the region without infringing on the area's natural splendor. Beware its spell: many visitors have been known to extend their stays indefinitely.

TRANSPORTATION

Direct **buses** to **Santa Elena** and **Monteverde** run from **San José** (4hr.; 6:30am, 2:30pm; ¢2350), **Puntarenas** (3.5hr.; 7:50am, 1:50, 2:15pm; ¢1235), and **Tilarán** (3hr., 12:30pm, ¢1400). From **Liberia,** you can take a San José-bound bus as far as **Lagarto,** and then take a bus to **Monteverde** (8:30am, 3:00pm; ¢1200). Alternatively, go to **Puntarenas** and catch a bus from there to Monteverde. To get to Monteverde Reserve, you must change buses in **Santa Elena** (approximately 20min., times listed under Monteverde Reserve; purchase tickets for ¢600 on the bus to the Reserve).

Leaving Monteverde, buses head to: **San José** (4hr.; 6:30am, 2:30pm; ¢2350), **Puntarenas** (3hr.; 4:30am, 6, 3pm; ¢1235), and **Tilarán** (3hr., 7am, ¢1400). Buy return tickets from Monteverde to Puntarenas the morning of your bus; if going to San José, purchase the day before at the **Transmonteverde B.S.A. ticket office,**

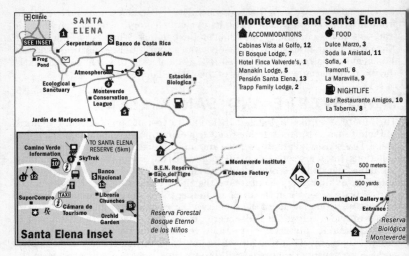

Monteverde and Santa Elena

ACCOMMODATIONS
Cabinas Vista al Golfo, 12
El Bosque Lodge, 7
Hotel Finca Valverde's, 1
Manakín Lodge, 5
Pensión Santa Elena, 13
Trapp Family Lodge, 2

FOOD
Dulce Marzo, 3
Soda la Amistad, 11
Sofia, 4
Tramonti, 6
La Maravilla, 9

NIGHTLIFE
Bar Restaurante Amigos, 10
La Taberna, 8

located across the street from Camino Verde in Santa Elena (☎2645 5159. Open M-F 5:45-11am and 1:30-5pm, Sa-Su 5:45-11am and 1:30-3pm.)

Many companies offer more adventurous ways to reach popular destinations. **Jeep-Boat-Jeep** (US$25) and **Horse-Boat-Car** are offered through Aventuras El Lago. **Taxis** wait outside the church in Santa Elena. Be wary of taxi-drivers looking to charge tourists unreasonable fares. Ask the tourist office what it should cost to take a taxi to your destination; it shouldn't be more than ₡5000.

⚡🔼 ORIENTATION AND PRACTICAL INFORMATION

Buses arrive in the town of Santa Elena, which has affordable local services, hotels, and restaurants. From here, an unpaved road heads 6km southeast to the Monteverde Reserve. The actual settlement of Monteverde is strung along this road, and has more expensive restaurants and hotels. Unless otherwise noted, the following services are in Santa Elena.

Tourist Information and Tours: Camino Verde Information & Reservation Center (☎2645 6304; www.exploringmonteverde.com), across from the bus stop, offers friendly assistance when arranging a tour. Open daily 6am-9pm. Those searching for tour companies will find no shortage along the main street; it's worth shopping around as commissions vary widely. **Cámara de Turismo** (☎2645 6565; fax 2645 6464), at the end of the street across from Supermercado La Esperanza, is the official tourist center. Both book reservations to the Santa Elena and Monteverde Reserve, nearby canopy tours, ATV rides, and more. Open daily 8am-8pm. Most accommodations have their own information and tour deals; often they do not receive commission and some offer refunds for tour cancellations.

Bank: Banco Nacional (☎2645 5027; www.bncr.fi.cr), around the corner from the bus station. Changes traveler's checks and US$ and gives cash advances on MC and V with passport. Open M-Sa 8:30am-3:45pm. ATM available. **Banco de Costa Rica,** up the main road toward Monteverde Reserve, next to Sapo Dorado. Open M-F 9am-4pm.

Supermarket: SuperCompro (☎2645 5068), south of the bus station, across the street from Camara de Turismo. Open M-Sa 7am-8pm, Su 7am-8pm. AmEx/D/MC/V.

Bookstore: Librería Chunches (☎2645 5147), across from Banco Nacional and Pensión Santa Elena. Overpriced and photocopied US newspapers (NY Times ¢5000) and plain overpriced magazines (US Weekly ¢5500), new and used books and music, local information, and coffee (¢600). Also sells souvenirs, batteries, blank CDs, and envelopes. Free Wi-Fi. Open M-F 8am-6:30pm, Sa 8am-6pm. MC/V.

Laundry: Most hotels and some hostels offer laundry services; more options line the main road. Available at **Librería Chunches** for ¢3000 per load.

Emergency: Red Cross (☎128 or 2645 6128).

Police: (☎2645 6248; emergency 911), across from SuperCompro, next to the Vitosi pharmacy.

Pharmacy: Vitosi (☎2645 5004), next to the police station. Open M-Sa 8am-8pm, Su 9am-8pm. AmEx/D/MC/V.

Medical Services: Clínica Monteverde (☎2645 5076), 50m west and 150m south of the sports field. Open M-F 7am-4pm, Sa-Su 7am-7pm.

Telephones: Public telephones are everywhere, including outside SuperCompro and in the Visitors Center at the Reserve.

Internet Access: Pura Vida Internet, 50m northwest of Banco Nacional. Internet ¢1600 per hr. Open daily 11am-9pm. **Atmosphera Internet Cafe** (☎2645 6555), halfway down the road to Monteverde Reserve from Santa Elena. ¢1740 per hr. Also has free coffee, gourmet meso-American food, an art gallery, and a licensed spa. Free internet for customers of the restaurant or art gallery. 12% discount for customers carrying *Let's Go* with them.

Post Office: Up the first hill on the way to Monteverde, beyond the Serpentarium. Open M-F 8am-4:30pm, Sa 8am-12pm. V. **Postal Code:** 5655.

⌐ ACCOMMODATIONS

With dozens of lodgings to choose from, travelers of all kinds can find a temporary home that fits their personality and budget in the cloud forests. Pricier hotels line the road to Monteverde, while most budget accommodations are in or near Santa Elena. Making reservations ahead of time is a good idea during the high season, but low-season visitors will find enterprising crowds waiting to solicit them at the bus stop. No need to be wary—most representatives are just trying to keep their businesses afloat. Prices are usually fixed. Most establishments list prices in US$ because the value of the *colón* is depreciating so rapidly, but most are happy to accept *colones* as well.

SANTA ELENA

☒ **Cabinas Vista al Golfo** (☎2645 6321; www.cabinasvistaalgolfo.com), 5min. walk down the dirt road heading away from time, past the police station. The extremely amicable owners Jorge and Anali and their extended family treat their fun-loving guests as close friends from the start. Sink into the snug beds and see the beautiful view of the Monteverde mountains from the enormous bedroom windows. If that's not enough, the communal kitchen, dining tables, and hammocks upstairs all boast some of the best panoramic views of the Nicoya Gulf. Many guests have hailed their stay at Vista al Golfo as their best experience in Costa Rica. Laundry and hot water available. Free Wi-Fi and internet, coffee, tea, and towels. Quiet after 10pm. Singles with shared bath ¢8700 (US$15), with private baths ¢11,600 (US$20); doubles ¢11,600/14,500 (US$20/25); quads ¢5800/6960 (US$10/12) per person. Apartments (with private bath, kitchen, fridge, and dining table): 2 people ¢29,000 (US$50), 3 or more ¢11,600 (US$20) each. AmEx/D/MC/V. ❷

Pensión Santa Elena (☎2645 5051; www.pensionsantaelena.com; shannon@pension-santaelena.com). Young, adventure-bound backpackers flock to this ultra-social hostel just down the street from Banco Nacional. Though some locals believe it to be some-what unsavory, it has one of the best communal kitchens around, dining tables in the reception area, and a hammock on the porch. Travelers live and mingle like family—even with the staff. Owners and siblings Shannon and Ran spend quality time with guests to answer questions, give frank suggestions, and offer words of wisdom. Early nights may not be an option as the guests tend to loosen up in the evening. Night guard makes sure only guests enter. Laundry and hot water available. Internet free for guests. Dorms ¢3480 (US$6); singles ¢6960 (US$12); doubles ¢12,760 (US$22), with private baths ¢15,080 (US$26); *cabinas* ¢20,300 (US$35). ❷

Hotel Finca Valverde's (☎2645 5157; www.verde.co.cr), down the road from Santa Elena's center en route to Monteverde. Take a small bridge over the creek to this upscale oasis, where spacious cabins are connected by stone walkways and metal bridges shaded by plantain and banana leaves. A small, private trail alongside a babbling brook provides an immediate escape. The reception area hosts a bar and restaurant serving tasty mixed drinks and affordable *tico* delights (¢4060-¢18,560/US$7-32). Cable TV, coffee maker, and fridge in every room. Complimentary breakfast. Parking available. Sin-gles ¢40,600 (US$70); doubles ¢23,200 (US$40); triples ¢19,720 (US$34); quads ¢16,820 (US$29); *cabinas* with bathtub ¢40,600 (US$70). AmEx/D/MC/V. ❸

Hostel Cabinas el Pueblo (☎2645 6192; www.cabinaselpueblo.com), pass the police station and take the dirt road down the hill. Family atmosphere plus a bang-for-your-buck deal, which includes hot water, a floral hammock area, a fully stocked communal kitchen, a lounge with cable TV, and a tourist center. Try to catch the sloth that fre-quents a tree just outside the hotel. Marlenny, who waits for guests at the bus stop, will point you to her mother's *soda*, **Soda La Amistad** (p. 99), just up the road. Breakfast included. Free Wi-Fi and internet. Parking available. Rooms ¢4350 (US$7.50), with private baths ¢5800 (US$10). AmEx/D/MC/V. ❶

Hostel El Tucan (☎2645 7590; www.hoteleltucan.net), located 50m from the Banco Nacional. The brightly painted sign welcomes backpackers to small simple rooms. Leave your upstairs room to hang out in the TV room where, instead of on couches, you can relax on one of several hammocks. Fully equipped kitchen. Breakfast included. Free inter-net. Offers tour information. Dorms ¢4060 (US$7); singles ¢8700 (US$15), with private baths ¢11,600 (US$20); doubles ¢11,600/14,500 (US$20/25). ❶

MONTEVERDE

Manakín Lodge (☎2645 5080; www.manakinlodge.com), about 1km from Santa Elena toward the Monteverde Reserve. 3rd-generation owner Mario and his children make guests feel like part of the family, offering town gossip, healthy veggies, and organic meals (homemade granola, omelettes, and special requests). The porches of these beautiful rooms face the edge of the forest, where white-faced monkeys wait for bananas from guests. Horse tours (¢17,400, US$30) and trips to local *fincas* available. Breakfast included. Private bath, hot water, cable TV, and fridge. Free internet. Singles ¢11,600 (US$20); doubles ¢17,400-23,200 (US$30-40); triples ¢26,100-34,800 (US$45-60); quads ¢34,800-46,400 (US$60-80). D/MC/V. ❸

Trapp Family Lodge (☎2645 5858; www.trappfam.com). The closest hotel to the Monte-verde Cloud Forest Reserve, though its distance from town necessitates transport by car, taxi (¢5000), or bus (¢600). With tall, A-frame ceilings, huge floor-to-ceiling windows, a warm orange lodge, spacious rooms, and a gorgeous location, it's easy to feel like you're already in the cloud forest. Watch the clouds roll in from the plush chairs in your room. Great restaurant on premises (entrees ¢4640-11,600, US$8-20). Parking available. Rooms with 2 double beds ¢49,300 (US$85); mountain suites (slightly higher elevation, TV, fridge, larger windows, and bathtub) ¢58,000 (US$100). AmEx/D/MC/V. ❺

El Bosque Lodge (☎2645 5221; fax 2645 5129; www.bosquelodge.com), behind Tramonti's, halfway between Santa Elena and the Monteverde Reserve. Private rooms are connected by a series of paths and bridges that weave through lovely landscaped gardens speckled with butterflies, hummingbirds, white-face monkeys, and *aguatis*. This lodge's apparent seclusion is an illusion—it is actually located right off the main road. All rooms have coffee maker, refrigerator, and hair dryer. Singles ¢26,100 (US$45); doubles ¢31,900 (US$55); triples ¢37,770 (US$65); quads ¢43,500 (US$75). D/MC/V. ❹

Nidia Lodge (☎2645 5236; www.nidialodge.com), on the way to the Ecological Sanctuary. This tranquil lodge is complete with restaurant and spa (offers massages, pedicures and jacuzzi time). Ask Eduardo, the hotel owner, to give you a rundown on the intricacies of the forest. All rooms have a private bath with hot water, iron, desk, and telephone. Deluxe rooms include bathtub, private balcony, and coffee maker (¢11,600, US$20 more). Meeting room holds 30 people. Parking available. Singles in the low season ¢23,300 (US$40), in the high season ¢29,000 (US$50); doubles ¢31,900/37,700 (US$55/65); triples ¢37,700/43,500 (US$65/75); junior suites ¢66,700/69,600 (US$115/120). ❹

🍴 FOOD

SANTA ELENA

🍴 **La Maravilla** (☎2645 6623), right across from the bus station. Serves *comida típica* to locals and tourists alike. Its convenient location and lightning-fast service make it easy to grab a ham and cheese omelet (¢1600) or a *casado* (¢2300-2850). Salads, sandwiches, soups, and seafood (fish fillet in garlic sauce ¢3450). Mango milkshake (¢800). Open daily 6:10am-9pm. AmEx/D/MC/V. ❶

🍴 **Soda La Amistad** (☎2645 6108), down the dirt road past the police station and next to Cabinas Vista al Golfo. Miss your *mama*? Your dynamic surrogate is waiting to serve you the most mouthwatering *tico* delights right from her personal kitchen. Cándida will plop herself down at one of the 3 tables in her home to offer warm advice and ask when she should expect you tomorrow. She can provide all of your meals: *gallo pinto* (¢1600) for breakfast, a *casado* for lunch (¢2500-3500), and vegetable spaghetti for dinner (¢1800). Open daily 6am-9pm. Cash only. ❶

🍴 **Coffee Bar** (☎2645 5757), in the alleyway across from the church on the main road, next to Bar Restaurante Amigos. It's all in the name: several hot coffee drinks are available (¢550-950); on warm days, the iced coffee is delightful (¢1350). Great deals include pizzas with various toppings (¢2150), burritos (¢1650), and fried garlic potatoes with bacon dressing (¢1450). Open daily 11am-10pm. ❶

Restaurante El Marquez (☎2645 5918), just past Pura Vida Internet. This eatery is designed to resemble the inside of a boat, so it's not surprising that seafood is always the special of the day. Gringos and *ticos* alike enjoy the signature *mariscada au Marquez* (¢5000), combining shrimp, fish, squid, clams, mussels, and crabs in one dish. Lunch buffet of *comida típica* ¢3500. Octopus in garlic butter ¢5000. Open M-Sa 11am-10pm. AmEx/D/MC/V. ❷

Morphos (☎2645 5607), across the street from the supermarket in Santa Elena. The restaurant has taken on the phosphorescent blue Morpho (a species of butterfly) as its namesake as well as the inspiration for its decor: huge hanging butterflies fill the jungle-themed interior. A godsend for those seeking a respite from rice and beans. Double hamburgers topped with bacon, avocado, and cucumbers ¢4000. Sea bass in avocado sauce ¢6500. Top off your meal with their signature Café Morphos, a frozen concoction with coffee, coffee ice cream, and coffee liqueur (¢3200). Blackberry milkshake ¢1000. Open daily 11am-9pm. MC/V. ❷

Trio Restaurant (☎2645 7254), past the Camara de Turismo, next to the SuperCompro. This classy and elegant restaurant serves gourmet food on glass tabletops. Start with a palm heart, tomato, avocado tower ¢2030 (US$3.50), move to a delectable chicken and mango sandwich ¢3770 (US$6.50), and end with fresh fruit glazed over with frozen margarita cream ¢2030 (US$3.50). Or come in for a quiet evening to sit at one of their tables that overlooks the town with mixed drink ¢2900 (US$5) in hand. Open daily 11:30am-9:30pm. ❷

MONTEVERDE

🔲 **Sofia** (☎2645 7017). Take a right at Atmosphera Internet C@fé and walk up 50m on the left. Indulge in creative *nueva latina* food while guitar instrumentals strum in the background. Mango-ginger mojitos ¢2900 (US$5) are a heavenly prelude to innovative fusion dishes like the Seafood Chimichanga with shrimp and tender sea bass, guacamole, sweet potato puree, and *chayote picadillo* ¢8120 (US$14). Appetizers are a cheap, delicious treat (skewered shrimp with fresh fruits and ginger, US$5). Entrees US$12-16. Open daily 11:30am-9:30pm. AmEx/D/MC/V. ❸

Pizza Tramonti (☎2645 6120), in front of El Bosque Lodge on the main road to Monteverde Reserve. Unlike many other pizzerias in town, this one maintains authenticity through its native Italian owner, Gianni. Savor Italian specialties made with imported ingredients like Pizza Tramonti with asparagus, mushrooms, ricotta, and gorgonzola cheese ¢8700 (US$15). *Spaguetti con Pesto* ¢5800 (US$10). Open daily for breakfast 6:30-8:30am, lunch 11:30am-10pm. MC/V. ❸

Dulce Marzo (☎2645 6568), next to Moon Shiva on the road to Monteverde Reserve. The kindly American owner visited the quirky cafe and was so enamored that she bought it and moved to Monteverde. Indulge in the tantalizing chocolate creations, including cheesecakes, staggeringly large cookies, or the specialty hot chocolate (a secret homemade blend of cocoa and spices; ¢1225) and you might want to buy the place too. To temper an anticipated sugar high, the small, inventive lunch menu offers daily specials of soups, pastas, and the popular curry (¢1500). Th salsa lessons with free chips, guacamole, and of course, salsa (2hr., ¢2000). Open daily 11am-7pm. ❶

Stella's Bakery (☎2645 5560), across from El Bosque Lodge. Though Stella now spends much of her time painting and selling her work, her bakery, which displays many of her paintings, is still popular with locals and tourists. Sandwiches are customized from a selection of breads, spreads, meats, cheeses, and fillings. A chicken ham sandwich on whole wheat bread with avocado and cheese comes out to ¢1700. Fresh pastries and cakes are also available (carrot cake ¢900). Open daily 11am-7pm. ❶

LOCAL FLAVOR. US$4 *casados* beyond your budget? Shop like a *tico* at the weekly farmer's market, *La Feria,* Sa 7am-noon at the Santa Elena School, 1 block past Restaurante El Marquez, on the road to Santa Elena Reserve. Grab 3 avocados for ¢580, 3kg of mangos for ¢1160, and homemade bread, all while supporting local farmers.

NIGHTLIFE

If you're too exhausted from your daytime excursions to hit the dance floors, don't feel guilty: you're not missing much. The nightlife in Monteverde is minimal. A few small-scale clubs host modest crowds where *ticos* and American tourists engage in awkward courtship rituals and heat up on hesitant dance floors. Even so, the few modest options can be entertaining.

La Taberna (☎2645 5883), 300m from Banco Nacional on the road to the Reserve. This hip *discoteca* strewn with Bob Marley and Beatles murals attracts a large crowd of *ticos* and travelers who hit the small dance floor in the main room, dancing to everything from rap to *merengue*. On quiet nights, a young crowd lounges in a room with large couches. Beer ¢800. Open daily 4pm-2am. MC/V.

Bar Restaurante Amigos (☎2645 5071), across from the church on the main road, about 20m down a small dirt road. Drawing the largest crowds in town on the weekends, Bar Amigos resembles a sports bar with some TVs, a full menu until 10pm (chicken nachos ¢1500), and a plethora of drink options. F night live salsa, merengue, and *marcao* (a tango-esque melody unique to Costa Rica). Open daily 12pm-2am. D/MC/V.

Chancho's Bar (☎2645 5926), connected from behind with La Taberna. This small, psychedelic hangout plays *trova* (Cuban protest music), alternative rock, reggae, and house, but not too loudly. A small space in the middle of the bar allows for some tico-turista grinding or salsa dancing (music requests accepted). During the dry season, BBQs are held in the firepit in back. If you're lucky, Chancho may invite your group to do a welcome shot. Daiquiris ¢2500; beers ¢800-1000. Open daily 7pm-3am. Wheelchair-accessible. AmEx/D/MC/V.

La Guarida del Sapo (☎2645 7010; www.sapodorado.com), next to Banco de Costa Rica, on the road to the Reserve. This enormous dark wood house with gorgeous stained-glass windows is home to beautiful restaurant and bar known as "The Lair of the Toad." Mosaic fauna, large booths, and a long bar. Festive drinks include the delicious Monteverde Sunset (fresh blackberry syrup, OJ, and vodka; ¢1500) and the Orgasm "El Sapo" (condensed milk, amaretto, Bailey's, and coffee; ¢3000). Live music M, W and F. DJs Tu, Th, Sa-Su. Open daily 6pm-3am. Food available until 2am. AmEx/D/MC/V.

Moon Shiva Bar (☎2645 7175; www.moonshiva.com), about halfway down the road to the Monteverde Reserve. Local Costa Rican bands play alternative rock M-Sa 7-9pm. Come for the good vibes and good drinks (imported beer ¢1500). Open M-Sa 6pm-3am. Salsa night Th.

THE RESERVES

RESERVA BIOLÓGICA MONTEVERDE

The reserve is 6km uphill from Santa Elena. Walk, take a taxi (¢3500), or take a public bus from Santa Elena outside Camino Verde (every 2hr.; 6:15, 7:40am, 1:20, 3pm; return buses 6:45, 11:30am, 2, 4pm; ¢600). The Visitor Center (☎2645 5122; www.cct.or.cr) provides general info, maps, and binoculars. ¢9860 (US$17), students or ages 6-12 ¢5220 (US$9), under 6 free. 2½hr. guided tours daily 7:30am, noon, 1:30pm; ¢9860 (US$17) per person; proceeds benefit an environmental education program geared toward rural communities, as well as a recycling program. Reservations a day in advance recommended during dry season. Many local hotels and hostels arrange private tours. The Reserve only lets in 180 people at a time; get there early if you don't want to wait for entry. Open daily 7am-4pm. Night hikes 7:30pm, ¢11,600 (US$20) with transportation; if you've already been to the reserve that day, you don't have to pay the fee again. The Visitor Center lodge has dorms *with 40 beds and 6 communal showers (3 female and 3 male). Prices include entrance fee and 3 meals. Private room and bath ¢37,120 (US$64), shared room ¢30,740 (US$53); includes entrance fee and 3 meals.*

Positioned directly on the continental divide, this enthralling private reserve encompasses 4025 hectares of land and provides protection for over 2500 plant species and over 400 animal species. The population of this wildlife sanctuary includes jaguars, mountain lions, peccaries, and the elusive quetzal. This last animal is a shimmering red-and-green-colored bird that falls backward off perches when startled. Though visitors frequently see animals like coatis and white-faced monkeys, spotting the other inhabitants of this dense forest can prove difficult; many visitors find that guides can prove invaluable as nature-translators or human binoculars, able to pick out creatures hidden in the trees and hear monkey calls from the ground. Other visitors find that these mystical forests cloaked in clouds and bathed in mist are best appreciated uninterpreted and are content to wander unaccompanied through the dwarf elfin woodlands and the towering canopies of the higher cove forests. Reserve highlights include **La Ventana lookout** (along the continental divide; take Sendero Bosque Nuboso directly to it) and a **long suspension bridge** (on the Sendero Wilford Guindon). At some points, it is possible to stand on either side of the continental divide, with one foot on the Caribbean slope and the other on the Pacific.

RESERVA SANTA ELENA

Reserva Santa Elena is 5km northeast of Santa Elena village. Walk on the road north from Banco Nacional, take a taxi (one-way ¢5000), or catch a minibus to the reserve in front of the bus stop (6:30, 8:30, 10:30am, 12:30pm; return buses 9, 11am, 1, 3, 4pm; ¢580). Make reservations for buses through Camino Verde after 6am (☎2645 6296). The reserve information center in town is 200m north of Banco Nacional (☎2645 5390); there is also a Visitor Center at the entrance. Open daily 7am-4pm. 3hr. guided tours 7:30, 11:30am; ¢8700 (US$15) not including entrance fee; must be arranged 1 day in advance. Entrance fee ¢8120 (US$14), students and ages 6-12 ¢4060 (US$7), under 5 free.

The often-overlooked **Santa Elena Reserve** was established in 1992 to diffuse Monteverde's tourism burden. During the dry season, Santa Elena makes for a less-crowded, equally beautiful alternative to Monteverde. Encompassing primary and secondary forests, it offers similar flora and fauna on more sparsely populated trails, where howler monkeys make a ruckus in the liana vines that dangle from the trees. There are **four main trails** in this old growth cloud forest, all short enough (1-5km) to be done as day hikes (45min.-5hr.). From some lookouts you can see **Volcán Arenal** 14km away. Morning hikes make for better weather (especially during the wet season), views, and animal watching. Informed professional guides help identify hidden animals and plants. Unlike the Monteverde Reserve, this Reserve is government-owned. Proceeds from the entrance fee go toward the local high school.

◎ 🏃 SIGHTS AND OUTDOOR ACTIVITIES

CANOPY TOURS. Canopy tours are one of Monteverde's ecotourism highlights. These tours lead potential Tarzans through forests with less intrusion than other activities. **Original Canopy Tour,** the pioneer of this arboreal activity, provides tours, but the newer tour companies offer larger coverage and cheaper prices. In addition to ziplines, suspension bridges crossing extensive distances of canopy immerse visitors in the forest while they scout for glimpses of spectacular birds, animals, insects, and plants. Five companies offer zipline tours. Three of these companies also offer walking canopy tours. The canopy tours lead visitors along a network of bouncing suspension bridges nestled in or near the canopy of the Santa Elena Reserve. **Aventura, Selvatura, Sky Trek,** and **Extremo** all offer similar packages with harrowing ziplines, though each company has its own style. Adrenaline junkies rave about the Aventura "Tarzan swings," the "Superman," mid-forest location, and rappelling apparatus, while others prefer mixing up various lengths and speeds on Selvatura or Sky Trek cables. Sky Trek boasts the highest and longest cable among its 11 (named for popular characters like "Speedy Gonzalez"). Though Sky Trek's iron platforms offer stunning vistas and combo packages with Sky Tram gondolas, some prefer tours with less-obtrusive infrastructure. In both zipline and walking tours, be prepared for sustained exposure to the elements, especially in the afternoon during the rainy season. *(Aventura ☎ 2645 6959. Zipline tour ¢23,300 (US$40), students ¢17,400 (US$30). Original Canopy Tour ☎ 2645 5243; www.canopytour.com. ¢26,100 (US$45), students ¢20,300 (US$35). Sky Trek & Sky Tram ☎ 2645 5238; www.skytrek.com. ¢34,800 (US$60), students ¢27,840 (US$48), children ¢23,200 (US$40). Selvatura ☎ 2645 5929; www.selvatura.com. US$40, students US$30, children US$25. Extremo ☎ 2645 6058; www.monteverdeextremo.com. ¢23,300 (US$40), students ¢17,400 (US$30), children ¢14,500 (US$25). Natural Wonders Tram ☎ 2645 5960; www. telefericomonteverde.com. Aventura, Selvatura, and Sky Trek have discounted packages for ziplines and walks on the same day. Aventura Bridges or Selvatura Walkway ¢14,500 (US$25), students ¢11,600 (US$20); Sky Walk & Sky Tram ¢29,000/23,200 (US$50/40).)*

SAN LUIS WATERFALL. Tired of tour guides and over-used trails? Be free at the Leiton family *finca* that maintains this natural marvel. Follow an enchanting trail (1.7km) through the rainforest that dances across the San Luis river and finish at the enormous waterfall that snakes down two ledges before it comes crashing down. Most likely, you will be able to enjoy the waterfall all by yourself. Climb around the right side of the rocks to get close, but don't jump in—it's off limits. *(Taxi to Catarata de San Luis ¢8120/US$14. Entrance fee ¢4640/US$8. Trail maps available.)*

ECOLOGICAL SANCTUARY. The banana and coffee plantations that once operated here have been transformed into private reserves. Four different loop trails pass stunning lookouts and several cascading waterfalls, taking anywhere from 30min. to 3hr. to hike. Because the climate is hotter here than in the reserves, there are more animals to see. The forest is home to coatimundis, three-wattled bell birds, sloths, monkeys. The sanctuary is also home to the quick-footed *agoutis*, a small barking mammal that seems to walk on tiptoe as it crosses the trails. Night visits offer a very different experience than daytime walks, frequently featuring porcupines, sloths, tarantulas, kinkajous, and lots of insects. *(The well-marked turnoff from the Monteverde road is right by Atmosphera C@fe, almost 1km from Santa Elena. ☎ 2645 5869; www.ecologicalsanctuary.com. Open daily 6:30am-5pm. Guides recommended. Call a day ahead. Guides ¢14,500/US$25 for 3hr. tour, entrance fee included. Night tour 5:30-7:30pm, arrive around 5pm; ¢8700/US$15 includes entrance fee. Free printed guides available at the Visitor Center. Entrance ¢5800/US$10, students ¢4640/US$8, Costa Rican nationals and children under 10 ¢2900/US$5.)*

COFFEE TOURS. Coffee lovers everywhere will gain a new appreciation for their morning cup-o-joe on a coffee tour. Start off this educational adventure at one of Monteverde's *fincas* to see how the beans are harvested, from the drying to the roasting process, in the olden days and now. At the end of the tour, visitors can taste the different types of coffee. *(Monteverde Coffee Tour; ☎ 2645 7090; www.cafemonteverde.com. Tours 8am and 1:30pm. Don Juan Coffee Tour; ☎ 2645 7100; www. donjuancoffeetour.com. Irapiche Tour; ☎ 2645 5271. Tours 9:45am and 2:45pm.)*

NORTHWEST COSTA RICA

CHEESE FACTORY. The most stable business in Monteverde was started by Quakers in 1953 as a logical way to preserve their milk, since plain milk would sour before reaching the bottom of the mountain. Tours of the factory tell visitors of Monteverde's beginnings. Visitors watch the cheese production process through an observation window as they enjoy the delicious ice cream, milkshakes (rum raisin, ¢1600), and 25 kinds of cheese (including chocolate cheese) sold in the store. Everything in the store is made at the factory. (*¾ of the way to Monteverde Reserve coming from Santa Elena, up the hill on the left and before the bridge.* ☎ *2645 7090; http://crstudytours.com. Tours M-Sa 9am and 2pm, ¢6380/US$11. Open M-Sa 7:30am-5pm.*)

HORSEBACK RIDING. There are many opportunities for horseback riding in the area. **Sabine's Smiling Horses** offers sunset and waterfall tours on well cared-for horses. (*Bear right 50m after Tina's Casitas, 200m down on the left.* ☎ *2645 6894; www.smilinghorses.com. Call ahead. 2½hr., US$35. For volunteer opportunities, contact info@horseback-riding-tour.com.*) **Caballeriza El Rodeo** also offers a local sunset tour (*Take the road past the police station and bear right 500m on your right.* ☎ *2645 5764. Usually 2hr., 4pm, ¢17,400/US$30. Open daily 8am-4:30pm. Offers special group rates; call ahead.*)

The **Jardín De Mariposas (Butterfly Garden)** focuses on the study of all sorts of insects, from the elegant to the nasty. Energetic young volunteers give 1hr. tours of four distinct butterfly habitats. Insects raised on-site include a colony of leaf-cutter ants, a variety of beetles, cockroaches, walking sticks, and tarantulas. Hold a praying mantis, stroke the fuzzy back of an elephant beetle, or release a newly born butterfly into its new habitat. While creatures vary by season, the garden promises a good selection year-round. (*Turn off the Monteverde road, about 1km from Santa Elena; signs will direct you.* ☎ *2645 5512; www.monteverdebutterflygarden.com. Open daily 9:30am-4pm. Call about volunteer opportunities. ¢5800/US$10, students ¢4640/US$8, children ¢2320/US$4. Tours included in entrance fee.*)

HUMMINGBIRD GALLERY. The patio hosts hundreds of hummingbirds—so many that the sounds of their fluttering wings combine to form a loud gushing sound. Up to 10 hummingbird species (of Monteverde's 30) fly boldly right in front of visitors' faces. (*About 50m before the entrance to the Monteverde Reserve.* ☎ *2645 5030. Free. Open daily 7am-5pm.*)

SERPENTARIO. Eleven of Costa Rica's 17 venomous snake species can be found in this display of Monteverde's reptilian population. The toxic eyelash viper is so well-adapted for camouflage that it often surprises hikers in the wild; here it is kept (along with its companions) in bounds and within sight. Try to see a feeding, which happens every 15 days. The complex also houses frogs, turtles, and iguanas. (*Just outside of the village, on the road to Monteverde.* ☎ *2645 5238. Open daily 9am-8pm. Entrance and guide ¢4640/US$8, students ¢3480/US$6, children ¢2900/US$5.*)

TILARÁN

The only travelers who don't breeze in and out of this gusty little transportation hub are windsurfers setting sail on **Laguna de Arenal**, 5km away. The man-made lake (initially small and natural) is the largest, most efficient hydroelectric project in Costa Rica, providing 40% of the country's energy. The lake also provides spectacular views of Volcán Arenal. High winds (up to 70kph) provide "clean energy," spinning a group of windmills at the best energy-producing wind turbine in the world. Many foreigners have made their homes here, but *ticos* still abound. The park in town is full of red benches where older *tico* couples talk quietly as the younger generations prowl the wide streets in search of wilder nights.

▗ TRANSPORTATION

The church is east of the *parque*. **Buses** leave half a block west from the *parque's* northwest corner to: **Laguna Arenal** (45min., 4 per day 7am-4:30pm, ¢400); **Cañas** (45min.; 7 per day M-Sa 5, 6, 10:30, 11:30am, 2, 5, 7pm; ¢350); **Monteverde/Santa Elena** (3hr.; 12:30, 4:30pm; ¢1400); **Puntarenas** (2hr.; 6am, 1, 6pm; ¢1300); **San Carlos/Ciudad Quesada** (4hr.; 7am, 1:45pm; ¢1700) via **Fortuna** and **Laguna de Arenal**; **Guatuso** (3hr., noon, ¢1200); **San José** (3hr.; 5 per day 5, 7, 9:30am, 2, 5pm; ¢3000). Bus tickets can be bought the same day. Bus stop open M-Sa 6:30-11am and 1-5pm. **Taxis** (☎2696 5324) line the west side of the *parque* by the phones.

▗ PRACTICAL INFORMATION

Tourist Office: No official information center. Ask hotel receptionists.

Bank: Banco Nacional (☎2695 5028), across the southwest corner of the *parque*. Open M-F 8:30am-3:45pm. **ATM** on-site.

Police: (☎2695 5001, emergency 911), a block west of the bus station. Open 24hr.

Red Cross: (☎2695 5256), 100m east of the *parque's* northeast corner.

Pharmacy: Farmacia Irva (☎2695 8210), across from the northwest corner of the *parque*, to the left. Open M-Sa 7am-8:30pm. AmEx/MC/V.

Hospital: (☎2695 5093), 200m west of the *parque's* southwest corner.

Internet Access: Cyber Cafe (☎695 3319), 50m north of the northeast corner of the *parque*. ¢500 per hr. Open M-Sa 9am-11pm.

Post Office: (☎2695 6230; fax 5387), 1 block north, 2 blocks east from the northeast corner of the *parque*. Open M-F 9am-4pm. **Postal code:** 5710.

▗ ACCOMMODATIONS

Hotel Tilawa (☎2695 5050; www.tilawa.com), 8km north of Tilarán. Designed in homage to Cretan palaces, its architecture is majestically imitative with "ancient" columns and hand-painted frescoes. Panoramic windows offer stunning views of Laguna Arenal and surrounding volcanoes. Hot tub, outdoor pool, Central America's largest skateboard park, tennis courts, and organic gardens. Check out the nearby **Tilawa Water Activity Center** for kayaks (¢5800, US$10 per hr.) and windsurfing. A jungle excursion on one of its 4 well maintained trails (0.60-1.70km) will reveal white-faced monkeys, toucans, butterflies, and iguanas, if you have not seen them from your window already. Free Wi-Fi. High season singles ¢40,600/US$70; doubles ¢46,400/US$80. Low season singles ¢20,300/US$35; doubles ¢23,200/US$40. Apartments with kitchen, couch, and hammock for 3-4 people low season ¢52,220/US$90, high season ¢63,800/US$110; each additional person ¢5800/US$10. AmEx/D/MC/V. ❺

Hotel Guadalupe Bed & Breakfast (☎2695 5943), 1 block south and 1 block east of the southeast corner of the park. Rustic wooden doors open up to spacious rooms with private bathrooms and cable TV. Breakfast included. Laundry US$1 per item. Free Wi-Fi. Singles ¢17,400 (US$30); doubles ¢26,100 (US$45); triples ¢34,800 (US$60); quads ¢40,600 (US$70). AmEx/D/MC/V. ❸

Hotel Mary (☎ 2695 5479), on the south side of the *parque*. Homey rooms with cable TV, hot water, and clean wall-to-wall carpeting. The restaurant and bar downstairs is popular with the locals and can get a bit loud on weekend nights. Laundry ¢300 per piece. Singles ¢5220 (US$9); doubles ¢12,180 (US$21); triples ¢15,080 (US$26); quads ¢20,300 (US$35). D/MC/V. ❷

⬛ FOOD

The town supermarket, **Almacén Samora** (☎2695 6227; open daily 7:30am-7:30pm), is located one block south of southeast corner of the *parque*. **Super-Compro** (☎2695 6050; open daily 8am-9pm) is on the south side of the *parque*. For those looking for fresher options, the **market** next to the bus station sells *comida típica* (*casados* ¢2000) along with produce. *Chorreadas* (creations that lie somewhere between tortillas and crepes, topped with cream or cheese) ¢700. Open daily, hours vary.

⬛ Taquería Las Leñitas (☎2695 8949), 50m north of the *parque*'s northeast corner. One of the few places in town that provides a break from *comida típica*. Sit inside or out and enjoy *quesadilla de honges* (tortillas filled with garlic mushrooms and cheese; ¢2200) or specialty nachos with beans, ground beef, cheese, and homemade corn chips (¢1800). Burrito Texano (flour tortilla with beef, refried beans, cheese, and guaca-mole) ¢2100. Open M-F 11am-9pm, Sa 1-9pm, Su 5-9pm. AmEx/MC/V. ❶

Restaurant Mary (☎2695 3281), underneath Hotel Mary on the south side of the *parque*. Serves a diverse menu from the diner-style bartop, including salads, fish, spa-ghetti, *comidas típicas,* and *comidas rápidas*. Get started with shrimp *ceviche* (¢2900), followed by the grilled chicken fillet (¢3000). Service may be slow when the place gets busy at night. Open daily 11am-2:30am. AmEx/D/MC/V. ❷

Restaurant Catalá (☎2695 3281), across from Hotel Mary, a bit past the south side of the *parque*. Don't let the dim lighting of this restaurant scare you off. The menu is full of pictures displaying options like their tenderloin with a special house sauce (¢5800) and the chicken breast stuffed with ham and cheese (¢4300). Fried ice cream (¢1800). Complimentary viewing of pop music videos on their big screen included. Open daily 11am-11pm. MC/V. ❷

⬛ NIGHTLIFE AND ENTERTAINMENT

Equss, 12km from Tilarán, accessible by car or bus heading toward Arenal. Walk through a small patch of jungle, down a hill to an open dance floor made with rugs. Filled with a mix of *ticos* and windsurfers. Sa night salsa, merengue, and cumbia. Open 8pm-3am or when the party dies down.

Ciudad Mágica, to the right of the church. Has several rides for young children and those who are still children at heart. Every ride, including the mini roller coaster and bumper cars, requires a ¢500 ticket (bought at the booth). Open daily 4-10pm.

⬛ OUTDOOR ACTIVITIES

On the skirts of the volcano, **Laguna de Arenal** is one of the world's premier wind-surfing spots, with a high season that runs from December to May and peaks in April. At the **Tilawa Water Activity Center** on the lakeshore, downhill 100m from Hotel Tilawa, instructors Tom and Evelio offer great windsurfing lessons. (Kay-aks ¢5800/US$10 per hr. Sailing 1hr. ¢11,600/US$20, half-day ¢20,300/US$35, full day ¢26,100/US$45. Windsurfing 1hr. ¢14,500/US$25, half-day ¢20,300/US$35, full day ¢26,100/US$45; 3-4hr. beginner lessons ¢26,100/US$45. Open daily 7am-5pm.) Taxis run to the Center from the *parque* (¢4000).

LIBERIA

As the commercial center of Guanacaste and the cultural heart of this dusty cowboy region, Liberia (pop. 40,000) is more visibly entrenched in history than many other Costa Rican towns. Paradoxically, it still strives to appease a trendier crowd; surfer stores and local *sodas* line the street in Spanish-style, white-washed colonial houses while a flag waves above the *parque central.* Guanacaste maintains a strong sense of regional autonomy and identity. In suit, Liberia celebrates Guanacaste Day, which commemorates the annexation of the "Partido de Nicoya," now known as Guanacaste, from Nicaragua in 1824. The eight-day festival, culminating on July 25th, features the traditional *tope* (horse parade). Constant fiestas, dancing, concerts, bullfights, and cattle auctions in front of the University of Costa Rica make this a highly anticipated week, drawing crowds from around the country. Apart from seasonal festivities, there's not much to see in Liberia; it's more of a transportation hub than anything else. The city also serves as an excellent base for visits to national parks like Rincón de la Vieja, Santa Rosa, and Palo Verde.

⌐ TRANSPORTATION

Flights: The **Daniel Oduber Quiros International Aiport (LIR),** 13km west of Liberia, can be reached by taxi or public transportation from the 200m north of Hotel Guanacaste. **Sansa** (☎+1-877-767-2672; www.flysansa.com). Flights to **San José** (1hr.; Nov. 20-Apr. 19 7, 10:22am, 1:13, 5:18pm; Apr. 20-Nov. 19 7, 10:22am, 1:10, 3:34, 4:54pm; round-trip ¢110,200/US$190).

Buses: Schedules often change but buses are reliable; check at either the **Pulmitán** or **Central station ticket booths.** Buy tickets in advance for **Playa Hermosa, Playa Panama, Playa Tamarindo, Playa Flamingo, Nicoya,** and all international buses. Otherwise, pay on the bus. Buses fill up quickly; arrive about 30min. early. Unless otherwise noted, buses leave from **Estación Central,** across from the market, to: **Cañas** (1hr., every hr. 5am-5:30pm, ¢550); the Nicaraguan border at **Peñas Blancas** via **La Cruz** (1hr., every 2hr. 5:30am-7pm, ¢1200); **Playa Tamarindo** (1hr., 15 per day 3:50am-6pm, ¢1180); and **Playa Flamingo** (1hr., 15 per day 3:50am-6pm, ¢1165); **Playa del Coco** (1hr.; every hr. 5am-11am, 12:30, 2:30, 6:30pm; ¢350); **Puntarenas** via **Cañas** (3hr.; 5am, every hr. 8:30am-3:30pm; ¢1125); **Nicoya** via **Santa Cruz** and **Filadelfia** (2hr., every 30min. 4:30am-7:30pm, ¢785); **Playa Hermosa** and **Playa Panama** (1hr., 9 per day 4:45am-5:30pm, ¢580). Three companies depart for Nicaragua from Hotel Guanacaste (☎2666 0085), 2 blocks south of Estación Central. **Rivas, Las Virgen San Juan del Sur, Nandaime, Granada, Masaya,** and **Managua** can be reached on **Central Line** (8:30am, ¢12,000) or **Transnica** (9:30am, ¢11,400). Transnica continues to **San Salvador, El Salvador** (¢45,700). Buses to **San José** via **Bagaces** leave from the **Pulmitán terminal** (☎2666 0458), 1 block south of the main terminal (4hr.; M-F every hr. 3am-8pm, Sa every hr. 4am-8pm, Su every hr. 5am-8pm; 9am and 3pm buses stop at Playa Coco; ¢2005).

Taxis: Line up at the north side of the *parque,* as well as by the Estación Central. **Taxi Liberia** (☎2666 7070 or 3330). **Taxi Porteadores** (☎2665 5050 or 5051).

Car Rental: Sol Rent-a-Car (☎2666 2222 or +1-800-SOL-RENT/2765 7368; www.solrentacar.com), 250m south of the Toyota dealership, on the Interamericana Hwy. in Hotel Bolero. From ¢23,200 (US$40) per day. Open daily 7:30am-5pm. Multiple rental options are also available on the road to the airport.

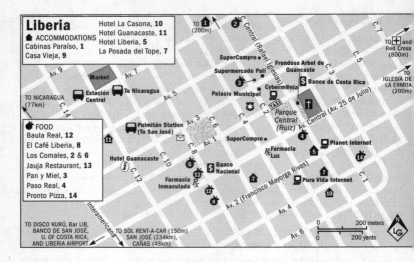

Liberia

♠ ACCOMMODATIONS
Cabinas Paraíso, **1**
Casa Vieja, **9**
Hotel La Casona, **10**
Hotel Guanacaste, **11**
Hotel Liberia, **5**
La Posada del Tope, **7**

♣ FOOD
Baula Real, **12**
El Café Liberia, **8**
Los Comales, **2** & **6**
Jauja Restaurant, **13**
Pan y Miel, **3**
Paso Real, **4**
Pronto Pizza, **14**

⚔ ⓘ ORIENTATION AND PRACTICAL INFORMATION

The city is built on a typical grid with **Avenida Central** (or Av. 25 de Julio) acting as the southern border of the *parque central*, officially known as **Parque Ruiz**. Streets, however, are not well marked. **Calle Central**, or **Calle Ruben Iglesias**, is split by the *parque*. The oldest *barrios* of **Cerros, Los Angeles, Condega**, and **La Victoria** do justice to Liberia's other name, Pueblo Blanco, with their white-washed colonial buildings. In front of the church in the main plaza sits the **Frondoso Arbol de Guanacaste**, the tree after which the province was named. The **Universidad de Costa Rica** is on the west side of town.

Tourist Information and Guided Tours: Most of the hotels in town offer info on the city and on tours of nearby national parks. **Hotel La Posada del Tope, Hotel Liberia, La Casona**, and **Hotel Guanacaste** offer transportation and, during the dry season, various activities in the national parks. La Posada del Tope offers rafting trips (¢26,100/US$45), trips to Palo Verde in the dry season (¢29,000/US$50), canopy tours (¢26,100/US$45), and full adventure tours (tubing, canopy tour, and horseback riding; ¢49,300/US$85). These hotels also provide bus service to **Rincón de la Vieja** (depart 7am, return 4pm; ¢12,600) and **Santa Rosa** (depart 6am, return 3pm; ¢12,600); arrange at least a day in advance.

Banks: Banco Nacional (☎2666 1036), 3 blocks west of the *parque*. Exchanges travelers' checks. Cash advances on V. **24hr. ATM.** Open M-F 8:30am-3:45pm. **Banco de San José** (☎2666 2020), across the Interamericana Hwy., 100m along on the left, under Bar LIB. Cirrus **ATM.** Cash advances on MC/V. Open M-F 8am-6pm, Sa 9am-1pm. **Banco de Costa Rica** (☎2665 6530), north of the church. Exchanges currency and traveler's checks. Cash advances on AmEx/MC/V. Open M-F 9am-4pm.

Police: (☎2666 0213, emergency 911), 800m south of the *parque*, on the Interamericana.

Red Cross: (☎2666 0016), 200m south of the hospital, east of the *parque*.

Pharmacy: Farmacia Lux (☎2666 0061), 100m west of the *parque*'s southwest corner. Open M-Sa 8am-10pm, Su 8am-4pm. AmEx/D/MC/V. **Farmacia La Inmaculada**, Av.

25 de Julio (☎2666 7657), 50m west of Banco Nacional. Open M-Sa 8am-9:30pm, Su 10am-12pm and 4-8:30pm. AmEx/D/MC/V.

Hospital: (☎2666 0011, emergency ext. 325, or 911), 1km northeast of the *parque.*

Internet Access:Ciberm@nia (☎2666 7237), on the north side of the *parque.* Printing (black and white ¢100; color ¢300), international calls (¢100 per min. to US), and internet (¢300 per 30min., ¢550 per hr.). Open daily 8am-10pm. **Planet Internet** (☎2665 3737), on C. Central south of the *parque.* Internet ¢400 per 30min., ¢600 per hr. Open M-Sa 8am-10pm, Su 9am-9pm. AmEx/D/MC/V.

Post Office: (☎2666 1649), 3 blocks west and 1 block north of the *parque.* Open M-F 8am-5:30pm, Sa 8am-noon. **Postal Code:** 5000.

ACCOMMODATIONS

There are many options in the city center. Some more luxurious hotels line the Interamericana Hwy. Rates may increase during the high season (Dec.-Apr.).

Casa Vieja (☎2665 5826), 2 blocks south and 50m east of the southwest corner of the *parque.* Offers the best lodging in town without hurting your wallet. Plush couches, a full kitchen, and a covered patio with snug chairs. Dark wooden doors open up into fresh rooms with elegant curtains, private bathrooms, and cable TV. Wi-Fi and internet. Reception 24hr. Singles ¢10,000; doubles ¢17,000; triples ¢21,000. Cash only. ❷

La Posada del Tope (☎2666 3876), 1 block south of the *parque.* Entering the rustic courtyard of this 150-year-old building is like stepping into a time warp. Beds come with mosquito nets (for decorative purposes only). All rooms have cable TV. No hot water. Wi-Fi. Offers tours during the dry season and transportation to Rincon and Santa Rosa (¢12,760/US$22). Singles ¢8000, ¢12000 with private bath. Cash only. ❷

Hotel Liberia (☎2666 0161), 1 block south of the *parque's* southeast corner. Simple rooms separated from the street by the hotel's tiled patio. Make time for a conversation with the owner, Beto. Backpackers gather around the TV in the common area, chatting, drinking beer, and lounging on hammocks. Tours during dry season and transportation to parks. Laundry ¢1200 per kg. Wi-Fi. Parking available. Reception 24hr. Check-out noon. Singles ¢6300, with private bath ¢7400-8600. MC/V. 16% charge for credit cards. ❶

Cabinas Paraíso (☎2666 3434), 500m north of the *parque* and 100m west of the fire station on a quiet dead-end street. Simple white rooms with large windows and balconies. The gate is not easily visible from inside, so if it's locked, yell loudly. Cable TV in some rooms (¢1000 extra). Singles ¢6000, with private bath ¢7500; doubles ¢7500/12,000; triples ¢15,000; quads ¢18,000. ❶

Hotel La Casona (☎2666 2971), 300m south of the *parque's* southeast corner. No-frills rooms with private bathrooms and cable TV. Fully furnished apartments with private bath, hot water, A/C, television, fridge, and kitchen. Laundry ¢1200 per kg. Transportation offered to nearby parks (¢11,600/US$20 per person, 7am-3pm). Singles ¢10,000, with A/C ¢12,000; doubles and triples ¢14,000/18,000; apartment for 1 person ¢15,000, for 2 people ¢20,000.❷

Hotel Guanacaste (☎2666 0085; www.higuanacaste.com), 500m west and 100 m north of the *parque.* Private rooms, as well as small shared rooms where you can fight with fellow backpackers over rights to the top bunk. No hot water. Tours to nearby volcanoes (¢11,600/US$20 per person) and national parks (¢11,600/US$20 per person to Santa Rosa, min. 4 people). Sells tickets for buses heading to Nicaragua. On-site restaurant; entrees ¢1800-4500. Wi-Fi. Shared room ¢4500; singles ¢6600; doubles ¢14,000; triples ¢19500. AmEx/D/MC/V. ❶

◤ FOOD

For an adventurous food experience, try the sweet traditional drink called *chan*, made from coyol or flower seeds, which can look like frog eggs in water. Also ask restaurants about the popular snack *chorreadas*—a corn pancake eaten with cream or cheese. Those shopping for supplies can browse the outdoor **street market,** five blocks west and three blocks north of the *parque.* (Open M-Sa 7am-5pm.) **SuperCompro** is one block west of the *parque*'s southwest corner. (☎2666 5242. Open daily 8am-9pm.) **Supermercado Palí** is in front of the Palacio Municipal. (☎2666 4730. Open M-F 8am-7:30pm, Sa 8am-8pm, Su 8am-6pm. AmEx/D/MC/V.)

🍴 **Los Comales** (☎2665 0105), 3 blocks north of the northeast corner of the *parque.* Coopeingua RL, a cooperative of 25 women striving to bring back regional traditions and improve the lives of females, runs this authentic place. Serves hearty Guanacaste *típico* to locals. It's easy to miss this hole-in-the-wall, as there's no sign outside. The *arroz de maíz* (¢1600) is not actually rice, but broken corn chips cooked with chicken. *Pollo de salchichon* (long sausage) ¢1300. Open daily 6am-10pm. Open M-Sa 7am-5pm. MC/V. ❶

🍴 **El Café Liberia** (☎2665 1660), a few blocks southwest of the *parque.* The only European-style cafe you'll find in Liberia. Serves freshly roasted Guanacastan coffee (roasted in an antique machine in the dining area) alongside homemade delicacies. Share hummus and olives (¢3000) with a friend or go solo with a toasted pesto, goat cheese, and tomato sandwich (¢3000). Finish up with some homemade cheesecake (¢1500). Breakfast combos of 100% natural juice, wheat toast with jam, coffee, and an omelette or yogurt with granola and fruit (¢3500) will fuel a day of hiking. Free Wi-Fi, multilingual book exchange, world music, and sporadic live performances. Themed movie showings (Th 7pm). Open M-F 8:30am-7pm, Sa 10am-6pm. Cash only. ❷

Pan y Miel (☎2666 0718), on the corner next to Palí and a Musamanni. The loaves of fresh bread stacked behind the counter are replenished often, as swarms of locals deplete the shelves of favorites like *pan danes* (¢1200). Pastries and cakes are also on sale. The 4 small tables don't allow much room for sit-down dining, so you may want to get your goodies to go. A less sweet but still popular option is the pan pizza topped with ham and cheese (¢1050). Open M-Sa 6am-8:30pm, Su 7am-5pm. AmEx/MC/V. ❶

Paso Real (☎2666 3455), on the 2nd fl. of a building overlooking the *parque.* A breezy outdoor balcony wraps around the high-ceilinged interior of this popular *marisquería.* Seafood and shellfish are their specialty and are prepared in every way possible. Shrimp cordon bleu fish fillet ¢6000. Shellfish casserole ¢5000. Wi-Fi. Open daily 11am-10pm. AmEx/D/MC/ V. ❸

Baula Real Bar & Restaurant (☎2666 0898), 300m south of the *parque*'s southwest corner. Decorations at this Mexican restaurant include Mexican flags, a disco ball, and sombreros. Karaoke Th-F 7-midnight. Go big with the Taco Baula (stuffed with chicken, ham, guacamole, and beans). *Fajitas* (¢3000). Open daily 4pm-2am. AmEx/D/MC/ V. ❷

Jauja Restaurant (☎2666 2061), 50m west of Banco Nacional. Cleanly presented and quickly delivered dishes served on bamboo tables. Offerings range from shrimp cocktail (¢5950) and bruschetta (¢2950) to Teriyaki tenderloin (¢7350) and pork ribs in BBQ sauce (¢5850). Finish the night with a crepe covered in chocolate, fruit sauce, and ice cream (¢2250). Live rock W 7:30pm. Wi-Fi. Open daily 7am-9pm. MC/ V. ❸

Pronto Pizza (☎2666 2098), corner of Av. 4 and C. 1. Watch the dough rise on your pizza in the clay oven. Over 26 different kinds of pizza include time-tested favorites and creative concoctions like peach pizza (tomato, cheese, peach, pineapple, honey;

¢4500). Small ¢4500-4700; medium ¢5700-6500; large ¢7800-8000. Pasta ¢4500.
Sandwiches ¢3000. Open daily noon-3pm, 6-11pm. AmEx/D/MC/ V. ❷

👁 SIGHTS

Iglesia de la Ermita, six blocks east of the *parque* along Av. Central, is the
oldest church in town (open daily 3-6pm, but hours vary). Enthusiastic
locals converge each weekend on **Rancho Santa Alicia,** 20min. from Liberia,
on the Interamericana Hwy. toward San José, where horse races, rodeos,
and unrelenting heat come together to form a unique and sweaty attraction.
The large horse statue at the entrance and the roaring of the crowd within
make it difficult to miss (☎2671 2513; open Tu-Su).

🎵 ENTERTAINMENT

Ticos hailing from surrounding villages compose the bulk of the minimal party
scene here. Even with the University of Costa Rica nearby, the young crowd
flocks to the beach towns for more exhilirating nights.

Disco Kurú (☎2666 0769), 300m past Burger King, across the Interamericana Hwy. One
of the busiest late-night spots in Liberia. Draws include 2 bars and a dance floor with
mirrors. Blasting tunes feature a mix of *merengue,* salsa, *cumbia,* and hip hop. Beers
¢1100. 18+. Open daily 9:30pm-6am. AmEx/MC/V.

Bar LIB (☎2665 0741), across the Interamericana Hwy., 100m on the left above the
bank. Quieter music makes for a more talkative crowd. Tropical beats on the dance floor
provide lively ambience for diners. Entrees (rice, meat, *ceviche*) ¢5000. Occasional live
music events. Cover ¢1000-2000. Open W-Sa 5pm-2:13am. AmEx/MC/V.

Bar de Luna (☎2665 5640), across the Interamerican Hwy. from Disco Kurú. Blasts
strictly electronica for busy weekend crowds. Mixed drinks from ¢2000. Imperial ¢1000.
Sa cover ¢1000. Open Tu-Su 9pm-6am.

Mall-Plaza Centro Liberia, off the Interamericana Hwy. Taxi from the bus station ¢1000.
This mall's new movie theater features recent American flicks with Spanish subtitles.
Adults ¢1600, children ¢1200. Showings 2-9pm.

PARQUE NACIONAL SANTA ROSA

Established in 1971, Santa Rosa preserves one of the largest remaining tropical dry forest in Central America. Encompassing most of the Península Santa
Rosa, this park has managed to keep its beaches, famous for great surfing and
turtle-watching, relatively tourist-free. In addition to its status as a **UNESCO
World Heritage Site,** the park is part of the **Area de Conservación Guanacaste (ACG),**
one of 11 conservation areas in Costa Rica. The unique flora here includes the
Guanacaste, Pochote, Naked Indian, and Caoba trees, as well as 115 species of
mammals, 9600 species of butterflies and moths, 460 species of birds, and more
than 30,000 species of insects. There are a number of enchanting *miradores*
(lookout points) on the natural and man-made trails.

The park also houses a famous historical site, **Hacienda Santa Rosa** (La
Casona). On March 20, 1856, a ragtag Costa Rican army defeated invading
troops sent from Nicaragua by American imperialist William Walker. Though
the event consisted of only 14 minutes of fighting, this battle is one of the most
famous in Costa Rican history. Invasions were again prevented in 1919 and
1955. Sadly, La Casona did not withstand its most recent invasion, on May 20,
2001, when two vindictive deer hunters snuck into the park and set fire to the
site, reducing over half of the fort to ashes. The arsonists, apparently angered

by recent hunting restrictions, were caught and convicted. Costa Ricans raised ¢200,350,000 to rebuild the fort. La Casona now stands restored, with roof tiles dating from 1886 and a state-of-the-art fire alarm system. Out front, you can watch cattle going through immersion baths in preparation for their truck journey from the *embarcadero* to the *corrales de piedra* (stone corrals).

TRANSPORTATION. About 12 **buses** per day pass along the Interamericana Hwy. and stop at the entrance station at La Casetilla. No buses run the 7km stretch to the administration center or along the dirt road to the beach, so those without wheels will need to find alternative means of transportation (walking takes about an hour). **Hotel Guanacaste** (p. 109) and **Hotel Liberia** (p. 109) arrange transportation but often require a minimum number of people (¢12,760/US$22 per person). Hotel Liberia is the only hotel that arranges transportation for solo travelers (¢20,300/US$35). It may be cheaper for groups to find their own **taxi** (¢34,800/US$60 round-trip).

ORIENTATION AND PRACTICAL INFORMATION. The national park's **entrance station** is 35km north of Liberia and 24km south of La Cruz, on the west side of the Interamericana Hwy. From here, a dirt road leads 7km to the park's **administration center** which houses **MINAE offices** and an **information center.** A bit farther to the left is the campground; to the right, past the cabins, is the *comedor* (cafeteria). Beyond the administration center is a four-wheel-drive road (often closed to traffic during the rainy season) leading to the coast, 12km away. The road forks after 7km; the left branch leads 4km to **Playa Naranjo,** a popular campsite and famed surfing beach; the right heads 8km to **Playa Nancite.** Access to Playa Nancite requires special permission given to formal researchers. Contact the park for volunteer opportunities, mostly available before and during the turtle-hatching (June-Dec.; reservaciones@acguanacaste.ac.cr).

The park's **Sector Murciélago,** spread over the isolated northern coast of Península Santa Rosa, isn't accessible from the rest of the park (open 8am-5pm). To visit, start at **Cuajuniquil,** 8km off the Interamericana Hwy., which can be reached by taking a bus from La Cruz or Liberia. You will either need to walk 7km down the dirt road to the sector's ranger station or traverse the bumpy stretch with a four-wheel-drive vehicle. Information is available at the **administration center** (☎2666 5051, ext. 219; www.acguanacaste.ac.cr). Open daily 8am-4pm. For reservations, contact reservaciones@acguanacaste.ac.cr. The park is open daily 8am-4pm. Entrance fee US$10; beaches US$15; camping US$2 extra. Discounts offered to those working on conservation efforts.

ACCOMMODATIONS AND FOOD. The park offers lodging in small houses near the main offices and decent meals in the *comedor.* An on-site snack bar selling sandwiches, drinks, and bagged cookies is open to all. Reserve lodging at least one month in advance. (☎2666 5051. Lodging US$12 per person. Meals US$6 per day. Breakfast 6:30-7:30am; lunch 11:30am-1pm; dinner 5:30-6pm. Ask in the morning to have your lunch or dinner prepared.) A campground near the administration center has drinking water, toilets, and cold-water showers. The campground at Playa Naranjo has toilets and non-potable water. Ask about camping at the administration center.

SIGHTS AND HIKING. La Casona, near the administration center (follow signs past the administration center to the left), is a museum featuring historic rooms with accompanying information and an exhibition about the

Area de Conservación Guanacaste. (Open daily 8am-11:30am and 1-4pm. Free.) The **Monument to the Heroes of 1856 and 1955** lies beside La Casona and offers a windy view of nearby volcanoes in Orosi, Cacao, and Rincón de la Vieja. The lookouts **Mirador Tierras Emergidas,** halfway to the administration center from the entrance on the way to the coast, and **Mirador Valle Naranjo,** starting 6km after the administration center on the way to the coast, feature stellar views of the mountains and the beach. All trails and points of interest are marked on a useful **map** available at the entrance (¢100). The short 1km **Sendero Indio Desnudo** (a.k.a. Gringo Pelado, or "Peeled Gringo") begins on the north side of La Casona next to the museum; it winds around an impressive array of regional flora. Many of the trees in this region lose their leaves during the dry season, so it's not unusual to see them bare. Look out for indigenous carvings and monkeys high in the trees. **Sendero Los Patos** (3km), 5km beyond the administration center on the road to the coast, is one of the best trails for spotting birds and the blue morpho butterfly, and features **Mirador al Cañon del Tigre.** The 2km **Sendero Palo Seco** lies 300m before Playa Naranjo. The 6km **Sendero Carbonal** also lies 300m before Playa Naranjo and leads to **Laguna El Limbo,** a crocodile hangout. On the coast, you can swim at **Bahía El Hachal, Bahía Danta** (temporarily closed), **Coquito** (temporarily closed), **Santa Elena,** and **Playa Blanca** (17km long), or hike the 600m **Poza del General** to view birds and monkeys. **Camping** is permitted in the area, but check with the park office to see if there is space, especially during *Semana Santa* (☎2666 5051). No potable water is available.

 BEACHES. The famous fast waves of **Piedra Bruja** (Witch Rock) break onto a stone off **Playa Naranjo.** Though there are great waves on the shoreline, serious surfers may want to seek out sandbars where the estuary meets the ocean at Piedra Bruja; these are best from December to April. Bring a mosquito net if you plan to use the **campground** at Playa Naranjo; beware of biting *chitras* on the beach at dawn and dusk. **Playa Nancite** hosts the country's second-largest population of Olive Ridley turtles. The nesting season, lasting from July to December, is at its height from October to November and reaches its zenith during the eight days of the crescent moon. During this time, thousands of turtles arrive at 800m of beach each night around 9pm. Access to Playa Nancite is granted by permission only, and swimming is not allowed. Bring water to these beaches, as there is none to drink. Lodging is open only to researchers and students ($10 per person, up to 20 people). Call the **administration center** (☎2666 5051, ext. 233) 20 days ahead to reserve **camping** near the beach (US$2 per day; max. 25 people per day). If you arrive at the park by car, keep in mind that driving to Nancite is not allowed. Drop the vehicle off at Playa Naranjo, where a guard will watch it for you.

> **TIP** **THIS BEACH WAS MADE FOR WALKIN'.** During the rainy season, the road may be impossible to drive, even with a four-wheel-drive vehicle. The most determined can hike the muddy trail on foot, leaving cars at the information center. Bring proper clothing for heavy mid-morning rains.

PEÑAS BLANCAS: BORDER WITH NICARAGUA
Liberia is only 1hr. away from the border at Peñas Blancas, a small frontier featuring a few houses and whole lot of police along the tree-lined road to Nicaragua. **Buses** run frequently from Liberia's **Estación Central** to the border (every hr. 5:30am-7pm, ¢1200). Buses from Liberia that continue into Nicaragua

stop in front of **Hotel Guanacaste** (5hr., 3 per day 7:30-9:30am, ¢12,180). To reach Peñas Blancas from **San José,** take a bus from C. 14, Av. 3/5 (every hr. 3am-7pm, ¢4600). If you are traveling into Costa Rica, buses run from Peñas Blancas to **La Cruz** (every hr. 5am-6:30pm, ¢550), **San José** (every 1½hr. 5:30am-5:30pm, ¢4600), or **San Carlos** (5hr.; 6:30am, 2pm; ¢2800).

Crossing the border into Nicaragua usually takes about 30min.; if arriving on a bus, the process is slightly more prolonged. After getting your passport stamped at the **Costa Rica Immigration Office** (☎2677 0230 or 0064; open 6am-10pm), drive or walk to the actual crossing about 100m down the road. **Banco de Costa Rica** (open M-F 9am-4pm, Sa 9am-1pm), next to the immigration office, can exchange money and traveler's checks. Agents that catch you right as you get off the bus can also exchange money; they often offer a better deal than the bank, but **watch out for counterfeit bills.** Rates for changing US dollars to *cordobas* are better on the Nicaraguan side of the border, while rates for changing *colones* to *cordobas* are worse. **Hotel Guanacaste** in Liberia will also change money. Snack vendors line the road to the border. **Restaurante de Frontera,** connected to the immigration office, serves more substantial food (hamburgers ¢1000; *casados* ¢2000-2500; AmEx/D/MC/V).

Buses from the Nicaraguan border run to **Rivas** (1hr., every 30min. 4am-5:30pm; ¢20) and continue to **Managua.** To get to **San Juan del Sur,** catch the **Rivas bus** and change in Rivas for San Juan (30min., every 30min. 5am-5pm, ¢20).

NICOYA

The trip can be long, and the roads difficult, but the gorgeous beaches, nature reserves, and world-class waves of the Nicoya Peninsula will convince most travelers that it's worth the trek. Surfers come from across the world to surf at Tamarindo and Playa Negra, while the reef at El Coco draws novices and experienced divers alike. Though the inland region is often overlooked by travelers, its villages offer a rugged charm, with streets full of ambling cowpokes and *pueblos* where the residents guard a proud history. Larger cities like Santa Cruz and Nicoya are frequently used as transportation jump-offs but can offer rich cultural performances and a chance to experience authentic *tico* lifestyle. Since activities in these towns are scarce, it's likely you'll find yourself itching for the crashing waves and vast expanses of sand farther west.

PLAYA HERMOSA

Known as a prime swimming and diving beach for its calm waters and diverse marine life, Playa Hermosa offers beach-goers the chance to see eels, octopi, and seahorses, as well as breathtaking sunsets. With its location just outside of the Papagayo Gulf and its designation as the next "it" spot for tourism, Hermosa is experiencing tremendous growth. More villas, beachside condos, and gated communities sprout up every day. Fights to prevent environmental damage have dominated the Supreme Court for years. Despite the chaos of continual construction, Hermosa offers a peaceful and relaxing experience described by travelers and locals alike as *muy tranquilo* (very calm)—particularly in comparison to its rowdy neighbor, Playa del Coco.

▆ TRANSPORTATION

Buses: Buses to Hermosa depart from **San José** on Av. 5/7, C. 12, one block north of the **Atlántica Norte Terminal** (6hr., 3:30pm, ¢2000) and from **Liberia** (1hr., 8 per day 4:30am-5:30pm, ¢1200). To get to San José from Hermosa, catch any bus to Liberia and transfer at the central bus station, or catch the **directo** (5am, ¢4000). Buses from **Playa Panamá** to Liberia stop in **Sardinal** (6, 7:30, 8:30, 10am, 2, 4, 5, 7:10pm; ¢1200).

Taxis: Taxis shuttle visitors from **Playa del Coco** to Playa Hermosa (15min., ¢5000).

◢ ▪ ORIENTATION AND PRACTICAL INFORMATION

Playa Hermosa has two entrances, both within walking distance of each other. From Playa Hermosa, **Playa Panamá** is a 3km walk along the main road to the north. **MiniSuper Dayi,** 150m south of the second Hermosa entrance, sells food products, basic amenities, beer, wine, and other liquor. (☎2672 0032; open M-Sa 7am-8pm, Su 7am-5pm.) **Lupero,** the closest *supermercado*, sits on the main road between the two entrances (☎2672 0303; open M-F 7:30am-8pm, Sa 7:30am-8:30pm, Su 8am-7:30pm). Most other services beyond those listed are available in **Sardinal**.

24hr. ATM: in the small complex of shops on the main road near the 1st entrance.

Telephones: 150m east of the beach, at the second entrance, next to **Pescado Loco**.

NICOYA

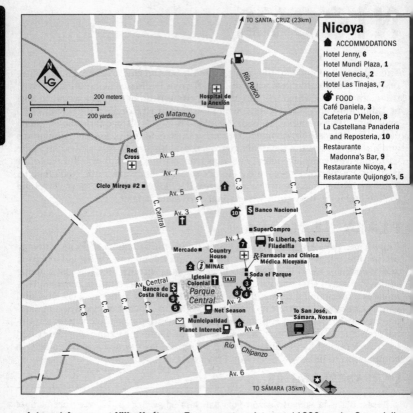

TO SANTA CRUZ (23km)

Nicoya

🏠 ACCOMMODATIONS
Hotel Jenny, **6**
Hotel Mundi Plaza, **1**
Hotel Venecia, **2**
Hotel Las Tinajas, **7**

🍎 FOOD
Café Daniela, **3**
Cafeteria D'Melon, **8**
La Castellana Panaderia
 and Reposteria, **10**
Restaurante
 Madonna's Bar, **9**
Restaurante Nicoya, **4**
Restaurante Quijongo's, **5**

Internet Access: at **Villa Huétares.** Two computers. Internet ₡1000 per hr. Open daily 7am-10pm. Many of the hotels and restaurants have free Wi-Fi.

🏨 ACCOMMODATIONS

▧ **Cabinas la Casona** (☎2672 0025), 500m west of the 2nd entrance and 20m north on the road before the beach. Friendly owners and spacious rooms with private baths, cable TV, and fully-equipped kitchens offer the best deal on the beach. Apartments for 2 with large beds, futons, and A/C provide temporary havens from the heat. Low-season singles ₡14,500 (US$25), high-season ₡17,400 (US$30); doubles ₡17,400/23,200 (US$30/40); 6-person rooms ₡43,500/49,300 (US$75/85); apartments for 2 ₡43,500/52,200 (US$75/90). Cash only. ❺

▧ **Villa Huétares** (☎2672 0052), 300m west of the 2nd entrance to the beach. Comfortable rooms. You will be pleased with the familial owners. A/C, cable TV, pool and jacuzzi, Wi-Fi, and internet. On-site restaurant. Low-season doubles ₡26,100 (US$45), high-season ₡37,700 (US$65); triples ₡52,200/72,500 (US$90/125); quads ₡81,200 (US$140). ❹

 Ecotel (☎2672 0175), walk 500m down the road from the 2nd beach entrance and turn left at the last road before the beach. The cheapest place to stay in town, suit-

NICOYA

able for nature-lovers or those willing to rough it. Options include bunk rooms, indoor lofts, and beds in the communal space. Snorkel and canoe use included. Bunk rooms and singles from ¢8700 (US$15); doubles from ¢14,500 (US$25). Camping ¢5800 (US$10) per tent, when available. ❷

Hotel El Velero (☎2672 0036; www.costaricahotel.net), on the beach. This beautifully decorated hotel has wide, whitewashed hallways, decorative fountains, bold draperies of Costa Rican fauna, and a small aquatic-themed pool. Common area on the 2nd floor has wicker rocking chairs and a book exchange. A/C and several rooms with beach views. Sailboat tours (5hr. sunset tour ¢34,800/US$60; day tour ¢46,400/US$80 per person; both include snorkeling and open bar). Massages ¢23,200 (US$40) per hr. Yoga classes ¢4060 (US$7). Doubles ¢43,500 (US$75), each additional person ¢5800 (US$10). Ask about student discounts. Prices jump in high season. Children 9 and under stay free. AmEx/D/MC/V. ❹

Playa Hermosa Inn (☎2672 0063), on the beach next to Aqua Sports, near the 2nd entrance. Rooms and apartments with full kitchens, A/C, and hot water. Borrow a book from the mini-library's random selection of fiction. Breakfast included. Rooms ¢14,500 (US$25) per person; apartment ¢34,800 (US$60) for 2 people, each additional person ¢5800 (US$10). Ask about student discounts. AmEx/D/MC/V. ❷

🔳🎵 FOOD AND ENTERTAINMENT

For once, *comida típica* is not the norm: restaurants are geared almost exclusively toward tourists and, accordingly, are pricier. Penny-pinchers will appreciate **Soda Dayi** right next to **MiniSuper Dayi**, where breakfast combos (¢2000-2500), burgers (¢1500), and other *comida rápida* leave both stomachs and wallets pleasantly full (open M-Sa 6am-7pm, Su 7am-3pm; cash only).

🔳 **Finisterra** (☎2672 0227; www.finisterra.net). At the 1st beach entrance, follow the signs to the restaurant by walking 700m toward the beach, taking a left, and walking 250m up the steep hill. Perched on a cliff, this popular Caribbean restaurant has some of the best views and food in town. Trained in Peru, the local-born chef cooks up creative dishes, including long-time favorites like purée of yucca with seared tuna, leeks, onion, and soy (¢5800) and Thai curry (¢81,200). Soak up your surroundings over the unforgettable passionfruit pie (¢2900). Free Wi-Fi. Open M and W-Su 5-10pm. AmEx/D/MC/V. ❸

Ginger (☎2672 0041), on stilts, off the main road. A delightful, unique tapas experience which purports to combine "all the flavors of the world on a small plate." In reality, the food is a hodgepodge of Asian and Mediterranean influences. The chef uses ample amounts of ginger, lemon-grass, cilantro, mint, and soy. Ahi Tuna (a pepper-crusted fillet served over ginger slaw and drizzled with citrus mayonnaise) ¢4000. Mojitico (guaro, passion fruit, basil, and soda) ¢2800. Large selection of wines. Open Tu-Su 5-10pm. MC/V. ❸

Pescado Loco Bar y Restaurant (☎2627 0017), 500m toward the beach (from the 2nd entrance), 50m to the right. Local food at reasonable prices served under a large wooden fish. Interesting options include squid in its own ink (¢4000), octopus *ceviche* (¢3800), and orange shrimp (¢6500). Frequented by beer-drinking locals. *Casados* ¢2800. Open daily 9am-10pm. ❷

El Velero (☎2672 1015), 600m west and 25m north of the 2nd beach entrance. Just back from the sand, watch the sunset at this restaurant while seafood experts prepare *ceviche* (¢3400) and whole red snapper (¢8000). W and Sa seafood BBQ, where fresh meat and seafood, cooked over glowing embers, are served a la carte. Chicken breast ¢4300. Filet mignon ¢7500. Daily happy hour offers 2-for-1 deals on selected drinks 4-6pm. Open daily 6am-9pm. AmEx/D/MC/V. ❷

Restaurant Aqua Sports (☎2672 0050), follow the signs from the 2nd beach entrance. Served next to Aqua Sport's extensive collection of kayaks, selections include *lomito* (tenderloin; ¢5690) and shrimp rice (¢4880). For a lobster with garlic butter, you'll have to shell out ¢13,820. Tequila sunrise ¢1870. Open daily 11am-9pm. AmEx/D/MC/V. ❷

Vallejos Bar Restaurant (☎2672 0187), 800m west of the 1st beach entrance. Brave souls can munch on jumbo shrimp in hot sauce (¢9000), while less adventurous eaters can enjoy chicken in mushroom sauce (¢4000) or filet mignon (¢8000). Entrees ¢3800-9000. Wine ¢2500 per glass. Open daily 10am-9pm. Cash only. ❷

Pizzeria Isabella (☎8302 3375), in front of the 1st beach entrance. Forget the *casado:* order a large pizza for the beach (¢8000-9000). Pastas ¢3800-7000. Calzones ¢5500. Salads ¢2000-4000. Open daily 5pm-10pm. Cash only. ❷

☕ WATERSPORTS

If it rains heavily the day before, don't plan on seeing many fish when snorkeling; Pacific tides wash phytoplankton toward the shores of the Nicoya Peninsula, which reduces visibility. By and large, however, Hermosa's calm, clear water is ideal for diving, kayaking, and waterskiing.

Diving Safaris (☎2672 1259; www.costaricadiving.net), 500m west of the second entrance to the beach. Specializes in diving and snorkeling tours. Morning dives and snorkeling 8:30am-1:30pm. 2-tank dives ¢55,100/US$95, includes equipment. Beginner day-long classes and dives ¢72,500/US$125. Snorkeling ¢23,200/US$40, includes boat. For equipment only, rentals are ¢2900/US$5 per 2hr. Arranges day sails and sunset sails with open bar and the option of snorkeling, jet-skiing, or sportfishing (from ¢58,000/US$100). Also books surfing trips to Witch's Rock and Ollie's Point (7:30am-3pm; ¢174,000/US$300, 5 person max.; experienced participants only). PADI certification course available. Open daily 7am-5pm.

Aqua Sport (☎2672 0500), follow the signs from the beach's 2nd entrance. Rents kayaks (¢5800/US$10 per 3-4hr.), pedal and paddleboats (¢5800/US$10 per person), boogie boards (¢2900/US$5 per 3hr.), and sailboats (¢17,400/US$30 for 2 people per 2hr.). Snorkeling gear and tours (¢17,400/US$30 per 3hr.; includes water, fruit, kayak, and guide). Trips to Witch's Rock (¢116,000/US$200 for 4 people per 8hr.). Fishing tour (¢116,000/US$200 per 5hr.; includes water, fruit and beer). Open M-Sa 6am-9pm.

Sea Life (☎8306 1807). Snorkeling (¢26,100/US$45 per 2½hr.); sunset cruise (¢26,100/US$45 per 3hr., 10 people max.); dolphin tour (¢26,100/US$45); jet skis (¢55,100/US$95 for 1-2 people per 1hr.); ATV tour of the mountains (¢55,100/US$95 per 2hr.); tour of waterfalls, canopy, and hotsprings (7:30am-4pm, ¢55,100/US$95); horse rental (¢29,000/US$50 per 2½hr.). Call or ask for reservations through **Villa Huétares** (p. 116). Open daily 6am-11pm.

Funsealand (☎2248 0615; www.funsealand.infca.com), in front Hotel Condovac on the main road. Specializes in ATV tours (¢29,000 (US$50) per 1½hr., ¢46,400 (US$80) per 2½hr.). The megacombo package includes waverunner (1hr.), ATV (2hr.), and canopy (2hr.) tours for ¢130,500 (US$225). Student discount 25% with ID.

🔲 DAYTRIP FROM PLAYA HERMOSA

PLAYA PANAMÁ
Buses from Liberia pass Hermosa and end their route in Panamá. Buses from Hermosa to Panamá (15min.; 5:30, 8:30am, 12:30, 2, 4:30, 6:30pm; ¢300). Buses from Panamá to Hermosa (15min.; 6, 7:30, 8:30, 10am, 2, 4, 5, 7:10pm; ¢300). The two beaches are

separated by 2km of well-paved road, so walking is also an option. The village of Playa Panamá lies a few kilometers beyond the beach itself.

At Playa Panamá, just 2km north of Hermosa, the arc of the coast makes for an impressively long beach. The tranquil, glassy waters are perfect for swimming, though the sand is a bit darker than on Playa Hermosa, and the vegetation is less cared-for. Budget accommodations on Panamá are non-existent; the **Four Seasons Hotel** and other luxury resorts such as **Alegro, Fiesta Premier,** and **Giardini di Papagayo** have claimed this stretch of beach. The sand, fortunately, remains free, which enables many *tico* families to sip coconut juice and sink into beach chairs on this pleasant strip. Outdoor showers, a camping zone, and a smattering of non-resort restaurants are available. Bring your own water.

NICOYA

Nicoya, 78km south of Liberia, is the main settlement on the peninsula. The town was named after Chorotegan Indian Chief Nicoya, who ruled the region and welcomed the Spanish in 1523. In many museums throughout Europe, Nicoya is one of the main places marked on early colonial navigation maps. Though it sees less traffic these days, Nicoya still has its charms. The *parque central* is home to ancient stone benches, cobblestone barriers, and one of Costa Rica's oldest churches. The city serves as a good base for spelunking in Parque Nacional Barra Honda. Nicoya also features more tourist services and transportation options than nearby towns, though many find that the city lacks the personality to be a destination in and of itself.

TRANSPORTATION

Buses: The **main station** is 200m east and 200m south of the *parque*. Buses leave for: **Nosara** (3hr.; 5, 10am, noon, 3, 5:30pm; ¢1000); **Playa Sámara** (1hr., every hr. 8am-9:30pm, ¢800); **San José** (4hr. via ferry, 8 per day 3am-5pm, ¢2430; 5-5½hr. via Liberia, 7:30am and 3pm, ¢4190). Buy tickets for San José at the window at least a day in advance to guarantee a seat. (☎2685 5032. Open daily 7am-5pm.) From another stop 100m north and 150m east of the *parque*, buses run to **Filadelfia** (1hr.; 10pm, additional bus Su and holidays; ¢680) and **Liberia** (2hr.; M-Sa 55 per day 3:30am-9pm, Su and holidays 9 per day 5am-7pm; ¢1000) via **Santa Cruz** (45min., ¢310).

Taxis: (¢17130/US$30 to Sámara) line up just about anywhere, including in front of the bus station, *parque,* and hospital.

ORIENTATION AND PRACTICAL INFORMATION

The two landmarks in the city center are the **parque central** and the main road, **Calle 3,** which runs north-south a block east of the *parque*. The bus might drop you off at various locations, so your best bet is to ask for the *parque central*. Once in the *parque*, Hotel Venecia is north, the *municipalidad* is south, Banco de Costa Rica is west, and Soda el Parque is east.

Tourist Information: MINAE (☎2686 6760), on the north side of the *parque*. Info on the national parks in Guanacaste. Open M-F 8am-4pm.

Banks: Banco de Costa Rica (☎2685 5010), on the west side of the *parque* with Visa/Plus **ATM,** cashes traveler's checks and gives Visa cash advances. Open M-F 9am-4pm. **Banco Nacional** (☎2685 3366), next to the Super Compro. Open M-F 8:30am-3:45pm. **24hr. ATM.**

Police: (☎2685 5559, emergency 911), 150m south of the bus station, near the airport.

Red Cross: (☎2685 5458, emergency 911), 500m north and 50m west of the *parque*.

Medical Services: Hospital de la Anexión (☎2685 8400), 100m east and 600m north of the *parque*. **Farmacia and Clínica Médica Nicoyana** (☎2685 5138), 100m east and 10m south of the northeast corner of the *parque*. Pharmacy open daily 8am-7pm, Sa 8am-6pm. Clinic open M-Sa 8am-5pm.

Internet Access: Planet Internet (☎2685 4281), 100m south of the southeast corner of the *parque*. Internet ¢500 per hr. Open M-Sa 8am-10pm, Su 10am-9pm. **Good Times Internet** (☎8893 8891), on the south side of the *parque*, has new flatscreen computers. Internet ¢400 per hr. Black and white copies ¢100, color ¢250-1000. Open daily 9am-10pm. **Cyber Center** (☎8886 0730), below Hotel Jenny. ¢500 per hr. Black and white copies ¢100, color ¢250 and up. **Cyber Plus Internet** (☎2686 7607), 100m south of the southeast corner of the *parque*, has webcams and headphones. Internet ¢400 per hr. Open daily 8am-10:30pm.

Post Office: (☎2686 6402), across from the southwest corner of the *parque*. Open M-F 8am-5:30pm, Sa 7:30am-noon. **Postal Code:** 5200.

ACCOMMODATIONS

Unless you're willing to completely empty your wallet for a room in the truly impressive **Hotel Tempisque,** lodging options here are not the height of luxury.

Hotel Mundi Plaza (☎2685 3535 or 6702), 50m north of Banco Nacional. Pastel pink hallway and mirrors lead to bright, comfortable rooms with blue tiled floors and matching toilet-sink sets; some have balconies with mountain views. A/C and cable TV. Breakfast included. Towels provided. Secure parking. Singles ¢14,276 (US$25); doubles ¢23,984 (US$42); triples ¢34,263 (US$60). AmEx/MC/V. ❷

Hotel Jenny (☎2685 5050 or 867 5309), 100m south of the southeast corner of the *parque*. Rattier than Hotel Mundi, but becomes a real bargain if you're traveling in a group. Simple rooms with small beds, decent baths, A/C, and cable TVs. Parking available. Singles ¢10,000; doubles ¢14,000; triples ¢18,000; quads ¢20,000. AmEx/MC/V. ❷

Hotel Las Tinajas (☎2685 5081), across from the bus station to Liberia. Simple but clean rooms with small desks, shelves, and cable TVs. Public telephone available. Singles ¢6950, with A/C ¢9965; doubles ¢9800/13,600; triples ¢13,400/17,300; quads with A/C ¢22,000; quints ¢25,000; 6-person rooms without A/C ¢22,400. MC/V. ❶

Hotel Venecia (☎2686 5325), on the north side of the *parque*. High ceilings. Basic rooms with shared baths and a fan. TV and A/C also available. If you don't need a TV or A/C, this is the most economical option, though not the most comfy or sanitary. If you're going to spring for these amenities, look elsewhere. Free Wi-Fi. Lockout midnight. Singles ¢7000, with TV ¢9000, with TV and A/C ¢12,200; doubles ¢9000/10,200/13,500; triples ¢11,000/12,700/15,500. Cash only. ❷

FOOD

Casados and Chinese food joints dominate Nicoya. Pick up groceries at **Super Compro,** next to Banco Nacional. (☎2686 6314. Open M-Sa 8am-8pm, Su 8am-noon.) **Country House,** north of the northeast corner of the *parque*, sells produce. (☎2686 4800. Open M-F 8am-7pm, Sa 7am-7pm.)

Café Daniela (☎2686 6149), 100m east and 50m south of the northeast corner of the *parque*. The most popular spot for *comida típica*, with vegetarian *casados* (¢1800) that come with large green salads—a rarity in *sodas*. Large meat *casados* (¢1800-2700) come with beans, salad, rice, tortilla, and pasta. The fresh lemonade (¢800) is incredible. Open M-Sa 7am-9pm. MC/V. ❶

Cafeteria D'Melon (☎2658 4674), 100m east of the *parque*, on Av. 2. Cute coffee shop with lime green and orange walls has 67 options for hot or cold coffee, tea, and hot chocolate. Creative drinks include the Shiver *café* (coffee, chocolate cookie, vanilla ice cream, and milk; ¢1600) and the mint choco-orange (¢1000). Breakfast combo (¢2900) served with pancakes, juice, and fruit. Free Wi-Fi. Open M-Sa 9am-7pm. ❶

Restaurante Nicoya (☎2658 5113), next to Café Daniela. With the best Chinese food in town, Restaurante Nicoya is a local favorite. Large portions of fresh seafood with various Asian and Indian flavors, like sweet-and-sour shrimp (¢3480) and chicken and shrimp with cashews (¢4000). Open daily 10:30am-3pm and 5-10:30pm. MC/V. ❷

Restaurante Madonna's Bar (☎2685 4142), on the west side of the *parque*. Don't cry for her, Costa Rica—Madonna has made it to small towns here, if only in poster form. Try the *casado* (¢1900) or the fried chicken with fruit and veggies (¢1600). Entrees ¢1500-2000. Open daily 11am-2am. ❶

La Castellana Panaderia and Reposteria (☎8861 4205), across from the Banco Nacional. Locals come for the pan pizza (¢800) and bread with pineapple and coconut (¢700). Americans feeling homesick will feel better after a slice of chocolate cake (¢600). There isn't much seating, so take it to go. Open M-Sa 5am-7pm, Su 6am-1pm. ❶

🔎 SIGHTS

Iglesia Colonial, on the northeast corner of the *parque*, is one of the oldest churches in Costa Rica. It was constructed in 1644 from stone, brick, and *cal*, a unique local sand. The church was damaged by earthquakes in 1822 and rebuilt in 1831. Several religious artifacts, including a baptismal font and a 16th-century confessional booth, are worth a look. (Open to visitors M-F 8am-4pm, Sa 8am-11pm, Su 8am-5pm.) The folks at **Ciclo Mireya #2,** 400m north of the northwest corner of the *parque*, rent bikes, the perfect way to explore the surrounding countryside. (☎2685 5391. Bikes ¢8000 per day; mountain bikes ¢15,000.) Nicoya is full of shops, selling imported Panamanian clothes at unbeatable prices.

OSTIONAL

This gritty strip of black-sand beach is Costa Rica's most important breeding ground for olive ridley turtles. During the moon's fourth quarter, female turtles flock here by the thousands to lay their eggs. During this time, the tiny town comes to life: the few modest hotels in the area fill up and the fires at the two restaurants remain lit. Luckily, daytrips to Ostional from Nosara, Sámara, and even Tamarindo are available.

🚌 TRANSPORTATION. The trip between Nosara and Ostional (8km) makes for a pleasant 1hr. **bike** ride over dirt roads lined with cow pastures; bring a buddy. Alternatively, hop on one of the many **buses** from the bigger hotels in the surrounding towns. One bus makes the bouncy 3hr. ride between **Santa Cruz** and Ostional, leaving from Cabinas Guacamaya in Ostional and stopping at all the small towns along the way. (5, 7am, 4pm; from the *mercado* in Santa Cruz 12:30 and 4pm. It passes through Restaurante Las Tucas in **Paraíso** at 1pm. ¢2100.) The bus can't make the trip during heavy rains. Some travelers report finding rides, though *Let's Go* never recommends hitchhiking. Inquire for a **taxi** at local businesses, like Soda Conchito.

🏠🍴 ACCOMMODATIONS AND FOOD. Cabinas Guacamaya ❶, 150m south of Soda La Plaza, is the best deal in Ostional, with spacious orange rooms that have private baths, fans, and large patios. (☎2682 0430. ¢4000 per person.) **Arribadas ❷**, across and slightly to the left of Soda La Plaza (p. 122), offers more amenities for a higher price. Each of the five rooms has a private bath with hot water and large windows. (☎8816 9815; www.hostcasaatmos.com. Breakfast included. Kitchen available. Two computers with internet available. Free Wi-Fi. Rooms ¢14,313/US$25 per person.) **Cabinas Ostional ❷**, across from Soda La Plaza, has simple triples and quads with private baths, a few hammocks, and small, private porches. The reception area is hidden, so just walk straight across from Soda La Plaza. (☎2682 0428. ¢5000 per person.) **Camping ❶** is allowed during the summer for ¢2,290/US$4 per day. You'll need to speak with the guard and pay at the ADIO booth, 150m to the left of Soda La Plaza when facing the beach. (Portable outdoor toilet.)

The central **Soda La Plaza ❶** is one of the few restaurants in town and has a menu of all the *típico* staples at bargain prices. (*Casados* ¢2500. *Batidos*—fresh fruit juice shakes—¢500. Open daily 7am-8:30pm.) An attached **pulpería** stocks snacks and very basic cooking supplies. (Open daily 6:30am-noon and 2-7pm.) **Tony ❷**, next door to Cabinas Guacamaya, is your only other option and a break from the ubiquitous *casado*. Favorites include the Thai chicken (¢3900) or one of the many pizzas (¢4200). Free Wi-Fi for customers. (Open daily noon-10pm.)

⚑ OUTDOOR ACTIVITIES. Turtles come almost every night in small numbers, beginning around 9pm. During the moon's fourth quarter is the **arribada** or **flota**, the synchronized arrival of thousands of turtles to a specific section of the beach. In those special periods (generally 3-8 days) when the *arribada* occurs, most turtles arrive at the beach between 3pm and 7am. They travel from as far away as Peru and Baja California to give their offspring a chance to begin life in the same place they themselves were born. This makes Ostional the second largest olive ridley sea turtle breeding ground in the world. During the *arribada*, the sand is barely visible beneath the massive number of turtles digging cozy holes for their eggs. With guides holding red lights, you can watch a mother turtle dig a hole, drop all her eggs, scramble to cover the hole, and then camouflage it. This fascinating process takes about 30min. Including the ascent to the laying spot and return to the water, expect a viewing to last about an hour and fifteen minutes. Sometimes the beach gets so full with turtles that they overflow onto the town's roads. To make sure you don't miss this event, contact biologist Rodrigo Morera (☎ 682 0470; www.ostionalcr.tripod.com/index.html) at **La Asociación de Desarollo Integral de Ostional,** 100m north of Soda La Plaza. The **National Wildlife Directorate** (☎8233 8112 or 8222 9533) can also provide information about the *arribada*. You can also check in with the tourist agencies in Nosara or Sámara. If you do miss the *arribada*, wait a few weeks to see the baby turtles make their way to the water. During the *arribada* and at night, **guides are required.** Contact Rodrigo Morera, who can refer you to a guide, or any tourist agency in the area. (¢5,725/US$10. 10-person maximum per group. Flash cameras, flashlights, and surfing are prohibited during the *arribada*.) You will not be able to see the many crabs that roam the beach in the dark, so wear closed-toed shoes. To learn more about the volunteer opportunities available here, contact Rodrigo Morera. Fore more information on volunteering in Costa Rica, see **Beyond Tourism,** p. 35.

MAL PAÍS AND SANTA TERESA

Don't be fooled by the name of this remote surfing village near the southern tip of the Nicoya Peninsula; with long, empty beaches, stunning rock formations, and scenic coves, Mal País is hardly a "bad country." Settled by a small community of locals and currently home to a growing contingent of foreigners, this area is slowly developing into a haven for excellent ethnic restaurants and unique accommodations. You'll find more hotels, restaurants, and shops clumped together in Santa Teresa. Bad roads can make travel to Mal País difficult and time-consuming, but the constant surf and peaceful vibe make the trip worth the effort.

TRANSPORTATION

Buses: Most travelers take the **ferry** from Puntarenas to **Paquera** and drive directly to Mal País, or take buses directly to **Cóbano** (2hr., 7 per day 6am-7pm, ₡1200). If you're lucky, there may be extra space on the **San José** bus coming off the ferry that will go directly to Mal País. You can also head first to **Montezuma** and then take buses to Mal País. From Montezuma, take the bus to **Cóbano** (15min., 6 per day 5:30am-4pm, ₡300) and catch a connecting bus from the same stop to **Santa Teresa** via **Mal País** (1hr.; 10:30am, 2:30pm;

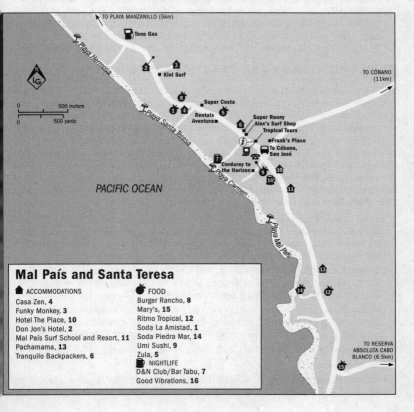

Mal País and Santa Teresa

ACCOMMODATIONS
Casa Zen, **4**
Funky Monkey, **3**
Hotel The Place, **10**
Don Jon's Hotel, **2**
Mal País Surf School and Resort, **11**
Pachamama, **13**
Tranquilo Backpackers, **6**

FOOD
Burger Rancho, **8**
Mary's, **15**
Ritmo Tropical, **12**
Soda La Amistad, **1**
Soda Piedra Mar, **14**
Umi Sushi, **9**
Zula, **5**

NIGHTLIFE
D&N Club/Bar Tabu, **7**
Good Vibrations, **16**

¢700). Return buses leave from Santa Teresa and pick passengers up at hotels and the main crossroads by Frank's Place before heading back to **Cóbano** (7:30, 11:30am, 3:30pm). Buses leave from Frank's Place to **San José** (M-F 5:45am, Sa-Su 5:45, 8:15am, 3:45pm; ¢6500). Ask your accommodation for more information about bus stops in town.

Taxis: Taxis drive around town but are not common. If you can't find one, call a local taxi (☎8819 9021). Taxis to **Cóbano** ¢8588 (US$15) leave from the intersection.

Private Transportation: Bad roads and infrequent public transportation make moving on from Mal País time-consuming and complicated, so transfer services, though expensive, may prove well worth it for the convenience. **Montezuma Expeditions** (☎2642 0919), which can be booked at **Tropical Tours** (☎2640 0384) by the crossroads, has shuttles to major destinations (Arenal, Jacó, Manuel Antonio, Monteverde, San José, Tamarindo; ¢22,900-25,763/US$40-45) and can arrange other shuttles. Most leave around 8am.

Car Rental: Alamo (☎2640 0526), on the right, on the road into town from Cobano. Rentals from ¢22,900 (US$40). 21+. Open daily 8am-5pm. **Budget** (☎2640 0500), 100m from Frank's Place on the road to Santa Teresa. Rentals from ¢25,763 (US$45). 21+. Open M-Sa 8am-6pm, Su 8am-4pm.

Bike and ATV Rentals: Getting around Mal País is easiest with a **bike** or **4WD vehicle. Alex's Surf Shop** (☎2640 0364), 600m toward Santa Teresa from the main intersection, rents bikes for ¢5725/US$10 per day and quads for ¢34,350/US$60 per day. Open daily 8am-6:30pm. MC/V. In Mal País, **Isla Red Snapper** (☎2640 0490), 400m south of Mal País Surf School and Resort. Look for a sign that says "bikes, sportfishing, snorkeling." Low-season bikes ¢4580 (US$8); high-season ¢5725 (US$10). **Tropical Tours** (☎2640 0384). ATVs for ¢25,763 (US$45) per 6hr., ¢31,488 (US$55) per 10hr., ¢42,938 (US$75) per 24hr.

✈ 🏋 ORIENTATION AND PRACTICAL INFORMATION

The area that most surfers and locals refer to as Mal País is actually three separate beaches stretching along 6km of shoreline on the southwest corner of the Nicoya Peninsula, 11km southwest of Cóbano. Buses from Cóbano stop first at the **crossroads,** which marks the center of the bumpy **dirt road** that runs parallel to the beaches. All accommodations and services are off this main drag. The closest thing you'll find to a town center is at this main crossroads and just to the right into **Santa Teresa,** which stretches 3km north. On the opposite end from the crossroads, **Mal País** stretches 3km south, ending at the tiny marina where fishermen unload their daily catch. Establishments are pretty spread out in Mal País. **Playa Carmen** is 100m west, down a gravel road in front of the bus stop.

Tourist Office: Tropical Tours (☎2640 0384 or 1900). 2 locations, 1 by Frank's Place and the other by Super Ronny. The most comprehensive tourist information center, offering private transportation, internet, and organized tours. Open daily 8am-8pm. Hotels and various surf shops are also glad to help with information and book tours.

Currency Exchange: Banco Nacional (☎2640 0640), in the Playa Carmen Mall, 50m north of the main intersection. **24hr. ATM.** Open M-Sa 1pm-7pm. **Banco Costa Rica** (☎2640 1019), to the left of Frank's Place. **Currency exchange** and **ATM.** Open M-F 9am-4pm.

Laundry: Many hotels and hostels do laundry for their guests, but locals often offer cheaper rates. Heading north toward Santa Teresa from the main intersection, look for the many signs on the right advertising laundry. Most places charge around ¢1000 per kg.

Gas Station: Tano (☎2641 0009), 3km toward Santa Teresa. Open M-Sa 7am-5pm.

Police: ☎911 or 117.

Pharmacies: Amiga Farmacia (☎2640 0539), next to the Banco Nacional. Open M-Sa 8am-8pm. AmEx/MC/V.

Medical Services: Costa Rica Medical Response (☎2640 0976 or 2417), in the Playa Carmen Mall. The only clinic in the area. English spoken. Open 24hr.

Telephones: Several along the main drag, at the crossroads, and at Super Santa Teresa. Super Ronny's (p. 126) sells phone cards.

Internet Access: Tropical Tours, next to Super Ronny's. ¢1500 per hr. Open daily 8am-9pm. **Frank's Place** has similar rates. Open daily 8am-6pm. Other options throughout Santa Teresa. Many restaurants offer free Wi-Fi with purchase of a meal.

Post Office: Closest full-service office is in Cóbano, but there's a **mailbox** at **Pizza Tomate,** 1.5km toward Santa Teresa.

ACCOMMODATIONS AND CAMPING

Santa Teresa is where you'll find most of the budget places, while Mal País has several newer and more upscale options. Many rooms come equipped with full kitchens to accommodate surfers, many of whom stay for weeks at a time. A few camping areas provide sandy grounds for the bare-bones traveler. **Zeneida's Cabinas y Camping ❶** is a good option on the beach. Sites have bathrooms, showers, and water. (☎2640 0118. ¢2000 per person.)

SANTA TERESA

Casa Zen (☎2640 0523; www.zencostarica.com), 1km down the road to Santa Teresa. The highlight of this peaceful palace is its centerpiece: a 2-story, octagonal common area and Thai restaurant with elephants painted on the walls. In high season, Zen offers massages and nightly shows, including live music, trapeze artists, and fire entertainment. Small climbing wall on-site. Th and Su free movie nights. Yoga classes ¢4015 (US$7) per class or ¢14,338 (US$25) for 5 classes. Laundry ¢800 per kg. Internet ¢1200 per hr. Dorms ¢6882 (US$12); private rooms for 2-5 people ¢13,764-27,528 (US$24-48); huge apartment with kitchen, satellite TV, and bath for 2 people ¢31,543 (US$55), can accommodate up to 14 for ¢83,158 (US$145). ❶

Funky Monkey (☎2640 0272; www.funky-monkey-lodge.com). One of the town's most popular surfer hangouts. Two-story, unpainted wooden dorms are spacious and include gardens, showers, and sinks. Bungalows are similar, with floor-length shutters that open up onto porches with hammocks. The lounge area has a pool table and mattresses for lying out on while you watch TV. Close to a good surf break. The on-site restaurant is open daily for breakfast and dinner and serves sushi Tu and Sa. Wi-Fi, a pool, and a communal kitchen also available. High-season dorms ¢9750 (US$17); bungalows ¢45,880 (US$80). Low-season dorms ¢6882 (US$12); bungalows ¢34,410 (US$60). Each additional person ¢5735 (US$10). Apartments for 4 with ocean view ¢57,350 (US$100), with A/C ¢68,820 (US$120). V. ❶

Tranquilo Backpackers (☎2640 0614; www.tranquilobackpackers.com), 400m down the road from Frank's Place in Santa Teresa. The rooms aren't fancy, but live music during high season, a communal kitchen, cable TV, free internet, a pool table, and plenty of hammocks draw a social bunch of backpackers. The young and helpful staff offers complimentary coffee and tea and flips free pancakes every morning. ¢2000 room key and linens deposit. Security guard 6:30am-6:30pm. Dorms ¢6309 (US$11), with bath ¢7456 (US$13); doubles ¢17,205/20,073 (US$30/35). ❶

Don Jon's Hotel (☎2640 0700), past Pizzeria Tomate on the road to Santa Teresa. Tight-fisted but simply can't live without A/C? You're in luck. This hotel boasts brand new, spacious dorms with log bunk beds, high ceilings, and, yes, A/C. Common room shows surf movies all day, and a restaurant serving breakfast and lunch is located on-site. Communal kitchen. High-season dorms ¢8603 (US$15), low-season dorms ¢6882 (US$12); triples and quads ¢25,808/22,940 (US$45/40). Two-bedroom apartment with kitchen, bathroom, and DVD payer ¢34,410/43,013 (US$60/ US$75). Cash only. ❶

MAL PAÍS

▨ **Hotel the Place** (☎2640 0001; www.theplacemalpais.com). Elegance and style don't have to come at prohibitive prices. The modern, outdoor lounge next to the swimming pool has low tables, chairs, and pillowed seats, all accented with African and Costa Rican masks and patterns. The private bungalows all have their own themes: from "Mediterranean Breeze" and "Out of Africa" to "El Nido de Amor" (The Love Nest). The chic bar serves just about any drink you could want. Rooms come with A/C, private baths, and Wi-Fi. Satellite TV in common area. Doubles ¢40,145 (US$70); quads ¢45,880 (US$80); bungalows for 4 ¢57,350 (US$100); 2-bedroom house ¢114,700 (US$200). Discounts in low season and for stays of 6 nights or more. MC/V. ❹

▨ **Mal País Surf School and Resort** (☎2640 0061; www.malpaissurfcamp.com), 500m down the road to Mal País. Prides itself on a relaxed surfer atmosphere. Has rooms for all budgets. Its 10 acres of land feature a bar, restaurant, 17m pool, gym, and pool and ping-pong tables. With a flat-screen TV showing surfing videos and a projection screen for movies at night, there's always something to watch. Surf lessons (¢22,940/US$40), board rental, tours, and laundry also available. Check-out noon. Surfer package with 3 meals, board rental, and basic accommodations ¢34,410 (US$60). High-season open-air dorms ¢8603 (US$15); cabins for 2 ¢20,073 (US$35); villas for 4 ¢48,748 (US$85); suite with kitchen and living room ¢86,025 (US$150). Low-season dorms ¢5735 (US$10); cabins for 2 ¢14,338 ($25); villas for 4 ¢37,278 ($65); suite with kitchen and living room ¢57,350 ($100). AmEx/D/MC/V. ❶

Pachamama (☎2640 0195; www.pacha-malpais.com), 1km from Frank's Place, toward Mal País. Lemon, mango, and papaya trees surround the buildings, while monkeys move in the treetops. A 30m trek up to the hotel's lookout point offers the most breathtaking sunset view in the area. The friendly Austrian owner, Franz, offers fishing trips, kitesurfing, and board rentals. Three bungalows sleep 2-5 and have private hot water baths, kitchens, and porches with hammocks. Bigger groups will love the 2-story house, which sleeps 5 and includes a kitchen, bath, BBQ pit, outdoor dining area, loft, and porch. Free Wi-Fi. Adjoining bungalows ¢34,410 (US$60); stand-alone bungalows ¢45,880 (US$80); house ¢80,290 (US$140). 3-floor tipi ¢5735 (US$10) per person. Cash only. ❹

▣ FOOD

The long road running through Mal País and Santa Teresa is sprinkled with cafes, restaurants, and *sodas*. Many keep unpredictable hours despite their "official" schedules. Additionally, some restaurants close entirely in the low season. Those looking to cook at home can go to **Super Ronny's,** about 750m down the road to Santa Teresa. (☎2640 0297. Open daily 7am-9pm.) Farther into Santa Teresa is **Treble Maya Super.** (☎2640 0645. Open daily 7am-9pm.) **Super Costa** is across the street from Casa Zen. (☎2640 0530. Open daily 7am-9pm.) An **organic produce market** is held every Saturday afternoon near the main beach entrance of Playa Carmen.

SANTA TERESA

Zula, 700m down from Frank's Place toward Santa Teresa. This Israeli restaurant comes highly recommended. Hummus served with falafel (¢3500) or chicken on homemade pita bread (¢3500) are fantastic. Vegetarians will drool over the delicious avocado pita (¢3000). Larger dishes come with salad and fries. If you're feeling adventurous, try the *shakshuka*, a traditional meal with eggs poached in tomato sauce (¢3600). Free Wi-Fi. Glass of house wine ¢2000. Shisha ¢2500 per tablet. Open M-F and Su 10am-4pm and 6:30-10pm. ❷

Umi Sushi (☎2640 0968), in the Playa Carmen Mall, at the intersection of the road to Cóbano. The cool Japanese decor and extensive sushi menu will make you forget you're in Costa Rica. Eat indoors or under an umbrella in the pebble-filled courtyard. Sushi (¢1750-2780) and sashimi (¢2650-5150) are made with both local and imported fish. Start with edamame (¢1900) or miso soup (¢1155), and sip on an imported Sapporo (¢2250). Open daily 11:30am-10:30pm. MC/V. ❷

Soda La Amistad (☎2640 0452), slightly past Casa Zen. This small soda comes highly recommended by surfers. Owner Stanley serves yummy *comida típica*. *Casados* ¢2000-2200. Rice with seafood ¢3000. Open daily 8am-10pm. ❶

Burger Rancho (☎2640 0583), 200m south from Funky Monkey, in front of the *futból* pitch. "Free Love" is listed on the menu, but chicken sandwich (¢2900) and hummus and pita (¢2600) are better bets. Daily specials listed on the black board. Belgian meatballs ¢4500. Free Wi-Fi for customers. Open daily 9am-11pm. ❷

MAL PAÍS

▣ **Mary's** (☎2640 0153), 3km down the road to Mal País. Hand-made lanterns made of pressed flowers hang over private booths. The wood oven bakes delicious red snapper; the seared yellowfin tuna is scrumptious as well. All of the fish are caught by fishermen in Mal País. Pizzas (¢5000-6500) are all made with their special tomato sauce. Entrees ¢4500-6500. Open M-Tu and Th-Su 5:30-10pm. ❷

▣ **Soda Piedra Mar** (☎2640 0069), 2km down the road to Mal País and then 200m down a dirt path toward the beach. Set back from the main road and nestled between the rocks and waves that crowd the beach, this quiet *soda* remains hidden from most travelers. The standard *típico* entrees are as scrumptious as they are affordable. Sit out on the patio and enjoy spectacular ocean views and picture-perfect sunsets. Ask about fishing trips and kite-fishing lessons. *Casados* ¢1800-2000. Chicken fajitas ¢3000. Breakfast pancakes with honey ¢1800. Fruit drinks ¢900-1000. Open M-Sa 8am-8pm. ❶

Ritmo Tropical (☎2640 0174), 700m down to the road to Mal País. Come here for good Italian food. Sit under the palm-leaf umbrellas and listen to the ocean in the distance. Pizza ¢3600-5200. Four-cheese pasta ¢4000. Open daily 8am-11:45am and 5-10:30pm. ❷

THE LOCAL STORY

TOP TEN WORDS YOU'LL HEAR AROUND THE SURFER SCENE

It is difficult to avoid the surfer scene on the Pacific coast. Surf shops are everywhere, and you'll probably look out of place without a board in hand. While you'll never fit in by simply throwing out some sweet lingo (you need to crush some real waves before earning any real respect), we can at least help you to understand what's going on. The next time you're chilling on the beach with some sweet bros, de-code their language by keeping the following glossary in mind:

1. A-Frame: large wave with double shoulders that can be surfed by two people.

2. Dropping in: standing up and taking off down a wave.

3. Filthy: sick; awesome.

4. Grom or Grommet: a young surfer, probably not looking very good.

5. Gnarly: intimidating, scary. Often shortened to gnar; occasionally lengthned to gnar gnar.

6. Hollow: a curling wave with a pocket to ride inside.

7. Overhead: a wave that's higher than the height of the surfer.

8. Point break: peeling waves breaking perfectly around a point.

9.   Shredding/Ripping/Shralping : tearing it up.

10. Smashed: wiped-out; laid out; f***** up.

NIGHTLIFE

In general, the surfer lifestyle makes for subdued nights in Mal País. That said, three main bars still get crowded on some nights.

La Lora (☎2640 0132), 3km up the road to Santa Teresa. The place to be on Th nights for reggae. Latin dance music separates the foreigners from the *ticos* on Sa. Cover ¢2000-3000 for live music events. Open daily in high season noon-2:30am, in low season 6pm-2:30am.

D&N Club (☎2640 0353), right off the beach, just south of the town center. Formerly Bar Tabu, D&N hosts full-moon parties with fire dancers, trapeze artists, and trippy techno music during the high season. M night reggae. W Latin night. Sa electronica. The club also holds BBQs on the beach and is planning to set up night lighting for surfers. Open daily 4:30pm-2am.

Good Vibrations (☎2640 0007), just south of the Playa Carmen Mall at the main intersection. Formerly Howling Monkey Sports Bar and Grill. Not much of a party scene unless the reggae (or Beach Boys) is blasting, but has a flatscreen TV permanently tuned to surfing or big sports games. Tasty bar food ¢3000-4800. F 10pm jam sessions. Beer ¢1000. Happy hour 5-7pm, beer ¢800. Open daily 11am-2am.

BEACHES AND SURFING

The Mal País area is known as a **world-class surf spot** with consistent waves and a faithful crowd. Its location between the Central Pacific coast and Guanacaste creates big southern swells in the rainy season and gnarly offshore breaks in the dry season. The currents are strong here, so swimming can be dangerous. There are several surf spots along the coast with slightly different conditions. South of the crossroads, **Playa Mal País** is inconsistent and better for tide pool exploration. Three kilometers south of the crossroads, **Punta Barrigona** at Bar Mar Azul develops great waves around the point when the swell is big. One kilometer farther south is **Playa de Los Suecos** (or Sunset Reef). The break here is shallow, inconsistent, and for high caliber surfers only. **Playa El Carmen,** directly ahead of the crossroad, has a long right wall. The best spot on **Playa Santa Teresa** is 3km north of the crossroad behind Cabinas Santa Teresa. The A-frame break here is more powerful and consistent than El Carmen; it also holds a better wave at low tide. **Playa Hermosa,** the next beach north of Santa Teresa, has almost no crowds and fast peaks rise along the beach. This beach is becoming increasingly popular for kite-surfing. The beach farthest north in the area is **Playa Manzanillo,** an idyllic spot 8km from the crossroads. It has an offshore reef and less hairy waves than its neighboring beaches. It's only accessible by 4WD or a 1hr. bike ride on rough roads and through shallow rivers. Still, it's worth the daytrip just to see the unspoiled scenery.

Several surf shops in Mal País and Santa Teresa rent boards and provide instruction. **Kina Surf,** 2.2km down the road to Santa Teresa, next to Pizzeria Tomate, is one the best-run surf shops, with plenty of boards and gear to pick from and a knowledgeable, friendly staff. It also sells pop art made from items found on the beach. (☎2640 0627; wwww.kinasurfcostarica.com. Surfboard rental ¢5735/US$10 per day; 2-3hr. surf lessons plus day board rental ¢20,073/US$35. Open M-Sa 9am-5pm, Su 10am-4pm.) **Alex's Surf Shop,** 200m toward Santa Teresa from Frank's Place, rents boards (¢5735/US$10 per day) and offers lessons (private ¢28,675/US$50, group ¢20,073/US$35), which include board rental. (☎2640 0364. Open daily 8am-6:30pm. MC/V.)

OUTDOOR ACTIVITIES AND GUIDED TOURS

Although the hollow beach break is what most people come to town for, the Mal País area offers an array of outdoor activities for non-surfers; even die-hard wave-riders might find themselves diverted by the plethora of beach activities. **Fishing** is the second-most popular activity around here. The small marina at the end of the road to Mal País is always bustling with fishermen and tourists counting their catches. The adventurous and bus-weary can walk 2.5km along the road to Mal País until they reach the fork in the road, then turn left and continue 9km more to the **Reserva Natural Absoluta Cabo Blanco.** Otherwise, rent a snorkel and explore the **tide pools** just behind Sunset Reef Hotel. To get there, walk 2.5km down the road to Mal País, turn right at the fork, and continue another 500m until you see the hotel at the end of the road. Those with a bit more cash can take one of the package tours or organized trips offered around town. Check out a wide range of options at **Tropical Tours.** They offer **canopy tours** (¢20,073/US$35), **snorkeling** at Isla Tortuga from Montezuma with BBQ and drinks (¢25,808/US$45), and daytrips to Monteverde and Arenal (☎2640 1900; www.tropicaltoursmalpais.com). Located on the beach next to D&N Club, **Adrenaline Surf and Kite School** offers kite-surfing lessons to beginners and advances surfers alike. (☎8324 8671. 2hr. beginner lesson ¢57,350 (US$100); 4hr. ¢103,230 (US$180). You can also talk to Franz, the owner of **Pachamama,** about kite-surfing tours up to Nicaragua; he also knows about some inexpensive **sportfishing** (☎2640 0195; www.pacha-malpais.com).

CENTRAL PACIFIC COAST

The Central Pacific shore is Costa Rica's poster child: snapshots of its sunsets grace the covers of travel brochures and postcards, man-sized marlin lure sportfishermen from all over the world, and rugged rainforests sprawl just steps from the region's soft, sandy beaches. From vacationing *ticos* and foreign backpackers to resort-hopping honeymooners, a diverse group of travelers flocks to costal towns where they can take advantage of a well-developed tourist infrastructure. Popularity brings inevitable drawbacks, and major beach towns like Jacó, Quepos, and Manuel Antonio are invariably more crowded and more expensive than Costa Rica's more remote Caribbean side. Diehard peace-seekers, however, need only move on to Playa Esterillos Oeste or Uvita for magnificent, unspoiled scenery and long stretches of deserted beach.

JACÓ

Swimmers might be intimidated by the waves that beat against Jacó's cinnamon-colored sands, but surfers from around the world flock here to enjoy the consistent conditions and energetic atmosphere. Beginners will find that this is a great spot to pick up surfing skills, as the waves are not as enormous as other Pacific beaches, and surfing lessons are almost as common as the *casado*. Even during the low season, the town bustles with activity as surfers hit the water and tourists enjoy the numerous shops on Jacó's main drag. On the weekends, *ticos* flock to Jacó for the parties and waves. Of course, all this popularity comes with a price: restaurants charge a little more, budget accommodations aren't quite as cheap, the streets are littered with tour agencies, the beaches are not as pristine as they once were, and drugs and prostitution grow more common with each passing year. The party scene is fast-paced and runs from dusk until dawn every night. To avoid trouble, always walk with friends or take a taxi at night. Travelers looking to relax can find more peace on the black sands of Playa Hermosa, a getaway just a few kilometers south.

▐ TRANSPORTATION

Buses: Buses to **San José** (Transportes Jacó S.A., ☎2290 2922; 3hr.; 5, 7, 9, 11am, 1, 3, 5pm; ¢1510) arrive and depart from Plaza Jacó, opposite the Best Western, 1km north of the town center on Ave. Pastor Diaz. Buy tickets early from the office at the southeast corner of the plaza. Other buses stop at various locations along the main road so ask around for the nearest stop; a good place to catch them is from the benches near the Más X Menos. Buses to **Orotina** (1½hr.; 4:30, 5:30, 7, 9am, noon, 2, 4pm; ¢1000) and **Puntarenas** (3hr.; 6, 9am, noon, 2, 4:30, 5, 7pm; ¢1350) stop on the east side of the street, and buses to **Quepos** (1hr.; 6:30, 9:30am, 12:30, 2, 4, 6pm; ¢800) stop on the west side.

Taxis: (☎2643 1919, 2643 2121, or 2643 2020) line up in front of Más X Menos (Playa Herradura ¢3500; Playa Hermosa ¢3000). Except for those coming from San José and Puntarenas, buses drop off passengers along the main road. Otherwise, buses passing

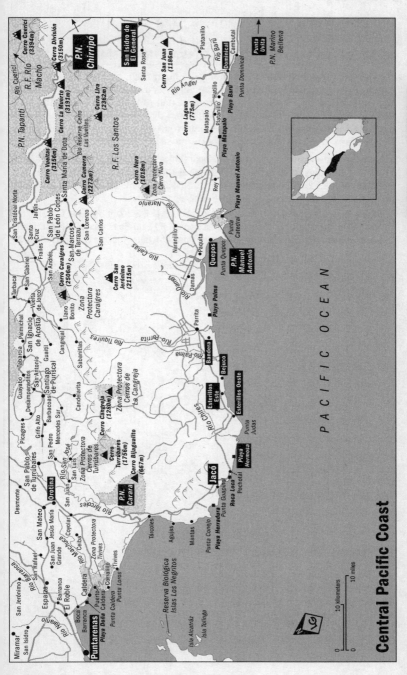

Central Pacific Coast

near Jacó along the Costanera Sur Hwy. stop at the south end of town. It is a 1km walk or a ¢600 taxi ride to Jacó center.

ORIENTATION AND PRACTICAL INFORMATION

Jacó center stretches about 1km along the main road, which runs northwest to southwest, parallel to the beach. For simplicity's sake, we describe the road here as north-south, with the northernmost end of town marked by the Best Western and bus station and the far south end by the post office. Several side roads and paths branch west off the main road and lead to the beach. Playa Herradura is 7km north of Jacó; Playa Hermosa is about 5km south.

Tourist Information: Jacó has no official tourist office, but many tour operators and shop owners are attentive and speak English. Maaike, the attendant at **Pacific Travel and Tours** (☎2643 2520; open M-F 9am-6pm, Sa 10am-1pm), arranges tours and transportation, and provides maps and other general information.

Banks: Banco Nacional, in the center of town. Open M-F 8:30am-3:45pm. **BAC,** ion the top floor of the Il Galeone shopping center. Open M-F 11am-6pm. **Banco Popular,** 100m north of Banco Nacional next to Il Galeone. Open M-F 8am-4pm, Sa 8:30-11:30am. All

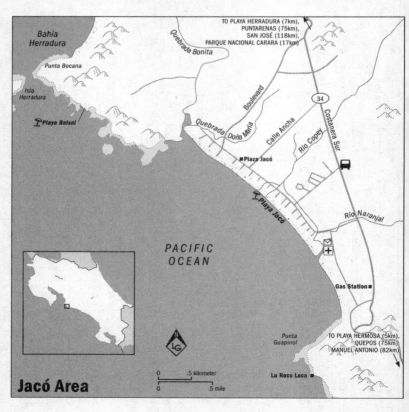

Jacó Area

TO PLAYA HERRADURA (7km),
PUNTARENAS (75km),
SAN JOSÉ (118km),
PARQUE NACIONAL CARARA (17km)

Bahía
Herradura

Punta Bocana

Isla
Herradura

Playa Balsal

Quebrada Bonita

Boulevard

Quebrada Doña María

Calle Ancha

Río Copey

Costanera Sur

34

Plaza Jacó

Playa Jacó

Río Naranjal

PACIFIC
OCEAN

Gas Station

Punta
Guapinol

TO PLAYA HERMOSA (5km),
QUEPOS (75km),
MANUEL ANTONIO (82km)

La Roca Loca

0   .5 kilometer
0   5 mile

have **24hr. ATMs.** A **Western Union** office is located next door to Mexican Joe's. Open M-Sa 9am-1pm and 2-6pm.

Car Rental:

Budget Car Rental (☎2643 2665; www.budget.co.cr), in the Pacific Shopping Center, 50m north of the Jungle Bar. 21+. Drivers 18-20 pay ¢11,600 (US$20) extra per day. ¢435,000 (US$750) deposit. Cars in high season from ¢578,600 (US$57) per day, ¢208,800 (US$360) per week; in low season from ¢19,100/134,560 (US$33/232). Open daily 8am-5:30pm. AmEx/D/MC/V.

Economy Rent a Car (☎2643 1719), on the north side of town across from W.O.W. Surf. 18+ for Costa Rican residents, 21+ for non-residents. ¢1,160,000 (US$2000) deposit. Open daily 8am-6pm.

Laundry: Lava Max (☎2643 1617), just north of Mexican Joe's. Self-service wash and dry ¢4000 per 5kg; full-service ¢5000 per 5kg. Pick-up and delivery service also available. Open daily 8am-5pm. AmEx/MC/V. **Aqua Matic Lavandería** (☎2643 2083), 50m south of Banco Nacional. Self-service wash and dry ¢3000 per 5kg; full-service ¢3400 per 5kg. Open M-Sa 7:30am-5pm. AmEx/MC/V.

Parking: in El Paso Parqueo on C. Bohio across from Hotel Poseidon. ¢600 per hr., ¢400 per hr. for 24hr.

Emergency: ☎911.

Police:(☎2643 3011 or 2643 1881), in front of the Plaza de Futbol. Take C. Bohio down to the beach and walk 50m north. Open 24hr. An office for the transit police is located next to Clínica de Jacó.

Red Cross: (☎2643 3090), 50m south of Más X Menos. Open 24hr.

Pharmacy: Farmacia Fischel (☎2643 2089; www.fischel.co.cr), on the ground floor of Il Galeone. Has a knowledgeable staff. Remedies for jellyfish stings and board burn. Open daily 9am-9pm. AmEx/MC/V.

Medical Services: Clínica de Jacó (☎2264 3176 or 2643 3667), a 5min. walk south of town along the main road, just past the post office. English spoken. Open daily for consultations 7am-4pm. Open 24hr. for emergencies.

Telephones: Most internet cafes offer international calls and Skype access. **Public telephones** are located near the beach at the end of C. Bohio and all over town.

Internet: Mexican Joe's Internet Café, next to Tabacon in the center of town. 2nd location on the north end of town near W.O.W. Surf. Internet ¢250 per 15min., ¢700 per hr. Wi-Fi ¢550. International calls ¢100 per min. Private rooms available for Skype. Open daily 7am-11pm. **Cafe Internet @** (☎2643 2089 or 2643 1518), just north of Banco Nacional. Internet ¢500 per 15min., ¢1000 per hr. International calls ¢80 per min.

Post Office: On the south side of town, near the clinic. Follow the main road south as it curves left and make a right in front of the *municipalídad;* turn right on the 2nd side-street. Open M-F 8am-4:30pm, Sa 8am-noon. **Postal Code:** 4023.

ACCOMMODATIONS

Jacó's main drag and its surrounding side streets are lined with small *cabinas* and hotels, the majority of which have budget or mid-range rooms located less than 200m from the beach. A few more luxurious places cluster around the northern and southern ends of town. Rooms fill quickly on weekends and during the high season; it's not a bad idea to reserve a few days in advance. In the low season, bargain down the prices for groups and extended stays.

Rutan Surf Cabinas (☎2643 3328), 400m north of the bridge. Turn toward the beach at Mexican Joe's; the cabinas are on the left just past Isaga. Formerly known as Chuck's Cabinas (and still known by that name to locals). Myriad surf-slang bumper stickers testify to the hundreds of surfers who have crashed here. There's always a handful relaxing in the courtyard and giving free advice to beginners. Rents beginner epoxy boards from

W.O.W. Surf across the street for ¢1740 (US$3) per hr., ¢8700 (US$15) per day. Free Wi-Fi. Dorms ¢5800 (US$10) per person; doubles ¢130,500 (US$15). ❶

Hostel Las Camas (☎8377 3459), 50m north of the bridge across from Plaza Coral. This 4-story complex with brightly painted walls and funky accents is a haven for backpackers. Well-equipped common area and rooftop patio with spectacular views of the mountains to the east and the ocean to the west. Each room has A/C, cable TV, and lockers. Wi-Fi. Check-out 11am. Dorms ¢8120 (US$14); doubles ¢17,400 (US$30). ❶

Cabinas Los Ranchos (☎2643 3070; fax 2643 1810), 100m down the first sidestreet south of the bridge. A beautiful complex just 50m from the beach with private patios, lazy-day hammocks, and a pool surrounded by towering palms. Simple, spacious rooms with comfy beds, overhead fans, and private hot-water baths. All rooms are quads. Wi-Fi available. Check-in 8am-10pm. Check-out noon. Rooms ¢26,100 (US$45); with kitchen ¢31,900 (US$55). Discounts for long stays and in the low season. AmEx/D/MC/V. ❷

Cabinas Sol Marena (☎2643 1124), next door to Rutan. High-ceilinged rooms with cable TVs, fridges, and private baths are kept cool by overhead fans or A/C. Internet available. Singles ¢10,000 with fan, with A/C and hot-water ¢20,000; doubles ¢15,000/18,000; triples ¢18,000/30,000. ❷

🍴 FOOD

A wide range of food options, from traditional *tico* fare to sushi and Argentinean steaks, are available in Jacó. This variety comes with a price: even the *sodas* in Jacó are more expensive than normal. Watch out for nightly tourist-trap promotions. For those looking to cook for themselves, the **Más X Menos** (☎2643 2528) supermarket, just south of Banco Nacional, is well stocked. (Open daily 8am-10pm. AmEx/MC/V.). A **Megasuper** (☎2643 2764) is also located in Plaza Coral just north of Budget Car Rental. Open daily 8am-10pm.

Soda Jacó Rústico (☎2643 1721), 50m down the south side of Pancho Villa's. Inexpensive, but tasty, *típico*. Filling buffet-style lunch and dinner with rice, beans, your choice of meat, salad, and drink ¢2000. Open daily 7am-7pm. ❶

Bar and Restaurant Isaga (☎2643 1467 or 2643 1412), on the north end of town, across from Rutan's Hostel. *Gallo pinto* ¢1500. *Ceviche* ¢2700. *Casados* ¢1600-2300. Beer ¢700. Free Wi-Fi. Open daily 10am-2am. ❶

Tsunami Sushi (☎2643 3678), upstairs in the Il Galeone complex, 100m north of Banco Nacional. Classic Japanese dishes like California rolls (¢3045), dragon rolls (¢6400), and shrimp and vegetable tempura (¢4900). Tu 2-for-1 tuna roll special. Watch your rolls being made in the open sushi-making area. Open daily 5-11pm. MC/V. ❷

Rioasis (☎2643 3354 or 2643 0119), 25m down C. Cocal, on the side street just north of Banco Nacional. Creatively topped wood-oven pizzas. Munchies pizza with ham, onions, sweet pepper, salami, and oregano ¢5209. Mexican burrito ¢3000. Tortellini alfredo ¢5890. Free delivery in Jacó for any order over ¢5000. Open daily 11:30am-10pm. ❷

Caliche's Wishbone Restaurant and Bar (☎2643 3406). Signed surf boards and a palm tree motif constitute the decor at this popular eatery. Stuffed potatoes with cheese and choice of chicken or broccoli ¢3300. Wishbone pizza (BBQ chicken, onion, cilantro, mozzarella; ¢6100). Guacamole and chips ¢3800. Open M-Tu and Th-Su noon-10pm. ❷

Jugos Naturales Pura Vida (☎2643 6221), in the Pacific Shopping Mall. This small juice shop concocts thirst-quenching drinks with fresh produce. Drinks ¢1000. Fruit salad topped with condensed milk, cornflakes, and granola ¢1600. Open daily 7am-8pm. ❶

GUIDED TOURS

King Tours (☎2643 2441, toll-free from the US 800 213 7091; www.kingtours.com), 150m north of Banco Nacional. Friendly, knowledgeable staff arranges tours to satisfy all manner of adventure cravings. Tours to Isla Tortuga (¢69,600, US$120), Manuel Antonio (¢51,600, US$89), Poas (¢72,500, US$125), and Volcán Arenal (¢72,500, US$125) include lunch and transportation. Canopy tours ¢49,300 (US$85). Rafting ¢69,600 (US$120). Dolphin-watching ¢40,020 (US$69). Horseback riding ¢43,500 (US$75). Open daily 8am-8pm. AmEx/D/MC/V.

Green Tours (☎2643 1984 or 2643 1021), directly across from Il Galeone. Extensive selection of tours and services. Canopy tours at Vista Los Sueños and crocodile tours ¢31,900 (US$55). Rafting near Quepos ¢58,000 (US$100). Rainforest ATV tours ¢40,600 (US$70). Meals, water, and A/C transportation included. Transportation services to Manuel Antonio ¢16,800 (US$29) per person. Full-day sportfishing tours with meals, drinks, bait, and transportation provided ¢377,000 (US$650). Open daily 8:30am-8pm.

Ricaventura ATV Tours and Motorcycle Rentals (☎2643 5720; www.ricaventura.com), just north of the bridge next to Subway. Arranges comprehensive ATV tours. Tours include waterfall views and swimming time in naturally formed pools. (2hr. tour ¢37,700/US$65; 3hr. ¢49,300/US$85; 4hr. ¢63,800/US$110). Scooters ¢17,400/US$30 per day. Motorcycles ¢34,800/US$60 per day. Open daily 8am-6:30pm.

An Xtreme Rider (☎2643 3130 or 8867 5089; www.axroad.com), just north of the Red Cross across from Pancho Villa's. Runs ATV tours and rents motorbikes, scooters, bicycles, and surfboards. Bicycles ¢5800 (US$10) per day, ¢17,400 (US$30) per week. Scooters ¢23,200 (US$40) per day. Motorbikes ¢40,600 (US$70) per day. Credit card required to rent. Open daily 8am-7pm.

NIGHTLIFE

Jacó has no shortage of clubs and bars: nightlife here is serious business. Be aware that Jacó's drug problems are on the rise and prostitutes linger in many bars at night.

Le Loft (☎2643 5846), across from Lappa Verde St. Up-and-coming bar with Asian-inspired decor. Plays all types of music, but if you want to salsa, head elsewhere. Open bar W midnight-2:30am. Cover for men only ¢3000. Open 9:30pm-2:30am.

Jungle Bar and Grill (☎8643 3911), 50m north of Payless Car Rental, above Subway. Live DJ plays mostly Latin and Reggaeton to accompany revelers on the enormous dance floor. Pool and beer pong tables. Tu and Sa Ladies nights 10pm-midnight (free tequila, vodka, and rum). W Latin night. Open 6pm-2:30am.

Tabacon (☎2643 3097), in the center of town opposite C. Bohio. Classy, relaxed atmosphere is a welcome break from the high-party feel of its peers. But that doesn't mean that you won't find a party here: live rock and reggae bands on weekends draw a dance crowd. Tasty drinks include the Jamaica banana (¢2500) and the mango and peach margarita (¢2200). Appetizers ¢2700-5800. M Ladies night 10pm-midnight. Open daily noon-midnight.

Pancho Villa's (☎2643 3571), toward the southern end of town across from the Red Cross. After the other bars close, a largely male crowd stumbles to this all-night joint for pricey grub and gambling on the in-house slot machines. Mariachis regularly stop by. Free Wi-Fi. Appetizers ¢2000-6500. *Casados* ¢2000. Lobster ¢16,500. Open 24hr. Loosely affiliated with **Divas Night Club** (☎2643 1978), an adult entertainment lounge located upstairs. Cover ¢4000; includes 2 beers. Open daily 8pm-3am.

Bar Oz (☎2643 2162), down a side-street across from Más X Menos. Large, airy bar. Pool tables, darts, and TVs playing American sports. Open daily 10am-2:30am.

◤ BEACHES AND SURFING

Long renowned as some of Costa Rica's best surfing, the waters around Jacó have some of the country's most consistently diverse waves. Jacó's main beach has gentler swells that mellow southward—ideal conditions for beginners and intermediates. Experts craving more challenging surf head to the mouth of the river, north past Plaza Jacó, or to La Roca Loca, a sizable right break about 1.5km south of Jacó that crashes over a large submerged rock on Punta Guapinol (read: no beginners). **La Roca Loca** is a 30-45min. walk from the center of Jacó Beach—just head south and climb out over the rocks. Or, make the 5-10min. drive and tiptoe down a gnarly cliff. Just 5km away, Playa Hermosa (p. 115) has a challenging beach break also popular with advanced surfers. Farther south of Jacó are **Esterillos Oeste, Esterillos Centro, Esterillos Este, Playas Bandera,** and **Bejuco.** North of Jacó is **Boca Barranca.** Most of these beaches have isolated surf spots.

Jacó is a popular daytrip for surfers from all over the country, and most surf tourists pay it a visit. The main road is loaded with surf shops that buy, rent, sell, trade, and repair boards. Most offer similar services and prices, but some unusual deals exist.

W.O.W. Surf (☎2643 3844 or 2643 1108; www.wowsurf.net), on the northernmost part of the main road, 50m past Beatle Bar. The largest selection of surfboards, boogie boards, and surf gear in town. Beginner epoxy boards ¢8700 (US$15) per 24hr., fiberglass boards ¢11,600 (US$20) per 24hr. ¢464,000 (US$800) credit card deposit. Surf lessons (¢37,700/US$65 for a 3hr. group lesson, ¢69,600/US$120 for a private lesson). Open M-Sa 8am-8pm, Su 8am-6pm. AmEx/MC/V.

El Pana (☎2643 2125), directly across from Tabacon. Great deals on board rentals (¢5800, US$10 per day). One of the most affordable places to buy a used board in good condition (from ¢58,000/US$100). Pana himself is almost always around to help you make the best selection. Open daily 7am-9pm.

El Roka Loka (☎2643 1806), 50m south from Pana. Good selection of used boards (from ¢87,000/US$150). Board rentals ¢8700/US$15 per 24hr.

Jacó Surf School (☎8829 4697 or 2643 1905 after 7:30pm; www.jacosurflessons.com). Operates out of a small tent on the beach at the end of Bohio Rd. Run by Gustavo Castillo, a pro who spent a decade with the Costa Rican national team, this school offers the best, most comprehensive surf lessons in town. If you don't stand up, you don't pay. All instructors are certified lifeguards and speak English and Spanish. 3hr. group lessons (¢29,000, US$50 per person) include water, fruit, and full-day board use. Private lessons ¢43,500 (US$75).

PARQUE NACIONAL CARARA

Encompassing over 5200 hectares, Parque Nacional Carara features the only remaining transitional rainforest in Costa Rica, where the drier rainforest of the North Pacific meets the humid rainforest of the South Pacific. The highly varied flora of these two distinct ecosystems provides homes for numerous rare and endangered species, including the giant anteater, the white-faced monkey, the scarlet macaw, and over 50 American crocodiles that lounge on the banks of the Río Tarcoles and the Meándrica Lagoon. Archaeological sites in the surrounding area have dug up artifacts of ceramic, rock, and jade. The park's well-maintained trail system also features **Acceso Universal,** the first and only wheelchair-accessible trail in any national park in Central America.

AT A GLANCE

AREA: 5242 hectares. Approx. 10% trail-accessible.

CLIMATE: Mean annual temperature 27˚C. Annual rainfall 2.8m. Highlights: Fully paved, wheelchair-accessible trail; several rare and endangered species; the only remaining transition forest in Costa Rica; crocodiles.

FEATURES: Río Tárcoles, Meándrica Lagoon.

GATEWAYS: Jacó (p. 130), Orotina

CAMPING: Not allowed in the park.

FEES: Admission ¢5735 (US$10), children 6-12 ¢574 (US$1), children under 3 free; Costa Rican nationals ¢1147 (US$2).

TRANSPORTATION

Buses traveling along the **Costanera Highway** pass by the reserve regularly. From **Jacó** or **Playa Hermosa**, take any Puntarenas-, Orotina-, or San José-bound bus (see **Transportation** sections), and ask the driver to let you off at the park entrance. In case your driver is forgetful, watch for the sign and large white ranger station. From **Puntarenas** or **Orotina,** take any Jacó- or Quepos-bound bus. **To return,** you'll have to rely on the buses that pass along the highway from San José or Puntarenas to Jacó or Quepos. A schedule of buses is posted on the information desk at the entrance to the park. Buses to Jacó and San José typically pass by every hour starting at 7am. Buses to San Jose pass by every 2hr., and to Jacó or Quepos every hour. Because buses pass by on different schedules, you may find yourself waiting anywhere from 10min. to 2hr. for the correct bus. (The park is open daily from Dec. to Apr. 7am-4pm; from May to Nov. 8am-4pm. Last tickets sold at 3pm.)

ORIENTATION

Located 17km northeast of Jacó and 90km west of San José, Parque Nacional Carara was originally created to facilitate scientific studies and investigations. Three of its trails leave from the main entrance and are good for casual hikers, as they are easily traversed, evenly sloped, and well-shaded. The fourth, **Sendero Laguna Meándrica,** is a bit more challenging, especially during the wet season.

WHEN TO GO. Because most of the trails take about 1-2hr. to walk, Carara is best visited as a short daytrip. Get an early start and bring insect repellent, food, and water. Birdwatching is best in the morning (as soon as the park opens). Crocodiles are most likely seen at midday; scarlet macaws and monkeys are usually visible between noon to 2pm on the Laguna Meándrica trail. The **ranger station** has bathrooms, a picnic area, and potable water but no food.

HIKING

Only 10% of Carara is accessible by trail, but these trails are all well-marked and maintained. One trail leaves from the main ranger station and connects with two others, while the fourth, Sendero Laguna Meándrica, leaves from a trailhead off the highway 2km north of the main entrance. Wheelchair-accessible **Acceso Universal,** or **Sendero Cemento,** is a flat, paved 1.2km loop that takes about an hour to hike. It begins at the ranger station, moves through primary rainforest, and connects to **Sendero Quebrada Bonita.** Bonita is 1.5km long and takes about 1hr. to complete. It begins after a small metal bridge and is linked to a third trail, the 1.2km loop of **Sendero Las Aráceas,** by another small bridge. While all trails pass through similar primary forest, you're more likely to see wildlife on the Bonita trail. The less-trodden fourth trail, **Sendero Laguna Meándrica,** begins at the yellow gates 2km along the Costanera from the ranger station, where even more animals are to be found. Meandering alongside the **Río Grande de Tárcoles** for 4km, Laguna Meándrica leads to a lagoon **viewpoint,** which is the best place in the park to spot monkeys, scarlet macaws and crocodiles. This trail, however, offers little shade and is muddy year-round due to the high waters of the lagoon, so the rangers recommend rubber boots (¢1000 for rental at the ranger station). When the lagoon floods in September the trail becomes impassable. All visitors to the park must **register** and buy their **tickets** at the **MINAE office** (☎8383 9953) before hiking. Freelance guides can be hired to spot creatures and help keep your feet dry; they are recommended for visitors taking the Laguna Meándrica path. (¢11,470/US$20 per person. Guides available in English, French, German and Spanish. Antonio Vindas, ☎2645 1064, is recommended by the park, and during the dry season he can guide overnight backpacking trips into the park for ¢57,350/US$100, up to 15 people.) Scouts will guard cars for tips (recommended contribution ¢2868/US$5). There is also a secure parking lot (guarded M-Sa 8am-2pm) lot near the station if you don't mind walking to the farther trails. Don't leave valuables in the car. Carrying them is no safer, as **muggings** have been known to occur.

SIGHTS

The **Río Tárcoles Bridge** is about 3km north of Parque Nacional Carara's ranger station on the highway to Puntarenas and San José. It is known more commonly as the **Puente de los Cocodrilos** (Crocodile Bridge) because of the scores of crocodiles that reside in the muddy waters of the river and doze along its banks. The rangers say that the crocodiles prey on farm animals that roam the surrounding pastures. While there have been a few (probably apocryphal) reports of people being eaten alive or having their limbs chewed off, the animals can be safely viewed from the edge of the bridge. If you're lucky, you might see a crocodile lumbering around or floating log-like down the river, but it's more likely you'll see 20-40 crocodiles lounging immobile by the water. Locals sometimes stir up activity by throwing plants or even live chickens into the water (not recommended). The bridge is hardly worth its own visit, but if you're passing by on the highway you might stop for a quick peek. Just look for several people peering off the edge. If you want a closer look, call **Jungle Crocodile Safari** (☎2236 6473 or 2385 6591; www.junglecrocodilesafari.com) in Tarcoles for a 2hr. tour down the Río Tárcoles, complete with a bilingual guide who will perform some daring crocodile tricks. (¢14,338/US$25. Tours at 8:30, 10:30am, 1:30, and 3:30pm.)

SOUTHERN COSTA RICA

With the notable exception of Parque Nacional Chirripó, this relatively isolated area doesn't really cater to tourists. In its small towns, which are either business hubs of fruit producers or gateways into the secluded wilderness of the region, foreigners often receive inquisitive stares, or an emphatic "hellooooo" and laughter from children practicing their English.

SAN ISIDRO

One hundred and thirty-eight kilometers southeast of San José, the city of San Isidro de El General, also known as Pérez Zeledón, is an urban centered circumscribed by rural villages. Though the urban streets are unusually clean and friendly, the attractions of the asphalt terrain pale in comparison to the living greenness of nearby parks. The city makes an ideal springboard for trips into the surrounding national parks and other areas of southern Costa Rica, where you can get away from the bustle of city life and relax amidst natural splendors. Shoe fanatics may find it difficult to leave San Isidro, however; *zapaterías* line every corner, making it likely that you will finally find those blue sneakers with neon green laces you've always known, deep down, that you needed.

▆ TRANSPORTATION

While finding the right **bus** out of San Isidro is complicated by the fact that the five different companies that share the town don't share destinations, all five have well-staffed and well-marked stations, which makes travel a bit easier. From the local bus terminal on the south side of the *mercado*, buses leave to nearby villages including **Quedabras** (15min., 11 per day 6:45am-7:25pm, ¢250) and **San Gerardo** (1hr., 2pm, ¢900). Another bus to San Gerardo leaves from the west side of the *parque* at 5am.

Musoc (☎2771 0414). Buses go to **San José** from the terminal on the Interamericana Hwy. between C. 2 and 4 (3hr., M-F 4:30am and daily every hr. 5am-6:30pm, ¢2190). Bathroom ¢150. Ticket office open daily 4:30am-6pm.

Transportes Blancos (☎2771 2550), on the curve between Av. 2 and Av. 4 on the east side of town. Marked by a Soda Quepos sign. Buses to: **Dominical** (1½hr.; 7, 9am, 4pm; ¢800); **Puerto Jiménez** (6hr.; 6:30am, 3pm; ¢2300); **Quepos** (3½hr.; 7, 11:30am, 3:30pm; ¢1300); **Uvita** (2hr.; 9am, 4pm; ¢950). Ticket office open daily 6:15-11am and 1:30-4pm.

Tracopa (☎2771 0468), on the corner of the Interamericana Hwy. and C. 3. Service to **Golfito** (3½hr.; 10am, ¢3760; 6pm, ¢5800); **San Vito** (3½hr.; 5:30am, 2pm; ¢3995); the Panamanian border at **Paso Canoas** (4hr.; direct at 10am, ¢7000; indirect at 2, 4, 7:30, 9pm, ¢3760). Ticket office open M-Sa 4:30am-7pm, Su 4:30am-3pm.

Gafeso (☎2771 0097), next to Transportes Blancos. Buses to **Buenos Aires** (1½hr.; direct at 5:15, 7:20, 10am, 12:15, 3, 5pm; indirect at 6, 8:30, 11:30am, 1:30, 4, 7:45, 10pm; ¢685).

Taxis: On the north and west sides of the *parque central*, south of Av. 6 between C. Central and C. 1. Next to the MUSOC bus terminal. To San Gerardo ¢10,000.

✦ ▌ ORIENTATION AND PRACTICAL INFORMATION

Unlike most other towns in Costa Rica, San Isidro has well-marked streets with signs on almost every corner. **Avenida Central** and **Calle 0** meet at the northwest corner of the *parque central*. Overlooking the eastern side of the *parque central*,

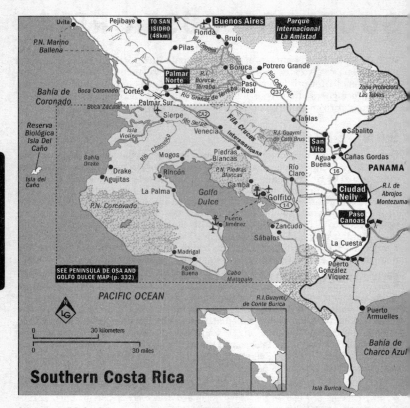

Southern Costa Rica

the spires of the large modern cathedral, visible from most places downtown, serve as useful landmarks. The Interamericana Highway forms the northern boundary of the *parque* and is a good reference for finding other streets.

Tourist Information:

CIPROTUR, Av. 1/3, C. 4 (☎2771 6096 or 2771 2003; www.camaradecomerciopz.com), in the back of the blue Coopealianza building. Provides free maps. Answers questions about San Isidro and offers information about tours and activities in the surrounding area. Internet ₡300 per hr. Open M-F 7:30am-noon and 1-5pm.

Selva Mar, Av. 2/4, C. 1 (☎2771 4582; www.exploringcostarica.com; www.selvamar.com). Information on kayaking, canopy, and snorkeling tours to Bahía Drake, Delfines, Golfo Dulce, Isla del Caño, Parque Nacional Chirripó, Parque Nacional Corcovado, and Tortuguero. Open M-F 7:30am-5:30pm, Sa 8am-noon. AmEx/MC/V.

Oficina Regional de Cultura-Zona Sur (☎2771 5273; dirculturazonasur@gmail.com), inside the *mercado* near the entrance to the bathrooms and buses. Works to support cultural activities within southern Costa Rica. Provides information on artisan groups and other cultural events in the area. Open M-F 8am-4pm.

Banks: All offer currency exchange and have **24hr. ATMs.**

Banco Nacional de Costa Rica (☎2785 1000), on the northeast corner of the *parque* at Av. Central, C. 1. Changes traveler's checks and gives V cash advances. Open M-F 8:30am-3:45pm.

Banco de Costa Rica, Av. 4, C. 0/2 (☎2770 9996). Open M-F 9am-6pm.

BAC San José, Av. 4, C. 0/1(☎2771 3080 or 2295 9797). Open M-F 9am-6pm, Sa 9am-1pm.

Western Union, Av. 2, C. 0/2 (☎2771 8535 or 2771 3534), on the 2nd fl. of the large yellow building. Open M-F 7:30am-4:30pm, Sa 7:30am-noon.

Bookstore: Libreria San Isidro (☎2771 7802; www.libreriasanisidro.com), next to the BAC San José on Av. 4. Office supplies and copying services available on the 1st fl. (black and white ¢12, color ¢290). 2nd fl. has books, magazines, and posters, mostly in Spanish. Open M-F 8am-7pm, Sa 8am-6pm. AmEx/MC/V.

Library: Biblioteca Municipal (☎2771 3816), on the corner of Av. Central and C. 2. Travelers can read in the pleasant, well lit library but cannot check out books. Open M-F 8am-7pm, Sa 8am-noon.

Laundry: Av. Central, C. 4 (☎2771 4042). ¢800 per kg. Open M-Sa 8am-6pm.

Public Toilets: On the north and south sides of the *mercado.* ¢150. Open M-Sa 6am-6pm, Su 6am-4pm. Additional location on the north side of the cathedral. Open M-F 7am-5:30pm.

Police: (☎2771 3608 or 2771 3447), less than 1km from the *parque;* walk 200m to a small bridge over Río San Isidro, then 300m farther on the left, or speak with one of the many officers on duty around town.

Red Cross: Emergency ☎911. Toll-free ☎128. Ambulance ☎2771 0481.

Pharmacy: Farmacia San Isidro (☎2771 1567), on Av. Central, north of the *parque.* Open M-Sa 7am-8:30pm. AmEx/MC/V.

Hospital: Hospital Clínica Labrador (☎2771 7115 or 2772 6464), 5 blocks south of the cathedral on C. 1. Open daily 7am-8pm for appointments and 24hr. for emergencies. Some English-speaking doctors.

Internet Access:

Connect@ Internet Café, Av. 10, C. 0/2 (☎2771 6023), across from the soccer stadium, 400m from the *mercado.* Computers are Skype-capable. Internet ¢350 per hr. Open daily 8:30am-10pm.

Fofo's Internet, Av. 1 & C. 4 (☎2770 1186), 1 block south of Hotel Diamante Real. Internet ¢350 per hr. Wi-Fi ¢200. International calls to the U.S. ¢50 per min. Printing services black and white ¢50, color ¢300. Open M-F 7am-10pm, Sa 7am-7pm, Su noon-8pm.

Post Office: Av. 6/8, C. 1 (☎2771 0346). Offers fax service. Open M-F 8am-5:30pm, Sa 9am-1pm. MC/V. **Postal Code:** 11901.

ACCOMMODATIONS

Most of San Isidro's budget and mid-range accommodations are clustered around the *parque central.* Other, more expensive accommodations line to the perimeter of town.

Hotel Chirripó, Av. 2, C. 0/1 (☎2771 0529), on the south side of the *parque.* Behind a small restaurant of the same name. Large windows light up pleasant, peach-walled and tiled hallways. Bright rooms have fans, cable TVs, and hot-water baths. Wi-Fi available. Singles with shared baths ¢6500, with private baths ¢9500; doubles ¢10,000/16,000; triples ¢20,000; quads ¢27,000. ❶

Hotel El Valle, Av. Central/2, C. 2 (☎2771 0246), 1 block west and 1 block south of the *parque's* northwest corner. Well kept establishment lined with signs commanding *"silencio,"* especially after midnight. A "no visitors, no exceptions" policy. Parking available. Singles with shared baths ¢6000, with private baths and cable TV ¢8000; doubles ¢9000/12,000; triples ¢18,500. ❶

Hotel Astoria (☎2771 0914), on Av. Central facing the north side of the *parque.* 2nd entrance on the Interamericana Hwy. across from the courthouse. Somewhat institutional feel. Small rooms with just as small armoires may lack windows, limiting ventilation to a small space near the ceiling. Singles ¢4000, with private baths ¢6000; doubles ¢13000; triples ¢12,000, with private bath and cable TV ¢18,000. ❶

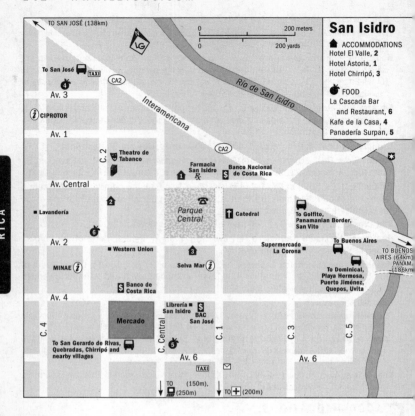

San Isidro

♠ ACCOMMODATIONS
Hotel El Valle, **2**
Hotel Astoria, **1**
Hotel Chirripó, **3**

♦ FOOD
La Cascada Bar
 and Restaurant, **6**
Kafe de la Casa, **4**
Panadería Surpan, **5**

SOUTHERN COSTA RICA

🪧 FOOD

In addition to *sodas* and restaurants, you can stock up on essentials at **Super-mercado La Corona** on Av. 2 between C. 3 and the Interamericana Hwy. (☎2771 5252; open M-Sa 7:30am-9pm, Su 8am-7pm; AmEx/MC/V) or at the even larger **Supermercado Central Coopeagri,** just south of the local bus terminal. (☎2785 0227. Open M-Sa 7pm-9pm, Su 8am-4pm.) Dominated by *sodas*, raw meat shops, and produce vendors, the **Mercado Municipal** smells of fish and fried food all day. (Located between Av. 4/6, C. 0/2. Open M-Sa 5am-6pm, Su 5-11am.)

   Kafe de la Casa, Av. 3 between C. 3 & 4 (☎2771 7000). Homey coffee shop. Extensive menu features everything from cinnamon pancakes (¢1800) and banana chocolate coffee (¢2000) to eggplant stuffed with meat (¢3500) and baked potatoes filled with spinach (¢3500). Leave your mark by writing your thanks on one of the walls. Open M-F 6am-9pm, Sa 6am-7pm, Su 8am-5pm. MC/V. ❷

   La Cascada Bar & Restaurant, Av. 2 and C. 2 (☎2771 6479). This open-air restaurant always hosts hungry customers munching on chicken kebabs (¢4000), Caesar salad (¢4200), or stroganoff tenderloin (¢5500). Mixed drinks and virgin daiquiris ¢2500-3000. Open daily 11am-2am. ❷

Soda Chirripó, Av. 2, C. 1 (☎2771 8287), on the southeast corner of the park. Catering mostly to locals watching sports on its small TV, this restaurant feels more like a diner than a traditional *soda*. Cheese and ham omelettes ¢1800. *Casados* ¢1950-3200. Also has a less expensive fast-food menu (¢1200-1850). Open daily 6:30am-6pm. MC/V. ❶

SIGHTS

COMPLEJO CULTURAL. This cultural center hosts local shows and performances. Dates and times posted on an announcement board just outside the building. *(On Av. 1, C. 2, next to the municipal library. ☎2771 2336 . ¢1500).*

FUNDACIÓN PARA EL DESARROLLO DEL CENTRO BIOLÓGICO LAS QUEBRADASN (FUDEBIOL). This reserve is managed by a group of devoted volunteers. Learn about conservation at Las Quebradas, hike through bird-filled trails to impressive waterfalls, visit the reserve's butterfly garden, or simply enjoy its streams and lagoon. Its isolated location makes this reserve as relaxing as it is educational. Up to 30 people can stay at the center's **mountain lodge** (¢7000 per night). Join the staff every Sunday for a traditional *tico* breakfast (Su 8-11am; ¢3000). Ask about volunteer opportunities. *(In the mountains above the Quebradas River Basin, 7km from downtown San Isidro. Take the bus to Quebradas from the main bus station (every hr., 15min. past the hr., starting at 8:15am) and get off at the last stop. Walk 2.5km up to the dirt road, turning right at the FUDEBIOL sign, and continue until the end of the road. ☎2771 4131 for information and reservations. Open M and W-Th 7am-3pm. US$2 entrance fee.)*

CHIRRIPÓ AND SAN GERARDO DE RIVAS

A popular destination for nature enthusiasts, Parque Nacional Chirripó is home to the tallest peak in Costa Rica and the second tallest peak in Central America, Cerro Chirripó (3820m). A well-marked route to the summit ascends through steep pastures before winding through cloud forest and into alpine-tundra-like *páramo*. The name Chirripó means "land of eternal waters" and is well-suited to the many rivers that originate from sparkling lagoons on its summit and rush down its glacial valleys to both the Pacific and Caribbean. If the weather cooperates (during high season Jan.-Apr., or very early in the morning), you can see both the Atlantic and Pacific Oceans from Cerro Chirripó. The 20km trip up the mountain is an manageable climb for the average traveler in three days, though the especially experienced and motivated can make it in two. Sports extremists and foolhardy masochists from around the world come to challenge the mountain every year for the Chirripó Marathon in February; the record to beat for the 29km to and from Base Crestones stands at just over 3hr. San Gerardo, the gateway to Parque Nacional Chirripó, although unavoidably situated on steep hills, is otherwise geared toward accommodating the sore legs and hungry bellies of visiting hikers. Since the park's opening in 1975, the families of San Gerardo have learned to embrace tourism while still maintaining their rural authenticity. To the weary hiker, the town offers natural hot springs, local trout and coffee, home-grown vegetarian food, and an abundance of hospitality.

TRANSPORTATION

The **bus** from San Isidro (5:30am or 2pm) will drop you off at the edge of town in front of the ranger station (2km from the trailhead), or at the town center in front of the soccer field. Catch the return bus at the ranger station (1½hr.; 7am, 4pm; ¢900) or from the church (5min. before the ranger station bus).

SOUTHERN COSTA RICA

✈ 🔓 ORIENTATION AND PRACTICAL INFORMATION

San Gerardo stretches for 2km along an uphill section of road from the ranger station at the bottom to the park entrance at the top. The town center consists of a large yellow church and a school with a soccer field across from the *pulpería* (small grocery store) **Las Nubes** (☎2742 5045; open daily 6:30am-8pm). Another smaller *pulpería* is at Hotel El Urán. The owner, Hans Arias, and his family can provide a wealth of information about San Gerardo and the national park.

Tourist Information: Extensive tourist and volunteer information can also be found online at www.sangerardocostarica.com.

Public phones: outside the ranger station and in front of Las Nubes. Both establishments also have free restrooms.

Internet Access: Reserva Talamanca (☎2742 5080), 1km uphill from the soccer field. ¢3000 per hr. Open M and W-Su 11am-10pm.

Taxis: ☎2770 1066.

🏠 🍴 ACCOMMODATIONS AND FOOD

After arriving in town, some travelers get dropped off at the ranger station, check in, and then find a nearby hotel. Most others prefer to find a hotel near the trail, stash their gear, and then walk down to check in at the ranger station. Reservations are recommended for those planning to stay at hotels near the trail during the high season (Jan.-Apr.).

🏨 **Casa Mariposa** (☎2742 5037; www.hotelcasamariposa.com), 50m from the trailhead. This unique stone and bamboo structure offers the closest beds to the trailhead. Cozy dorms have great window views of the rainforest and the surrounding mountains. All rooms have access to shared hot-water showers, a communal kitchen, and a relaxing gazebo with hammocks. The owners, John and Jill, are a wonderful source of information on the area. Free tea and coffee complement the priceless hospitality. Provides transportation to and from the ranger station upon request. Laundry ¢2500 per load. Internet ¢350 per hr. Dorms ¢6000 (US$12); singles ¢8000 (US$16); doubles ¢12,500 (US$28). ❶

Hotel El Urán (☎2742 5003 or 2742 5004; www.hoteluran.com), 25m below Casa Mariposa. Picks up visitors from the ranger station for free. The on-site **restaurant** ❶ offers hearty *comida típica* (*casados* ¢2000-2400, sandwiches ¢850-1200, pancake breakfast with fruit ¢1200, coffee ¢350; open 4:30am-8pm), while the attached grocery store sells bread, eggs, milk, spaghetti, beans, and snacks for the trek up. Free pick-up from the ranger station. Free internet for guests; for others, ¢600 per hr. Free parking. Sleeping bag rentals ¢1500 per night. Stoves ¢1500. Dorms ¢6000; singles ¢11,300; doubles ¢16,950; triples ¢23,000. ❶

Cabinas El Descanso (☎2742 5061). Small, pastel rooms with cramped, shared hot-water baths. The owner, Francisco, has run the race up the mountain 21 times (check out his impressive trophy cabinet). On-site **restaurant** ❶ (open daily 5am-9pm) serves coffee (¢500), vegetarian dishes made with homegrown produce (spaghetti with vegetables ¢2000), and fresh *batidos* (milkshakes ¢800). Free parking and complimentary rides to the trail entrance after 5am. Trail maps provided upon request. Laundry ¢400 per item. Internet ¢1000 per hr. Sleeping bags ¢2000 per night. Stoves ¢3000 for 2 nights. Camping on the lawn or on Francisco's nearby coffee farm ¢2320. Rooms ¢5800 per person, with private baths ¢8700 per person. ❶

Cabinas El Bosque (☎2742 5021), across from the ranger station. Basic cement-floored rooms with access to hammocks on the 2nd fl. balcony. The attached **restaurant** ❶ serves *comida típica* (open daily 10am-9:30pm; earlier upon request). Breakfasts ¢1600-1800.

Arroz con pollo ¢2300. Salads ¢2400-2700. Chicken fingers ¢2600. Rents sleeping bags for ¢2000 per night. Doubles ¢5000; each additional person ¢5000. ❶

Hotel El Marin (☎2742 5091), next to the ranger station. Transportation to the park at 5am. Restaurant open 5am-10pm. *Casados* ¢2500-2700. Omelettes ¢1200. Doubles ¢14,000. ❶

OUTDOOR ACTIVITIES

PARQUE NACIONAL CHIRRIPÓ. Hikers almost always stay at **Base Crestones,** a rugged, well-equipped lodge at the base of the peak, as a layover point on their way to the summit. Reservations are required as only 40 spaces are available, but cancellations are frequent. You may be able to nab a spot from the San Gerardo rangers. It's usually easier to reserve in the rainy season (May-Nov.). Reservations can be made one month in advance by calling the San Gerardo ranger station (☎2742 5083; M-F 6:30am-4:30pm) and then making a direct deposit into a P.N. Chirripó Banco de Costa Rica account. Reservations can also be made in person one day in advance. (Ranger station open daily 6:30am-4:30pm. Park admission ¢8700 per night plus ¢5800 for lodging at Base Crestones and ¢3000 for camping.)

> **!** **CLOSED GATES.** During two weeks in May and the entire month of Oct., the park closes to allow for trail and facility maintenance. Visitors can still check with the rangers in San Gerardo to find out if any trails are open.

Most hikers take two or three days to summit the mountain and return using Base Crestones as a stopping point. The 14.5km to Base Crestones is almost entirely uphill and takes a good hiker anywhere from 6-10hr. To ensure that hikers get an early enough start to reach the shelter before night falls, the park entrance is open only between 5am and 10am, and rangers suggest starting as early as possible. Make sure you keep an extra keen lookout for the park entrance on the right; you will have gone too far if you hit the Cloudbridge research station. Rangers also discourage hiking in the dark because of jaguars and other dangerous wildlife that emerge at night. When hiking in the wet season, it is especially important to start early, as rain can begin as early as noon and often continue throughout the afternoon.

Base Crestones, officially named Centro Ambientalista el Páramo, is a top-of-the-line facility, located 500m vertically below the summit. It offers dorm beds with mattresses, bathrooms with running water and extremely cold showers, a communal kitchen with cooking utensils (but no stoves), a phone, and high-speed internet. The facility is powered by solar energy and has electrical light beginning at 6pm. One thing it doesn't have is heat—the temperature at the base can drop to 3°C (45°F) at night from May to December and as low as 0°C (32°F) from January to April—so plan accordingly. The lodge can provide blankets and stoves in an emergency, but in general, sleeping bags and stoves should be rented from hotels in San Gerardo. Most offer rentals for around ¢2000 per night.

DAYHIKES FROM BASE CRESTONES. The trail up Chirripó is not the only hike from Base Crestones. **Cerro Crestones** is another popular summit located 1.7km from Base Crestones. Topped by towering exposed rock, it is the most recognizable rock formation in the park. A popular day-long route is to climb Cerro Chirripó early to watch the sunrise, and then take the other turn at Valle de Los Conejos that leads over **Cerro Terbi** (3760m) and to Los Crestones for the sunset. Hikers may then stay in a shelter nearby and hike down to Base Crestones in the morning. Other hikers may opt to take the extremely steep hike up from

Base Crestones (2hr., 2.5km) and try to scale La Aguja ("The Needle"), a 60m vertical face for advanced rock climbers. Sendero Ventisqueros (6km) leads to the *cerro* of the same name. Other trails include the flatter hike to the Valle de Las Morenas (Valley of the Moraines; 7km), where lagoons reflect the mountains, Sabana del Los Leones (The Lion's Savannah; 3.9km) flanked by paramo flowers in the wet season (May-Nov.), and Laguna Ditkebi (3.3km).

AN ALTERNATIVE ROUTE. Serious hikers—only about 80 per year compared with the 8000 others who hike Chirripó—have recently begun exploring a three-day, 40km hike along the **Cordillera Talamanca,** the highest mountain range in the country (Chirripó is one of its peaks). This range divides the Atlantic and Pacific sides of the country, and 80% of the trail (about two days) consists of a ridge path that offers stunning views of both coasts. Some say that Cerro Urán, a distinctive two-peaked mountain, provides an even more beautiful view of the country than Chirripó does. The trail, **Urán Chirripó,** originates in the village of Herradura, 3km uphill from the San Gerardo Ranger Station. The rangers require that hikers take a guide from Herradura with them. Contact Rudalfo Elizondo of Herradura (☎2742 5006), a knowledgeable, kind man who can set you up with guides and lodging in Herradura. (Up to 10 people US$50; 11-16 people US$65.)

BEYOND CHIRRIPÓ. Although the more athletic or motivated can make a round trip in two full days, most overnight trekkers spend three days in the park: the first to hike to **Sirena,** the second to explore using Sirena as a base (the route to Los Patos is most popular), and the third to hike out. Rangers arrange lodging options and meals. (Breakfast US$10. Lunch and dinner US$15. Dorm beds US$8; bring sheets and mosquito net. Camping US$4 per person; only allowed in designated areas at the stations.) Where the *colectivo* truck stops in Carate, there are last-minute meals (coffee ¢300; *gallo pinto* ¢1500; steak and eggs ¢2000). A public restroom is available for ¢300.

If your legs have enough energy left for a bridge crossing on Río Blanco and another steep hike, you'll be rewarded by soothing *aguas termales* atop a nearby hill, where hot water (32.5˚C/97˚F) from a natural spring bubbles up into two stone pools. These **thermal waters** are popular in the dry season (Jan.-Apr.) but often under-touristed during the wet season. Take the road that forks left at the large cement bridge for 100m. Proceed uphill about 500m to a bridge well-marked as the entrance to Aguas Termales. Don't forget your towel! The ¢1500/US$3 entrance fee is collected at the small *soda* at the top of the hill run by Gerardo Alvarado and his family (☎2742 5210. Open daily 7am-5pm.). Gerardo also has three small *cabinas* for rent (¢15,000 per night).

Francisco Elizondo of Cabinas El Descanso (p. 144) and his family offer guided treks in English through their Finca El Mirador **coffee farm,** complete with views of the entire valley and a lesson on coffee harvesting and production (3hr., ¢11,600 per person). Francisco will also guide Chirripó hikes for small groups (¢23,200), although you may have to ask him to take it slowly: he has run the Chirripó Marathon over a dozen times. He can also arrange **horseback rides** and other tours throughout the area (price varies depending on duration and group). **Truchero los Cocolisos,** a short walk up the left fork 200m past the church, offers **trout fishing** at its farm. Visitors can take fish to cook later, or, on weekends, the owner will fry them up for you. Arrive before 4pm to be guaranteed trout action. (☎2742 5054 or 2742 5023; ¢3,000 per person; open Sa-Su 9am-6pm.)

For less-adventurous nature enthusiasts and those exhausted from Chirripó's relentless inclines, the **Cloudbridge Reserve** (www.cloudbridge.org) offers mellower hikes. The Reserve's goal is to preserve and reforest former pasture lands. Researchers study the ecology of the surrounding cloud forest at the reserve year-round. Ask for volunteer opportunities through the website. For hiking, follow the main road 1km past the Chirripó trailhead until it ends at the Cloudbridge Station. Hikes make 1hr., 3hr., and day-long loops. Eric, a Seattle native at the first house past the Chirripó trailhead, is available to guide tours. It is best to contact him in advance through the Cloudbridge website. For those who only have one day but want to experience both Chirripó and Cloudbridge, a solid 5-6hr. day hike starts at the park entrance and ends 7km at the Refugio Llanto Bonito, a resting point with a bench table and some toilets. On the return from this point, about 150m past the 4km mark, you can take the more scenic trail on your right into Cloudbridge Reserve, which leads back to the main road and affords several waterfall sightings.

GOLFITO

Golfito (pop. 18,000), former home of the United Fruit Company headquarters, sits on the northeast coast of the Golfo Dulce. Drastic banana production cutbacks in 1984 led officials to revive a weakening local economy by establishing a duty-free zone in the northern end of the city. This well-known shopping area fills the hotels year-round (especially on the weekends) with *ticos* who come to buy appliances, clothing, and alcohol without tariffs or taxes, while industrial ships bring in fertilizer and export palm oil from surrounding farms. Unlike in surrounding surfing towns, Golfito's numerous bars compete for the loudest music until they are shut down at midnight. Watch your back when walking near the park at night. Beyond the duty-free zone, the city is filled with dirty streets and slightly dilapidated buildings. Water taxis and private boats in the harbor ferry tourists to more hospitable locales like Pavones, Zancudo, Cacao, or Puerto Jiménez. Its convenience, however, makes Golfito a worthy stopping point for a few days—it's a great base for touring the bays and beaches of Golfo Dulce, or for exploring nearby nature reserves and Parque Nacional Piedras Blancas.

TRANSPORTATION

Flights: Sansa (☎2775 0303) has flights daily between **San José** and **Golfito** (1hr.; ¢55,300). Flights depart San José at 6am, noon, and 2:14pm. Flights depart Golfito at 7:13am and 1:40pm. The Sansa office is 100m north of *muellecito,* on the other side of the street. **Golfito Vive Information Center** near the hospital also arranges tickets.

Buses: Depart from the **TRACOPA** bus terminal (☎2775 0365) to **San José** (7hr.; 5am, 1:30pm, ¢6800) via **San Isidro** (4hr., ¢3520). Ticket office open daily 4:30am-4:30pm. Down the main street, 200m north of TRACOPA, buses go to **Neily** (1hr., 6am-7pm, ¢520) via **Río Claros** (30min.; ¢420) before continuing on to the Panamanian border at **Paso Canoas,** 17km beyond Neily. These buses also stop at the covered bus stops throughout the main road in **Golfito.**

Boats and Ferries: For connections in the high season, plan to arrive early to secure a seat. From the *muellecito* (between Hotel Golfito and the gas station), ferries run to **Puerto Jiménez** (30min.; 5:30, 10:30am, 4pm; ¢2000). Private taxi boats can also be arranged at the *muellecito* with the numerous captains hanging around during the day. Taxis run to **Playa Zancudo** (¢17,400/US$30), **Playa Cacao** (¢7000/US$12), **Casa Orquídeas** (¢46,400/US$80), **Pavones** (¢70,000/US$120), **Playa Azul** (¢17,400/US$30), and other locations. A daily taxi boat runs to **Zancudo** (1hr., noon, ¢2000) leaving from the dock at the Hotel Samoa. Other private boats can be found about 1km north near the gigantic *muelle bananero.*

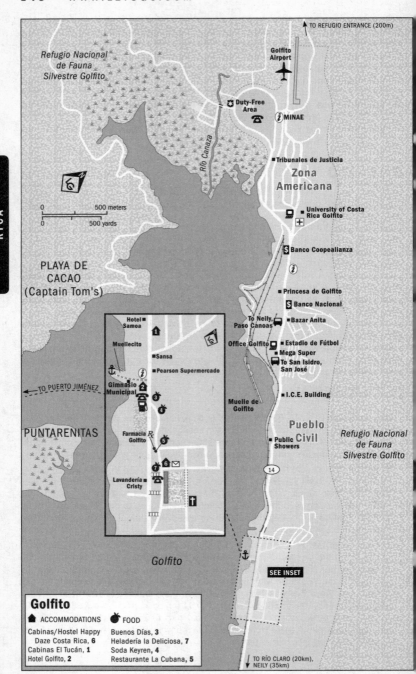

SOUTHERN COSTA RICA

TO REFUGIO ENTRANCE (200m)

Refugio Nacional
de Fauna
Silvestre Golfito

Golfito
Airport

Río Canaza

Duty-Free
Area

☎

ⓘ MINAE

■ Tribunales de Justicia

Zona
Americana

0   500 meters

0   500 yards

PLAYA DE
CACAO
(Captain Tom's)

■ University of Costa
Rica Golfito

$ Banco Coopealianza

ⓘ

■ Princesa de Golfito

$ Banco Nacional

■ Bazar Anita

To Neily,
Paso Canoas

Office Golfito

■ Estadio de Fútbol
■ Mega Super
To San Isidro,
San José

Hotel ■
Samoa

Muellecito

TO PUERTO JIMÉNEZ

PUNTARENITAS

1

ⓘ

■ Sansa

■ Pearson Supermercado

Gimnasio
Municipal

2

3

4

Farmacia
Golfito

5

Muelle de
Golfito

■ I.C.E. Building

Pueblo
Civil

Refugio Nacional
de Fauna
Silvestre Golfito

■ Public
Showers

7 **6** ✉

Lavandería ■
Cristy

✝

14

Golfito

⚓

SEE INSET

TO RÍO CLARO (20km),
NEILY (35km)

Golfito

⌂ ACCOMMODATIONS

Cabinas/Hostel Happy
  Daze Costa Rica, **6**
Cabinas El Tucán, **1**
Hotel Golfito, **2**

🍎 FOOD

Buenos Días, **3**
Heladería la Deliciosa, **7**
Soda Keyren, **4**
Restaurante La Cubana, **5**

Taxis: (☎2775 1170 or 2775 2020). Line up next to the gas station and can be flagged down anywhere on the main road (¢500 anywhere on the map, ¢350 if split with another party). **Local Bus:** Run along the main drag from 5:30am-10pm and stops on either side of the road at the bench. Bus stops every 20min. (¢155 anywhere on the main road).

🛠 🏧 ORIENTATION AND PRACTICAL INFORMATION

Golfito runs along a 4km north-south stretch of beach road, with the gulf to the west. The city is physically and economically divided into two sections. The swankier **Zona Americana** lies near the duty-free zone and airport and includes everything north of the hospital. It's home to a mix of US retirees and well-to-do *ticos*. The bus terminal, the Puerto Jiménez ferry dock, called *muellecito* or "little dock," and many smaller businesses and *sodas* occupy the shabbier **Pueblo Civil** to the south. Red, white, and blue buses marked "Golfito Centro" (¢155) and taxis (¢500) run up and down Golfito between these two areas.

Tourist Office: Cámara Ecoturística de Golfito (☎2775 1820), just north of the *muellecito*. Friendly staff offers information on transportation, lodging, and tours in Golfito and the surrounding area. They also have maps and free internet. Open M-F 8am-noon and 1-4pm. The **Golfito Vive Information Center** (☎2755 3338), south of the Banco Coopelianza. Provides general information and can arrange flights from Golfito and guided tours. Open M-F 8am-5pm, Sa 8am-noon.

Guided Tours: It is more convenient to hire tour guides in Puerto Jiménez, but if you want to stay in Golfito, adventure trips are available. The best option is **Dolfin Quest** (☎2775 0373; www.dolphinquestcostarica.com), run by an expat named Ray who owns 700 acres of virgin rainforest in San Josécito. He offers horseback tours of his land and butterfly farm (¢5800/US$10 per hr.), snorkel trips and jungle hikes (¢2900, US$5 per hr.), and 4hr. dolphin tours (¢116,000/US$200 for a group of up to 15). All equipment included. Water taxis can take you directly to his farm (¢11,600-23,200/US$20-40). The main **MINAE** office (☎2775 2620 or 2775 0075) is located in the large white and blue building just south of the airport. Better information can be obtained from the office at the Golfito Refuge park entrance 800m down the gravel road south of the airport. Open M-F 8am-4pm.

Bank: Banco Nacional (☎2775 1101), 100m north of the TRACOPA bus terminal. Has a **24hr. ATM,** changes traveler's checks, and gives cash advances. Open M-F 8:30am-3:45pm. **Banco Coopealianza** (☎2775 0025 or 2775 0800) also has an **ATM** and a **Western Union** office inside. Open M-F 8am-5pm, Sa 8am-noon.

Laundromat: Lavandería Cristy (☎2775 0043), inside the Hotel Delfina on the flat road south of the gas station. Go up the stairs and ring the bell. A load takes a few hours. ¢1000 per kg. Open 24hr.

Police: (☎2775 1022), located on the west side of the duty-free zone.

Pharmacy: Farmacía Golfito (☎2775 2442), across the street from Lavandería Cristy. Open M-Sa 8am-noon and 1-7pm. MC/V.

Hospital: (☎2775 1001), 2km north of the *muellecito*. It's the complex of green buildings with red roofs.

Telephones: Available outside the gas station, in the duty-free zone, next to Heladería La Deliciosa, and at regular intervals along the main road.

Internet Access: Free internet is available at the **Cámara Ecoturística de Golfito.** Open M-F 8am-noon and 1-4pm. For access at night and on weekends, try **Office Golfito**

(☎2775 0718), just north of the MegaSuper. ¢600 per hr. Open daily 8:30am-8:30pm. An unnamed office across from the University of Costa Rica (☎2775 0570) also has internet for ¢500 per hr. Photocopies ¢25. Open M-Sa 8am-7pm.

Post Office: (☎2775 1911; fax 2775 0373), uphill from the *muellecito* and the 2nd left before the soccer field. Offers fax services. Open M-F 8am-noon and 1-4:30pm, Sa 8am-noon. **Postal Code:** 60701.

ACCOMMODATIONS

There are numerous cheap, simple accommodations in and around Pueblo Civil. Quieter accommodations away from the bustle of the city can be found both north and south of town, but these tend to be a bit pricey.

Cabinas El Tucán (☎2735 0553), 50m north of the *muellecito* on the right. Doña Daisy offers simple rooms with private cold-water baths and fans. Charming garden in the back. Parking available. Singles ¢5000, with A/C ¢7500. MC/V. ❶

Cabinas y Marisquería Princesa de Golfito (☎2775 0442), across the street from the Banco Nacional. This cozy 2-story white house with red roof and trim has a well-kept garden and comfortable rooms. Each comes with a small private bath, fan, TV, and lacy sheets. Laundry service available. Singles ¢7500, with A/C 12,000; doubles ¢9500/12,000; quads ¢13,000/16,000. Hot water is an extra ¢1000. MC/V.❶

Hotel Golfito (☎2775 0047), just south of the *muellecito*. Some of the nicest, cleanest and most reasonably priced rooms in town. Bright rooms have soft beds, showers with hot water, and A/C; some have waterfront views. Doubles with fans ¢7000, with A/C ¢12,000; triples ¢18,000. ❶

FOOD

You can grab a meal anywhere along the road between the pharmacy and the Banco Nacional. *Sodas* are your go-to option here; prices hover consistently between ¢1500 and ¢2500 for a full meal. Alternatively, go to **MegaSuper** across from the soccer stadium. It has all the necessities, from fresh fruit to hygiene products. (☎2775 2274. Open M-Th 8am-8pm, F-Sa 6am-9pm, Su 6am-7pm. AmEx/MC/V.) **Supermercado Pearson** is closer to the Pueblo Civil. (☎2775 0054. Open M-Sa 8am-8pm, Su 7am-6pm. AmEx/MC/V.)

Buenos Días (☎2775 1124), just south of the *muellecito* in the center of Pueblo Civil. This unusually clean, air-conditioned diner is a local favorite. The bilingual menu features a full beer selection as well as enormous *casados* (¢2500-3250) and *gallo pinto* breakfasts (¢1500-2550). Pancakes ¢2500-2950. Banana split ¢1980. Open daily 6am-10pm. MC/V. ❷

La Casona de Marisco (☎2775 0671). Seafood joint dishes with heaping entrees, such as Filet of Dorado stuffed with shrimp in jalapeño sauce (¢5000) and squid rings with tartar sauce, plantains, and salad (¢3500). Meals for two (jumbo shrimp ¢11,000). Open daily Tu-Su 10am-10pm. MC/V. ❷

Soda Keyren (☎2775 1880). Great for ill-timed hunger pangs, this *soda* is one of the most convenient and friendly restaurants around. Substantial *casados* with chicken, beefsteak, or ribs (¢1600-1800) are served from the cozy kitchen. Open 24hr. ❶

Heladería La Deliciosa (☎2775 1674), entrance opposite of the main road and up the stairs. Known around Golfito for unbeatable desserts. Flavors include vanilla caramel and rum with fruit. Cones ¢600. Banana splits ¢2000. Flan and rice pudding (each ¢500) are unfrozen favorites. Open daily 2-10pm. ❶

⚡ DAYTRIPS FROM GOLFITO

The "outdoors" lies deceptively close to the edges of town: just minutes outside Golfito, the sometimes depressing city life easily gives way to clear streams cutting through the expanse of greenery. And though the beaches and forests feel remote, their proximity to the city makes them susceptible to many of the same threats as the surrounding urban environment. Travelers should be wary of exploring these areas alone at night.

PLAYA DE CACAO. Though this beach is easily accessible from Golfito, it's rarely crowded. The vegetation reaches all the way down to the water in many places, but there are plenty of smooth sandbars as well. Here, the warm water of the Pacific calmly caresses the shore. Because the Cacao peninsula and Puntarenitas island make a natural marina of Golfito Bay, the water here is extremely calm and rarely rises more than a foot with the tide. Cacao is known locally as Captain Tom's, so beachgoers should ask the taxi to drop them there. Tom's wrecked ship remains a point of interest on the southern edge of the main beach. *(6km north around the bay from Golfito; a pleasant 1hr. walk. Taxis cost about ¢6000, but the water taxis from the muellecito or muelle bananero are a cheaper, more enjoyable option, especially during the rainy season when the road can become impassable. 10min. ¢3000.)*

REFUGIO NACIONAL DE FAUNA SILVESTRE GOLFITO. Poorly publicized Refugio Nacional de Fauna Silvestre Golfito protects the steep, lush hills of primary rainforest above Golfito, encompassing distinct terrains that are home to 125 species of trees. This forest area is visible from the town, and extends from the edges of its residential areas to Playa Cacao. The reserve has the advantage of remaining fairly dry even during the rainy season and offers relaxed alternatives to more demanding routes in **Parque Nacional Corcovado.**

The park includes four principal **trails** beginning at various locations throughout Golfito. The main park entrance provides access to the easiest and best-marked trail just north of the Golfito airport. Take any of Golfito's local buses and get off at the entrance to the duty-free zone near the airstrip. Walk past the airstrip to the marked trailhead. The park office is located 800m down the dirt road. A short, well-marked trail begins behind the park office and leads through impressive primary rainforest to a small waterfall about 20min. away. *(Follow the main trail for about 10min. until the trail encounters a stream. Follow the stream the rest of the way to the waterfall.)*

Another waterfall trail begins near the police station on the road toward Playa Cacao. The **waterfall** is on the property of the public water supplier, so to take this trail you must have a note from the park office or a guide. Take the gravel road on the south side of the police station and follow it straight through the neighborhood of Llano Bonito. The road winds through beautiful countryside with flower-covered pastures on one side and trees on the other for 30min. before reaching a fork. Bear left there and follow the road for another 15min. Here you'll reach a small house where the guard for the water supply lives, and you'll have to present permission to continue. Behind the house the trail narrows before crossing a stream and climbing uphill for another 10min. The waterfall here is more impressive than the one near the park entrance, and has several cascades. The hike should take about 2hr. round-trip.

Another trail through more difficult territory begins behind the Banco Nacional. Nicknamed **"Las Torres,"** this trail (2hr.) leads uphill through the forest to the radio towers at the top of the hill, and offers spectacular views of Golfito and all of the Golfo Dulce from the top. To find the trailhead, take the side road just south of the Banco Nacional and follow it through the residential area. At the point where the road starts to loop back around, there is a small dirt road leading uphill on the right marking the beginning of the trail. Because the trailhead can be tricky to find, a guide is recommended for visitors. This hike is not recommended at night or for solo travelers, as the urban location makes it susceptible to crime. There are very few facilities within the park and none for overnight stays. *(Entrance fee US$10 per person. For more information, contact Susan at the MINAE office in Golfito. ☎ 2775 2620 or 2775 0075. Open M-F 8am-4pm. For guided tours the park recommends Pedro Caballo (☎ 2775 2240, 8876 7357, or 2732 1229), who offers 6hr. horseback tours of the refuge and Playa Cacoa. Don Martin of the Ecotour Development Foundation (☎ 2775 1813 or 818 2433) will also guide hiking or horseback tours of the waterfalls. 3 days of hiking ₡34,800/ US$60 per person. 8hr. horseback tour ₡55,100/US$95 per person. 5 person min.)*

CARIBBEAN LOWLANDS

PARISMINA

Drier, dustier, and even more secluded than its northern neighbor, Tortuguero, the tiny island hamlet of Parismina (pop. 400) attracts hundreds of leatherback, green, and hawksbill turtles every year, along with surprisingly small numbers of tourists. Where Tortuguero has developed an ecotourism industry based on short-term stays and guided tours, Parismina has created several volunteer programs that allow visitors to become "park rangers," doing 4hr. night watchman shifts while living with local families in homestays. Visitors looking to enjoy the island's calm ambience for only a few days will also find Parismina a welcoming stop; locals drink with tourists at the Mono Carablanca Lodge, and everyone who can stand the heat joins in the impromptu soccer games that pop up continually on every flat surface available.

TRANSPORTATION

Buses: From the Gran Terminal Siquirres, where the bus drops off, walk to the old bus station on the north side of the soccer field and catch a bus to Caño Blanco, from where a boat heads to Parismina (2hr.; M-F 4am and 1pm, Sa-Su 6am and 2pm; ¢300).

Boats: Parismina has no roads and is only accessible by boat. From Caño Blanco, a public boat meets the bus and shuttles passengers to Parismina (8min., ¢1000). If you arrive at Caño Blanco from Siquirres by taxi (¢17,400, US$30) or private car, you can hire a private boat from the Caño Blanco dock to Parismina (¢14,500, US$25) or take one of the public boats leaving that day (8min., ¢1000). Be sure to arrive at Caño Blanco at least 30min. before 6pm as boats leave the dock early and there are no overnight facilities. Coming from farther south, hop on a boat from Moín to Tortuguero and tell the captain you only need to go to Parismina. Jumping on an already hired boat should run about ¢14,500 (US$25) to Moín and ¢11,600 (US$20) to Tortuguero. The tourist info center can arrange a pick-up for 5pm; notify them by 3pm that day. Public boats usually pass by each day in each direction between 10:30am and noon. Private boats organized on Parismina will cost upwards of US$100 for the trip; as usual, the best way to go is to buddy up or join another traveling group. To return to Siquirres, take the boat from Parismina to Caño Blanco (open M-F 5:30am and 2:30pm, Sa-Su 8:30am and 4:30pm; ¢1000) and catch the bus back to Siquirres (open M-F 6am and 3pm, Sa-Su 10am and 5pm).

Tour agencies: From Parismina, the easiest way to continue onto Tortuguero or south to Moín is to contact one of the Tortuguero tour agencies, most of which arrange round-trip transportation from Moín to Tortuguero. The agencies will notify the boat captains heading in each direction that they should stop for passengers at Parismina.

ORIENTATION AND PRACTICAL INFORMATION

Though the island of Parismina is quite long, the town itself is small and easy to navigate. There are two main docks in town; both are 100m west of the main path. Just south of town, the first docks service boats to Caño Blanco, while the second dock, about 250m north, services private boats including those going to Moín and Tortuguero. The main path stretches from the Caño Blanco docks in the south and ends at Sayleen del Caribe, where a right turn leads east toward the waterfront and the soccer field. There is a *pulpería*, 100m east and 50m south of Sayleen del Caribe (open daily 7am-5pm). There are **no banks or ATMs in town,** and the only place that accepts credit cards is **Mono Carablanca Lodge and Restaurant** (MC/V), so plan accordingly.

Tourist Office: The **Parismina Information Center,** located 200m north of the Caño Blanco docks, has a poster board with up-to-date info about traveling to and from the island as well as volunteer opportunities. The center also has a English and Spanish **book exchange** (open M-Sa 2-5pm).

Internet: The information center houses the only computer with internet in town (¢1500 per hr.; be prepared for lines).

Medical Services: There is no clinic in town, but a **doctor** visits every few days; details of the visits are posted in the Information Center.

Telephones: in front of both docks.

ACCOMMODATIONS

Though most visitors to Parismina are students on school trips or long-term volunteers participating in homestay programs, the town has several good value budget options for short-term, independent travelers.

▨ **Carefree Ranch Lodge** (☎2710 3149), east of the Information Center. This small B&B-style lodge feels like home, with peach-colored sideboards and forest-green doors. Offers some of the most comfortable accommodations in town, with high ceilings, private hot-water baths, and wide balconies. A charming on-site restaurant serves family-style meals. Rooms ₡5800 (US$10), with 3 meals ₡15,660 (US$27). ❶

Cabinas La Iguana Verde (☎2798 0828), 100m east of Salon Naomi. The yard of this small hotel looks like a jungle: the resident parrot erratically spouts greetings to passersby, and massive beetles hang continually from tree branches near the fence. The rooms, however, are animal-free, with private hot-water baths and large beds. Rooms ₡5500, with A/C ₡10,000. ❷

Mono Carablanco Lodge (☎2798 1031), 200m east of Sayleen El Caribe, just past the soccer field. The stark blue block of rooms is easily outshined by the *cabana*-style bar and restaurant, small blue pool, and palm-tree-filled lawn. All rooms have fans and private cold-water baths. ₡5000 per person, with A/C ₡7000. ❶

⬗🞔 FOOD AND NIGHTLIFE

Because most visitors to Parismina have meals with their home-stay families, the options for food and nightlife are pretty basic. Expect a lot of *comida típica* and not much else.

Restaurante Mono Carablanca (☎2798 1031), in the Mono Carablanca Lodge. Serves upscale versions of staples. Popular for locals and tourists looking for a beer between soccer games (₡500-1800). Breakfasts ₡3000. *Casados* and rice dishes ₡3000. Open daily 8am-8:30pm. MC/V. ❷

Rancho La Palma (☎2798 0259), in front of the docks where boats depart for Tortuguero. An older crowd enjoys Parismina's cheapest, most basic eats in this open-air dining area. *Casados* ₡2500. Sandwiches ₡1200. Open daily 5am-7pm. ❶

Carefree Ranch Restaurant (☎2710 3149), in the Carefree Ranch. Home-cooked, family-style meals. Drop by during breakfast hours for scrambled eggs, fruit, fresh bread, cheese, coffee, and orange juice (₡2500). Lunch and dinner ₡3000. ❷

Salon Naomi, in the center of town. The Salon is the only disco in Parismina, though the size of the local population means that the cavernous building only starts to fill on weekends or when a particularly large tourist group is in town. Beer ₡700. Mixed drinks ₡1000-2000. Dancing on Sa night. Open daily 11am-10pm. ❶

Soda Xine, in the center of town near Salon Naomi. *Casados* ₡2400-3600. Hamburgers ₡1500. *Gallos* ₡1000. Rice and beans ₡2800. Open daily 8am-7pm. ❶

🏔 OUTDOOR ACTIVITIES

There are no official tourist agencies with offices in Parismina, but you can get information and phone numbers for tour guides at the Information Center. Parismina's biggest tourist attraction is the *deshove* (turtle nesting), whose high season runs between March and September, though turtles nest sporadically throughout the year. Green turtles primarily nest between June and October, leatherbacks from February to June, and hawksbills at various times. Visitors can explore the wildlife-filled canals around Parismina village and go whitewater rafting, hiking, fishing, and horseback riding.

Rainforest World (☎2556 0014 or 2556 2678; www.rforestw.com). Runs 2- and 3-day all-inclusive rafting and turtle-watching trips down the Reventazon to Parismina, where guests stay in Rainforest World guide Rick Knowles's hotel Iguana Verde. 2-day, 2-night packages start at ₡150,800 (US$260). Whitewater rafting on the Pacuare or Reventazon ₡52,500-72,500 (US$90-125) per day.

La Asociación de Boteros de Parismina. A small, private group of boat captains that offers tours of the river canals from Caño Blanco. Several captains are bilingual and excellent at spotting the wide variety of wildlife lurking on the river banks. Prices range from ¢2900 (US$5) for the short ride to Parismina to ¢87,000 (US$150) for a round-trip ride to Tortuguero. Look for the boat captains at the Caño Blanco docks; be sure to get there by 5:30pm at the latest.

Mola Fish (☎2798 1034 or 8308 5518; www.molafish.com). Daniel, the owner, has offered sportfishing trips for the past four years in Parismina. 1-day trip US$580 (¢336,400) for 1 person, US$780 (¢457,000) for 2-people. All equipment is provided. English spoken.

Paradise Island (☎2298 0989; www.junglejessietours.com), near Mono Carablanca. Jorge Alberto has 30 years of experience offering sportfishing (¢145,000/US$250) and wildlife tours at sea (¢11,600/US$20; min. 6 people). English spoken.

TORTUGUERO VILLAGE

Famed for the vast number of turtles that nest on its beaches every year, the small village of Tortuguero has managed to parlay its ecological wealth into a thriving tourism industry that has both improved the local economy and reduced the impact of poaching. Completely separated from the mainland by a maze of canals and situated on the shores of the Caribbean, Tortuguero cannot be conveniently accessed from San José or any of Costa Rica's major transport hubs, but the effort required to get here is entirely worth it. Though the village is charming and the sunbathing quite pleasant, the real reason for visiting Tortuguero is a night-long event: the *deshove* (turtle nesting). From June to September, visitors to Tortuguero can witness the impressive efforts of nesting leatherback, green, and hawksbill turtles on the shores of Tortuguero village and the adjacent Tortuguero National Park. For those who don't get their fill of animal watching at the *deshove*, Tortuguero has many opportunities for boat, canoe, and kayak trips in its surrounding canals, where visitors can get practically face-to-face with caimans, monkeys, turtles, and a fantastically diverse array of birds.

Though thousands of tourists follow the turtles to Tortuguero's beaches each year, the onslaught of *cabinas* and tourist information centers has not completely destroyed its small-town appeal. Here, ecotourism has truly taken hold, and many of Tortuguero's residents are employed in the tourism industry. The influx of tourist money that comes from the nightly *deshove* has stabilized the local community and helped to decrease the prevalence of turtle poaching in the area.

▐ TRANSPORTATION

Flying from San José (p. 57) to the airstrip, a few kilometers north of Tortuguero, is the most convenient way to get to the village, but it is also the most expensive. **Sansa** offers flights from San José and from Juan Santa María International Airport in Alajuela. (☎2221 9414; www.flysansa.com. Approx. US$100.) **NatureAir** departs from Tobías Bolaños Airport in Pavas. (☎2220 3054, reservations from US +1-888-535-8832. Approx. US$100/¢58,000.) Except for flying, all routes into Tortuguero require a boat trip, as the island is separated from the mainland by a network of canals. There are two main starting points for transport into Tortuguero: **Cariari,** in northeastern Costa Rica, and **Moín,** next to Limón on the Caribbean coast.

From Cariari: Buses leave each morning for Cariari from the **Terminal de los Caribeños** in San José (☎2221 2596; 2hr.; 9 per day). Once in Cariari, there are 2 options for transport to Tortuguero. The cheapest route from Cariari is by bus to Pavona (1hr.; 6,

11:30am, 3pm; ¢1100). Take this bus to the end of the line at the river's edge, where **lanchas** (small boats) will speed you through a swampy river to Tortuguero's main docks (1hr.; departs upon bus arrival; ¢1600, buy tickets on board). If you are traveling by **car,** park your car in Pavona and then take the boat to Tortuguero.

From Moín: The trip to Tortuguero from Moín is completed entirely in a boat and is known for providing opportunities for crocodile, bird, and monkey sightings. *Lanchas* depart early in the morning for Tortuguero from Moín's small dock behind **Restaurante Papá Manuel** (10am and 3pm, but try to arrive at least 1hr. early to bargain prices and get a captain). The *lancha* trip is 3-5hr. through canals teeming with wildlife (¢20,300/US$35). It's best to arrange in advance, either at the docks or through a hotel or tour company in Tortuguero. If you're traveling alone, a tour guide may request up to ¢87,000 (US$150) for the trip; arrive early to buddy up with other travelers (see **Tour Smart,** p. 160).

From Tortuguero: Private boats depart from Tortuguero at almost any hour desired, though boats are only allowed to travel in the area's waterways from 6am to 6pm. Most tour companies in Tortuguero organize return trips to Moín, Parismina, and Cariari via Pavona. To schedule a trip, talk to any of the tour companies listed; prices should run about ¢14,500 (US$25) per person to **Moín,** ¢11,600 (US$20) per person to **Parismina,** and ¢5800 (US$10) to **Pavona** and on to **Cariari.** Boats depart regularly for Pavona from the main docks at 6am, 11:30am, and 3pm, where a bus waits to travel the rest of the way to Cariari. Make sure to book in advance to ensure an available boat, and be aware that prices may become much steeper if traveling alone. By booking in advance, you can join a group and pay a significantly lower price.

Tour Companies: Most tour companies in Tortuguero can arrange transportation from San José or cities along the Caribbean coast to Tortuguero. However, there are several companies throughout Costa Rica that offer pre-arranged trips to the park. **Fran and Modesto Watson's tours** (☎2226 0986; www.tortuguerocanals. com) on their riverboat, *Francesca,* are highly recommended. Their most popular trip to Tortuguero includes round-trip transportation from San José to Moín in a van and from Moín to Tortuguero in a boat, in addition to 2-day, 1-night lodging at the Laguna Lodge, 5 meals, a canal boat tour, a turtle tour, a visit to Caribbean Conservation Center, and park entrance fees (¢95,700-113,100/US$165-195) per person. **Turtle Beach Lodge** (☎2248 0707; info@turtlebeachlodge.com) also offers transportation from San Jose (7½hr.; 6am; ¢20,300/US$35).

◢ ▐ ORIENTATION AND PRACTICAL INFORMATION

The main village of Tortuguero is only about 500m long, with sandy gravel paths winding their way through the scattered buildings. The airstrip is a few kilometers north of town and is only accessible by boat. Most travelers arrive at the dock in the center of town. From the docks, with your back to the water, north is to your left and south is to your right. The docks lead on to the canals and rivers, and across the island, only about 200m from the docks, is the Caribbean Sea. The main path, **Calle Principal,** runs from the **Caribbean Conservation Center** at the far north end of the village all the way to the **ranger station** at the park entrance on the southern end of town. If you are walking around at night, you should consider bringing a flashlight; there are very few streetlights, and the paths through town beyond the main road near the docks are mostly dark and covered by trees.

Tourist Office: Tortuguero boasts an impressive number of buildings along the river's edge purporting to be "free information centers," each of which adjoins a for-profit tour company. Information guru Victor Parientes runs the ▨**Tortuguero Information Center** (☎2709 8015), opposite the church, 100m north of the docks. At the **Sansa Ticket Office** (☎2709 8015 or 8838 6330), in the same building, you can arrange plane, bus, and boat reservations, as well as rafting, hiking, and turtle-watching excursions. Open daily 8am-1pm and 2-7pm.

Banks: There are no banks or ATMs in Tortuguero, so try to stock up on *colones* before you arrive. If you are in a bind, the **Super Morpho,** located in the town center across from the docks, gives cash back on credit card or debit card purchases. (Open daily 7am-9pm. AmEx/MC/V.)

Police: The **police station** (☎2767 1593), in the blue building, 75m north of the dock to the left of the C. Principal.

Medical Services: For medical emergencies, call ☎8841 8404 or 8304 2121. For serious emergencies, the Sansa ticket office can arrange charter flights to the hospital in San José.

Telephones: Available at **Miss Junie's,** the Super Morpho in front of the docks, and in front of the **ICE office,** 25m south of the police station. Local calls ¢20 per min. International calls require a calling card; some phones require a calling card regardless of destination.

Internet Access: Internet Cafe, 150m north of the main dock on the right. Offers 6 computers with sometimes-slow internet (¢2000 per hr.). Open daily until 9pm.

ACCOMMODATIONS

Despite its remote location, Tortuguero Village has an extensive selection of accommodations, most of them well within a student traveler's means. Hot-water baths and fans are standard fare on the island, and many *cabinas* have on-site breakfasts and hammocks available. Because of the large number of tourists visiting the island, it is important to make reservations in advance if you wish to stay at a particular place, especially during the Tortuguero's high season (July-Oct.). Those who aren't too fond of bugs should remember that the buildings near the canals, where the water is slow-moving, are much more mosquito-friendly than those closer to the drier air and quicker currents of the beach. **Camping** is not allowed on the beach. Backpackers can pitch tents for US$12 (¢6960) per person at the **Jalova ranger station** (includes park entry, accessible only by boat; p. 161) in Tortuguero Village (includes access to kitchen and hot-water showers).

Cabinas Aracari (☎2709 8006). From the docks, head south on the path and take the 1st left after the mini shopping center; Aracari is at the end of the path. Though its prices are relatively low, the *cabinas* scattered throughout the tropical garden are spotless, with tile floors, private hot-water showers, fans, and porches. Singles ¢5800 (US$10); doubles ¢9260 (US$16); triples ¢13,920 (US$24). ❶

Casa Marbella (☎8833 0827 or 2709 8011), between the Tortuguero Information Center and Dorling's Bakery. Beautiful views and a friendly owner make it a charming option, but swarming mosquitoes detract from the experience. Each of the 10 rooms has high ceilings, soft beds, and hot water. Breakfast included, as well as access to the fridge and microwave. Free Wi-Fi. Singles ¢17,400-29,000 (US$30-50); doubles ¢20,300-31,900 (US$35-55); triples ¢26,100-37,700 (US$45-65). ❸

Miss Miriam's (☎2709 8002), on the soccer field, next door to Miss Miriam's Caribbean restaurant. A 2-story house with sunny, yellow-walled rooms with private, but temperamental, hot-water baths and fans. Across the soccer field, at **Miss Miriam's II,** 9 slightly larger cabins with similar amenities are just as close to the ocean but farther from the traffic. Singles ¢11,600 (US$20); doubles ¢14,500 (US$25); triples ¢17,400 (US$30). ❷

Cabinas y Restaurante La Casona (☎2709 8092 or 8860 0453), on the northeast corner of the soccer field. The best deal at this popular complex is the *casita,* a 3-bedroom apartment with its own kitchen, hot-water bath, and open-air porch with stellar views of the Caribbean beach. Breakfast included. Free Wi-Fi and internet. Reserve in advance.

CARIBBEAN LOWLANDS

Casita ¢4060 (US$7) per person for up to 8 people; singles ¢13,340 (US$23); doubles ¢17,400 (US$30); triples ¢23,200 (US$40). AmEx/D/MC/V. ❷

🍴 FOOD

Though a small town, Tortuguero has a fair number of restaurants, most of which are on the expensive side as they cater to an almost entirely tourist clientele. To pick up your own trimmings, head to **Super Morpho,** directly opposite the docks (open daily 7am-9pm; AmEx/D/MC/V), **Super Las Tortugas** (☎27098022), 200m north of the docks (open daily 7am-9pm; AmEx/D/MC/V), or **Super Bambu** (☎2709 8108), 200m south of the docks (open daily 7am-9pm; AmEx/D/MC/V).

🍽 **Miss Junie's,** 250m north of the docks. When it is not overrun by tourist groups, this Caribbean restaurant conjures up fresh and flavorful regional specialties. Breakfast ¢1160-4060 (US$2-7). Entrees ¢5220-8120 (US$9-14). Open daily 7am-10pm. ❸

🍽 **Miss Miriam's** (☎2709 8002), next door to Miss Miriam's *cabinas* on the north side of the soccer field. Serves family-style "make your own *casado*" meals with coconut-simmered rice, salad, *gallo pinto*, french fries, and a variety of Caribbean-flavored proteins including whole fish, chicken, steak, and pork chops (¢4400 per person). Stop by in the morning for a traditional *tico gallo pinto* breakfast with a kick of coconut flavoring (¢3300). Call out if no one is in sight. Open daily 7:30am-9pm. ❷

Cabinas y Restaurante La Casona, on the northwest corner of the soccer field. Nestled in a thatched-roof porch in the gardens of Cabinas La Casona, this relaxing restaurant prepares a variety of tasty dishes for customers at picnic-style wooden tables. Hanging plants and the sweet smell of burning incense add to the intoxicating vibe. Delicious *casados* ¢3200, heart of palm lasagna ¢4200, and garlic and butter grilled shrimp with rice ¢5600. Open daily 7:30-11am and 1:30-8:30pm. AmEx/D/MC/V. ❸

Buddha Bar (☎2709 8084), 50m north of docks. Though its prices are a bit higher than those of other restaurants in town, the lounge-like atmosphere, spacious riverside terrace, and pleasant ambient music bring a fair-sized crowd to the relaxed Buddha Bar. Guests can relax on couches in the night-club-style interior or enjoy their meal *al fresco* at the dock-side tables along the river. *Batidos* ¢2000-2800. Pizza ¢4000-8000. Lasagna ¢3800. Crepes ¢3700-4300. Sangria ¢2800. Desserts (¢2000-2700) are tasty, though tiny. Reservations recommended for after 6pm. Open daily 11:30am-8:30pm. AmEx/D/MC/V. ❷

🎵 NIGHTLIFE

Punto Encuentro, 100m north of the docks. Look for writing on the left side of the wall. The hippest place in town, right on the water's edge. Just try not to fall in after too many cold *Imperiales* (¢1000). Large screen displays music videos showcase old-school Caribbean music and Latin pop. Rice and shrimp ¢2500. Open daily 11am-2am. AmEx/D/MC/V.

Mala Culebra, across from the SuperMorpho at the docks. Not as busy as Punto Encuentro. Groups of tourists gather to show off their moves to the reggae-heavy soundtrack. *Imperial* ¢1000. Open daily 11am-2am.

👁 SIGHTS

CARIBBEAN CONSERVATION CORPORATION NATURAL HISTORY VISITOR CENTER. Before going to see the turtles, check out the non-profit Caribbean Conservation Corporation Natural History Visitor Center (CCC). Founded by Archie Carr, who later prompted the creation of Tortuguero National Park, the CCC specializes in research and education on sea turtles. The center has videos, exhibits, and information on the decimation of the sea turtle population and the efforts taken by conservationists to save the endangered animals. In the 50 years since its inception, the CCC has tagged over 50,000 turtles, making it the world's largest green-turtle-tagging program. Visitors can "adopt" a turtle with a ¢14,500 (US$25) donation and, in turn, receive an adoption certificate, photograph, turtle fact sheet, and information about the tagged turtle when it is found. Those who want to get up close and personal with the turtles can sign up for the center's internship positions, where interns hole up in research facilities and aid the center's scientists in their work. Interns can pick which type of turtle they want to research. Prices for internships run ¢816,000-1,573,800 (US$1400-2700) for 1-3 week programs. The center's admission fee is used to further the efforts of the CCC. *(At the north end of town. Head north on the main path for about 200m, where you will see the center's signs; turn right and follow the path a few hundred meters farther until you reach the center. ☎ 2709 8091; www.cccturtle.org. Open M-Sa 10am-noon and 2-5:30pm, Su 2-5:30pm. US$1/¢580. MC/V.)*

TOUR SMART. While tourism has certainly reinvigorated the local economy in Tortuguero, it has also resulted in a wave of new tour agencies, some of which hire unqualified guides and require travelers to patronize certain establishments. To ensure that you are getting your money's worth, ask about a guide's qualifications before signing up for a tour and try to compare the offers of several individuals or companies before making a decision. Keep in mind that tours that uncover the sand where eggs are located disrupt the hatching process, kill the newly hatched baby turtles, and are illegal.

PARQUE NACIONAL TORTUGUERO

Sheltering the most important nesting site for marine turtles in the Western Hemisphere, Parque Nacional Tortuguero encompasses 261 sq. km of coastal territory and 501 sq. km of marine territory 84km north of Limón. It is almost exclusively accessible and navigable by boat. The park's 35km beach, where thousands of turtles return each year to lay their eggs, has brought the park international fame and thousands of visitors. Not content to surrender the show, howler monkeys echo in the treetops, toucans coast overhead, and caimans glide through the canals that flow into the park's swampy regions.

Despite decades of research, scientists still do not know why the turtles flock in such numbers to Tortuguero or how they are able to find their way back here to nest over 30 years after they first hatched. They do know that as the turtle leaves the beach, it records the details of the beach and its location relative to its next destination. Despite an extinction scare in the 1960s brought on by poaching and egg-stealing, conservation efforts have tremendously helped the turtle population, and the famous green turtles continue to nest in the park (from the end of June to Sept.), along with leatherbacks (Mar.-July), hawksbills (May-Sept.), and loggerheads (June-Oct.). All of these species are endangered, though the recent focus on ecotourism in the area has helped the turtles considerably; they are now worth more as a tourist attraction than as an ingredient in turtle soup. However, the turtles still face an immense number of natural predators. If they make it to the sea, baby turtles are prime meat for sharks, big fish, and other sea creatures. In the end, only one out of 1000 sea turtles will make it. To help save the baby turtles from human predators, proceeds from designated turtle stickers ¢2320 (US$4) sold at souvenir shops and tourist booths fund the guards who watch over the eggs.

Today, researchers tag turtles and use satellite tracking to determine patterns of birth dates, routes, and travel patterns in an attempt to uncover the mystery behind these forever-returning females. Tagging turtles has revealed amazing information about their migratory and mating habits: one turtle tagged near Tortuguero was found just one month later on the coast of Senegal, Africa, and many reports show that female turtles, after visiting hundreds of beaches around the world, return to their birth site to nest 30 years later.

TRANSPORTATION. Tortuguero Village is the gateway for Parque Nacional Tortuguero. See p. 156 for transportation to and from Tortuguero. The entrance to the park, at the Cuatro Esquinas Ranger Station, is a 400m walk south of the main docks in Tortuguero Village. The less-frequented Jalova Ranger Station is accessible by a 1½hr. boat ride—arrange transportation at the main docks.

WHEN TO GO. Tortuguero has an average yearly rainfall of 5-6m. The rainy season is officially June-Oct., but expect it to rain a lot year-round. The driest months are Feb.-May. Unlike most of Costa Rica, high season in Tortuguero is during the rainy season, when the four different species of turtles come for the *deshove* (turtle nesting). The famous *tortugas verdes* nest on Tortuguero's 35km beach June-Sept.; leatherbacks nest Mar.-July; hawksbills nest May-Sept.; and loggerheads nest June-Oct. Be sure to bring good, waterproof footwear (rubber boots work well), rain gear, sunblock, insect repellent, a hat, and cash. Frequent blackouts in rainy season make a flashlight highly advisable.

PRACTICAL INFORMATION. Most journeys into the park begin at the **Cuatro Esquinas Ranger Station,** where rangers sell entrance tickets, provide maps, and answer visitors' questions. The entrance is open daily 5:30am-6pm. Although the park closes at 6pm, tickets must be purchased before 4pm, and the last entry is at 4pm. If planning a boat trip, remember that many of the canals around Tortuguero are part of the national park and thus are only open daily 6am-6pm. Most of the canals also have speed and motor restrictions; check with the park rangers (☎2709 8086) for more details. Entrance ₡5800 (US$10); children ₡580 (US$1).

HIKING AND GUIDED TOURS. There are two official land hikes in Tortuguero National Park. Starting from the Cuatro Esquinas Ranger Station, **Sendero El Gavilán** (1hr., 2km) used to be the only hike available, but it is currently under construction. Though it is not a difficult hike, it can be muddy and buggy. The trail winds through the forest and ends on the beach, where you can take a left and walk back to town. Rubber boots are required for the hike and can be rented for ₡580 (US$1) per person at a hotel or tourist center. If it is still under construction, you can take the **Sendero Jaguar,** a 4 km (1½hr.) circular hike that both begins and ends at the Ranger Station. Venomous snakes can be found on both trails, but will not attack unless aggravated. **Caño Harold** is one of the best waterways in the Park for caiman, turtle, monkey, and kingfisher sightings.

The best way to explore the park is by canoe or kayak on its numerous canals and rivers. Although it's possible to go alone, hiring a guide makes for a much more informative and fun experience. Keep in mind, however, that guides abound in Tortuguero, and the competition between guides can be fierce. If you want a particular guide, stick with them, even if competitors try to mislead you. Most guided boat tours cost about ₡8700 (US$15) per person, plus park entry fees. The hike to the top of Cerro Tortuguero offers one of the most spectacular views of Parque Nacional Tortuguero, but is under-frequented due to its location across the canals from the village. Guided tours of the hike last about 3hr. and include transportation (¢11,600, US$20 per person).

Tinamon Tours (☎2709 8004 or 8842 6561; www.tinamontours.de), in the purple house 100m past Cabinas Tortuguero. Owner Bárbara Hartung leads canoe, hiking, and village tours in English, French, German, and Spanish. She prefers groups of 4-5 people. Tours ¢2900 (US$5) per hr. per person. Book several days in advance as tours fill up quickly.

Mundo Natural Tours (☎8341 1359 or 8811 7919), next to the cafe. Owners Jorge and David offer canoe trips (¢8700, US$15), turtle night walks (¢11,600, US$20), a frog night tour on private trails (¢8700, US$15), and an 8hr. "extreme adventure" tour (¢34,800, US$60).

Bony Scott (☎2709 8139 or 8320 5232), 50m south of the docks. Offers canoe tours each morning (3hr.; ¢145,000, US$25, includes park entrance fee). Kayak rentals ¢9800/US$18 per day; includes park entrance fee.

TURTLE WATCHING. The park's feature presentation is the nightly *deshove*, when turtles come to lay their eggs. The female turtle emerges from the sea and makes her way up the sand, pausing frequently to check for danger. When she finds the perfect spot, she uses her flippers to dig a body pit about 1ft. deep, and then a smaller pit for her eggs. After laying her eggs and using her flippers to bury them in the sand, she leaves them, never seeing the final product. The intriguing process lasts about 2hr.

Visitors must be with a guide certified by the park (ask to see a license). The beaches are guarded by 18 rangers whose sole job is to find and protect the turtles; if you try to watch the *deshove* without a guide, they will throw you out. (Tours leave nightly around 8 and 10pm. ¢11,600/US$20 per person. Park entrance ticket required for beaches south of Cuatro Esquinas Ranger Station.)

Talk to any of the guides mentioned above to arrange a tour or ask around town to find an experienced local guide. It is best to find a guide in town before 4pm because the guides must purchase permits before the park closes. Wear good walking shoes and dark clothing (light clothes may scare the turtles). Flashlights are useful for the hike to the beach, but cameras and flashlights cannot be turned on once at the beach, as the light disturbs the turtles and causes them to stop the nesting process. Make sure to bring a bottle of water along with you, as some of the hikes are upwards of 2km long, and you may end up waiting up to an hour for the first turtle to arrive. Official park rules state that once a tour group has seen the egg-laying process, they must leave, regardless of whether or not the two hours have elapsed. The park rangers take any offenses very seriously and may deny future entry to any visitor who violates the rules.

ECO-FRIENDLY TOURS. Visitors should always exercise responsibility and sensitivity when exploring the wildlife. Official park rules require boats to switch from gas to electric motors, which do not disturb the animals as much as the roar from loud gas engines. Tour boats should also glide along the canals extremely slowly to avoid causing wakes, which disrupt animal and insect life on the shores. Most tour guides observe these rules, but some ignore them for financial reasons. As an informed and eco-sensitive tourist, do your best to ask non-rule-abiding guides to slow down and be quiet.

 CERRO TORTUGUERO AND CAÑO PALMA BIOLOGICAL STATION. Located just off the canals en route to Tortuguero Village from Pavona, **Caño Palma**

Biological Station offers similar naturalist attractions and fauna to Tortuguero without the large numbers of tourists. Staffed by a small group of employees and volunteers from the non-profit **Canadian Organization for Tropical Education and Rainforest Conservation (COTERC),** the station has numerous hiking trails for day visitors and opportunities for long-term volunteer work. Though technically part of Barra del Colorado Wildlife Refuge, the entrance to Caño Palma is more easily accessed from Pavona or Tortuguero. (☎2709 8052; www.coterc.org. 1st week ₡145,000/US$250, each additional week ₡104,400/US$180; includes dorm-style lodging, meals, hiking, and pickup from Cariari or Tortuguero. Station admission ₡1160/US$2.)

From Pavona, take the boat heading for Tortuguero and ask to be dropped off at the station (30min.; 9am, 1:30pm; ₡1600). From Tortuguero, catch any of the boats heading back to Pavona and ask to be dropped off at the station (30min.; 6, 11:30am, 3pm; ₡1600).

NICARAGUA

Nicaragua, known as the "land of lakes and volcanoes," is a dream come true for many travelers: a tropical paradise largely undiscovered by tourists, complete with picturesque colonial towns, spectacular natural phenomena, and a vibrant, welcoming population. At peace for more than a decade, Nicaragua is shedding its reputation from the Contra War of the 1980s, and you'll find that outside the messy urban jungle of Managua, the country clearly deserves recognition as one of the most beautiful and fascinating places on the continent.

Though Nicaragua is the most populous country in Central America (with 5.5 million people), its land mass (also largest in the region) makes it one of the least densely populated. More than 90% of citizens live in the Pacific lowlands and less than 15% of its territory. Unfortunately, it also remains the poorest country in the region, in part due to political unrest over the past few decades, and also because of the devastation unleashed by Hurricane Mitch in November 1998. As the tourism industry is practically nonexistent in many parts of the country, exploration requires initiative and courage. Volcanoes on the Pacific coast, beaches on the Caribbean, and tracts of rainforest dwarf even Costa Rica's park system, and yet remain largely untouched. Those willing to leave the tourist trail and tolerate fewer amenities will find Nicaraguan destinations extremely rewarding.

ESSENTIALS

PASSPORTS, VISAS, AND CUSTOMS.
Passport. Required of all visitors. Must be valid for a full 6 months after arrival.
Visa (p. 6). Not required of citizens from the US, UK, EU, Canada, Australia, New Zealand, and Ireland. However, a tourist card (US$5) is required of all visitors; good for 30 days.
Onward Ticket. Required of all visitors.
Work Permit. Required for all foreigners planning to work in Nicaragua.
Required Vaccinations. Travelers who have visited nations with endemic yellow fever need proof of vaccination.
Driving Permit. Valid driver's license from your home country or an International Driving Permit required.
Departure Tax. US$32.

EMBASSIES AND CONSULATES

For a list of embassies in Nicaragua, see the **Practical Information** section for Managua (p. 178).

Canada: Consulate, 4870 Doherty Avenue, Montréal, PQ H4V (☎+1 514-484-8250).

NZ: Consulate, 50 Clonbern Road Auckland, 1005 (☎+64 9373 7599).

UK: Embassy, Suite 31, Vicarage House, 58-60 Kensington Church Street London W8 4DP (☎+44 020 7938 2373).

US: Embassy, 1627 New Hampshire Avenue NW, Washington DC 20009 (☎+1 202-939-6570). **Consulates** located in Houston, Los Angeles, Miami, New York, and other American cities.

VISA INFORMATION

All visitors must purchase a **tourist card** (US$5) upon entering Nicaragua. Countries with which Nicaragua has a *visa librado* agreement (US, UK, select European countries) may then stay up to 90 days. Citizens of Canada, Australia, and New Zealand may only stay for 30 days with a tourist card. However, extensions are often permitted upon arrival. The often dysfunctional website of the **Ministry of Immigration and Foreign Affairs** (www.migracion. gob.ni) can provide more details.

For those wishing to **work** or **study** in Nicaragua, a **resident visa** is required. To apply for residency, travelers may enter with a passport and obtain a letter from the school or employer. This, plus a medical certificate, birth certificate, and police record should be submitted to the Immigration Office in Managua.

NICARAGUA

TOURIST OFFICES

The **Instituto Nicaragüense de Turismo (INTUR; ☎**+505 254-5191; www.intur.gob.ni or www.visitnicaragua.com) offers resources for travelers to Nicaragua, including suggestions on destinations and accommodations. The websites aren't very good; it might be worth a trip to the office in Managua.

MONEY

CÓRDOBAS(C)	AUS$1 = C15.3	C1 = AUS$0.07
	CDN$1 = C17.5	C1 = CDN$0.06
	EUR€1 = C27.1	C1 = EUR€0.04
	NZ$1 = C12.2	C1 = NZ$0.08
	UK£1 = C31.0	C1 = UK£0.03
	US$1 = C19.1	C1 = US$0.05

The currency chart above is based on August 2009 exchange rates. The Nicaraguan unit of currency is the **córdoba** (C). There are 100 **centavos** to one *córdoba*. Colloquially, *córdobas* are sometimes referred to as *pesos* and 10 *centavos* are referred to as one *real*. Coins come in 1 and 5 *córdoba* pieces. Large bills are hard to break. US dollars are usually accepted and welcome at larger banks, hotels, stores, and even street vendors or markets. Changing dollars to *córdobas* is never a problem, and most banks will exchange at the official rate. Nicaragua's **coyotes,** guys on street corners with a calculator in one hand and a wad of bills in the other, will also change dollars at comparable rates. This is technically illegal. Though the black market is usually not dangerous, *Let's Go* does not recommend you interact with *coyotes*. Avoid changing currency at night, and make sure bills are genuine.

Many Nicaraguan cities have at least one bank that changes **traveler's checks.** Watch out for long lines, forms, and service charges. Most hotels and restaurants do not accept traveler's checks, though some take credit cards. Coyotes are less willing to change traveler's checks than cash. Most cities have **Western Union** offices, but some still route their orders by phone to Managua, sometimes with a one-day delay. **ATMs** are found in Managua and most other big cities. ATMs are linked to Visa, Master Card, American Express, and Cirrus. There's no withdrawal charge, but there is a 2000C maximum withdrawal per day. Tipping policies vary—use discretion. For more info, see **Tipping and Bargaining,** p. 9.

PRICE DIVERSITY

Our researchers list establishments in order of value from best to worst, honoring our favorites with the Let's Go thumbpick (🖐). Because the cheapest price is not always the best value, we have incorporated a system of price ranges based on a rough expectation of what you will spend. For **accommodations,** we base our range on the cheapest price for which a single traveler can stay for one night. For **restaurants,** we estimate the average amount one traveler will spend in one sitting. The following table tells you what you'll *typically* find in Panama at the corresponding price range, but keep in mind that no system can allow for the quirks of individual establishments.

ACCOMMODATIONS	RANGE	WHAT YOU'RE *LIKELY* TO FIND
❶	Under C118 (Under US$6)	Hammocks and rented mattresses in some hostels; you'll be providing the sheets.
❷	C118-237 (US$6-12)	Dorms at hostels in tourist-heavy areas and single rooms in lower-end family hotels. Bathrooms are usually shared.
❸	C257-395 (US$13-20)	Nicer family hotels and some singles at larger hotels. You should definitely expect a private bathroom, and amenities such as cable TV and complimentary breakfast.
❹	C415-890 (US$20-45)	Large rooms with all the amenities as a ❸; possibly phone access or Wi-Fi.
❺	Over C890 (Over US$45)	Large, upscale hotels and chains. This should be the best of the best. Sizeable rooms, big beds, and all the perks you could want.

FOOD	RANGE	WHAT YOU'RE *LIKELY* TO FIND
❶	Under C59 (Under US$3)	Probably street food or smaller meals from local *comedors* (street vendors). You aren't going to get high quality foodstuffs or particularly exotic flavors, but these establishments are a good idea if you're hungry and low on cash.
❷	C59-99 (US$3-5)	Meals from local restaurants, usually serving typical Nicaraguan fare or regional dishes.
❸	C118-178 (US$6-9)	Local favorites and fast food restaurants imported from the US or elsewhere. A greasy, oversized, American hamburger? Yep, it's a bit more down here.
❹	C198-257 (US$10-13)	More upscale restaurants that have a wider selection of dishes and more exotic flavoring. You should also be able to find international options.
❺	Over C257 (Over US$13)	This should be gourmet, exquisitely prepared food in a restaurant that prides itself on ambiance. A dress code may be imposed, and there's likely to be an extensive bar. Enjoy!

NICARAGUA

COSTS

Accommodations in Nicaragua are notably more expensive than those in other parts of Central America. While basic rooms and dorms can certainly be found for under 100C, more safe and comfortable lodgings are 150C-200C. Food is cheap, with *típico* (a standard meal) usually 15C-30C. While the assiduous traveler may be able to scrape by on 200C-300C per day, a safer bet would be 400C-500C, excluding transportation.

TRANSPORTATION

Buses are the primary mode of transportation in Nicaragua. Most of Nicaragua's bus fleet is composed of **"chicken buses,"** yellow school buses retired from North America. Buses usually leave from one main terminal in town (except Managua, where there are five terminals), and each terminal has a small office with info on schedules. Nearly every town and certainly every city has a local bus system.

For more information on driving in Nicaragua, see **Essentials,** p. 5. Within cities, **taxis** are the easiest mode of transport.

La Costeña (☎+505 263-2142; www.lacostena.com.ni) offers flights to several destinations in Nicaragua, including Bluefields, the Corn Islands, Puerto Cabezas, and San Carlos. The main office is in Managua, but most travel agencies sell tickets.

BORDER CROSSINGS

Travelers can cross into Nicaragua by land or sea. Remember to carry enough money to pay any entrance or exit fees.

COSTA RICA. There is one land crossing. **Peñas Blancas/Sapoá** is 36km southeast of Rivas, near Liberia, Costa Rica (p. 107). There is also a river crossing at **Los Chiles,** south of San Carlos.

HONDURAS. There are three land crossings. **Guasaule** is 77km north of Chinandega, near Choluteca, Honduras. **San Marcos/El Espino** is 25km west of Somoto, near Choluteca, Honduras. **Las Manos** is 25km north of Ocotal, and 150km east of Tegus, Honduras. It's also possible to cross by boat via the Caribbean port town of **Puerto Cabezas.**

SAFETY

As always, you should stay alert and check the latest travel advisories before departing. Managua, like any large city, demands a certain degree of caution and common sense, especially to avoid pickpockets. Touristed areas see a lot of petty crime; poorer neighborhoods and political demonstrations are best avoided entirely. Avoid traveling alone in rural areas. Sporadic armed violence is reported throughout the country, and bandits have been known to operate on the roads, especially in the rural northeast. See **Safety and Health,** p. 168, for more info.

HEALTH

Prophylaxis for **malaria** is recommended for travelers going to the outskirts of Managua and other rural areas.

LIFE AND TIMES

HISTORY

FROM INDIGENOUS TO INDEPENDENT (PRE-COLUMBIAN–AD 1838). Before the arrival of the Spanish, three distinct cultural groups inhabited the territory known today as Nicaragua: the **Niquirano**, the **Chorotega**, and the **Chontal**. Columbus was the first European to visit, coasting by in 1502. In 1524, the rival towns of Granada and León were founded, marking the beginning of permanent Spanish settlement. The Spaniards also gave Nicaragua its name, likely after powerful Niquirano chief Nicarao. Great Britain entered the scene in 1655 when it claimed authority over the Caribbean-facing **Mosquito Coast** (named both for the local Miskito tribe and for the pesky blood-sucking insects). Nicaragua remained a Spanish colony until 1821, when a wave of revolutions swept through Central America. It was then that Nicaragua joined the United Provinces of Central America. Only with the collapse of that union in 1838 did Nicaragua gain full autonomy.

ANGLO-AMERICAN ADVENTURING (1838–1857). After the Spanish departed, British and American influence grew in Nicaragua. In 1847, American transportation magnate **Cornelius Vanderbilt** established the Accessory Transit Company, which carried thousands of prospectors through Nicaragua to California during the Gold Rush of the 1850s. In 1855, American freebooter **William Walker** took advantage of domestic Nicaraguan strife. Invited by liberals in León to help capture the conservative capital at Granada, Walker decided to stick around. Soon, he had taken control of the national army and declared himself president. But in 1857 when Walker drew Vanderbilt's ire by seizing property from the transit company, the combined forces of the British Navy and four Central American governments expelled him from Nicaragua.

AUTOCRATS AND ASSASSINATIONS (1857–1979). The city of Managua, a geographic compromise between León and Granada, was selected as the capital after Walker's forced departure. Conservatives held power in Managua until an 1893 liberal revolt installed dictator José Santos Zelaya in power. Zelaya's actions included driving the British out of the Mosquito Coast and offering Japan canal-building rights in Nicaragua, drawing the ire of the US government, which proceeded to consequently sponsor the first of many rebellions in 1909 to overthrow Zelaya. US Marines remained in the country from 1912 until 1933, when they departed after a gruesome six-year struggle against revolutionaries under General Augusto Sandino. In their wake, they left the brutal US-trained militia, the **Guardia Nacional,** in the hands of **Anastasio Somoza García** (a.k.a. "Tacho"), who had Sandino assassinated in 1934 and promptly assumed dictatorial power. The Somoza family ruled brutally for the next half century, repressing their opposition through torture, murder, and "disappearances." In 1972, a major earthquake struck, killing some 10,000 Nicaraguans and destroying 90% of Managua. Sadly, the ruling Somoza dictator, Anastasio Somoza Debayle, embezzled most the international aid dollars: his estimated worth rose to US$400 million as his country sunk further into poverty. Finally, in 1979, a popular revolution against the Somozas began in earnest. The revolt was led by the socialist **Frente Sandinista de Liberación Nacional (FSLN),** which took its name after the assassinated Sandino. By the time the Sandinistas took the capital on July 19, 1979, the revolution had cost around 50,000 lives and left 500,000 homeless.

SANDINISTAS AND CONTRAS (1979–1990). In the depths of Cold War anxiety, US President Ronald Reagan envisaged communist trouble lurking behind the Sandinista government. US money and CIA expertise began pouring in to assist the actions of counter-revolutionary groups, known as the **Contras**, against the leftist Sandinistas. The struggle plunged Nicaragua back into chaos. Over 30,000 were killed amid rampant human-rights violations, food and supply shortages, and staggering 30,000% inflation. Despite more than US$100 million of US aid and CIA agents mining Nicaraguan harbors, the Contras failed to overthrow the government. The election of opposition candidate **Violeta Chamorro** in 1990 over incumbent Daniel Ortega ended Sandinista rule democratically, and the majority of the Contras disbanded.

NICARAGUA

TODAY

Though Nicaragua still suffers today from the physical and economic destruction of the 20th century, it appears to have secured a modest level of domestic tranquility. Chamorro's presidency saw an effective restoration of peace in the early 1990s after she reintegrated former fighters into society with unconditional amnesties and an extensive campaign to buy back and destroy weapons used in the war. The end of the fighting also brought relative economic stability. Unfortunately, this stability did not lead to prosperity. In 1998, Hurricane Mitch dealt the country another devastating blow by wreaking a billion dollars of damage, killing 3000, and displacing 870,000 Nicaraguans from their homes. Though **President Arnoldo Alémán** managed to lead the country through the storm, he was convicted after leaving office of embezzling US$100 million with the help of his family and was sentenced to 20 years in prison in 2003.

In 2006, Daniel Ortega was re-elected President at the head of the still-powerful Sandinista party. Though Ortega had run as the Sandinista candidate in every presidential election since 1990, this marked the first time he and his party had captured the nation's highest office since the end of the civil war. Despite gaining only 38% of the vote, Ortega held a ten-point lead over his closest opponent, a margin that enabled him to narrowly avoid a runoff, one of the electoral reforms introduced in 2000.

As his commitment to the capitalist economic status quo demonstrates, the socialist Ortega has moved towards the political center since the 1980s. Such policies have not, however, removed this president from the scrutiny of the United States: his friendly overtures to Iran and socialist Venezuela have invited deep suspicion in Washington. Ortega has endeavored to craft a more prominent international persona for Nicaragua in other ways as well. In June 2008, he led a failed diplomatic bid for Nicaragua to assume the presidency of the United Nations General Assembly.

Ortega's international ambitions have done little to quell domestic tensions. Only a few months after the failed UN maneuver, riots erupted in the streets after opposition parties claimed that the Sandinistas had rigged hundreds of mayoral elections across the country. The governing party incited further controversy in January of 2009 when the Nicaraguan Supreme Court overturned former President Alémán's corruption conviction. Opponents claimed the ruling had been rigged in a political deal which let Alémán off in exchange for congressional support from his Liberal Party.

ECONOMY AND GOVERNMENT

Despite a massive influx of international aid in the 21st century, Nicaragua's economy is still on the rocks. Unemployment afflicts more than half of the country's population. The per capita income of the country is one of the lowest in the Western Hemisphere, with Haiti's falling just above. The **Heavily Indebted Poor Countries Initiative** provided around US$4.5 billion in debt relief for Nicaragua in 2004, followed by more help from a **Poverty Reduction and Growth Facility** program headed by the International Monetary Fund in 2007. Agriculture remains important, employing a third of the country's working population even after the damage reaped by human and natural disasters from 1980 to 2000. Coffee exports and tourism constitute the nation's top two industries. The textile and clothing industry—together comprising almost 60% of Nicaragua's exports—round out the list of Nicaragua's most profitable economic endeavors.

The political scene in Nicaragua is currently dominated by the socialist **Sandinistas**, who hold the presidency and a plurality of seats in the legislative

National Assembly. Their main rivals are the two liberal parties, the **Constitu-
tionalist Liberal Party (PLC)** and the **Nicaraguan Liberal Alliance (ALN).** The latter split
from the PLC in 2005 over controversy concerning Alémán's continued power
despite his corruption conviction and the political alliance (named "El Pacto")
with Ortega. Recent proposals to transform the Nicaraguan government into a
parliamentary government with a separate president and prime minister may
enable both men to run Nicaragua simultaneously.

PEOPLE

DEMOGRAPHICS

Nicaragua has a population of 5.7 million people whose racially and ethnically
diverse composition reflects nation's rich history. *Mestizos*, who compose
almost 70% of the country's population, almost exclusively occupy the western half of the country, living in and around urban centers. Descendents of
European settlers make up about 17% of the population, while descendents
of African slaves comprise another 5%. Only 5% of the modern-day citizenry is
accounted for by the nation's indigenous peoples, the largest groups of which
are the Miskito, Rama, and Sumu.

LANGUAGE

Like most countries in Central America, Nicaragua's primary language is Spanish—or **Nicañol**, as Nicaraguan Spanish is sometimes called—which is spoken
by 90% of the population. Although there is some English along the Caribbean
coast due to lingering British influences and American commercialization, it is
better to be safe than sorry and always have your translator—human, diction-
ary, or otherwise—at hand. The Nicaraguan accent and dialect are different
from those of other Spanish-speaking nations. *Nicas* are likely to drop the "s"
from many words, making it harder for you to understand but easier for them to
speak. Though much less common, the indigenous languages of Somo, Rama,
and Miskito are still used, the latter being the most prevalent of the three.

RELIGION

Religion, predominantly **Roman Catholicism**, is an important part of Nicaraguan culture. Aside from Catholics and indigenous peoples, who follow their own religions, the rest of Nicaragua's inhabitants are largely
Protestant. Though still very much a minority religion, Protestantism has
expanded rapidly in Nicaragua since the 1990s.

CULTURE

MUSIC. An important trade stop, Nicaragua is home to a blend of cultures
and nationalities. Nicaragua's music and dance hail from a wide array of cultural origins including traditions of indigenous tribes, European settlers, and
African slaves. Surprisingly, all musical genres are not only accepted but also
embraced in this country. Home to such popular singers as Reggaeton artists
Torombolo and J. Smooth, Nicaraguans listen primarily to modern Latin American music as well as Reggae groups like Kali Boom. One is likely to see people
dancing to another nation's popularized beats, like Colombia's *cumbia* or the
Dominican Republic's *bachata*, in addition to the *salsa* and *mambo*, but there

is no shortage of local musical flair. The *marimba*, a percussion instrument with keys arranged like a piano, is a staple of native bands whose music style embodies the soulful ethnic core of Nicaraguan culture.

LITERATURE. Nicaragua's literary history can be traced to pre-colonial times where its oral traditions of myth and folklore originated. The most famous Nicaraguan story, first orated by an anonymous author, was passed down from the 16th century until it was finally recorded in the early 1900s. This satire, called "El Güegüense," depicts Nicaragua before Columbian settlement. The story is a masterful rendering of indigenous dance, customs, and music. Literacy rates have jumped in recent decades thanks to the Sandista's literacy campaign of the 1980s. Few modern Nicaraguan writers gain international literary recognition. Modernist poet Rubén Darío (1867-1916), whose poetry started the "Modernismo" movement in Nicaraguan literature, is an exception to this trend, as is Pedro Joaquin Chamorro (1924-1978), whose activism against the Somoza dynasty led to his assassination in 1978.

VISUAL ARTS. Nicaragua's art history has experienced remarkable change with the country's political revolutions. Its native arts are essentially unpracticed now, except for a few remaining rituals observed in isolated indigenous areas. Most of the art one sees today is of a style pioneered by Ernesto Cardenal, a Sandinista priest and leader. He created a small community on the island of Solentiname, where he encouraged Nicaraguans to create experimental and imaginative paintings and murals. While the creative styles of these pieces were not traditional, Cardenal's technical influence did include some features typical of indigenous art such as strong emotion and bold colors. Though much of this art was censored and eventually burned by the National Guard after the 1979 Revolution, this inventive, colorful painting style became Nicaragua's most popular form of visual art.

LAND

GEOGRAPHY. It may be the largest country in Central America, but Nicaragua is only about the size of New York State. The country has three distinct regions: the **Pacific Lowlands**, the **North-Central Highlands**, and the **Atlantic lowlands.** The Pacific Lowlands are hot, fertile plains punctuated by the bubbling volcanoes of the Marrabio mountain range. The North-Central Highlands are marked by rugged mountain terrain and mixed oak and pine forests. The Atlantic lowlands are fondly and all-too truthfully known as La Costa De Mosquitos (the Coast of Mosquitos). As well as the majority of its pesky, blood-sucking insects, these lowlands contain the majority of Nicaragua's famously stunning rainforests.

WILDLIFE. The wildlife of Nicaragua is unlike that of any other country. Perhaps best known for its sea turtles, thousands of whom lay eggs on the country's beaches each year, Nicaragua is also inhabited by about 700 bird species, jaguars, Tamandus anteaters, and fresh-water bull sharks. Nicaragua is also home to the three-toed sloth, a creature that moves so slowly that it is literally impossible to miss.

WEATHER. Nicaragua's climate is primarily tropical, especially during the dry season which lasts from December to May, when the temperature can reach 100°F. Though you'll still be hot and sweaty from June to November, the temperature will drop toward the 80s. The northern mountain regions boast a much cooler climate, but one still warm enough to allow frolicking in Nicaragua's beautiful outdoors.

NICARAGUA

CUSTOMS AND ETIQUETTE

GREETINGS

Nicaraguans are friendly people, but they cherish their personal space. A simple handshake will suffice between men and generally between men and women as well. A brief hug and a single cheek kiss are usually reserved for close friends and family. Depending on whom you are interacting with, don't be offended if they don't look you in the eye or try to shake your hand. Typically, people of lower classes will not make eye contact upon formal introduction. But don't be frightened if you catch some staring at you, especially in rural areas; *Nicas* people-watch with the best of them.

GESTURES AND MANNERS

Don't be afraid to use the finger! No, not *that* one—a finger wag is a common way to motion toward something, such as a taxi or a passing bus, and rubbing fingers together usually signifies you want to pay for something.

Nicas value politeness and avoid conflict whenever they can. Try not to say "no" if you can handle the consequences of saying "yes," and never take off your shoes unless you are told to do so.

FOOD AND DRINK

Nicaraguan cuisine is based on rice, beans, meat, and tortillas. Nicaragua is not for the heart-healthy or carb-wary, as everything is cooked in oil and fried into oblivion. Though this may seem scary at first, it is undeniably delicious. These starch-heavy loads are balanced with an abundance of tropical fruit and *ensaladas* of cabbage, tomatos, and beets. Even fruit can be fried, and plantains are no exception—they are often served greasy and sweet as *maduros* or crispy and brittle as *tostones*. For the thirsty, national beers can be found everywhere, and it wouldn't be surprising if they came dripping out of your faucet. **Flor de Cana**, the favorite local rum, is produced from evaporated sugarcane and will add an extra punch to any drink.

BEYOND TOURISM

VOLUNTEERING

Building New Hope, 106 Overton Lane, Pittsburgh, PA 15217, USA (☎412-421-1625; www.buildingnewhope.org). Volunteers must be able to commit to the organization for at least a month, and should have an intermediate knowledge of Spanish. You may work as a teaching assistant, animal technician, chef, or tutor to a teenage student. For details on volunteering, email donna@buildingnewhope.org.

Experiential Learning International (ELI), 2828 N. Speer Blvd. Suite 230, Denver, CO 80211, USA (☎+303-321-8278; www.eliabroad.org). Offers Spanish language immersion programs for students of all levels. ELI offers fun and low-key Spanish lessons in Granada, as well as a 2-week "Expanded" Spanish program including both practical and theoretical lessons. 1-week Spanish lessons US$250; 2-week Expanded Spanish US$725; each additional week US$200-380.

NICARAGUA

Proyecto Mosaico, 3a Av. Nte. #3, Casa de Mito, Antigua, Guatemala (☎502 7832 0955; www.promosaico.org). A German nonprofit organization offering volunteer programs in Nicaragua and Guatemala. Project Mosaic Nicaragua (PMN) works to combat the poverty in Nicaragua, a nation politically aligned with Germany. Volunteer projects include working with the elderly and undernourished or disabled children. Visit the "Volunteering" section of the website to request information.

VISA INFORMATION. To visit Nicaragua, you must have a valid passport, and will have to pay US$5 for a tourist card upon arrival. If you plan to stay for more than 90 days, you need permission from Nicaraguan immigration authorities. Also, there is a departure fee of US$32 that may be included in the price of the airline ticket.

STUDYING

AMERICAN PROGRAMS

Helping Hands in Health Education, 948 Pearl Street, Boulder, CO 80302, USA (☎303 448 1811; www.helpinghandsusa.org). An organization that works to reduce the child mortality rate in Nicaragua, offering volunteer programs in both summer and winter. Volunteers work in a local health clinic. US$2700 (includes travel, room and board, and scheduled excursions).

NICARAGUAN PROGRAMS

The Institute for Central American Development Studies (ICADS), Dept. 826, P.O. Box 025216, Miami, FL 33102-5216, USA (www.icads.org). In Nicaragua, ICADS has a field course in resource management and sustainable development, as well as a semester-long internship and research opportunity. Tuition, room and board (without lunch included) US$9850. Programs also available in Costa Rica.

LANGUAGE SCHOOLS

La Mariposa Spanish School and Eco-Hotel (☎505 418-4638; www.mariposaspanish-school.com). A truly unique learning environment for Nicaraguans and expats, La Mariposa offers a relaxed learning environment where you choose the duration of your stay. Offers a variety of outings on foot, public transportation, and horseback. Information on volunteer opportunities is also available on the website. US$300 per week per person; US$1000 per month per person.

Viva Spanish School, (☎505 2 270 2339; www.vivaspanishschool.com). Owned by an American living in Nicaragua, Viva Spanish School in Managua offers intensive and semi-intensive Spanish language courses. Homestays are offered for US$115 per week. Provides a fixed schedule of affordable activities and tours (US$2-10). Spanish courses US$90-175 per person per week. Also offers online Skype courses for US$11 per hour.

THERE'S MORE? For more information on volunteer and study abroad opportunities in other areas of Central America, see **Beyond Tourism, p. 35.** To learn more about opportunities all over the world, visit our website at ▧ **www.letsgo.com**.

MANAGUA

With a series of massive, disorganized *barrios* in place of tall buildings, the city feels more like an overgrown suburb than the capital of Central America's largest country. Downtown Managua was leveled by an earthquake in 1972; what remained was then left to the mercy of the revolution. Today, empty dirt lots surround shopping centers and bustling markets border gutted buildings. Nonetheless, Managua remains the entertainment, commercial, and transportation hub of Nicaragua. Although it is less safe than other parts of Nicaragua and its cultural life is suffering—many museums and galleries have closed due to inadequate funds—Managua does have bright spots: the famous Teatro Rubén Darío and the impressive Palacio Nacional.

✈ INTERCITY TRANSPORTATION

FLIGHTS

Managua International Airport (Augusto Sandino International Airport), 12km east of the city. Accessible by bus. All buses headed to Roberto Huembes pass by the airport, just ask the driver to drop you off on the way. **International** airlines include: **Aerocaribbean** (☎2277 5191); **Aeroméxico** (☎2266 6997); **American** (☎22559090); **Contitnental** (☎2278 7033); **Copa** (☎2267 0045); **Delta** (☎2254 8130); **Helinica** (☎2263 2142); **Iberia**(☎506 441 2591); **Nature Air** (506 358 2395); **Serper AA** (☎2270 7863); **Spirit** (☎2233 2884 86); **Taca** (☎2266 3136). **Domestic flights** are all on **La Costeña** airlines. Open M-F 7am-6pm, Sa 7am-3pm, Su 8am-3pm. Counter M-F 5am-5pm, Sa 5am-3pm, Su 5am-3pm.

INTERNATIONAL BUSES

International buses can be found at the **Ticabus Bus Station** (www.ticabus.com. two blocks east of the Antiguo Cine Dorado, Barrio Bolonia). Buses travel to: **San José, Costa Rica** (9-10hr., 6am, C480) via **Granada** (9-10hr., noon, C480); **San Pedro Sula, Honduras** (12-13hr., 5am, C780); **San Salvador, El Salvador** (11-12hr., 5am, C730); **Tegucigalpa, Honduras** (7-8hr., 5am, C480).

DOMESTIC BUSES

Buses depart from four scattered markets: **Mercado Roberto Huembes** and **Mercado Israel Lewites** in the southwest part of the city, and **Mercado Ivan Montenegro** and **Mercado Mayoreo** in the eastern part of the city. It's best to take a taxi or a local bus from one station to another. Note that fares and times for buses change often, so you should always double check with the driver when you board.

Ivan Montenegro: (☎2253 2879). To **Bluefields** (6¾hr., 9pm, C350) and **El Rama** (5hr., 9pm, C150).

Israel Lewites: To: **Carazo** (1¼hr., every 20min. 5:10am-7pm, C18); **Chinandega** (2hr., every 30min. 4:30am-6pm, C50); **Corinto** (2¾hr., 6:30am, C65); **Jinotepe** (1¼hr., every 20min. 5am-7pm, C18); **León** (2½hr., every 45min. 5am-7pm, C30); **Masatepe** (1¾hr.; 1, 3, 5:30, 6:10pm; C20); **Pochomil** (1¼hr., every 20min. 5:10am-7pm, C22).

Mayoreo: Buses bound for the northern half of Nicaragua can be caught from the **Rigoberto Cabezas** bus station, more commonly known as **Mercado Mayoreo** (which is the name of the market surrounding the station). To: **Boaco** (every 30min. 5:30am-6:30pm, C30); **Estelí** (every hr. 5:45am-5:45pm, C60); **Jinotega,** (every 1½hr. 4am-5:30pm, C75); **Matagalpa** (every hr. 3:30am-6pm, C60); **Nueva Guinea,** (every hr. 3:30am-9:30pm, C150); **Rama** (every 2hr. 5am-10pm, C120); **Somoto** (7:15, 9:45am, 12:45, 1:45, 3:45, 4:45pm; C78); **Uigalpa** (every hr. 5:30am-5:30pm, C30).

Roberto Huembes: To: **Rivas** (1½hr., every 30min. 4am-6pm, C50); **Granada** (1½hr., 6am-8pm, C20); **Masaya** (1hr., 6am-8pm, C14); **Masatepe** (1hr., 6am-8pm, C16); **Tipitapa** (30-45min., 6am-8pm, C8).

OTHER TRANSPORTATION

Rental Car Companies: All rental car company offices can be found inside the international wing of the Managua International Airport.

Avis (☎2233 3013; www.avis.com.ni). Open daily 5am-last flight. AmEx/D/MC/V.

Alamo (☎2244 3718; www.alamocentroamerica.com). Open daily 6am-9:30pm. AmEx/D/MC/V.

Dollar Rent a Car (☎2233 2192; www.dollar.com.ni). Open daily 5am-9pm. AmEx/D/MC/V.

Hertz (☎2233 1237; www.hertz.com). Open daily 5am-9pm. AmEx/D/MC/V.

Budget (☎2263 1222; www.budget.com.ni). Open daily until last flight.

▟ ORIENTATION

UPON ARRIVAL

Arriving by air, you'll land at the **Managua International Airport,** also known as the **César Augusto Sandino International Airport,** 12km east of the city on the **Carretera Norte.** Taxis from the airport to hotel-rich barrio **Martha Quezada** cost between C200 and 400, with prices rising after dark. For a less expensive ride to your hostel, walk 100m right or left after exiting the terminal and head toward the highway where you can get a non-airport certified taxi; these guys are much cheaper (C200-300). This is not suggested if you arrive after dark, as Managua can be dangerous at night. Arriving by international bus from another Central American capital, you'll most likely be at the well-situated **Ticabus** terminal in Martha Quezada, just a few blocks from **Plaza Inter** and numerous hotels. **Sirca** buses from San José arrive in the south part of the city on **Avenida Eduardo Delgado.** Arriving by **domestic bus,** you'll find yourself at one of four markets scattered about the city. Crowded local buses go between the markets and the hotel areas; taxis are usually easier to find (C30-50).

 WATCH OUT! Managua is far from the world's safest city. Theft and muggings are common, and as a tourist you look like a walking wallet. This goes for the whole city, although the Barrio Martha Quezada is relatively safe. The city's parks and crowded streets host pickpockets and grab-and-run thiefs, so hold on to your belongings. Be especially careful at the bus stations and markets, as they are always packed with people. After sunset, the safest way to get around is by taxi, especially for women traveling alone.

LAYOUT AND ADDRESSES

Managua doesn't have street names; helpful, we know. "Addresses" are given in terms of proximity to landmarks—a Texaco station, a statue, where a cinema used to be—and their proximity to the **Rotunda. Al sur** means south, **al lago** is toward the lake and north, **arriba** is east, and **abajo** means west. For example,

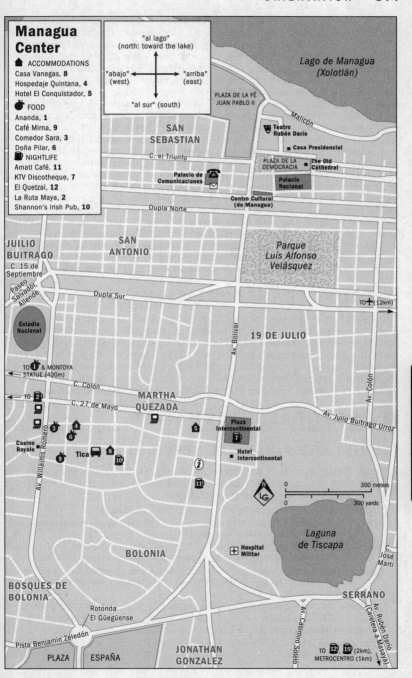

Managua Center

ACCOMMODATIONS
Casa Vanegas, 8
Hospedaje Quintana, 4
Hotel El Conquistador, 5

FOOD
Ananda, 1
Café Mirna, 9
Comedor Sara, 3
Doña Pilar, 6

NIGHTLIFE
Amatl Café, 11
KTV Discotheque, 7
El Quetzal, 12
La Ruta Maya, 2
Shannon's Irish Pub, 10

"al lago"
(north: toward the lake)

"abajo"
(west)

"arriba"
(east)

"al sur" (south)

Lago de Managua
(Xolotlán)

PLAZA DE LA FÉ
JUAN PABLO II

Malicón

SAN
SEBASTIAN

Teatro
Rubén Darío

Casa Presidencial

C. el Triunfo

PLAZA DE LA
DEMOCRACIA

The Old
Cathedral

Palacio de
Comunicaciones

Palacio
Nacional

Centro Cultural
(de Managua)

Dupla Norte

JUILIO
BUITRAGO

C. 15 de
Septiembre

SAN
ANTONIO

Parque
Luis Alfonso
Velásquez

Paseo Salvador Allende

Dupla Sur

Estadio
Nacional

TO ✈ (12km)

19 DE JULIO

Av. Bolívar

Av. Colón

TO ⑧ & MONTOYA
STATUE (400m)

C. Colón

MARTHA
QUEZADA

C. 27 de Mayo

Plaza
Intercontinental
⑦

Av. Julio Buitrago Urroz

TO ②

③ ④
⑥

⑤

Hotel
Intercontinental

Casino
Royale

⑨ Tica ⑧
⑩

ℹ

⑪

MANAGUA

Av. Williams Romero

0   300 meters
0   300 yards

Laguna
de Tiscapa

BOLONIA

Hospital
Militar

C.
José
Martí

BOSQUES DE
BOLONIA

SERRANO

Rotonda
El Güegüense

Av. Casimiro Sotelo

Av. Rubén Darío
Carretera a Masaya

Pista Benjamín Zeledón

PLAZA
ESPAÑA

JONATHAN
GONZALEZ

TO ⑫ ⑮ (2km),
METROCENTRO (1km)

"Del Tica Bus una cuadra abajo y media cuadra al lago," means from the Tica Bus Station walk one block west and half a block toward the lake (north).

Managua lies on the south shore of **Lago de Managua;** the locals call it **Lago Xolotlán.** Managua expands in all directions away from the lake. Near the *malecón* (lakefront), you will find many of Managua's sights. El viejo Catedral, La Casa Presidencial, Teatro Nacional Rubén Darío and the Rubén Darío monument are all located lake's shores. The effective center of the city is the pyramid-like Hotel Crown Plaza. Just north of the hotel is **Plaza Inter,** a US-style shopping mall complete with specialty stores, a cinema, and a food court. Just west of the Inter, **Avenida Bolívar** runs north to south 1km north from the hotel to the lakeshore and the old city center, where it meets **Teatro Rubén Darío.** Along the way, it passes the **Asemblea Nacional,** the **Bank of America** skyscraper, the **Palacio Nacional,** and the **Santo Domingo Cathedral.** Across Av. Bolívar from the Inter is the **Intur** tourist office of Managua. **Martha Quezada** is the neighborhood that houses most of Managua's budget hotels and *hospedajes.* Situated in the center of this *barrio* is the **Ticabus Station. Avenida Williams Romero,** with the now-defunct **Casino Royale,** forms the western border of Martha Quezada. The northern border of the *barrio* is formed by **Calle 27 de Mayo.** Both of these streets are larger and busier than the bumpy byways of Martha Quezada. Eight blocks south of C. 27 de Mayo, on Av. Williams Roberto, is the **Plaza de España,** home to a number of banks, several travel agencies, and a supermarket. Most of the discos, chain restaurants, and the **Metrocentro Mall** are located on the **Carretera a Masaya.**

☐ LOCAL TRANSPORTATION

Transportation in Managua is unreliable and often unsafe. Your best bet is to grab a cab, especially at night. Should you need to take a bus within the city, don't take anything valuable with you; keep what small amount of cash you do carry in a money belt or in you shoe. No matter where you go within the city limits, be sure there is a way for you to get back to your accommodation; ask your driver when and from where the last bus back departs. Getting stuck in an unfamiliar neighborhood after dark in Managua almost guarantees disaster.

◪ PRACTICAL INFORMATION

TOURIST AND FINANCIAL SERVICES

Tourist Offices: Ministerio de Turismo INTUR (☎2254 5191; www.intur.gob.ni), 2 blocks south and 1 block west of Plaza Inter. English spoken. Sells a variety of maps and guides. Open M-F 8:30am-12:30pm and 1:30-5pm.

Tours: Most sights in Nicaragua are safer when visited through tours.

Ecotours de Nicaragua, 123 Del Hotel Crowne Plaza (☎2266 8523; www.centralamericanexcursions.com), 2 block south and half a block west.

Tours Nicaragua, 110 Shell Plaza El Sol (☎2252 4035; www.toursnicaragua.com), 1 block south and 120m. Offers a variety of tour packages from ecotourism to beach vacation packages.

Ecole Travel, Planes de Altamira (☎2278 2572 or 6919; www.carelitours.com). Offers several different organized tours of Nicaragua. Packages include History and Culture, Adventure, Ecotrips, and Beaches.

Embassies: For more information see, **Essentials** p. 5. **U.S. Embassy,** Carretera Sur (☎2252 7100). Ask for the American Citizens Services Unit. Open 7:30am-4:15pm. **Canadian Embassy,** Costado Oriental de la Casa Nasareth, Una Cuadra Arriba, C. El Noval. (☎2268 0433 or 3323) Open M-F 7:30am-4:30pm, Fri 7:30am-1pm. The **Brit-**

ish Embassy in Nicaragua closed in 2004, but you can contact the **British Honorary Consul** (in Managua) in case of emergency; **Dr. José Evenor Taboada,** Taboada & Asociados, Av. Bolivar 1947, del Hospital Militar (☎2254 5454 or 3839).

Currency Exchange and Banks: There are banks located throughout Managua; almost all have **ATMs.** You can also find ATMs in most busy, commercial centers. The Plaza Inter, next to the Barrio Martha Quezada, has several ATMs outside the shopping center on the ground floor.

BanPro, Plaza Inter (☎2255 9595). Open M-F 10am-6pm, Sa 10am-noon.

BDF, Av. Bolivaracross (☎2240 3001), across the street from Plaza Inter. Open M-F 8:30am-4:30pm, Sa 8:30am-12:30pm. **24hr. ATM.**

Citibank (☎2271 9212), inside the MetroCentro Mall. Open M-F 8:30am-4:30pm, Sa 8:30am-12:30pm. **24hr. ATM** located next to the food court.

Western Union, Plaza Inter, ground floor. Open daily 10am-7pm.

SHOPPING

Markets and Malls: Metrocentro Mall, across the street from La Nueva Catedral. This is *the* mall of Managua. You can find brand name stores and eat from one of the many food court options (McDonald's, Pizza Hut, Burger King, Subway, and Quizno's). There are also ATMs.

Centro Comercial Las Américas, in Barrio Bello Horizonte. Another big shopping center, complete with food court, a multi-level shopping area, grocery store, and movie theater.

EMERGENCY AND COMMUNICATIONS

Police: (☎2277 4130, emergency 118), across the street from the MetroCentro Mall, at the Plaza del Sol. Open M-F 8am-5pm, although there is always an officer present at the station. There are 8 different Police districts within the city of Managua; in case of an emergency, contact the dispatch nearest you.

District 1: **Ciudad Sandino** (☎2269 9290 or 9318).

District 2: **Linda Vista** (☎2266 4718 or 1427).

District 3: **Altagracia** (☎2265 0651 or 0659).

District 4: **Mercado Oriental** (☎2249 8340-41 or 8342).

District 5: **Colonia Centroamérica** (☎2278 8934).

District 6: **La Subasta** (☎2233 1118 or 1621).

District 7: **San Rafael del Sur** (☎2293 3319 or 3231).

District 8: **Tipitapa** (☎2295 3229).

Pharmacy: Farmacia del Buen Pastor (☎2222 6462), 1 block north and half a block west from Ticabus. Open M-Sa 8am-6:30pm. AmEx/D/MC/V. **Medco Pharmacy** (☎2254 1000), on the bottom floor of Plaza Inter. Open daily 10am-9pm. AmEx/D/MC/V.

Hospital: Hospital Bautista (☎2249 7070 ext. 4002; www.hospitalbautistanicaragua. com), Barrio Largaespada. **Hospital Privado Salud Integral** (☎2266 1707; www.hospitalsaludintegral.com.ni), Barrio Javier Cuadra Montoya, 1 block north and 1 block west.

Internet: Western Union Internet Cafe, inside the Plaza Inter, bottom floor. Internet C30 per hr. Open daily 10am-9pm. Cash only. **Cyber A. J.** (☎2222 7030), Barrio Martha Quezada, 1 block north from Cafe Mirna. Internet C11 per hr. Open M-Sa 9am-9pm. Also offers international calls. Cash only.

Post Office: Correos Central (☎2222 1060). Edificio Jorge Navarro, to the west of Teatro Nacional Rubén Darío. Open M-F 8am-5pm, Sa 8am-noon.

⌂ ACCOMMODATIONS

Managua is a big city, so we've narrowed our search for the best accommodations to the central neighborhood of **Martha Quezada**. It's a quiet, residential neighborhood full of family-run restaurants and small- to medium- sized hotels. Here you can find everything from a backpacker's hostel for C140 to an upscale hotel for C1000. The neighborhood is close to Ticabus station, the Plaza Inter shopping center, and the tourist office INTUR. While Martha Quezada is relatively safe by Managua's standards, you should still be careful, especially at night. Bear in mind when hunting for hotels or hostels here that the Nicaraguan address system still applies—you'll be placing everything in perspective from the Ticabus. Just remember, *al lago* (to the lake) is north, *abajo* (down) is west, *arriba* (up) is east, and *al sur* (south) is to the south.

BETWEEN LOS HEROES AND THE UNIVERSITY

▨ **Hostal Dulce Sueño** (☎2228 4125), 75m west of Ticabus. Nicer than most of the hostels near the station. The common area, with yellow and green walls, has free purified water and a TV. Kitchen use. Laundry C40. Check-out noon. Rooms C160 per person. Cash only. ❷

▨ **Casa de Huespedes Santos** (☎2222 3713 or 8962 4084; www.casadehuespedes-santos.com), 1½ blocks east of Ticabus. A giant, 2-story building with great patios. All rooms have fans, baths, and small TVs. Breakfast C30-50. Internet. Check-out 10am. Rooms C140 per person. Call a day in advance to reserve. Cash only. ❷

Hotel Los Cisneros (☎2222 3535; www.hotelloscisneros.com), 1 block north and 1½ blocks east from Ticabus. All of the rooms here are essentially small apartments, and come with private bath, cable TV, a kitchenette, and Wi-Fi; some have patios with hammocks. Breakfast C60. Checkout 11am. Singles with fan C600, with A/C C900; matrimonial C800/1100. Also rents by the week and month. AmEx/D/MC/V. ❹

Hotel El Conquistador, 1 block west from INTUR. With all the hand-painted jungle murals and a garden in the courtyard, it almost feels like you've left Managua. Clean rooms, each with hot-water bath, cable TV, and a mini-refrigerator. Breakfast included. Free Wi-Fi. Checkout at noon. Singles C1100, doubles C1300, triples C1500. AmEx/D/MC/V. ❺

Hospedaje Casa Blanca (☎8637 1350), 10m north from Ticabus, right off the street from the bus station. All rooms with baths and cable TVs. Checkout 9am. Doubles C100 per person. ❶

Hospedaje El Molinito, is half block north from Ticabus. Singles with shared bath C120, doubles with shared bath C240, triples with private bath and TV C300. Cash only. ❶

Hospedaje El Viajero (☎2228 1280), half a block west from Ticabus. A light pink building, Traveler's Hostel offers basic accommodations. Singles C140 per person; the apartment (really just a large room with multiple beds) costs C200 per person. Cash only. ❷

⊙ FOOD

Nicaraguan cuisine is made out of basic ingredients—beans, rice, and corn tortillas. The *fritangas* (food joints) often offer the same dishes as the traditional Nicaraguan restaurants. There's certainly enough *gallo pinto* (rice and fried bean mixture) to go around. Still, Managua also has its fair share of international eateries. There's also a food court at the Metrocentro for those who miss their happy meals.

There is a **supermarket** on Av. Central, C. 11/13. (Open daily 6:30am-midnight. AmEx/MC/V.) You can also try **La Colonia,** in Centro Comercial Las Américas, Barrio Bello Horizonte. (☎2277 7710. Open daily 8am-9pm.)

▨ **Doña Pilar** (☎2222 6016), 1 block west and half a block north from Ticabus. A Nicaraguan culinary experience. Come by Doña Pilar's restaurant on Sunday at noon for *Baho,* a steaming hot conglomeration of all things good (meat, eggplant, yucca, plantains, and salad all cooked together in a single bowl). Large plate C40, with rice C50. Cash only. ❶

Cocina de Doña Haydée (☎2249 5494), Carretera Nte., 1 block east of La Rotunda Bello Horizonte. One of Managua's most popular traditional food spots decorated in a rancho style. Delicious House specialty *Enchiladas Doña Haydée* C45. Entrees C45-170. Open daily 7am-10pm. AmEx/D/MC/V. ❷

El Grillito 1 (&2) (☎2266 8567 or 8958 4706), across the street from INTUR. A spacious open-air porch decorated with murals of masks, faces, and half-naked women. Hot wings C70. Mixed plates C189. If it's too crowded when you arrive, don't worry—just head up the block to its twin, **El Grillito 2.** Open daily 3pm-6am. Cash only. ❷

Restaurante del Rey (☎2222 4475), 1 block west and 1 north from Ticabus. Spanish soft rock and ranchero music sets the mood here. Fruit salad C40. Open M-F 10am-10pm, Sa-Su 10am-midnight. Cash only. ❷

Bar Los Chepes (☎8649 0083), 1 block north and 2 west from Ticabus. A tin roof over a few plastic tables on the sidewalk, Bar Los Chepes doesn't have a menu—you'll just have to look at the handpainted signs on the walls. Catering to the backpacker crowd, this bar offers pancakes, french toast, and omelettes for breakfast. Steak in Jalapeño sauce C46. Open M-Sa 9am-9pm. Cash only. ❶

◎ SIGHTS

The sights in Managua surround the **Plaza de la Democracia** (formerly Plaza de la Revolución), on the northern end of Av. Bolívar, near the lake. From Martha Quezada to the plaza, walk 12 blocks north or take bus #109 from the corner of Av. Bolívar and C. Julio Buitrago. Head to the plaza for the **colorful light** show choreographed to classical music in the central fountain at 6 and 9pm nightly.

EL VIEJO CATEDRAL. This cathedral is a testament to Nicaragua's volatile geology. Nearly destroyed by the 1972 earthquake that ravaged Managua, it's now closed to the public, and for good reason—it looks as if it could fall at any moment. Despite being cracked, it remains a beautiful and poignant spot to visit. *(Plaza de la Democracia, next to La Casa Presidencial and El Palacio Nacional.)*

MUSEO NACIONAL. Occupying the first floor of the Palacio Nacional, Nicaragua's national museum showcases the country's geology, paleontology, and cultural heritage. There are some great fossils, pre-Colombian statues unearthed near Juigalpa, and costumes used in Nicaraguan folk festivals. *(Plaza de la Democracia. ☎2222 3845; www.inc.gob.ni. Open T-Sa 9am-4pm, Su 9am-3:30pm. C80. Camera use C20. Video use C40.)*

RUBÉN DARÍO MONUMENT This monument commemorates Nicaragua's national poet. A white-marble Rubén Darío stands atop a stone pillar with an angel, harp in hand, behind him. Swans and a boat with women blowing trumpets occupy the fountain below. Lines of Darío's poetry decorate the sides of the pillar upon which he stands. *(In a quiet plaza, right next to the Casa Presidencial.)*

CATEDRAL DE LA INMACULA CONCEPCIÓN. This new cathedral has certainly departed stylistically from its Gothic predecessors. An enormous, concrete box, it looks a bit like an open egg-carton, with a ceiling full of egg-shaped domes. These same domes, when viewed from the inside, have small skylights at their tops. The sign inside commemorates those who helped fund the construction of the cathedral. *(Across from the Metrocentro Mall. Open daily 7am-6pm. Mass Su 8, 11am, and 6pm.)*

TEATRO NACIONAL RUBÉN DARÍO. The largest theater in Central America, Teatro Rubén Darío is a multi-level edifice with the *salón de las cristales*, named for its pair of enormous crystal chandeliers. *(Down on the edge of Lake Managua, across from the Malécon. ☎ 2222 7426; www.tnrubendario.gob.ni. Box office open M-F 9am-5pm, or until 7pm if there's a show, Sa-Su 10am-3pm. Tours of the theater in the afternoon C20. No shorts, flip-flops, or tank tops.)*

ARBORETUM NACIONAL. Come sit and read on one of the many benches situated throughout this verdant park. An oasis in an otherwise cold and concrete city, the Aboretum is especially beautiful in March with the national flower, the *sacuanoche*, is in bloom. *(Av. Bolivar, 2 blocks north of Plaza Inter. ☎ 2222 2558. Guided tours available, call in advance. Open M-F 8am-5pm.)*

▚ NIGHTLIFE

ZONA 1

- **Bar & Restaurante Irlandés** (☎2222 6683), 1 block east and 1 south from Ticabus. A reincarnation of the once popular Shannon Bar. Fried mozzarella sticks C80. Guinness C85. Grolsch C40. An extensive liquor selection.

- **Casa de los Mejía Godoy** (☎2222 4866), on the west side of the Hotel Crown Plaza, next to Plaza Inter. A open-air bar and restaurant for musical and cultural events. Nicaraguan artists perform on stage here Th-Sa 9pm-midnight. Sit down at a table, grab a beer, and enjoy the music. Open M-W 8am-11pm, Th-Sa 8am-midnight. AmEx/D/MC/V.

PACIFIC LOWLANDS

The Pacific lowlands stretch from Chinandega in the north to Rivas in the south. A long string of volcanoes along the coast has made the lowlands the most fertile farmland in the country. Shielded from the Caribbean rains by the mountains, the lowlands are hot and dry. For a breeze, migrate to any body of water—Lago de Nicaragua or the Pacific. León, where student radicals keep things lively, and Granada, a tourist favorite for its architectural wonders, are both steeped in history.

LEÓN

The streets of León (pop. 130,000) blend colonial with modern at every step. Horse-drawn carriages and liberal students fill the streets, while bells from the 19 churches compete with taxi horns and *camionetas*. Prayer to saints is never far from town parties where spirituality is easily forgotten. Despite the constant mixing of eras, echoes of the town's Spanish founders ring loud and clear.

León Viejo was founded on the shore of Lake Xolotlán in 1524. Destroyed by an earthquake in 1610, León (full name: León Santiago de los Caballeros) was rebuilt 30km to the west. After a slow beginning, the new León soon became a cultural and intellectual stronghold, and acted as the capital of Nicaragua for more than 300 years. The heady atmosphere fueled the imagination of its favorite son, Rubén Darío, whose poetry launched the Modernist movement in Latin America. As bumper stickers on many cars proclaim, León is *orgullosamente liberal* (proudly liberal). The Universidad Nacional Autónoma de Nicaragua (UNAN), the country's first university, sharpens León's politics to a keen radical edge.

⌐ TRANSPORTATION

Buses: The main terminal is 6 blocks north and 7 blocks east of the *parque central*. To get there take a taxi (C15) or a camioneta (C3). To: **Chinandega** (1hr., every 15min. 4:30am-6pm, C12-15); **Estelí** (3hr.; 5:20am, 12:45, 2:15, 3:30pm; C60); **Managua** (1½hr., every hr. 4am-4pm, C24); **Matagalpa** (2hr.; 4:20am, 7:30am and 2:45pm; C24). Buses also leave from "El Mercadito," on the western side of town, to the beaches of **Poneloya** and **Las Peñitas** (1hr., every hr. 6am-6pm, C10).

✈ 🔂 ORIENTATION AND PRACTICAL INFORMATION

One of the few cities in Nicaragua where street names are used in directions, León is surprisingly easy to navigate. Like many other cities in Nicaragua, León's center is the **parque central.** If you're standing in the *parque* with the fountain of lions, the massive **cathedral** is to the east, and the imposing **ENITEL** antenna is to the west. León's *calles* run east and west and its *avenidas* run north and south. **Calle Central Rubén Darío** fronts the north side of the parque. **Avenida Central,** León's main thoroughfare, runs north-south straight through the city, broken only by the *parque central*. León's nineteen churches dot the landscape every few blocks and are frequently used as reference points for directions farther away from the *parque* and the cathedral. **La Iglesia de La Merced,** one block north of the *parque's* northwest corner, and **La Iglesia de La Recolección,** 1 block east and 2 blocks north of the *parque's* northeast corner, are useful landmarks. The **bus terminal** sits on the edge of town, 6 blocks north and 7 blocks east of the *parque central*. To get to town from the bus station, take a right onto the main street that you came in on, walk past the market, and continue for several blocks before taking a left on 1 Av. Noreste. The walk to the center of town can be a hot and dusty 20min. trek, but it's manageable. Take advantage of the shade provided by overhangs, or hop in a taxi to skip the whole thing for C15.

Tourist Office: Intur (☎2311 3682), 1½ blocks north of the *parque*. Provides tourist information and brochures. Open M-F 8am-noon and 2-5pm. **Office of Tourist**

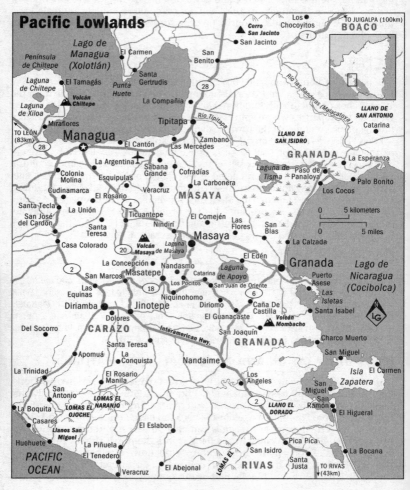

Pacific Lowlands

Information (☎8647 4521), 20m north of the Cathedral. English spoken. Open M-F 8:30am-7pm, Sa 9am-5pm.

Tours and Agencies:

Tierra Tour (☎2315 4278 or 8966 3482; www.tierratour.com), 3 blocks north of the northwest corner of the *parque central*. Offers a wide array of excursions, from a simple tour of León City (C300-400) to sandboarding the Cerro Negro (C560) and exploring the Isla Juan Venado. Tours generally depart twice daily: once in the morning and once in the afternoon. Open M-F 8am-7pm, Sa-Su 8am-6pm.

Quetzal Trekkers (☎2311 6695; www.quetzaltrekkers.com), 1½ blocks east of Iglesia La Recolección. A non-profit tour company specializing in hikes of the surrounding volcanoes. All proceeds go to help **Las Tías**, an organization dedicated to helping orphans and homeless children. Volunteer opportunities available. Open M-Sa 9am-5pm, Su 1-5pm.

Nicasí Tours (☎8414 1192 or 8999 4754; www.nicasitours.com). An alternative to conventional tour companies, offering a variety of social and cultural tours. Cooking workshop with a local family C400 per person. History of the Revolution tour. Most tours leave from ViaVia hostel.

Vapues Tours (☎2315 4099; www.vapuestours.com), half a block east of the north side of El Laborio Church. Offers maps tours of León and the surrounding area, as well as a León-Granada shuttle service.

Pathways Tour Co. (www.greenpathways.com), across the street from Bigfoot hostel. 3-day whale watching tour in Cosigüina C3000 per person, min. 4 people. 1-day combination Cerro Negro, León Viejo, and Laguna de Asososca tour C1000 per person. 6hr. Isla de Juan Venado tour C600 per person. Bike rentals C200 per day. Open M-Sa 10am-6pm.

Banks: BanCentro (☎2311 0991), half a block south of the cathedral. **24hr. ATM.** Open M-F 8:30am-4:30pm, Sa 8am-noon. V only. **BanPro** (☎2311 3445), 30m south of the Iglesia La Recolección. **24hr. ATM.** Open M-F 8:30am-4:30pm, Sa 8:30am-noon. AmEx/D/MC/V. **Banco ProCredit**, 2½ blocks east of the *parque central*. Open M-F 8:30am-4:30pm, Sa 8:30am-1pm.

Beyond Tourism: Metropolis Spanish School (☎8932 6686; www.metropolisspanish. com), 30m north of the northeast corner of *parque central*. One-on-one instruction, homestays, and activities.

Police and Tourist Police: (☎118 or 2311 3137), 1 block east and 2 blocks north from the northeast corner of the *parque central*.

Pharmacy: Farmacia Lopez (☎2311 3363), 1½ blocks west from El Calvario Church. Open daily 8am-noon and 1-5:30pm.

Hospital: (☎2311 6990 or 2311 6934), 2 blocks south from the southeast corner of the *parque central*.

Internet Access: Cyber La Cegua (☎8895 1116), 1 block north and 1½ blocks west of the *parque central*. Internet C10 per hr. Open M-F 8am-6pm. **Cyber Fast,** 2½ blocks north of Parque de las Poetas. Internet C8 per hr. Open M-Sa 9am-8pm. **Cyber Home. net,** 1½ blocks west from the southwest corner of the *parque central*. Internet C10 per hr. Open M-F 8am-9pm, Sa 8am-6pm.

Post Office: (☎2311 6655), 3½ blocks north of Iglesia San Francisco. Open M-F 8am-5pm, Sa 8am-noon.

ACCOMMODATIONS

León has more hotels and hostels per square mile than any other city in Nicaragua, with an abundance of great hostels and several luxury hotels. Larger hostels have tourist information and offer tours of the surrounding area. If you arrive in León and don't like the look of the first place you stop at, keep moving: chances are you'll find something better around the corner.

▨ **Hostal Colibri** (☎2311 3858; iguana.colibri@yahoo.com), half a block left of La Iglesia de la Recolección. Large rooms. Free kitchen access. Breakfast and unlimited coffee included. Free internet and Wi-Fi. The shaded patio area in front and the hammocks

PACIFIC LOWLANDS

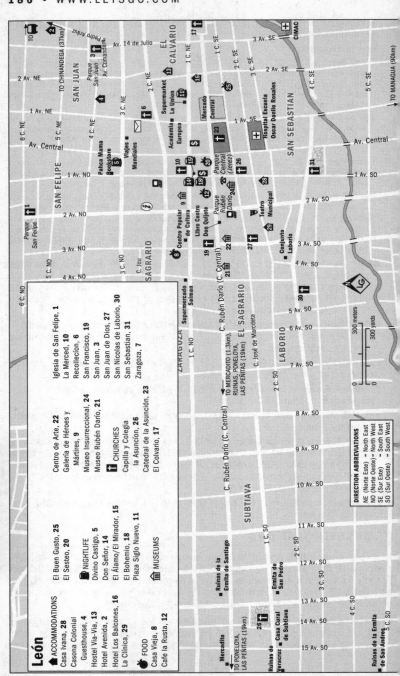

under the thatched palm hut out back are great places to enjoy the free coffee. Reception 24hr. Singles C200, doubles C260-280, triples C360. ❷

Hostal Tortuga Booluda (☎2311 4653; www.tortugabooluda.com), 3½ blocks west of the southwest corner of the *parque central*. Winner of hostelworld.com's "best hostel in Nicaragua 2008" award, Tortuga Booluda lives up to its reputation by providing clean, cheap accommodations and plenty of perks. Free kitchen use and coffee. Breakfast included. Internet available. One-on-one Spanish instruction C100 per hr. Dorms C120, singles C200-480. ❷

Hostal El Nancite (☎8834 2256 or 2311 4117), 2½ blocks south of the Iglesia San Juan. More like a hotel than a hostel, Hostal El Nancite is brand new, and has the sparkling bathrooms and glossy, comfortable bedspreads to prove it. Only the prices make it seem like a hostel. Check-out 11am. Singles and doubles C300, suites for up to 4 people C900. Cash only. ❸

ViaVia (☎2311 6142; www.viavia.com), 75m south of Banco ProCredit. Clean dorms. The lively bar (open until 11:30pm) is a great place to connect with fellow travelers in León. F nights live music. Dorms C100, private rooms with bath C300-500. Cash only. ❸

Hostal El Albergue (☎8894 1787; www.hosteltrail.com/elalbergueleon), 50m west of the Petronic. A locally owned and operated hostel, this is your ultimate budget stop. Free coffee and kitchen use. Talk to the owner about city tours and volunteer opportunities. Check-out 11am. Dorms C60-120. Cash only. ❶

Bigfoot Hostel (☎8977 8832; www.bigfootnicaragua.com), 75m south of Banco ProCredit. Another backpacker favorite. Mini-park, complete with mini pool in back. Dorms C120, singles C260. ❶

Lazybones Hostel (☎2311 3472; www.lazybonesleon.com), 1 block west and 2½ blocks north from the northwest corner of the *parque central*. Comfortable dorms. Amenities include a pool, pool table, and TV. Free internet and Wi-Fi. Dorms C160, private rooms C380-560. Check-out 11am. Cash only. ❷

Casona Colonial (☎2311 3178), half a block west of Parque San Juan. A perfect spot for couples or honeymooners, the Casona Colonial takes its name to heart. Rooms feature elaborate furnishings and beautiful bed frames. Checkout 11am. Singles with private bath C400, doubles C600. Cash only. ❸

Hotel La Posada del Doctor (☎2311 4343; www.laposadadeldoctor.com). Lovely inner courtyard with stone pathways and even a fountain. Free Wi-Fi. Singles with fan C800, with A/C C1000; 5-person suite C1400/1700. AmEx/D/MC/V. ❹

Hotel La Perla (☎2311 2279 or 2311 3125), 2½ blocks north of the *parque central* on the right. A completely converted and restored colonial mansion, Hotel La Perla is now the lodging of choice for travelers wishing to indulge. Impeccably clean rooms come with enormous beds, private bathrooms, A/C, and flatscreen TVs. Free access to the pool. Free Wi-Fi. Rooms C1400-3600. AmEx/MC/V. ❺

Casa Marbella (☎2833 0827 or 2709 8011), between the Tortuguero Information Center and Dorling's Bakery. Beautiful views and friendly owners make this small bed and breakfast a charming and comfortable option. Each of the 4 rooms has high ceilings, soft beds, and solar-powered hot water. Breakfast included. Singles in high season C700, in low season C600, doubles C800/700, triples C1000/900. ❹

FOOD

Like any college town, León has plenty of pizza joints. Thankfully, most restaurants here also provide an equally enjoyable atmosphere and quality food. Try the traditional Nicaraguan eateries on the south side of the market and by Bigfoot Hostel for a cheap and tasty meal. For groceries, visit **Salman Supermer-**

cado, 1 block north and 3 blocks west of the *parque central.* (☎2311 5027. Open M-Sa 7am-9pm, Su 8am-8pm.)

▨ **Comedor El Buen Gusto,** on the south side of El Mercado. Serves great food in enormous quantities on the cheap. Heaping plate of *típico* with a coke C45-80. Open M-Sa 10am-10pm. Cash only. ❷

▨ **Cocinarte** (☎2315 4099 or 8854 6928), a bit of a hike from the center of town, on the south side of El Calvario Church. Vegetarians rejoice: finally, a restaurant catering specifically to you that offers more than rice and beans. Entrees like Bami Maní, an Indonesian noodle plate with steamed veggies and peanut sauce, cost C90-130. Natural fruit juice C15-20. F nights live music. Open daily 11am-10pm. ❸

Mediterraneo (☎8895 9392), 2½ blocks north from the Parque de las Poetas. Great ambience matched by great food. *Espagueti* Doña Petrona with prawns in a white wine sauce C160. Extensive international wine list. Open T-Su 5:30-11pm. AmEx/D/MC/V. ❸

Comedor Lucia (☎2311 4932), ½ block south of Banco ProCredit, next to both Bigfoot hostel and ViaVia. Buffet style breakfasts and lunches (C35-60) are tasty and filling. Open M-F 7am-9pm, Sa 7am-4pm. Cash only. ❶

El Sesteo (☎2311 5327), on the NW corner of the *parque central.* Open-air restaurant makes a great vantage point for people-watching. *Nactamales* C88. Burgers and hotdogs C64-110. Cool down with a banana split, C60. Open daily 8am-10pm. AmEx/D/MC/V. ❷

La Terraza M (☎8458 1374), 2½ blocks north of Parque de las Poetas. Mediterraneo's little brother, La Terraza M caters to the cafe crowd with sandwiches (hot or cold, C45) and crepes. Palm trees, dim lighting, and a fountain with goldfish make for a pleasant atmosphere. Open T-Su 7:30am-11pm. AmEx/D/MC/V. ❶

Café La Rosita, half a block west of the *parque central.* Grab a bagel (C25) or donut (C12), and wash it down with one of La Rosita's coffee concoctions. Cappucinos C22. Open M-Sa 7am-10pm, Su 11am-2pm. Cash only. ❶

⊙ SIGHTS

CENTRO DE ARTE. Housed in two colonial buildings, this private collection, owned by the Ortiz Guardian Foundation, has a wide selection of art on display. From pre-Columbian ceramics to European religious paintings to modern art, the Centro is a must-see. *(Two blocks east and 15m south of the northeast corner of the parque central. ☎ 2311 7225; www.fundacionortizguardian.com. Open Tu-Su 10:30am-6:15pm. C20.)*

CATEDRAL DE LA ASUNCIÓN. This cathedral is the largest in Central America, a reputation the imposing facade won't let you forget. Rubén Darío rests here; his tomb is guarded by one of the cathedral's enormous lion statues. Cathedral de la Asuncíin is also famous for the *Stations of the Cross*, a series of paintings by Antonio Sarria. At the time of publication, these paintings were being restored by local art students. *(On the east side of the parque central. C40 to climb the stairs to the top of the church.)*

MUSEO ARCHIVO RUBÉN DARÍO. This museum, honoring the country's favorite and most respected poet, Rubén Darío, is befittingly housed in Darío's former abode. The museum has collected are some of his clothes, paintings of his family, his death mask, many of his manuscripts, and first editions of several of his works. Unfortunately, there is not much information given about these items; the little info available is entirely in Spanish. With permission, you can read the books in the archive. *(3 blocks west of the parque. ☎ 2311 2388; www.unanleon. edu.ni. Open Tu-Sa 9am-noon and 2-5pm, Su 9am-noon. Donations encouraged.)*

MUSEO ENTOMOLOGICO. Featuring rotating exhibits of both native and foreign insects, this museum allows you to get up close and personal with everything from incandescent butterflies to giant pincer beetles. *(1½ blocks from El Calvario Church. ☎ 2311 6586; www.bio-nica.com. Open M-Sa 8am-noon, 2-5pm. C10.)*

MUSEO DE LEYENDAS Y TRADICIONES. Through the pleasant garden in front may lead you to believe otherwise, this building was a prison for Somoza's political enemies from 1921-1979. Converted into a museum in 2000, it now contains a mixture of superstitious tales and artifacts from León's violent past. Paintings on the prison walls depict various scenes of guard brutality. Ask one of the guides to explain the history of the prison. *(Three blocks south and ½ block east of the cathedral's southwest corner, across from San Sebastián Church. Open Tu-Sa 8:30am-noon and 2-5:30pm, Su 8:30am-3pm. C10.)*

LEÓN VIEJO. "Old León" lies 30km southeast of León, on the shores of Lago de Managua. Founded in 1524 by Francisco Hernández de Córdoba, it was the colonial capital of Nicaragua until early 1610, when Volcán Momotombo, standing at the edge of town, caused an earthquake that destroyed the city. Hurricanes have since taken their toll on the partially-excavated ruins. To prevent further damage, UNESCO has covered the remaining brick foundations so only footprints of buildings remain. A Spanish-speaking guide will relate the story of their past splendor. Tours take 45min. and begin at the foundations of the cathedral, a 5min. walk past the museum, where a statue marks the spot of Hernández de Córdoba's beheading. Córdoba's remains were exhumed from the Iglesia de La Merced in May 2000 and are now entombed below the statue. *(From León, take a bus to La Pax Centro (1hr., every 35-40min. 5:50am-6:40pm, C8). Then, catch a bus for the town of Momotombo and ask to be let off at "Las Ruinas" (30min., 9 buses per day 6:30am-5pm, C6). From Managua, take a bus from Mercado Israel Lewites to La Paz Centro (1¼hr., every 20min. 4am-6pm, C10). Buses return to La Paz Centro every 1-2hr (8 buses 8am-5pm, C5). Once in Momotombo, follow the blue-and-white signs to Las Ruinas de León Viejo; the walk takes 10min. Open daily 8am-5pm. C10, with ISIC C5.)*

NIGHTLIFE AND ENTERTAINMENT

León really comes alive at night. University students spend weekend nights dancing until dawn—or at least until authorities shut the clubs down (at 1 or 2am), after which the party moves to bars. Popular areas are well lit and patrolled by vigilantes (local watchmen hired by the town). The larger hostels host frequent parties: Quetzal Trekkers hosts a combination party and fundraising raffle on select weekends. The local tourist board sponsors **Tertulias Leonesas** in the *parque* every few Saturdays. The events—part concert, part culture, and part fiesta—are free to the public and draw huge crowds. Artisans and street vendors set up mid-afternoon, and a music show starts around 6:30pm.

Bar y Restaurante "Baro" (☎8820 4000), 1 block west of the *parque central*. Popular with both tourists and locals. Serves more than 50 mixed drinks, such as the *Despertador* (alarm clock). Fish fingers and fries C80. The owner, an Israeli ex-pat, swears that his hummus (C115) is the best in Central America.

ViaVia (☎2311 6142; www.viavia.com), 75m south of Banco ProCredit. The bar at ViaVia is a happening place, but people staying there shouldn't worry: it shuts down early. Specialty nights include M trivia night, W themed music night, and F live music. Open daily 7:30-11:30pm. Cash only.

Oxygene (☎2311 0748), 75m west of the *parque central*. Despite having a name that sounds like a pair of aerated Levis (it's French), Oxygene is the club du jour for dancing. Pulsing electronica fills the place with people on the weekends. Beer C20. Mixed drinks C30-40. Oxygene Margarita C55. Cover F-Sa C30. Open Tu-Su 4pm-2am. D/MC/V.

Don Señor (☎2311 1212) 1 block north of the northwest corner of the *parque central*. Bar bordering the street downstairs; disco and dance floor upstairs. Salsa dominates the playlist. Cover up to C40. Open Tu-Su 8pm-2am. AmEx/D/MC/V.

Restaurante Cactus (☎2311 3591), 15m west from La Merced Church. A great place to scope out local music and dance. W-Sa nights live music, ranging from Nicaraguan rock to folklore. The enormous open-air space and sparsely arranged tables make getting a good view easy. Hamburgers and chicken sandwiches C60. Cactus plate C150. Open M-Sa 10am-2am. AmEx/D/MC/V.

Malibu Bar & Restauarante (☎2311 6327), 2½ blocks north of the Parque de las Poetas. Decorated with model sailboats and lit by revolving beer signs. W 3-6pm beer C16. Mixed drinks C50. Open Tu-Th 4pm-midnight, F-Su 4pm-2am. AmEx/D/MC/V.

SANDBOARDING THE CERRO NEGRO

Take advantage of one of several tour companies that do sandboarding tours, including **Tierra Tours** (p. 185) and **Bigfoot Hostel** (p. 187). The drive each the volcano takes 1hr. each way. At the entrance point, you will have to pay C100 (some tours cover this fee). You'll then grab the boards and begin the trek to the rim of the crater. The hike itself isn't too step, but the loose rocks can make things difficult. It can get extremely windy at the top, so be careful. From the top you can see the entire Maribos Volcano chain. Look into the sulfurous, still-smoking crater of the Cerro Negro, whose last eruption was in 1993. Then, when you're ready, head over to the "sandy" side (on the opposite side of the volcano) and get ready to throw yourself down the mountain. You can ride standing up or sitting down. No matter how you ride, you're bound to get covered in dust. It's also possible to get some serious road rash if you fall, so wear jeans and a tucked in shirt.

VOLCANOES

León is situated near several breathtaking volcanoes, all of which can be scaled in guided treks. Treks range from half-day walking tours to three-night camping excursions. Your best bet is to go with the **Quetzaltrekkers** (p. 185), a group of friendly international volunteers who donate all of their proceeds to a local charity. Try a relatively untaxing overnight trip to **Cerro Negro.** A pleasant hike up **Telica** includes swims in volcanic pools. More hard core camping and trekking tours to **Cosiguina** (3 days; minimum donation C1300) and **Momotombo** (2 days; minimum donation C1100) are only for travelers in decent shape. Local tourism offices and hostels can arrange other treks and guides.

GRANADA

Granada's prime location makes it hands-down the most touristed city in Nicaragua. Worlds away from the chaos and grime of neighboring Managua, Granada is a peaceful city with astonishing beauty. Palm trees share wide boulevards with colorful colonial houses, ribboned horse-drawn taxis rattle by, and vendors hawk eccentric wares in the *parque central.*

▐ TRANSPORTATION

Buses: Express buses leave for **Managua** from just beyond the *parque central* on C. Vega. Buses leave for **Masaya** across from El Mercado on C. Atrevesada. Buses leave for **Rivas** just past El Mercado on C. Atrevesada.

Bike Rental: Bearded Monkey, C. 14 de Septiembre (☎2552 4028), 1 block from La Libertad. C100 (US$5) per day.

✈ 🛈 ORIENTATION AND PRACTICAL INFORMATION

Granada is built around the attractive *parque central.* The major streets **El Consulado, Real Xalteva, La Libertad,** and **La Calzada** all begin on the *parque's* edges. Many of the tourist hostels, hotels, and restaurants are clustered on and around La Calzada. **Bus stations** and **El Mercado** are both located to the south of town. When in doubt, simply ask someone to direct you to your destination. If they don't know, have them point you back to *parque central* and try again.

Tourist Office: Intur (☎ 2552 6858; www.visitanicaragua.com). From the *parque central,* walk to the end of the Plaza de la Independencia. From there, walk 2 blocks to the right. Open M-F 8am-12:30pm and 2-5pm.

Tours: Nica Adventures (☎2552 8461; www.nica-adventures.com), on La Calzada, 1½ blocks from the Cathedral. Runs a daily shuttle to Managua airport, San Jorge, and San Juan del Sur. Offers tours of the surrounding area, including a kayaking trip on Lake Nicaragua. Also exchanges dollars and euros. Open M-Sa 8am-6pm. AmEx/D/MC. **Tierra Tours** (☎2552 8723; www.tierratour.com), on La Calzada, 2 blocks from the Cathedral. Tour of Granada C300 (US$15). Open M-F 8am-7pm, Sa-Su 8am-5pm. AmEx/D/MC/V.

Bank:Banco America Central (BAC), on the corner of Atrevesada and La Libertad. Open M-F 8:30am-4:30pm, Sa 8:30am-noon. **24hr. ATM.** AmEx/MC/V. **Banpro,** on the corner of El Consulado and La Atrevesada. Open M-F 8:30am-4:30pm, Sa 8:30am-noon. **24hr. ATM.** MC/V.

Beyond Tourism:

Centro de Arte (☎8616 7322; www.nicasagas.com), 25m up La Calzada from the Cathedral, on the left. Owned and operated by American artist Amy. Painting classes W, F, and Su 9am-noon; C100 (US$5). Mosaic classes M-Sa 1-4pm; C100 (US$5) per hr. Cash only.

One on One Spanish and English tutoring (☎2552 6771; www.1on1tutoring.net), 5 blocks down La Calzada from the Cathedral. Offers a personalized schedule of Spanish classes. C400 (US$20) per day; C1900 (US$95) per week. Open daily 8am-noon, 1-8pm. Cash only.

Nicaragua Mía Spanish School (☎2552 8193 or 2755; www.nicaraguamiaspanish.com), 3½ blocks east, down El Caimito from the *parque central.* Open daily 8am-noon and 1-5pm. C100 (US$5) per hr. lesson; C2000 (US$100) per week.

Spanish School Xpress (☎2552 8577), 2½ blocks from the northwest corner of *parque central.*

La Esperanza Granada (☎2432 5420; www.la-esperanza-granada.org), half a block east from the corner of C. La Lib-

THE WICKED WITCHES OF NICARAGUA

The wicked witch **La Ceuga** is a well-known figure in Nicaragua legend. She is said to wear a dress of plantain leaves while her long, dark hair cloaks her ghoulish face. She passes through the jungle at night, unbounded by the laws of physics, floating or passing through objects on her mission to haunt the unfortunate. Sometimes La Ceuga goes naked, using her seductive silhouette to lure men into the jungle. La Cegua's whispers are so ghastly that the men to whom she speaks go crazy and never recover.

Those who manage to escape La Ceuga's grasp must still be wary of **La Mocuana.** She is the beautiful daughter of a local chief, who once fought the Spaniards. The chief hid his treasure and shared the secret with his daughter before defeating the enemy. Some time later, a Spaniard who had fought against the villagers settled peacefully in the area and fell in love with La Mocuana. The enamored chief's daughter took the treasure to help her start a new life with her lover. The Spaniard, however, preferred the gold to La Mocuana, and made off with it after sealing La Mocuana in a cave. The heartbroken girl escaped and began to roam the landscape in sorrow. She wanders around, exacting vengeance on the lustful, unfaithful, and unsuspecting men who make her acquaintance.

ertad and C. Miguel de Cervantes. Help local school systems by donating your time, skills, or money. Open M-F 9am-5pm.

English-Language Bookstore: Mockingbird Books (☎2552 2146), on La Libertad just off the *parque central*. Used books in English from C80 (US$4). Open M-Sa 9am-5pm, Su 11am-5pm.

Laundromat: Mapache Laundry Service (☎2552 6711). Open M-F 7:30am-6pm, Sa 7:30am-4:30pm. Under 5lb C70 (US$3.50); up to 20lb. C200 (US$10). Extensive assortment of free flyers, brochures, and maps.

Emergency: Cruz Roja (☎552 2711), on La Calzada, just past Iglesia de Guadalupe.

Police: (☎552 2977 or 552 2929), 1½ blocks east of the Parque Sandino.

Pharmacy: (☎552 5726 or 552 7679), on C. Xalteva, 2 blocks from the *parque central*. Open M-Sa 7am-7pm, Su 7:30am-7pm. AmEx/D/MC.

Hospital: (☎552 2719).

Internet Access: Cyber Games, on C. Estrada, 10m east of C. Atrevesada, across the street from Hostal Oasis. Internet C20 (US$1) per hr. International calls C1 (US$0.05) per min. Open 8am-10pm daily. **Internet Transfer and Tours** (☎2552-441; hewleto8@ hotmail.com), on the corner of La Libertad and C. Miguel de Cervantes. Internet C15 (US$0.75) per hr. International calls C1 (US$0.05) per min. Cash only.

Post Office: (☎2552 2776), from the Iglesia San Francisco, half a block down C. el Arsenal. Open M-F 8am-noon and 1-5pm, Sa 8am-noon.

ACCOMMODATIONS

Hotels and a scattering of hostels line C. La Calzada, the long road that runs east from the *parque* to the lake shore. Wander up and down it long enough and you're bound to find something.

Hostal Oasis, C. Estrada (☎2552 8006 or 8005), half a block from C. Atrevesada. Spotless high-ceilinged dorms and small, but functional, private rooms. Quiet, out-of-the-way location. Exchange for books and movies. Free daily 10min. international phone call. Free internet and Wi-Fi. Reception 24hr. Dorms C160 (US$8). Cash only. ❷

Hotel America, (☎2552 3914), 3 blocks down C. La Calzada on the left. Warm colors and polished wood furniture make for attractive decor and great ambience. Singles with bath C500 (US$25), with A/C C560 (US$28); doubles C700/760 (US$35/38); triples C900/960 (US$45/48). D/MC/V. ❹

Hotel Colonial, (☎552 758 182), 25m from the *parque central* on La Libertad. As luxurious as accommodations come in this touristed city. All rooms feature fans, cable TVs, and lockboxes. Pool. Free Wi-Fi. Singles C1200 (US$60); doubles C1500 (US$75); suite C2400 (US$120). ❺

The Bearded Monkey, C. 14 de Septiembre (☎2552 4028), 1 block from La Libertad. A lively social center with every amenity a backpacker could hope for. Great place to share stories with fellow travelers. Bulletin boards full of brochures and flyers for things to do in Granada, including Spanish lessons and volunteer opportunities. Free Wi-Fi. Bike rental C100 (US$5) per day. Hammocks C80 (US$4); dorms C120 (US$6); singles C220 (US$11); doubles 380 (US$19); triples C520 (US$26). ❶

Hospedaje Cocibolca (☎2552 7223), 3 blocks down La Calzada, on the right. A favorite of backpackers. Free Wi-Fi and kitchen use. Singles with bath C300 (US$15); doubles 360 (US$18); quads C560 (US$28). AmEx/D/MC/V. ❸

FOOD

Tired of eating *gallo pinto* and fried plantains? Fortunately for you, Granada is home to an international restaurant scene. For groceries, visit supermarket

Palí, just past El Mercado on C. Atravesada. (☎2552 7110. Open M-Sa 8am-8:30pm, Su 8am-5pm. Cash only.)

Imagine Restaurant and Bar (☎2454 1602), 1 block from the *parque central*. The owner, a native New Englander, grows produce in his own private garden. Vegetarians will love the Vegetable Fantasy Spectacular, and with dishes like the Pacific Coast Mahí Mahí in a papaya lime cilantro salsa, carnivores are in good hands. Entrees from C220 (US$11). Open daily 5-11pm. ❷

El Zaguán (☎2552 2522), 1 block down La Calzada street. Try the *brocheta el bramadero*, or beef kebab (260C, US$13). Drinks 40C (US$2). Open noon-11pm daily. AmEx/D/MC/V. ❸

Nuestra Casa (☎2552 8469), 1½ blocks down C. El Consulado. The bull horns above the door don't lie: this is the South in the... uh, other South. Jimmy, Alabama native and owner, does his ribs right. Entrees from C140 (US$7). Open 6-9:30pm daily. Cash only. ❷

O'Shea's Irish Pub and Restaurant, 2 blocks down La Calzada on right. The Irish flag outside is no gimmick: the fish and chips C90 (US$4.50) are authentic. Open 10am-late. Cash only. ❶

Chocolate Cafetería (☎2552 3400), 1½ blocks up Calzada on the left from the Cathedral. Coffee from C15 (US$0.75). Salads C80 (US$4). Sandwiches and hamburgers C60-100 (US$3-5). Open 24hr. AmEx/D/MC/V. ❶

👁 SIGHTS

We thought we'd change it up here and give you a sort of walking tour through Granada. This should take you about two hours to complete; wear comfortable shoes, because you'll be covering about 20 blocks of the city.

Begin your tour of the city at **Iglesia La Merced.** The outer facade of this building is a testament to Nicaragua's volatile history. Climb the bell tower for the best view in town; you'll see the lake, Volcán Mombacho, and Granada's school children playing soccer in church's concrete plaza (Open 5am-7pm daily. C20/ US$1) Next, head down Real Xalteva until you get to La Atrevesada. Then, turn right, and walk two blocks to **El Mercado Municipal;** you'll find bootleg wares and fresh fruit and vegetables here. When you're done shopping around, pack up your purchases head back toward Atrevesada. Walk about four blocks to C. El

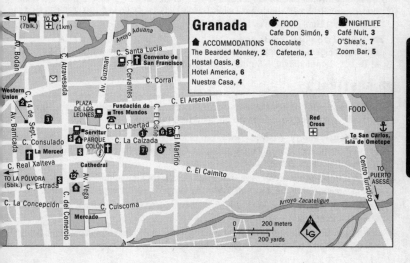

Artesenal. Turn right and follow Arsenal for two blocks until you reach **La Igle-sia San Francisco,** commissioned by the filibuster William Walker in 1856. The stunning **Antiguo Convento San Francisco** (☎2552 5535), right next door, is a must-see. The building is a piece of art in and of itself, with a grand staircase and a set of bells. Inside, surrounding palm tree courtyards, is an impressive collection of art. Some of the pieces, including statues taken from the surrounding islands, date all the way back to AD 800. (Open M-F 8am-5pm, Sa-Su 9am-4pm. C40/US$2. Cash only.) After a long afternoon at the museum, head across the street to **Kathy's Waffle House** where you can take down some tasty Belgian Waffles. Enjoy a complimentary coffee with your meal. (☎2552 8401. Open 7am-2pm daily. C81-102/US$4-5.) Heading back down El Arsenal, take a left at **Plaza de la Independencia.** Be sure to stop off at **Casa de los Tres Mundos** (☎2552 4176; www.c3mundos.org), a multicultural center that provides music and art lessons and info on upcoming events in the city. The *parque central* is right at the end of the Plaza. You'll notice the beautiful yellow and white **Cathedral.** Walk down C. La Calzada (right next to the Cathedral), stop in at one of the many cafés, and grab a scrumptious espresso. End your tour at **Iglesia de Guadalupe** (about five blocks down C. La Calzada), which was originally built as a fort.

NIGHTLIFE AND ENTERTAINMENT

Café Nuit (☎2552 7376; www.granadaparty.com), on C. La Libertad, 2½ blocks from the *parque central*. A cafe turned discoteque. The DJ and live music (merengue anyone?) will have you dancing all night long. Mixed drinks from 40C (US$2). Beer from 25C (US$1.25). Open M and W-Su 8pm-3am. Cover F C10 (US$0.50), Sa C20 (US$1). Cash only.

Be Karaoke (☎2552 4209; www.begranada.com), on the corner of C. Atrevesada and C. La Libertad, across the street from the Banco America Central. Chances are you'll hear this place before you get to it. More than 40 mixed drinks (from C30, US$1.50) provide ample liquid courage. Open T-Su 7pm-6am. AmEx/D/MC/V.

Roadhouse Drinks and Food (☎2552 8459), C. La Calzada, 2 blocks from the Cathedral. Baseball themed sports bar. Drinks C20-80 (US$1-4). Food C120-220 (US$6-11). Open daily 11am-2am. AmEx/D/MC/V.

Zoom Bar, (☎89 858 0913), on La Calzada 3 blocks from *parque central*. A Sports Bar with a great location. Claims to serve the best hamburger in Granada C80 (US$4). Open M-Th 11:30am-midnight, F-Su 8am-midnight. Cash only.

FESTIVALS

With its beautiful colonial buildings and tourist-friendly atmosphere, Granada is a wonderful place to celebrate Nicaragua's culture.

International Poetry Festival (www.festivalpoesianicaragua.com). Since 2005 celebrated poets from many different countries have been getting together in Granada for a week of readings, presentations, and poetry.

Hípica. A once-a-year occurrence, the Hípica is a celebration of the patron saint of each city. In Granada, that means an all-day party for La Virgen Concepción de María.

Día de la Independencia, Sept. 14-15. Nicaragua and Central America celebrate their liberation from Spain.

La Gritería, Dec. 7-8. A celebration of the Virgin Mary's conception. Nicaraguans light off enough fireworks to worry a pyrotechnic teenager.

⚡ DAYTRIPS FROM GRANADA

VOLCÁN MOMBACHO

To get to Volcán Mombacho, head down past the market in Granada and hop on a bus to Rivas. Let your driver know that you wish to be let out at "el volcán." From there you'll have to catch one of the park's transport services, or else suffer the 3hr. hike to the visitors center. Transport runs M-W at 10:30am, and Th-Su at 8, 10am, and noon.

Three main hikes await visitors to Volcán Mombacho. The crater hike (2hr.; C100, US$5) takes you for a loop around the crater. The "Tigrillo" hike (2½ hr.; C200, US$10) takes you to a higher elevation than the crater hike. The Puma hike (4hr.) is the most physically demanding. It takes you around both craters and to higher elevations still for some of the best views of the surrounding area. Tack on an extra C100 (US$5) for a bilingual guide.

LAS ISLETAS

There are many "unofficial" tour guide companies down at the Malecón that are willing to take you on a trip through Las Isletas. 📷Zapatera tours (☎ 2479 9944; www.zapatera-tours.com) is a more "off the beaten path" option.

Kevin will take you out on his boat for a tour of any part of the surrounding area. Take a half-day trip to Las Isletas and stop on a beach for lunch. If you want something a little more adventurous, have him show you around **Isla Zapatera,** an important archaeological site, to see the ancient petroglyphs. For the truly intrepid, he's even willing to take you on an overnight trip to camp on the lake itself. Prices range from C200 (US$10), depending on the size of the group and the length of the trip.

SAN JUAN DEL SUR

In the days of the gold rush, before the Panama Canal, San Juan del Sur served as a transportation hub for prospectors shuttling between the Atlantic and the Pacific. No longer a layover for money-hungry sailors, modern San Juan del Sur is a relatively undiscovered beach town. A popular surfer hangout for decades, this humble beachfront town has a lot to offer, even if your itinerary does not include riding the waves. The city's beach forms a large half circle, with beautiful cliff faces framing either side. Come here to grab a cheap drink and watch a spectacular beach sunset. Prices drop progressively with added distance from the sand; the small, local eateries and accommodations located inland from the beach are a budget traveler's best bets.

🚌 TRANSPORTATION

Despite its history, San Juan del Sur is no longer a major transportation hub.

Buses: The **bus station** is on Av. Central, across the street from El Mercado. To: **Managua** (5, 6, 7am) and **Rivas** (every 30min. 7am-5pm).

Shuttles: Hostel Casa Oro offers a daily shuttle to **Playa Maderas** (departs 10am, 12:30, 3:45pm; returns 10:45am, 1, and 5pm).

Taxis: To **Granada** C1000 (US$50). To **Rivas** or **San Jorge** C300-400 (US$15-20).

🔲 ❓ ORIENTATION AND PRACTICAL INFORMATION

Located on the Pacific ocean and boasting some of the best waves around, San Juan del Sur is a surfer's dream. Unsurprisingly, the town revolves around the coast. **El Paso del Rey** runs along the shore; *avenidas* **El Albinal, Central and Real** branch inland.

Tourist Office: San Juan del Sur has no official tourist office, but check out **Casa de Oro Hostel** (below) for tourism opportunities. Open 8am-8pm.

Bank: Banco America Central (BAC) ATM, on the beachfront, in front of the Casablanca Hotel. Open 24hr. AmEx/MC/V. **Banco de Finanzas (BDF),** on the coastal end of C. Real. Open M-F 8:30am-noon and 1-4:30pm, Su 8:30am-12:30pm. **24hr ATM.**

Beyond Tourism: Playas del Sur Spanish School (☎8668 9334; www.playasdelsur-spanishschool.com), about 50m south on beachfront from Banco de Finanzas. 1 week with 20hr. of class C2000 (US$100), with homestay C3500 (US$175). Also offers activities such as dancing, cooking, and trips to the beach. Open M-Sa 8am-5pm, Su 8am-noon. **Spanish School House Rosa Silva** (☎8682 2938; www.span-ishsilva.com), 30m seaward from Market. 1hr. lesson C140 (US$7); 1 week with 20hr. of class C2500 (US$125), with homestay C4500 (US$225). **Nica Spanish** (☎505 832 4668; www.nicaspanish.com), on the corner of Av. Real and C. Vander-bilt. 1week with 20hr. of class and homestay C2000 (US$100). Collaborates with volunteer organizations throughout Nicaragua.

English-Language Bookstore: El Gato Negro (☎8678 9210; elgatonegronica.com), 1 block inland from El Albinal. New and used English-language books. Open daily 7am-3pm.

Laundromat: Nica Spanish Laundry Service (☎832 4668), on the corner of Av. Real and C. Vanderbilt. 12 pieces C70 (US$3.50).

Red Cross: (☎2563 3415).

Police: (☎2563 3732).

Pharmacy: Farmacianic (☎8411 3330), half a block south of Texaco. Open M-Sa 8am-5pm.

Hospital: (☎2563 3301, 3615, or 3415).

Internet Access: Cyber Cool Welcome, Av. Central (☎2568 3037), half a block inland from the shore. All computers have webcams and Skype. Internet C40 (US$2) per hr. Interna-tional calls to most places C1 (US$0.05) per min. most places. Also sells camera memory cards and data disks. **Cyber Leo's,** C. Vanderbilt, south of C. El Albinal. Internet C20 (US$1) per hr. International calls to the US C2 (US$0.10) per min. Open daily 7am-9pm..

Post Office: (☎2568 2560), on the southern end of the beachfront. Open M-F 8am-4pm.

ACCOMMODATIONS

Accommodations in San Jan del Sur are geared toward the beach-loving back-packer crowd. As expected, the closer you are to the beach, the more expen-sive your hotel is going to be.

Casa Oro Hostel (☎2568 2415; www.casaeloro.com), on the corner of C. Vanderbilt and C. Real. A hostel and tourist office all in one, Casa Oro is your hookup to goings-on in San Juan del Sur. With surfing lessons, beach transport (including a cheap shuttle that runs 3 times daily), sea turtle expeditions, and canopy tours, they've got you covered. Dorms C150-170; singles C340-380; doubles C500. Discounts to local establishments available. ❷

Hostal South Seas, C. Tropezón (☎2568 2084; www.thesouthseashostal.com), just beyond the fork of C. Tropezón with C. Albinal. This completely refurbished building boasts clean, comfortable rooms, spotless shared bathrooms, and a small but refresh-ing pool. Rooms C300. Discounts for a stays exceeding 1 week. AmEx/D/MC/V. ❸

Hostel Esperanza (☎8423 6869; www.hostelesperanza.com), half a block down the beachfront from the Banco de Finanzas. This clean and friendly newcomer offers the cheapest beachside accommodations around, and locals and travelers alike know it: the hostel is almost always full. Free water, coffee, kitchen use, and internet. Hammocks and tents C100; dorms C200-300; private rooms C400. Cash only. ❶

Hotel La Estación (☎2568 2304; www.laestacion.com.ni), on the corner of C. Paseo del Rey and C. Central. A sparkling hotel right on the beachfront with numerous amenities. Large, air-conditioned rooms with cable TV, private baths with hot water, and balconies overlooking the beach. Breakfast included. Free Wi-Fi. Singles C1100-1200; doubles C1400. AmEx/D/MC/V. ❺

Hospedaje Delfin (☎2568 2373), 1½ blocks north of the market. Another reasonable option close to the beach. Free kitchen use. International calls available, with discounts for guests. Checkout 1pm. Rooms with private bathroom C140; with TV C200. Cash only. ❷

🍴 FOOD

As with accommodations, the closer your restaurant is to the beach, the more likely it is to be expensive. Whether or not they boast beachfront views, international options are plentiful. For groceries, visit the **town market,** on the corner of C. Gaspar García Laviana and C. Central.

El Gato Negro (☎8678 9210; www.elgatonegronica.com), 1 block inland, on El Albinal. An eclectic cafe with more personality than you'll know what to do with. The food is organic and local whenever possible. Extensive selection of tasty vegetarian options. In-house bookstore sells brand-new English-language books (C100-500). Vegetable sandwich (avocado, tomato, onion, cucumber, lettuce and melted cheese) C95. Local, organic coffee C30. Decadent specialty drinks (Dark Chocolate Raspberry Truffle Latté; C50-60). Open 7am-3pm daily. ❷

Big Wave Dave's (☎2568 2151), just before El Gato Negro, on El Albinal. With its international American fare, Big Wave Dan's is apparently where the Americans who live in San Juan del Sur come to hang out. Hamburgers with mashed potatoes or fries (C90). Chicken and beef nachos (C45). Vegetarian options include fresh Caesar salad. Open 7:30am-11pm daily. AmEx/D/MC/V. ❷

Soda Mariel (☎2568 2466), half a block towards the shore from El Mercado. Definitely one of the cheapest options in town. The pink and purple interior will grow on you when you realize how much cash you are saving. Vegetarian tacos C30. Entrees C65-90. Soda C10. Open M-Sa 8am-8pm, Su 10am-3pm. Cash only. ❶

Restaurante El Globo (☎505 568 2478), across the street from the Banco de Finanzas. One of many beachfront options, El Globo provides a great view, though it isn't cheap. Chicken *cordon bleu* C170. Lunch special C85. Open M-F 10am-10pm, Sa-Su 10am-midnight. AmEx/D/MC/V. ❸

🏄 OUTDOOR ACTIVITIES

Arena Caliente Surf Shop, C. Gaspar García Laviana (☎8815 3247; www.arenacaliente. com), half a block north of the Market. The oldest surf company in San Juan del Sur. 1hr. lesson, 24hr. board rental, round-trip transportation, and rash guard shirt C600. Boogie board C100 per day; skimboard C120 per day. Cash only.

San Juan Surf and Sport, Av. Central (☎2984 2464 or 8402 2973; www.sanjuandelsurf. com), 20m west of the market. Although all the hype would have you to believe that you're in for a rowdy excursion, San Juan Surf and Sport's "Booze Cruise" (daily 3:30-5:30pm, C300) is actually more of a lesson in ecotourism than a party. A combination of sightseeing and sportfishing, passengers scout for sea turtles and watch the sunset over the ocean. After you've made your catch, guides are happy to direct you to restaurants where you can have it seasoned and cooked. Open 8am-6:30pm daily. AmEx/D/MC/V.

Nica Surf, C. Vanderbilt (☎2568 2626), just south of Av. Central. Offers 3hr. surf lessons with board rental included C800. Transportation to surf spots C100. Open M-Sa 8am-6pm. AmEx/MC/V.

Good Times Surf Shop, C. Vanderbilt (☎8976 1568), just south of Av. El Albinal. 1hr. lesson, 24hr. board rental, and transportation C600. They'll take you to the beach; you decide when to come back. Surfboard rental C200. Transportation C100.

CHINANDEGA

Chinandega (pop. 120,000), 36km northwest of León, is located in one of Nicaragua's hottest, driest, and flattest regions. A bustling commercial center, it has little to offer tourists save its chaotic *mercado* and ample stock of the famous rum, *flor de caña*. The only compelling reason to linger is to climb San Cristóbal, the country's tallest volcano.

📧 TRANSPORTATION. From the terminal in León, take the **bus** (1¼hr., every 15min. 4:30am-6pm, C12-15). For a faster and more comfortable trip, take the **minibus,** which departs from the terminal in León throughout the day as soon as it fills (40min., C20). Once you arrive in Chinandega, take a taxi or bus to the center of town.

All **buses** from Chinandega leave from the "El Bisne" bus terminal. Buses go to: Ciudad Darío (5:20am and 2:14pm); Corinto (every 15min. 4:30am-6pm); Guasaule, Honduras (every hr. 4am-5pm); León (every 15min., 4:30am-6pm); Managua (every hr. 4am-5:20pm); Matagalpa (4:20, 5:20am, 2:45pm). **Minibuses** depart when full for Managua, León, Guasaule, and Corinto (daily 4am-5pm).

🔼 PRACTICAL INFORMATION. The tourist office, **Intur,** is located 1 block east and half a block south of the *parque central.* (☎2341 1931. Open M-F 8am-12:30pm, 2-5pm.) **Farmacia Lisseth** is 2½ blocks east of the *parque* (open M-Sa 8am-6:30pm.) **Internet access** is available at **Satcom,** 2 blocks east of the *parque.* (☎2241 8481. C10 per hr. Open daily 8am-8pm.)

🏨 ACCOMMODATIONS. Hotel Cosigüina ❹, 2 blocks east and ½ block south from the SE corner of the *parque,* is the nicest (and most expensive) hotel in Chinandega. All rooms come with cable TV, hot water, and private bathrooms. (☎2341 3636; www.hotelcosiguina.com. Free Wi-Fi. Singles C800; doubles C1000; triples C1250. AmEx/D/MC/V.) In front of El Gallo más Gallo, **Hotel Casa Grande ❷** offers basic rooms. The owner speaks English and offers tours of San Cristóbal, where he owns a farm. (☎2341 4283. Free laundry service. Checkout 11:30am. Singles and doubles C200-400; triples C300-500. Cash only.) **Hotel Glomar ❷,** 1 block south of the *mercado central,* has well-lit rooms with fans. Some come with cable TV and private baths. (☎2341 2562. Checkout 2pm. Singles C200-300; doubles C300-500; triples C450-600. Cash only.)

🍴 FOOD. Chinandega is not exactly a thrill-ride for your taste buds. The best food here is the *fritanga* (fried food), served from a line of small huts on the east side of the *parque central.* **Fritanga La Parrillada ❶,** 1 block south of the SE corner of the *parque,* serves delicious *comida corriente* for C30-75. (☎2341 2132. Open daily 10am-10pm. Cash only.) For groceries, visit **Palí,** on the east side of the *parque.* (☎2341 1007. Open M-Sa 7:30am-8pm, Su 8am-6pm.) **Deliburguer ❶,** a small white and green hut on the east side of the *parque,* serves cheap eats; and, yes, that's actually how the name is spelled. (☎2341 2779. Jumbo hot dog C22. Open daily 11am-midnight.) At **Buffet Doña Jilma ❶,** Chinese rice and a drink will set you back C65. (3 blocks east and half a block south from the *parque,* in Chinandega's small food court. ☎2341 0378. Open M-Sa 11:30am-3pm. Cash only.)

📷 OUTDOOR ACTIVITIES

SAN CRISTÓBAL VOLCANO

From Mercado Bisne in Chinandega, take the bus headed toward Guasaule on the Hondu-ran border. Ask to be let off at the Campusano stop in El Ranchería (40min.; every 30min. 4am-7:30pm, return every 30min.; C8). Buses leave for El Bolsa from El Mercadito in Chinandega (30min., every hr. 5am-6pm, C6).

The highest volcano in Nicaragua (1786m), San Cristóbal affords amazing views. From **Chinandega** (p. 198), the climb is difficult. It's likely that you will have little time to look around if you want to get up and back before nightfall. **Hiring a guide is a must,** since following a random trail will likely take you nowhere. The 8-10hr. round-trip hike is steep and mostly above the tree line. There are two routes to the top, the first via **El Ranchería.** From the bus stop in Chinandega, walk along the highway toward Guasaule. Turn right where you see the few houses in the area and ask locals to show you where the *guardabosque* responsible for the area lives. He should be able to find you guide and horses. Come early, or the guide will probably refuse to take you to the top because hiking past nightfall is not advisable. (Guide and horses C110-140, plus tip).

The other route to the volcano is via **Las Bolsas.** From Las Bolsas, it's 11km up the road to **Hacienda Rosas,** at the foot of the volcano. No buses pass this way, so if you don't have a car you'll either have to walk or borrow a horse from **Socorro Pérez Alvarado** (☎8883 9354) who lives at the Las Bolsas stop. It's best to go with a guide to the summit. **Vincente Pérez Alvarado** (Socorro's brother) is knowledgeable and can arrange to meet you. The walk from Las Bolsas to the summit takes 9hr.; from the base of the volcano, the climb takes 5hr. round-trip. There is no water on either route, so bring plenty.

LAGO DE NICARAGUA

Fed by more than 40 rivers, streams, and brooks from Nicaragua and Costa Rica, Lago de Nicaragua is the largest lake in Central America and the tenth-largest freshwater body in the world. Hundreds of islands—430 to be exact—dot the lake's surface, notable as much for the water's wildlife as for the myths of the pre-Columbian petroglyphs. The lake is home to the bullshark, the only freshwater shark in the world. Many years ago these animals migrated up Río San Juan from the Caribbean Sea and slowly adapted to the freshwater environment.

Farther south, the Archipiélago de Solentiname is renowned for both its natural beauty and the minimalist paintings it has inspired. On the southeastern side of the lake sits San Carlos, where the Río San Juan begins its lazy trek toward the Caribbean. Four hours from Granada, some of Nicaragua's most treasured spots—two enormous volcanoes and the paradise of the Isla de Ometepe—sit in waiting.

ISLA DE OMETEPE

In Náhuatl, the ancient language of the Aztecs, *ome* means "two" and *tepetl* means "hills" or "volcanoes." Ometepe is the highest freshwater island in the world. The island has twin volcanoes, the active Volcán Conceptión (1610m) and the extinct **Volcán Maderas** (1394m), which houses an exquisite crater lake.

Ometepe is certainly one of Nicaragua's jewels, with pre-Columbian petroglyphs, fresh fish dinners, and above all, natural beauty. An adventure junkie's dream, Ometepe teems with energy. Homegrown tour agencies, which bombard tourists arriving from the port at Moyogalpa, offer activities ranging from hikes up the volcano, to tours on horseback, to kayaking on the lake. After you've come back to your hotel, grimy, sweaty, and smiling, know that this island is no stranger to nightlife. Although you won't find the techno discoteque that prevails in Granada, there are plenty of bars.

The only thing more inspiring than the scenery is the fact that local nature reserves are making conscious efforts to preserve it; you'll find more signs here urging you to clean up after yourself than you will in Managua. Even if you've always had an aversion to the outdoors, come to Ometepe and you'll be sure to find something that will amaze you.

⊏ LOCAL TRANSPORTATION

The easiest way to get around the island is to grab a **taxi** or **bus** from the station, just past the port as you walk in. Buses coordinate with the local **ferries** and head around the island, leaving from Moyogalpa hourly throughout the day. Taxis are bound to be more expensive, but offer the perks of faster travel and comfort. For the truly adventureous, there are many **dirtbike** rental places clustered around the port at Moyogalpa.

Car and Bike Rentals: UGO (☎8901 5587). Manual C700 per 12hr. Automatic C900 per 12hr. **OmetepExpeditions** (☎8933 4796). Dirtbikes C700 per 12hr. Scooters C900 per 12hr. **Parradero Tours** (☎8363 5796). Bikes C500 per 12hr.

✈ ORIENTATION

La Isla de Ometepe's imposing skyline can be intimidating from the ferry. Fortunately, it's not too complicated to get around. All of the island's towns and roads are situated on the edges of the island, and roads traverse the gap between the two volcanoes. All parts of Ometepe can be reached in close to two hours by taxi. **Moyogalpa,** on the western side of the island, has a spectacular view of **Volcán Concepción. Altagracia** and **Santo Domingo** also populate the western half of the island, while the incredible ▨**San Ramón waterfall** and **Volcán Maderas** occupy the eastern portion. On the whole, moving around is fairly easy, despite the often poor road conditions. Just know that if you do decide to ride the bus, or even the faster and more comfortable taxis, you are in for a bumpy ride.

⁊ PRACTICAL INFORMATION

MOYOGALPA

Tour Companies: Several different tour companies are located just inside the port of Moyogalpa, but "unofficial" guides can be found all around the island. Ask around for the best price.

UGO: Unión Guías de Ometepe (☎8901 5587; www.ometepeguides.com). UGO hands out a large map of the island and a helpful brochure. It also runs 10 different guided tours of the entire island. Tours of Volcán Concepción (up 1000m to a lookout point) C300 each for a group of 6. Hikes to the summit of Volcán Maderas (9hr.) C400 each for a group of 6. Horse tours around the island C120 per hr. 4hr. kayak tour C400 per person. Manual motorcycle C700, automatic C900. Open daily 9am-6pm.

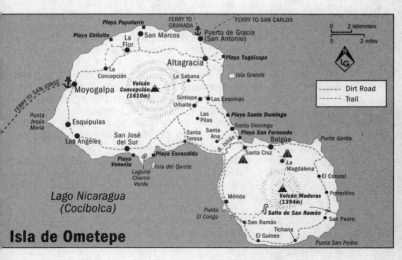

GALLO PINTO

Nationalist rivalries come to fore in the celebration of *gallo pinto* ("painted rooster"), the official dish of both Nicaragua and Costa Rica. Though both countries claim to have created the dish, it is not known which country's version came first.

Nicaraguan *gallo pinto* consists of fried red beans and fried brown rice, mushed together and fried again with vegetables and spices such as onions, peppers and cilantro. The shade the beans dye the rice is similar to the red crest and coloring of a rooster, explaining the origin of the dish's name. Costa Rican *gallo pinto* is nearly identical, though with slight local variations. A fairly simple recipe, it is made using ample amounts of oil and is cooked over a wood fire, making its taste difficult to replicate in a modern kitchen.

The dish is eaten for breakfast, lunch, dinner, or all three meals, sometimes with sides of meat, bread, or cheese. If a meal fried three separate times doesn't satisfy your saturated fat craving, it can be served refried for extra crispiness.

In fall of 2008, Nicaragua competed with Costa Rica for the honor of the world's largest gallo pinto at Pharaoh's Casino. The event, which took place on Nicaragua's annual **Gallo Pinto Day**, provided enough *gallo pinto* to feed 22,200 attendees.

OmetepExpeditions (☎8933 4796), just off the port on the left. 3-4 person tour of Volcán Maderas C600. Fishing tour C400 per hr. per person. Kayak and horse tours. Dirtbike rental C700. Scooter rental C900. Open daily 9am-6pm.

Parrandero Tours (☎836 35796), across the street from UGO and OmetepExpeditions. Fun, laid-back tours in English or Spanish. Just tell them what you want to do. Trip up to the lookout on Concepción C200. Motorcycle C500 per day.

Bank: Banco ProCredit (☎883 6393 or 883 8786), 3 blocks up from the Port, just past Cyber Arcia. **24hr ATM.** Open M-F 8:30am-4:30pm, Sa 8:30am-1pm.

Pharmacy: Farmacia Jany, 3½ blocks up from the port, on the left. Open M-F 8:30am-noon, 2-6pm.

Internet: Arcia Cyber Cafe (☎2569 4110), 2½ blocks from the port, on the right. Internet C10 per 30min. Open M-Sa 8am-8pm.

Post Office: Half a block left of the *parque central.* Open M-F 8am-noon, 1-4pm.

ALTAGRACIA

Internet: Hotel Castillo, 1 block south of the *parque central,* has the only reliable internet in town. Internet C25 per 30min.

Pharmacy: Farmacia Jany, on south side of the *parque central.* Open M-F and Su 7:30am-10pm.

🖸 FOOD

Food on Ometepe does not stray far from the Nicaraguan norm. Here, your culinary experience is enhanced with fresh ingredients. Chances are that your fish came directly from the lake. Most vegetables sold are grown locally and organically in Ometepe's nutrient-rich volcanic soil. For groceries, head to **Comercial Hugo Navas.** It's no Palí, but it covers the basics (☎2569 4244; open M-Sa 7:30am-5:30pm).

MOYOGALPA

🖼 **Los Ranchitos** (☎2569 4112), 3 blocks up from and half a block to the right of the port. Dirt floor and a lovely thatched roof with wicker lampshades. Recommended by every local around. Breakfast C45-75. Lunch and dinner C110-150. Open 7am-9:30pm daily. Cash only. ❸

Chidos (☎8359 7546), 3 blocks up, and a half block to the left of the port. Watch sports on the big screen TV inside or enjoy the fresh air on the patio. Personal pizza C80; extra large pizza C260. Calzones C100. Beer C20. Cash only. ❷

Comedor Mar Dulce (☎8667 5261), 2½ blocks up from the port, right before Banco ProCredit, on the left. Red and white tablecloths and multicolored plastic lawn chairs. A classic family restaurant serving hearty homecooked meals. Open daily 7am-7:30pm. Cash only. ❷

ALTAGRACIA

▨ **Comedor Nicarao,** across from the *parque central.* Big plates heaped with fresh, flavorful Nicaraguan fare. Beef, chicken, or fish with *gallo pinto* C45. Open 7am-10pm. ❶

SANTO DOMINGO

The best way to grab cheap beach grub on Santo Domingo is, unsurprisingly, to make your way to the beach. Walk along it in either direction and chances are you'll quickly find a good *comedor.*

Comedor Gloriana, just down the beach from Finca Santo Domingo. This little lakeside eatery serves standard fare, but it's cheap and the view can't be beat. Entrees C40-120. Drinks C10-25. Open 7am-9pm. Cash only. ❶

👁 SIGHTS

▨**SAN RAMÓN WATERFALL.** Located on a private ecological preserve, the *cascada* (waterfall) is well known around the island: local guides will know how to reach it. Pay C60 to enter and make the 1½ hour trek up as early as possible, both to beat the heat and avoid the crowds. Getting there takes you through some pristine jungle, where you can hear howler monkeys calling and see exotic birds flying overhead. It's bound to be hot and humid in any season, so bring lots of water. The hike itself is fairly easy going; it's only the last quarter of the 3km jaunt that the trek gets rocky and steep. It's worth all the effort, however, when you get there. Turning a corner, you suddenly come upon the San Ramón waterfall. A sheer, gray cliff face rises seemingly out of nowhere. Water, falling down and crashing off the rocks, collects in a small pool at the bottom. The best part is that you can simply walk right up to the edge of the waterfall and cool off under its spray. The pool never gets deeper than around 3 ft. The hike back down only takes about two-thirds of the time needed to ascend.

VOLCÁN MADERAS. Reaching Maderas's summit requires an early start: it's 5-8hr. (closer to the 8hr. end) of fairly steep hiking to the top and back, not including stops. The hike passes through tropical dry forest, then dense tropical rainforest, and finally cloud forest, so be prepared for muddy and physically taxing conditions. Hiking down into the lagoon in the crater, you may see howler and white-faced monkeys alongside colorful wildflowers. Be prepared: the higher you get, the colder it gets, so bring a jacket, even if you think you're not going to need it. It is possible to continue down into the crater with a rope to assist you, though this is better attempted with a guide. Unless you're planning on staying overnight, get started early. Ask the bus driver to drop you off at the entrance to Magdalena, from which a 15min. walk up the path leads to **La Finca Magdalena** ❸ (☎8855 1403; www.fincamagdalena.com), an organic coffee farm with spectacular views that sells quality cups of joe and pure bee honey. Workers live off the ecologically friendly solar energy system. It has a *hospedaje,* where tourists can stay in their hammocks or campgrounds (C60), or upgrade to a three-person dorm (C320) or a four-person wooden cabin (C1110). The restaurant serves delicious, traditional food (C60-100), and you can get 1lb. of roasted, ground coffee for C120.

VOLCÁN CONCEPCIÓN. The taller of the two volcanoes (1610m), Concepción is said to have the most perfect conical shape of all the volcanoes in Cen-

GIVING BACK

ISLAND SCHOOL

For those looking to contribute to the communities they visit during their stay in Nicaragua, the bilingual school on Ometepe may provide the perfect opportunity for their efforts.

The school is located in the small town of Mérida, on the slopes of Volcán Maderas. Founded in 2007 by Alvaro Molino, proprietor of the Hacienda Merida, the school requires a minimum committment of two weeks. The school offers free langue courses to the 50 students enrolled. Volunteers can expect to teach as many as three 2hr. English classes to 10 or more students each day; there is no school on Sunday. Sometimes class involves kayaking, hiking, or other field trips; these trips engage kids in discussions regarding local biodiversity. In this way, the school promotes the preservation of habitats and wildlife on Ometepe.

The fee for volunteers is US$150 for two weeks, which covers lodging in the hacienda as well as three meals per day. You do not have to be able to speak Spanish to participate as a volunteer.

Interested in helping out? Send your basic information and work experience details via email to **Alvaro** (alvaronica@gmail.com); be sure to include the dates you can work and the reasons why you are interested in volunteering.

tral America. Concepción is still active and the terrain near the top consists primarily of loose rocks and sand, making it less popular than Maderas for climbing. Low visibility, especially during the rainy season, often makes reaching the crater challenging (and pointless). If you do plan on hiking Concepción, bear in mind that it is very steep, and you need to be just as careful coming down as going up. The lower half of the volcano is covered with tropical dry forest. **Floreana** (about 2hr. to the top) is a good destination and offers the first clear, breathtaking vista from the volcano. Most hikes begin at **La Flor,** 6km northeast of Moyogalpa and reachable by bus (6:30, 10am, 1:30pm; returns every hr. 12:10-5:10pm.) Trails also start at **Cuatro Cuadras,** 2km from Altagracia; **La Concha,** 4km from Moyogalpa on the road to La Flor; **La Sabana,** a 1km walk from Altagracia; and **San Ramón.** A guide is essential; paths on Concepción are unmarked and hard to find.

MUSEO DE OMETEPE Sadly, Altagracia's one real claim to fame is in a sad state of disrepair. What should be an interesting, engaging collection of ancient ceramic and *petroglyphs* (rock carvings) is in need of a good cleaning and some serious reorganization. It's still worth a peek if you're in town. *(1 block west of parque central, Altagracia. Open M-F 8am-noon, 1-4:30pm, Sa 9am-3pm, Su 9am-1pm. C30, permission to take photos of the exhibits C35.*

SALA ARQUEOLOGICA, MOYOGALPA. This salon exhibits a private collection of pre-Colombian pieces found all over Ometepe, including ancient ceramics and grindstones. Some objects date back as far as 300 BC. *(2½ blocks from the port on the right.* ☎ *2569 4225. Open daily 9am-9pm. C40)*

PLAYA SANTO DOMINGO. Come to Ometepe to explore; come to Playa Santo Domingo to rest afterwards. With its long stretches of white sand, a lake with amazing views, and cheap eats, Santo Domingo is a wonderful place to relax. This long beachfront is home to several different hotels and hostels, including **Finca Santo Domingo.** The lake water is warm, comfortable, and safe to swim in.

CHARCO VERDE. Charco Verde, or the "green lagoon," is another tourist hotspot on Ometepe located in a private nature reserve. A hotel with lakefront beach access awaits all those who come to see the lagoon and discover they just can't leave. As an added bonus, the C10 entrance fee to the park is waived for guests of the hotel. Walking around, check out massive termites hard at work and iguanas lurking in tree tops. A quiet, shady trail circles the lagoon. There is also a hike to a nearby hill to witness it from above, where its green color is supposedly at its most vibrant. After you've explored the lagoon, grab a beer and enjoy the hotel's spacious table seating, or cool off by jumping in the lake.

Hotel y Restaurante Charco Verde (☎8927 2892; www.charcoverde.com), on the route to Altagracia from Moyogalpa. Rooms with private baths and A/C. Checkout at noon. Doubles C910, triples C1110. AmEx/D/MC/V.

PETROGLYPHS. Affording a unique glimpse into the pre-Columbian world, most of the petroglyphs lie between Balgüe and Magdalena on the Maderas side of the island. Another group is located near El Porvenir, a 30min. walk from Santo Domingo and 10min. from Santa Cruz and La Palma. Carved between the 11th and 13th centuries, these simple etchings contain spirals and circles of unknown significance. Find them yourself by renting a bike or car and asking around (most children will be willing to show you the way for a few córdobas), or hire a guide.

RÍO SAN JUAN

The gorgeous Río San Juan runs over 200km, connecting Lake Nicaragua and its river tributaries to the Caribbean Sea. It also marks the border between Nicaragua and Costa Rica. Swirling, expanding, and churning from San Carlos to San Juan del Norte, its waters have washed away history and legends since the 16th century. Since its days as a conduit between the Atlantic and the Pacific for slave-trading ships, the region's growing ecotourism market has blossomed. While some might cry foul at the commercialization of this natural wonder, nearly all of the tours are geared toward a better appreciation of the area's beauty, with an eye for helping preserve its pristine condition.

The Río San Juan has counted many admirers, including the American author Mark Twain. The lucky visitor who makes it out to see this wonder will find a mini-Amazon full of untouched flora and fauna, including the *Sábalo Real* (a giant fish, known in English as the Tarpon) and endless tropical flora like *lechuga*, a type of lettuce that grows on floating vegetation. Apart from the main attractions, there are many hidden places along the river—farms, mountains, pueblos, and *comarcas* like Boca de Sábalos and Raudal del Toro. Travel down the Río San Juan and experience some of Nicaragua's most remote settlements, namely Boca, El Castillo Viejo, and San Juan del Nicaragua.

⊟ LOCAL TRANSPORTATION

BOCA DE SÁBALOS

Boats: Take any of the boats heading from San Carlos to El Castillo; they all make a stop at Boca de Sábalos. C65. Daily departures at 6:30, 8, 10am, noon, 12:30, 3:30, 4:30pm.

Water Taxis: C5-10 depending. Ask one of the people waiting at the docks for someone to take you across the river in a wooden canoe.

EL CASTILLO

Boats: Boats leave from San Carlos to El Castillo daily (6:30, 8, 10am, noon, 12:30, 3:30, 4:30pm; C75). Boats returning to San Carlos (2hr. 20min; 5, 6, 7am, 2pm; C80; express 1hr. 20min.; 5:20am, 11am, 3:30pm; C120).

SAN JUAN DE NICARAGUA

Boats: Public *lanchas* come and leave town only twice a week from San Carlos (9-12hr.; Tu and F 6am, return Th and Su 5am; 160C) and El Castillo (Tu and F 10am, return Th and Su 2pm).

ORIENTATION

The Río San Juan runs from its southwestern joining point with Lago de Nicaragua at the dull city of **San Carlos,** and flows east all the way through to the Atlantic Ocean and **San Juan de Nicaragua.** The towns of **Boca de Sábalos** and **El Castillo,** as well as **Refugio Bartola** and the **Indio Maíz nature preserve,** lie along the river between these two points. Boca de Sábalos comes first, sitting on the mouth of a tributary ("boca" meaning mouth). El Castillo, an additional 15-30min. upriver by boat, is all located on one bank and sits on top of a large hill. Six kilometers farther upstream takes you to Refugio Bartola, located on the edge of the Indio Maíz nature preserve. From there, it's a straight 8hr. boat ride to San Juan de Nicaragua.

PRACTICAL INFORMATION

BOCA DE SÁBALOS

Tourist Office: (☎8123 3190), in a small shack on the docks. Ask for Julío Murillo. Offers 12 different tours, including a hot springs tour (C700 for a group of 5); a steamboat tour, where you can observe the remains of an over 200-year-old steamboat abandoned on the Río San Juan (2½-3hr.; C850 for a group of 5); and an epic, 6-day kayak trip to San Juan de Nicaragua (C5050 per person). Open M-Sa 7am-noon, 1-5pm.

Tour Companies: Hotel Sábalos, across the river from the Tourist Office. Canoe tour up the Río Sábalos in a traditional wooden canoe C200. 2hr. horseback tour C400. Steamboat tour C700. San Juan Plantation tour C900. 2hr. Caymen tour C300 per person. Tour of Cocoa Plantation (price varies). Full-day tour of El Castillo and Reserva Indio Maíz, which takes you first to El Castillo to see La Fortaleza Immaculada de la Concepción, and then continues on an into the nature reserve; C3000 for a group of 4-5.

Pharmacy: "Farmacia Flor de Liz," 1½ blocks up the hill on the left. Open M-Sa 7:30am-10pm, Su 7:30-11:30am.

EL CASTILLO

Tourist Office, 20m from the docks. Provides information about the town and the surrounding area, and offers several different tours. Caymen night tour (C800 for a group of 4). Tours of Reserva Indio Maíz (4hr.; C1300 for a group of 6). This tour showcases the natural beauty of the area, with virgin forests, birdwatching, monkeys, and medicinal plants. Trails are very well marked. Fishing tours also available: consult office for prices. Guides speak some English.

Pharmacy: Venta Social de Medicamentos Inmaculada Concepción, 3 blocks south of the docks. Take a right at the playground; its on the left. Open M-F 8am-noon, 2-5pm.

Internet: Hotel Albergue. Internet C15 per hr. **Border's Coffee.** Internet C20 per hr. International calls to the US C10 per min.

LAGO DE NICARAGUA

⛏ ACCOMMODATIONS

When exploring the Río San Juan, you'll most likely end up staying at one of the area's two river towns, Boca de Sábalos and El Castillo. There are plenty of small hostels and family hotels in both cities, although El Castillo is more tourist-oriented than Boca de Sábalos. For groceries, head to **Mini Super San Antonio** in El Castillo, 2 blocks south of the docks. This small shop sells basic produce, snacks, and toiletries. (☎8690 0681. Open daily 6:30am-9pm.)

BOCA DE SÁBALOS

▧ **Hotel Sábalos** (☎8659 0252 or 2894 9377; www.hotelsabalos.com), at the entrance to Boca de Sábalos, on the opposite bank of the Río San Juan. The impressive deck, strewn with chairs and hammocks, will make you want to stay here just so you can hang out outside. Clean and comfortable rooms with fresh linens and hot water. The owner, Rosa Elena, is a great source of information about the surrounding area, and the hotel offers various tours. Breakfast included. Singles from C300, doubles from C600. AmEx/D/MC/V. ❸

Hotel Kateana (☎8633 8185 or 2583 0178), about 1½ blocks up from the dock on the left. A smaller and less expensive option than Hotel Sábalos. A small market downstairs means you can get all your snacks for the day before you head out. Check-out 10am. Singles with shared baths C150, with private baths C200; doubles C200/250. Cash only. ❷

EL CASTILLO

▧ **Hotel El Albergue** (☎8924 5608; mrcrsls116@yahoo.com), from the dock, 1 block east up the stairs. Spacious, open interior filled with comfortable wood-paneled rooms. Breakfast included. Internet C15 per hr. Wi-Fi C20 per hr. Singles C300. Cash only. ❸

Hotel Richarson (☎8644 0782), 350m east of the docks. Basic, clean rooms, each with a private bath and fan. Breakfast included. Singles C200, doubles C400. ❷

Hospedaje Marantial (☎8843 7033), 75m from the docks. Breakfast C35. Singles C80. Discounts available for groups. ❶

Hotel Refugio Bartola (☎8880 8754; refugiobartola@yahoo.com), 6km downriver from El Castillo. On the edge of the Bartola nature reserve, next to La Reserva Indio Maíz. For those who really, really want to "get away from it all." Large "rancho" space available for group events. Breakfast included. Individual cabins C1000 per person. ❻

SAN JUAN DE NICARAGUA

Tío Poon's Place, on C. Primera across from Disco Fantasía. Offers rooms with shared baths for a low C60. ❶

🍴 FOOD

Small *comedors* (diners) and *sodas* (cafés) constitute the majority of the food options on the Río San Juan. Your best bet is to opt for some fresh fish—the local favorite is tarpon—and have it cooked to your liking.

BOCA DE SÁBALOS

Comedor Gomez (☎8446 7447), half a block up from the docks, on the right. A Mom and Pop establishment. Serves a quick plate of whatever's hot with a soda (C50). Open daily 6am-8pm. ❶

Soda "El Buen Gusto" (☎8991 1158), 1 block up from the docks, on the left. Cheap, classic Nica food. Entrees C40-100. Sodas C10. Beer C20. Open daily 7am-8:30pm. Cash only. ❶

EL CASTILLO AND SAN JUAN DEL NICARAGUA

▨ **Border's Coffee** (☎2583 0110 or 8408 7688; borderscoffee21@yahoo.com), off of the docks on the right. Try the vegetarian pasta (C120) or a milkshake made with real, locally grown cocoa (C40). Owner Yamil Obregón is a wonderful resource for information on the town and boat schedules. Open daily 7am-10pm. Cash only. ❷

Comedor Vanessa (☎8408 0279 or 8447 8213), about 4 blocks south of the docks. Entrees C120-C220. *Comidas rápidas* C20-80. Beer C20. Open daily 7am-8:30pm. ❷

Bar y Restaurante los Delicias del Indio, on C. Primera in San Juan de Nicaragua. Serves cheap corriente (C20) under a gazebo along the Río Indio. ❶

👁 SIGHTS

EL CASTILLO

LA FORTALEZA INMACULADA DE LA CONCEPCIÓN. Constructed in the 17th century by the Spanish at a strategic point on the *El Diablo* rapids, this fortress is now a national landmark. No tourist excursion down the Río San Juan would be complete without a stroll around its ancient walls. Climb up the stairs and cross over the drawbridge (yes, it has a drawbridge) of this 300-year-old structure. The top of the fortress, where the Nicaraguan flag proudly flies, is a perfect spot for taking photos of the surrounding area. The public library for El Castillo is located in the Fortress. *(Open M-F 8am-noon, 2-5pm. C40.)*

LA FORTALEZA INMACULADA DE LA CONCEPCIÓN MUSEUM. At the top of a hill, just before the final push to the fortress, is the fortress's museum. This new building features several attractive displays, holding artifacts ranging from ancient grinding stones to glass bottles and pistol handles pulled out of the river. Each display is accompanied by an elaborate explanation in Spanish and a smaller explanation in dubious English. Stroll through before heading up to the monument and to get a crash course in the history of the region. *(On the top of the hill, just before the monument. C40, pictures C25 extra.)*

REFUGIO BARTOLA AND THE INDIO MAÍZ NATURE PRESERVE. Up river from El Castillo, toward San Juan de Nicargua, lies El Refugio Bartola and La Reserva Indio Maíz, a nature preserve that houses some of the most pristine wilderness in the world. The hot, steamy jungles of the Río San Juan are filled with exotic flora and fauna. A stay at the **Hotel Refugio Bartola** (p. 207), 6km downriver from El Castillo, affords travelers an opportunity to immerse themselves completely in these jungles.

▨**FESTIVALS.** On March 19th, El Castillo celebrates its patron saint, San Jose de la Montaña, with *hípica* (horse parades), dancing, and parties. From September 13-15, the town hosts an international fishing tournament for *Sábalos Real* (Tarpon).

CENTRAL HIGHLANDS

The central highlands are a region of rugged mountains accessible by steep, curving, scenic roads. They were the political stronghold of the Contras during the late 1980s, and fighting continued here long after it had died out in the lowlands. Nearly every individual over age 25 has a story to tell about the war's impact. The fiercely free-thinking highlanders have always been difficult for the government to control, with passionate viewpoints spanning the political spectrum.

Estelí, the largest city in the north, has some compelling reminders of the war and is easily visited en route from Managua to the Honduran border along the Interamerican Hwy. South of Estelí is a turnoff for the beautifully situated town of Matagalpa, gateway to Selva Negra, one of Nicaragua's most accessible forest preserves. A separate highway running east from Managua toward the Caribbean coast passes near Boaco, a mountainous cowboy town, before reaching Juigalpa, a good place to stop if you're making the trip all the way to the coast.

ESTELÍ

The agricultural town of Estelí (pop. 201,000), about halfway between Managua and the Honduran border, is a welcome escape from the heat of lowland cities. While it is the largest town in northern Nicaragua, its cobbled streets turn to dirt roads just a few blocks from the Avenida Central, and the nearby countryside remains fairly unsettled. The colonial Cathedral, Nuestra Señora del Rosario, towers over the surrounding streets, providing an excellent example of the past that this town zealously tries to preserve. Estelí is the tobacco center of Nicaragua, producing volumes of hand-rolled cigars that rival the quality of those made in Cuba. The town also has a lively coffee industry. Fiercely patriotic, Estelí celebrates its own revolution on the 16th of July, three days before the rest of the country, with an enormous party in the *parque central* full of music, flags, and screaming people.

▛ TRANSPORTATION

Buses: Cotran Norte, on the PanAm highway, on the south side of town. To: **Managua** (3hr.; 5:20, 6:20, 11:20am; C60); **León** (2hr. 20min., 3:10pm, C60); **Masaya** (3hr., 2 and 3:10pm, C60); **Jinotega** (3½hr.; 4:45, 7:30, 8:30am; C45); **Ocotoal** (2¼hr., every hr. 6-11am, C25); **Somoto** (2hr., every hr. 5:30-10:30am, C25); **Jalapa** (5½hr., 4:10am, C76); **Wiwili** (8hr.; 3, 4, 5, 7:35, 8:30am; C85). **Cotran Sur,** on the PanAm highway, about 200m south of Cotran Norte. To **Managua** (regular: 3hr. 10min., C45; express: 2hr. 10min., every 30min. 3:30am-6pm, C60), **León** (2½hr., 6:50am, C60), and **Matagalpa** (1¾hr., every 30min. 5:20am-5:30pm, C25).

◢ ▟ ORIENTATION AND PRACTICAL INFORMATION

Avenidas run north-south and *calles* run east-west. **Avenida Central,** which spans the length of the city, and **Calle Transversal** run near the center of town one block south of the *parque*. The **Interamerican Highway** runs along the eastern edge of

Central Highlands

town, six blocks east of Av. Central. The **Esquina de los Bancos** (financial district) sits at the intersection of Av. 1 SO and C. Transversal. The town is divided into **quadrants (NO, NE, SO, SE)** that originate from the four corners of the **parque central.** The **Terminal Norte** is at the south end of town; three blocks up is **Terminal Sur.**

Tourist Office: Cafe Luz (☎8405 8919; www.cafeluzyluna.com) has the best tourist information in Estelí. **Intur** (☎2713 6799; www.visitanicaragua.com), half a block south of the western corner of the *parque central*. Has some tourist information and brochures. Open M-F 8am-noon and 2-5pm.

Tours: UCA Miraflor (☎2713 2971 or 8855 0585), 2 blocks east and half a block north of the eastern corner of the *parque*. Has information and makes reservation services for the Miraflor reserve.

Banks: BanPro, BDF, ProCredit, and BAC are located on the *esquina de los bancos* (bank corner), 1 block south and 1 block west of the *parque central*. All have **24hr. ATMs.** All are open M-F 8:30am-4:30pm, Sa 8:30am-noon.

Beyond Tourism: Cenac Spanish School (☎2713 5437; www.spanishschoolcenac.com), by the stoplights on the PanAm highway. Offers 4hr. Spanish classes. **Texoxel Spanish School** (☎8487 4106), 5 blocks east on right from the Shell Estelí. C100 per hr. or C3430 per week. Funds go to help support a cancer research group based in Managua.

Emergency: Cruz Roja (☎2713 2330 or 119).

Police: (☎2713 2616 or 118).

24hr. Pharmacy: Farmacia Las Segovias (☎2713 6654), 1 block south and half a block west from the southwest corner of *parque central*. Open M-Sa 8am-8:30pm. Cash only. **Farmacia Estelí** (☎2713 2531), 1 block south on C. Central from *parque central*. Open daily 8am-8pm. Cash only.

Hospital: (☎2713 6305).

Internet Access: Conectate, half block west from the southwestern corner of the *parque central*. Internet C12 per hr. Open daily 8am-10pm. **Estelí@Net,** across the street from Farmacia Las Segovias. Internet C12 per hr. Open daily 8am-10pm.

Post Office: Av. 2nd NE, between 5a SE and 6a SE. Open M-Sa 8am-noon and 1-4pm.

ACCOMMODATIONS

▧ **Hospedaje Luna** (☎8405 8919; www.cafeluzyluna.com), 1 block east of Hotel Mesón. Guests of the hotel get free tea and coffee at Cafe Luz (below). Attentive staff provides you with tourist info and gives tours of the city's murals and cigar factory. Wi-Fi available. Dorms C140; singles C200, with bath C240; doubles C340/400; triples C420/480. Cash only. ❷

Hotel El Mesón (☎2713 2655), 1 block north from the Cathedral on the *parque central*. Eye-catching bright blue and maroon exterior. Rooms come with private baths, hot water, fans, and cable TVs. Pleasant garden courtyard with tables and palm-thatch huts. Wi-Fi in lobby. Check-out 2pm. Singles C300, with A/C C500; quads C640. AmEx/MC/V. ❸

Hotel Los Arcos (☎2713 3830). This is Estelí's luxury option. Convenient location only half a block away from the *parque central*. Large rooms, each with TV, bath, hot water, and complimentary candy. Lovely garden. Singles C800, with A/C C1000; doubles C900/1100; Presidential Suite C1700. AmEx/D/MC/V. ❸

Hotel Nicarao (☎2713 2490), 1½ blocks south of the *parque central*. Well-decorated rooms, some with TVs. Sells tasty-looking donuts all day in the lobby. Dorms C140, rooms C200-600. Cash only. ❷

FOOD

Estelí has some of the best *comida extranjera* (foreign food) in Nicaragua. For groceries, visit **Palí,** 3½ blocks south on C. Central. (☎2713 2963. Open M-Sa 7:30am-8pm, Su 8am-7pm. Cash only.)

▧ **Cafe Luz** (☎8405 8919; www.cafeluzyluna.com). Café Luz is not to be missed. The varied menu contains several flavorful vegetarian options. Smoothies, made with milk and fresh house yogurt, come in a variety of fruit flavors (C30-35). The inside of this eclectic cafe is filled with shelves selling local chocolate, coffee, and handicrafts. All profits from the cafe go to the Miraflor foundation. ❶

▧ **Casa Italia** (☎2713 5274), 3 blocks north and half a block east of Hotel El Mesón. Sit down for authentic Italian cuisine in the chef's house and play complimentary pool, darts, cards, or dominos while you wait for your food. Delicious pizzas (C100-150) and appetizers (garlic bread; C20), handmade from scratch. Open Tu-Su noon-2pm and 4-10pm. Cash only. ❸

▧ **La Casita** (☎2713 4917), 500m south down the highway past the curve. Healthful, tasty food. Try a *merienda* (a small loaf of homemade whole wheat bread) with hummus and cucumber for C26. Fresh fruit juices and coffee. Open M 2-7pm, Tu-Su 9am-7pm. Closed 1st M of every month. Cash only. ❶

Rincón Pinareño (☎2713 0248), 1½ blocks south from the southeastern corner of the *parque central*. Specializes in Cuban food. Get your pork fix here. Smoked roasted pork leg

CENTRAL HIGHLANDS

C100. Roasted pork sandwich on a crispy baguette half C55, whole C75. Refresh yourself after the meal with a *mojito cubano* (C55). Open Tu-Su 10am-11pm. AmEx/D/MC/V. ❷

La's Carreta Buffet (☎8608 3783), next to Farmacia Las Segovias. A traditional Nica buffet and lunchtime hangout. 3-course plate C30. Open M-Sa 7am-4pm. Cash only. ❶

Yúsvar (☎8412 3713), half a block west from the *parque central*. This small juice bar serves fresh smoothies. Cooling cucumber, watermelon, and mint leaves C25-35. Fruit salads C15. Open M-Sa 8am-7pm. Cash only. ❶

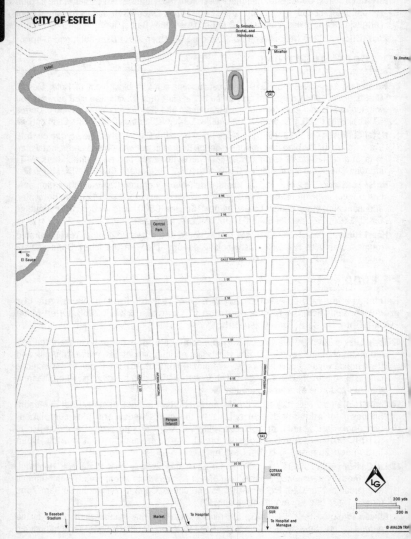

CITY OF ESTELÍ

Café Repostería Mamilou (☎2713 2878), 20m south of Bancentro. Secluded cafe with fountains, prompt service, and multiple comfortable seating areas. Coffee and soda C5-28. Pies C5-25. Small meals C45. Open M 10am-7pm, Tu 10am-5pm, W-Sa 10am-7pm, Su 1-7pm. ❶

📻 🎵 NIGHTLIFE AND ENTERTAINMENT

Rincón Legal (☎8438 6336 or 8423 3721), on the PanAm highway, on the south end of Estelí. This bar is a standing tribute to the revolution, with murals of Sandino, Fonseca, and other heroes, as well as Che Guevara. The entryway is decorated with war relics, including helmets and machine guns. Beer C20. Rum C50. Open Th-Sa 5pm-3am. Cash only.

Cinema Estelí (☎2713 2293), on the south side of the *parque central*. Shows recently released movies. Showings M-Th 6 and 8pm; Sa-Su 3, 6, and 8pm. C30.

Los Semáforos (☎2713 3659), on the south side of town, 400m south of the hospital. 2 dance floors and 2 bars make this discotheque popular with locals. F-Sa live music. DJs spin when the bands aren't playing. Beer C24. Rum shot C20. Open Th-Su 7pm-2 or 3am. Cash only.

👁 SIGHTS

CIGAR TOUR. The tour guides explain the cigar-making process in great detail. Walking through the factory, you'll see tobacco in its multiple stages, from being "cured" in great stacks (to make it flexible for rolling) to being rolled by workers into cigars. You'll also see the workers who roll the cigars. For real cigar aficionados, the company sells its product in any size or brand (C20 per cigar). Grab a box to take home. *(The easiest way to go on a tour of the cigar factory is to inquire at Café Luz. The tours leave at 9am and take about 2hr. Includes guide, tour, taxi ride, and a free stogie. C100.)*

CATEDRAL NUESTRA SEÑORA DEL CARMEN. Built in a modern style, this cathedral has floor tiles, colorful windows, and wooden ceiling panels that are worth a look. *(On the east side of the parque central.)*

OTHER SIGHTS. Casa de Cultura showcases local art. Wander the gallery downstairs to see if any of the artists are at work. La Casa de Cultura also runs dance and theater classes; call María (☎8362 5294) for more info. The **Museo de Heroes y Martínes** covers history of the revolution of 1979 through photographs and soldier memorabilia. *(1 block south of the parque central. ☎2713 3021. Both are open M-F 8am-noon and 1-4pm. Free. Donations encouraged.)*

🏔 OUTDOOR ACTIVITIES

EL SALTO DE ESTANZUELA. This sight may be reason enough to come to Estelí. The waterfall is spectacular, spilling over the edge of the cliff and filling a small pool perfect for swimming. The area on the cliff around the water is covered in green moss, which makes for a great photo opportunity. Visitors can swim right up to the waterfall and feel the water crash down around them. There is also a small overhang to the left of the waterfall in case you want to stay up close but avoid the spray. The pool under the waterfall drains into a small stream that heads off into the jungle. *(Take the bus from Terminal Norte (1hr., 6:30am and 1:30pm, C20) all the way to the waterfall, or take a taxi to the hospital south of town and then walk 5km up the dirt road. 1½hr. C15.)*

MIRAFLOR. Just outside of Estelí is the nature reserve Miraflor, a collection of 44 different communities, all of them populated by subsistence farmers and

CENTRAL HIGHLANDS

coffee producers. Five of the communities are open for tourist homestays, and some offer *cabaña* accommodations. The outdoor opportunities around Miraflor are endless: with jungles, waterfalls, and caves, you won't be a bored hiker here. The real joy in visiting Miraflor, however, lies in getting to know the people that live there. Staying with a family in a simple cement and wood home and experiencing their day-to-day activities is a once-in-a-lifetime experience. *(Arrange a reservation at the UCA Miraflor office—see Practical Information, p. 209. Homestays C30; meals included. Cabañas C100.)*

MATAGALPA

Matagalpa (pop. 77,000) has an extraordinary location in the heart of coffee country. Those arriving from hotter climates will be refreshed by the pleasantly cool days and downright chilly nights. Originally settled in the 19th century by European immigrants, Matagalpa was an FSLN (Sandinista National Liberation Front) stronghold during the revolution and the birthplace of Carlos Fonseca— a founding member of the FSLN. As a result, locals take their politics seriously. The majority of visitors come to Matagalpa for the spectacular Selva Negra National Park, a short bus ride from the city, but visitors should also check out El Castillo de Cacao, the chocolate factory just outside of town.

TRANSPORTATION

Buses: 2 blocks south and 5 blocks west of Parque Rubén Darío. To: **Chinandega** (2½hr., 2pm, C60); **Estelí** (2hr., 2 per hr., C25); **Jintogea** (1½hr., 2 per hr., C25); **León** (2½hr., 3 and 4pm, C60); **Managua**, (2hr., every hr., C60); **Selva Negra** (45min.-1hr., C15)

ORIENTATION AND PRACTICAL INFORMATION

Matagalpa has two *parque centrals:* **Parque Rubén Darío** in the south and **Parque Morazán** in the north, across the Cathedral. The downtown area lies between them. The main street, **Calle de los Comercios,** begins at the northwestern corner of Rubén Darío and continues north for seven blocks before ending in the middle of Parque Morazán. One block east, **Avenida de los Bancos** (Avenida Central) also connects the two parks and contains most banks. The **bus terminal** is five blocks west and two blocks south of Parque Darío, along the river.

Tourist Office: Intur (☎2772 7060; www.visitanicaragua.com), 1½ blocks from Citibank. Attentive staff answers questions about the surrounding area. No English spoken. Great map of Matagalpa C50. Open M-F 8am-5:30pm.

Tours: Matagalpa Tours (☎2772 0108 or 8647 4680; www.matagalpatours.com), 1 block south and half a block east from Parque Morazán. A great tour company that specializes in ecotours and hikes of the surrounding area. Offers visits to cacao and coffee farms, as well as trips to the indigenous village of "Chile" 30km away. City tour (C740) focuses on Nicaraguan social life. Hike in the cloud forests of Cerro El Arenal nature preserve (3-5hr., C700 per person). Ask about more intense, week-long hikes up into the untouched rainforests near Siuna. Open M-F 8am-6pm, Sa 9am-2pm.

Bank: Banco ProCredit (☎2772 6501), 2 blocks east from Parque Morazán. Open M-F 8:30am-5:30pm, Sa 8:30am-1pm. **24hr. ATM.**

Beyond Tourism: Escuela Español Matagalpa, inside Matagalpa Tours. One-on-one language classes. C140 per hr. Homestay packages available.

Police: (☎2772 3870), on the south side of Parque Morazán. **Red Cross:** (☎2772 2059), across the river from the bridge, near Parque Morazán.

Hospital: Cesar Amador Molina (☎2772 2081), on the north end of town.

Pharmacy: Farmacia Arevalo (☎2772 0988), half a block from the southwestern corner of Parque Darío. Open M-Sa 7am-9pm, Su 7am-1pm.

Internet Access: Excell Cyber (☎2772 3173), on the west side of Parque Morazán. Internet C14 per hr. Open daily 8am-8:30pm. **Cyber G-Net** (☎2772 2214), 1 block north from the northwest corner of Parque Darío. Internet C12 per hr. Open M-Sa 8am-9pm.

Post Office: (☎2772 2004), 1 block south and half a block east from Parque Morazán. Open M-F 8am-5pm, Sa 8am-noon.

▮ ACCOMMODATIONS

There is no shortage of accommodations in Matagalpa. Expect clean, family-run hotels and a mostly Nicaraguan clientele.

▨ **Hostal El Rey** (☎2772 3435 or 2772 3762). A new hostel and a great budget option. All rooms with TVs. Kitchen available. 2-person dorms C100 per person; private rooms with baths and hot water C200 per person. Cash only. ❶

▨ **Hotel Apante** (☎2772 6890), next to Gallo más Gallo, on the west side of Parque Darío. Family-run hotel with free coffee and purified water (score!). Incredible views from the 2nd floor. Singles with bath and hot water C150; doubles C220; triples 350. Cash only. ❷

Hotel Alvarado (☎2772 2830). Owned by a nice elderly couple. Each room comes with a fan, but more importantly, a bedspread that you might actually need. Curfew 10:30pm. Checkout 10am. Singles have shared baths; all other rooms come with private baths. Singles C150; matrimonials C300; doubles C350; triples C400. Cash only. ❷

Hotel Soza (☎2772 3030 or 8928 1941), 2½ blocks from the northwest corner of Parque Darío. Tight hallways and low head clearances. Clean and comfortable rooms. Checkout 10am. Rooms C140 per person, with TV C200 per person. Cash only. ❷

Hotel 24 Horas (☎8607 6164), 1 block south of Juan Morales. One of the newest hotels in Matagalpa. Clean and modern rooms. Be warned: guests have been known to get locked out at the not-so-late-hours of the night. TV in common room. Balcony on the 2nd floor. Checkout 9am. Matrimonials C200; doubles C300. Cash only. ❷

▮ FOOD

For groceries, visit **Supermercado La Matagalpa**, 2½ blocks from the northwest corner of Parque Darío (☎2772 2664 or 2772 5312; open daily 8am-9pm). You're in the heart of coffee country, so enjoy it! There are several small cafes scattered about Matagalpa where you can get a cup of freshly brewed joe.

▨ **Comedor Oasis** (☎2772 3833), 1½ blocks east of Parque Darío. Tasty and filling 3 course meals, complete with corn tortilla and *refresco* (juice drink; C40). Try the Maracuya and carrot drink. Open M-F 7am-8:30pm, Sa 7am-3pm. Cash only. ❶

La Vita é Bella (☎2772 5476), 2 blocks east and 1½ blocks north from northeast corner of Parque Morazán. Great homemade pasta and pizza await at this tucked-away restaurant. Pizzas small C40-60, large C130-160. Try the Pasta Vita Bella (with your choice of spaghetti, penne, or bowtie noodles), with bacon, tomato sauce, olives, and mushrooms. All pastas come with homemade garlic bread. Open Tu-Su noon-10:30pm. AmEx/D/MC/V. ❷

Casa Grande (☎2772 0988), 1½ blocks from Iglesia San Jose. A local favorite. Balcony seating available. Try *Caballo Ball* (a platter with chicken, beef, pork, green and ripe plantains, tortillas, cheese, *gallo pinto*, and salad; C350). Beer C15-40. Appetizers C80. Main plates C150-205. Open daily 11am-11pm. AmEx/D/MC/V. ❸

Maná del Cielo (☎2772 5686), 1½ blocks south of Av. de los Bancos. Convenient buffet and breakfast joint. Plates of ham and cheese C50. Open daily 7am-10pm. AmEx/D/MC/V. ❶

CENTRAL HIGHLANDS

CAFES IN MATAGALPA

◪ **Simo's Cafe** (☎2772 0020), 75m west of the southwest corner of Parque Darío. A modern cafe, with padded chairs, comfy couches, A/C, and great coffee. Wi-Fi available. Cup of joe C12. Arabic coffee and cappuccino C20-25. Sandwiches and breakfast plates C30-50. Open daily 8am-9pm. AmEx/D/MC/V.

Cafe Barista (☎2772 6790), on the north side of the cathedral. Espresso C15. Mocha frappe C30. Nutella crepe C40. Daily paper and Wi-Fi available. Open M-Sa 8:30am-9pm, Su 9am-9pm. AmEx/D/MC/V.

☜ SIGHTS

◪**EL CASTILLO DEL CACAO.** Nicaragua's chocolate company offers a tour of its headquarters that covers the history of cacao and describes the process of turning the tiny beans into a sweet, finished product. Five women produce 400-500 candy bars by hand each day. The best part about the tour, however, is that when you're done, you'll receive the best brownies of your life, accompanied by coffee and juice. (4 blocks north of Esso Las Marías on the carretera to Tuma. Taxi ride C20. ☎2772 2002. C100. Call ahead for tours in English.)

◪**MUSEO CASA CUNA CARLOS FONSECA AMADOR.** Located in the house of Fonseca Amador's birth, this museum pays tribute to the local hero, martyr, and revolutionary. Fonseca Amador was one of the founding fathers of the Sandinista National Liberation Front and a key member of Nicaragua's revolution, which he didn't live to see—he was killed in a gunfight in 1976. The museum displays several of his personal items, including his typewriter and machine gun. Check out the newspaper articles, published by the Somozan government, that chronicle his death, albeit with a serious bias. (☎8655 6304. Open M-Sa 8:30am-8pm.)

MUSEO DEL CAFÉ. El Museo del Café showcases old coffee roasting equipment and exhibits photos of past mayors of Matagalpa. (Av. del Comercio, 1½ blocks south of Parque Morazán. ☎2772 0587. Open M-F 8am-noon, 2-5pm.)

CATEDRAL SAN PEDRO. The cathedral in Matagalpa must be one of the most freshly-painted cathedrals in Central America. It features intricate ceilings and a beautiful wooden altar. (On the north side of the Parque Morazán. Open daily 5:30am-9pm. Mass M-Sa 6am and 7pm, Su 6, 10am, 4, 7pm.)

▣ ♫ NIGHTLIFE AND ENTERTAINMENT

Matagalpa has a social scene that far exceeds its small-town status. Even though the movie theater closed down, you can still catch a documentary at the **Centro Cultural Guanuca** on Friday nights. In terms of bars and discotheques, Matagalpa has its fair share. **Artesanos Bar,** next to Matagalpa Tours, is the most popular bar in town. **Rancho Escondido,** a disco to the west of Parque Darío, also gets packed on the weekends. On the last weekend of every month, the local restaurants set up shops at one of the *parques* for **Noches Matagalpinas,** a weekend full of traditional dance and music (Sa-Su 5-11pm). Local festivals include the **Fiesta Patronales de la Merced** on September 24, and the **Festival de Polkas, Mazurcas y Jamaquellos** during the last weekend of September.

◪ **Artesanos Café Bar,** C. La Calzada (☎2552 8459), 2 blocks from the cathedral. Baseball themed bar with blasting A/C. Entrees C115-215. Drinks C20-80. Open daily 11am-2am. AmEx/D/MC/V.

DJ's Sports Bar (☎8601 0219), 25m west from the northwest corner of Parque Darío. Watch the game on this sports bar's flatscreen TV while you enjoy a refreshingly cold beer (C20-35). Try the Alitas Buffalo Wings, C80. Open daily 11am-11pm. Cash only.

Centro Cultural Guanuca (☎2772 3562). A women's center that encourages equality between the sexes. F documentary screenings. Sa live music. Open F from 7:30pm until the end of movie, Sa 8pm-midnight.

El Rancho Escondido (☎2772 6432), 2 blocks west of the southwest corner of Parque Darío. A bar and dance floor decorated with palm fronds. Beer C20. Rum shots C20. Half-bottle of rum C130. Open Th-Su 6pm-2am.

▶ DAYTRIPS FROM MATAGALPA

◼ SELVA NEGRA

While it's possible to get private transportation with a tour company (such as Matagalpa Tours), getting to Selva Negra on your own isn't that difficult. Take a Jinotega-bound bus from Matagalpa (45min.-1hr., 2 per hr., C15) and tell the driver that you want to be let off at the entrance to the park. You'll know you're there when you see the old tank, now covered in rainbow graffitti, that was abandoned by the Somozan army during the revolution. From there, it's about a 1km walk to the entrance of the hiking area. C25, with dessert and coffee C50.

The "Black Jungle," 12km north of Matagalpa, is a coffee plantation and forest reserve. Nearly 80% of the 2000-acre estate is protected and has a network of labeled hiking paths. Vibrant toucans, howler monkeys, and even the elusive quetzal inhabit the 150m of dense foliage. If you're spending the night, try the **Selva Negra Ecolodge** ❹, a family-run ecolodge with excellent rooms and cabins, the largest of which feature spiral staircases and fireplaces. Each room comes with a private bath, hot water, fresh towels, and complimentary bottled water. The larger cabins boast upstairs lofts with lots of natural sunlight. The dorms are also comfortable and are decorated with murals painted by local artists. (☎2772 3883 or 2772 5713; www.selvanegra.com.ni. Dorms C600; double cabins C1240; 12-person suites C3615. AmEx/D/MC/V.) To experience the jungle mists at the park's second highest point, try the **Peter and Helen** trail (1¾hr.). Bear in mind, however, that the higher you go in this humid jungle, the muddier it gets. In other words, be careful where you step and be prepared to get dirty. All of the hikes can be completed alone; however, *Let's Go* warns against hiking alone, especially for women. Signs are in English, and a free map of the trails is available at the hotel desk. If there is one disappointing thing about the Selva Negra Ecolodge, it's that the food from the **restaurant** ❹ doesn't come cheap. Entrees exceed C200, and the seafood is even more expensive. However, you can get a delicious dessert, such as an orange-chocolate cake, for C50-60. (Open 9am-9pm. AmEx/D/MC/V.)

CARIBBEAN COAST

Nicaragua's Caribbean coast is unlike the rest of the country, and the fact that it is only reachable by boat or plane only broadens this gap. The region is part of a geographical area known as the Mosquitia (Mosquito Coast), a sparsely populated expanse of rainforest, plains, and coastland extending the length of Nicaragua's east coast and north into Honduras. The Mosquitia is home to the country's largest group of indígenas, the Miskitos, who maintain their own language and have a semi-autonomous government system. Other indigenous groups, including the Sumos, Garífunas, and Ramas, also reside here. Most Caribbean-coast residents identify more strongly with their West Indian heritage or indigenous community than with a Nicaraguan identity.

Travel here is tricky, as there are almost no roads. Unless you're flying, getting from one place to another involves a great deal of puttering around in small boats. The extra effort is rewarded by relaxing beaches and colorful villages. Be aware that the remote nature of the Atlantic coast means little policing in some areas, so exercise extra caution.

BLUEFIELDS

Bluefields (pop. 48,000) is Nicaragua's most important Caribbean port, though the port itself is actually across the bay in Bluff. The city is a fascinating urban jungle: the streets are full of a delightful mix of Caribbean-tinged English, Spanish, and Miskito. Since Bluefields lacks beaches for swimming and big tourist attractions, it is most often used as a launch pad to the Corn Islands or other remote points on the Caribbean coast. You can fly in from Managua or Puerto Cabezas, or take the road to Rama, and follow that with a boat ride to Bluefields. Unfortunately, the area is plagued with a large drug problem: bags of drugs abandoned by smugglers in the Gulf of Mexico have been known to wash up on shore. Be safe, keep a watchful eye on your belongings, and always take a taxi at night.

▐ TRANSPORTATION

Flights: The airport at Bluefields is located about 3km south of the city center. **La Costeña** airline flies from Managua to **Bluefields** (1hr.; M-Sa 6am and 2pm; one-way C1165, round trip C2560). To **Managua** (50min.; daily 7:10, 8:40, 11:10am, 1:10, 4:10pm), **Puerto Cabezas** (50min., M, W, F 11:10am) and **Corn Island** (20min.; daily 7:40am and 3:10pm; one-way C1300, round trip C1990). From **Puerto Cabezas** to **Bluefields** (50min.; M, W, F 12:10pm; one-way C1950, round trip C2990). From **Corn Island** to **Bluefields** (20min., daily 8:10am and 3:40pm).

Buses: Managua Bus Station Rigoberto Cabezas (otherwise known as **Mercado Mayoreo**). Buses go to **Rama** at 5, 6, 7:30, 8:45, 11:30am, 2, 6, and 10pm (C150).

Boats: At the small docks a few blocks north of the Moravian Church. To **El Rama** (6hr., daily at 4am, C150) and **Big Corn Island** (Tu 9am, C4300).

✳🄝 ORIENTATION AND PRACTICAL INFORMATION

Tourist Office: (☎2572 0221), 1 block west, half a block north of Hotel South Atlantic II. Brochures describing the area and hotel information. Open M-F 8am-noon and 1:30-5pm.

Bank: BanPro, across the street from the Moravian Church. **24hr ATM.** Open M-F 8:30am-4:30pm, Sa 8:30am-noon. MC/V.

Police: (☎2572 2448), 1 block south of Hotel Caribbean Dream .

Pharmacy: Farmacia Nueva Lucha (☎8628 1377), across the street from Hotel Costa Sur. Open daily 7am-9pm.

Internet Access: (☎2572 1900), half a block west of Cima Club and Karaoke Bar. C10 per hr. International calls available. Open M-Sa 8am-8:30pm.

Post Office: 1 block west of Los Pipitos. Open M-F 8am-5pm, Sa 8am-noon.

🄝 ACCOMMODATIONS

During high season (January-May), it's a good idea to make reservations: the nicer hotels in Bluefields become considerably crowded and prices rise.

▣ **Mini Hotel Cafetín Central** (☎2572 2362), half a block south from the Moravian Church. The best deal for your buck. Large, comfortable rooms, all with A/C, fans, private baths, and Wi-Fi. The 2nd fl. patio above the street is charming as well. Rooms C200-250. Cash only. ❷

Hospedaje Los Pipitos (☎2572 1590; terezaperezmai@yahoo.com), from the Moravian Church, 1½ blocks south. A cozy family-run hostel. Clean rooms with spring mattresses. Private bath and A/C available in the pricier rooms. Offers 2 smaller rooms with a shared living space. Rooms C200-500; rooms with shared living space C160 per person. Cash only. ❷

Hotel Caribbean Dream (☎2572 0107; reyzapata1@yahoo.com), the big green building 2 blocks south of the Moravian church on the right. Spacious rooms come with A/C, cable TVs, and private baths. Check-out noon. Singles C550; doubles C650; triples C750. MC/V. ❸

Oasis Hotel and Casino (☎2572 0665 or 2572 2812; www.oasiscasinohotel.net). Cornered from the docks is Bluefields' (and possibly eastern Nicaragua's) most luxurious hotel. Each spotless, well-decorated room boasts an enormous, apartment-like space with a huge balcony, full kitchen, A/C, flatscreen TV, Wi-Fi, and private bath with hot water. Casino downstairs. Free transport to the airport is provided for all guests. Check-out noon. Singles C1275; doubles C1860; Presidential Suite C3700. AmEx/D/MC/V. ❺

Hotel South Atlantic II (☎2572 1022), next door to the Moravian Church. All rooms have A/C, cable TVs, and private baths. If you can ignore the unattractive furniture in the lobby, it's a comfortable place to stay the night. Singles C500-560; doubles C1000; triples C1200. AmEx/D/MC/V. ❸

Hotel Costa Sur (☎2572 2452), half a block west from Mini Hotel Cafetín Central. Your diehard budget option. 13 small rooms with tiny TVs, shared baths, and lumpy mattresses. Singles C160; matrimonial suite C200. Cash only. ❷

🄝 FOOD

For groceries, visit the **market,** a group of small booths two blocks east of Los Pipitos, each with a different selection of fruits and vegetables.

▣ **Comedor Arlen** (☎2572 2741), half a block west and half a block north from the post office. This hole-in-the-wall is a local favorite for delicious, cheap meals. C50 gets you a

FROM THE ROAD

NICARAGUA BY NUMBERS

As I move across Nicaragua, five weeks into my trip, I thought it would be appropriate to compile a little numbers list, a collection of the hard facts that have made this trip what it is.

0: The number of hotels or hostels I've been at where the internet hasn't crashed or cut out at least once.

1½: The number of times I've "washed" my clothing.

3: Volcanoes climbed.

4: The sum total of all of my articles of clothing.

6: The number of once-a-week anti-malarial tablets I've taken, starting from one week before I left.

8: The highest number of people I've had to ask when trying to find a building.

15: The number of hours since I last took a shower.

30: The SPF of my sunscreen.

68: The number of geckos crawling along the walls of my hostel.

1000: The average temperature in Nicaragua.

Countless: Miles I've walked.

- Asa Bush

heaping plate of steaming Nica food. Open M-F 11:30am-2pm and 5-9pm. Cash only. ❷

Salón Siu (☎2552 2511), across the street from Intur. A relaxing place to hang out and grab some cheap eats—nothing on the menu here is more than C70. Breakfast (eggs, sausage, and pancakes) C50. Open daily 7am-8pm. Cash only. ❷

Restaurante La Ola (☎2572 2779), 2 blocks south and 1 block west from the Moravian church. Fresh fish plates complete with rice, salad, and french fries for C90. Yes, you're eating your meal at a plastic chair and table, but the food is tasty and the restaurant is out of the sun. Open daily 8am-midnight. V. ❷

⬡ SIGHTS

MUSEO HISTÓRICO CULTURAL (BLUEFIELDS INDIAN & CARIBBEAN UNIVERSITY). This government-sponsored museum showcases exhibits from private donations. Highlights include the interesting display of the Caribbean and missionary influenced culture as well as the collection of old currency. *(Located in Barrio Punta Fría, by the police station and half a block south of Pesca Frita. ☎2572 2735 or 8658 5607; museobicu@yahoo.com. Open M-F 8am-noon and 2-5pm. Free. Donations appreciated.)*

▣ NIGHTLIFE

Cima Club and Karaoke Bar, 1 block inland from Hotel South Atlantic II. 2-story discoteque and karaoke bar. Open Th-Su 7pm- 3am.

▶ DAYTRIP FROM BLUEFIELD

LAGUNA DE PERLAS
Pangas leave the main pier each morning for Laguna de Perlas (1hr., 3 boats per day 6-10am, 70C). Pangas return to Bluefields at 6am, noon, and occasionally 10pm; C70.

Pearl Lagoon is a small community on the southern edge of a large lagoon of the same name, 80km north of Bluefields. The 1-2hr. trip is an excellent way to get a look at Caribbean coastal culture and local **wildlife.** The pearl cayes—18 uninhabited, white-sand tropical islands with coral off the coasts—are ideal for **snorkeling.** There is also a waterfall in the area, and tour companies offer hikes to go swim in its pool. Contact Canadian Ray Beloin (☎780 956 3334) to organize your own tour. **Green Lodge Guesthouse ❷**, has basic, clean rooms with fans and outside baths (C85) and excellent food (shrimp C30). Electricity is limited. Bring your own snorkeling equipment, food, and drinks. In the village, local boats can take you to even smaller villages around the lagoon (C1600-1920 for the *panga*). About 1hr. south from Bluefields by boat, **Ramaqui** is a small island community home to descendants of the Rama. Corrugated metal buildings stand next to traditional bamboo huts, and canoes pull up next to more modern fishing vessels. Though the island sees few visitors, local families are usually willing to host guests for a negotiable price. (You'll have to hire your own boat; it's a good idea to recruit a group to split the cost. C600-700.)

CARIBBEAN COAST

THE CORN ISLANDS

The Corn Islands, 70km off the coast from Bluefields, offer white sand beaches, warm turquoise water, and a uniquely untouristed Caribbean atmosphere. Most visitors stay on Big Corn Island (pop. 10,000), with a small but reasonable selection of hotels and restaurants. With no resorts and no cars or roads, splendid Little Corn Island (pop. 700), 18km away, feels even more untouched and noticeably safer. The islands, populated by English speakers of British West Indian descent, have excellent fishing and colorful coral reefs, but most of all they simply offer the chance to curl your toes in pure Caribbean sands and do absolutely nothing. Unfortunately, safety is as much of a concern on the Corn Islands as in Bluefields; violence and robbery are both common. Paying more for increased security is a good idea, and absolutely worth it.

BIG CORN ISLAND

The Corn Islands are an undiscovered oasis of Caribbean beauty lazing off Nicaragua's east coast. It's also an oasis of beautiful deals—it's still possible to find a hotel for C200 (US$10) per night and to get your meals for even less. The larger of the two islands, Big Corn Island, is home to a small airstrip, roads, and cars. Although it may seem more accessible, it's also more polluted and dangerous than Little Corn Island. Whichever Corn you're drawn to, beautiful beaches and pleasant accommodations await you.

▐ TRANSPORTATION

Flights: La Costeña airlines. Open M-F 5am-5pm, Sa-Su 5am-3pm. From **Managua** to **Corn Island** (1½hr.; daily 6:30 am and 2pm; one-way C2140, round trip C3300). From **Corn Island** to **Managua** (1½hr., daily 8:10am and 3:40pm). From **Bluefields** to **Corn Island** (20min.; daily 7:40am and 3:10pm; one-way C1300, round trip C1980). From **Corn Island** to **Bluefields** (20min., daily 8:10am and 3:40pm).

Boats: Boats leave from **Bluefields** to **Big Corn** Tu 9am (C250). Pangas from **Big Corn** to **Little Corn** daily 10am and 4:30pm. From **Little Corn** to **Big Corn** daily 7am and 2pm (C110).

 WET AND WILD. The boat ride over to Little Corn can jar even the steadiest of sea legs. Locals know that the best places to avoid being thrown up and down by the waves and getting soaked by the spray are the middle seats, preferably on the left side.

◆ ▐ ORIENTATION AND PRACTICAL INFORMATION

Big Corn Island is approximately 6 sq. km. The island's main road runs all the way around its coast, and a few dead-end drives branch off either inland or out to the ocean. The **airstrip** runs southwest to northeast, marking off **Brig Bay** and the western quarter of the island, where most of the businesses and hotels are located. In the eastern part of the island are the beach communities of **North End** and **South End,** with **Sally Peachie Beach** in between. Pick up maps of the island at **Nautilus Ecotours,** about 5 blocks north of Fisher's Cave Restaurant.

Tours: Nautilus Water Sports (☎2575 5077; divebigcorn.com), just north of the Enitel. Come here for tourist info about the island. Scuba courses: basic PADI instruction and dive (C1600), 2 dives (C1300-1900), 1 night dive (C1200), 10 dives package (C6000). Offers 3-day open-water PADI dive course (C5600) and 2-day advanced course (C4650). Snorkeling on Big Corn (2hr., C400) and Little Corn (1hr., C900). Glass-bottomed boat tour: 3 shipwrecks and coral reef (2hr., C400). All equipment included. V.

Bank: BanPro, Barrio Brig Bay (☎2575 5107). Open M-F 8:30am-4:30pm, Sa 8:30am-noon. **24hr ATM. Western Union,** Brig Bay (☎2575 5074), in front of Reggae Palace. Offers **currency exchange.** Open M-Sa 8am-5pm.

Police: Brig Bay (☎2575 5201), a few blocks north of Fisher's Cave restaurant.

Pharmacy: Taylor Drugs Store (☎8417 7247), just south of the airport. Open M-Sa 7am-7pm, Su 7am-noon.

Internet: Cyber Cafe Island Spring (☎2575 5053), a few blocks north of the Police station. C30 per hr. International phone calls to USA C3 per min., Europe C10 per min.

ACCOMMODATIONS

Expect to spend more on Big Corn than on the mainland. Hotels here run from C200-1000 per night, and chances are you'll want a hotel somewhere in the middle of the island.

Hotel & Restaurante Morgan (☎2575 5052 or 8835 5890), at the North End. A beautiful hotel with handmade pillars and courtyard. Large and comfortable rooms all with TVs and fans; some with A/C and private baths. Singles C300, with A/C and bath C500; doubles C600/800. Internet. Check-out 2pm. Additional 5% tax. AmEx/D/MC/V. ❸

Sunrise Hotel (☎8828 7835 or 8420 5468; southendsunrise@yahoo.com), at the South End, across the street from Casa Canada. It may not be *right* on the beach (it's actually across the street), but if it's comfort you're looking for, the Sunrise Hotel will meet all of your expectations. Spacious and immaculate rooms with white tile floors and modern baths. Each room comes with cable TV, A/C, and a private bath. Rooms C700-1100. Check-out 2pm. ❹

Hotel G&G (☎2575 5017 or 8824 8237; hotelg.gcornisland@hotmail.com), at Brig Bay, next to the Pasanic. Big rooms with fresh, clean linens, high water pressure, and (best of all) a bottle opener attached to the wall of every room. Bar and restaurant right next door. Rooms C600. MC/V. ❹

Casa Canada (☎8644 0925), on the south side of the island. Casa Canada is a resort-like hotel. Each room has a private bath, hot water, cable TV with DVD, A/C, and a minibar. Unfortunately, it also comes with a resort price. Restaurant and bar on the premises. Check-out 2pm. Singles C1800, doubles C2000. Additional 5% tax. AmEx/D/MC/V. ❺

Hotel Creole (☎8356 4719), at Brig Bay, just north of Cyber Cafe Island Spring. For those on a tight budget, Hotel Creole rents basic rooms with baths for C150-200. Call in advance—the rooms are often full with long-term boarders. ❸

FOOD

Food on the islands is generally good, and the seafood is always excellent. Try the Caribbean-influenced dishes, such as the "Run down," a combination of fruits (plantain, breadfruit, and coconut) and seafood (lobster or shrimp) stewed together in a big pot so that the flavors "run down" into the dish. Fresh and usually cheap lobster and shrimp can also be found at most restaurants, and it's up to you how you want them prepared. Impatient personalities beware: Big Corn's "relax, take it easy" attitude often applies to its leisurely restaurant service. For **groceries,** visit supermarket Miscelanea Aquileo Martinez, just after the big runway loop, at Brig Bay. (☎2575 5126. Open M-Sa 6am-6pm, Su 6am-midnight).

🦀 **Fisher's Cave,** right off the docks, Brig Bay. Decked out in crabs and coconuts, Fisher's Cave is a favorite of tourists and locals waiting for the panga to Little Corn. Try the "Fisher's Cave" breakfast (ham or bacon, bread, butter, a pancake, *gallo pinto, huevo entero*, and coffee or juice; C125). Open daily 7am-11am. Cash only. ❷

Hotel and Restaurante Morgan (☎2575 5052 or 8835 5890), at the North End. Classy restaurant with fresh, tasty food. The owner is ready to answer any questions you might have about the area. Filet mignon C270. Pasta with lobster C180. Check out the 6 ft. tall baseball trophy inside. Open daily 7am-9pm. AmEx/D/MC/V. ❸

🍸 NIGHTLIFE

Nico Bar (☎8827 1894), at the South End. A nondescript yellow wooden building overlooking the beach. Handpainted pictures of Bob Marley and a small balcony over the ocean make for a fun atmosphere. Don't miss this local favorite. Beer C20. Rum shots C30.

🏞 OUTDOOR ACTIVITIES

A walk around the island is worthwhile and takes about 4½hr. Be careful around **Bluff Point,** on the south side of the island: the area is known for drug-related crimes and is unsafe for walking. The **Picnic Center** should also be avoided. **Long Bay,** just south of South End, is a sweeping crescent of white sand, turquoise water, and coconut palms, perfect for sunbathing and relaxing. Water currents, however, make the swimming less than ideal. The best snorkeling site is **Sally Peachie Beach,** on the east side of the island: swim among schools of iridescent fish and drift over reefs teeming with marine life. Be sure to explore the sunken ships on the west side of the island. A number of places rent snorkel equipment. Remember to check equipment for quality. Half-day guided hikes around the island run about C64; boat excursions cost C1040-2000.

Marcus Gómez at Hospedaje Sunrise, in Sally Peachie (see Accommodations, p. 223). Rents new gear C60 per day, C160 deposit.

Yellow Tail House, in Sally Peachie. Rents gear C80 per day, C160 with a 2hr. tour.

Nautilus Ecotours (☎ 285 5077), 5 blocks north of Fisher's Cave Restaurant. Activities for experienced divers. 2 tank dive C720. Rents snorkel gear (half-day 64C, full day C110), new bikes (C60-C95), and horses (half-day C190).

LITTLE CORN ISLAND

A thirty minute *panga* ride from Big Corn Island takes you to Little Corn island, where there are no cars, no bikes after dark, and pristine beaches all around. Add to this local islanders who are community-oriented and kind to visitors, and you've got the new hotspot in Nicaraguan tourism. Dirt footpaths wind through lush palm forests and reach uninhabited beaches where coral reefs sit just offshore. The swimming and snorkeling are great, and there are several dive companies on the island where you can get cheap PADI certification. On the far side of the island, a shipwrecked fishing boat—just visible above the surface of the reef—awaits exploration. The 50 ft. lighthouse on the island's highest point yields a gorgeous vista. Sportfishing is excellent: snag some giant barracuda (or even just a few yellowtails) and get a free dinner. Little Corn

Island as a general rule is very safe, but be wary of your surroundings after dark, especially on the more remote eastern side of the island.

▐ TRANSPORTATION

Boats: 4 daily *panga* rides run daily between the islands. From **Little Corn** to **Big Corn** 7am and 2pm. From **Big Corn** to Little Corn 10am and 4:30pm (30min, C110).

✈ ⁊ ORIENTATION AND PRACTICAL INFORMATION

Little Corn island is essentially divided into three different areas. The majority of the island's hotels and restaurants are on its **western side.** There is a collection of assorted beach cabins on the quieter, more deserted **eastern side.** Additional accommodations are scattered across the northern tip of the island, including **Farm Peace Love** and **Derek's Place.** It's hard *not* to find a beautiful beach, but there are some particularly impressive ones on the north side of the island— **Otto's Beach** is a favorite. Just make sure to ask Otto if you can have some of his coconuts before you take them.

Tours and Agencies: ▨**Dolphin Dive** (☎8690 0225 or 8917 0717; info@dolphindi-velittlecorn.com), 2 blocks south of the dock. Wide variety of scuba-diving activities, including recreation as well as PADI courses. Offers 1 tank dives (C700), 2 tank dives (C1300), 5 dive packages (C3000), 10 dive packages (C5650), and refresher dives (C1300). PADI courses (C1300-12,800). 4 night hotel stay plus PADI certification C800 per person. Underwater digital camera rental C400; includes a day's use and a CD with your pictures. **Dive Little Corn** (www.divelittlecorn.com), just south of the dock. PADI scuba certification C6870. Snorkel trips C300, C200 with your own gear. Bike rental C300 per 24hr. All instructors speak English and Spanish.

Hospital: Just south of Los Delfines. Open M-F 8am-4pm. Always open for emergencies.

Internet: Upstairs of the Los Delfines Hotel, next to the restaurant. C60 per hr. Open 11am-7pm.

▐ ACCOMMODATIONS

Little Corn Island has some surprisingly great budget options. Most hotels with modern amenities can be found on the western side of the island. Looking for a little cabaña on the beach? Head to the more remote eastern side.

▨ **Sunshine Hotel** (☎8495 6223; www.sunshinehotellittlecornisland.com), just north of the docks. Each dorm and room with private bath has cable TV and A/C. Guests get full access to the game room with pool, ping pong, card tables, and video games. DVD player with movie rental (C100 per day), snorkel gear rental (C60 per day), and snorkel trips (C200 per person, min. 4 people). Dorms C100; rooms C200. ❷

Elsa's Place Hotel and Restaurant (☎8333 0971), on the eastern half of the island. Collection of brightly-colored beach *cabañas* on a beautiful, quiet stretch of beach. Restaurant on site. *Gallo pinto*, eggs, coconut bread or pancakes, and coffee C60. Singles C200, with bath C500; doubles C600. Cash only. ❷

Hotel Los Delfines (☎8836 2013), south of the docks, on the western side of the island. A series of *cabañas*, each comprised of 2 rooms stacked on top of one another. Rocking chairs on the porch or patio. All rooms have private baths, cable TVs, and A/C. The green and white paint job goes well with the park-like atmosphere. Singles C600-700; doubles C1000. AmEx/D/MC/V. ❹

Lobster Inn (☎8847 1736 or 8927 0710), about 2 blocks south of the docks on the western side of the island. Lives up to its name with a color scheme that could only be described as Pepto-Bismol pink. Clean rooms with private baths and balconies with

THE CORN ISLANDS

ocean views. Restaurant downstairs. Rooms for C400-500, with cable TVs C500-600. Discounts for groups. ❸

Grace's Place Cool Spot (☎8948 7725), on the eastern half of the island, right next to Elsa's place. Basic beach *cabaña* option. The rooms are small, and if you got one in the back without the ocean breeze, they feel like tin incubators. Kitchen use C100. The shared bathrooms are 2 tiny shacks that share a small outside sink. The "mosquito nets" are really just old tarps tied above the beds. Singles and doubles with shared bath C300; matrimonial with private bath C500. ❸

🔲 FOOD

Food on the island is generally fresh, if a bit unimaginative. You'll get lots of great fish, but you'll be hard-pressed to find it prepared any way other than the island's preferred method—deep fried. That being said, there are a few fantastic restaurants, and asking the locals is always an effective way to figure out where to head for dinner. For groceries, visit **Comercial Los Delfines,** just past Dive Little Corn, south of the docks. As well as having fresh and canned goods, this small supermarket also carries a large selection of hardware and a building supplies section (open daily 6:30am-7:30pm).

Mango's Pizza (☎8495 9268), just past Los Delfines, south of the dock. Serves tasty pizzas at a great price underneath palm huts. Try a calzone, with toppings like fresh pineapple and a flaky crust (small C100, large C150). Grab a pizza and add the toppings (C7-18) at your leisure. ❷

Sweet Oasis, 50m south of Dive Little Corn, right next to Comercial Los Delfines. If you're into big breakfasts, you'll be in heaven at this bright restaurant. Get a typical island breakfast: a generous portion of *gallo pinto,* a pile of plantain chips, and an entire fried fish (C120). Coffee C12. There are also delicious, cheap hot dogs at the little stand across the sidewalk. Open daily 7am-9pm. AmEx/D/MC/V. ❸

Restaurante Glorieta ("La Sabrosicima"; ☎8354 5716 or 8354 5715), 1 block north of the Sunshine Hotel. A kitchen surrounded by plastic tables under a tin roof. Great food for a decent price. Meat plates C150-180. Try the *espaguety* (with fish or lobster; C130-180). Open daily 6am-9pm. Cash only. ❸

🔲 🎵 NIGHTLIFE AND ENTERTAINMENT

Las Aguilas, a few blocks north of the Sunshine Hotel on the western side of the island. This small dance club-billiard hall is popular with locals on the weekends. Show up on Mother's or Father's day to witness (or take part) in the impromptu boxing matches. Seriously. Beer C25.

PANAMA

True, the Panama Canal might be one of the greatest human-made wonders of the world. Put that aside for the moment and consider Panama's other wonders: lush mountain forests, Caribbean beaches surrounded by coral reefs, a thriving and skyscraping metropolis, vast ranches of highland villages. Panama's 2.5 million people create a diverse culture, including vibrant indigenous groups and recent international immigrants. Far east in San Blas and Darién, dugout canoes provide access to hidden remote villages and images of Western pop culture's fashions are replaced by Kuna molas, traditional patched cloth panels. Pristine Caribbean shores and untouched forests are within a few hours' drive of Panama City, Central America's most modern city. The political situation in Panama is stable and the tourist and national park infrastructure is unmatched.

ESSENTIALS

PLANNING YOUR TRIP

PASSPORTS, VISAS, AND CUSTOMS.
Passport. Required of all visitors. Must be valid 3 months after arrival.
Visa (p. 6). Not required of citizens from the UK or EU. For others, visa is valid for 30 days, with possible 60-day extension. In place of a visa, tourist cards (US$5) are available upon arrival.
Onward Ticket. Required of all visitors.
Work Permit. Required for all foreigners planning to work for a Panamanian business in Panama. Employees of international corporations do not need a permit.
Required Vaccinations. Travelers coming from nations with endemic yellow fever need proof of vaccination.
Driving Permit. Valid driver's license from your home country or an International Driving Permit required.
Departure Tax. US$20.

EMBASSIES AND CONSULATES

For embassies in Panama, see the **Practical Information** section for Panama City (p. 242). The following are Panamanian embassies and consulates abroad.

Australia: Consulate, 1/234 Slade Road, Bexley North NSW 2207 (☎+61 02 9150 8409; fax 02 9150 8410). Open M-F 9am-3pm.

Canada: Embassy, 130 Albert Street, Ottawa, Ontario K1P 5G4 (☎+1 613-236-7177).

NZ: Consulate, 61 High Street, Auckland Central, Auckland (☎+64 9379 8550).

UK: Embassy, 40 Hertford Street, London W1J 7SH (☎+44 20 74934646).

US: Embassy, 2862 McGill Terrace NW, Washington, DC 20008 (☎+1 202-483-1407). Open M-F 9am-5pm.

VISA INFORMATION

Citizens from the EU and UK can travel in Panama for 30 days without a visa. Residents of other nations must obtain a multiple-entry visa from the nearest consulate before arriving, or purchase a US$5 **tourist card** upon arrival. It is possible to extend your stay another 60 days through an application at any immigration office. To stay past 90 days, you must apply for a **change of migratory status.** You will be charged US$250 and will probably need the help of a Panamanian lawyer.

If you are working for a foreign company in Panama, you do not need a **work permit.** If you are hired by a Panamanian company, you will need a permit from the Ministry of Labor. These are good for one year and are renewable. You must also have a passport, a police record notarized by the nearest Panamanian Consulate, an original birth certificate, six passport-sized photos, and a negative HIV test. If married, you must show a certificate. Alternately, if you live in Panama legally for five years, you can become a resident alien with working rights.

TOURIST OFFICES

La Autoridad de Turismo Panamá (☎507 526 7000; www.visitpanama.com) runs the tourism show in Panama. They offer maps and a wealth of information about what to do and where to go. They also have a ton of helpful info on Panama's national parks.

MONEY

US DOLLARS ($)	
AUS$1 = US$0.80	US$1 = AUS$1.24
CDN$1 = US$0.92	US$1 = CDN$01.09
EUR€1 = US$1.41	US$1 = EUR€0.71
NZ$1 = US$0.64	US$1 = NZ$1.56
UK£1 = US$1.62	US$1 = UK£0.62

The currency chart above is based on August 2009 exchange rates. All prices in this section are quoted in US dollars, as the Panamanian currency, the **balboa,** is directly linked to the dollar. Panama uses actual US bills but mints its own coins. A huge 50¢ piece, known as a *peso*, is used regularly, and a nickel is often called a *real*.

ATMs (marked by red Sistema Clave signs) are everywhere in Panama City and throughout David. Though uncommon in rural areas, they are also found in a number of towns west of Panama City. Note that these machines don't always accept foreign cards.

There are several **Western Union** offices around the country. Some more pricey hotels and department stores accept **traveler's checks,** but few budget establishments or businesses will honor them. Many banks are willing to exchange American Express checks and sometimes other types. Bring proper ID and be prepared to pay a fee unless you are exchanging at the AmEx office.

Outside Panama City, national banks satisfy money needs, but at border crossings, money is exchanged at bad rates; bring US dollars. **Visa** and **Mastercard** are easier to use than other cards, but many hotels and restaurants only accept cash. Visitors can often obtain AmEx/MC/V **cash advances,** and there are a number of US banks (Citibank, Fleet, HCSB) where commissions and fees may be less substantial. All international debit cards work, but PINs should be

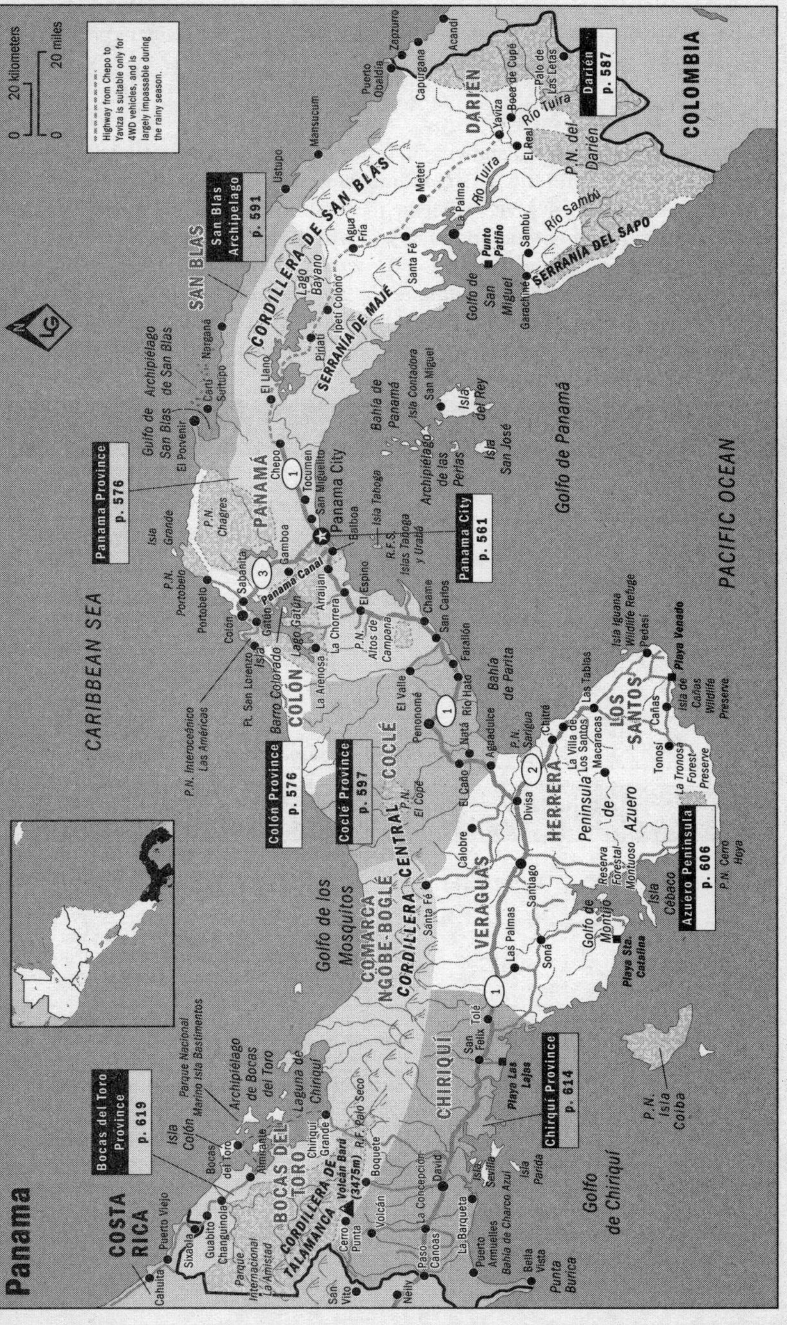
Panama
0 20 kilometers
0 20 miles
Highway from Chepo to Yaviza is suitable only for 4WD vehicles, and is largely impassable during the rainy season.
CARIBBEAN SEA
PACIFIC OCEAN
COSTA RICA
COLOMBIA
Bocas del Toro Province p. 619
Chiriquí Province p. 614
Colón Province p. 576
Coclé Province p. 597
Panama Province p. 576
Panama City p. 561
San Blas Archipelago p. 591
Darién p. 587
Azuero Peninsula p. 606
BOCAS DEL TORO
CHIRIQUÍ
COMARCA NGÖBE-BOGLÉ
VERAGUAS
COCLÉ
COLÓN
PANAMÁ
SAN BLAS
DARIÉN
HERRERA
LOS SANTOS
CORDILLERA DE TALAMANCA
CORDILLERA CENTRAL
CORDILLERA DE SAN BLAS
SERRANÍA DE MAJÉ
SERRANÍA DEL SAPO
Volcán Barú (3475m)
Cahuita
Puerto Viejo
Sixaola
Guabito
Changuinola
Bocas del Toro
Almirante
Isla Colón
Archipiélago de Bocas del Toro
Parque Nacional Marino Isla Bastimentos
Laguna de Chiriquí
Chiriquí Grande
Parque Internacional La Amistad
Cerro Punta
Volcán
Boquete
R.F. Palo Seco
La Concepción
David
Paso Canoas
La Barqueta
Puerto Armuelles
Bahía de Charco Azul
Punta Burica
Bella Vista
San Vito
Neily
Isla Sevilla
Isla Parida
Golfo de Chiriquí
Playa Las Lajas
San Félix
Tolé
Golfo de los Mosquitos
Santa Fé
Las Palmas
Soná
Santiago
Calobre
Golfo de Montijo
Playa Sta. Catalina
Isla Cébaco
P.N. Isla Coiba
P.N. Cerro Hoya
Reserva Forestal Montuoso
Península de Azuero
El Caño
Divisa
P.N. El Copé
Penonomé
Natá
Aguadulce
P.N. Sarigua
Chitré
La Villa de Los Santos
Macaracas
Las Tablas
Tonosí
La Tronosa Forest Preserve
Cañas
Isla de Cañas Wildlife Preserve
Playa Venado
Pedasí
Isla Iguana Wildlife Refuge
Bahía de Parita
Río Hato
El Valle
Farallón
San Carlos
Chame
P.N. Altos de Campana
La Chorrera
Arraiján
El Espino
La Arenosa
Lago Gatún
Isla Barro Colorado
Ft. San Lorenzo
P.N. Interoceánico Las Américas
Colón
Gatún
Portobelo
P.N. Portobelo
Sabanita
Panama Canal
Gamboa
Balboa
Panama City
P.N. Chagres
Isla Grande
R.F.S. Islas Taboga y Urabá
Isla Taboga
San Miguelito
Tocumen
Chepo
Bahía de Panamá
Archipiélago de las Perlas
Isla Contadora
San Miguel
Isla del Rey
Isla San José
Golfo de Panamá
El Porvenir
Golfo de San Blas
Archipiélago de San Blas
Cartí
Sulitupo
Narganá
El Llano
Pintati
Ipetí Colono
Lago Bayano
Agua Fría
Santa Fé
Metetí
La Palma
Río Tuira
Punto Patiño
Golfo de San Miguel
Garachiné
Sambú
Río Sambú
El Real
Yaviza
Boca de Cupé
Palo de las Letras
P.N. del Darién
Ustupo
Mansucum
Puerto Obaldía
Zapzurro
Capurganá
Acandí

PANAMA

in combinations to accommodate letter-less keypads. Tipping, 10% at least in the big cities, is generally expected. "Free" travel guides usually expect a tip. For more info, see **Tipping and Bargaining,** p. 9.

PRICE DIVERSITY

Our Researchers list establishments in order of value from best to worst, honoring our favorites with the Let's Go thumbs-up (🖾). Because the best *value* is not always the cheapest *price*, we have incorporated a system of price ranges based on a rough expectation of what you will spend. For **accommodations,** we base our range on the cheapest price for which a single traveler can stay for one night. For **restaurants,** we estimate the average amount one traveler will spend in one sitting. The table below tells you what you'll *typically* find in Panama at the corresponding price range, but keep in mind that no system can allow for the quirks of individual establishments.

ACCOMMODATIONS	RANGE	WHAT YOU'RE *LIKELY* TO FIND
❶	Under US$5	Campgrounds and dorm rooms, both in hostels and actual universities. Expect bunk beds and a communal bath. You may have to provide or rent towels.
❷	US$5-15	Hostels in heavily-touristed areas or shabby hotels. Sometimes private bathrooms, but most likely communal facilities. May have a TV.
❸	US$16-25	A comfortable room with a private bath. Should have decent amenities such as A/C and TV. Breakfast may be included.
❹	US$26-50	Bigger rooms than a ❸, with more amenities, and often in a more convenient location. Breakfast may be included.
❺	Over US$50	Large hotels or upscale chains. If it's a ❺ and it doesn't have the perks you want, you've paid too much.

FOOD	RANGE	WHAT YOU'RE *LIKELY* TO FIND
❶	Under US$2	Probably food stalls, university cafeterias, and rural Panamanian eateries. It's yummy and cheap, but you'll be reaching for the Panamanian version of Tums post pig out.
❷	US$2-4	National restaurant chains and some international fast food. Expect typical Panamanian platters and sandwiches, food at a bar, and low-priced entrees. The average Panamanian eatery is a ❷.
❸	US$8-11	Mid-priced entrees, seafood, and exotic pasta dishes. More upscale Panamanian eateries. Check the menu to see if tax is included in prices.
❹	US$8-15	The cheapest entrees at an upscale restaurant. Entrees tend to be heartier or more elaborate, but you'll mostly be throwing down for ambiance. Few restaurants in this range have a dress code, but you'll feel out of place in a T-shirts and sandals.
❺	Over US$15	Your meal might cost more than your room, but there's a reason—it's something fabulous, famous, or both. Extensive drink options. Only found in big cities or the most heavily-touristed areas.

PANAMA

COSTS

The most significant costs for travelers in Panama will be accommodations. While basic rooms or dorm beds can usually be found for under US$7, more elaborate lodgings are US$10-15. Private singles with some amenities cost at least US$20. Food is cheap, with easily-found *típico* (a standard meal) US$1-3. While the assiduous traveler may be able to scrape by on US$15-20 per day, a safer bet would be US$25-30, without transportation.

TRANSPORTATION

The major domestic airline is **Aeroperlas** (☎507 315 7500; www.aeroperlas.com). There are a few smaller airlines connecting Panama City to San Blas and Darién. **Buses** are the major means of budget transport and the only means of reaching remote locations. Bus quality is generally good, and long trips tend to be served by luxury coaches. Other intercity routes are run by **mini-buses,** while in remote areas, **vans** provide service. A bus' destination is almost always written on the front. If there's no terminal, many buses linger around the *parque central.* Pay when getting off, but confirm the fare before embarking. Consider taking warm clothes on board to protect yourself from the chilling air-conditioning or the constant breeze from open windows. Travelers say **hitchhiking** becomes easier the farther one gets from the Pan-American Highway, but *Let's Go* does not recommend it. Truck drivers have been known to offer *"un lif"* from gas stations.

BORDER CROSSINGS

Travelers can cross into Panama by land or (occasionally) sea. Remember to carry enough money to pay any entrance or exit fees. Border crossings in Panama are bolded, and adjacent border towns are always listed alongside their respective country names.

COSTA RICA. There are three land crossings. **Paso Canoas** (p. 302) is 50km west of David, near Ciudad Neily, Costa Rica. To get there, catch a bus from David (p. 298). **Sixaola/Guabito** (p. 313) is on the Caribbean coast 15 minutes from Changuinola, near Puerto Viejo de Talamanca, Costa Rica. **Río Sereno,** at the end of the Concepción-Volcán road, is rarely used.

COLOMBIA. The Darién gap, the only break in the Pan-American Highway, prevents land travel to Colombia. The **ferry** service between Colón and

FROM THE ROAD

GETTING AROUND

You can tell a lot about a place by its different forms of transportation. Whether you are riding up a river in a dugout canoe or cruising the roads in a retrofitted school bus, transportation in Panama depends on the environment you're in and the needs of the people trying to get around. Here's my take on the transportation offered in different parts of the country:

Darien: The dugout canoe and well—your two feet. There aren't too many roads in the Darien, so hollowed-out logs are used to navigate wide, muddy rivers.

San Blas Islands: The only way to get around here is by boat or the infrequent propeller plane.

Panama Province: The school bus dominates transportation here. These aren't just any old yellow mobiles; they have quirky paint jobs, whistles and all sorts of other noise makers.

Azuero: Residents of the Azuero Peninsula still use horses. Most of the peninsula is hilly and has few roads. It's not uncommon to see people riding their horses with a drink in each hand; it's probably best that there are little to no cars around here.

Chiriqui: The wealthiest province in the country has the nicest buses—unfortunately, A/C is unnecessary at an altitude of 2000m. The best way to get around here is by scooter. You'll look really cool and save a few bucks while you're at it.

Cartagena has been discontinued, but occasional passage can be found on cargo ships from Panama. One land-sea route involves island-hopping through the San Blas Archipelago via **Puerto Obaldía,** but this is also considered unsafe due to paramilitary and criminal activity.

SAFETY

The regions west of Panama City are politically stable and safe. In Panama City, standard big-city rules apply; some neighborhoods are best avoided at night, and a few are best avoided altogether (see **Panama City: Orientation,** p. 240). Outside the free trade zone, Colón is generally unsafe—take taxis from the bus station and don't walk in the city (see **Colón,** p. 257). Guerrillas and paramilitaries are active in the **Darién** area along the Colombian border, especially since the US military left in 1999. Both US and Panamanian governments warn travelers not to enter the region. **Women travelers** will find the same *machismo*, catcalls, and stares as in the rest of Central America, though Panama is no worse than other countries (see **Women Travelers,** p. 31). While public displays of homosexuality are not accepted anywhere in Panama, **gay and lesbian travelers** shouldn't have major problems as long as they keep a low profile.

HEALTH

Malaria is a particular concern in Panama, as there are strains of mosquitoes that resist basic malaria medication. If traveling east of Panama City, be sure to take an alternative anti-malarial. Malaria risk is greatest in rural areas like Bocas del Toro, San Blas, and the Darién. **Yellow fever vaccination** is recommended.

LIFE AND TIMES

HISTORY

FROM PRE-DEPENDENCE TO INDEPENDENCE (PRE-COLUMBIAN—AD 1821). Some eleven thousand years ago, hunter-gatherers made their first appearance on the Panamanian isthmus and eventually settled in villages such as those of the Monagrillo culture, whose pottery dates back to 2500-1700BC. When Columbus landed at present-day Portobelo in 1502, he came across indigenous cultures thousands of years old. Vasco Nuñez de Balboa followed him a few years later to conquer those cultures, establish the first Spanish colony in the New World, and appoint himself governor. Most importantly, in 1513, Balboa "discovered" the Pacific Ocean just on the other side of Panama: a finding which would soon transform the isthmus into a major route for shipping stolen Inca gold to Spain. Dutch and English pirates began to attack these trade routes in an attempt to get their hands on the precious cargo. In spite of such riches, the Spanish Empire in the New World collapsed in 1821, and Panama became part of the independent Gran Colombia, a republic that also included present-day Colombia, Venezuela, and Ecuador.

A MAN, A PLAN, A CANAL: PANAMA (1821-1914). Transportation in Panama took off with the construction of the US-sponsored Panama Railroad in 1855, the world's first transcontinental railroad. From 1880 to 1889, the French engineer Ferdinand de Lesseps made the first attempt to dig a canal through Panama, but was ultimately defeated by the fatal triad of yellow fever, malaria, and landslides. US President Theodore Roosevelt decided to take on the challenge again in 1902. Faced with a recalcitrant Colombian government, Roosevelt sent US warships to encourage Panama to declare independence from Colombia. The result of this gunboat diplomacy was the establishment of an independent Republic of Panama in 1903. Two weeks later, the Hay-Bunau Varilla Treaty gave the US ownership of the Canal Zone, and the great Panama Canal was completed, after much effort, in 1914.

INTERVENTION CENTURY (1914-1999). The new Republic of Panama not only gave the US permission to dig the Canal, but it also gave the US the right to protect it. Although Franklin D. Roosevelt officially renounced the US's authority to intervene in 1936, the US did its fair share of "protecting" in the 20th century. The quasi-fascist President Arnulfo Arias, who had formerly been Panama's ambassador to Italy, was deposed by a US-backed coup in 1941; he returned to power in 1948, only to be ousted again later that year. In 1964, riots broke out when Panamanian students were prevented by US forces from raising a Panamanian flag over a Canal Zone high school, leaving some 25 people dead and causing Panama to break diplomatic relations with the US for three months. Arias was elected for a third term in 1968, but his political ambitions were frustrated yet again, after only eleven days in office, when he was overthrown by a third military coup. His replacement, General Omar Torrijos, negotiated a treaty with Jimmy Carter to give Panama complete control over the Canal by the year 2000. Torrijos, however, died in a mysterious plane crash in 1981 and was succeeded by former CIA operative General Manuel Noriega. Noriega granted himself dictatorial powers and backed US interests in Nicaragua against the Sandinistas. He soon lost US support by becoming involved in drug-trafficking, and in 1989, the US launched "Operation Just Cause," sending 27,000 troops into Panama to take Noriega down. When the dictator fled into the Vatican embassy, US soldiers assailed him with a bizarre form of psychological torture: they blared "Voodoo Child" and other rock tunes into the compound 24 hours a day to flush him out. (We couldn't make this up even if we wanted to.) Noriega surrendered and was sentenced in Miami to 40 years in prison.

TODAY

In 1999, Panama elected its first female president, **Mireya Moscoso,** the widow of Arnulfo Arias. Despite entering office with high hopes, Moscoso's selection of officials to government positions were dogged with charges of nepotism and she ended her term with extraordinarily low approval ratings. She was succeeded by Martin Torrijos in 2004, the illegitimate son of **Omar Torrijos** who headed the helm of Panama's government thirty years earlier. Elected on a platform of reducing corruption and fostering economic growth, the younger Torrijos' presidency focused on fiscal and social reforms; however, such reforms were frustrated by significant opposition from both labor unions and the Catholic Church. Torrijos also issued several controversial decrees intended to strengthen Panama's internal security forces, which some feared would lead to a renewed influence of the military in government affairs. Opposition candidate **Ricardo Martinelli** is the favorite to win election in 2009 for a Presidential term slated to last until 2014.

Panama has made significant progress in reversing its reputation as a safe haven for drug-smugglers and money-launderers. The construction of the new **Centennial Bridge,** which opened in 2004, has markedly improved the country's infrastructure. Spanning the Panama Canal at the Gaillard Cut, the bridge now carries the six-lane **Pan-American Highway:** an impressive architectural achievement, which, along with the decrease in drug-related violence, has led to a significant increase in tourism.

Since gaining absolute sovereignty over **the Canal** in 2000, the Panamanian government has been planning to massively expand the World's Greatest Ditch. In 2006, a national referendum approved a proposal to build a third set of locks, which would enable even larger ships to cross the isthmus. At a projected cost of around US$5.25 billion, the project is expected to nearly double the capacity of the Canal. The new locks are scheduled to open in 2015, just after the Canal's centennial.

ECONOMY AND GOVERNMENT

Panama's economy is one of the fastest-growing in the region, pulling in an impressive 8.3% of GDP growth in 2008. Nearly 80% of the country's income comes from its highly developed services' sector, which includes the **Panama Canal** and the **Colón Free Trade Zone.** The Canal **expansion project** in particular is expected to fuel economic growth over the next decade. Despite these positive achievements, however, income remains unevenly distributed throughout the country, and nearly one-third of the population lingered below the poverty line in 2008. The nation's currency is technically the **balboa, fixed to equal the US dollar;** however, no *balboa* bills exist and US dollars are used for all daily money transactions.

Political parties in Panama today are more polarized by personalities than platforms. The major players include the **Panameñista Party,** long known as the Arnulfista Party in honor of its leader **Arnulfo Arias,** and the **Democratic Revolutionary Party of Torrijos,** which won the presidency and more than half of the National Assembly seats in the 2004 election. The up-and-coming **Democratic Change Party,** founded in 1998, owes its rising popularity to the charisma of its leader Ric1ardo Martinelli and his credible message of change as a candidate free from connections with Panama's political past.

PEOPLE

Ever since the Spanish conquest, the population of native populations in Panama has been declining. Though some early settlers tried to defend indigenous rights, many of the native populations fell victim to persecution and enslavement. Today the indigenous populations reside mostly in remote areas of the countryside, and constitute just 6% of the overall population. The overwhelming majority of Panama's inhabitants are **mestizo,** of mixed Spanish and native origin; they make up 70% of the population. The next largest ethnic group, at 14%, is comprised of predominantly black **West Indians.** This segment of the population grew during the first half of the 20th century, when thousands of laborers migrated to Panama from the Antilles. Many worked on the construction of the Panama Canal, while others worked on banana plantations. A tenth of Panamanians are made up of foreigners or Americans who, for the most part, have stayed in the country since the Canal was completed.

Like most former Spanish colonies, Panama has a strong **Roman Catholic** heritage. In the early stages of colonization, many efforts were made to convert the native population to Catholicism. As a result, **Christianity** is by far the most dominant faith: Catholics account for 85% of the Panamanian population, while **Protestants,** mainly hailing from the British West Indies, make up the rest.

The official language of Panama is **Spanish.** However, many Panamanians also speak English, so you needn't worry if your high school Spanish classes have failed you—someone who is able to interpret is probably close by.

CUSTOMS AND ETIQUETTE

Because the United States was politically involved in Panama during the construction of the Canal, Panamanians are familiar with North American customs and gestures. If you are a guest in someone's house, make sure to bring a gift for your host, and when eating a meal, do not begin until all are seated and your host has started. Also, it is important to note that because Panama has a strong Roman Catholic tradition, dressing conservatively is always the way to go. Beachwear must be strictly limited to the beach, as even shorts are considered inappropriate in restaurants and on the city streets.

When greeting people, remember to address men as Señor, married women as Señora, and unmarried women as Señorita. If you do strike up a conversation, baseball is a favorite Panamanian topic. It's best to avoid talking about politics, especially regarding foreign involvement in the construction of the Canal.

FOOD AND DRINK

Panamanian cuisine reflects the flavors of Latin America, with **rice, beans,** and **tortillas** serving as the basic ingredients for many popular dishes. Panama's significant West Indian population has brought Western Caribbean influences to the cuisine, especially to the coastal regions. One of the most popular dishes is **ropa vieja,** literally "old rope," which consists of shredded beef and peppers with plantains and rice. We recommend include **gallo pinto,** a dish of pork, rice, and beans.

Fresh **chichas,** or juices, include the ever-popular orange as well as more exotic varieties such as watermelon and pineapple. If you still want local flavor but juice isn't exactly what you had in mind, try **seco,** an alcohol distilled from sugarcane and served over milk and ice. **Beer** fans will not be disappointed in the selection of Panamanian brands: Balboa, Atlas, Panamá, Soberana, and Cristal are all popular options.

CULTURE

ART

Though indigenous people only make up a small piece of the Panamanian population, they are responsible for much of the country's art. The indigenous **Kuna,** an Amerindian people who reside mainly in the eastern regions of Panama and on islands off the Caribbean coast, create beautiful and colorful, handmade *molas*. *Molas* are intricate, embroidered garments worn by women as part of the traditional wardrobe on the front or back of a blouse. Some *molas* take up to 100 hours to complete, and feature geometric designs that originated in the traditional art of body painting. Today, *molas* may also feature designs reflecting the local wildlife. Other indigenous crafts include hand-woven baskets, carvings, and elaborate masks.

LITERATURE

Any account of the history of Panamanian literature must begin with the **oral tradition,** passed down to new generations through the ancient art of storytelling. The Kuna people in particular are well known for their myths, songs, and fables, many of which have now been compiled into books.

Panamanian literature came into its own when the nation gained independence from Colombia in 1903. Since then, Panamanians have produced an abundance of poetry, short stories, and novels. The **Modernist** movement took off in post-independence Panama and found a champion in the poet **Darío Herrera**. During the 1930s, under the leadership of the poet **Rogelio Sinán**, *Modernismo* gave way to new styles like **Surrealism** and **magical realism**. Much of the country's 20th-century literature reflected the contemporary political and social situations in Panama, including the controversy surrounding the canal.

MUSIC

Rubén Blades ranks far above the rest as Panama's biggest musical superstar. The popular **salsa** and **Latin jazz** musician has won multiple Grammy Awards for his Afro-Cuban rhythms and politically charged lyrics. On top of his wildly successful musical career, Blades has appeared in several films and actually ran for president in 1994, garnering 18% of the vote.

The Panamanian folkloric style of music is known as **típico** and features vocals and the accordion. Other styles of music, including Colombian **vallenato** and Puerto Rican **bachata** and **calypso**, are also quite common. Today, **reggaeton** and **rock and roll** can be heard alongside these more traditional styles.

LAND

Panama is an isthmus connecting North and South America. It lies between Costa Rica on the west and Colombia on the east, and between the Caribbean Sea to the north and the Pacific Ocean to the south. As the narrowest stretch of land standing between these two great bodies of water, Panama is of great strategic importance to many nations. As such, it attracted considerable controversy in the early 20th century during the construction of the Panama Canal, which spans 48 miles and bisects the country. Today, over 300 million tons of cargo pass through annually. International commerce aside, Panama's 1540 miles of coastline are also strategic for those seeking beautiful beaches. The interior of this narrow country is dominated by mountains formed along the continental divide.

Panama is a tropical paradise, hot and humid year round. The Pacific coast tends to be cooler than the Caribbean and temperatures are notably cooler at higher elevations inland. The length of the rainy season varies, but it usually extends from April to December. This climate supports an abundance of flora and fauna, in habitats ranging from **cloud forests** at high elevation to **rainforests** and **mangrove swamps** closer to sea level. Panama is home to a host of tropical flowers including **bromeliads** and over 1000 species of **orchid**. Highlights of native wildlife include the **giant anteater, the capybara,** and several different monkey species. Among Panama's more colorful residents are **macaw parrots** and **toucans.**

BEYOND TOURISM

VOLUNTEERING

SEAS, TREES, AND CLOUDS

School for International Training (SIT) Study Abroad, 1 Kipling Rd., P.O. Box 676, Brattleboro, VT 05302, USA (☎+1-888-272-7881 or 802-258-3212; www.sit.edu/studyabroad). Semester-long program in Panama entitled, "Tropical Ecology, Marine Ecosystems, and Biodiversity Conservation," costing approximately US$13,000 for the semester.

The Lost and Found Lodge Eco Resort (☎507 6581 9223 or 507 6636 8863; www. lostandfoundlodge.com). In the Panama Cloud Forest, this resort is perfect for the nature-loving backpacker. The lodge offers several volunteer opportunities, including maintaining organic farms, teaching English, and leading tours. Email info@lostand-foundlodge.com for further details on volunteer opportunities.

COMMUNITY OUTREACH

Global Volunteer Network Ltd., P.O. Box 30-968, Lower Hutt, New Zealand (☎+1 800-963-1198 from the US or Canada, 0800 032 5035 from the UK; www.volunteer. org). Founded in 2000, the Global Volunteer Network helps communities in need by supporting local organizations. Several volunteer opportunities are available in Panama, including working with children, teaching adults and children to read, and helping at a center for disabled people of all ages. Alternatively, you may help out at a local animal refuge or join a community recycling project.

Volunteers for Peace, 1034 Tiffany Road, Belmont VT, 05730, USA (☎+1-802-259-2759; www.vfp.org). Check website for volunteer programs in countries throughout the world, including Panama. Volunteers needed in Kuna, Panama to teach English to children and adults.

FOR HIGH SCHOOL STUDENTS

Rustic Pathways, P.O. Box 1150 Willoughby, Ohio, 44096, USA (☎+1-800-321-4353; www.rusticpathways.com). Offers summer programs in Panama, Costa Rica and Nicaragua for high school students. In the 9-day Panama program, students will be immersed in the Kuna culture. Community service activities hosted in the coastal paradise of Carti Yantupu. Nine-day Panama program US$1295.

STUDYING

AMERICAN PROGRAMS

Institute for Tropical Ecology and Conservation (ITEC, Inc.), 1023 SW 2nd Ave., Gainesville, FL, 3260, USA (☎352 367 9128; www.itec-edu.org). A research and conservation organization that operates the Bocas del Toro Biological Station in Panama. During summer and winter break, ITEC offers field courses to graduate and postgraduate students (18+). Coral reef ecology, primate ecology, and adventure photography are just a few of the courses offered. ITEC is a private institution; students will have to contact their respective universities to ensure that they can receive credit for this program. Tuition US$1650 (3 weeks) to US$1950 (4 weeks).

PANAMA

PANAMA CITY

Few cities in the world have a history, fortune, and character so intimately and singularly related to their geography. Permanently marked by the canal and the commerce it brings, not mention a century of partial US occupation, Panama City (pop. 800,000) is unlike anything else you'll find in the country or in the rest of Central America. It's a surprising and welcoming combination of the historic and ultra-modern, where Spanish and indigenous traditions coexist with immigrant cultures from the world over. The result is a metropolis that defines "cosmopolitan."

Panama City's location, a calm harbor on a narrow bridge between two continents, has made it a transit point for people and currency for over 300 years. Originally the gateway for all the gold from Spain's Pacific colonies, the first Panama City, known as Panamá Viejo (Old Panama), was founded by the Spanish in 1519 on the site of an Indian village. In the late 17th century, pirate invasions, infertile swamps, and numerous fires forced residents to move 8km west, to modern-day San Felipe. There, the city flourished under

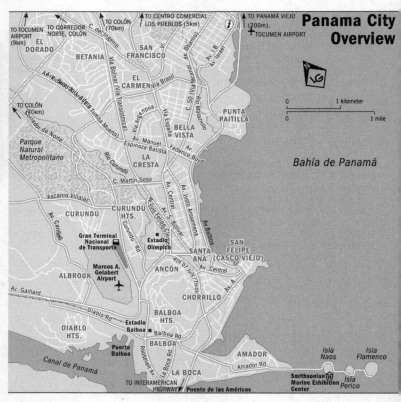

Panama City Overview

Bahía de Panamá

Spanish, French, and American occupations. During the California Gold Rush, hordes of prospectors flowed in from North America, fattening the pockets of steam-ship barons and resulting in the construction of the first railway joining the Pacific and Atlantic Oceans. The French dreamed of more ambitious inter-oceanic connection; their attempt to build a canal at the end of the 19th century ended in failure. By the early 20th century, US plans for a water passage were complete. During the canal's construction the city began to expand and spread eastward, moving to its current site. The first ship passed through the canal's Miraflores Locks in 1914. Since then, Panama has gained control over the canal, and its favorable tax regulations have made Panama City an international banking and commercial center. Today, Panama's relative stability compared to other Latin American countries continues to attract people and money. The low cost of living here has drawn retired Americans by the thousands. This influx of wealthy residents is reflected across the city, from the international cuisine to the rapidly expanding skyline.

With its first-world infrastructure, diverse population, continuing international influence, and lively nightlife, Panama City boasts all the advantages of a large, modern city. Be sure to take time and explore Panama's rainforests, Indian villages, and beautiful beaches, which are all just an hour from the city.

◼ INTERCITY TRANSPORTATION

Flights: Tocumen International Airport (☎238 2600) lies 30min. east of the city and can be reached by cab (US$15-20) or any bus marked Tocumen Corredor (US$0.35), which leave from the bus terminals at Albrook, C.50, Vía España, and Plaza 5 de Mayo. Airport serves: **American** (☎269 6022); **Continental** (☎263 9177); **Copa** (☎227 0116); **Delta** (☎214 8118); **KLM** (☎264 6395); and **Taca** (☎360 2093). **Marcos Gelabert Airport** (☎526 7990) handles all domestic flights and is a US$2 taxi ride from the Santa Ana neighborhood. **Aeroperlas** (☎315 7500; www.aeroperlas.com) has flights to **Bocas del Toro, Darien, David,** and **the San Blas islands. Air Panama** (☎316 9000; www.flyairpanama.com) serves roughly the same destinations. Flight prices and schedules change often, depending on demand. Flights are often canceled, combined, or re-directed. Trips to smaller destinations will often involve 2 or more stopovers.

Buses: Gran Terminal de Transporte (☎232 5803), is next door to the Albrook mall and near Marcos Gelabert Airport. Tickets can be bought at the booths lining the terminal. Station employees can point you in the right direction, though few of them speak English. Information booth (☎303 3040) open 24hr. The terminal has food courts, ATMs, internet, and luggage storage. Schedules are flexible; buses may wait to fill up. To: **Bocas del Toro** (10hr., 8pm, US$24) via **Almirante** (9½hr.); **Chitré** (4hr., every hr. 6am-11pm, US$7.50); **Colón** (1½hr., every 30min. 4am-midnight, US1.80; express service 1hr., 14-17 per day, US$2.50) via **Sabanitas** (1hr.); **David** (7hr., every hr. 5:30am-8:30am, US$12.60; express night service 6hr., 10:45pm and midnight, US$15), with some continuing on to **the border** with Costa Rica at Paso Canoas (9 per day 6:30am-midnight); **El Valle** (2hr., every 25min. 6am-7pm, US$3.50); **Metetí** (6hr., 14 per day, US$9); **Penonomé** (2hr., every 20min. 4am-11pm, US$4.35); **Santiago** (3½hr., every hr. 3am-1am, US$7.50,); and **Yaviza** (7hr.; 4:15, 5:15, 5:45, 6:30, 7:30am; US$14). **Tica Buses** (☎314 6385) sends buses to **San José, Costa Rica** (16hr.; 11am, 10, 11pm; US$25-35).

⚓ ORIENTATION

From the international airport, take a taxi (30min.; US$28, shared taxi US$11). To find a bus, walk out of the parking lot where the cars exit, and walk through the roundabout. On the other side of the road is a bus stop. Take the Tocumen Corredor bus (45min., US$0.35), which will drop you off on C. 50. The domestic airport is a US$2 cab ride from the center; alternatively, take a bus (US$0.25) from the airport to the central bus station nearby. From the bus station, there are buses to almost everywhere in the city. For Bella Vista, take the "Vía España" bus and ask the driver to let you off in Bella Vista.

Parts of Panama City are laid out in grids. Many streets have two or three names: one is often a person's name, the second some a combination of numbers and letters (i.e. C. 49A Este). As such, directions in the city are generally given in terms of landmarks and blocks. The city sprawls west to east along the **Bahía de Panamá** (Panama Bay). The **Peninsula of San Felipe** (also known as **Casco Viejo**), on the west side of the bay, is home to magnificent crumbling old buildings, some of the swankiest new restaurants, and many of the city's historical sites. At the heart of Casco Viejo is **Plaza Independencia**, from which the city's largest street, **Avenida Central**, extends northeast into **Santa Ana** (often pronounced "Santana"). Between the Plaza de Santa Ana, just north of San Felipe and **Plaza 5 de Mayo**, in the heart of Santa Ana, Av. Central becomes a pedestrian mall lined with budget shopping. Beyond the Plaza, the road runs east through Calidonia before becoming **Vía España**. Further on, the road enters **Bella Vista**, which is quickly becoming the cosmopolitan center of the city. **Avenida Balboa** intersects with Av. Central in Santa Ana, and stretches along the bay with a new park on the right and the city's fanciest skyscrapers on the left. Passing through **Marbella**, which borders Bella Vista, Av. Balboa continues through a bulge in the bay known as **Punta Paitilla** and **Punta Pacífica**, which are home to some of the most expensive apartment buildings and the best hospital in town.

SAFETY. Though Panama City is welcoming to visitors, all cities have their dangers, and Panama definitely has its share. Problems have been reported in San Felipe, Santa Ana, Panamá Viejo, and Calidonia neighborhoods, especially at night. **After dark, avoid walking long distances, try to stick to busier roads, and don't flaunt your wallet, watch, camera, or any other item that marks you as a tourist.** Women traveling alone will probably feel most comfortable in Bella Vista. The city's poorest and most dangerous section, El Chorillo, borders San Felipe and Santa Ana to the west. Panamá Viejo basically shuts down at night. Americans in particular are advised to avoid Panamá Viejo, since US troops burned many area residences to the ground during the 1989 invasion, stirring up anti-American sentiment. Curundu, San Miguel, and Santa Cruz, north of Santa Ana and Calidonia are all best avoided. If traveling long distances, take a taxi.

⚏ LOCAL TRANSPORTATION

Buses: Stops are often unmarked, and there aren't any route maps. Still, buses are the cheapest way to get around. **City buses** (old American school buses with loud mufflers) have their final destination painted on the front windshield; to wave one down just stick out your hand. Most buses run through **Plaza 5 de Mayo**, or along **Avenida Perú, Calle 50**, or **Vía España**. Buses marked "*directo*" make fewer stops. It's a good idea to let

Panama City Center

🏠 ACCOMMODATIONS

Casa Grande, **11**
Hotel California, **1**
Hotel Caracas, **16**
Hotel Centroamericano, **2**
Hotel Colón, **18**
Hotel Herrera, **17**
Hotel Riazor, **9**
Pensión Las Tablas, **5**
Residencia Turística
 Volcán, **4**

🍎 FOOD

Café Asís, **8**
Café Caribe, **6**
Café CocaCola, **14**
Raspados de Chico, **15**
Rest. La Victoria, **13**
Rest. Luna Llena, **12**
Rest. Mercado
 de Mariscos, **7**
Rest. Pizzería
 Romanaccio, **3**
NIGHTLIFE
844, **10**

your driver know your destination. The cost within the city is always US$0.25 (Tocumen Airport US$0.35); pay the driver or the bus jockey as you get off. **Express buses** (US$0.75-1) have *"corredor"* marked on the front next to their destination; these buses are more expensive because they take toll roads and sometime have A/C. If the bus doesn't stop where you want, yell *"¡Parada!"* Buses run from 4am-11pm.

Taxis: Taxis can be found everywhere. Fares are based on a six-zone system spanning from **Balboa** to just beyond the **Río Abajo**. Rides within a zone for 1 person should cost no more than US$1.35; every zone boundary crossed adds US$0.15. Each additional passenger costs US$0.25. A US$0.40 surcharge applies for called cabs (**Radio Taxi Express** ☎221 3142; **Radio Taxi Rey** ☎254 1880). These rules are loosely followed. A trip from San Felipe to Vía España costs around US$1.50. To Albrook Airport, the mall, or the bus station US$2-3. To Amador Causeway US$3-5. Taxi drivers can be picky;

depending on traffic or destination, you may have to try another cab. Always settle on a price before getting in; tourists are prime targets for scams.

Car Rental: Prices range from US$40-100 per day, depending on car size and insurance. At major chains, drivers must be 25 or older, although some go as low as 23 if you pay with a credit card. Website reservations are usually easier; you can sometimes get a better deal online. All chains have locations near or along Vía España in Bella Vista. Companies include **Alamo** (☎229 5257; www.alamopanama.com); **Avis** (☎278 9444); **Budget** (☎263 8777; www.budgetpanama.com); **Dollar** (☎270 0335); **Hertz** (☎260 2111; www.rentacarpanama.com); **Thrifty** (☎264 2613).

🔢 PRACTICAL INFORMATION

TOURIST AND FINANCIAL SERVICES

Tourist Information: Autoridad de Turismo Panama (ATP; ☎526 7000; www.visitpanama.com). National office in a large black building on Av. Samuel Lewis, in front of the Comosa building, though this office is basically useless. Their website serves as a good database of phone numbers and services. Other branches, at Albrook (☎526 7990; open 6am-6pm everyday) and Tocumen (☎238 8356; open daily 8am-midnight) airports and in Plaza Concordia (open M-F 8am-4pm, Sa 8am-1pm) are more useful. The **Autoridad Nacional del Ambiente (National Environmental Authority),** known commonly as **ANAM,** (☎500 0839) has an office housing its Areas Protegidas (protected areas) division near the Albrook Airport. They have limited info about the parks. More thorough info is available at regional offices and at the park headquarters. Open M-F 7:30am-3:30pm.

Travel Agencies and Tour Companies: Ancon Expeditions, C. Elvira Méndez at C.49A Este (☎269 9415; www.anconexpeditions.com), in Edificio El Dorado. A wide range of options for ecological trips throughout the country. Prices run about US$100 per day per person. Open M-F 8am-5pm, Sa 9am-1pm. **Viajes y Destinos** (☎264 8461; www.viajesydestinos.com.pa), across the street from the Hotel Continental and the Banco Transatlantico on C. Manuel Maricasa. Popular travel agency with English-speaking staff. Books everything from international flights to domestic tours. Open M-Sa 8am-5pm. **Mirador Adventures** (☎6401 6278; www.miradoradventures.com), operates out of La Jungla Hostel, and is an outfitter for everything outdoors.

Embassies and Consulates: Canada, Edificio World Trade Center, 1st fl. (☎264 9731; www.panama.gc.ca), in Marbella, C.53 Este near C.50. Open to public M-F 8:30am-1pm. **Costa Rica** (☎264 2980), on Av. Samuel Lewis, behind El Rey on Av. España. Open 8am-1pm. **UK** (☎269 0866; www.britishembassy.gov.uk/panama), in Marbella in the MMG buiding on C.53. Open M-Th 7:30am-3:30pm and F 7:30am-12:30pm. **US,** 783 Av. Demetrio B. Lakas (☎207 7030; www.panama.usembassy.gov), in Clayton. Open M-F 8am-noon and 1:30pm-3:30pm. Closed last Th of each month and on US holidays.

Banks: The city is littered with banks, especially in Bella Vista along Vía Espana. **Sistema Clave** 24hr. **ATMs** accept the most debit and ATM cards, and can be found throughout the city, and in many pharmacies and grocery stores. **Banco General,** in Santa Ana, in the pedestrian mall on Av. Central. Open M-F 8am-3pm. **HSBC,** on Vía España across from Hotel Panama. English-speaking staff. Cash advances on major credit cards. Open M-F 8am-8:30pm, Sa 9am-noon.

American Express: (☎264 2444), in Centro Commercial, Vía Pacífica, in Punta Paitilla next to Lumi Centro. Open M-F 8am-5pm, Sa 8am-10:30am.

Western Union: Plaza Concordia, across from the Supermercado El Rey in Bella Vista. Open M-Sa 8am-7pm. Another in the Albrook Mall. Open M-Sa 10am-7:30pm, Su 10:30am-7pm.

PANAMA CITY

LOCAL SERVICES

Luggage Storage: In the bus terminal. Walk out the end of the terminal on the side that buses enter, take a left, and then another left into a narrow hallway; it's on the left. US$1.50-4 per day depending on size. Open M-Sa 7am-9pm, Su 8:30am-7pm.

Bookstores: Exedra Books (☎264 4252), on Vía España and Vía Brazil. The best bookstore in Panama, with a large selection of English-language books. Nice cafe with Wi-Fi. Open M-F 9:30am-8:30pm, Sa 9:30am-7pm. **Gran Morrison** (☎202 0029), next to El Rey in Bella Vista, across from Plaza Concordia. Limited English-language selection relative to the rather large Kama Sutra section.

Laundromats: Most hostels offer laundry service for a small fee (US$3.50-5), but there are also *lavamáticos* (machine laundromats) and *lavanderías* everywhere. **Lavamático,** on C.13 between Av. A and Av. B, just off the plaza in Santa Ana. Full service US$4. Wash US$1; dry US$0.75. Soap US$0.30. Open M-Sa 7:30am-3pm, Su 8:30am-2pm. **Milena Lavandería & Lavamático,** just next to the Blockbuster on Vía España in Bella Vista. Wash and dry US$2. Open M-Sa 7:30am-8pm, Su 9am-4pm.

EMERGENCY AND COMMUNICATIONS

Emergency: ☎104.

Police: Tourist Police (☎211 3365); **National Police** (☎511 7000); **Bella Vista** (☎511 9439); **Calidonia, San Felipe, Santa Ana** (☎511 9427).

Red Cross: ☎228 2187.

Pharmacy: Pharmacies are everywhere in Panama City. **Farmacia Arrocha** (☎223 4505), in Bella Vista, just off Vía España, near HSBC. Open daily 7:30am-11pm. Another branch (☎262 1068) on Av. Central on the Pedestrian Mall in Santa Ana. Open M-Sa 7am-8:15pm, Su 8:30am-4:45pm.

Hospital: Hospital Punta Pacífica (☎204 8000), near the Multiplaza. English spoken.

Telephones: Public phones are everywhere, though they may not always work. **Phone cards,** for sale at supermarkets and pharmacies, are a good option since public phones rarely give change.

Internet: Internet cafes are common in most parts of the city, especially Calidonia and Bella Vista. Internet around US$1 per hr. **Internet Panama Cafe,** in Santa Ana on the plaza, at the end of the pedestrian mall. Internet US$0.75 per hr. Open daily 9am-9pm. Another cafe in Bella Vista in Plaza Concordia. Internet US$0.50 per 30min. Open M-F 8am-8pm, Sa 9am-5pm.

Post Office: (☎511 6232), inside Plaza Concordia. Open M-F 7:15am-4:45pm, Sa 8:15am-12:45pm.

▚ ACCOMMODATIONS

Accommodations in Panama City run the gamut, from dark and dreary *pensiones* that do business by the hour to glitzy glass high-rises catering to the jetset crowd. Quality hostels and establishments on the backpacker circuit lie in Casco Viejo and the neighborhoods east of Bella Vista; these are on opposite sides from the center of the city, but within walking distance. Hotels closer to the city center, in Santa Ana and Calidonia, cost more and have fewer amenities. It's advisable to book in advance, especially during the high season (December-March).

SAN FELIPE (CASCO VIEJO)

San Felipe, popularly know as Casco Viejo, is in a constant state of transition. Crumbling colonial buildings lay vacant next to beautifully restored buildings. Lodgings in Casco Viejo reflect this duality, offering the most bohemian hostels and some of the shadiest hotels. During the day, it's safe to walk around, but at night the neighborhood is sort of a ghost town, so it is a good idea to either stick to main roads (Av. Central) or take cabs.

▣ **Luna's Castle,** C. 9NA, Este 3-28 (☎262 1540; www.lunascastlehostel.com). From Av. B and C.9, walk east toward the water. From the public market, walk up the ramp; it's the 2nd house on the right. Housed in a beautifully renovated old mansion and chock-full of modern art, sofas, and hammocks, this place is a backpacker's paradise. A popular bar, a movie theater, and views of the ocean and the glamorous high-rises across the bay round out the deal. Breakfast and lockers included. Laundry US$5. Free internet. Reservations recommended. Dorms US$12; doubles with shared bath US$28; triples US$36. ❷

Hospedaje Casco Viejo, C. 8a and Av. A (☎211 2027; www.hospedajecascoviejo. com). Walk west away from the plaza; it's on the left. A renovated colonial mansion, this new hostel lacks the homey atmosphere and the amenities of its competitors, but its hard to beat the price. Very little communal space and clean, standard rooms. Bathrooms very small and a bit dirty. Kitchen and lockers available. Free Wi-Fi. Dorms US$9; singles US$16, with bath US$18. ❷

Casa Grande, C.8 and Av. Central (☎211 3316), in an old yellow and white building. Cheapest rooms in Casco Viejo. Common baths, tiny showers, and high ceilings with fans. Many of the guests are long-term, so it can be hard to get a room. Private rooms US$6, with balcony US$7. ❶

SANTA ANA

Noisy, bustling Santa Ana is closer to the city center, and has a number of good hotels, but nothing nearly as charming or bohemian as Casco Viejo. Streets are a lot more crowded, and considered by most to be a little more dangerous, so stick to Av. Central if you stay here. Most of the hotels are within a block or two of Plaza de Santa Ana and the Pedestrian mall on Av. Central.

Hotel Colón, C.B and C.12 (☎228 8506). From the pedestrian mall at Plaza Santa Ana, follow the trolley tracks 1 block toward San Felipe and turn right. Peeling paint and a general air of neglect add to the mystique of this enormous 5-story hotel that's been around since 1915. Large, beautiful common rooms and a rooftop terrace with views over Casco Viejo and the bay. Rooms come with fans. Singles US$11, with bath US$15.40, with A/C and bath US$10.90; doubles US$13.20/18.70/24.20. ❷

Hotel Caracas (☎228 7229). When facing the church in Plaza Santa Ana, it's on the left. Three floors of big rooms. Singles US$10, with A/C US$15; doubles US$12/16; triples US$18/24. ❷

Hotel Riazor, C.16 and Av. 1 (☎228 0777), around the corner from the Banco Nacional building in the pedestrian mall. A good deal in a central, though noisy location. Forty-six comfortable and spotless rooms, each with a fan, hot water, towels, and free coffee. Singles US$25; doubles US$28; triples US$40. ❸

CALIDONIA

Calidonia, running east of Playa 5 de Mayo along Av. Central, has many options, but don't expect the best values in town. US$12 will get you a queen size bed with a fan a shared bath. Expect to pay twice as much for a private bath and air-conditioning.

Mamallena, C. 38 and Av. Central (☎6676 6136; www.mamallena.com). Head toward Plaza 5 de Mayo on Av. Central and turn right at the Govimar building. Closer to downtown but far from some of the sights. Friendly, English-speaking staff. Rooms are a little rough around the edges, but all have A/C. Breakfast included. Laundry US$3.25. Free internet and Wi-Fi. Singles US$11; doubles with shared bath US$27.50. ❷

Hotel Backpacker Inn (☎225 7283, reservations 227 1522), north of Av. Justo Arosemana on C. 33, near Hotel Roma. The closest thing to a hostel in Caladonia and the best value in the area. Rooms are simple but clean; all come with private bath, hot water, A/C, and cable TV. Free transportation to the international airport. Free Wi-Fi. Singles US$25; doubles US$35. MC/V. ❸

Pensión Las Tablas, Av. Perú between C. 28 and C. 29, across from Machetazo. Small, clean rooms with fans, TVs, and an uncommonly festive paint job. Rooms on Av. Perú are noisy. Rooms US$12, with bath US$15; doubles US$18. ❷

Residencia Turística Volcán (☎225 5263), on C. 29 between Av. Perú and Av. Cuba. Recently renovated, Volcán's woodwork, tiles, and bright paint job brighten up the otherwise basic and clean rooms. The mattresses are a little stiff. All rooms have A/C. Singles US$25; doubles US$30. ❸

BELLA VISTA

The Bella Vista district is a large swath of land east of the city center. This area encompasses a number of smaller neighborhoods that stretch along Vía España, including (from west to east) Bella Vista, El Congrejo, and El Carmen. Not quite as old and charming as Casco Viejo, nor as glamorous as the buildings along the waterfront, Bella Vista is home to some of the best restaurants and nightlife in town.

▨ **Hostal La Casa de Carmen** (☎263 4366; www.lacasadecarmen.net), on C.1 in El Carmen. It's on the street parallel to Vía España, off Vía Brazil. A beautiful backyard garden, a spacious lounge, and homey rooms make this a pleasant respite from the bustle and heat of the city. All rooms have A/C. Showers, kitchen, and library on-site. Breakfast included. Wash US$1; dry US$1. Free Wi-Fi. 6-bed dorm US$12; singles US$30, with bath US$38; studio US$55. ❷

La Jungla (☎6668 5076; www.miradoradventures.com), on C. 49A west of Vía Arentina, 3 buildings up the hill from Hotel Las Huacas, on the 5th fl. A new, welcoming hostel with a laid-back environment in a quiet residential neighborhood. People congregate on the balcony to sip on beer and discuss their escapades. The owner is an outdoorsman and a valuable resource for anyone looking to head into the jungle. Dorms US$16; singles US$26; quads with A/C and bath US$80. ❸

Voyager International Hostel (☎260 5913). From Vía Argentina, turn right at the Subway restaurant; the hostel is on the 2nd fl. Great location on the Vía Argentina is the main selling point, but a full array of amenities adds to the appeal. Rooms comes with cable TV and hot water. Bathrooms are a little dirty. Kitchen available. Breakfast included. Free Wi-Fi. Reception 24hr. 12- and 5-person dorms US$10; 4-person dorm with A/C US$13; private doubles US$27. ❷

◩ FOOD

Given the variety of cultures that have left their mark here, it isn't surprising that Panama City is the capital of international cuisine in Central America. Prices are diverse, from the cheap (US$1-2) *comida típica* found in cafeterias, to the international flavors of Bella Vista, Marbella, and El Congrejo. Throughout the city, street vendors sell hot dogs, *empanadas, frituras,* fresh fruit,

ON THE MENU

TOP 10 PLACES TO GET YOUR HOT TAMALE FIX IN PANAMA

1. **El Trapiche** (p. 249) combines sweet cornmeal, chicken, and vegetables in their **tamal de olla** for a late breakfast of champions. You'll never settle for pancakes again. (Vía Argentina at Av. 2a B Nte., in the El Cangrejo district of Panama City. ☎+507 269 4353.)

2. A savory tamale after a late night out is always a good choice. **Niko's Café** in **Panama City** serves up spicy tamales that are cheap and tasty. (C. 50. ☎+507 270 2555.)

3. Try a vegetarian tamale at the **Casa Vegetariana,** a buffet-style restaurant owned by a Taiwanese family that serves over 20 meat-free, Asian-inspired Panamanian dishes each day. (Center C. Ricardo Arias, Av. 3, Panama City. ☎+507 269-1876.)

4. Little known fact: Panamanian prison food is delicious! While it hasn't been an active prison since the 17th century, the Spanish dungeon in **Casco Viejo** is now home to **Las Bóvedas,** a high-end restaurant serving French-influenced Panamanian cuisine. (Plaza Francia in Panama City. ☎+507 228 8068.)

5. At **Manolo Caracol,** pay the chefs a flat fee of around US$17 for 12-courses carefully handcrafted right in front of you. While your tamale may be slow in its creation, it's sure to be eaten in a

and *chichas* (a sweet fruit juice concoction). You can find most vendors around C. 13, the pedestrian mall, Playa 5 de Mayo, in the *mercadito* at Av. Perú and C.34, or at the grand **market** on Av. Alfaro.

Panama City is filled with supermarkets. **El Rey** is a popular chain; there's one on Vía España across from the Plaza Concordia in Bella Vista (open 24hr.). **Machetazo,** a gargantuan five-story department store, has a supermarket inside. There is one on the Pedestrian Mall near Plaza Santa Ana (open M-Sa 8:30am-7pm) and another on Av. Perú between C.29 and C.30 (open M-Sa 8:30am-8pm).

The **seafood market** on the coast at Av. Balboa and C. 24E is worth a visit; there's nothing like the sound of hundreds of butcher knives gutting the day's catch. (Open daily from dawn until the early afternoon.) Just up the hill on Av. Balboa is **El Mercado Público,** a large warehouse with stalls selling meat and vegetables. The market is surprisingly clean and sanitary considering the bloody cow parts. Food starts coming in from the countryside as early as 3:30am; the place empties out by 4pm.

SAN FELIPE (CASCO VIEJO)

Food options in San Felipe range from chic gourmet cafes to cafeteria-style *típicos*, with little else in between. Restaurants are spread fairly evenly throughout the area. If you're really on a budget, it may be worth a trek up to Santa Ana for more affordable options.

René, on Plaza Catedral. High-class, 5-course meals at affordable prices. The kitchen is open, allowing you to watch the chef prepare each course. The fixed 5-course meal (from US$8.25) comes with salad, appetizer, rice, your choice of entree, and dessert. Open M-Sa 11:30am-3pm and 6:30-10pm. ❸

Casablanca, at Av. B and C.4, on Plaza Bólivar. Grab a table on the historic plaza at this classy establishment. Their specialties, ribs and seafood, are probably a little pricey for most. Cheaper options like veggie burgers (US$6) and sandwiches (US$5) are also available. Casablanca is also a great place to grab a beer (US$2.75). Be sure to try 1 of their 10 different mojitos (US$5). Open daily 10am-1am. MC/V. ❷

Cafe Perdue, on Av. A and C.4. Probably the most affordable non-*típico* restaurant in Casco Viejo. Throwback tunes (Ace of Base, anyone?) and the best pizza (US$4-6) in the neighborhood. Breakfast US$2-4. Subs US$3.50. Open Tu-Sa 8:30am-10pm. ❷

Habana Club, at the corner of Av. B and C.5. Looks like a Havana saloon from the playboy 50s. Does more business as a bar than a restaurant, but the food is good, the portions decent, and the prices agreeable.

Hamburgers US$6.50-9. *Ceviche* US$7-8. Sandwiches US$7-8. Restaurant open daily 8am-4pm. Bar open 4pm-midnight. MC/V. ❸

Conajagua, on Av. B between C.11 and C.12. Though its just one of the many *fondas* in the neighborhood serving cafeteria-style *típico*, Conajagua is a bit friendlier and cleaner than the rest. Grab a tray and point to what you want. Large portions US$1.50-2.00. Open daily 4am-4pm. ❶

SANTA ANA

More crowded and less historic Santa Ana has many more budget options than San Felipe. A variety of street stall offerings, ice cream, pizza, and fast food (God bless America), as well as plenty of cheap *típico*. Most of the eateries line the Pedestrian mall from Plaza Santa Ana to Plaza 5 de Mayo.

Restaurante Mercado de Mariscos, part of the Seafood Market where Av. Balboa hits the San Felipe entrance. Head indoors and up the stairs. Seafood that practically crawls off the boats and onto your plate. Seafood cocktails US$4. Fish US$5-8. Shrimp and calamari US$7-10. Lobster US$20-30. Open M-Sa 11am-7pm, Su 11am-4pm. ❸

Café CocaCola, Av. Central and C.12, across from Plaza Santa Ana. Supposedly the oldest cafe in Panama, this is a gathering spot for old men wearing Panamanian caps and *guayaberas* (the traditional 4-pocket shirts). Seafood cocktails US$3.50. Spaghetti US$2.50. Fish US$4-7. Open daily 7:30am-11:30pm. ❷

Restaurante Cheyi, on the pedestrian mall on Plaza Santa Ana, directly across from the church. Cafeteria-style *típico* with a little bit of Chinese flair. Cheap and hearty portions. Large order of *patacones* US$0.50. Fried chicken with rice US$1-2. Open daily 6:30am-8pm. ❶

CALIDONIA

Calidonia's establishments serve similar fare as those in Santa Ana, though many close a bit earlier. Eateries cluster on C.28-32, between Central and Arosemana.

Café Caribe, on C. 28 and Av. Perú, inside Hotel Caribe. A popular place with locals, Caribe is one of the only non-cafeteria establishments in the area. Cheap *típico* made all the better by A/C. Sandwiches US$3-5. Fish US$8. Open M-Sa 7am-9pm, Su 7am-3pm. AmEx/MC/V. ❷

Restaurante Pizzería Romanaccio, on C. 29 and Perú. Delicious pizza popular with locals. Mini pizza US$4, for 2 US$6. Whole pizza US$11. Open daily 11am-11pm. MC/V. ❷

flash. (C. 3 at Av. Central Sur, Panama City. ☎+507 228 4640.)

6. At **Miraflores Restaurant** located in the **Miraflores Panama Canal Visitors Center,** you can take down your delicious tamale while watching the ships going through the canal locks below. (☎+507 232 3120, Miraflores Locks, at the Panama Canal, on Amador Causeway.)

7. Las Tinajas, a sit-down restaurant featuring Panamanian folklore and dance shows every Tuesday through Saturday, serves tamales. Enjoy their famous chicken pot tamale. (C. 51 #22 Bellavista. ☎+507 263 7890.)

8. Become one with nature and your tamale at **Rincon de Filo,** a family-style Spanish restaurant 25min. outside of Panama City. Drive from Panama City on the main road through Veracruz. (☎+507 250 1728.)

9. Place your order at **La Cascada,** where the 16-page menu is almost as big as the portions. (Av. Balboa, C. 24 in Panama City. ☎+507 262 1297.)

10. Viso 52 Restaurant's polenta tamale with ossobuco and spicy shrimp is incredible. It's no secret that Viso cooks up one of the best tamales in Panama, so be sure to call ahead and make a dinner reservation. (Galerias Punta Paitilla, Locales 5/6, on the corner of Av. Balboa and Via Italia. ☎+507 215 0349.)

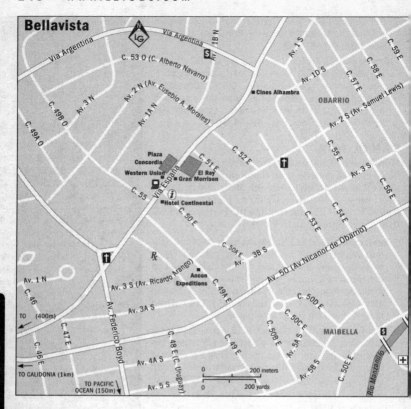

Bellavista

BELLA VISTA

Bella Vista is dubbed the "restaurant district" for a reason. The thriving culinary scene here caters to the thousands of resident expats. From sushi and crepes to tacos and gelato, you can find almost anything here. The greatest concentration of restaurants is on Av. Argentina, up the hill from Vía España. Be prepared to shell out for anything but fast food.

New York Bagel Cafe. Heading up Vía Argentina, turn right at the Subway restaurant; pass Voyager, it's 10m up on the right. The closest thing to a New York deli this side of the Tropic of Cancer, this delicious diner serves hearty omelettes (US$6) and a large selection of bagels (with cream cheese US$2; dozen US$9). Free Wi-Fi with purchase. Open M-F 7am-8pm, Sa 8am-8pm, Su 8am-3pm. MC/V. ❷

La Novena, up Vía Argentina near C. 49B. Sophisticated, friendly, and vegetarian. Watch your food be prepared in the open kitchen. Enjoy your meal while listening to classical music and admiring the fabulous local art. Soups US$4-5. Entrees US$6-8. Open M-Sa 10am-10pm. MC/V. ❷

Dolce, on Vía Argentina, a few blocks up from Vía España. The Canadian owner, Angel, boasts that there is no internet, TV, or even a cash register. Come here to devour delicious meals, brownies, beer, and participate in the booming book exchange. Breakfast US$2-4. Sandwiches US$4-5. Open M and W-Sa 8am-10pm, Su 8am-6pm. ❷

Beirut, Ricardo Arias at C. 52, near the Marriott Hotel. Great Middle Eastern fare with hookah (US$10.50) and live performances F and Sa night 9pm-midnight. Appetizers US$4-6. Entrees US$8-15. Beer US$3. Open daily 11am-4am. AmEx/MC/V. ❸

El Trapiche, on Vía Argentina, 1½ blocks from Vía España. An upscale sampling of traditional dishes from around Panama, popularly believed to be the best Panamanian food in the city. The *criollo* breakfast (US$1.60-4.50) is excellent. If you want a little bit of everything, share a *Fiesta Panameña* (US$11). Entrees US$6-10. Beer US$2. Open daily 7am-11pm. MC/V. ❷

Pita Pan Kosher (☎264 2786), in Bal Harbour shopping mall on Av. Italia off Av. Balboa. From the Multiplex shopping center, head up the street with a Popeyes on the corner; it's 2 blocks up on the left. Located in the city's Jewish neighborhood, this bakery cooks up a variety of kosher meals, sushi, and a wide assortment of fresh bread. Sushi US$6-8. Pasta US$6-10. Salad US$6-10. Open M-Th 7am-8pm, F 7am-5pm, Su 9am-9pm. ❷

Casa Vegetariana, on C. D in front of the Veneto Casino. Might be the cheapest place to fill up in the whole city. Simple cafeteria-style vegetarian dishes (US$0.50 per serving) and fresh juice (US$0.50). Open M-Sa 7am-11pm, Su 8am-9pm. ❶

Niko's Cafe, on C.51B just off Vía España, across the street from El Rey supermarket. Reliable, cheap cafeteria-style meals. Late night you'll run into droves of tipsy Panamanians on their way home from clubs and bars. Try *sancocho* (US$2), the national hangover remedy. Sandwich with soda and fries US$5. Gyros US$3. Pizza combo US$3. Open 24hr. ❷

👁 SIGHTS

Most travelers pass through Panama City to see other parts of the country, but for history buffs and art-lovers Panama City is the place to be. Casco Viejo has the greatest concentration of museums, ruins, and art galleries. With beautiful colonial churches, the fabulous Canal Museum, and splendid views of the new city across the bay, Casco Viejo alone deserves a day of wandering around. A trip to the new Museo Antropológico Reina Torres De Araúz, just a few minutes outside of the city, is also well worth the trip.

SAN FELIPE (CASCO VIEJO)

The second "Panama City" was founded on January 21, 1673, after pirate greed and a fire destroyed the original city. Known today as Casco Viejo, this area is a striking blend of beautifully restored colonial buildings and crumbling, decrepit buildings. Old Spanish colonial churches blend in among the houses with iron balconies, inspired by the French when they undertook the initial Canal construction effort. In 1997, UNESCO declared the area a **World Heritage Site** for its rich architectural diversity. Though the whole neighborhood seems to be under endless renovation, it's loaded with worthwhile memorials, ruins, and museums. Begin at **Plaza de la Independencia** (Plaza Catedral), on Av. Central and C. 7, which honors Panama's founders, among them the first President of the Republic, Manuel Amador Guerrero.

CATHEDRAL. Facing the Plaza de la Independencia is the huge Cathedral, which features a chiseled stone facade enclosed by whitewashed towers. The inside is simple, but be sure to check out the intricate sacrament. The cathedral has been around since 1798 and was one of the few buildings in the city to survive the 1882 earthquake. *(If the front is closed, try one of the side entrances. Open daily 8am-2pm. Su services 10:30am.)*

MUSEO DEL CANAL INTEROCEÁNICO. Though rivaled by the exhibit at Miraflores, this is probably the best museum in Panama. Housed in what used to be the headquarters of the French company that first worked on the Canal, the building itself is fascinating. The museum explains in detail the canal's construction, history, and operations; in tracing the early history of the Canal, it also manages to cover the history of the colonization of Panama. The museum has a vast collection of primary artifacts, from a Panama Railway depot's original benches to the colonial weapons from the *Camino de Cruces* (see **Portobelo Sights,** p. 262). Displays are well organized and informative, accompanied by videos and diagrams. All descriptions are in Spanish—even if you can't read them, though, there's plenty to see. *(With your back to the cathedral, the museum is on your right. ☎211 1650; www.sinfo.net/pcmuseum. Open Tu-Su 9am-5pm. US$2, students with ISIC card and children US$0.75. English-language tours available, but book in advance; US$5 per person.)*

PASEO LAS BÓVEDAS. This walkway, with fabulous views of the Pacific, was once used as a buffer against pirates and prisoners. Today the arbor-covered footpath offers shade and a great place to stroll. At the end of the Paseo lie the *bóvedas*, vaults which once held prisoners but now house a fancy restaurant and the small **Instituto Nacional de Artes Visuales** (National Institute of Visual Arts), which showcases rotating exhibits by local artists. The gallery faces **Plaza Francia,** built in honor of the Frenchmen who died during the 19th-century canal attempt. Walk around the semicircle to learn more about the history leading up to the Canal's construction and the men who came to build it (keep in mind it's all in Spanish). Chamber orchestras occasionally play in the park's small plaza. *(From Plaza de la Independencia, walk south away from the Cathedral along Av. Central unti the street winds past the Pacific. Free. Gallery open M-F 9am-5pm. Free.)*

CHURCH AND CONVENT OF SANTO DOMINGO. Dating back to 1678, the church's **Arco Chato** was famous for its mortar construction and lack of internal supports—right until it collapsed in 2003. Panamanian leaders used the arch's age to prove the country was earthquake-proof, important in the campaign to get the Canal built there. Connected to the old church ruins, the **Museo de Arte Religioso Colonial** contains a gigantic altar, sculptures, and religious paintings. *(Av. A and C. 3, 1 block south and 2 blocks east of the Plaza de la Independencia. At the time of publication, both were undergoing renovation, but they are slated to reopen at the end of Dec. 2009. ☎228 2897. Open Tu-Sa 9am-4:30pm. US$0.75, students US$0.25.)*

TEATRO NACIONAL. The Neoclassical theater was built at the turn of the century by an Italian architect; it was reconstructed after part of the ceiling caved in. Stunning frescoes on the ceiling were painted by Panamanian Roberto Lewis. During the day, you're allowed to walk around the theater. Someone is usually practicing on stage; be sure to pause and listen from the lush balcony seats. Performances in the theater range from folk and classical music to ballet and tango. *(Av. B and C. 3. From the Plaza, stand with your back to the Cathedral and walk left (north) 1 block and then right (east) 3 blocks on Av. Central. ☎262 3525. Open M-F 9:30am-5:30pm. Call for a schedule of upcoming concerts and shows. Tickets US$5-20.)*

OTHER SIGHTS. Parque Simón Bolívar features a monument honoring the namesake liberator with friezes depicting his feats. *(1 block east and 1 block north of Plaza de la Independencia.)* There are a number of cafes here with seating arranged on the square (see **Food,** p. 245). The Moorish-style **Palacio Presidencial,** also known as the "Palace of Herons," is home to Panama's president; you won't be able to get anywhere near it. *(On Av. Alfaro, 2 blocks north of Plaza de la Independencia.)* The **Iglesia de San José** houses the **Altar de Oro.** According to legend, a priest covered the magnificent golden altar in mud to disguise its worth from pirate Henry Morgan, who sacked Panama Viejo in 1671. The Church was built just a few years later. *(Av. A and C. 8, 1 block south and 1 block west of the Plaza.)* **Casa Góngora**, built in 1756, is one of the oldest buildings in Panama and the only one with a preserved interior. The building has been beautifully restored with its original architecture and floor. The wall space is used for rotating art exhibits. *(C. 4 and Av. Central. ☎ 506 5836. Open M 8am-4pm, Tu-Su 10am-6pm. Free.)* For everything from fresh fruit to Spanish textbooks head to **Sal Si Puede** (literally "get out if you can"), which runs from Av. Alfaro to the pedestrian mall at the Plaza de Santa Ana. Note the name and take precautions against pickpockets and thieves.

OUTSIDE CASCO VIEJO

Most of the museums outside of San Felipe are concentrated around **Plaza 5 de Mayo**, connected to San Felipe via the busy pedestrian mall. The mall itself is a piece of history, erected in honor of firemen who battled the flames from a gunpowder warehouse that exploded in 1914. Although none of the museums are particularly eye-opening, wandering through them is a nice way to while away a day.

MUSEO DE ARTE CONTEMPORÁNEO. This museum houses a small rotating exhibition space for modern artists from around the world, with a focus on Latin America. The first floor is child-oriented. *(West of Plaza 5 de Mayo on Av. de los Mártires. ☎ 262 8012. Open Tu-Su 9am-5pm. US$3, students US$2, children US$1.)*

MUSEO AFRO-ANTILLIANO. Housed in a tiny gray church, this stand-out one-room museum was once the chapel of the Christian mission, around which Panama's Afro-Indian population first organized. The small museum expertly recounts their history with photos, antiques, and parts of the old Panamanian railroad, the construction of which attracted immigrants looking for work. The museum also pays tribute to the important cultural, religious, and economic contributions these cultures have made to Panama. *(From Plaza 5 de Mayo, continue east 1-2 blocks along Av. Justo Arosemana. ☎ 501 4130. Open Tu-Sa 8:30am-3:30pm. US$1, students US$0.75.)*

MUSEO DE CIENCIAS NATURALES. Though it's no Smithsonian, the museum offers small exhibits on paleontology, geology, and vertebrate taxonomy. One exhibit on indigenous wildlife has a wide variety of stuffed birds and mammals. This might be the only way to experience the Panamanian outdoors without mosquitoes, but unless you're a biology or taxidermy buff, the Museo de Ciencias Naturales might be worth a pass. *(Av. Cuba, C. 30 Este. ☎ 225 0642. Open M-F 9am-3:30pm. US$1.)*

MUSEO ANTROPOLÓGICO REINA TORRES DE ARAÚZ. Recently moved from its prime location on the Plaza 5 de Mayo, this museum now occupies a large modern building outside of town, complete with an outdoor amphitheater and an indoor auditorium. Though at the time of publication some of the exhibits were being modified, the museum does a decent job documenting Panamanian ethnography from pre-Colombian times and is home to 15,000 pieces of art-work made of gold, ceramic, and stone. *(Near the Albrook bus station. Take any directo bus heading to the terminal and ask to get off at Curundu (or the University of Panama at Curundu), then walk up the street toward an Esso station; it's just past the station. ☎ 501 4743. Open M-F 9am-3:30pm. Free. Free English-speaking tours available; call ahead to schedule.)*

PANAMA VIEJO

Founded in 1519, Panamá Viejo—the original Panama City—was the first European New World city on the Pacific coast. As the starting point for Spanish expeditions to the rest of the continent, the city quickly became linked to international transport and trade. It flourished as the Pacific terminus of Spain's **Camino Real.** The Camino functioned as the transisthmian pipeline for

Spain's Pacific colonies. This importance was short-lived, however, and after near-destruction at the hands of pirate Henry Morgan in 1671 and the fire that followed, Panamá Viejo was abandoned. Today, it offers an intriguing peek into a 16th-century city. The modern **museum** has two floors with materials on the city's history and archaeology; a fair amount of the information is in English. The first floor even has a surprisingly lighthearted exhibit on pirates.

Panamá Viejo includes ruins, a fort, several convents, a hospital, and other structures sprawled along a lovely 1km boardwalk that follows the bay. The stretch is conveniently delineated by two impressive landmarks, the 15m **cathedral tower** at the far end, and the Bridge of Kings, one of the oldest bridges in the Americas, just before the modern museum. At the end of the road is the **Mercado Nacional de Artesanías,** which houses loads of touristy mini-shops that all seem to sell the same stuff, though they claim it comes from different regions around the country. *(Take any city bus with the "Panamá Viejo" sign from Casco Viejo on Av. B and C. 12, just in front of the police station, and along Av. Balboa. 30min., 7am-11pm, US$0.25. Info center ☎ 226 8915. Open daily 9am-5pm. Entrance to the museum and ruins U$6, ruins US$3, under 17 US$0.50. Market open daily 9am-6pm.)*

🎵 ENTERTAINMENT

Theater: Teatro Nacional (☎202 3525), in San Felipe. A beautiful old theater with 3 floors of balconies and stunning frescoes. Everything from classical concerts to folk dance and ballet. Call for a schedule. Tickets US$5-20. Open M-F 9:30am-5:30pm. **Teatro Anita Villalaz** (☎501 4020), inside the grand Instituto Nacional de Cultura on Plaza Francia, at the tip of Casco Viejo. Additional shows on weekends. Visit during the day and you can probably watch rehearsal. Office open M-F 9:30am-5:30pm.

Cinema: Movie theaters abound; most show the latest Hollywood hits with subtitles. **Extreme Planet** (☎214 7022), on Av. Balboa next to MultiCentro. **Alhambra** (☎264 3217), on Vía España near the intersection with Vía Argentina. **CineMark** (☎314 6001), inside the Albrook Mall. Tickets US$4. **Cine Universitario** (☎223 9324), on the campus of Universidad Nacional de Panamá, behind Iglesia del Carmen. Tickets US$2.

🌙 NIGHTLIFE

Whether you're looking to strut your stuff on the dance floor or to just sit back and watch the locals, Panama City has it all. Panamanians dress well most of the time, especially so for nightlife: men wear long pants and collared shirts. Around here, women aren't afraid to show some skin. Jeans and short-sleeve shirts are acceptable for bars and discos, but shorts and sandals are not. You must be 18 or over to enter; be ready to show ID, though most places don't card.

Trendy San Felipe can be a blast, but take extra care at night—if you're alone, stick to taxis and avoid walking. Bella Vista's happening scene, concentrated around C. Uruguay and Vía Argentina, is considerably more safe. **Calle Uruguay** is the undisputed nightclub zone. If you aren't looking to dance, Vía Argentina has a more bar-oriented scene. On the Amador Causeway, there are a number of bars where you can sit at a table, grab a few drinks, and admire massive yachts. The action in clubs usually picks up around 11pm, but they tend to stay open as long as there are people, and there usually are. Panamanians don't consider it a night without some serious dancing. On average, beer costs US$2, mixed drinks US$4-5, and a bottle of Panamanian alcohol US$30.

For live music, head to **Restaurante Las Bóvedas** on Plaza de Francia. This spot is housed in a 17th-century fort turned torture chamber turned classy jazz club.

(☎228 8058. Open W and Sa 9pm-midnight.) For traditional *típico* music, **Las Tinajas,** Av. Frederico Boyd and Av. 3 Sur, has traditional performances Tu-Sa at 9pm. (☎263 7890. Cover US$5. Open M-Sa 11am-11pm. AmEx/MC/V.)

El Pavo Real, 3 blocks up Vía Argentina. A hugely popular bar that attracts locals and expats alike. Recently relocated, the loyal clients were so attached that they brought pieces of the old bar to the new location. Free pool tables. F-Sa live music. Open M-Sa 5pm-late. MC/V.

People (☎263 0104; www.peoplepanama.com), on C. Uruguay. One of the many trendy, pumping nightclubs on the block. Outdoor patio to cool off and a 2nd floor deck that overlooks the dance floor. They play "crossover" music, which is essentially electronic, salsa, hip hop, or anything else that keeps people dancing. Th women free before 11pm. If you're in a group, call ahead and see if you can get the cover waived. Cover US$10. Beer US$3. Mixed drinks US$4-7. Open 9pm-5am or late. MC/V.

The Londoner, on C. Uruguay. A haven for expats and travelers. With authentic English ambience (one of the owners is from the UK) and anywhere from 12-15 types of imported beer (US$5), this place attracts a slightly older crowd looking to have a good time. 70s and 80s rock, with an occasional live performance. Beer US$3. Open M-Sa 5pm-2am. AmEx/MC/V.

Relic, inside of Luna's Castle (see p. 244). Appropriately named, this new bar is housed in the basement and courtyard of a 1905 mansion. Unlike other places in the area, drinks are cheap (beer US$1; drinks US$2). Not the place to go if you're looking to meet locals, but a great place to share stories and drinks with some eccentric travelers. Open F-Sa 7pm-late.

Baños Publicos, on Plaza Herrera. Epitomizes Casco Viejo, reclaiming the old public bathrooms (hence the namesake) as a laid-back bar with a small stage for performances. Live music F-Sa. Music ranges from hip hop to Latin and rock. Beer US$1. Open W-F 6pm-late, Sa-Su noon-late.

Sahara. Walk through the shipping container on C. 48, just off C. Uruguay. One of the most popular places for backpackers, but still a mostly local crowd. This loud bar-nightclub is a welcome change from the chic places on C. Uruguay. Live music on weekends. F-Sa cover US$5 includes 1 drink. Local beer US$2.50. Bar food US$2. Open Tu-Sa 5pm-late. AmEx/MC/V.

Kiyuico, on the Amador Causeway, behind the Flamenco Yacht Club. A great place to grab a drink, listen to loud rock, and drool over huge boats you'll never see close up. Despite its high-rolling location, the place is surprisingly cheap. The boisterous local crowd stays until late. Local beer US$1.50. Pitcher of sangria US$18. Open daily 9am-late.

Rockin' Gorilla (☎399 6500), on Vía Argentina, about 2 blocks from Vía España. Although the large gorilla outside and the cheesy wooden tables inside make it feel a little like a roadside attraction, this place is bumping at night with a local crowd. W live rock. F karaoke. Billiards US$3. Beer US$1.75. Open M-F 5pm-8am. AmEx/MC/V.

La Casona (www.enlacasona.com), in Plaza Herrera, Casco Viejo. Housed in a former Art Deco bank and filled with art, La Casona is the artsy night club mecca. Their wall space displays pieces by artists from around the world. They showcase and sell crafts from around the country. F night live music and a large crowd. Events on other days of the week, like film festivals; check the website to see what's going on. Beer US$2. Open W-Sa 9:30pm-late.

Zouk (☎393 2155), on Vía Argentina, just behind the Blockbuster on Vía España. Complete with techno lights and some groovy furniture, this spot is home of the afterparty. Zouk pumps electronic and reggaeton starting in the wee hours of the morning, with the peak hours around 4am. 2 performances per month (US$10); otherwise no cover. Open W-Su 8am-4pm. AmEx/MC/V.

PANAMA CITY

⚠ OUTDOOR ACTIVITIES

PARQUE NATURAL METROPOLITANO

Metropolitano is within walking distance of the Albrook Mall and the bus station, and is easily accessible by bus. Take any Albrook Station bus headed for the Gran Terminal (US$0.25) and ask the driver to let you off at the Universidad de Panamá at Curundo, just before the station. Facing the forest across the street, turn left. Walk along the road for 100m and go right at the 1st fork. The ranger station will be on your left. Taxis cost about US$2-3. Park and ranger station open daily 7am-5pm. Early morning and late afternoon are the best times to watch wildlife. During the rainy season, come in the early morning. ☎ 232 5516 or 5552; www.parquemetropolitano.org. Trails US$2. Map US$1.50. Guides US$5 per person with a minimum of 5 people.

Panamanians claim this is "the most accessible rainforest in the world," which just might be true. Metropolitano occupies 232 hectares (almost a square mile) of forest within the city limits, 75% of which is fragile Pacific dry forest, an ecosystem almost extinct in the region. The park is just minutes from downtown and is somehow still home to hundreds of plant and animal species like the ▧**two- and three-toed sloth,** trogon, toucan, and Geoffrey's tamarin. Without the drone of cars whizzing by on the nearby highways, this urban escape might as well be in the Darién.

There are five **trails** in the park. In order of increasing difficulty, trails include: **Los Momótides** (900m, 30min.), named after the motmot bird; **El Roble** (700m, 30min.), named for the oak tree; **Los Caobos** (900m, 1hr.), named for the *Caoba* (mahogany) tree; **Mono Tití** (1.1km, 1½hr.), named for the *tití* monkey; and **La Cienaguita** (1.1km, 1hr.), named for its swamp. This last trail leads you to the top of a hill, 150m above sea level, that offers spectacular views of the city, canal, and bay. From the ranger station, you can make a loop including almost all of these routes (1½-2hr.).

PANAMA CITY

PANAMA AND COLÓN PROVINCES

PANAMA PROVINCE

PANAMA CANAL

The Panama Canal is the world's greatest shortcut, chopping 8000 miles off the voyage from the Pacific to the Caribbean. Although the locks are designed to raise and lower two boats at the same time, for logistical reasons they tend to move boats in the same direction and alternate every hour. On the Pacific side, boats go through a series of two locks, the Miraflores and Pedro Miguel, that elevate the ships a total of 26m above sea level, to the altitude of the Gatún Lake. From the locks, the boats pass through a narrow section of highland rainforest known as the Gaillard Cut, and finally enter the expansive Gatún Lake before they are lowered on the Atlantic side by the Gatún Dam. Boats use their own propulsion, but when passing through the locks, electric locomotives align them and keep them in position. Ships are charged based on their weight; the average cost to pass is around US$90,000. Around 36 boats pass through every day. More than a technological marvel, the Canal has also determined much of Panama's history, from its colonial exploitation to its recent economic growth. Today it continues to be a central part of the Panamanian economy.

▟ TRANSPORTATION. To get to the canal, you can take a taxi (US$5-6) or take a bus from the Gran Terminal just outside Panama City toward **Gamboa** (M-F 14 per day 5am-10:30pm, Sa-Su 9 per day 5:45am-10:30pm; US$0.65) or **Paraíso** (M-F 12 per day, Sa-Su fewer; US$0.35) and ask the driver to stop at Miraflores. Buses to **Chilibre** also pass by Miraflores.

▟▟ ORIENTATION AND PRACTICAL INFORMATION. From the bus stop, turn left toward the canal and cross the bridge. It is about a 10min. walk to the air-conditioned **visitor center.** (☎276 8617. Entrance US$5, with access to the museum and theatre US$8; students US$3/5. Open daily 9am-5pm. AmEx/ MC/V.) Partial boat tours of the canal run by **Canal and Bay Tours** leave Saturdays at 7:30am from Isla Flamenco on the Amador Causeway behind Mi Ranchito. (☎209 9000. US$115 per person, full tours first Sa of every month US$165.)

◪ SIGHTS. Few people pass through Panama without paying tribute to the canal at the **Miraflores Locks,** the largest on the canal and the closest to the Panama city. The visitor center includes a four-story museum, a film about the canal, an expensive restaurant (entrees US$18-30), a souvenir shop, and a fourth-story deck with a commanding view over the impressive operation. When boats pass, presentations in English and Spanish on the viewing deck explain how it works. When boats are not passing, a 10min. film alternates between English and Spanish to recount the history of the canal. The best (though priciest) way to see the canal is to experience it yourself by taking a partial or full tour. Panama City travel agents book the tour, but the main operator is **Canal and Bay Tours** (p. 255).

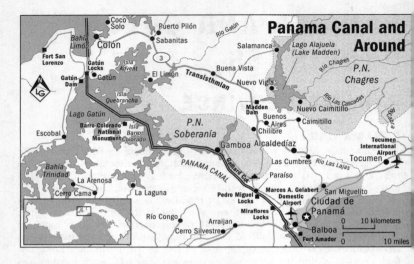

THE ROAD TO GAMBOA

Traveling along the canal out of Panama City, you'll eventually come to **Gamboa,** where Río Chagres feeds into Gatún Lake. A short hike in Soberanía or a stop in Summit Gardens makes a great daytrip from Panama City. Unless you want to camp or shell out some serious cash, spending the night in the area is difficult.

To access the area, take a Gamboa-bound bus from the Gran Terminal in Panama City (40min.; M-F 14 per day 5am-10:30pm, Sa-Su 9 per day 5:45am-10:30pm; US$0.65) or you can take a Chilibre bus and ask to get off at the ANAM station at the entrance to Gamboa. If your first stop is Miraflores, you can also take a Paraíso bus. These also leave from the terminal frequently.

Nine kilometers from the city is the turnoff to the Miraflores Locks (p. 255). Another 2.5km along the road are the Pedro Miguel Locks, which are harder to see and less tourist-friendly. Beyond these lies the small town of Paraíso, the last town before the birdwatching paradise of **Parque Nacional Soberanía** (p. 257). Following the cut-off for Gamboa, the road skirts along between the canal and the park, passing the Summit Botanical Gardens and Zoo on the continental divide. The road crosses the Río Chagres and then finally enters the sleepy town of Gamboa, the entrance to one of the park's best hikes and a point of departure for boat trips on the Río Chagres or Lago Gatún.

The ritzy **Gamboa Tropical Rainforest Resort** (take a right after the bridge in to town or stay on the bus while it passes through the town and loops around to the resort) is a good (if pricey) place to arrange tours of the park trips up the Chagres or activities on Lago Gatún. (☎314 5028; www.gamboaresort.com. 2hr. rainforest tram US$52, 40min. river tour US$15.) Another destination is **Barro Colorado,** a densely forested island in Lago Gatún operated by the Smithsonian Tropical Research Institute. (Follow the road straight through town. When it bends right, continue straight; it's a 5min. down on the left. ☎212 8903. Trips to the island including the boat launch, a guide, and lunch. Call in advance to make a reservation. US$70 for a full day up to 5 people.)

PARQUE NACIONAL SOBERANÍA

Spanning 19,540 hectares on the canal's east bank and encompassing the Río Chagres, part of Lago Gatún, and rich tropical rainforest, Soberanía is a fantastic day trip from Panama City, just 25km from Panama City. In addition to several good trails, it protects the canal's watershed and harbors an abundance of wildlife and birds. The park also hosts 105 species of mammals, 79 reptiles, 55 amphibians, and more than 1300 species of plants.

Buses going to Chilibre pass the park. You'll need to get off at the ranger station, pay the entrance fee, and wait for another bus or alternate transport to the trailheads. Or, head off on foot; the zoo is about a 25min. walk. If you're on a bus to Gamboa, you can get off the bus to pay the entrance fee and a collect a map, but the buses to the trailheads come rather infrequently (about every hour in the morning, longer in the afternoon); disembarking could mean a long wait before you get to the trailheads. From the road, Chilibre is to the right and Gamboa to the left. Guides can be arranged in advance through the ranger station or with outfitters in Panama City. (Ranger station ☎232 4192. Open daily 7am-5pm. Park US$5, students US$3. Camping US$3 per day.)

About 5min. down the road by bus is **Summit Gardens.** Another 7min. and you'll come to the first trailhead for the **Plantation Loop.** The trail takes you past the funky **Canopy Tower** (www.canopytower.com), a former US radar station, now a pricey hotel and birdwatching mecca. The moderately difficult trail leads 4 mi. into the forest and terminates in the middle of the **Camino de las Cruces** (p. 257). Another few minutes by car down the road lies the short and easy **El Charco** trail, a short but well-maintained loop through the forest. It follows a creek and ultimately leads to a waterfall and pond where you can swim. The walk takes an hour at a leisurely pace, but is quite crowded on weekends. The **Camino de Oleoducto** (Pipeline Road), which traces the path of a pipeline built by the US in WWII to transport oil from the Caribbean, is said to be one of the best places to birdwatch in all of Panama. To get there, get off the bus in Gamboa, another 10min. down the road (passing over the Río Chagres), and continue straight through the town. When the road bends right, stay straight to get to the trailhead. Although the trail is technically the longest in the park, you can only head up 6km through secondary and primary rainforest. Strikingly colorful butterflies, howler monkeys, and phenomenal bird life inhabit the hilly forests around the path.

In Soberanía, you can also hike one of the only remaining and maintained sections of the historic **Camino de Las Cruces,** which was constructed by the Spanish in the 16th century to transfer goods, primarily gold, across the isthmus. The difficult 6.2-mile (10km) trail has stone steps and terminates at the ruins of **Venta de Cruces,** a former resting spot along the Río Chagres. The trailhead is along the road to Chilibre, so after checking in at the ranger station, catch one of the frequent buses towards Chilibre and get off about 7km up the road. Unless you do a difficult round-trip hike (12.4 miles), you will need to arrange a boat on the Chagres to pick you up from the ruins. If you hire a guide, this will be taken care of for you. Felipe Cabezoni, a local Embera man, offers tours, though he only speaks Spanish (US$40). Elvira Cabrera, a local Embera woman who also only speaks Spanish, can also arrange a boat. (☎6704 0380. one-way US$3.50, round-trip US$7.)

COLÓN ☎981

Mention Colón to most Panamanians and they'll tell you not to go there. If you choose to come anyway, most people will advise you to leave. Colón has been in a downward spiral since its splendor in the early 20th century. Today the city is plagued by poverty and the highest crime rates in the country. Muggings occur in broad daylight despite the numerous armed policemen who patrol the streets. Aside from shopping in **Colón 2000**, the cruise port, or the **Zona Libre** (the second largest free trade zone in the world), there is not much to do in Colón. If you don't mind the real possibility of getting mugged, however, wandering the streets (with all your belongings locked in your room) can be an interesting experience. Despite the squalor, Colón has its own color and gritty vibrancy. Whether it's kids playing baseball in the streets, men playing checkers in the alleys, women fixing their hair, or drunk homeless men picking through trash, everyone seems to be outside, yelling, joking, and bringing the streets alive.

⌨ TRANSPORTATION

Buses: Leave from the bustling terminal on C. 13 and Av. Bolívar. Buses to: **Coco Solo** (35min., every 30min. 6am-7pm, US$0.30); **La Guaira** (2hr.; M-Sa every hr. 9:30am-3:30pm, fewer Su; US$2.50); **Panama City** (1½hr., every 30min. 4am-midnight, US$1.80; express service 1hr., every hr. M-F 4:45am-10pm, Sa-Su 7am-9pm, US$2.50); **Portobelo** (1½hr.; every 20min. M-F 4:30am-6pm, Sa-Su 7am-6pm; US$1.30); **Sabanitas** (45min., every 30min. 5am-12am, US$0.35).

Trains: By far the classiest way to travel. Vintage train complete with wood paneling and an open-air viewing deck. Runs through the jungle and skirts the canal. Trains (☎317 6070; www.panarail.com) leave from the **Albrook station** in Panama City and arrive near the **Cristóbal Colón port** in Colón. (1hr. Leave from Panama City weekdays at 7:15am; return from Colón at 5:15pm. One-way US$22.)

Boats: From the port at **Coco Solo** you can try to get a boat to the San Blas Archipelago and on to Colombia. These trips are negotiated with the vessel captains. They can be dangerous as this route is frequented by drug traffickers. For the best info about safer boat travel, inquire at hostels in Panama City.

Car Rental: Located in Colón 2000. **Hertz** (☎441 3272, open M-F 8am-5pm and Sa 8am-4pm). **Budget** (☎263 8777, open M-Sa 8am-12:30pm and 1:30-5pm).

◀▦ ⁊ ORIENTATION AND PRACTICAL INFORMATION

Colón is laid out in a north-south grid pattern. The city is situated on a roughly square piece of land that was once an island. In general, *avenidas* run north-south, connected by numbered east-west *calles*; C. 1 is to the north, while C. 16 is to the south. Very few of the roads are labeled, but **Avenida Central** runs through the center of the island with a wide median—stick to this *avenida* for the safest walking routes. West of Av. Central is **Avenida Guerrero** and then **Avenida Bolívar**. The **Zona Libre** (closed Sunday) occupies the southeast corner; the **Port of Cristóbal** is in the southwest. The **Colón 2000** shopping complex is on the far east side of town at the ends of C. 9-11. The **airport** is reached by a bridge from the Zona Libre. Outside of the Zona Libre, most of the neighborhoods are unsafe. There is a cluster of budget eating and lodging options between C. 9 and C. 11 on Av. Guerrero.

Tourist office: ATP (☎475 2301), in a small building on the waterfront facing C. 1 just west of Av. Central. Provides basic information on the city. Little English spoken. Open M-F 7:30am-3:30pm.

Banks: Although there are banks and **ATMs** all over Colón, the safest options are in Colón 2000 and Zona Libre, where a bank is on almost every block. If you need a bank closer to the center of town, you can try the **HSBC** on C. 11 and Av. Barboa, which has an **ATM;** open M-F 8am-3:30pm, Sa 9am-noon. For safety reasons, have a taxi waiting for you. **Western Union,** C. 13 and Av. Central (☎441 1309), on the 2nd floor. Open M-F 8am-5pm, Sa 8am-1pm.

Laundry: Most hotels will do laundry (usually around US$5). Numerous *lavamáticos* and *lavanderías*. **Luis N-2,** near a cluster of cheap hotels and restaurants on Av. Guerrero south of C. 11. Open daily 7am-5pm.

Police: (☎473 0365, emergencies 104), temporarily at Fuerte Davis; main branch is under renovation.

Pharmacy: Farmacia Itzel (☎441 7940) is one of 2 pharmacies at the intersection of C. 11 and Av. Guerrero. Open M-Sa 7am-11pm, Su 8am-10pm.

Hospital: Amador Guerrero (☎475 2211), next to Colón 2000 on C. 11, is clean.

Internet: Dollar Rent-A-Computer, on the 2nd floor above **Cafetería Nacional** (p. 259).

Post Office: (☎475 3043), in a particularly seedy section of C. 9, west of Av. Bolivar. Open M-F 7:15am-4:45pm and Sa 8:15am-12:45pm.

ACCOMMODATIONS

Let's Go recommends that you make Colón a daytrip from Panama City or stop by on your way to Portobelo. If you decide to stay, there are two good options with decent amenities and security; neither is particularly budget-friendly.

Hotel Carlton (☎447 0111), on C.10 2 blocks east of Av. Central, a few blocks north of Zona Libra. Clean and basic rooms come with TV and A/C. You're mostly paying for proximity to the Zona Libra and amenities: in-house laundry, pharmacy, and restaurant. Staff speaks English. Singles US$39-44; doubles US$44-50; triples US$55; quads US$66. Higher prices for rooms with a balcony. ❹

Hotel Internacional (☎445 2930), near the bus station on C.11 and Av. Bolivar. Similarly basic rooms with internet, TV, and A/C. Also has its own restaurant-bar (open M-F 7:30am-10:30pm, Sa 8am-11pm). They offer a free shuttle to the Zona Libre in the morning. Singles US$35; doubles US$45. ❹

FOOD

There is no shortage of places to eat in Colón, although it's probably a good idea to eat at or near your hotel if possible. The main dishes are *criolla*-style chicken or fish, but other cheap standbys like American fast food and Chinese food are easy to find. Supermarkets abound throughout the city, many of which are open 24 hours. Try **El Rey** on C.7 and Av. Central and **Super 99** in Colón 2000. Both have ATMs.

La Cabanita, on Av. Central and C.8. Serves local *criolla*-style fried chicken ($3.50), shrimp ($6), and fish ($6-8). Decked out in strange animal remains, including giant sets of jaws, snake skins, and stuffed heads. Open M-Sa 11am-5pm. ❷

Restaurante Dominicano, next to Pensión Acropolis. Offers up cheap, delicious Dominican chicken ($3) and meat ($4). Open M-Sa 7am-7:45pm. ❷

Cafetería Nacional, south along Av. Guerrero at the intersection with C.11. A strange combination of Chinese and local food. Heavily air-conditioned. Breakfast US$1.50. Sandwiches US$1.75-3.50. Full meals US$3-6. Open daily 9am-9:30pm. ❷

DAYTRIP FROM COLÓN

GATÚN LOCKS. Just 10km south of Colón, the Gatún Locks and Dam may be the best place to see the Panama Canal in operation; together they make for a great half-day trip from Colón. The **Gatún Locks,** the longest of the three sets of locks, raise and lower ships 26m between the Caribbean and Lago Gatún. The two sets of locks are designed to allow boats to come in and out at the same time. Boats going in the same direction move together, alternating every hour. For a better idea of how massive the locks really are, you can walk across the small bridge at the bottom of the lowest lock and come within meters of the massive iron walls. It's less glamorous than its Miraflores counterpart, but the **visitor center**, a tower above the middle of the three locks, has some of the best views of the canal operation. The guides speak perfect English and are eager to share all there is to know about the canal. Observe as the electric locomotives, known as *mulas*, guide the ships steadily through the canal. Jump on one of the original, retired *mulas* at the visitor center exit. *(From the main bus terminal in Colón, catch a bus to Cuipo or Costa Abajo (both 15 min., every hr. 5am-10pm, US$0.75) and let the bus driver know you want to get off before crossing the locks or a few min. down the road at the dam. From the bus stop at the locks, go left up the hill, keeping the canal on your right until you reach the visitor center, a white building with an ATM in front of it. ☎ 443 8878. Open daily 8am-4pm. US$5).*

GATÚN DAM. Two kilometers up the road from the locks is the massive **Gatún dam.** When it was constructed in 1906, it was the largest earth dam in the world and created the largest artificial body of water to date, Lago Gatún. The dam's construction caused the Rio Chagres to flood, covering villages, the Panama Railroad, and 262 hectares of forest. Today, the dam actively regulates the water level of the lake and generates enough power to operate the entire canal system. If you're lucky, some of the 14 spillways will be open; you can watch as millions of gallons of water flow out, changing the water level and powering one of the greatest engineering feats in the world. *(To reach the dam, you can catch the bus ($0.25) across the locks, or walk 20min. If you choose to walk, go left after crossing the locks and bear right when the road forks. Beware that the Canal Police are not always excited to have people walking near the locks or the dam, so they may ask you to take the bus. Buses return to Colón at least once an hr., though they do not stop if they are full. If you get tired of waiting for the bus, there are usually taxis ($10-15) that will pick you up.)*

PORTOBELO   ☎ 981

Lush hills gently bend through Spanish colonial ruins to meet crisp Caribbean waters here in alluring Portobelo (pop. 8000). For 200 years after its founding in 1597, Portobelo was a commercial center of the Spanish colonies. It hosted famous fairs mingling the Old and New Worlds, where Spanish traders came to collect gold and silver in exchange for European goods to be introduced into the Americas. For several weeks a year, the streets of Portobelo would host these huge exchange markets whose spirit of commerce and vigorous enterprise is today echoed in the **Colón Free Trade Zone**. Forts were built to protect outgoing gold supplies against pirates and the English Navy. Eventually though, the fort failed, and the port met its demise. Today, this laid-back, economically depressed town comes to life twice a year for some of the best festivals in all of Panama. Ruins, diving, snorkeling, and mangrove tours draw crowds on the weekends and in the dry season, but in the low season Portobelo enters a lull; most establishments close during this time.

▉ TRANSPORTATION

To get to Portobelo, take any **bus** from Panama City toward Colón and ask your driver to let you off at **Sabanitas** (look for shops with "Sabanitas" signboards, or for the McDonald's on the left side of the road. From the turnoff in front of El Rey supermarket, catch a **Portobelo** or **Costa Arriba** bus (1hr.; every 30 min. 5:30am-7pm, fewer on Su; US$1), though these buses are often standing-room only. In Colón, buses to Portobelo leave from the **bus terminal** (1½hr.;

every 30min. 4:30am-6pm, less on Su; US$1.30). From Portobelo, buses leave
for Colón (1½hr.; every 45min. 4:30am-6pm, less on Su; US$1.30) and stop in
Sabanitas, where you can catch buses headed for Panama City all day. There
are buses east to **Guaira** (30min., every 2hr. 11am-5pm, US$2), the jump-off
point to **Isla Grande.** Be sure to check with the driver before boarding, as onlt
a few Costa Arriba buses stop at Guaira. There are **taxis** waiting in town; a trip
to the resorts on the outskirts of town will cost US$2, but on the way back
you'll have to take a bus ($0.25).

⬛🔲 ORIENTATION AND PRACTICAL INFORMATION

Portobelo town lies on the south side of the tranquil Bay of Portobelo,
34km east of Sabanitas. All the watersport activities and high-class establishments are located a few kilometers before town on the main road. To
skip town and go directly to one of these places, get off the bus when you
see the "Scuba Portobelo" or "Coco Plum" signs on your left. From **Scuba
Portobelo,** the small town is a 40min. walk east along the main road through
the **Santiago de la Gloria ruins.** The town itself is centered around two squares.
The first, the **parque central,** is in front of the **Aduana,** the distinctive historic
building with arches. The main road continues on to the main square, which
sits in front of a large white church, **El Nazareno.**

Tourist Office: IPAT (☎448 2200), located in a new building 20m west of the **Aduana,** across the street from the municipal offices. Open M-F and Su 7:30am-3:30pm.

Police: ☎448 2033, 2km west of the town in front of Pirate's Cove resort.

Medical Services: Ministerio de Salud (☎448 2033), runs a **clinic** in Barrio Guinea. From the main road, take a right up the hill. There is another clinic, **Caja de Seguro Social** (☎448 2729), just outside of the town, on the main road heading east. Neither are open at night, so you may have to go to Sabanitas in case of a nighttime emergency.

Internet: A cafe just after the IPAT office. Internet US$1.50 per hr. Open M-F 8am-4pm. **Internet Enilda** (☎448 2439), across from Restaurante Ida (p. 262). Internet US$1.25 per hr. Open M-F 8:30am-9pm, Sa-Su 10am-8pm.

🏠 ACCOMMODATIONS

Although the bulk of the places to stay are on the road on the way into Portobelo, the town proper has three options. If you can't afford resort prices but
want to stay outside of town, a family rents out a few **basic rooms** ❷ with fans
and baths just past Coco Plum. (☎448 2400. Rooms US$15-20.)

Mercado Andy (☎448 2332), in front of El Nazareno. Rents out 4 clean rooms with fan and shower. Rooms US$15. ❷

Hospedaje Saigu (☎448 2204) on the main road up a hill to the east. Putting the "bare" in "barebones." Rooms with fans have beds on a concrete floor. Angel, the friendly owner, is willing to negotiate his already low prices. Rooms US$7-10. ❷

Hospedaje Aduana (☎448 2925), next to the *aduana,* above a bar. A few basic, if damp, rooms with floor fans. Doubles US$12, with bath US$14, with A/C US$20. ❷

Coco Plum Eco-Lodge and Resort (☎264 1338; www.cocoplum-panama.com). The best resort outside of town with large, overly decorated rooms. It's situated among a beautiful grove of palms, with plenty of hammocks and a small beach. All rooms have A/C, private bath and TV, and there is an adjoining restaurant. Rooms US$45 plus 10% tax; US$10 for each additional person. ❹

Scuba Panama (☎261 3841 www.scubapanama.com), further down the road. Nice rooms with A/C and bath for typical resort rates. A full array of aquatic activities offered, including rides to nearby pristine beaches ($4-10), snorkel rental ($10), dives (starting at US$18; equipment US$21), and an incredible value 4-5 day PADI certification class that includes equipment and lodging ($175). Doubles US$50; 4-person cabana US$61. ❹

🍴 FOOD

All the budget eateries are in town; nicer places with more options lie on the outskirts. In town, both **Restaurante Arith** ❶ on the *parque*, and **Restaurante Ida** ❶ near El Nazereno, serve cheap and delicious local food. Try the fried meat, chicken, or fish with rice, beans, and plantains ($3). On the edges of town, prices double. There are several **mercaditos,** one on each square, and one on the outskirts of town before the dive shop.

> **Restaurante Los Cañones** (☎448 2980), a few feet west of Scuba Portobelo. Superb place for conch and other Caribbean delights. Named after the rusting cannons that dot the Portobelo region, the restaurant has a great bay view. Fish *ceviche* US$4. Seafood with salad and rice US$8-10. Beer US$1.50. Open 9am until empty, usually around 6:30pm. ❷
>
> **Restaurante El Torre** (☎448 2039), just west of the police station. A great lunch spot with fantastic fresh juices ($1.50), *empanadas* (6 for US$4), and typical seafood dishes ($8-11). ❷

🎊 FESTIVALS

The **El Nazareno statue** first arrived in Portobelo in 1646 en route to Cartagena, Colombia. During a furious storm, the ship captain tossed everything overboard, including a statue of Christ. Miraculously, the cholera epidemic that had been ravaging Portobelo disappeared at the same time that fishermen recovered the lost statue. On October 21, after the outbreak had ended, the 40 men left carried the statue to town on a heavy platform. This same procession, now ritualized, occurs throughout the year, notably for **Cristo Negro** on October 21, when thousands of Panamanians sporting purple robes descend on Portobelo to celebrate what is one of Panama's most important religious traditions. Another lively festival celebrates **congo,** an upbeat Afro-Caribbean dance performed during **Carnaval** (February). The dance commemorates the liberation of the thousands of slaves brought from Africa. Women wear long dresses and men decorate themselves with odds and ends: bottles, old radios, just about anything they can find. They then take their turn dancing with the appointed *rey* and *reina* (king and queen) of Carnaval.

👁 SIGHTS

FORTRESSES AND RUINS. Gold from Spain's South American colonies was carried by mule from Panama City to Portobelo on the Camino de Cruces and down the Rio Chagres. The gold made Portobelo a prized target for pirates and the British Navy, so the Spanish built (and constantly rebuilt) a number of castles, battlements, and forts on either side of the bay. Built in the 1600s, **Santiago de la Gloria** is located on the left as you enter the town. Across the street, climb on top of what is left of the 18th-century **Castillo de Santiago** for a beautiful view of the bay. From the dock next to Santiago de la Gloria, catch a boat to **San Fernando,** an impressive three-tiered battlement built in 1753. The highest tier commands the best view of the whole bay. Be sure to arrange a pick-up time to return; allow at least 30min. for exploration. *(round-trip $5.)* The statue of **San Felipe** once guarded the entrance to the harbor, but was dismantled early in the 20th century to provide stones for the Gatún Locks (p. 259) of the Panama Canal and the breakwater at Colón. The hillside above Portobelo is dotted with other ruins including **La Trinchera** and **La Batería de Buenaventura.** The jungle seems to have reclaimed the path to these ruins, so making your way extremely difficult at best. In town, **San Gerónimo,** with cannons, vultures, and a view of the harbor, rests behind the **Aduana.** In a famous surprise attack in 1668, the Welsh pirate Henry Morgan (the namesake of your favorite spiced rum) stowed his boats on the other side of the mountain in Buenaventura, marched his men over the mountain and took Santiago de la Gloria. Morgan took priests and nuns hostage in exchange for the San Gerónimo Castle. **El Nazareno** (p. 262), the sacred statue of Christ carrying the crucifix, rests in the large, white church of San Felipe.

ADUANA. The royal customs house, built in 1630 out of the same coral reef used for the forts, was used to store gold. For a century, more than one-third of the world's gold passed through this building. The building underwent a joint Panamanian-Spanish renovation in 1998. There are two museums on the first floor: one houses historical artifacts and the other features an informative video and helpful diagrams about the history of Portobelo. *(Materials in English and Spanish. Both open daily 8am-4pm. US$1, provides entry to both.)* Entry also gets you access to the **Museum of Negro Cristo** behind the church of San Felipe, which displays scores of the purple cloaks worn by El Nazareno; the statue is dressed in a new cloak each year.

ISLA GRANDE   ☎981

Just 100m off the coast, Isla Grande is a quiet Caribbean island that comes to life on the weekend, attracting a crowd of Panamanians on vacation. The island offers lovely beaches and great surfing. This is a great place to lay back and enjoy a drink with friendly locals, *extranjeros* (foreigners), and *capitalianos* (those from Panama City).

▐ TRANSPORTATION

During daylight hours, **boats** travel frequently between Isla Grande and **Guaira,** its sister town on the mainland (5min., US$1.50). **Buses** go to Guaira from Colón (M-Sa every 2hr. 9:30am-3:30pm, fewer Sunday; US$2.50) via **Sabanitas** (connections to and from Panama City) and **Portobelo.** They return on the same route (6:30, 7:30, 9am, 12:30pm).

✈ ⁂ ORIENTATION AND PRACTICAL INFORMATION

All the hotels and restaurants spread across a short 2km strip on the southern face of the island. Opposite the **main dock** sits the small but whimsically-named market **Bodega Super Jackson.** The store has a large selection of alcohol and a small selection of groceries. Facing inland, walk 100m to the right (east) for a medical clinic, the **Sub-Centro de Salud** (open M-F 8am-3pm, Sa-Su 11am-6pm; no emergency service). There is a public **phone** two houses past the clinic.

⚲ ACCOMMODATIONS

A number of great hotels are sprawled along the coast, with prices ranging from US$20 for rooms with a fan, to US$75 for a little more. **Nido del Postre** (see **Food,** p. 264) rents out a few rooms in an old thatched building (doubles and triples US$75). The cheapest, but certainly not the safest, option is to camp on the beach. (Free. Bring a mosquito net.) Try the point just beyond the neglected **Hotel Isla Grande.** Extreme caution is recommended if you camp on the beach; it is not advisable to do it alone.

Hotel Sister Moon (☎236 8489; www.hotelsistermoon.com), at the eastern end of the island. Sister Moon rents a number of private *cabañas* overlooking some of the best surf on the island. The beach is rocky, but the hostel has a small fresh water pool with a tiled deck. Each room comes with a hammock. Doubles US$50; triples US$75. ❹

Cabañas Cholitas (☎448 2962; cholitas@cwpanama.com), about half the distance to Sister Moon. Probably the best bang for your buck, with clean and simple rooms. One of the most lively places on the island. All rooms have A/C. Singles US$20; doubles US$25. MC/V. ❸

Cabañas Candy Rose (☎448 2947), right next to Bodega Super Jackson. Rents out a number of colorful rooms. The friendly, enterprising owner is willing to negotiate when business is slow. Doubles with fan US$30, with A/C US$40. ❹

FOOD

The scrumptious *comida típica* of Isla Grande is fresh fish fried with coconut rice. A dozen or so places dotting the coastline serve some combination of chicken, meat, or fish; most of them are affiliated with one of the hotels. A cut above the rest is ▨**Nido del Postre** ❺ (☎448 2061). Though expensive by local standards, the savory gourmet Mediterranean food (dinner US$18-25) is a welcome change of pace from the local restaurants. Call ahead, so Olga can spend the afternoon preparing your meal. If dinner here is out of your budget, stop by in the morning for a cappuccino and some fresh fruit with yogurt and granola (US$5). Olga's French husband, François, speaks a little English and is full of stories from his travels around the world. The best value is **Restaurante Teletón** ❷, where they serve chicken ($3) and seafood served with *patacones* ($7). Built on stilts, **Restaurante-Bar El Congo** ❷ has good food, two parrots, and smooth Caribbean music. Their well stocked bar attracts a crowd on the weekends. (Seafood meals US$7-10. Open 11am-8pm, later on weekends.) Sip on a piña colada ($5) without even getting out of the water at **Cabañas Cholitas** ❸ (see above). They also cook fabulous fish (US$8). In the high season (Dec.-Feb.), **Restaurante La Punta** ❷, in the wooden shack on the sandy spit near Hotel Isla Grande, serves drinks and cheap lunches (US$3-4).

SIGHTS

For the best **beaches**, turn left from the dock and head west for 10min. For a pleasant **hike**, turn left up the hill before you get to Hotel Sister Moon. The trail takes you through the thick forest, so it's a good idea to bring sturdy shoes—a must in the rainy season. It's a 20min. hike to the top of the mountain, which is marked by a cell tower and an abandoned lighthouse. If you walk past the lighthouse, a **lookout** materializes over the expansive Caribbean. If you're still feeling adventurous, find the trail heading down the other side. Its a hazardous 20min. walk along the ridgeline down to a secluded **cove**. The rocky beach and strong surf make it too dangerous to swim, but you can cool off in the tidal pool. From the cove, the safest route is to retrace your way back.

NIGHTLIFE

Nightlife on Isla Grande consists of sitting, talking above loud music, and downing mixed drinks. During the week in the low season, the bars are empty and sometimes don't even bother to open, but in the winter and during the weekends they're open late. Side-by-side **Cholitas** (p. 264) and **Ensueño** are popular places on the water, as is **El Congo**. Decorated like a shrine to Bob Marley, **Pupy's**, just before El Congo, plays reggae until the wee hours and attracts a more local crowd. It's usually only open on the weekends, or whenever Pupy feels like it.

◣ OUTDOOR ACTIVITIES

Surfing is possible on the eastern part of the island, in front of Hotel Sister Moon (p. 264). **Snorkeling** is another popular activity, especially on the reef in front of Villa Ensueño, where schools of fish gather around the striking white crucifix in the water. The crucifix stands near a breach in the reef where the current is strong, so be careful. The best reefs are on the western part of the island. Walk west to the beach point and then swim 200m across the inlet toward the pink house on the hill. Beware: this can be a hard swim. Unless you're fit, it's probably not worth it. In front of the house are the best reefs on the island. **Villa Ensueño** (☎448 2964) rents snorkeling equipment ($1.50 per hr.). **Isla Grande Diving Center** (☎775 9127 or 570 0500; www.panamadive.com), a blue and yellow house west of the dock, just past a small bridge, has quality snorkeling gear (US$10 per day), snorkeling trips (US$35 for a 3hr. tour), and scuba trips (US$85-125). Andres, the English-speaking owner, also offers a four-day course (US$350; call in advance). **Kayaking** is another option; **Hotel Isla Grande** (☎448 2019) rents two-person kayaks (US$10 per hr.). **El Congo** has the cheapest kayaks on the island (US$5 per person).

DARIÉN

The Darién is quite literally the end of the road, the only gap in the entire Interamerican Highway from Northern Alaska to Tierra del Fuego in Argentina. It's a vast expanse of wild virgin jungle and one of the last few unexplored places on earth. Many who come are lured by the mystique and risk associated with crossing the dangerous Darién Gap into Colombia. *Let's Go* strongly discourages any attempt to cross the gap, which is home to, aside from two indigenous groups, a motley collection of drug smugglers, paramilitary groups, and bandits—not to mention the poisonous animals. Travelers in the gap have been abducted and murdered as recently as 1994. That said, it is also home to **Parque Nacional Darién,** one of the most biologically rich areas in the world, part of which is safe to explore.

The Interamerican Highway leads from Panama City through Metetí and ends near **Yaviza,** from where you can get a *piragua* (a wooden canoe) to **El Real** and hike into Parque Nacional Darién. Alternatively, you can turn off at Metetí, take a side road and a short boat ride to **La Palma** on the Golfo de San Miguel on the Pacific Ocean. Between the reserve and La Palma is the village of **Mogué,** which is remarkably touristy for a traditional village. On the other side of the reserve on the way to Garachiné is the **Río Sambu,** lined with indigenous villages. South along the Pacific coast from the Garachiné coast lie **Casa Vieja** and the isolated village of **Playa Muerto.** Even farther south is **Bahía Piña** and then, practically in Colombia, **Jaqué.**

Traveling in the Darién requires a lot of patience, money, or luck, and more often than not, a bit of all three. There are few roads, so almost all transport is by boat, either on rivers or on the Pacific Ocean. Buses and boats rarely run on a timetable, and even if they do, they are subject to change at any moment—ask around to make sure you won't be stranded. Issues of safety, transportation, and local knowledge make planning a trip here difficult, so it might be wise (if pricey) to take a guided tour of the region. **Ancon Expeditions** has extensive experience in the region. If the areas of Garachiné and Sambú are what interest you most, fly in directly and avoid the hassle of waiting for a boat.

YAVIZA

The Interamerican Hwy. comes to an unceremonious end at Yaviza, the beginning of the infamous 150km-long Darién gap. Yaviza remains the best starting point for intrepid, fearless souls looking to cross the gap, although we can't emphasize enough how dangerous and suicidal this would be. If civil unrest and guerrilla warfare aren't enough to dissuade you, the border police will not permit you to go any farther than **Boca de Cupe,** 30km farther along; good luck finding a guide to take you the rest of the way. If you bring camping equipment, the trek to Boca de Cupe is considered safe.

▐ TRANSPORTATION. Buses arrive in Yaviza from **Panama City** if there are enough passengers; otherwise, they let you off in Metetí and pile you into an overcrowded minibus for the last hour of the journey. **Minivans** leave Yaviza (1hr., every 30min.-1hr., US$5). Between Yaviza and **El Real,** *piraguas* (1hr., US$5) pass throughout the day, but your best bet is in the morning. If you're lucky, you might get a faster *panga* (fiber glass boat; 20min.). Special trips cost US$30, but are usually unnecessary unless you arrive in the late afternoon. Boats and buses meet at the dock.

⚑ PRACTICAL INFORMATION. Continue straight and turn left at the **post office** (open M-F 8am-noon and 1-2:45pm, Sa 8am-noon), which has **internet,** to get to the **police station,** where you should check in upon arrival. Past the police office is the **ANAM office,** where you will need to stop if you want to go to the **Pirre Station** of **Parque Nacional Darién** (see p. 269). (☎299 4495; open M-F 8am-4pm; call during the week if you plan to come during the weekend). If you instead turn right at the post office, cross a narrow suspension bridge and turn left to find the **hospital.** (Open 24hr.; pharmacy open 8am-4pm.) Behind the basketball court in the center of town is the **Visitor Center,** which has lots of information about surrounding communities and events. They can arrange a guide for nearby hikes (US$5) and volunteer opportunities in villages. (☎299-4469; www.cegel.com. Open daily 8am-4pm.)

⌂ ☐ ACCOMMODATIONS AND FOOD. If you have to spend the night, the new **Hotel Yadarien ❷,** a yellow building just past the dock, offers spare, clean rooms with private baths. (☎299 4334. Doubles US$15; with A/C US$20; triples US$20/25.) A decent enough option is **Pensión Americas ❷,** across from the basketball court. They have four rooms with a shared bath. Sheets are provided, but it's probably a good idea to bring your own. (☎299 4439. Rooms US$12, with A/C US$15.

There are **restaurants** clustered around the dock, all serving basically the same *típico* for US$2 during the day. They open for breakfast around 6am and stay open for dinner, closing around 7pm.

EL REAL

El Real (pop. 1500) is the gateway to Parque Nacional Darién and the Pirre station. The main part of town the town is a built on a small grid of paved paths around a decaying plaza with a church. Most of the services are on a paved path leading out from the river.

☐⚑ TRANSPORTATION AND PRACTICAL INFORMATION. Coming from the river, you will enter through one of two ports: **El Mercado** is for larger boats and is used all day, while **Gallital** is on a small stream and can only accommodate dugout canoes at high tide. Boats leave town throughout the day, but not on any regular schedule; ask around near the docks for departure times. In the morning you won't have to wait more than an hour, but you'll have a harder time in the afternoon.

Along the path leading outside the town (turn right when you get off the boat), you will find a **Centro de Salud** with a small **pharmacy.** (☎299 6589. Open 24hr. Pharmacy open 7am-3pm.) Farther along you will find a **post office** and the **police station,** where you should check in before and after you go to Pirre.

⌂ ☐ ACCOMMDATIONS AND FOOD. If you spend the night, **Hotel El Nazareno ❶,** an attractive blue and white building one block from the central plaza, is your only option. Rooms have fans and private baths, but the town has serious water problems, so don't expect water after noon; they have a bucket full of water for rinsing off. (☎299 5033. Singles US$7; doubles US$10; triples US$15; quads US$20.)

There is a **restaurant** around the corner serving the dish of the day—usually fried chicken, rice and beans (US$2).

LA PALMA

La Palma (pop. 6000) is the province's capital and largest town, but don't get the wrong idea—it's little more than a few houses strewn over a hillside or on stilts above the water. Though it offers scenic views, it's not a destination in and of itself, and most travelers stay a single night on their way through. From La Palma, you can access the villages along **Río Tuira**, the most prominent of which is the traditional Emberá village of **Mogué**. Its tourist infrastructure is more extensive than that of other villages in the region, but you'll probably still be the only guest.

TRANSPORTATION. There is an airstrip 20min. outside of town in **Miraflores**, which is served by **Air Panama** on Tuesday and Saturday if there is demand. The booking agent, Serafina Sugasti (☎6529 6446) has an office at the airstrip, but she is usually in town. She can also give you a lift to the airport for US$1. La Palma can be reached by **bus** to **Metetí** (6hr.), by **minibus** to **La Quimba** (25min., every 20-30min. 5am-5pm, US$1.50), and by **boat** (20min., every hr. 5am-5pm, US$3). Onward transportation to Sambú or Garachiné is difficult to find; ask around about hiring a boat (US$150-250). Boats head to **Garachiné** (M, W, F 10am). If you want to leave on a day without scheduled departures, the best thing to do is wake up early (5:30-6am) and head for the dock to see where boats are leaving for. The only way to get reliable information is to ask on the day of; if you want to get to Garachiné or other towns directly, look into direct flights, which are often cheaper. Private boats to **Mogué** cost US$100.

IT'S ALWAYS BETTER WHEN WE'RE TOGETHER. Hiring a private boat by yourself can be terribly expensive. Chat up your hostel-mates and other travelers you encounter and see if they're heading to the same place; splitting the trip can save you a lot of money.

PRACTICAL INFORMATION. You will arrive on a concrete ramp, which serves as the dock. Walking right from the dock, you'll encounter the **ANAM office** (☎299 6373; open 8am-4pm), though the tourist office, **ATP**, inside the Ministerio de Comercio e Industrias (☎299 6337; open M-F 8am-4:30pm) farther down the road is much more helpful. They also have free **internet**. Across the street, the **Banco Nacional** has an **ATM**. (Open M-F 8am-3pm, Sa 9am-noon.) Earlier on the same path is the **police station**. To get to the **hospital** (☎299 6219) and **pharmacy**, hop on the minibus (US$0.25) that passes through town in the direction right from the dock, and they will drop you off.

ACCOMMODATIONS. To the left, you'll find **Hotel Guacamayra ❷**, unmarked above the mini-market Ramaldy. It offers wood-paneled and attractive rooms on the second floor with two open-air lounges, one with a hammock overlooking the water and one with satellite TV looking down on the street. Rooms and baths are clean and have free drinking water. (☎299 6224. Singles US$10, with A/C and private bath US$20; each additional person US$5.)

SAMBÚ

The muddy waters of the Río Sambú open up to the Pacific between Garachiné and Punta Patiño. The river is lined with traditional Emberá villages that form the backbone of the **Comarca Emberá Sambú**, the first of which is the village of **Puerto Indio** and the neighboring village of Sambú. From these two joined villages (connected by a narrow suspension bridge), adventurous souls trek up the jungle's river.

TRANSPORTATION. By far the easiest way to get to Sambú is by plane. **Air Panama** flies in (T, Th, Sa; US$60). To make a reservation on a flight, show up the night before or morning of at 8am. You can also take a **boat** from **La Palma**, though finding a boat directly to Sambú is difficult. You're more likely to find a boat to **Garachiné** (1hr., US$10), from where some travelers hitch a ride (1hr., US$3) on the road that connects them; *Let's Go* never recommends hitchhiking. You can also book a private boat for around US$200 between Sambú and La Palma.

⚐ PRACTICAL INFORMATION. Sambú, connected to Puerto Indio by a narrow suspension bridge, has a **police station** and **medical clinic** (open 24hr.), both visible from the runway that cuts through the middle of town. There's also a **public phone** at the end of the runway, but you'll need to bring a phone card.

⚑ ACCOMMODATIONS. Villa Fiesta ❸, at the end of the runway, has pleasant rooms and an affable English-speaking owner. Rooms have two queen size beds and clean private bathrooms, sheets, and towels. (US$20, with A/C US$25.)

◪ SIGHTS. For a trip up the Río Sambú, arrange for a guide and a *piragua* in Sambú. The journey is hot and tiring and modern amenities, such as mattresses, electricity, and running water, are virtually non-existent. Make sure to bring water. Guides can arrange for a place to spend the night, but you will need a hammock or a sleeping pad, and a mosquito net is recommended. The farthest village up the river is **Pavarandó.** A trip there and back will cost US$100-150, including the guide, boat, and gasoline. If you spend the night, expect to pay US$10-15 for food and a place to sleep for you and your guide.

PARQUE NACIONAL DARIÉN

The Rancho Frío ranger station is a 3hr. walk from El Real, depending on conditions on the trail. Another option is to hire a piragua (US$30-50) to take you to the village of Piji Basal, where you can find the trail for the last hour. Guides are a must—ask around El Real, or at the ANAM office in Yaviza. There is a dormitory at the station (US$15 per person) and a campsite (US$10). The park is accessible at Rancho Frío, Sambú, and Garachiné. These entry points are generally safe, though check on the current status at one of the many police stations in the region. There is a little solar electricity and a propane stove, as well as an outhouse with running water, but you need to bring your own food, flashlight and sleep sheet. The water is safe to drink, but bring a filter or purification tablets to be safe. Entrance fee US$5. Wear hiking boots at all times—there are snakes.

With 576,000 hectares of old-growth tropical forest, Parque Nacional Darién is so dense that the midday sun looks like dusk. The Park's neotropical biodiversity is bested only by the Amazon, and more migrating birds cross the isthmus through its boundaries than any other place in the world. Among the 450 species of birds are the toucan, parrot, and Harpy Eagle, the national bird of Panama. The Park is most easily accessible at **Rancho Frío,** though it's still a hike just to enter. At Rancho Frío, there are enough trails to keep a hike-happy visitor busy for days. One of the highlights is a summit of the **Cerro Ridge,** which is best done over two days, so bring a tent. Whether you have a day or a week, be sure to go to the nearby ⛲**waterfall,** just 20min. from the station. Crisp, pure water flows off the rocks into a serene pool, while the thick canopy opens above just enough to let in a few direct rays of light—it's a true jungle oasis, especially after the sweaty walk in, and you can slide down the waterfall. A few friendly rangers run the station. They each spend a month there at a time with little to do, so they will be happy to see you.

SAN BLAS

SAN BLAS ISLANDS ☎981

With traditional, indigenous tribes, pristine beaches, and an abundance of coco-nuts, fish, and hammocks, the San Blas Archipelago (pop. 32,000) may be the closest anyone can come to true paradise. Formally known as the *Comarca Kuna Yala* ("Land of the Kuna"), the Caribbean archipelago stretches between Colón and Colombia, and is one of two autonomous political regions in Panama. The Islands are owned and operated entirely by the region's indigenous inhabit-ants, the Kuna. Although they use the mainland for corn, mangos, *Yucca*, and other agricultural products, almost all the Kuna are concentrated on the islands. The near-absence of mosquitoes and wild animals makes for a healthy and safe environment. Although you'll have to shell out a little extra cash to stay here, it's well worth it. Come get a tan and learn more about the culture of one of Central America's most independent indigenous peoples while you're at it.

HISTORY

By the 1500s, the Kuna had migrated into Daríen from Colombia. By the 19th century, war with the Spanish and the rival Emberá tribe had forced the Kuna onto the San Blas Islands. Here, the Spanish left them in comparative peace. In the early 20th century, however, a newly independent Panama launched attempts to "civilize" the Kuna. Fed up with mistreatment, on February 25th, 1925, the Kuna revolted against the Panamanian police force in the **Nele Kantule Revolution** (named in honor of their leader) and, with the help of a US battleship offshore, successfully gained autonomy. In 1938, Kuna land was further secured by the organization of the *comarca*, or district; in 1952 San Blas was officially recog-nized by the Panamanian government as a self-governing entity.

The Kuna are not subject to Panamanian taxation, they own the entire region, and they send two representatives to the National Assembly. Even so, the older generation is fighting once again (this time without violence) to preserve tra-ditions in the face of growing Westernization. In many Kuna town congress halls, banners proclaim, "People who lose their tradition lose their souls." Still, modernization continues to infiltrate the islands. While the Kuna once survived by trading coconuts with Colombian ships, today the *balboa* (US dollar) reigns supreme, with tourists as the new trading partners. As a result, the number of amenities and establishments on the Archipelago is constantly on the rise. Although it appears that each generation is becoming more Westernized, most of the Kuna lead simple, traditional lives.

CULTURE AND CUSTOMS

The *comarca* is governed by three *Cacinques*, who are the equivalent of provincial governors and act as elected intermediaries between the Kuna and the Panamanian government. Every village has its own smaller **Congress**, the *"Casa de Congreso,"* which is headed by the **Sáhila**. The community celebrates religious ceremonies, resolves disputes, and makes important decisions in the *Casa de Congreso*.

The Kuna have their own language, but many speak at least some Spanish. Men typically wear Western clothes, while women wear distinctive clothing styles with golden earrings, nose piercings, bright colored bracelets, and skirts with blouses featuring the famous *mola*. The *mola* is a piece of colorful cloth stitched by hand. Although traditional *molas* have only abstract designs, modern ones are often decorated with animals and scenes from daily life. One of the most sophisticated and sought-after handicrafts in Latin America, the *mola* is sold to tourists everywhere in Kuna Yala (prices depend on quality, size, and age; US$5-10 per small panel).

With few exceptions, the Kuna live on the beach, only using the inland as a sort of grocery store for fresh produce and wood. Despite the presence of Christian missionaries, most of the Kuna maintain traditional piety. Kuna theology revolves around a divine human, **Iboorgum,** sent to teach them how to live based on the principle of sharing within a community. More recent events, such as battles fought against the Emberá, the Spanish, and the Panamanian army, have become part of semi-mythic Kuna cosmology. Kuna Yala culture includes customary puberty rituals, marriage ceremonies, funeral rites, and traditional medicine. If you hang around long enough, you could run into a **chica fuerte** feast. *Chica fuerte* is an alcoholic drink made from sugarcane juice and maize and flavored with *cacao;* like the name suggests, it's not recommended for the faint of heart. The biggest parties of the year are in February: the 25th of the month is the anniversary of the 1925 Kuna revolution.

Travelers, particularly if visiting the more isolated islands, should learn about the Kuna before coming. Those arriving on an island that has no hotel need to see the **sáhila** to ask permission to stay (an entrance fee of US$1-3 is typically charged, irrespective of duration). Meeting the *sáhila* also provides an opportunity to ask about meals or accommodation options on the island. If you want to spent the night on an uninhabited island (an amazing experience), you should arrange a trip through one of the hotel owners, who may be able to talk with the owner of the island and work out a deal.**And don't forget to arrange a pick up.**

VISITING SAN BLAS

Due to its remoteness and the high price of gasoline and commodities, San Blas is not the easiest place in which to stay within a budget. Thanks to a newly improved road and growing budget accommodation options, it is becoming relatively more accessible to the student traveler. (Round-trip jeep US$50, boat transfer US$15; US$20 per night.) **Lodging** options are extremely limited. A stay on a densely populated island with vibrant Kuna life is just a short boat ride away from the mainland. Staying on an uninhabited, fairly remote island filled with nothing but coconuts, hammocks, and a few Kuna huts for you to rent, is more expensive to access. Most accommodations include three meals and many include tours of nearby islands. At higher prices, you are mostly paying for a little more comfort: Western-style toilets, a shower, and better, larger quantities of food. Although almost everywhere has a solar panel for electricity, only the higher-end places have lights inside the rooms.

There isn't much value in doing a highlights tour of the islands; the attractions on each are fairly similar, and picking one or two nearby will give you a good sense of what Kuna Yala is all about. **Guided tours** of the archipelago are best booked in Panama City (p. 238), but are only worth the expense if you're looking for a specific bonus, such as sailing or fishing. All visitors should keep in mind that most Kuna islands require visitors to pay a US$1-3 fee; this may be paid at governmental offices or with the local *Sáhila*. Even uninhabited islands are privately owned, and often require a fee. There's also a rule in most towns prohibiting walking around with only bathing suits on. In addition, photographers will normally be charged US$1, sometimes per shot.

▐ GETTING THERE AND AROUND

FLIGHTS
Flights to the San Blas Islands are easy, short, and fairly cheap, though prices depend on the price of fuel. Beware, destinations vary almost daily. At the time of publication, **Aeroperlas** and **Air Panama** were the only two airlines flying to San Blas. Flights go to **Cartí** or **Porvenir** (usually alternating depending on the conditions of the runway), **Corazón de Jesus** and **Playon Chico**, and **Puerto Obaldía** near the Colombian border. For more information, see **Panama City: Transportation,** p. 239. Since planes make multiple stops in the islands, they are occasionally available for island hopping, depending on demand. If you're planning to island-hop by plane, check with the airline before you arrive. Note that airports are often not on the destination itself; if you know where you are staying, arranging connection transportation with your hotel is the easiest and cheapest way to get where you are going. Alternatively, every arriving plane is met with enthusiasm by **boats** and **guides** from as far as an hour away. It is usually not that difficult to get where you are going—just be very clear on the name of the island and the specific accommodation. Agree on the price before you get on the boat. Boat rides largely depend on distance, from US$1 for an island that you could swim to versus US$10-15 for an hour-long trip. For much longer trips expect to shell out some serious cash. Since there is little chance of sharing a boat, you will be expected to pay for the gas need to travel to your destination and back, whether or not you return (up to US$75).

JEEPS
Thanks to new improvements, the once impassible Llano-Cartí Road can now be navigated by jeep. Jeeps from Panama city cost US$25 in each direction (3hr.); they'll pick you up at your hotel. The easiest way to book this is through your hotel or hostel; La Jungla, Mamallena, and Luna's (see **Accommodations,** p. 243) are all known to book jeeps.

BOATS
There are two options for long-distance boat travel: one is expensive and usually safe and the other is cheap and less safe. Wealthy travelers take yachts from Panama, usually embarking near Colón at Puerto Lindo, passing through the San Blas islands and ending in Cartagena, Colombia. Similar trips can be arranged through travel agents or hostels. The best hostels have extensive information about boats. Prices usually run around US$350-450 for a five-day, all inclusive tour.

▐ THE ISLANDS

It seems as though there is a picturesque island for every day of the year in the San Blas Archipelago. Surrounded by reefs ideal for scuba-diving and snorkeling, and almost entirely isolated, these sandy gems make for perfect getaways. Keep in mind, however, that the islands farther afield are notorious stopping points for drug runners from Colombia. Arrange your visit with a hotel owner who knows which islands are safe—Arnulfo Robinson of **Cabañas Robinson** (p. 275) is one of many who would be happy to help.

The most densely populated islands tend to be the closest to larger pieces of land (the population is dependent on it for most of its food), and those farther afield are usually uninhabited—though few are more than a few kilometers from the mainland. Almost every island has two names: one Kuna and one Spanish; some even have an English name. For example, **Achutupu** is the same as **Isla Perro** which is sometimes called **Dog Island**. **Leading to even more confusion, some of the islands have the same name—make sure you and your boat captain are talking about the same place.** The western part of the archipelago has the greatest density of islands and the most accommodations. This area is the most easily accessible thanks to the road connection and the two airports on Cartí and Porvenir.

WESTERN ISLANDS. El Porvenir, the farthest west access point, is right next to the well-touristed **Wichub Wala** and **Nalunega,** both densely populated and rather traditional. Twenty minutes south, Cartí, is a group of four similarly dense and slightly less traditional islands. Among them, **Cartí-Sugtupu** offers the most services, including a clinic. East of Cartí are **Río Sidra** and **Nusadup,** also densely inhabited and just off the coast. Directly north lie the budget-friendly islands of **Naranja Chico** (Narasgandup) and **Dupasenika.** Also north is the more expensive **Kuanidup.** Farther north lies **Isla Pelicano,** with just four huts for rent. Still farther north, and a bit west, lies another group of islands. These are mostly uninhabited, though there are *cabañas* for rent on **Isla Diablo** and **Achutupu** (also known as Isla Perro). Note there is another Achutupu halfway to Colombia; don't get the two confused. Between Isla Diablo and Achutupu there is an easily accessible shipwreck perfect for snorkeling. To the west **Coco Blanco** has a few simple accommodation options. All of these islands, plus many more uninhabited ones, make up the western *comarca*, and are reasonably accessible from one another (at most 1½hr.).

OTHER ISLANDS. Farther northeast, the **Cayos Holandéses** (Holland Cayes) is a large group of completely uninhabited, picturesque islands popular with Yachties. A trip here is expensive (round-trip US$45-70). Farther east (up to 2½hr. by boat) are the fairly Westernized **Corazón de Jesús** and **Narganá.** The more traditional **Isla Tigre** and **Tikantiki** even farther east. From there, in order of increasing distance, are **Playón Chico, Yandup, Isla Tupile, Achutupo,** and the **Port of Obaldía.**

EL PORVENIR

Just barely large enough to fit an airstrip, Porvenir serves as a popular jumping-off point to the western archipelago. This island is also a required stop for any boat passing on its way to or from Colombia; as a result, it tends to be flanked by yachts. The island itself has little to offer—this is not the place to see a Kuna village and the beaches are better elsewhere—but it is practically within a stone's throw of Wichub Wala and Nalunega, which each offer comfortable accommodations among densely populated bamboo and thatch huts.

⌐ TRANSPORTATION. Although it is not official policy, it seems that the airports at Cartí and Porvernir alternate as the local airport. At the time of publication, the Porvenir airport was closed, but slated to open shortly (when the Cartí airport was closing). Flights coming in from Panama City arrive around 6:45am or later depending on what stops they make first. Make reservations a day in advance to fly to other islands; internal flights are subject to demand. Go to the government building a day before your flight and put your name on the list of people leaving, especially if you haven't bought a ticket. Hotels often take care of this for guests. When arriving by plane, sign in with immigration or the police official who meets each flight. (Entry fee US$6.) **Boats** to **Wichub Wala** cost US$1-2, though hotels will often pick you up for free.

▦ ▨ ORIENTATION AND PRACTICAL INFORMATION. Directly in front of the docks, a government building houses the **police station** (☎299 9124), **immigration**

office (theoretically open 9am-4pm, though you may have to go look for the officer), **marine office,** and **public phones** (☎299 9000). To get any of the offices by phone, call the public phone and someone will try to find who you are looking for. The **airport** serves as a **post office;** give letters to the pilot heading out on the morning flight to Panama City (he'll buy stamps, if necessary).

▐▜ ▐▛ **ACCOMMODATIONS AND FOOD.** The only hotel on the island is **Hotel Porvenir ❶**, practically on the tiny airstrip. This hotel offers contiguous concrete rooms with private baths. (Local cell ☎6692 3542, in Panama City 221 1397. Daytrips and meals included. US$45 per person). Hotel Porvenir also operates a small snack bar with surprisingly cheap bottles of liquor. A brand new restaurant, **Nan Magriya ❶**, is owned by Congreso General Kuna, the unified government of the different Kuna Villages. Its a great place to grab a coffee (US$0.35) or a mid-afternoon snack (fish and rice US$3) before your early morning flight. (Open from 7am until last customer.)

WICHUB WALA

This small, densely populated island is not a beach destination. If it's a Kuna village you seek, this charming assembly of traditional homes will suit you fine. Join local kids playing basketball with hoops attached to palm trees, or watch women put in long hours on their *molas*. The island has a **health center** (open M-F 7:30am-3:30am, Sa-Su 8am-noon), but in a bigger emergency you will need to go to Cartí. There are a number of small markets, including a community-run **store** just past the public docks. (Open daily 6am-9pm.) There are two good accommodations for those visiting Wichub Wala; only one is actually on the Island. **Hotel Ukuptupu ❺** is a 5min. canoe ride farther west, on a tiny island, halfway to Nalunega. The island is actually manmade. A former Smithsonian research island, this island is now occupied by the family of Juan García, an amiable man who speaks English. The hotel here has clean, breezy rooms, and common bathrooms constructed on stilts over water. García and his wife go out of their way to make you feel welcome, especially when it comes to food; you can even handpick the lobster you want for dinner. Rates include three meals, tours of other islands, and all-night electricity. (Panama City ☎290 6650, cell 6514 2788; www.ukuptupu.com. US$55 per person.) Among the cluster of thatch houses on the main island of Wichub Wala, **Kuna Niskua Lodge ❹** has a beautiful two-story bamboo-thatch building. All rooms have private baths, and there is electricity all night. Rooms include three meager meals and tours. (☎6029 6255 or 6662 2239. Snorkeling equipment US$6 per day. US$50 per person.)

NALUNEGA

A short trip west from Wichub Wala, Nalunega is slightly more spread out, but equally populated. It is home to the well-known **Hotel San Blas ❹**, the oldest hotel on the Archipelago, which offers Kuna-style cabins with sand floors as well as a newer concrete building. Luis Burgos, the aged owner, speaks English and Spanish. The place has ample hammocks and benches. If you are not staying at the hotel, you can still go on the daily tours for US$25. The hotel rents snorkeling masks (US$3) and flippers (US$6). (☎344 1274, cell 6661 4609. Rooms US$10. Tour and 3 meals an additional US$40.) There is a small one-room **museum** marked by a door made of washed up cans and bottles. Inside is a collection of impressive wood carvings. Teodoro Dorez is the creator of most of the work. Dorez is deeply disturbed by the amount of trash found in the water; for this reason, he dedicates himself to collecting trash in his museum. He hopes to some day construct a new building from the trash he gathers.

CARTÍ-SUGTUPU

Cartí is a group of four densely populated islands just off the mainland. **Cartí-Sugtupu, Cartí-Tupile,** and **Cartí-Yantupu** are the three largest ones. Of these, Cartí-Sugtupu (pop. 2000) is the largest and the most thickly settled, and offers the most services.

◰ TRANSPORTATION. Daily flights from Panama City arrive in Cartí airport when it is not closed, which appears to be about half the time. The airport is on the mainland, a 5min. boat ride from the island. The airplanes land on the northern terminus of the El Llano-Cartí road, the only overland road to the entire Archipelago. Although the road has recently been upgraded, don't expect actual pavement; the trip still requires good four-wheel-drive vehicle and possibly a snorkel. Jeeps making the journey daily from Panama City can be booked by most of the hostels (one-way US$25).

◰◰ ORIENTATION AND PRACTICAL INFORMATION. The busy island is crossed by **two east-west footpaths.** The **public docks** are on the north side, near the middle of the island; walk straight on a nearby path to run in to the two main footpaths. The town's **health center** is one of the biggest in the whole archipelago, though the competition isn't that steep; in an off-hours emergency, you may have to find the medics in town. (☎6041 3611. Open M-F 7:30am-12pm and 1pm-3:30pm, Sa-Su 8am-noon.) There are **public phones** next to the dock (☎299 9002).

◰◰ ACCOMMODATIONS AND FOOD. If you head right on the first footpath, you will find the **Cartí Homestay Backpacker Inn,** one of the cheapest places in the area. The second floor has a number of beds, separated by partition walls; it's essentially one big dorm with plenty of hammocks. Eulogio Pérez, the English-speaking owner, runs **San Blas Adventures,** where you can book reasonably-priced tours thoughout the islands, though tours and food are included in the price of a room at the inn. (Panama City ☎257 7189, cell 6517 9815. US$30 per person.) Cartí-Sugtupu boasts a friendly community-run **dormitorio** and **cafeteria,** though at the time of publication it was undergoing renovations. Rooms do not include food. The bathroom is built in the Kuna style: a toilet seat over a hole in the floor. (☎6065 0098. Open 7am-10pm. Meals US$3.50. Rooms US$8.) There are no fewer than four *tiendas* in town, all of which sell basic items such as soap, toilet paper, and beer.

◰ SIGHTS. Also in town is the one-room **Kuna Museum,** 5min. east of the public dock on the northern road. The room is filled with Kuna artifacts, in an attempt to preserve and educate about Kuna life. Owner, curator, and guide José Davies leads visitors through the Kuna artifacts and his own illustrations of Kuna myths and rituals. Tours are in Spanish, and, if necessary, broken English. If he is not there or your Spanish is limited, his son (who speaks perfect English) can direct you. (☎6732 1899 or 6668 6821. Open daily 7am-10pm.)

NARASGANDUP PIPI (NARANJO CHICO)

Naranjo Chico is a beautiful island with a plethora of pristine beaches and palm trees, sparsely populated by four large Kuna families. The families rent different enclaves of *cabañas,* though it's difficult to find many differences between them. On the southern part of the island lie two of the best value spots in the archipelago, **Ina Cabins ❸** (☎6034 9655 or 6970 5988) and **◰Cabañas Robinson ❸** (☎6721 9885 or 6026 2609). These two accommodations are operated by relatives and are virtually indistinguishable. Together, they are the unofficial backpacker enclave of the San Blas, always home to an eclectic group of travelers. Both offer traditional bamboo-thatch huts with sand floors and foam mattresses. Electricity is available for a communal area and charging devices (US$1). Rooms do not lock, and they share a "Kuna toilet" on the backside of the island (far from the beach). Although there are no showers, the accommodations offer a bucket of water for rinsing off. The US$20 rooms include three modest meals and tours to nearby islands. **Arnulfo Robinson** of Cabañas Robinson is a master of world history; he can go on and on about anything from the conflict in the Middle East to the Gettysburg Address, but you'll need to speak Spanish to soak up his wealth of information. On the other side of the narrow island is **Cabañas Narasgandup ❺**, which offers slightly more removed cabins with locking doors and proper bathrooms. The main draw here is the food. Ausberto, the hospitable owner can get whatever seafood you want. (Panama City ☎256 6239, cell 6501 6033. All-inclusive low season US$45, high season US$55.)

DUPASENIKA

This tiny, attractive island is home to two sets of tightly packed *cabañas*. With cheap prices and basic services, Dupasenika is also quite popular with backpackers. To the confusion of many a traveler, it used to be called Isla Robinson. Indeed, many still call it by its old name. The main difference between Dupasenika and Robinson is that Dupasenika only has employees living on it. On one side of the island are **Senidup Cabañas ❸** (☎6801 1251; www.kunayala. info), which has bathrooms and showers for its Kuna-style huts. Tony, the English-speaking administrator, offers a four-day, three-night trip including food, tours, a Jeep from Panama City, and boat transfers for US$200. If you prefer to organize everything on your own, its US$20 with food and US$10 for a one-way airport transfer. (Tours not included.) Next door, **Cabañas Dupasenika ❸** has the cheapest prices in the area, and includes a bathroom with running water, showers, and a volleyball court. Room prices include food, but no tours. Airport transfers cost US$10 each way. Cabins have three beds; if you want a private cabin for less than three people you may have to pay more. (☎299 9058. US$17.50 per person; camping US$8.50.)

ISLA PERRO (DOG ISLAND) AND ISLA DIABLO

If all you want is beaches, palm trees, and a roof to lay under during the rain, search no farther than these tiny islands. Isla Perro is occupied by a single family (☎6042 0778 or 6684 9762) that has one large **cabin** where they will set up a hammock for US$11 without food, or US$20 with food. Just about 20m off the shore is a shipwreck that partially sticks out of the water and offers some cool snorkeling. Within easy swimming distance is Isla Diablo, where you can stay for US$35 with **Kuna Tours** (☎6740 7538 or 6500 0016), which operates out of Cartí. Make sure to reserve through them, as there are no permanent beds on the island. (US$35 with food, tours, and boat transfer.) Just a few minutes north by boat is a tiny island with one tree surrounded by flawless beaches.

◾ISLA PELICANO

Short of renting an island for a night and bringing your own hammock, this is the most secluded you can get. The gorgeous island has only four **cabañas,** situated along the water with hammocks hung between idyllic palm trees. (☎6088 2436, ask for Ricardo Bonilla.) There is a semi-modern bathroom (that is, it isn't over the water, but still flushes into the ocean through a pipe) and an extremely primitive shower. The US$20 includes tours and food. A transfer to Cartí costs US$15 round-trip.

NUSATUPO AND RÍO SIDRA

Nusatupo is small island packed with traditional bamboo-thatch huts. The one stand-out, three-story concrete building houses the **Hotel Kuna Yala.** This structure, with a rooftop terrace, has striking views of the village below and islands nearby. The community here is more Westernized than that at Wichub Wala. The people are friendly to tourists, making this island a rather accessible location to experience Kuna culture. The hotel offers 24hr. electricity in all the rooms and shared flushing bathrooms with running water. (☎315 7520. Food and tours included. US$50 per person.) Nearby is the larger and more populated **Río Sidra.** Although there are not any rooms for rent, the island has one of the biggest **medical clinics** in the area (open daily 7am-noon and 1pm-3pm; 24hr. for emergencies) on the opposite side of the island from the main port. There is also a small **pharmacy.** Near the basketball court, at the entrance of the northern port, **Refresquería Betty ❶** serves cakes and other savory snacks. (Special meal of the day US$3.50. Coke US$1. Slice of cake US$0.25. Open daily 6am-8pm.) On the same plaza, next to the turquoise building, there's a **public phone** (☎299 9058), which seldom works.

COCLÉ AND VERAGUAS

EL VALLE DE ANTÓN

It's no wonder that Panamanians flock here on the weekends. The main attraction of El Valle (pop. 6200), which is surrounded by mountains and fields of flowers, is the climate. A tranquil town situated 600m up on the crater floor of an ancient volcano, El Valle has temperate weather year-round, a godsend in the sweltering summer. Nearby attractions include hot springs, hikes, and waterfalls.

▐ TRANSPORTATION

Buses: Buses in El Valle fill up quickly, so it's best to pick them up at the market. You can usually get them to stop anywhere along the main road leading east of town. They head to **Panama City** (2½hr., every 45min. 3:30am-4pm, US$3.50). For later departures, take the bus to **San Carlos** (40min., every 20-25min. 4am-6pm, US$1.50); from there you can go just about anywhere. Buses to **La Mesa** (10min., every 25-30min., US$0.75) head west of town passing by **El Macho** (US$0.25).

Public Transportation: There is 1 local bus, labeled **"La Compañia El Halto,"** which loops through the town's few streets (US$0.25)

Taxis: Around town. Fares around US$2.

⬛ ▐ ORIENTATION AND PRACTICAL INFORMATION

El Valle is about 40min. up a twisty road off the Interamerican Highway from the cut-off at Las Uvas. The **main road** enters town from the east and runs west; almost everything is either along this road or a short walk off it. The open **mercado** is in the middle of town. Generally, sights are outside of town to the west; lodgings are to the east of town.

Tourist Office: (☎983 6474), in a small pavilion in front of the market. Free maps and basic info about transportation and nearby activities. Some English spoken. Open Tu and Th-Su 7:30am-3:30pm. **ANAM** (☎983 6411). Take a left about 1½km before town at the sign. Info about nearby hikes in Monumento Cerro Gaital and the surrounding areas. Open daily 8am-4pm.

Tours: Proyecto de Eco-Turismo (☎983 6472), about 500m before town. Turn left following signs for the Orchid Center. Take any bus (US$0.25) heading east from town back toward the highway. Based out of the Orchid center, they offer guide services for nearby attractions. English guides available. Prices include transportation, and range from US$10 for a guided trip to El Macho to US$35 for longer hikes.

Library: After the market and before the church. Terminals and Wi-Fi US$1 per hr. Open M-F 8:30am-4:30pm, Sa 8:30am-3pm, Su 9:30am-12:30pm.

Laundromat: Lavamático La Libertad, about 500m before town on the main road. Wash US$0.75. Dry US$1. Tips appreciated. Open M-Sa 8am-4pm.

Public Toilets: In the market. US$0.25.

Police: (☎983 6216), on the way in to town. Turn right as if going to El Níspero.

Pharmacy: Mi Farmacia, 500m before town, next to Lavamático La Libertad. Open M-Sa 8am-4pm. MC/V.

Medical Clinic: Centro de Salud (☎983 6112), behind the church. Open M-F 7am-3pm. **24hr. emergency care.**

Internet Access: FSR technology Systems (☎908 7003), before town next to the Lavamático and pharmacy. Wi-Fi US$1 per hr. Open M-Sa 8am-6pm, Su 11am-3pm.

Post Office: Behind the market. Open M-F 8am-4pm. **Postal Code:** 1001.

ACCOMMODATIONS

El Valle is a weekend retreat for wealthy Panamanians, but there are plenty of options for budget travelers, too. Since the town is temperate year-round, hot water is standard, but A/C isn't. Some hotels jack up their prices on the weekends.

La Casa de Juan (☎6453 9775), about 1.5 km before town; take a left at the sign. Señor Juan rents out a few rooms in his funky house. Under the large roof is an outdoor kitchen and and eating area where backpackers sit around and sip beer. Rooms are clean and have private baths with hot water. Old mountain bike rentals US$5. 6-person dorms US$10; private rooms US$20. Cash only. ❷

Cabañas Potosi (☎983 6181). Follow the road west of town. After it curves right, turn left at the store and continue straight for 10min. Some of the most affordable cabins in the valley, situated in a beautiful park-like atmosphere. The charcoal grill is perfect for an afternoon picnic. Rooms are simple, sleep up to 3, and have hot water, mini-fridges, and fans. Rooms US$43. Cash only. ❹

Santa Librada (☎6591 9135), in Restaurante Santa Librada. The cheapest private rooms in town are small and have a bit of a bug problem, but they come with private bathrooms and towels. Singles US$12; doubles US$20; triples US$30. Cash only. ❷

Don Pepe (☎983 6425), in the 3-story yellow and green building just before town. A good deal for a big group. Rooms are clean and have hot water baths and TVs. Laundry US$6. Internet US$2 per hr. Bikes US$2 per hr. Don Pepe can also arrange nearby tours (US$10 per hr.) and horseback riding (US$8 per hr.). Singles US$35; doubles US$40; 6-person room US$70. MC/V. ❹

FOOD

Food in El Valle is more expensive than in Panama City, but it's still possible to get cheap *típico* without breaking the bank. If you have access to a kitchen, your best option is to buy some produce from the market. For groceries, visit **Supercentro Yin,** across the street from the market. (Open daily 7am-1pm and 2-7pm.)

Pinocchio's (☎983 6715), just past town. Mario, the grandson of Italian immigrants, carries on the tradition in delicious pizzas (US$5-8) and pasta (US$5-6). The weekend crowd raves about the food. Open W-Su noon-9pm. Cash only. ❷

Hotel Anton Valley (☎983 6097), across the street from the church. This cute, American-owned B&B opens its doors to the public for breakfast. The dining room (the "Orchid Room") has a fountain and cozy seating. Coffee US$0.50. French Toast US$3.50. Wi-Fi. Open daily 7am-9:30am. MC/V. ❷

Restaurante Santa Librada (☎6591 9135), 100m before town on the right. An appealing little restaurant with outdoor seating. Specializes in seafood and meat dishes *al carbón*. Entrees US$6-8. Open daily 7am-9pm. Cash only. ❷

Restaurante Mar de Plata (☎983 6425), just before town, across from Supercentro Yin and inside Hotel Don Pepe. Serves a wide variety of *típico* and a selection of Peruvian dishes. Try the *sancocho* (traditional Panamanian chicken soup with rice; US$4). Entrees US$4-8. Open M-Th 7am-9pm, F-Su 7am-11pm. MC/V. ❷

Doña Nella (☎9087 0075), across from the market. Cafeteria-style *típico* attracts the locals from the market across the street. Open daily 7am-3:30pm. Cash only. ❶

👁 SIGHTS

MUSEO DEL VALLE. The museum is a large room with ancient artifacts and local crafts, accompanied by an explanation of the geological events that created the valley. Some explanations are in English. *(Behind the church. ☎6437 8639. Open during business hours. US$0.50)*

MERCADO EL VALLE. El Valle is known for its Sunday market, one of the most popular in Panama. Indigenous artisans gather from surrounding farms to sell sculpted pots, carved soapstone figurines, wooden toys, and woven baskets. There is also a large selection of delicious fruit, wholesome vegetables, and gorgeous plants; it's a pity that customs agents don't look kindly on botanical imports. Between August and October, the national flower—**Flor de Espíritu Santo** (Flower of the Holy Spirit)—is on sale. *(In the middle of town. Open 7am-5pm.)*

EL NÍSPERO. A well-maintained zoo and botanical garden, El Níspero makes for a lovely afternoon stroll. Animals include ocelots, titi monkeys, iguanas, scarlet macaws, giant sleeping tapirs, and jaguarundi. *(Take a right about 500m before town by the ATM. From there, walk straight and take a right after the fire station. ☎983 6142. Open 7am-5pm. Adults US$3, children US$2.)*

POZOS TERMALES. El Valle is one of the few places in Panama cool enough to make hot springs attractive. The pleasant grounds include natural pools, mudbaths, and hot springs. Admission includes a packet of mineral-rich mud for your face. *(☎6621 3896. Turn left following the signs when the road curves right outside of town; it's about 7min. farther down the road. Open 8am-5pm. US$1.)*

EL MACHO. An impressive 85m rainforest waterfall over black volcanic rock, EL Macho is one of El Valle's greatest attractions. It's a 5min. hike via bouncy suspended walkways, overlooking Río Guayago and Amarillo (El Valle's two water sources) and lush virgin forest. The viewing station is 20m away; it is forbidden to bathe or get too close to the waterfall. There is a 2hr. hike through the surrounding **Refugio Ecológico Chorro El Macho** that loops above the waterfall and comes down the other side. Guides are required for the hikes. The *refugio* also runs **Canopy Adventures,** which operates a system of ziplines that crisscross in front of the waterfall and through dense forest *(☎983 6547. Follow the main road west of town for 30min.; there are plenty of signs. Or, take the La Mesa bus (US$0.25). Open daily 8am-5pm. US$3.50, children US$1.75. Natural bathing pool US$3.50. Guided hike for wildlife observation US$35. Ziplines US$52.50 per person with a guide.)*

PIEDRA PINTADA. One of El Valle's most prized sights is a bit underwhelming unless you are a petroglyphs buff, but it's a nice walk regardless. Nearby is a splendid waterfall. Less famous but more accessible than El Macho, hiking Piedra Pintada is free. Some travelers jump into the crisp pool at the bottom.

It's also the beginning of the trail up the India Dormida. *(Follow the road out of town to the west. Continue as it bends to the right and turn left at the sign. Continue straight until the road comes to a T, then turn right; it's through an open gate to the left. The 10m rock is 5min. past the road. For the waterfall, continue up the path keeping the river to your left. Except during school hours, you will find little boys waiting to guide you; US$1 tip recommended.)*

INDIA DORMIDA. You can't spend a day in El Valle without someone pointing out La India Dormida. Legend has it that when the *indígena* maiden daughter of legendary Indian Chief Urracá, Flor del Aire, fell in love with a conquering Spaniard, her previous lover Yaraví killed himself. The girl, tormented and disgraced, wandered into the hills to die, lying down to stare forever at the skies. With a little imagination, her silhouette can be deciphered by visitors in the hills to the west of El Valle. *(The more difficult of two trails passes through incredible rainforest. Follow the signs to Piedra Pintada (p. 280) and continue up the trail keeping the river to your left. The hour-long hike is steep and slippery. The signs in town for La India Dormida lead to the other way up, a less exciting route. Follow the road west out of town; when it turns right, hang a left. At the 1st street take a right, and then at the next street, a left. It is a 15min. walk from town to the start.)*

SANTA FÉ

Santa Fé is a picturesque mountain town. Almost the entire community is affiliated with a *cooperativo*, one of many groups working in town to better the community. The main attractions are the surrounding mountains, valleys, organic farms, and waterfalls.

TRANSPORTATION

Buses: Run between Santiago's main bus terminal and the town center in Santa Fé (1½hr., every 30min. 5am-7pm, US$2.40).

Bike Rentals: Panama Dream Finders (☎945 0250), across the street from the sign reading "Bienvenidos a Santa Fé." Rentals US$2 per hr., US$10 per day. Open daily 8am-5pm.

ORIENTATION AND PRACTICAL INFORMATION

The town is laid out in a rough V-shape along the top of a ridge, with Cerro Tute looming on the western side and a deep, lush valley to the east. The **Santiago-Santa Fé road** enters along the ridge from the southeast and splits into 3 roads at the "Bienvenidos a Santa Fé" sign. The **left branch** heads off toward the forested area of Alto de Piedra and the Hotel Jardín Santa Fereño (p. 282). The **central branch** leads uphill 500m to the town's modest church and the cluster of Santa Fé-Santiago buses. The **right branch** takes you toward the Orquideario (p. 283). No amount of directions is likely to save you from having to ask for help.

Tourist Offices: ANAM. Follow the left road at the fork, then take your 1st left and another left at the Antenna. For good info, you're better off talking to the ANAM office in Santiago or to the owners of Hostal la Quía (p. 282). Open M-F 8am-4pm.

Police: (☎954 0905). Follow the left road at the fork, then take your 1st left; take another left at the Antenna.

Medical Services: Centro de Salud (☎954 0898), 50m before the fork. Open 7am-3pm.

Internet Access: Info Plaza (☎954 0737), part of the Fundación Hector Gallego (the tourist collective). Just up the hill from Hostal La Qhía. Wi-Fi. Internet US$0.75 per hr. Open 8am-8pm.

COCLÉ AND
VERAGUAS

Post Office: (☎954 0955), across from the ANAM office. Open M-F 7am-6pm, Sa 7am-5pm. **Postal Code:** 0921.

ACCOMMODATIONS

Hostal La Qhía (☎954 0903 or 6952 5589; www.panamamountainhouse.com). Follow the central road into town and take a left at the sign across the street from the cooperativo market and restaurant. Qhía is 20m up the hill. Just 4 years old, this hostel may be single-handedly putting Santa Fé on the backpacker circuit. Beautifully situated on a scenic slope, it has an indoor lounge area for watching movies and an outdoor shelter for relaxing. The owner Stephanie has valuable maps, directions, and recommendations for hiking. Bathrooms have hot water. Breakfast US$3-5. Dinner US$6. Dorms US$10; doubles with shared bath US$28; triples US$34, with private bath US$48. Cash only. ❷

Hotel El Sol de Santa Fé (☎954 0941). Walk 5min. before the fork at the entrance to town. The rooms, situated in a square around a small lawn, are immaculate and come with private baths, even if they're a little short on character. The friendly owner Miryan can contact guides and arrange hiking tours. She also cooks an excellent breakfast (US$5). Doubles US$20-25; triples U$25-35; quads US$35. Cash only. ❸

Hotel Jardín Santa Fereño (☎6799 1622). Follow the left fork and take the 1st left. Follow the road past the antenna; there's a sign on the left. On a hilltop overlooking the town, this hotels offers a few colorful concrete *cabañas* with private baths. Its location next to a bar makes it a little noisy on weekends. Call ahead. Cash only. ❷

FOOD

There are a lot of good places to get *típico* in town. If you want international cuisine, Hostal Qhía and Hotel Sol de Santa Fé are the best options. For groceries, visit **Mini-super Cooperativo Esperanza de Los Campesinos,** which has two locations along the central road: one is across from the *artesanías* market, and the other is 200m farther up the hill. (Open 6am-9pm).

Restaurante de la Cooperativa (☎6756 4099). Take the central road; it's 250m up the hill on the right, in the basement of a building with bamboo siding. Cafeteria-style *típico* (US$2) is the main offering, though they cook up other dishes for US$3-4. Fresh juice US$0.50. Open 5:30am-8pm. Cash only. ❶

Fonda La Nuestro (☎954 0777), on the central fork just beyond the *artesanías* market. A series of neat thatch huts are a great place to sit back and enjoy the fresh mountain air. *Típico* ranges from US$2 for cafeteria food to US$3 for special dishes. Open daily 5am-9pm. Cash only. ❶

SIGHTS AND ACTIVITIES

Despite the town's size, there's plenty to do in Santa Fé. In town, the coffee plant and *orquideario* are worth visiting, but the stunning landscapes here are the real draw. Around the town are organic farms, mountain communities, scenic mountain tops, and an endless number of waterfalls. It rains nearly every day from March to December, so be prepared for mud and slippery rocks. For *artesanías* and fresh fruit, stop by the **Mercado de Artesanías**, in the center of town, on the central street.

HIKING. There are miles upon miles up hiking trails in the region, but most of them are completely unmarked. The best way to see them is to arrange a guide, which costs US$10-20 per day. **Hostal La Quía** and **Hotel Santa Fé** can find guides; Quía provide its guests with detailed maps and directions for most of the trails. You can also arrange to do most of these trails by **horse**; contact **Cesamo** (☎954 0807 or 6792 0571) for information. **Cerro Tute** is a popular trail to the top of a nearby peak with views over the town. There are a number of routes, but the shortest starts just after the small bridge south of town. Walk down the road about 30min. and turn right after the bridge. It's about a 3hr. hike round-trip from there.

Alto de Piedra is a community west of town. From the ANAM office, continue straight on the steep, windy road. It's a 30min. walk to the community, but from there you can access Cerro Tute and nearby waterfalls. Children in town are usually eager to show you the way for a small tip. To get to **Las Lajas**, a lovely swimming spot, follow the right branch of the road from the entrance of town and continue straight for 30min. A longer walk leads to **El Salto.** The walk here takes you through a nearby community, an organic farm, and breathtaking waterfalls. From town, it is best to hop on a bus for the 10min. ride to El Salto—ask for the *puente grande.* Once you cross the large bridge, get off, turn left, and follow the signs for El Carmen. On the trail, keep to the right at the fork; it's about a 2-3hr. hike in.

TUBING. If you'd rather save your legs, float down the Santa María in an inner tube. **William** (☎6583 5944) rents tubes for US$5 at his house just across the bridge, east of town. To get there, walk 20min. past the Orquideario; it's on your right past the bridge. Most people float to the bridge south of town (about 1hr.), where it's easy to catch a bus back to town, though William can also arrange transportation.

CASA DE ORQUIDEARIO. Santa Fé's original attraction, this mesmerizing orchid garden is run by Berta de Castrellon, who until recently also served as the town's mayor. To get there, follow the right fork and take your second left. Walk past a small artisan stand on the right; it will be a small dirt driveway on the right. Somebody is usually around to let you in. Walk to the gate and call out, though they appreciate it if you call ahead. There is also a yearly orchid fair in August; call Berta or the ATP office in Santiago to find the date. *(☎954 0910.)*

COFFEE TOURS. In the northern part of town is the Café Tute factory, a part of the local cooperative, La Esperanza de Los Campesinos ("The Hope of the Farmers"). Local farmers grow delicious coffee, which is processed here and sold for export. If you stop by the factory, they can usually give you a tour of the operation, but it is best to call ahead. You can also arrange a more comprehensive guided coffee tour through the tourist cooperative. *(To get to the factory, walk past La Quía Hostal for 5min. ☎954 0801. Open 8am-5pm. Tourist cooperative ☎954 0737; ask for Lilia.)*

SANTIAGO

Halfway between Panama City and David, along the Interamerican Highway, Santiago (pop, 74,680) is a convenient base for forays into the fabulous province of Veraguas. Filled with waterfalls, wilderness areas, beaches, and small traditional villages, this area is gorgeous. Aside from the *Fiesta Patronal de Santiago Apóstol* (July 22-25), Santiago itself doesn't offer much to visitors.

▟ TRANSPORTATION

Situated on the Interamerican Highway, Santiago is a transportation hub, so you'll probably have to pass through whether you want to or not.

Buses: Transportes David-Panamá (☎998 4006), next to Hotel Piramidal on the Vía Americana, east of the fork. To **David** and **Panama City** (3hr., every hr. 9am-11pm, US$7.50). Buses leave from the main terminal on C. 10 halfway between Av. Central and the Interamerican Hwy. to: **Atalaya** (20min., every 30min. 6am-9pm, US$0.75); **Las Palmas** (1½hr., every hr. 5:15am-6:45pm, US$2.60); **Puerto Mutis** (45min., every 20min. 5:15am-10:10pm, US$1.10); **San Francisco** (30min., every 25min. 6:05am-8:15pm, US$0.75); **Santa Fé** (1½hr., every 30min. 5am-7pm, US$2.40); **Soná** (1hr., every 20min. 5:40am-9:20pm, US$1.25).

Taxis: Rides around town US$1.25.

Car Rental: Budget Rent-a-Car (☎998 1731), next to the McDonald's on the Interamerican Hwy., near the fork. Open M-Sa 8am-5pm. AmEx/MC/V.

◤✦◥ 🛈 ORIENTATION AND PRACTICAL INFORMATION

The main road, **Avenida Central,** branches off from the Interamerican Highway and runs west about 2km to the cathedral and the town's **parque central.** *Calles* run north-south between Av. Central and the Interamericana, starting with C. 1 beyond the cathedral and C. 10 about halfway between the **cathedral** and the fork. To get to the *parque* from the main bus terminal, turn right on C.10 in front of the terminal and continue for about 4 blocks; turn right at Av. Central and continue straight to the cathedral.

Tourist Office: ATP (☎998 3929), in Plaza Palermo on Av. Central. No English spoken. Open M-F 7:30am-3:30pm. **ANAM** (☎994 7313), across from the Hotel Gran David on the Interamerican Hwy. They operate cabins on Isla Coiba; call in advance to reserve one. Open M-F 8am-4pm.

Bank: HSBC, on Av. Central and C. 7. **24hr. ATM.** Open M-F 8am-5pm, Sa 9am-noon. There is **Western Union** (☎998 5431) inside Servicios Martinez on C. Eduardo Santo, across the street from the Escuela Normal. Open M-F 8am-5:30pm, Sa 8am-5pm.

Luggage Storage: In the main terminal on C. 10. US$0.75-6.50 per day. Open 24hr.

Laundromat: Lavamático La Espuma, 4 blocks north of Av. Central on C. 9. Wash US$0.50; dry US$0.50. Full service US$1.50. Open M-Sa 8am-8pm.

Police: (☎958 2400), 500m east of the fork on the Interamerican Hwy.

24hr. Pharmacy: Farmacia Veraguas (☎958 6844), in the same bus stop as Restaurante Tucanes on the Interamerican Hwy.

Hospital: (☎999 3070 and 3146), about 4km east of town on the Interamerican Hwy.

Internet Access: F1 Computers, across from the bus station on C.10. Internet US$0.60 per hr. Open M-F 8am-6pm, Sa 8am-1pm

Post Office: (☎998 4293), on C. 8, 8 blocks north of Av. Central. Open M-F 7am-5:45pm, Sa 7am-4:45pm. **Postal Code:** 0923.

◤ ACCOMMODATIONS

Most people pass through Santiago without spending the night. If you do have to spend the night, there are plenty of options, ranging from comfortable (along the highway) to basic and a bit dodgy (in the middle of town).

Hotel Gran David (☎998 4510), west of the fork on the Interamerican Hwy. One of Santiago's best hotels. Comfortable rooms have phones, private baths with hot water, and access to a 24hr. restaurant and pool. Internet US$1 per hr. Singles US$11, with cable and A/C US$20; doubles US$15/26, triples with A/C US$34. MC/V. ❷

Hotel Piramidal (☎998 3124), next to the David-Panama bus terminal on the Interamerican Hwy., just east of the fork. The surprisingly chic lobby has Wi-Fi, and there is a large pool in back. Plain rooms come with hot water, A/C, and cable. Singles US$25; doubles US$33; triples US$37. AmEx/MC/V. ❸

Hotel Santiago (☎998 4824), 1 block south of the southwestern corner of the Cathedral. With your back to the rear of the cathedral, turn left and walk 20m. A step up from the group of sketchy accommodations downtown. Don't be tricked by the attractive facade—the rooms in back are seriously neglected. Rooms have private baths, but the plumbing doesn't always work. Singles US$7.70; doubles US$11, with A/C US$17. Cash only. ❷

FOOD

You can find *típico* all over town. Fast food joints cluster around the Interamerican. For groceries, visit **Super99,** on C.10, just off Av. Central. They also have a **24hr. ATM** and a **pharmacy.** (☎998 3939. Open 24hr. MC/V.)

Cocina del Abuelo (☎933 4041), 1km east of the fork on the Interamerican Hwy., inside the Hotel Plaza Gran David (not to be confused with Hotel Gran David). Although it's a bit touristy, this restaurant serves delicious international cuisine, difficult to find in Santiago. People come for live performances Sa-Su night. The attached tavern is a sports bar. Entrees US$6-12. Beer US$1.50. Open daily 11am-11pm. Tavern open daily 5pm-1am. MC/V. ❷

Los Tucanes (☎958 6490), just west of the fork on the Interamericana. A popular stop for long-distance buses. Basically a large cafeteria with cheap sandwiches (US$1.25) and *típico* (US$1.25-2). Open 24hr. Cash only. ❶

SIGHTS

There isn't much to explore in Santiago, but the ■**Escuela Normal Juan Demóstenes Arosemana** is worth a stop. Built between 1936 and 1938, this school for teachers boasts dazzling architecture, sculptures, and paintings. The facade is a gorgeous hodgepodge of stone carvings hiding miniature figures of *pollera*-clad girls. Head through the archway of the entry hall, framed by the Allegory of Time and Philosophy (Plato and Aristotle lean on the clock) and through the doors to the Aula Máxima. This huge room was painted by **Roberto Lewis,** the famous painter who decorated the Palacio Presidencial in Panama City. (*On C.7, 4 blocks north of Av. Central. Shorts and sleeveless shirts prohibited. Open 7am-3pm. Free.*)

DAYTRIPS FROM SANTIAGO

■**IGLESIA SAN FRANCISCO DE LAS MONTAÑAS.** Thirty minutes down the road to Santa Fé is the small town of San Francisco, built around a pretty square and this beautiful church. Unlike the abundant white-washed churches in the rest of the region, this 18th-century masterpiece has a stone exterior with a single white steeple and an ornate wooden interior. If you're headed to Santa Fé and have a little time to kill, it's certainly worth the stop. (*Take a bus to San Francisco or Santa Fé from Santiago. Turn right off the main road after the Protecíon Civil building on the left. The entrance to the church is on the side. Open Tu-Sa 10am-6pm.*)

SANTA CATALINA

Santa Catalina, recognized as one of the best year-round surfing spots in the Americas, is a small fishing town 110km south of Santiago. Today it is fighting fiercely against developers and businessmen to maintain its small-town atmosphere. For the most part it has kept its laid-back feel. People from all over the world come to Panama and hop on a bus for six to seven hours to get straight to Catalina. Although the vast majority of these crazies are surfers, nearby fishing, diving, and snorkeling attract other nature-lovers. It's also a good leap-off point to Pacific islands like Cébaco, Gobernadora, and ■Coiba.

TRANSPORTATION

To get to Santa Catalina by **bus,** you have to travel through Soná. From the terminal, **buses** leave for **Santa Catalina** (1½hr., 4 per day 5am-6pm, US$3.80). Though Soná is closer to David than it is to Santiago, you'll probably have to pass through Santiago to get to Soná. Within Santa Catalina there is no public transportation. Fortunately, nothing is much more than a 30min. walk. For a **taxi,** talk to David (see **Ocean Tour,** below).

ORIENTATION AND PRACTICAL INFORMATION

There are only **two main roads** in town. The one from Soná leads to the heart of town and ends at the town's beach. The other, a dirt track, takes you to **Playa Estero.** Between the cut-off for Estero and the beach, there are **four side roads** on your right that also lead to the water. Services are extremely limited in town. There are still **no landlines here,** and cell phone service is only availiable a few kilometers up the road. There is **no bank,** so bring plenty of cash.

Tours:

Scuba Coiba (☎6575 0122; www.scubacoiba.com), on the beach. A professional full-service, PADI-certified scuba outfitter. Runs frequent trips to Isla Coiba. Open 8am-6pm. Full-day trip to Coiba with 2 dives US$100. Two-day trip US$420 (min. 2 people). You can hop on daytrips as a non-diver for US$60.

Fluid Adventures Panama (☎832 2368; www.fluidadventurespanama.com), on the beach next to Scuba Coiba. If nobody is there, check at the home next to Big World Villas; the owners are usually only in town Dec.-May. A young Canadian couple, one a former Outward Bound instructor and the other a yoga instructor, run this kayak, surf, and yoga outfit. They offer all sorts of different packages from kayaking in Coiba (US$85 per person with 4 people; overnight US$200 per person, minimum 4 people) to a combination surf and yoga camp.

Ocean Tour (☎6915 5256; www.2oceanpanama.com; david2670@gmail.com), next to Restaurant Tropical Beach, on the left on the way down to the beach. David takes people out on fishing, surfing, and snorkeling adventures. Fishing trip US$50 per hr. A trip to Coiba is US$280 or US$50 per person. A surfing trip to Cébaco is US$200 for up to 10 people. David also has a taxi service; a trip to Soná is US$30. As his cell phone rarely works, it's best to use email.

Laundromat: 20m from the main road toward Playa Estero. Two washing machines under a shelter. US$1. Open 24hr.

Police: Across the street from Rolo's, in the heart of town.

Internet Access: Big World Villas, in town across the street for the turn off for Playa Estero. The office for a nearby real estate development lets people use its satellite Wi-Fi connection. Bring your laptop. Free. Available 10am-6pm.

ACCOMMODATIONS

There are more than a dozen places to stay in this small town. Most accommodations are located along the road to Playa Estero. For travelers on a tight budget, there are a few reasonably priced dorm rooms (US$10). Those looking for more seclusion and comfort can get excellent lodgings for US$40-50. Most places are operated by foreigners, so English is widely spoken. From December through March, reservations are recommended.

☒ **Oasis Surf Camp.** From town, take the road to Playa Estero all the way to the end; it's across a small stream that you can cross in a car, except at high tide. A series of removed *cabañas* are strewn across an extensive black sand beach. There is a volleyball court, a communal area with satellite TV and Wi-Fi, and a restaurant serving exquisite Italian food. Every *cabaña* has its own thatch *ranchito* out front. Surfboard rentals US$10-15. Surfing classes US$25 per hr. Singles US$15; doubles US$25; triples US$45; room for 6 US$70. US$10 for A/C. Prices rise in high season. Cash only. ❷

☒ **Hibiscus Garden** (☎6615 6097; www.hibiscusgarden.com), a 7min. drive outside town down a dirt road (follow the signs). A series of beautiful new buildings lining a tranquil bay. Rooms combine chic style with natural wooden touches. For their impeccable style and quality, they're a great deal. Shared kitchen available. Breakfast US$3-5. Dinner US$7-10. Slow internet available. Shuttle service into town round-trip US$3.50; 3 or more US$1.50 per person. Singles US$15; doubles US$25. Large double with its own porch, A/C, and private bath US$39. Cash only. ❷

La Buena Vida (☎6635 1895; www.labuenavida.biz), in town 50m before the road to Playa Estero. A young American couple has 3 *cabañas* and a restaurant. Though a bit pricier than the other options in town, you won't find attention to detail and craftsmanship like this for a better price anywhere. All the finishes were done by the couple; it's apparent that they've put a lot of love into their business. Detached private rooms have private baths, A/C, and hot water. Rooms US$55-75. ❺

Boarder's Paradise, next door to La Buena Vida and operated by the same people. One of the best deals in town. There are just 2 rooms, each with 2 beds; there's a good chance you'll have the place to yourself, especially in the off-season. They have a communal kitchen and clean shared baths with hot water. Their restaurant is worth the few extra dollars, so stop by for a hearty bowl of fruit topped with yogurt and homemade granola (US$5). Rooms US$10 per night. Cash only. ❷

Campin' (☎6579 1504), along the road to Playa Estero; head down the small driveway marked "Campin" just after the turn off for Los Piebes. After turning right, turn right again at the 2 CDs hanging on the post. Someone from the Camarena family will most likely be there to great you. This extraordinarily friendly family opens up their rustic home to backpackers and campers. The bathroom is a tiny building made from palm leaves; you'll have to bathe from a bucket. The cute, old mother cooks dinner for a few dollars. Camping US$3 per person; thatched hut US$5 per person. Cash only. ❶

Cabañas Rolo (☎6598 9926), at the end of the road in town. One of the most popular places for surfers. A surfer himself, the owner Rolo is also one of the most influential people in the community, constantly fighting to fend off development and preserve the laid-back environment. Clean dorm rooms have fans and outdoor shared baths. There is a communal kitchen and plenty of hammocks. Rolo also arranges reasonably priced tours in a safe, comfortable boat. Dorms US$10; doubles US$40; triples US$45. Cash only. ❷

Surfer's Paradise (☎6709 1037). Take the 3rd right along the road to Playa Estero. This spot, situated on a bluff overlooking the best break in town, has the best views by far. They also offer the best access to the break and an easy walk to a good beach. As of summer 2009, this accommodation was in the process of being remodeled. The basic rooms come with A/C and baths. Shared rooms US$15 per person; private rooms US$22. Cash only. ❷

⚑ FOOD

For a small fishing town with a few surfers, Santa Catalina offers impressive cuisine, with everything from seafood to pizza. Entrees are reasonably priced. Many of the hotels cook decent meals. By law, places have to close by 10pm;

establishments more removed, like those along the road to Playa Estero, often disregard this rule when there's a crowd. There is one small grocery store with minimal offerings, **Mini-Super Elisa,** at the turn off for Playa Estero in town, below Hotel Costa America. (Open daily 7am-9:30pm.)

▨ **Los Pibes.** From the road to Playa Estero, follow the sign at the 2nd right. The Argentinean owner grills up burgers and other savory delights, served at open-air tables under a small roof. Non-stop surfing videos to entertain the crowd. Try the famous #3 burger, with bacon, cheese, and peppers (US$6). Fish special US$7-9. He'll also grill up your day's catch for free. National beers US$1. Open 6:30-10pm. Cash only. ❷

Donde Viancka, along the road to Playa Estero before the turn off for Los Pibes. Viancka, the bubbly former Panamanian surfing champ, serves delicious fresh seafood caught in the waters offshore. Vegetarian options available. Entrees US$5-7. Open daily in low season 2-10pm, in high season earlier for breakfast. Cash only. ❷

Pizzeria Jammin. From the road to Playa Estero, take the 2nd right. Pizza cooked in a wood-burning oven brings gringos and other expats here by the dozen. They have a few *ranchitos* out on a lawn and a lively area under the main roof where people hang out until late. The hammocks are perfect for sleeping off the booze. Pizza US$5-8. Open 4-10pm or later. Cash only. ❷

The Dive, just before the end of the main road, in front of Rolo's. The newest spot in town is a great place to grab a beer and meet other travelers. Beers are a bit steep (US$2), but they come with a shot. Drink up, since closing time is early. They also serve good tacos, burritos, and other Mexican food for US$3-5, with plenty of vegetarian options. Open until 10pm. Cash only. ❷

Restaurante Tropical Beach, on the main road from Soná, 60m up from the beach in an unmarked building advertising fresh fruit and vegetables. A popular spot with locals and backpackers alike. Delicious *típico.* You can get 2 small fried whole fish for just US$2. Open 7am-8pm. Cash only. ❶

◉ SURFING

There are five breaks within walking distance of Santa Catalina. The most famous break, known simply as **La Punta,** is a rocky break left of the town's main beach. You can get there by going left from town or by going right from Surfer's Paradise. **Playa Estero** is a long sandy beach with intermediate waves, good for beginning surfers. To get there, take the dirt road left from the main road all the way to the end; it's about a 30min. walk. Left along the beach from Estero is **Punta Brava.** Between Estero and La Punta and below Surfer's Paradise is **Indicador,** another rocky break. **Punta Roca** is right of the town's main beach.

▶ DAYTRIPS FROM SANTA CATALINA

▨**ISLA COIBA.** The gem of Panama's Pacific Coast, Isla Coiba, named a **UNESCO World Heritage site** in 2004, is home to the best snorkeling, diving, and fishing in Panama. Coiba is a tropical paradise, almost completely untouched by humans, thanks to the fact that until recently it was a notorious penal colony (think *Lord of the Flies*); the most violent and undesirable were sent to the island, and the name Coiba struck fear in the hearts of Panamanians. Today there are only four prisoners remaining on the island. Don't worry—not only are they far from the ANAM cabins, they're also probably the most laid-back prisoners you've ever met, employed to maintain the island and sell crafts and fruit to tourists. There are three trails on the island. The **observatory trail** starts at the main beach and leads to a lookout point less than an hour away. **Sendero (Monkey Trail)** is about an hour-long hike, and the new **Sendero del Parque (Park Trail)** is a 3hr. trek across the island. You need a boat to access all but the observatory trail. Tourism is just starting to pick up there; few services exist on the island, and it's expensive to get to. On the island, there are a series of recently renovated **cabins** with A/C operated by ANAM. They charge US$20 per night in addition to the US$20 entry fee. *(Leave from Puerto Mutis or Santa Catalina. From Puerto Mutis, you may be able to arrange a fishing boat, but you will most likely need to hire a private boat. Sr. Camarena (☎ 999 8103) charges US$135 per day plus gas, which runs around US$100 each way. In Santa Catalina, there are a number of tour organizers that charge around US$50 per person per day for a group of 8. To find a group, call in advance to see if they have any trips going out. Your best chances are on weekends and during the high season (Dec.-Mar.). See Santa Catalina Practical Information, p. 286, for outfitters.)*

AZUERO PENINSULA

The Azuero Peninsula is Panama's heartland. It is the home of *típico* music, the *pollera* (traditional Panamanian dress), and Panama's grandest fiestas, which involve bullfighting, drinking, traditional music, drinking, religious processions, and drinking. The peninsula is still heavily agrarian, with large green pastures filled with herds of cattle that frequently impede the flow of traffic. Many people travel by horse, the men often wear *guayaberas* (traditional 4-pocket shirts) and old-style straw hats, and the biggest crowd on a Saturday night is at the local cockfight. When a festival is not taking place—which doesn't seem to happen often—travelers are lured by the natural attractions. The peninsula has over 270km of mostly undeveloped beaches, perfect for seclusion in the sun. Off Isla Iguana, the snorkeling and diving is top-notch; Playa Venado has world-class surfing; thousands of sea turtles nest on Isla Cañas; and in a country known for its fishing, the nearby waters are believed to be among the best. The towns of interest—Chitré, Las Tablas and Pedasí—all lie on the eastern side of the peninsula and are linked by the Carretera Nacional, which branches off the Interamerican Hwy. at Divisa. Santiago is farther west along the highway, inland from the peninsula, and halfway between David and Panama City.

CHITRÉ

The largest town on the Azuero Peninsula (pop. 42,467), Chitré itself doesn't offer much, but it's an important jumping off point for nearby villages, where you can watch locals make traditional crafts, taste some scrumptious local bread, or, if you time it right, party until the sun rises. Many travelers continue farther down the peninsula to Las Tablas and from there visit the endless expanses of unexplored Pacific beach. Chitré explodes during the Fiesta Patronal de San Juan on June 24th, to celebrate the feast day of John the Baptist. They close all the main streets for a seemingly endless procession of horses, bands, and icons of the saint, all the while carousing and dancing to live music.

◧ TRANSPORTATION

The Carretera Nacional cuts right through the city center, making Chitré an excellent transportation hub.

Buses: Leave from a station 15min. south of town. To town, taxis run US$1.50, local buses US$0.15. **Tuasa** (☎996 2661) operates buses to **Panama City** (4hr., every 1½hr. 2:45am-6pm, US$7.50) via **Penonomé** (1½hr., US$4). Other buses go to: **Aguadulce** (1hr., every 20min. 6am-5:40pm, US$2.50) via **Divisa** (30min., US$1.25); **Las Tablas** (40min., every 10min. 6am-9pm, US$1.25) via **Guararé** (30min., US$1); **Monagre** (25min., every 40min. 6am-6:30pm, US$1); **Ocú** (1hr., every 30min. 6am-6:30pm, US$2.50); **Parita** (15min., every 20min. 6am-6pm, US$0.70); **Santiago** (1¼hr., every 30min. 4am-6:30pm, US$2.30); **Tonosí** (2hr., every 1½hr. 10am-4pm, US$4). Some buses run less frequently on Su and holidays, so check in advance. Local buses south to **Los Santos** (5min., US$0.25) and west to **La Arena** (5min., US$0.25) can be found at the bus terminal and in town on C. Manuel Correa, 2 blocks north of the cathedral. Any buses heading in those directions will drop you off for the same fare.

Taxis: (☎996 8700). Fares around town run US$1-2.

◼✦▮ ORIENTATION AND PRACTICAL INFORMATION

All cars and buses arrive in Chitré from the west along the **Carretera Nacional,** (Highway 2), which becomes **Calle Manuel Correa** as it comes into town. Near the center of town, C. Manuel Correa intersects **Avenida Herrera** (or **Avenida Central**), which runs north-south. Just about everything in town can be found along these two roads. Two blocks south of the intersection is the **cathedral,** next to the **parque.** Three blocks farther south, Av. Central bends southeast onto **Los Santos** and **Las Tablas.** To reach the *parque* from the bus terminal, turn left out the front parking lot and continue 500m. Turn left on the Carretera Nacional, passing by the hospital on the right. About 200m farther, take a right at the fork and the cathedral and *parque* are three blocks up.

Tourist Office: ATP (☎974 4532; www.visitpanama.com), near the industrial park south of the Carretera Nacional in La Arena. Take any bus for La Arena and tell the driver you are going to IPAT (the old name for ATP), or ask for Parque Industrial. Open M-F 8am-4pm. **ANAM** (☎996 7675), northeast of town near the Universidad de Panama. Local buses stop at the university; get off just before at Mini-super Zheng. It's on the left. Open M-F 8am-4pm.

Bank: Citibank, on Plaza de Las Banderas, 1 block west and 1 block north of the *parque.* **ATM.** Open M-F 8am-pm. Sa 9am-noon.

Laundry: Lavamático Azuero (☎996 7411), 1 block east and 3 blocks south of the cathedral, just off Carretera Central east of town. Wash US$0.50. Dry US$1. Full service US$2.50. Open M-Sa 7:30am-7pm, Su 7:30am-1pm.

Police: Policia Nacional: (☎996 2810), between Chitré and La Arena on the Carretera Nacional.

Pharmacy: Farmacia Universal (☎996 4608), across the street from the cathedral. Open daily 8am-8pm.

Hospital: Hospital Cecilio Castillero (☎996 4444), along the Carretera Nacional east of town. Follow Av. Central south behind the cathedral and take a left at the Carretera Nacional; it's 100m up on the left. Open 7:30am-3:30pm. Open 24hr. for emergencies.

Internet Access: Sanchi Computer Internet, (☎996 2134). Half a block north of the cathedral on Av. Central. US$0.50 per hr. Open 8am-midnight.

Post Office: Heading west on C. Manuel Correa, walk past the Museo de Herrera (on the left) and take a right on the next street. Its inside the Cable and Wireless building on the right. Open M-F 7am-6pm, Sa 7am-5pm. **Postal Code:** 0601.

▮ ACCOMMODATIONS

Hotels in Chitré aren't anything to write home about, and you'll have a hard time finding anything cheaper than US$15. Prices rise during festivals, so it's a good idea to call ahead. Most of the hotels crowd around the center of town in front of the cathedral.

Hotel Bali Panama (☎996 4620; www.balipanama.com), half a block north of the cathedral. Not the cheapest in town, but definitely the best value. The rooms lack character and could use a bit more lighting, but come with cable TV, private baths with hot water, desks, and A/C. Wi-Fi. English and Indonesian spoken. Singles US$20; doubles US$27; triples US$34. ❸

Hotel Versalles (☎996 4422; www.hotelversalles.com), a 15min. walk west of town on the Carretera Nacional. Walk or take the La Arena bus (US$0.15). A tropical, festive, white-washed motel. Rooms open onto a garden with beautiful flowers and a pool. Wi-Fi, hot baths, and cable TV in all the rooms. Singles can sleep 2 if you don't mind sharing a bed. Singles US$33; doubles US$50. ❹

Pensión Central (☎992 0059). Might be the cheapest place in town. Rooms have A/C and private baths, but are dark, dreary, and a tad dirty. The Wi-Fi only works in the lobby. Solo travelers are better off elsewhere, but it's a good deal for groups. Doubles US$18; triples US$23. ❸

🍴 FOOD

Food in Chitré is decent and cheap. Nearby La Arena is famous for its bread, so *panaderías* are a common sight. For groceries, visit **Supercentro Willians,** half a block north of C. Manuel Correa on Av. Central. (Open daily 6:30am-9pm.)

🍽 **Restaurante Chiquita** (☎996 2411), half a block north of C. Manuel Correa on Av. Central. This restaurant's offerings are anything but *chiquita*. It's basically a long counter, with stations for *típico*, bread, pizza, sweets, and ice cream. It's easy to get addicted to their fruity empanadas (US$0.30), baked fresh throughout the day. Open daily 5am-10:30pm. Cash only. ❶

Restaurante El Prado (☎996 4620), inside Hotel Bali Panama (p. 291). Globalization at its best, this restaurant is the product of a Panamanian-Indonesian marriage, serving Indonesian specialties with local spices mixed in. Meals aren't huge. Try the *sate ayam* (chicken kebabs with peanut sauce; US$3.50). Open daily 7am-8pm. Cash only. ❷

La Estrella (☎996 7811), on the corner across the street from the cathedral. Similar to Chiquita, but with a greater emphasis on *típico*. Its central location and cheap prices make it popular with the locals. Open daily 6am-9pm. Cash only. ❶

Restaurante El Aire Libre (☎996 3639), on the opposite side of the *parque* from the cathedral. Friendly restaurant with a wide variety of *típico*. Fish US$4-5. Sandwiches US$1-2. Entrees US$2-4. Open 6:30am-10pm. Cash only. ❷

📷 SIGHTS

IGLESIA SAN JUAN BAUTISTA. The cathedral in town features a beautiful gilded mahogany altar. On the 24th of June, it's the center of festivities for the feast day of John the Baptist. *(On Av. Central.)*

EL MUSEO DE HERRERA. The town's museum has exhibits on the archaeology, history, and traditions of the Herrera province. *(☎966 0077. On Av. Manuel Correa, 2 blocks west of Av. Central and on Plaza de Las Banderas. Open Tu-Sa 8am-4pm.)*

🔎 DAYTRIP FROM CHITRÉ

GUARARÉ. For a full dose of traditional Azuero music, stop by this otherwise sleepy town on September 24th for the the **Festival de la Mejorana.** The festival features many traditional instruments, including the accordion, tambourines, and the *mejorana* (a small guitar-like instrument made from mango wood). Guararé's **Semana Santa** festivities are more intricate than most. Dancing and singing form the backdrop for an Easter story reenactment, culminating in a bonfire where an effigy of Judas is burned amid great celebration. If you happen to be there when Guararé returns to its usual state of tranquility, visit **Casa-Museo Manuel F. Zárate,** former home of the festival's creator. It is filled with *polleras*, masks, costumes, and a photo of the chosen *reína* (queen) from each year of the festival's 59 years. *(Take a bus to Las Tablas, which leave every 30min. (US$1); and ask to be dropped off. From the road, take a left; the main plaza is 2 blocks down.)*

PEDASÍ

A small fishing town in the southeast corner of the Azuero Peninsula, Pedasí (pop. 3620) is a great place to spend a few days. Despite its small-town charm and quiet *parque central*, most people come here to fish, hoping for the catch of a lifetime. Even for the least experienced fishermen, it's a thrill: there's a good chance you'll come back with a fish half your size. The town is the birthplace of Panama's first female president, Mireya Moscoso. Pedasí has been a well-kept secret until recently, but today the word is getting out, and the town has seen millions of investment dollars pour in. Fortunately, the development hasn't yet spoiled the town—the only indication of it is the billboards along the road.

Pedasí is walking distance from miles of empty of Pacific beaches, and is the main jumping-off point for the picturesque Isla Iguana. Good surfing is another 30min. farther at Playa Venado, which has some of the best waves in the Americas. Even farther is Isla Cañas, where thousands of turtles go to lay eggs from July to November.

▄ TRANSPORTATION

Buses: Buses to **Las Tablas** head up Av. Central (40min., every 25min. 6:30am-5pm, US$2). Note that not every bus from Las Tablas to Cañas passes through Pedasí. One bus passes through to **Cañas** around 7am and returns at 10am; another passes around 2pm and returns are 3pm. These buses pass by the entrance to **Playa Venado,** but stop short of Isla Cañas (not to be confused with the town of Cañas).

Taxis: Go to nearby beaches (US$2.50), to Playa Venado (US$15-20), and to the port for Isla Iguana (US$20-25).

▄ ▄ ORIENTATION AND PRACTICAL INFORMATION

From Las Tablas, the Carretera Nacional hugs the east coast of the peninsula for 41km before entering Pedasí, where it becomes **Avenida Central,** the main north-south strip in town. The **parque central** is one block east of the main road. Most streets have signs, making it perhaps the best-labeled town in the country.

Tourist Office: IPAT/ATP (☎995 2339). Take the 2nd left after entering town; it's in a barely marked 2-story building on the right on the road to Playa El Arenal. Open M-F 8am-4pm.

Tours: Dive-N-Fish Pedasí (☎995 2894; www.dive-n-fishpanama.com), on Av. Central behind Pedasí Sports Club. A variety of services from fishing, spear fishing, and scuba diving to kayaking and horseback riding. Spearfishing trip US$85 per person (2 person minimum). Kayaks US$40 per day. Horseback riding US$55 per day.

Bank: Banco Nacional, just before town in the large white building on the right. **24hr. ATM.** Open M-F 8am-3pm, Sa 9am-noon. Plan ahead, as people withdraw cash to pay the fishermen and the machines sometimes run out.

Police: (☎995 2122), before the Banco Nacional building just outside of town, on the right.

Pharmacy: Centro Commercial Pedasí (☎995 2182), on Av. Central across from Dim's Hostel. Open M-F 7am-9:30pm. Sa-Su 7am-10pm.

Medical Services: Centro de Salud, C. Las Tablas (☎995 2127). Take a left off Av. Central. It's 3 blocks down past the *parque*. Open daily 7am-3pm; 7am-7pm for emergencies. After hours, seek medical attention in Las Tablas.

Internet Access: Los Macaraquenos #2, C. Agustin Moscoso (☎6788 4352). Take a left off Av. Central; it's 10m up on the left. Internet US$1 per hr. Open M-Sa 8am-8pm, Su 8am-2pm.

Post Office: (☎995 2221). Turn left after Centro Commercial Pedasí on to Av. Central. Open M-F 8am-3pm, Sa 8am-1pm. **Postal Code:** 0749.

ACCOMMODATIONS

In the past few years, the number of accommodations in Pedasí has doubled, and it seems that prices have followed suit. During Carnaval, most places hike up their prices, and you have to call far in advance to get room. The cheapest, but definitely not the safest, place to sleep any time of the year is on the beach; be sure to bring a tent and mosquito net.

Dim's Hostel (☎995 2303). One of the original spots and still the one of the coolest. Rooms are on the 2nd floor of a building decorated with logs and branches. The backyard has a thatch hut built around a tree, and although it may look like an unsuspecting spot, it's apparently ground zero for millions of dollars in local real estate deals. All rooms have A/C and hot water baths. Breakfast included. Free Wi-Fi. Singles US$33; each additional person US$15. Cash only. ❹

Hotel Residencial Pedasí (☎995 2490 or 6747 5363), on Av. Central, on the left as your enter town. Clean, brightly painted rooms open onto a large lawn with a few hammocks. Rooms have A/C, hot-water baths, and Wi-Fi. Singles US$25-30; doubles US$30-40; triples US$50. Cash only. ❸

Hostal Doña Maria (☎995 2916; www.hostaldonamaria.com). Charmingly decorated rooms with perfectly upholstered furniture. The best part is the large backyard, which has an open-air *cabaña*, hammocks, lounge chairs, and a BBQ for grilling your day's catch. Rooms have hot water baths and TVs. Breakfast US$5. Free Wi-Fi. Singles US$39; doubles US$44; triples US$54. Cash only. ❹

Hospedaje Moscoso (☎995 2203), on Av. Central just past C. Las Tablas. Sra. Moscoso is a relative of the former president Mireya Moscoso. More importantly, she rents out the cheapest rooms in town. They're nothing special, but they are clean and come with all the necessary amenities, including A/C, private baths, and TVs. Rooms along the road can be a little loud. Doubles US$25; triples US$30; quads US$35. Cash only. ❸

FOOD

Restaurants pop up overnight here, but unlike with hotels, it's still possible to eat well for cheap. *Típico* is the cheapest option, but you can get fresh fish for just a little more. For groceries, visit **Centro Commercial Pedasi** on Av. Central across from Dim's Hostel. (☎995 2182. Open daily M-F 7am-9:30pm, Sa-Su 7am-10pm.) **Abernathy's** is the best fishing supplies store in town, just across from the Centro de Salud, past the *parque* on C. Las Tablas. (☎995 2779. Open daily 8am-5pm. MC/V.)

Dulcería Yely (☎995 2215), off Av. Central. Take a right on C. Ofelia Reluz. A huge assortment of fresh, delicious cakes (US$0.35). They also have renowned *flan*, cheap sandwiches (US$1.50), and spectacular empanadas (US$0.30). Ask for the *chicheme*, a delicious sweet corn drink popular all over Panama. Open daily 8am-9pm. Cash only. ❶

Restaurante Angela (☎995 2207), on Av. Central just past Dim's Hostel. One of the original restaurants in Pedasí, Restaurante Angela serves fast, delicious, and cheap food. Granola and yogurt US$1.25. Be sure to try the day's catch. Fish US$4. Open M-Sa 7am-9pm, Su 7am-7:30pm. Cash only. ❷

Restaurante Pedasieño (☎6707 9945), next to the Accel gas station on Av. Central. A friendly spot serving great, cheap *típico*. Fast food US$2. Fish US$3.50. Open daily 6am-7pm. Cash only. ❶

Pizzeria Tiesto (☎995 2812), on the east side of the *parque*. A lovely spot with *arte-sanía*-covered walls and seating that opens up to the plaza. Pizzas (US$3-4) are a good deal. Open M and W-Su 8am-10pm. Cash only. ❷

◢ BEACHES

Although Pedasí itself is not on the beach, it is only a few kilometers from endless expanses of secluded sandy beaches. Most people head for **Isla Iguana** or **Playa Venado**, but on the weekends these can be more crowded. If all you're looking for is a wide stretch of your own, **Playa El Toro** and **La Garita** are just 3km from town. The water isn't as sparklingly clear here as on Isla Iguana, but these beaches are cheap and accessible. A taxi will charge you US$3 to get there, and if you want a pick-up you will have to arrange it,. The walk is also an easy 45min. jaunt.

◢ FISHING

The waters around Pedasí are a goldmine of wahoo, tuna, mahi mahi, marlin, and other delicious fish. People come from all around the world to fish off the coast. **Pedasifishing.com** arranges complete tours, while **Dive-N-Fish Pedasí** has a wide array of day trips. If you want to spearfish, you'll have to book through one of them. A cheaper option is to go directly through local fisherman. They will take you out for US$50 per day, plus gas, which usually runs another US$50. You can comfortably fit 5 people in the boat, and if you get a good catch, you'll come home with enough fish to feed you for a few days. Everyone who comes to Pedasí has their favorite fisherman, but not all of them have equipment. **Avidel** (☎6509 3783) comes highly recommended. He'll supply all the equipment and has a jeep, so he can pick you up. If you think you might get seasick, bring dramamine. It's also a good idea to bring plenty of sunscreen, snacks, and drinks because you'll probably be out all day. Make sure not to bring bananas on board, as the superstitious fishermen believe it's bad luck.

◢ DAYTRIPS FROM PEDASÍ

ISLA IGUANA. Pedasí's big draw is nearby **Refugio de Vida Silvestre Isla Iguana**, a diving, snorkeling, and fishing hotspot 7km from Pedasí's nearest beach. The island has two pristine beaches with crystal water, and lies within feet of one of the largest coral mass on the Pacific Coast, which covers an impressive 16 hectares. The rest of the coast is made up of dark rocks that look like baked sandcastles. The island is home to huge flocks of birds; a recent study has identified at least 20 different species. Boats let you off on the larger **Playa El Cirial**, where you pay to enter. Boats can also bring you 200m to the opposite side of the island to **Playita El Faro**, a smaller, more secluded beach with better snorkeling. There are two short paths, teeming with iguanas (hence the island's name). Those paths are surrounded by occasional bomb holes left over from the days when it was occupied by the US navy during WWII. The new **ANAM visitor center** has a pleasant view of the beach below; it also has information about the local plants and animals and a good map of the island. *(Hotels in Pedasí can arrange transportation to the island. The ANAM park ranger on the island, Analio, is also more than happy to bring you over. ☎6654 4716. The price of transportation to the island is US$50 (up to 8 people). The boats all leave from Playa El Arenal (also called El Bajadero), a 5min. car ride from the gas station at the northern end of Pedasí or a 45min. walk. From the beach it's a 20min. ride by boat. As soon as you disembark on the island, you will be asked for the entry fee; US$10,*

Panamanians US$4. There is an outhouse and a roof over a concrete floor where you can string up a hammock or post a tent; US$10, Panamians US$4.)

PLAYA VENADO. Thirty minutes southeast of Pedasí, "Playa Venado" (as the locals call it) has one of the best surfing breaks in all of Panama. Despite its fame, Playa Venado remains uncrowded. Even on a weekend there are only a few dozen people around, and there is almost no infrastructure to speak of. Venado's waves are big (2-3m, breaking both ways), so casual swimming is sometimes impossible. The 1.5km crescent of dark sand is flanked by two land points and backed by endless green hills, making for a stunning drive in.

At of 2009, there were no formal accommodations on the beach. Many choose to camp out in their cars or along the beach. If you choose to string up a hammock, make sure to bring a mosquito net. **Restaurante Playa Venado ❷** is along the beach at the entrance, and serves cheap fish (US$3) with rice and beans or fries. You can also get *sancocho* (US$2.50), a chicken, yucca, and vegetable stew. (Open daily 6:30am-9pm.) About 1km up the road toward Cañas is ⊠**Hospedaje Eco Venao ❷**, on top of a green hill. They have a volleyball court, an outdoor kitchen, and a game room. Bunked dormitories filled with surfers are surrounded by hammocks. You'll sleep well on the thick mattresses knowing that the hostel is part of a reforestation project for the surrounding 346 acres. (☎832 0530; www.venao.com. Dorms US$11; private rooms with shared bath US$27.50; private *cabañas* US$35. Campsite US$5 per person.) *(Buses from Las Tablas to Cañas are infrequent; there are 2 per day (30min., US$2) that arrive in Pedasí between 7-8am and 2-3pm. Ask to get off at Venao. It's a 5min. walk from the road to the beach. For current info ask at the gas station. The easiest way to get there is to hire a taxi (US$15), or hitchhike, though Let's Go does not recommend hitchhiking.)*

ISLA DE CAÑAS. West of Pedasí, Playa Venado, and the town of Cañas lies Isla de Cañas, an island off the southern coast of the Azuero. The sugarcane-covered island is scarcely populated. You arrive on the island's north side, a stone's throw from the mainland; the main beach is on the opposite side, a short 5min. walk away. It is on this beautiful 14km beach where five of the world's eight species of sea turtles come to lay eggs. The reproductive antics climax in **arribadas,** when more than 10,000 turtles hit the beach in just two or three nights to lay eggs. The main egg-laying season is July-November; most of the *arribadas* occur in October. Apart from the *arribadas*, there are many nights in the egg-laying season when 100 or more turtles spawn on the beach. The island is managed cooperatively by ANAM and the local community, which subsists mainly on turtle egg sales. The community has a nursery program: 1.5km of protected land on the beach means that about 15,000 nests are left untouched. The rest of the eggs are given to those who work with the program for profit.

Since the turtles are only around at night, you'll probably have to stay on the island. Unfortunately, the only accommodation is pretty unappealing. On the walk toward the beach, there is a **yellow house ❶** on the left. Ask for Neri Perez, who rents two bare rooms in an unattractive concrete structure behind her house. Each room has four beds and a private bath. (☎6918 3204. US$5 per person, with A/C US$10 per person.) A better option is to bring a tent, but high tide makes the beach a bad campsite. Boats let you off at an unmarked **restaurant,** where you will often find loud music and a few drunk men. Fulvilla, the cook, serves whatever they have—usually you'll have the option of beef, pork, or some sort of seafood. (☎6971 2957. US$2.50-4, including rice and a small salad. Open 6am-10pm.) She can also get in touch with a local **tour guide** (US$10-15). The **ANAM office,** in the middle of the island, can also arrange tours. Open M-F

8am-4pm. They answer the public phone in front of the office (☎995 8002). *(The easiest transportation is to take a taxi from Pedasí (US$20-25 each way). Alternatively, take a bus from Las Tablas toward Tonosí and get off at the entrance to the dirt road for the port. It is a 3km walk along the road; some travelers report that you can catch a ride from a passing car (though Let's Go does not recommend hitchhiking). There are 3 buses a day from Las Tablas directly to the port, leaving at 6, 10am and 2pm, and returning at 7:30, 11:45am, and 3pm; all these buses pass through the town of Cañas. Check with the bus drivers in Las Tablas for the latest schedule. Buses pass through Pedasí for the town of Cañas (see Pedasí Transportation, p. 293). Island admission US$10, for Panamanians US$4. The ANAM office is closed on the weekends.)*

CHIRIQUÍ PROVINCE

Located on the southwest extreme of Panama, Chiriquí is the Central American traveler's dream: enticing rainforests, endless beaches, and sky-scraping volcanoes. Choose your own kilometer of beach on Playa Las Lajas or head to the Golfo de Chiriquí and see some impressive wildlife. The northern highlands have striking views of Volcano Barú, the highest point in Panama. In these cloud-covered hills above the valley hold hot springs, lakes, and the elusive quetzal. Remote villages, only a few hours north from the provincial capital **David,** sit at the base of gorgeous mountain trails. Even if you're not a hiker, Boquete and **Cerro Punta** are pleasant spots to spend a few days. After a grueling day outside, you can sit down to world-renowned coffee, mounds of strawberries, and locally-grown beef. *Chiricanos* are proud of their land and their origins, and it's easy to see why.

DAVID

David (pop. 124,500) is the second largest city in Panama and the capital of the rich commercial and manufacturing province of Chiriquí. Hot and humid year-round, with impressively few tourist attractions for its size, David functions for most as a pit stop to Bocas del Toro, the Chiriquí highlands, and San José, Costa Rica. Fitness gyms, low-rider trucks, and a Top-40 radio station hint at the town's cosmopolitan aspirations, though its nightlife and cuisine pales in comparison to Panama City. David wakes from its slumber for 10 days in mid-March for the rowdy festival of its patron saint, La Feria de San José. Visitors from other provinces and Costa Rica join to celebrate.

▐ TRANSPORTATION

David is the transportation hub of the region. The large, bustling bus station has bathrooms, restaurants, internet, and luggage storage.

Flights: Aeropuerto Enrique Malek, 4km south of the city. **Aeroperlas** (☎721 1195), on C. Central between Av. A and Av. B Este. Open M-F 8am-5pm, Sa 8am-3pm. Flights to **Bocas del Toro** (30min.; M, W, F 11:20am; US$52) and **Panama City** (1hr.; M-F 7:55am, 12:55, 5:35pm; US$98). **Air Panama** (☎721 0841) on Av. 2 E and C.D N. Open M-F 8am-5pm, Sa 8am-3pm. Flights to: **Panama City** (1hr.; M-F 7:45am, 1:15, 5:15pm, Sa-Su 10:30am, 5:15pm; US$98); **San Jose** (45min.; M, W, F 10:30am; US$175).

Buses: North of Av. Obaldía on Av. 2E. From the main terminal, buses leave for: **Almirante** (4hr., every 30min. 3:30am-7pm, US$7); **Boquete** (1hr., every 30min. 5am-7pm, US$1.50); **Cerro Punta** (2hr., every 15min. 5:30am-8pm, US$2.90) via **Volcán** (1½hr., US$2.50); **Changuinola** (4½hr., every 30min. 3:15am-6:30pm, US$8) via **Chiriquí Grande** (2½hr., US$5); **Divisa** (3½hr., US$7.85); **Panama City** (7hr., every hr. 5:45am-8pm, US$12.60; express 6hr., 10:45pm and midnight, US$15) via **Santiago** (3hr., US$7.50); **Penonomé** (5hr., US$9.90); **Puerto Armuelles** (1½hr., every 15min. 3:45am-10:30pm, US$3) via the **Costa Rican border at Paso Canoas** (1¼hr., US$2.25); **San José, CRA** (8hr., daily 8:30am, US$16). PADAFRONT (☎774 9205) has a terminal on Av. 1E (9 de Enero), just south of Av. Obaldía. Buses go to **Panama City** (7hr., every 1½hr. 7:30am-7:45pm, US$12.50; express 6hr., 10:45pm and midnight, US$15).

Car Rental: Most major rental agencies have offices at the airport 4km outside of the city. **Budget** (☎775 5597; open M-Sa 7am-7pm, Su 8am-11am) and **Hertz** (☎775 8471) next to the Super 99 in San Mateo. **National** (☎721 0000) and **Thrifty** (☎721 2477) have better rates online. Cars from US$20 per day.

⚞ ⁊ ORIENTATION AND PRACTICAL INFORMATION

David is laid out in a grid, cut off from the *parque central* by the busy diagonal **Av. Obaldía** and to the northwest by the **Interamerican Highway**. North-south *avenidas* are numbered with *oeste* (west) and *este* (east) designations, starting on either side of **Avenida Central**. East-west *calles* have similiar *norte* (north) and *sur* (south) designations with letters increasing to the north and south from **Calle Central**. Many of the streets are now labeled by names instead of numbers—for example, Av. 3E is now Av. Bolivar, Av. 1 E is 9 de Enero, and C. A Sur is called Ruben D. Samudio, but locals stick to the old alphanumeric combinations. Few of the roads are actually labeled. The *parque central*, **Parque**

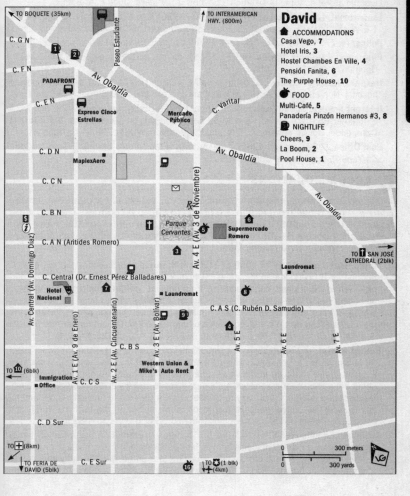

David

🏠 ACCOMMODATIONS
Casa Vego, **7**
Hotel Iris, **3**
Hostel Chambes En Ville, **4**
Pensión Fanita, **6**
The Purple House, **10**

🍴 FOOD
Multi-Café, **5**
Panadería Pinzón Hermanos #3, **8**

🍸 NIGHTLIFE
Cheers, **9**
La Boom, **2**
Pool House, **1**

Cervantes, lies between Av. 3/4 E. and C. A/B N. Most services are south of the *parque*, while the bus terminal and most of the shopping are north.

Tourist Office: ATP (☎775 2839), on C. Central between C. 5E and Av. 6E. Has some maps. Little English spoken. Open M-F 7:30am-3:30pm. **ANAM** (☎775 3163), on the road to the airport. Turn left onto Av. 8E at the Delta gas station. The main office for Parque Internacional La Amistad and Volcán Barú. May be able to arrange a guide at some of the ranger stations. English spoken. Open M-F 8am-4pm.

Consulate: Costa Rica C. B N. and Av. 1 E. (☎774 1923), 2 blocks west of the *parque*, across the street from the Policlinica on the 2nd floor. Open M-F 8am-12pm and 1-3pm.

Bank: Citibank, Av. Central and C. B N. (☎775 3988). Open M-F 8am-3pm, Sa 9am-noon. **24hr. ATM. Western Union,** inside Supermercado Romero in San Mateo. Open M-Sa 9am-1pm and 2-6pm.

Luggage storage: At the bus station. US$0.50-2 per piece. Open 6am-8pm.

Laundromat: Lavamático Los Primos (☎6908 3926), C. E N. between Av. Central and Av. 1 E. Wash US$0.75; dry US$0.75; soap US$0.25. Open M-Sa 7am-8pm, Su 9am-8pm.

Police: (☎775 2210), on C. F Sur and Av. 4 Este (Av. 3 de Noviembre).

Pharmacy: Farmacia Revilla (☎777 8515), on the northeast corner of the *parque*. Open daily 7am-11pm. AmEx/MC/V.

Hospital: Hospital Chiriquí, C. Central and Av. 3 Oeste (☎774 0128). A modern, private hospital. Non-emergency service M-F 9:30am-1:30pm and 2:30-6:30pm, Sa 9am-1pm.

Internet Access: Speed Explorer, C. Central (☎730 3541), between Av. 2 E and Av. 3 E. Internet US$0.75 per hr. Open M-Sa 8am-midnight, Su 10am-11pm. **Río Internet Cafe,** on Av. Bolívar between C. D N. and C. C N. Internet US$0.75 per hr. Open 24hr.

Post Office: C. C N. (☎775 4261), 1 block north of the *parque*. Open M-F 7am-5:30pm, Sa 7am-4:30pm. **Postal Code:** 0426.

ACCOMMODATIONS

There are numerous sleeping options in David, especially around the *parque central*. They range from expensive hotels to cheap *pensiones*. The two good hostels in town are both a bit of a hike from the town center in safer, more residential neighborhoods. Make reservations in advance if visiting during March, when the city's festival takes place.

Purple House Hostel (☎774 4059 or 6428 1488; www.purplehousehostel.com), on C. C Sur and Av. 6 Oeste. True to its name, this homey building is completely covered in purple—even the staff wears purple clothing. It's a popular spot for people passing through, and offers Wi-Fi, TV, free coffee, a book exchange, a public kitchen, cheap laundry service, luggage storage, and huge binders of information about destinations around Panama. The friendly American owner is a good source of info herself. Watch out for her mischievous dog, Cutsie. Dorms US$7.70; private room US$20, with A/C US$25. MC/V. ❷

Bambu Hostel (☎730 2966; www.bambuhostel.com), on C. Virgencito. With the Super 99 in San Mateo to your back, walk right and bear left at the gas station. Turn left after a junkyard and then right at the small store. Whew. A long walk from the city center and about 5min. from nearby services, but a nice place to stay if you're just passing through. The backyard pool is a great way to combat David's year-round humidity. Other amenities include free coffee, pancake mix (cook them yourself in the kitchen), Wi-Fi, and computers. Dorms US$8; private rooms with A/C US$25, with bath US$30. ❷

Chambres En Ville (☎6404 6203), Av. 5 E, between C. B and C. A Sur. A friendly family has opened up a number of rooms onto their large backyard, which is home to an outdoor public kitchen and a pool. Clean rooms sleep up to 3 and come with hot water, private baths, and Wi-Fi. Rooms US$15-25, with A/C US$20-30. Prices rise in high season. ❸

Hotel Iris (☎775 2251), on the south side of the *parque*. Iris has been around for more than 30 years, longer than most of the buildings in the area. Clean but unremarkable rooms come with hot water and TVs. Doubles US$18, with A/C US$25; triples US$25/40. MC/V. ❸

Pensión Fanita (☎775 3718), on C. B N., just off Av. 5 E. A green facade masks a labyrinth of rooms, a sheltered courtyard, and an attached restaurant (*comida corriente* US$2). Conveniently located near the *parque*, this *pensión* has the cheapest rooms in David. Fan US$1. US$5 per person, with bath US$7.50, with A/C US$9. ❶

🍴 FOOD

Comida típica is everywhere, but there isn't too much in the way of international cuisine aside from the occasional pizza shop or Chinese place. You can buy groceries at **Supermercado Baru,** Av. 3 Oeste and C. D N. (☎774 4344. Open M-Sa 7:30am-11pm, Su 8am-9pm. MC/V.) There is also a 24hr. **Super 99** (☎777 3694) in San Mateo with a pharmacy, bank, and several **ATMs.**

Java Juice (☎730-3794), on Av. Francisco Clark north of the bus station, and in San Mateo across from the Super 99. Great health food. On the menu are salads (US$1.60), burgers (US$1.80-3), and all-natural veggie-burgers. Amazing *batidos* (shakes) are made with 100% natural ingredients. Wi-Fi. Open M-Sa 10am-11pm, Su 10am-2pm. ❶

Restaurante Multi Café (☎775 4695), on the *parque*, underneath Hotel Occidental. Very popular, very cheap *típico*. Eclectic—the food is a blend of Chinese (chicken lo mein US$1.80) and Panamanian dishes. Try *guacho*, a local soup with rice (US$1.50). Open daily 6am-10pm. AmEx/MC/V. ❶

Panadería Pinzón Hermanos #3 (☎775 5194), on Av. 5E across from Pensión Costa Rica. By day a mild-mannered bakery (pastries US$0.50), by night a happening sandwich and burger joint (US$1.30-2.50), with a few *típico* options (US$1-2). Open M-Sa 7am-9pm, Su 9am-7pm. ❶

Restaurante Casa Vegetariana (☎6903 4465), on C. Central and Av. 2E. Super cheap cafeteria-style vegetarian dishes. Servings US$0.30. Open M-Sa 6:45am-4pm. ❶

Tambu Country (☎774 4951), on the corner of Av. 4 Este and Av. E Sur. A popular local pizza place serves all kinds of pasta, light salads, and sandwiches. Recently renovated with indoor and outdoor seating. Entrees US$4-8. Delivery available. Open daily 11am-11pm. AmEx/MC/V. ❸

🎵 🎭 ENTERTAINMENT AND NIGHTLIFE

If you don't feel like hitting the dance floor, catch a movie at **Multicines Nacional,** on Av. 1 E, C. A Sur, adjacent to the Hotel Nacional. (☎774 7889. Tickets US$3.50, M-W US$2.50.)

Opium (☎775 2849), at Av. 4 Oeste and C. Miguel A. Brenes, across the street from the Crown Casino. The swankiest club in David, popular with university students. The music is loud, and covers everything from electronica and reggaeton to salsa and merengue. Wear long pants and shoes. Cover men US$5, women US$3. W ladies night; free entry 9-11pm. F university night; US$1 for students. Open W, F, Sa 9pm-4am. Cash only.

Top Place Billars (☎774 2129), on C. Miguel A. Brenes across from the Super 99. Second-floor billiards bar that consistently attracts a local crew. Drinks are cheap and pool tables plentiful. Beer US$0.60. Mixed drinks US$1. Open 11am-late. Cash only.

Crown Casino (☎775 4447), at Av. 4 Oeste and C. Miguel A. Brenes, across the street from Super 99 in San Mateo. Panamanians love to gamble, and this is the hottest spot to roll the dice. They also have a popular sports bar. Beer US$1. Open 24hr. AmEx/MC/V.

✦ BORDER CROSSING: COSTA RICA

PASO CANOAS: BORDER WITH COSTA RICA Unappealing Paso Canoas, on the Interamerican Highway, is the principal crossing between Panama and Costa Rica. To get to the border, take one of the frequent **buses** from David, 50km east of Paso Canoas. They may ask you to show proof of onward travel; either an onward plane or bus ticket will suffice. They also may ask for proof of sufficient funds, so you may have to show that you have at least US$300; this can be done with cash or a bank statement.

Entering Costa Rica, you first need to stop at the Panamanian **Servicio Nacional de Migración** (☎727 6508; open daily 7am-11pm), the large building in the middle of the road where the bus lets you off. They will ask to see your **passport** and the **tourist card** you received upon entering Panama. Then you must walk 100m along the road to the Costa Rican Equivalent, **Dirección General de Migración** (☎2732 2150; open 6am-10pm), where you will need to present your **passport, proof of onward travel,** and **proof of sufficient funds.** If you do not have an onward ticket from Costa Rica, you will need to buy a bus ticket, so it is best to prepare for this beforehand. For proof of funds, a bank statement with US$300 is best, though cash will also do. Entering Panama, the process is the same, but you must buy a tourist card for US$5 at the **Autoridad de Turismo** (☎727 6524; open 7am-11pm) inside the same building as immigration. Customs may ask to search your bags on either side of the border.

In Panama, the **police** are a few feet from the border. (☎727 6521.) **Bolsijeros,** identifiable by the leather purses slung across their chests, congregate around the *Migración* building on the Panamanian side and offer good rates for currency exchange. There are also numerous **ATMs.** To get to **Banco Nacional de Panamá,** turn left before the crossing and walk 50m. They have a **24hr. ATM.** (☎727 6522. Open M-F 8am-3pm, Sa 9am-noon. MC/V.) The Panamanian **post office** is on the second floor of the main building. (Open M-F 8am-5pm, Sa 8am-4pm.) On the Panamanian side, just before the border, **Tourist Travel Internet,** above Café Raúl, has Wi-Fi and computers. (☎727 7220. US$0.75 per hr. Open 8am-midnight.)

In Costa Rica, the police are just across the border. (☎2732 2402.) Next to the police building is a bank, which offers *colones* (right machine) and US dollars (left machine). On the left is the Costa Rican post office. (Open M-F 8am-noon and 1-5pm.)

There aren't many places to spend the night, but **Cabinas Familiares ❷,** tucked away across the street from the Costa Rican Migración building, has a group of rooms opening onto a surprisingly nice garden. Parking available. Rooms hasve private baths. (☎732 2653. Singles ¢5000; doubles ¢10,000, with A/C ¢18,000; triples ¢15,000. US dollars accepted.) There is an overabundance of *típico* and men hawking fried food and fruit. For some tasty bread and a quick escape from the bustle of the border, try **Musmanni,** a small bakery behind the Costa Rican post office. (☎2732 1782. Empanadas ¢375. Open 5am-9pm.)

BOCAS DEL TORO PROVINCE

North of Chiriquí Province, the archipelago of Bocas del Toro (pop. 89,000) gives its name to the province and capital. Drawing travelers with an entirely different siren song than its southern neighbor, Bocas del Toro doesn't promise cool temperatures or high-altitude thrills, but rather its own distinct Caribbean allure. You'll hear Spanish give way to a dense mix of English creole and indigenous languages known as *Guari-guari*. Watch rugged forests and ranchlands melt into beaches, mangroves, and mossy docks that frame island life. The banana industry made Bocas del Toro a point of entry for immigrants and money in the 19th century. Today it attracts foreigners with its natural wonders: white sand islands, coral-rich underwater views, hikes through untouched vegetation, and great surfing spots. In addition to the Ngöbe (NO-beh), Bribrí, and Naso tribes, inhabitants include a mix of Latino and Afro-Caribbean peoples. Many islands, reflecting the local multi-lingual stew and Columbus's overzealous naming practices, have more than one name.

The archipelago is made up of six large islands (Colón, Bastimentos, Cristóbal, Popa, Cayo Nancy, and Cayo Caranero) and several smaller ones. Called "Bocas Isla" by the *bocatoreños*, Isla Colón is the main base for visiting the archipelago. It is also ground zero for Panama's backpacker scene. If you're looking for all-night partying, an international crowd, great cuisine, and hostels, look no further. If you prefer a laid-back Caribbean vibe, Bastimentos, just a few minutes away by boat, is the place to go.

BOCAS DEL TORO AND ISLA COLÓN

Bocas is equal parts Caribbean village and international backpacker destination. The island gives off a lazy island vibe, but still offers some of the best nightlife, food, and hostels in Panama. The slow pace of life here is infectious—Bocas is notorious for persuading visitors to put their travel plans on hold. Ambitious travelers can work in a few side trips during their stay, to Isla Bastimentos, Boca del Drago, and other nearby islands. The town swings its hips a little on November 16, when a parade celebrates the founding of the province.

▶ TRANSPORTATION

Flights: The airport is on Av. F and C. 6. From the park, walk 1 block north and 3 blocks west. **Nature Air** (☎6692 1983; www.natureair.com) flies to **San Jose** (1hr.; W, F, Su 12:30pm; US$158). **Air Panama** (☎757 9841; open 6:45am-5pm) has daily flights to **Panama City** (1hr., 8am and 4:45pm, US$98). **Aeroperlas** (☎757 9341, open 7am-5pm) has flights to **Changuinola** (15min., daily 7:30am and 4pm, US$22) and **Panama City** (1hr., daily 9am and 5pm, US$98). Call ahead to check schedules, as they change frequently.

Ferries: (☎6615 6674). Leave from the southern tip of town (1½hr., M-Sa 4pm, US$1.50).

Local Boats: Locals with boats hang out at the public docks south of the police station or at the Bocas Marine Tours pier on C. 3. Most fares are set. To: **Isla Carinero** (US$1) and **Old Bank** (US$3). Prices higher at night. Armando (☎6439 7439) is reliable, friendly, and fair.

Water Taxis: Bocas Marine Tours (☎757 9033), on C.3 between Av. B and C. **Taxi 25,** next to the police station on C.1. Water taxis go to Almirante (30min., every 30min. 6am-7:30pm, US$4).

Ground transportation: Getting around the island can be done by taxi or *colectivo*. Taxis charge US$0.50 per person within town, but special trips across the island cost upwards of US$15. *Colectivos* leave from the *parque* to **Bocas del Drago** (35min., 7 per day 5am-5:30pm, US$2.50). **Caribe Shuttle** (☎757 7048; www.caribeshuttle) runs daily trips from Bocas to **Puerto Viejo, CRA** (daily 8:30am, US$32). Caribe Shuttle also offers door-to-door service for any of the nearby islands. Book a day in advance with your destination hotel and passport.

Rentals: Ixa's Bicycle World (☎6717 5379), on Av. H Nte. Bikes US$2 per hr., US$10 per day. Open M-Sa 8am-6pm. **Lau's Bicycles and Scooters,** on C. 3 across from the park. Bikes and rusting scooters US$15 per hr., US$45 per day. **Bocas Water Sports** (☎757 9541; www.bocaswatersports.com), on C. 3 near Bocas Marine Tours. Single kayak US$3 per hr., US$10 per half-day, US$18 per day. Double kayak US$5 per hr., US$20 per ½-day, US$35 per day. MC/V.

✈ 🛈 ORIENTATION AND PRACTICAL INFORMATION

Bocas is laid out in an L-shaped grid. Numbered *calles* run north-south and lettered *avenidas* run east-west, though you won't find too many street signs. Directions are usually given by landmarks. With the docks behind you, north is to the right and south is to the left. Just about everything is on **Calle 3,** the wide main street, or on **Calle 1,** farther east. The water cuts across the grid from C. 3 at the south end of town to C. 1 at the east end. A small park lies between C. 2 and 3 and Av. D and E. **Avenida G,** at the northern end of town, is the main strip leading to the rest of the island.

Tourist Office: (☎757 9642), near the police station in a large yellow and white wooden house on C.1. Maps of the city and some information exhibits. English spoken. Open M-F 7:30am-3:30pm. **ANAM** (☎757 9244), next to Barco Hundido on C.1. Runs the Parque Nacional Marino Isla Bastimentos. Entry US$10, students US$5. Camping US$10.

Bank: Banco Nacional Panama, C. 4 and Av. E (☎757 9230). **24hr. ATM.** Open M-F 8am-2pm, Sa 9am-noon. There is also a 24hr. ATM next to the police station.

Laundromat: Lavamático Don Pardo (☎757 9487), next to Mondo Taitú on Av. G. Wash and dry US$3.50 per load. Open M-Sa 8am-8pm.

Police: (☎757 9217), on the southern end of C.1 before it ends at the water.

Pharmacy: Farmacia Rosa Blanca (☎757 9566), on C. 3 south of the *parque* near Bocas Marine Tours. Open M-Sa 8:30am-9pm, Su 10am-noon and 7-9pm. Cash only.

Hospital: Av. G (☎757 9201). From the park, walk north to Av. G (Hostal Mondo Taitú), then turn left and walk a few blocks west. Open M-F 7am-4pm. Emergency service 24hr.

Internet: Bocas Internet Cafe (☎757 9390), on C. 3 next to the supermarket Isla Colón. Internet US$0.50 per 15min. **Internet Micro,** next to La Buga. Skype, Wi-Fi, and new computers. US$2 per hr. Open M-Sa 9am-10pm, Su 9am-7pm. **Boca's Cyber Shop** (☎757 7035), across the street from the police. US$1 per hr.

Post Office: (☎757 9321), inside the government building on the northern side of the *parque.* Open M-F 8am-noon and 1-3pm.

🏠 ACCOMMODATIONS

Bocas is blessed with excellent hotels, not to mention the best hostels in Panama. Dorm rooms range from US$10-12, and private rooms start at US$20. Accommodations fill up in the high season (Dec.-Apr.), so make reservations. If you can't find a room, many families will rent out rooms in their house, so ask around.

Casa Max (☎757 9120), north of town at the beginning of Av. G and across from Mondo Taitú. Attractive, well-kept wooden rooms and ample outdoor space. All rooms have private baths with hot water. Splurge for the Caribbean-style deck with a hammock. Free Wi-Fi. Doubles US$25, with decks US$35; triples US$35. D/MC/V. ❸

Mondo Taitú (☎757 9425), north of town at the beginning of Av. G. B. A maze of wooden rooms and staircases built around a tree, Mondo has a cult following among backpackers. Free bike rentals, make-your-own pancake sessions every morning, and one of the most popular bars in town all ensure that the legacy lives on. If you want a good night's sleep, it might not be the best spot. Next-door, they have quieter rooms with A/C. Free Wi-Fi. Dorms US$10; rooms US$12. ❷

Hostal Gran Kahuna (☎757 9038 or 6732 2345; www.grankahunabocas.com), on C. 3 south of the *parque*. This recently remodeled hostel has a less party-oriented atmosphere. Probably the best spot for a good night's sleep. Large common area has computers (US$1.75 per hr.), games, and a kitchen. Shell out for the upstairs rooms, which are breezier and have balconies. Lockers included. Free Wi-Fi. Rooms US$10-12. Cash only. ❷

Hostal Heike (☎757 9708), on C. 3 just off the park. Mondo Taitú's cleaner, somewhat quieter sister hostel has a great rooftop deck with a lounge area and computers. Downstairs is a kitchen and a book exchange. All rooms are dorm style, with shared baths and lockers. Ask about their free Spanish lessons. Free Wi-Fi in lobby. Rooms US$10, with A/C US$12. ❷

Hotel del Parque (☎757 9008), on the eastern side of the *parque*. One of the quietest spots in town, despite its central location. A step above the rest. A pleasant front garden complements a back deck with hammocks. Rooms have A/C, fans, hot water, cable TV, and large orthopedic mattresses. Kitchen available. Free Wi-Fi. Doubles US$50; triples US$55. ❹

FOOD

Bocas has everything from fast-food and *típico* to classy Italian and Asian fusion. The prices might inspire a little sticker shock—even the produce and supermarkets are a bit more expensive than on the mainland. The cheapest food is local *bocatareño* food, usually seafood or chicken with coconut-lime sauce and coconut rice. Bocas doesn't have clean tap water, though some places have filters. For groceries, visit **Isla Colon**, on C. 3 just south of the *parque*. (☎757 9591. Open daily 7am-11:30pm.) Around the corner, they also operate a produce stand. (Open daily 8am-10:30pm.)

La Casbah, next to Mondo Taitú at the northern end of C. 3. Fresh food cooked with Mediterranean flair. Though the prices may not be the friendliest, they could easily charge more for the quality. Fish of the day US$9. Entrees US$8-12. Open Tu-Sa 6pm-10pm. Cash only. ❹

Lili's Café (☎6829 4600), near the police station along the water, on the diagonal connecting C. 1 and C. 3. Breakfast all day—try Lili's Omelette (US$7.50), the house special, with "killin' me, man" sauce. Open M-F 7am-11pm, Sa 7am-4pm, Su 7am-1pm. Cash only. ❸

Om Café (☎6624 0898), behind the municipal building between C. 1 and C. 3. Locally celebrated by long-term gringo residents, Om deserves the attention. Authentic Indian cuisine and ambience—feels closer to Goa than Bocas. Entrees US$7-11. Beer US$1.50. Open Tu and F-Su 8am-noon and 6pm-10pm. Cash only. ❹

Lemongrass Restaurant and Bar, next to Lili's Café near the police station. Asian fusion (like Thai tacos) on the breezy deck of a wooden building. The chef uses fresh produce and fish, so the menu changes daily. Dinner (US$10-12) is pricey, but lunch (US$5-6) is a good value. Cash only. ❸

Starfish Coffee, on the southern part of C. 3 along the water, next to La Buga. The best coffee shop in town has a cozy interior with books and a large selection of National Geographics. They serve the best breakfast in town. Coffee US$1.25. Salads US$7. Sandwiches US$5. Entrees US$8-12. Open M-Sa 8am-10pm, Su 9am-10pm. Cash only. ❹

The Reef (☎757 9336), at the southern end of C. 3. Tasty *bocatareño* food right by the sea. Excellent seafood is accompanied by rice, potatoes, or *patacones* (US$6-8). Beer US$1.25. Open daily 10am-10pm. Cash only. ❸

Golden Grill (☎757 9650), on C. 3 next to the *parque*. If food prices around town have got you on the bread diet, Golden Grill will be your salvation. The best value in town—cheaper than a lot of *típico* options. Free Wi-Fi. Fast food US$4. Open daily 7am-10pm. Cash only. ❷

🄖 SIGHTS

From Bocas town, Av. G leads west and eventually bends right across a small isthmus to the main body of the island. From here, the road forks: the left side leads 15km through the middle of the island past La Gruta to Boca del Drago, while the right side follows the eastern coast, passing through Big Creek, Playa Paunch, and Playa Bluff along the way. Many of these beaches are infested with *chitras* (tiny sandflies with an irritating bite), especially in the late afternoon. Biking is a great way to get around the island, though you should make sure your wheels are in working order, as the roads are hilly and often muddy. There are also *colectivos* and minibuses that go to Bocas del Drago and back a few times per day.

EASTERN BEACHES. Just north of town is a string of relatively easily accessible beaches. **Playa Paunch** is a surf spot, popular with locals, who can be territorial about the waves. The best of these beaches, farther north, is relatively *chitra*-free **Playa Bluff**. The sandy beach stretches almost 2km, with good surfing and casual swimming when the surf isn't too strong. Between May and July, the beach attracts sea turtles laying their eggs; ask ANAM (p. 304) for information. *(Playa Bluff is about 8km north of Bocas town; biking takes around 45min. Taxis US$10-15.)*

BOCA DEL DRAGO. On the western side of the island, 8km past La Gruta on a hilly road, you'll find laid-back Boca del Drago. Beautiful beaches and a coral reef are just a few meters from shore. There are only a few buildings along the water, and almost no services. For parts of the year, you may be able to stay overnight at **Cabañas Estefany.** From May 15 to August 15 and from December to January, the *cabañas* are generally rented out to the Institute of Tropical Ecology, but you may be able to scrounge an extra room of camp on the property. *(Minibuses leave for Boca del Drago. 35min., 7 per day 5am-5:30pm, US$2.50. Biking takes more than an hour, and it's a hilly ride. Cabañas Estefany ☎6624 9246; ask for Chino or Fátima. Camping US$5; dorms with separate bath US$15; private cabins with bath and kitchen US$35.)*

ISLA DE PÁJAROS OF SWAN CAYE, WRECK ROCK, AND SAIL ROCK. About 15min. by boat from Boca del Drago, Isla de Pájaros, part of the greater Swan Caye, attracts hundreds of seabirds which circle a huge rock and a few hardy trees. There's a coral reef with excellent deep-water snorkeling right off the island, but the water isn't always clear, especially after it rains. Just past Pájaros are two smaller rocky islands: Wreck Rock, which looks like the wreck of a ship, and Sail Rock, a phallic rock sticking straight out of the water. *(Tour operators in Bocas all offer trips here; contact them for transportation.)*

LA GRUTA CAVE. A series of two long, dark caves with plenty of bats and even more bat guano, La Gruta is a religious shrine and the site of an annual pilgrimage celebrating Nuestra Señora de la Gruta, la Virgen del Carmen. The celebration of the Virgin occurs on July 16th, with the procession to the cave on the following Sunday. *(La Colonia Santeña, where a short trail leads to the cave, is about 6km*

from town. Bring a flashlight and good boots. If you haven't had enough after the first cave, a dark,
wet 50m walk, there is another one about 30min. farther along the trail. US$1 per person.)

ISLA CARENERO. Just a few hundred meters east of Bocas town, *chitra*-infested
Isla Carenero is practically on Isla Colón. On the eastern point of the island,
black rock is a popular surfing break good for beginners. Most of the restaurants on the island are rather expensive and cater to the yachting crew, but if
you need to grab something to eat, the prices at **Restaurante Doña Maria ❸** are
fairly reasonable. (☎757 9551. Sandwiches US$5. Salads US$7. Entrees US$7-10.
Open 7am-10pm. MC/V). Most backpackers come to the island for **Aqua Lounge**
(see **Nightlife,** below), which throws the biggest parties around. Believe it or
not, people also stay here, though you probably won't get much sleep if you do.
(www.bocasaqualounge.com. Dorms US$10.) They have a diving board and a
waterside trampoline. *(Local boatmen take you to the isle; US$1.)*

NIGHTLIFE

Bocas town is one of the biggest party destinations in Central America for
backpackers, especially between December and February. That said, there are
only a few spots in town where it really goes down. It's a small island, so those
spots won't be hard to find. If you're looking for something more relaxed, most
restaurants have full-service bars. On Sunday night, there's usually a drum
circle in the park. You might catch the locally-famous Beach Boys de Bastimentos, a calypso band rumored to have once played for 15hr. straight. Ask
around to see if they are playing.

Aqua Lounge (www.bocasaqualounge.com), on Isla Carinero. Boats to the island US$1.
Parties every night. Crowds of people, mostly gringos, take the short boat ride and dance
until the wee hours of the morning. The dance floor is along the water. There's even a
diving board (maybe try it before the 3rd drink). Beer US$2.

Barco Hundido, on C.1 just east of the park near Taxi 25. Keeps the party going until
late. Most of the serious dancing is done on land, but you can also head off onto the
series of interconnected floating docks surrounding a sunken boat just off the shore.
When the party really gets crazy, it sometimes moves onto *Barco Loco,* a party boat
(well, a platform on top of 2 canoes). Beer US$2. Mixed drinks US$3. Open M-Tu and
Th-Su 9am-3am.

Mondo Taitú (see **Accommodations,** p. 304). This hostel has one of the most popular
bars in town. It's a great spot to meet fellow travelers, and beer is cheap (US$1). Happy
hour 7-8pm; beer US$0.50. Cocktail hour 8pm-9pm; US$1 off. Open until midnight.

Bar El Encanto, across the street from Hostal Gran Kahuna. A wooden building over the
water attracts a local crowd. A good place to meet townies, though women may feel a
little too welcome. Beer US$0.70. Open M-F 12:30pm-midnight, Sa-Su 12:30pm-3am.
Cash only.

WATERSPORTS AND GUIDED TOURS

DIVING AND SNORKELING. As the local economy is almost entirely dependent
on tourism, nearly every hotel, restaurant, dock, shack, and patch of grass
offers some form of rental. The archipelago is covered in dive spots. For beginners, the closer spots are best. **Hospital Point** is a great spot for divers and snor-
kelers alike, with a 100 ft. deep wall to explore. **Barco Hundido** is an artificial
reef the Smithsonian Institute created by sinking a boat near Isla Colón. Just
south of Bocas town is **Punta Manglar.** The **Playground** is the nearest dive, though
its proximity means that it's often crowded, and the fish are better elsewhere.
Around Bastimentos, **La Covita,** on the north side, has underwater caverns.

South of Cayo Nancy (Isla Solarte) is a huge coral reef with great visibility. One of the best dives around, **Tiger Rock,** is on the far eastern side of Bastimentos.

There are many dive schools in town, with prices generally around US$60 for a half-day, two-tank dive, as well as certification and trips for non-certified divers. The newest, PADI-certified **La Buga,** on C.3 between Av. A and B, has good instructors and new equipment. For certified divers, a half-day two-tank dive costs US$60, and a night dive (1 tank) is US$50. They also offer a certification course for US$265 and a full-day discovery crash course for non-certified divers for US$90. Dives change daily depending on time of year and conditions, though they try to accommodate diver requests. (☎757 9534; www.labugapanama.com. AmEx/MC/V.) For snorkeling, most dive shops run tours (US$20-25) with gear included.

SURFING. Crowds of surfers come to Bocas for the large waves, which are best in the winter months. On Isla Colón, **Playa Bluff** is the most popular spot for tourists, while **Playa Paunch,** a bit closer, has a territorial local crowd. On the eastern side of Isla Carenero, **Black Rock** can be a good place for beginners. **Wizard's Beach** and **Playa Larga,** on the northern side of Bastimentos, have some of the biggest waves, though they are not recommended for beginners, as the riptides are strong. **Hostal Gran Kahuna** (see **Accommodations,** p. 304) offers lessons and rents boards (US$10-15). La Buga Dive Center also runs classes. Ask for Panama's national champ Juan Pi Caraballo. (Full day US$89, half US$49.)

CATAMARAN SAILING AND SNORKELING. One family runs daily catamaran tours that stop at some of the best destinations for snorkeling and fishing. Boats leave from Av. Sur at the southern tip of the island at 9:30am and return at 5pm. Prices include lunch, fruit, and a drink. (☎757 9710 or 6464 4242; www.bocassailing.com. US$40 per person or US$33 for students.)

ISLA BASTIMENTOS

If the flood of party-oriented backpackers on Bocas doesn't appeal to you, Bastimentos offers a sample of authentic Caribbean life with a lot fewer tourists. Most boats arrive in the small town of Old Bank, from which it is a short walk to kilometers of beautiful beach. The island is also home to a Ngöbe village and Parque Nacional Marino Bastimentos, the region's best protected natural area, though getting there is either an expensive boat ride or a very long walk.

▐ TRANSPORTATION

Getting to Isla Bastimentos from Bocas del Toro is easy. Local **boats** leave from the pier of Bocas Marine Tours on C. 3 and head to Old Bank (6am-6pm, more frequent in the morning; US$2 per person, after dark US$5). To reach **Cayos Zapatillos** or the other side of the island, your best bet is the tour operators, who generally leave in the morning between 9-10am.

▐ ▐ ORIENTATION AND PRACTICAL INFORMATION

The village of Old Bank has no roads, only a semi-paved footpath running along the water. With your back to the water, east is to your right and west to the left. The little park is toward the western end, as are most of the docks, where you can catch a boat to the end. The island is crisscrossed by trails, most of which are hard to follow and poorly marked.

Tours: The Dutch Pirate (☎6567 1812; www.thedutchpirate.com), at the far eastern end of the trail over the water. Leads scuba tours and certification courses in Dutch, English, German, and Spanish. 2-tank dive US$55. Certification course US$225, includes 2-tank dive at the end. Surfboard rental US$10.

Police: (☎757 9757), in front of the main dock.

▮ FOOD

▦ **Island Time Thai Restaurant** (☎6844 7704; islandtimethairestaurant.com), up a hill 7min. from town. Follow the signs from the town center. Authentic Thai cuisine up in the hills overlooking nearby jungle and the ocean. All meals are US$6, a steal for the high quality. Wash it down with some soothing Thai tea (US$1). If you would like to stay (and you probably will), they rent 2 handsome wooden cabins (US$35 per night) with private baths, hot water, decks, and TVs. Open M-Sa noon-8pm. ❷

▦ **Up in the Hill Shop** (☎6570 8277; www.upinthehill.com), just past Island Time Thai. An amazing find in a garden paradise. An Argentinean-Scottish couple do every-thing home-style, from the organic farm and the hand-built house to the beautiful craftsmanship. They sell all-natural body products like insect repellents and soap. Many people just stop by for some organic coffee (US$1) and the unbelievably good cacao-brownies (US$2.50). ❷

Bar and Restaurant Roots (☎6754 1624), over the water across from Hotel Midland. Locals and gringos kick back to reggae, sip on cold beers, and enjoy some delicious local coconut rice and fish. Chicken US$4. Beer US$1. *Cuba libre* US$2. Open daily noon-9pm. ❷

Tacos by Face. Follow the signs from the western end of the path, situated on the wind-ward side of the island. This breezy spot is a great place to cool off. The owner, Face, cooks fish tacos (US$6.50), chicken burritos (US$6), and quesadillas (US$3.50), though beer (US$1.50) is probably the most popular order. Occasional live music. Open daily noon-last customer. ❷

◎ SIGHTS

BEACHES. The island's beaches lie in a string on the northern and eastern coast, and are connected by a series of poorly-marked trails. To get to **Playa Primera,** or "Wizard Beach," follow the sign from the eastern part of Old Bank's main concrete path and proceed 20min. over the island and down the other side. You can also get there along the path that passes Island Time Thai Restaurant and Up in the Hill Shop. The next beach is **Playa Segunda,** also known as "Red Frog Beach" for its amphibian inhabitants. This is a favorite tour destination from Bocas and a good surfing spot in the dry season (30-40min. past Wizard Beach). The next beach is **Playa Polo,** followed by the extensive **Playa Larga,** part of the **Parque Nacional Marino** (p. 311). Beware: extremely strong currents make swimming dangerous at all of these beaches. Furthermore, these beaches are known for harboring thieves, especially Wizard Beach. Leave your watch and other valuables at home and always keep your belongings within sight.

At the opposite end of the island from the town of Old Bank lies **Punta Vieja,** a secluded beach with astonishingly clear water and awesome snorkeling. Many turtles nest here during the night. *(Tour operators in Bocas generally run tours to both the reef and Salt Creek for US$20-25. Entry to Salt Creek US$6 per person.)*

CAYO NANCY. Isla Solarte (or Cayo Nancy) is south of Old Bank. It is most famous for Hospital Point, named after the United Fruit Company hospital that was once located there, and one of the best, most accessible places for snorkel-ing in the area. You'll find a variety of corals, some barely submerged, others 100 ft. deep. Many tours go to Hospital Point, but any boat can take you there. There are a few good places to snorkel in the protected waters between Bocas,

Isla Carenero, Isla Bastimentos, and Cayo Nancy. If you go by boat, make sure you have a ride back, as all of these sites are in open water.

NIGHTLIFE

Cantina La Feria. Bastimentos' main party spot and the best place in the archipelago to hang out with locals. F is reggae night, but "Blue Monday" is when the party really goes down. Beers US$0.75. Party starts at 9pm.

ALMIRANTE

People visit small, run-down Almirante either to hop on a boat out to the Bocas del Toro archipelago or to take a bus to Changuinola or David. Bananas are a big business in this small town. In recent years, the famous banana train has been cast to the wayside in favor of a flood of banana trucks, bringing the harvest from Changuinola to be loaded onto banana ships. There's not much to do in town, but if you have some time to kill waiting for a ferry, enjoy the view of the Almirante while throwing back a few bananas.

TRANSPORTATION

Buses: There are 2 terminals in Almirante. Buses to and from **Changuinola** (45min. every 20min. 5:50am-9pm, US$1.20) leave from the station near to town. With your back to the docks, turn left, and when the road dead ends walk to the right 100m. Buses to **David** (4hr., every 30min. 4am-7pm, US$7) and **Panama City** (11hr., 8am and 7pm, US$23) leave from a bus station about 10min. outside of town on the road between Chiriquí Grande and Changuinola. To get there, instead of turning right after walking from the docks, turn left and continue straight; the station is on the left. Buses to Changuinola also pass by this station.

Ferries: (☎6615 6674). Leave from the opposite side of town (M-Sa 8am, US$1.50).

Water Taxis: Taxi 25 (☎757 9028) and **Bocas Marine Tours** (☎758 4085) go to **Bocas del Toro** (30min., every 30min. 6am-7pm, US$4).

Taxis: Charge US$0.50 within town, and US$1 between the David station and the docks.

ORIENTATION AND PRACTICAL INFORMATION

The main strip in town runs east-west. It begins west of town at the intersection with the road between Chiriquí Grande and Changuinola and ends in the east at the Puerto de Almirante. The bus station to David, at the western intersection, is a 10min walk from town. With your back to the station, turn right and continue straight into town. To get to the dock, take another right about 10min. down the road before a roadside inspection station. If you continue straight and then take the second right after the Changuinola bus station at the large blue Movistar sign, you will arrive in the center of town. Most of the services are within a block of the center.

Bank: Banco Nacional de Panama (☎758 3718). Turn right into town, then take your 1st left and walk 2 blocks. **24hr. ATM.** Open M-F 8am-2pm, Sa 9am-noon.

Police: (☎758 3714), next to the port at the far eastern part of town.

Pharmacy: Farmacia San Vicente (☎758 3535), 2 blocks south of the main road in town just past the supermarket. Open M-Sa 8am-8pm, Su 9am-5pm. MC/V.

Hospital: (☎758 3754), at the southernmost point of town. Turn as if going in to town and continue straight for 3 blocks. Open 7am-3pm. Emergency service 24hr.

Post Office: (☎758 3650), 1 block past the bank. Open M-F 7am-6pm, Sa 7am-2:30pm. **Postal Code:** 0104.

ACCOMMODATIONS

Hostal Puerto Almirante (☎758 3786), across from the bank. If for some reason you can't get to Bocas, Almirante offers adequate, if barren, rooms with wooden floors, private baths, and TVs. Some water and electricity problems, so don't count on either. Doubles US$15; triples with A/C US$25. ❸

FOOD

There are plenty of *típico* options and fruit markets in town. Since groceries are expensive on Isla Colón, it may be worth stocking up at **Supermercado 888,** in the center of town, one block south of the main road. (Open daily 6am-9pm.)

Restaurante Bocas Marina (☎6697 6175). Walk to the far eastern part of town along the main road. With the port in front of you, turn right. A great place to pass the time while waiting for the ferry, with arguably the best view of Almirante Bay. Sandwiches US$1-3. Entrees US$4-6. Open daily 8am-midnight. ❷

SIGHTS

PARQUE NACIONAL MARINO ISLA BASTIMENTOS

Covering 13,156 hectares, of which only 1,630 are land, Parque Nacional Marino Isla Bastimentos comprises much of the interior of Basimentos, all the mangroves to its south, the two precious Cayos Zapatillos farther southeast, and all of the surrounding open water. The park is on the opposite end of the island from Old Bank, and although it is possible to hike to it in 3-4 hours (each way), the trail can be complicated without someone who knows the way. The best way to see the park is on one of the many tours that leave from the docks in the morning. **Playa Larga,** a spectacular 14km beach on the northern part of the park, is an important turtle nesting site from April to September. The interior of the island is home to some fantastic wildlife, including monkeys, sloths, and crocodiles. Farther south is a forest trail that leads to golden beaches and underwater cave formations. There are two ranger stations, one on the more southern of the two Cayos Zaptillos and one on Playa Larga. Camping is allowed (US$10 per night), though you will need to bring everything, including mosquito nets, water, and food. For more professional tours, talk to **ANCON Expeditions** (☎757 9600; www.anconexpeditions.com) on Av. G in Bocas. They run expensive tours to the park as well as to a nearby Ngöbe village.

CHANGUINOLA

Changuinola is hot and dirty, but is home to the border crossing into Costa Rica. It's a good place to run errands and complete any necessary paperwork. The city survives off merchants and banana plantations, many of which offer tours.

TRANSPORTATION

Flights: The airport is at the north end of town; turn right past the gas station. **Air Panama** (☎758 9841) flies to **Panama City** (1hr.; M-Sa 7:15am and 3:50pm, Su 3:50pm; US$98) via **Bocas del Toro** (15min., US$22.40). **Aeroperlas** (☎758 7521) also flies to Panama City (1hr., 8:35am and 4:40pm, US$98).

Buses: Changuinola has 2 bus terminals within 300m of each other on opposite sides of the street. Terminal La Piquera, next to the Shell station in the center of town, handles short-distance travel. There's no timetable, but buses come frequently. Buses to: **Almirante** (45min., every 20min. 5:40am-9:45pm, US$1.20); **Chiriquí Grande** (1½hr., every hr. 7am-2pm, US$5.50); **El Silencio** (20min., every 20min 6am-8:40pm, US$0.65); **Las Tablas** (30min., every 25min. 5:30am-8pm, US$0.80) via the **Costa Rican border at Guabito.** Terminal Urraca (☎ 758 8455), north of Terminal La Piquera. To **David** (4hr., every 30min. 3:15am-7pm, US$8) and **Panama City** (12hr., 7am and 6pm, US$24).

Taxis: *Taxis colectivos* next to Terminal La Piquera. A faster, more comfortable option. To **Guabito** (20min., US$1.20).

⚔🔋 ORIENTATION AND PRACTICAL INFORMATION

Changuinola is strung along the road from the Guabito border in the northwest to Almirante in the southeast. The road to Almirante curves along a traffic circle and turns left to intersect with the main strip. The center of town is marked by the Shell gas station, right next to the Terminal La Piquera. Facing the gas station from **Avenida 17 de Abril**, the town's main street, north is to the left and south is to the right.

Tourist Offices: ANAM (☎758 6603). Head 2 blocks north of La Piquera and turn left at the Western Union sign. Turn left again at the 1st intersection and then right at the mosque. They run the San-San wetlands and the Wetzo entrance to Parque Internacional La Amistad. Open M-F 8am-4pm.

Bank and Currency Exchange: HSBC (☎758 6163), between the 2 terminals. **24hr. ATM.** Open M-F 8am-3:30pm, Sa 9am-noon. Most of the large stores lining the main road will change *colones* for you. **Almacen Zona Libre** (☎758 5468), just south of the terminal. **Western Union** (☎758 9155), inside Super Deportes Sammy, just past the HSBC. Open M-F 8:30am-7:30pm, Sa 8:30am-8:30pm, Su 9:30am-2:30pm. MC/V.

Police: (☎758 2800), at the traffic circle east of the main strip.

Hospital: (☎758 8232). Facing the police station, go right 1 block.

Internet Access: Foto Centro Arco Iris (☎758 8457), across from the terminal on the north side. US$1 per hr. Open M-Sa 8am-7pm. MC/V.

🏠 ACCOMMODATIONS

Changuinola has no shortage of digs, but none of them is spectacular. Electricity and water in Changuinola can be erratic.

Hotel Carol (☎758 8731), 2 blocks south of Terminal La Piquera. Some of the cheapest rooms in town. They seem a bit unfinished, with partially concrete floors and other touches missing, but they all have private baths and much needed A/C. Singles US$14; with TV and hot water US$23; doubles US$16/25. Cash only. ❸

🍴 FOOD

Cheap *típico* dominates the menus, but there are a few surprises mixed in. For groceries, visit **Romero,** just south of the traffic circle, 1 block east from Hotel Carol. (☎758 9834. Open 24hr.) They also have a bakery and pharmacy.

🍽 **El Buen Sabor** (☎758 8422), hidden behind some foliage across the street from Paraíso de Batidos, between the 2 bus stations. This bakery is the best Changuinola has to offer. A wide variety of flaky, fresh-from-the-oven treats neatly sorted into wooden boxes—all for less than a dollar. They also sell pizzas (US$3.25), and a large variety of cool shakes. Cash only. ❶

✕ GUABITO: BORDER WITH COSTA RICA

Guabito is 16km from Changuinola (30min. by bus and 20min. by taxi); Sixaola is across the border in Costa Rica. *Taxis colectivos* (US$1.20) are the fastest way to travel between the two. The Panamanian side of the border is open daily from 8am-6pm and the Costa Rican side is open daily from 7am-5pm. The difference is due to the change in time zones at the border. When entering Panama, you must get an **exit stamp** from the Panamanian immigration, then go across a rickety bridge (the border is technically halfway along the bridge), and get an entrance stamp from the other side at the Costa Rican Immigration (☎2754 2044). When entering Panama, the process is the same, but on the Panama side, you need to buy a **tourist card** from the tourist office (☎759 7985; next to the Immigration Office). Both countries require that you show proof of onward travel; make sure to bring an onward bus or flight ticket. They also may ask you for a copy of your passport and proof of sufficient funds for travel—a bank statement with at least US$300 is best.

For those entering Panama, frequent buses run to Changuinola (30min., every 25min., US$0.80). Catch one at the junction 200m past the border next to the police station. *Taxis colectivos* (US$1.20) are faster. **El Caiman Internacional** and **Mini Super El Poderoso,** both on the left side of the border crossing, change money. The **immigration office** is just before the bridge, and the **police station** is 200m farther down the road. Before the police station on the left is **Abby's Internet.** (US$1 per hr. Open 9am-9pm, Su 10am-3:30pm.) The **post office** is across from the police station. (☎759 7997. Open M-F 8am-5pm, Sa 8am-noon.). On the Costa Rican side, the **police station** (☎2751 2160) is just over the bridge. Guabito has no accommodations and almost no restaurants; Sixaola, just across the border, has better options.

PARQUE INTERNACIONAL AMISTAD (WEKSO) AND NASSO VILLAGES

Getting to Wekso and Bunjik is difficult. Take one of the frequent buses to El Silencio from Changuinola. From El Silencio, both Bunjik and Wekso will arrange transport if you call ahead (US$60 roundtrip for up to 5 people). During the week, public transportation up the river can often be found in the morning. Alternatively, you can walk the 6km up the river. Fortunately, there is a road leading to Bunjik. Many travelers walk or catch a ride with one of the construction-company vehicles that shuttle up and down the dirt road, though Let's Go does not recommend hitchhiking. To walk, head down to the water in El Silencio and pay a boatman US$0.25 to get across the river. From there, follow the road straight and Bunjik will be on the left. To get to Wekso, ask someone in Bunjik to take you back across the river, or call Wekso to arrange for transport. The park entry fee can be paid at the ANAM station, but if they are not there, someone from the communities will collect it. US$10, students US$5.

Although Bocas del Toro contains a considerable chunk of Parque Internacional La Amista (PILA), this side is much less developed and takes a lot of effort to reach. If you are interested in extensive hiking within the park, Chiriquí is a better option (see **Chiriquí,** p. 298). On the Bocas side, the approach to the park begins at Bunjik or Wekso, two villages on opposite sides of the Río Teribe, 6km from El Silencio. From these towns, it is about 1½hr. to the edge of the park. Most people visit in a 5-7hr. full-day trek. Trails are poorly marked and getting lost would be disastrous, so you'll need to take a guide (US$20-30 depending on distance). Bring water, food, sturdy shoes, and insect repellent.

BOCAS DEL TORO PROVINCE

WEKSO. Wekso is not a village at all, but rather the ruins of former dictator Manuel Noriega's notorious Panajungla military training camp. It was used to train soldiers in survival skills. With no use for the land after he was overthrown, the government made it an annex to Parque Internacional Amistad. There is one well-maintained path around Wekso, the 2km **Sendero Las Heliconias.** If you are lucky, you might spot a few monkeys or colorful birds. Although nobody lives at Wekso, **ODESEN,** a cooperative run by the local community, has built a few concrete and wooden cabins among the eerie military ruins. It is best to call in advance as there is not always someone there—ask for Edwin Sanchez. In addition to housing, ODESEN offers a full array of activities including hikes and visits to Nasso communities. (☎ 6574 9874 or 6452 5429; www.odesen. org. Camping US$5. Lodging and three meals US$40 per person.)

BUNJIK AND OTHER NASSO COMMUNITIES. The indigenous Nasso people live in a group of 11 communities around the Río Teribe. Interestingly, the Nasso have the only monarchy left in the western hemisphere; the king resides up the river from Bunjik, the nearest community to El Silencio, 6km up the Teribe. A few hundred Nasso live in wooden houses on stilts. Although tourism is a recent phenomenon for these people, they have a concrete building with running water (but no electricity) and tiled floors where you can sleep. Contact Raúl, the friendly coordinator of tourism program, who can arrange tours to other Nasso communities, nearby hikes, or longer trips into PILA. They can also build a balsa raft to float you back to Silencio on the Teribe, though you and most of your things will get drenched. (Raul ☎ 6569 3869; http://ocen.bocas.com. Dorms US$15. Local meals US$3.50.)

APPENDIX

CLIMATE

AVG. TEMP. (LOW/ HIGH), PRECIP.	JANUARY			APRIL			JULY			OCTOBER		
	°C	°F	mm	°C	°F	mm	°C	°F	mm	°C	°F	mm
Managua, Nicaragua	20-31	68-87	5	23-34	73-93	5	22-31	71-87	134	22-31	71-87	59
San José, Costa Rica	14-24	57-75	15	17-26	62-78	46	17-25	62-77	211	16-25	60-77	300

MEASUREMENTS

Like the rest of the rational world, Costa Rica, Nicaragua, and Panama use the metric system. The basic unit of length is the **meter (m)**, which is divided into 100 **centimeters (cm)** or 1000 **millimeters (mm)**. One thousand meters make up one **kilometer (km)**. Fluids are measured in **liters (L)**, each divided into 1000 **milliliters (mL)**. A liter of pure water weighs one **kilogram (kg)**, which is divided into 1000 **grams (g)**. One metric ton is **1000kg.**

MEASUREMENT CONVERSIONS	
1 inch (in.) = 25.4mm	1 millimeter (mm) = 0.039 in.
1 foot (ft.) = 0.305m	1 meter (m) = 3.28 ft.
1 yard (yd.) = 0.914m	1 meter (m) = 1.094 yd.
1 mile (mi.) = 1.609km	1 kilometer (km) = 0.621 mi.
1 ounce (oz.) = 28.35g	1 gram (g) = 0.035 oz.
1 pound (lb.) = 0.454kg	1 kilogram (kg) = 2.205 lb.
1 fluid ounce (fl. oz.) = 29.57mL	1 milliliter (mL) = 0.034 fl. oz.
1 gallon (gal.) = 3.785L	1 liter (L) = 0.264 gal.

APPENDIX

LANGUAGE

PRONUNCIATION

The letter **X** has a baffling variety of pronunciations: depending on dialect and word position, it can sound like English "h," "s," "sh," or "x." Spanish words receive stress on the syllable marked with an accent (´). In the absence of an accent mark, words that end in vowels, "n," or "s" receive stress on the second to last syllable. For words ending in all other consonants, stress falls on the last syllable. Spanish has masculine and feminine nouns, and gives a gender to all adjectives. Masculine words generally end with an "o": *él es un tonto* (he is a fool). Feminine words generally end with an "a": *ella es bella* (she is beautiful). Pay close attention—slight changes in word ending can cause drastic changes in meaning. For instance, when receiving directions, mind the distinction between *derecho* (straight) and *derecha* (right).

PHONETIC UNIT	PRONUNCIATION	PHONETIC UNIT	PRONUNCIATION	PHONETIC UNIT	PRONUNCIATION
a	ah, as in "father"	rr	trilled	ñ	ay, as in "canyon"
e	eh, as in "pet"	h	silent	Mayan ch	sh, as in "shoe"
i	ee, as in "eat"	y and i	ee, as in "eat"	gü	goo, as in "gooey"
o	oh, as in "oh"	j	h, as in "hello"	g before e or i	h, as in "hen"
u	oo, as in "boot"	ll	y, as in "yes"	gu before e	g, as in "gate"

PHRASEBOOK

ESSENTIAL PHRASES

ENGLISH	SPANISH	PRONUNCIATION
hello	hola	O-la
goodbye	adiós	ah-dee-OHS
yes/no	sí/no	SEE/NO
please	por favor	POHR fa-VOHR
thank you	gracias	GRAH-see-ahs
you're welcome	de nada	deh NAH-dah
Do you speak English?	¿Habla inglés?	AH-blah een-GLESS
I don't speak Spanish.	No hablo español.	NO AH-bloh ehs-pahn-YOHL
Excuse me.	Perdón/Disculpe.	pehr-THOHN/dee-SKOOL-peh
I don't know.	No sé.	NO SEH
Can you repeat that?	¿Puede repetirlo?/¿Mande?	PWEH-deh reh-peh-TEER-lo/MAHN-deh
I'm sorry/forgive me.	Lo siento	lo see-EN-toe

SURVIVAL SPANISH

ENGLISH	SPANISH	ENGLISH	SPANISH
good morning	buenos días	How do you say (dodgeball) in Spanish?	¿Cómo se dice (dodgeball) en español?
good afternoon	buenas tardes	What (did you just say)?	¿Cómo?/¿Qué?/¿Mande?
goodnight	buenas noches	I don't understand.	No entiendo.
What is your name?	¿Cómo se llama?	Again, please.	Otra vez, por favor.
My name is (Jessica Laporte).	Me llamo (Jessica Laporte).	Could you speak slower?	¿Podría hablar más despacio?
What's up?	¿Qué tal?	Where is (the bathroom)?	¿Dónde está (el baño)?
See you later.	Hasta luego.	Who?/What?	¿Quién?/¿Qué?
How are you?	¿Qué tal?/¿Cómo está?	When?/Where?	¿Cuándo?/¿Dónde?
I'm sick/fine.	Estoy enfermo(a)/bien.	Why?	¿Por qué?
I am hot/cold.	Tengo calor/frío.	Because.	Porque.
I am hungry/thirsty.	Tengo hambre/sed.	Go on!/Come on!/Hurry up!	¡Ándale!
I want/would like...	Quiero/Quisiera...	Let's go!	¡Vámonos!
How much does it cost?	¿Cuánto cuesta?	Look!/Listen!	¡Mira!
That is very cheap/expensive.	Es muy barato/caro.	Stop!/That's enough!	¡Basta!
Is the store open/closed?	¿La tienda está abierta/cerrada?	maybe	tal vez/puede ser
Good morning.	Buenos días.	How do you say (I love Let's Go) in Spanish?	¿Cómo se dice (I love Let's Go) en español?

INTERPERSONAL INTERACTIONS

ENGLISH	SPANISH	ENGLISH	SPANISH
Where are you from?	¿De dónde viene usted?	Pleased to meet you.	Encantado(a)/Mucho gusto.
I am from (Europe).	Soy de (Europa).	Do you have a light?	¿Tiene luz?

I'm (20) years old.	Tengo (veinte) años.	He/she seems cool.	Él/ella me cae bien.
Would you like to go out with me?	¿Quiere salir conmigo?	What's wrong?	¿Qué le pasa?
I have a boyfriend/girl-friend/spouse.	Tengo novio/novia/esposo(a).	I'm sorry.	Lo siento.
I'm gay/straight/bisexual.	Soy gay/heterosexual/bisexual.	Do you come here often?	¿Viene aquí a menudo?
I love you.	Te quiero.	This is my first time in Mexico.	Esta es mi primera vez en Mexico.
Why not?	¿Por qué no?	What a shame: you bought Lonely Planet!	¡Qué lástima: compraste Lonely Planet!

YOUR ARRIVAL

ENGLISH	SPANISH	ENGLISH	SPANISH
I am from (the US/Europe).	Soy de (los Estados Unidos/Europa).	What's the problem, sir/madam?	¿Cuál es el problema, señor/señora?
Here is my passport.	Aquí está mi pasaporte.	I lost my passport/luggage.	Se me perdió mi pasa-porte/equipaje.
I will be here for less than six months.	Estaré aquí por menos de seis meses.	I have nothing to declare.	No tengo nada para declarar.
I don't know where that came from.	No sé de dónde vino eso.	Please do not detain me.	Por favor no me detenga.

GETTING AROUND

ENGLISH	SPANISH	ENGLISH	SPANISH
How do you get to (the bus station)?	¿Cómo se puede llegar a (la estación de auto-buses)?	Does this bus go to (Guanajuato)?	¿Esta autobús va a (Guanajuato)?
Which bus line goes to..?	¿Cuál línea de buses tiene servicio a...?	Where does the bus leave from?	¿De dónde sale el bús?
When does the bus leave?	¿Cuándo sale el bús?	How long does the trip take?	¿Cuánto tiempo dura el viaje?
Can I buy a ticket?	¿Puedo comprar un boleto?	I'm getting off at (Av. Juárez).	Me bajo en (Av. Juárez).
Where is (the center of town)?	¿Dónde está (el centro)?	Please let me off at (the zoo).	Por favor, déjeme en (el zoológico).
How near/far is...?	¿Qué tan cerca/lejos está...?	Where is (Constitución) street?	¿Dónde está la calle (Constitución)?
I'm in a hurry.	Estoy de prisa.	Continue forward.	Siga derecho.
I'm lost.	Estoy perdido(a).	On foot.	A pie.
I am going to the airport.	Voy al aeropuerto.	The flight is delayed/canceled.	El vuelo está atrasado/cancelado.
Where is the bathroom?	¿Dónde está el baño?	Is it safe to hitchhike?	¿Es seguro pedir aventón?
Where can I buy a cell-phone?	¿Dónde puedo comprar un teléfono celular?	Where can I check email?	¿Dónde se puede chequear el correo electrónico?
Could you tell me what time it is?	¿Podría decirme qué hora es?	Are there student dis-counts available?	¿Hay descuentos para estudiantes?

ON THE ROAD

ENGLISH	SPANISH	ENGLISH	SPANISH
I would like to rent (a car).	Quisiera alquilar (un coche).	north	norte
How much does it cost per day/week?	¿Cuánto cuesta por día/semana?	south	sur
Does it have (heating/air-conditioning)?	¿Tiene (calefacción/aire acondicionado)?	public bus/van	bús
stop	pare	slow	despacio
lane (ends)	carril (termina)	yield	ceda

APPENDIX

entrance	entrada	seatbelt	cinturón de seguridad
exit	salida	(maximum) speed	velocidad (máxima)
(narrow) bridge	puente (estrecho)	dangerous (curve)	(curva) peligrosa
narrow (lane)	(carril) estrecho	parking	estacionamiento, parking
toll (ahead)	peaje (adelante)	dead-end street	calle sin salida
authorized public buses only	transporte colectivo autorizado solamente	only	solo
slippery when wet	resbala cuando mojado	rest area	área de descansar
danger (ahead)	peligro (adelante)	do not park	no estacione
do not enter	no entre	do not turn right on red	no vire con luz roja

DIRECTIONS

ENGLISH	SPANISH	ENGLISH	SPANISH
(to the) right	(a la) derecha	near (to)	cerca (de)
(to the) left	(a la) izquierda	far (from)	lejos (de)
next to	al lado de/junto a	above	arriba
across from	en frente de/frente a	below	abajo
(Continue) straight.	(Siga) derecho.	block	cuadra/manzana
turn (command form)	doble	corner	esquina
traffic light	semáforo	street	calle/avenida

ACCOMMODATIONS

ENGLISH	SPANISH	ENGLISH	SPANISH
Is there a cheap hotel around here?	¿Hay un hotel económico por aquí?	Are there rooms with windows?	¿Hay habitaciones con ventanas?
Do you have rooms available?	¿Tiene habitaciones libres?	I am going to stay for (4) days.	Me voy a quedar (cuatro) días.
I would like to reserve a room.	Quisiera reservar una habitación.	Are there cheaper rooms?	¿Hay habitaciones más baratas?
Could I see a room?	¿Podría ver una habitación?	Do they come with private baths?	¿Vienen con baño privado?
Do you have any singles/doubles?	¿Tiene habitaciones simples/dobles?	I'll take it.	Lo acepto.
I need another key/towel/pillow.	Necesito otra llave/toalla/almohada.	There are cockroaches in my room.	Hay cucarachas en mi habitación.
The shower/sink/toilet is broken.	La ducha/la pila/el servicio no funciona.	(The cockroaches) are biting me.	(Las cucarachas) me están mordiendo.
My sheets are dirty.	Mis sábanas están sucias.	Dance, cockroaches, dance!	¡Bailen, cucarachas, bailen!

EMERGENCY

ENGLISH	SPANISH	ENGLISH	SPANISH
Help!	¡Socorro!/¡Auxilio!/¡Ayúdeme!	Call the police!	¡Llame a la policía!
I am hurt.	Estoy herido(a).	Leave me alone!	¡Déjame en paz!
It's an emergency!	¡Es una emergencia!	Don't touch me!	¡No me toque!
Fire!	¡Fuego!/¡Incendio!	I've been robbed!	¡Me han robado!
Call a clinic/ambulance/doctor/priest!	¡Llame a una clínica/una ambulancia/un médico/un padre!	They went that-a-way!	¡Se fueron por allá!
I need to contact my embassy.	Necesito comunicarme con mi embajada.	I will only speak in the presence of a lawyer.	Sólo hablaré con la presencia de un(a) abogado(a).

MEDICAL

ENGLISH	SPANISH	ENGLISH	SPANISH
I feel bad/worse/better/okay/fine.	Me siento mal/peor/mejor/más o menos/bien.	My (stomach) hurts.	Me duele (el estómago).

APPENDIX

I have a headache/stom-achache.	Tengo un dolor de cabeza/estómago.	It hurts here.	Me duele aquí.
I'm sick/ill.	Estoy enfermo(a).	I'm allergic to (nuts)	Soy alérgico(a) a (nueces)
Here is my prescription.	Aquí está mi receta médica.	I think I'm going to vomit.	Pienso que voy a vomitar.
What is this medicine for?	¿Para qué es esta medicina?	I have a cold/a fever/ diarrhea/nausea.	Tengo gripe/una calen-tura/diarrea/náusea.
Where is the nearest hospital/doctor?	¿Dónde está el hospital/ doctor más cercano?	I haven't been able to go to the bathroom in (4) days.	No he podido ir al baño en (cuatro) días.

OUT TO LUNCH

ENGLISH	SPANISH	ENGLISH	SPANISH
breakfast	desayuno	Where is a good restau-rant?	¿Dónde está un restau-rante bueno?
lunch	almuerzo	Can I see the menu?	¿Podría ver la carta/el menú?
dinner	comida/cena	Table for (one), please.	Mesa para (uno), por favor.
dessert	postre	Do you take credit cards?	¿Aceptan tarjetas de crédito?
drink (alcoholic)	bebida (trago)	I would like to order (the chicken).	Quisiera (el pollo).
cup	copa/taza	Do you have anything veg-etarian/without meat?	¿Hay algún plato vegetari-ano/sin carne?
fork	tenedor	Do you have hot sauce?	¿Tiene salsa picante?
knife	cuchillo	This is too spicy.	Es demasiado picante.
napkin	servilleta	Disgusting!	¡Guácala!/¡Qué asco!
spoon	cuchara	Delicious!	¡Qué rico!
bon appétit	buen provecho	Check, please.	La cuenta, por favor.

MENU READER

SPANISH	ENGLISH	SPANISH	ENGLISH
a la brasa	roasted	frijoles	beans
a la plancha	grilled	leche	milk
al vapor	steamed	legumbres	legumes
aceite	oil	licuado	smoothie
aceituna	olive	lima	lime
agua (purificada)	water (purified)	limón	lemon
ajo	garlic	limonada	lemonade
almeja	clam	lomo	steak or chop
arroz (con leche)	rice (rice pudding)	maíz	corn
birria	cow brain soup, a hang-over cure	mariscos	seafood
bistec	beefsteak	miel	honey
café	coffee	mole	dark chocolate chili sauce
caliente	hot	pan	bread
camarones	shrimp	papas (fritas)	potatoes (french fries)
carne	meat	parrillas	various grilled meats
cebolla	onion	pastes	meat pie
cemitas	sandwiches made with special long-lasting bread	pasteles	desserts/pies
cerveza	beer	pescado	fish
ceviche	raw marinated seafood	papa	potato
charales	small fish, fried and eaten whole	pimienta	pepper
chaya	plant similar to spinach native to the Yucatán	pollo	chicken

chorizo	spicy sausage	puerco/cerdo	pork
coco	coconut	pulque	liquor made from maguey cactus
cordero	lamb	queso	cheese
(sin) crema	(without) cream	refresco	soda pop
dulces	sweets	verduras/vegetales	vegetables
dulce de leche	caramelized milk	sal	salt
empanada	dumpling filled with meat, cheese, or potatoes	sopes	thick tortillas, stuffed with different toppings
ensalada	salad	tragos	mixed drinks/liquor
entrada	appetizer	Xtabentún	anise and honey liqueur

NUMBERS, DAYS, & MONTHS

ENGLISH	SPANISH	ENGLISH	SPANISH	ENGLISH	SPANISH
0	cero	30	treinta	weekend	fin de semana
1	uno	40	cuarenta	morning	mañana
2	dos	50	cincuenta	afternoon	tarde
3	tres	60	sesenta	night	noche
4	cuatro	70	setenta	day	día
5	cinco	80	ochenta	month	mes
6	seis	90	noventa	year	año
7	siete	100	cien	early	temprano
8	ocho	1000	mil	late	tarde
9	nueve	1,000,000	un millón	January	enero
10	diez	Monday	lunes	February	febrero
11	once	Tuesday	martes	March	marzo
12	doce	Wednesday	miércoles	April	abril
13	trece	Thursday	jueves	May	mayo
14	catorce	Friday	viernes	June	junio
15	quince	Saturday	sábado	July	julio
16	dieciseis	Sunday	domingo	August	agosto
17	diecisiete	day before yesterday	anteayer	September	septiembre
18	dieciocho	yesterday	ayer	October	octubre
19	diecinueve	last night	anoche	November	noviembre
20	veinte	today	hoy	December	diciembre
21	veintiuno	tomorrow	mañana	2010	dos mil diez
22	veintidos	day after tomorrow	pasado mañana	2011	dos mil once

SPANISH GLOSSARY

aduana: customs

agencia de viaje: travel agency

aguardiente: strong liquor

aguas frescas: cold fresh juice/tea

aguas termales: hot springs

ahora: now

ahorita: in just a moment

aire acondicionado: air-conditioning (A/C)

al gusto: as you wish

almacén: (grocery) store

almuerzo: lunch, midday meal

altiplano: highland

amigo(a): friend

andén: platform

antro: club/disco/joint

antojitos: appetizer

arena: sand

arroz: rice

artesanía: arts and crafts

avenida: avenue

azúcar: sugar

bahía: bay

balneario: spa

bandido: bandit

baño: bathroom or natural spa

barato(a): cheap

barranca: canyon

barro: mud

barrio: neighborhood

bello(a): beautiful

biblioteca: library

biosfera: biosphere

birria: meat stew, usually goat

bistec: beefsteak

blanquillo: egg

bocaditos: appetizers, at a bar

bodega: convenience store or winery

boetería: ticket counter

boleto: ticket

bonito(a): pretty

borracho(a): drunk

bosque: forest

botanas: snacks, frequently at bars

bueno(a): good

buena suerte: good luck

burro: donkey

caballero: gentleman

caballo: horse

cabañas: cabins

cajero automático: ATM

cajeros: cashiers

caldo: soup, broth, or stew

calle: street

cama: bed

cambio: change

caminata: hike

camino: path, track, road

camión: truck

camioneta: small pickup-sized

campamento: campground

campesino(a): person from a rural area, peasant

campo: countryside

canotaje: rafting

cantina: bar/drinking establishment

capilla: chapel

carne asada: roasted meat

carnitas: diced, cooked pork

caro(a): expensive

carretera: highway

carro: car, or sometimes a train car

casa: house

casa de cambio: currency exchange establishment

casado(a): married

cascadas: waterfalls

catedral: cathedral

cenote: fresh-water well

centro: city center

cerca: near/nearby

cerro: hill

cerveza: beer

ceviche: raw seafood marinated in lemon juice, herbs, vegetables

cevichería: ceviche restaurant

chico(a): little boy (girl)

chicharrón: bite-sized pieces of fried pork, pork rinds

chuleta de puerco: pork chop

cigarillo: cigarette

cine: cinema

ciudad: city

ciudadela: neighborhood in a large city

coche: car

cocodrilo: crocodile

colectivo: shared taxi

colina: hill

coliseo: coliseum, stadium

comedor: dining room

comida corrida: fixed-price

comida del día: daily special meal

comida típica: typical/traditional dishes

computador: computer

con: with

concha: shell

consulado: consulate

convento: convent

correo: mail, post office

correo electrónico: email

cordillera: mountain range

corvina: sea bass

crucero: crossroads

Cruz Roja: Red Cross

cuadra: street block

cuarto: room

cuenta: bill, check

cuento: story, account

cueva: cave

cuota: toll

curandero: healer

damas: ladies

de paso: in passing, usually refers to buses

desayuno: breakfast

descompuesto: broken, out of order; spoiled (food)

desierto: desert

despacio: slow

de turno: a 24hr. rotating schedule for pharmacies
dinero: money
discoteca: dance club
dueño(a): owner
dulces: sweets
duna: dune
edificio: building
ejido: communal land
embajada: embassy
embarcadero: dock
emergencia: emergency
encomiendas: estates granted to Spanish settlers in Latin America
entrada: entrance
equipaje: luggage
estadio: stadium
este: east
estrella: star
extranjero: foreign, foreigner
farmacia: pharmacy
farmacia en turno: 24hr. pharmacy
feliz: happy
ferrocarril: railroad
fiesta: party, holiday
finca: farm
friaje: sudden cold wind
frijoles: beans
frontera: border
fumar: to smoke
fumaroles: holes in a volcanic region that emit hot vapors
fundo: large estate or tract of land
fútbol: soccer
ganga: bargain
gobierno: government
gordo(a): fat
gorra: cap
gratis: free
gringo(a): Caucasian
habitación: a room
hacer una caminata: take a hike
hacienda: ranch
helado: ice cream
hermano(a): brother (sister)
hervido(a): boiled
hielo: ice
hijo(a): son (daughter)

hombre: man
huevo: egg
iglesia: church
impuestos: taxes
impuesto valor añadido (IVA): value added tax (VAT)
indígena: indigenous person, refers to the native culture
ir de camping: to go camping
isla: island
jaiba: crab meat
jamón: ham
jarra: pitcher
jirón: street
jugo: juice
ladrón: thief
lago/laguna: lake, lagoon
lancha: launch, small boat
langosta: lobster
langostino: jumbo shrimp
larga distancia: long distance
lavandería: laundromat
lejos: far
lento: slow
librería: bookstore
licuado: smoothie, shake
lista de correos: mail holding system in Latin America
llamada: call
loma: hill
lomo: chop, steak
lonchería: snack bar
loro: parrot
madre: mother
malo(a): bad
malecón: pier or seaside boardwalk
maletas: luggage, suitcases
manejar despacio: to drive slowly
manzana: apple
mar: sea
mariscos: seafood
matrimonial: double bed
menestras: lentils/beans

menú del día/menú: fixed daily meal often offered for a bargain price
mercado: market
merendero: outdoor bar/kiosk
merienda: snack
mestizaje: crossing of races
mestizo(a): a person of mixed European and indigenous descent
microbús: small, local bus
mirador: an observatory or lookout point
muelle: wharf
muerte: death
museo: museum
música folklórica: folk music
nada: nothing
naranja: orange
niño(a): child
norte (Nte.): north
nuez/nueces: nut/nuts
obra: work of art, play
obraje: primitive textile workshop
oeste: west
oficina de turismo: tourist office
oriente (Ote.): east
padre: father
palapa: palm-thatched umbrella
pampa: a treeless grassland area
pan: bread
panadería: bakery
papagayo: parrot
parada: a stop (on a bus or train)
parilla: various cuts of grilled meat
paro: labor strike
parque: park
parroquia: parish
paseo turístico: tour covering a series of sites
pelea de gallos: cockfight
peligroso(a): dangerous
peninsulares: Spanish-born colonists
pescado: fish

picante: spicy
plátano: plantain
playa: beach
población: population, settlement
poniente (Pte.): west
policía: police
portales: archways
pueblito: small town
pueblo: town
puente: bridge
puerta: door
puerto: port
queso: cheese
rana: frog
recreo: place of amusement, bar-restaurant on the outskirts of a city
refrescos: refreshments, soft drinks
refugio: refuge
reloj: watch, clock
requesón: cottage cheese
río: river
ropa: clothes
sábanas: bedsheets
sabor: flavor
sala: living room
salida: exit

salto: waterfall
salsa: sauce
scabé: paved, elevated roads found in many ruins.
seguro(a): lock, insurance; adj.: safe
selva: jungle
semáforo: traffic light
semana: week
Semana Santa: Holy Week
sexo: sex
SIDA: AIDS
siesta: mid-afternoon nap; businesses often close at this time
sillar: flexible volcanic rock used in construction
sol: sun
solito(a): alone
solo carril: one-lane road or bridge
soltero(a): single (unmarried)
supermercado: supermarket
sur (S.): south
tarifa: fee

tapas: bite-size appetizers served in bars
telenovela: soap opera
termas: hot mineral springs
terminal terrestre: bus station
tienda: store
timbre: bell
tipo de cambio: exchange rate
tortuga: turtle
trago: mixed drink/shot of alcohol
triste: sad
turismo: tourism
turista: tourist, tourist diarrhea
valle: valley
vecindad: neighborhood
vegetariano(a): vegetarian
volcán: volcano
zócalo: central town plaza
zona: zone

APPENDIX

INDEX

INDEX

INDEX

MAP INDEX

MAP INDEX

HELPING LET'S GO. If you want to share your discoveries, suggestions, or corrections, please drop us a line. We appreciate every piece of correspondence, whether a postcard, a 10-page email, or a coconut. Visit Let's Go at **http://www.letsgo.com,** or send email to:

feedback@letsgo.com, subject: "Let's Go Costa Rica, Nicaragua & Panama"

Address mail to:

Let's Go Costa Rica, Nicaragua & Panama, 67 Mount Auburn St., Cambridge, MA 02138 , USA

In addition to the invaluable travel advice our readers share with us, many are kind enough to offer their services as researchers or editors. Unfortunately, our charter enables us to employ only currently enrolled Harvard students.

Maps by Let's Go Copyright © 2010 by Let's Go, Inc.

Distributed by Publishers Group West.
Printed in Canada by Friesens Corp.

ISBN-13: 978-1-59880-587-1
ISBN-10: 1-59880-587-8
First edition
10 9 8 7 6 5 4 3 2 1

Let's Go Costa Rica, Nicaragua & Panama is written by Let's Go Publications, 67 Mount Auburn St., Cambridge, MA 02138, USA.

Let's Go® and the LG logo are trademarks of Let's Go, Inc.